MANAGEMENT & ORGANIZATION
2ND ED.

ANDREW J. DuBRIN

College of Business
Rochester Institute of Technology

R. DUANE IRELAND

Hankamer School of Business
Baylor University

COLLEGE DIVISION South-Western Publishing Co.

Cincinnati Ohio

Acquisitions Editor: Randy G. Haubner
Developmental Editor: Alice C. Denny
Production Editor: Rebecca Roby
Production House: WordCrafters Editorial Services, Inc.
Cover and Interior Design: Craig LaGesse Ramsdell
Top Cover Photograph: © Robert Mizono
Bottom Cover Photograph: © Walter Hodges/Westlight
Background Cover Photograph: © Jim Herity
Marketing Manager: Scott D. Person

GC65GA
Copyright © 1993
by SOUTH-WESTERN PUBLISHING CO.
Cincinnati, Ohio

ISBN: 0-538-81585-X

1 2 3 4 5 6 7 8 9 0 KI 0 9 8 7 6 5 4 3 2

Printed in the United States of America

Library of Congress Cataloging-in-Publication Data

DuBrin, Andrew J.
    Management and organization / Andrew J. Dubrin. R. Duane Ireland.
  —2nd ed.
      p.   cm.
    Rev. ed. of Management & organization. c1989.
    Includes bibliographical references and indexes.
    ISBN 0-538-81585-X
    1. Management.   2. Organization.   I. Ireland, R. Duane.
  II. Title.   III. Title: Management & organization.
  HD31.S57 1993
  658—dc20   92-22116
                                                                    CIP

Preface

Today's managers are confronted with important challenges. The broadest challenge is surviving in an extremely competitive economic environment while continuing to follow an acceptable ethical code. More specific challenges include competing effectively in a global marketplace, achieving high productivity and quality with fewer employees, and managing cultural diversity effectively. *Management and Organization* describes concepts and techniques that will help managers deal successfully with these challenges.

Written for use in the undergraduate principles of management course, *Management and Organization* is organized around the four management functions: planning, organizing, leading, and controlling. The comprehensive text introduces the student to important aspects of successful managerial activities. It examines all levels of management from first- to top-level, and the practices described in the text are appropriate for all types of organizations: profit firms, nonprofit organizations, and government agencies.

The text is action-oriented, with many applications materials and useful pedagogical features. The many examples depict how today's U.S. firms are managed successfully and effectively in both the domestic and international markets. The second edition of *Management and Organization* features ample use of colorful illustrations and photographs to enhance the written presentations.

CHANGES FOR THE SECOND EDITION

The second edition is easier to read as a result of tightening the presentation and shortening the average sentence length. Ethical awareness is promoted by presenting questions about ethical issues in the margins of each chapter. All six comprehensive cases and many of the chapter opener and concluding cases are new. The book has been completely updated and reflects the current managerial emphasis on quality, productivity, employee empowerment, cultural diversity, and ethical behavior.

A major addition to the second edition is coverage of the total quality management approach. Under TQM, product quality is defined by a firm's customers. *Management and Organization* integrates TQM throughout: from a manager's perspective in Chapter 11, from an operations or production viewpoint in Chapter 17, and from an organizational standpoint in Chapter 22. Chapter 17 is new to this edition and explores how, under TQM, every aspect of design, production, and distribution is affected by a customer's definition of quality. Detailed descriptions of these impacts are presented, along with explanations of how they must be monitored through the controlling function.

Chapters 5 and 6 have been heavily reworked to provide optimum integration of planning, strategic planning, and strategic management. Other emerging management trends and concepts are also included in the second edition of *Management and Organization*. New material reflects:

- Environmental adaptation (Chapter 5), which is explained and broken into three aspects: entrepreneurial, engineering, and administrative.
- The use of work teams (Chapter 7) for improved productivity and quality.
- Employee empowerment (Chapter 8): the benefits of employee involvement and accountability for decisions.
- The organizational design triangle (Chapter 9): an innovative approach to organization structure and *new* insights into organizing work.
- Managing with cultural diversity (Chapters 10 and 13).
- The role and benefits of entrepreneurship (Chapter 19) in firms of all sizes and society as a whole.
- Organizational culture (Chapter 22) and the effects of change.

ORGANIZATION

In Part I of *Management and Organization*, the nature and challenge of management are explored. A brief history of management is presented, along with a description of the ethical and social responsibilities of management. The focus of Part II is the decision-making and planning function. Coverage includes how managers make decisions; develop and implement strategic, tactical, and operational plans; and use strategic planning and strategic management processes.

Part III concerns the organizing function, and describes the activities through which tasks and authority are assigned. The use of power in the workplace is discussed, and an overview of human resources management (the staffing function) is presented.

Part IV examines the leading function, and the focus shifts to approaches and techniques used to lead, motivate, and communicate with employees at all levels. Current information is presented to enhance understanding of leadership and motivation, insights about interpersonal communication, and how a manager can improve the productivity of ineffective performers. An important new feature of Chapter 11 is a description of the manager's role in achieving total quality management.

Part V covers the controlling function and begins by presenting the underlying principles of control. Methods and techniques to control a firm's activities so that its objectives can be achieved are also described. Operations management, a key part of effective controlling, is highlighted in a new chapter. The use of management information systems as an element of control is also included in this part.

Part VI presents two examples of managing in special settings. One chapter covers entrepreneurship and the role of intrapreneurship in larger firms. The second chapter discusses how the basic functions of management are applied in an international environment. Part VII concerns individual and organizational development and presents tactics and strategies for managing one's career. This part also includes coverage of a topic mentioned throughout the text, organizational culture. Finally, approaches designed to bring about planned organization change, including a shift to total quality management, are summarized.

A group of cases that students can work by using the *Decision Assistant* software follows the last chapter. The cases may be used as individual or group assignments for certain text chapters. The cases are followed by a complete glossary and subject, name, and organization indexes.

KEY FEATURES OF THE TEXT

In addition to the features retained and updated from the previous edition, the new edition includes several new pedagogical features to encourage learning.

Learning Objectives

Each chapter begins with clearly stated learning objectives. These objectives help students identify the key learning goals of the chapter before studying the chapter material. The objectives are reviewed in the end-of-chapter discussion questions.

Opening Case

In addition to the learning objectives, each chapter begins with an opening case that describes a situation relevant to the chapter. At one or more places in the chapter, Back to the Opening Case segments are presented to illustrate the concepts relevant to the opening case.

Key Terms

Key terms are set boldface in the text of each chapter, and a complete listing of the terms appears at the end of the chapter. A complete glossary of all key terms is located at the end of the book.

Examples

The text is filled with current, interesting, real-world examples that clearly illustrate key concepts. Manager in Action and Organization in Action boxes and textual materials provide detailed and current examples of applied theory in real companies.

Ethics in Management

Ethics and corporate social responsibility are the focus of text Chapter 3. In addition, throughout the text, questions involving ethical issues are presented in the margins. The purpose of the questions is to sensitize students to the ethical implications of managerial actions. The issues suggested by the questions will help students apply their own viewpoints to some of the many ethics-based matters facing managers today.

International Management

The importance of the global marketplace is emphasized throughout the text. In addition to Chapter 20, "International Management," examples illustrating international applications of management appear in many chapters. A global icon appears in the margin to indicate material that relates to management practices in global situations.

Learning Checks

Periodic Learning Checks ask the student to summarize information presented up to that point in the chapter. These instant reviews serve to enhance comprehension.

Cases

At the end of each chapter are two Problems for Action and a Concluding Case. The problems and concluding case provide opportunities to apply information from the chapter to solve real managerial problems. Longer, more comprehensive cases appear at the ends of Parts I through VI. All six cases are new for the second edition. Each Comprehensive Case reinforces learning because it requires students to apply concepts, techniques, or approaches from several chapters. Ten additional cases for use with the *Decision Assistant* software are located at the end of the text.

Summary and Review Questions

Also at the end of each chapter are a Summary and Questions for Discussion and Review. These questions serve as a review of the chapter learning objectives. They may be used in class to assess the students' grasp of the material or by the students on their own to test their comprehension of important concepts.

Computer Software

A stand-alone software package called *Decision Assistant* has been developed to illustrate the use of five analytical techniques useful to managers. Ten cases in which the *Decision Assistant* might be used appear at the end of the text.

Glossary and Indexes

A Glossary containing all key terms provides easy reference for study and review of important concepts introduced in the text. Organization, name, and subject indexes are included to help students find examples and information quickly.

SUPPLEMENTS

Management and Organization is supported by a comprehensive package of supplementary learning aids and teaching resources.

Study Guide

Each chapter in the Study Guide contains chapter learning objectives; a chapter overview; review questions including matching, true/false, and multiple choice; activities designed to increase comprehension of information in the text; and suggested readings. The readings may be used to further explore topics described in the text or as resources for term papers.

DECISION ASSISTANT SOFTWARE. The instructor may place the *Decision Assistant* software in the computer lab for student use, or the text may be ordered with the software already packaged with it.

Instructor Supplements

INSTRUCTOR'S RESOURCE GUIDE. The *Instructor's Resource Guide* for *Management and Organization* has been expanded. Written by the authors of the textbook, the manual contains detailed materials for each text chapter. First the chapter learning objectives and the key terms, with definitions, are presented. Following are a detailed chapter outline and lecture notes. Special emphasis is placed on how and when major points can be reinforced with transparencies, discussion questions, and additional lecture materials.

Each manual chapter includes an Experiential Exercise to give students the opportunity to apply concepts presented in the chapter. Questions, and their answers, about the Opening Case and the Back to the Opening Case segments are also included for each chapter. Answers to the end-of-chapter Questions for Discussion and Review and suggested solutions for the Problems for Action and the Concluding Case questions are given for each chapter.

Suggested solutions for the questions that accompany each Comprehensive Case are also included. Finally, the *Instructor's Resource Guide* includes operating directions and suggestions for use of the *Decision Assistant* software and cases.

TEST BANK. Also prepared by the text authors, the *Test Bank* contains over 2,200 questions including multiple choice, true/false, and discussion. Each question is keyed to the text page where the answer appears. Thorough solutions to the discussion questions are provided.

COMPUTERIZED TEST BANK. The entire test bank is available on easy-to-use disks. The MicroSWAT III software includes pull-down menus that allow users to edit, add, delete, or randomly mix test bank questions for customized tests. Users may choose from a variety of print options. The computerized version of the test bank is available on 5¼-inch disks for use with IBM-compatible computers.

TRANSPARENCIES AND VIDEOS. Also available to adopters are full-color overhead transparencies. These transparencies include illustrations from the chapters as well as new information. Videotapes of selected management topics are also available to adopters of the text.

ACKNOWLEDGMENTS

We owe a special debt of gratitude to the professors, students, and managers who provided feedback regarding the first edition. We also thank our colleagues who served as reviewers for this new edition of *Management and Organization*. The following individuals made helpful comments and suggestions that have strengthened this book.

Leonard Ackerman,
Clarion University of Pennsylvania

Gerald Biberman,
University of Scranton

James C. Cotham,
Belmont College

Manual J. Coya,
St. Thomas University

Daphne S. Friday,
Belmont Abbey College

Philip C. Grant,
Husson College

Toby J. Kash,
Pittsburg State University

Herff L. Moore,
University of Central Arkansas

Mary Nicastro,
Capital University

Thomas J. Quirk,
Webster University

Robert C. Vaught,
Southwest Missouri State University

Adelle W. Ziemer,
Lehigh County Community
College

Roger K. Baker,
Illinois Central College

Allen Bluedorn,
University of Missouri-Columbia

Taylor Cox, Jr.,
University of Michigan

Norman H. Deunk,
Central Michigan University

Edwin A. Giermak,
College of DuPage

Cooper Johnson,
Delta State University

Clyde E. Kobberdahl,
Cincinnati Technical College

Wayne E. Nelson,
Central Missouri State University

Pamela S. Porter,
University of Cincinnati

Charles I. Stubbart,
Southern Illinois University at
Carbondale

Jack W. Wimer,
Baylor University

Writing a text of this nature is a team effort. We are fortunate in this respect, for we could not have asked for a better team than the one that supported the development and production of this edition of our book. While it is impossible to name everyone who played a role in bringing this edition to life, there are several people who deserve special recognition.

A number of individuals at South-Western Publishing Co. were important members of the team. Our developmental editor, Alice Denny, went far beyond all reasonable expectations in working with us to develop our product successfully. She worked tirelessly to make certain that we presented our ideas in an effective, as well as creative and appealing, manner. Important also were her supportive words and efforts as deadlines approached faster than we could have imagined. Although he joined the team at the very end of the project, our acquisitions editor, Randy Haubner, was also very supportive. Special thanks, too, go to marketing managers Scott Person and Tania Hindersman for keeping us attuned to needs of the marketplace throughout the development process. We also appreciate the guidance production editor Rebecca Roby provided for the actual production of the text and supplements.

Both of our universities provided intellectual environments that allow academic and teaching ideas to become published products. At Baylor University, Dean Richard Scott provided the support and encouragement faculty members need to complete many kinds of projects. Others who were involved at different stages of the product's development include Joyce Gunn, Lisa Walker, and Val Warren. We deeply appreciate the contributions of each to this endeavor.

We also want to acknowledge our families for their understanding throughout the long writing schedule. Their committment was critical to our efforts to develop a quality product. Thanks to Carol Bowman and the DuBrin family—Drew, Douglas, Melanie, Molly, and Rosemary—as well as Mary Anne, Rebecca, and Scott Ireland for their encouragement and support.

Andrew J. DuBrin
R. Duane Ireland

ABOUT THE AUTHORS

Andrew J. DuBrin is Professor of Management in the College of Business at Rochester Institute of Technology, where he teaches courses and conducts research in management, organizational behavior, and career management. He received his Ph.D. in Industrial Psychology from Michigan State University.

Dr. DuBrin has prior business experience in personnel and human-resources management and does consulting for organizations and individuals. His specialities include career counseling and management development.

Dr. DuBrin is also a widely published author of both textbooks and trade publications. He has written textbooks in management, organizational behavior, and human relations. His trade books cover many current issues including office politics, coping with adversity, and overcoming career self-sabotage.

R. Duane Ireland holds the Curtis Hankamer Chair in Entrepreneurship at Baylor University. Previously chair of the Management Department, he is currently Associate Dean for Research and Scholarly Activities in Baylor's Hankamer School of Business. Dr. Ireland is also associate editor of the *Academy of Management Executive.*

Dr. Ireland's research interests focus on strategic planning and strategic management practices in both large and small firms. His work has been published in a variety of scholarly journals including *Academy of Management Journal, Strategic Management Journal, Business Horizons,* and *Journal of Management.* As a consultant, he also specializes in strategic planning, as well as performance counseling and effective product management.

At Baylor University, and earlier at Oklahoma State University, Dr. Ireland has remained actively involved with teaching. In addition to principles of management, he has taught strategic management, organizational behavior, and small business management.

Brief Contents

Contents

PART V
CONTROLLING   377

15 Principles of Control   378

16 Controlling Methods and Techniques   401

17 Operations Management and Controlling   425

OPERATIONS MANAGEMENT, OPERATIONS SYSTEMS, AND OPERATIONS ACTIVITIES 427

OPERATIONS MANAGEMENT IN MANUFACTURING AND SERVICE FIRMS 430
Manufacturing Firms 431   Service Firms 431   The Importance of Service Firms in Today's Economy 432

OPERATIONS SYSTEMS 432
Product Design and Development 432   Facilities Location 435   Capital Equipment 437   Facilities Layout 438   Planning and Scheduling 440   Materials Management 440   Inventory Management 440

MANAGING PRODUCT AND SERVICE QUALITY 443
The History of Product Quality 444   Total Quality Management (TQM) 444 Managing Quality: Past and Future 446

18 Information Systems and Controlling   451

DEFINING DATA AND INFORMATION 453

THE IMPORTANCE OF INFORMATION SYSTEMS 455
Improving Productivity 456   Gaining Competitive Advantage 457 Information Systems and Computers 458

DIFFERENT TYPES OF COMPUTERS 459

TYPES OF INFORMATION SYSTEMS 460
Transaction Processing Systems 460   Office Automation Systems 460 Knowledge Work Systems 461   Management Information Systems 461 Decision Support Systems 461   Executive Support Systems 462   Expert Systems 462

PRIMARY INFORMATION SYSTEM COMPONENTS 463
Hardware 463   Software 464   Human Resources 465

IMPLEMENTING INFORMATION SYSTEMS 466
Step 1: Plan the Implementation Process 466   Step 2: Announce and Explain the Implementation Process 466   Step 3: Organize the Information System Staff 467 Step 4: Select the Hardware 468   Step 5: Prepare the Database 468   Step 6: Educate End-Users and Participants 468   Step 7: Prepare the Physical Facilities 468   Step 8: Convert to the Information System 468

HUMAN REACTIONS TO INFORMATION SYSTEMS 469

INFORMATION SYSTEMS IN THE 1990S 470
Managing Interdependence 470   Centralization Versus Decentralization 471 Outsourcing 472

COMPREHENSIVE CASE FOR PART V: CONTROLLING OPERATIONS AT THE ASAP CLINIC 478

22 Organizational Culture and Change   570

PART VIII
CASES USING
DECISION ASSISTANT
SOFTWARE   601

Acknowledgments

Cover © Jim Herity

Part I © Julie Houck/Westlight
7   © Rivera Collection/SuperStock International, Inc.
10   © Richard Braine/TSW-CLICK/Chicago
14   © S. Barth/H. Armstrong Roberts
31   Historical Pictures
34   Historical Pictures
38   Culver Pictures
57   Historical Pictures
59   © Tom Prettyman/PhotoEdit
61   © Lee Holden/Courtesy of Ben and Jerry's

Part II © Gregory Heisler/The Image Bank
84   © W. Rosin Malecki/PhotoEdit
87   Courtesy of Food Lion
89   © Tony Freeman/PhotoEdit
107   Courtesy of Kraft General Foods
111   (top) Courtesy of Cadillac Motor Division
111   (bottom) Courtesy of Chevrolet Motor Division

119   © Tony Freeman/PhotoEdit
135   © Michael Newman/PhotoEdit
139   Courtesy of Domino's Pizza
145   © Tony Freeman/PhotoEdit

Part III and Cover © Robert Mizono
162   © Charles Orrico/SuperStock International, Inc.
166   © Rivera Collection/SuperStock International, Inc.
172   © Mauritius/SuperStock International, Inc.
194   © Bruce Ayres/TSW-CLICK/Chicago
200   © Tim Brown/TSW-CLICK/Chicago
202   © Chuck Keeler/TSW-CLICK/Chicago
215   © Mark Richards/PhotoEdit
222   © Robert Llewellyn/SuperStock International, Inc.
230   © Herb Levart/SuperStock International, Inc.
243   © Charles Orrico/SuperStock International, Inc.
246   © David Young-Wolff/PhotoEdit

Part I
Introduction
to
Management

Chapter 1

The Nature and Challenge of Management

OPENING
CASE

Professor
Christine
Morrison's
Tuesday
Morning

7:55:   Christine Morrison, chair of the management department in a business school, arrived at her office, turned on her personal computer, and checked the day's appointment calendar.

8:00:   Made telephone calls to two people whom the management faculty wanted to hire. In response to inquiries, told both people more about the department's plans to develop internships for management majors.

8:12:   Learned from Shirley Bealls, the department's head secretary, that Professor Foster was often unavailable to students during his posted office hours. Scheduled an appointment with Foster to discuss the matter.

8:16:   Talked with a student who was dissatisfied with her business policy professor. Asked the student to prepare a written list of her concerns.

8:26:   Congratulated Sam Marquez on having his article accepted by a major academic journal.

8:30:   Worked on the department's schedule of classes for the fall semester. Penciled in classes for the two people who had interviewed for faculty positions, even though they had not formally accepted the department's offers.

8:45:   Saw Jack Crawford, head of the accounting department, in the hallway. Crawford asked for Morrison's support for his department's proposed 155-credit-hour, five-year accounting degree. Told Crawford that she would read his proposal and discuss it with the management faculty.

9:00:   Opened her Principles of Management class with a story about the successful practices of a local business firm. During class, remembered that she left material at home that she needed for an afternoon meeting.

9:58:   Arrived back in her office. Answered messages via her personal computer's electronic mail system. Made four telephone calls to organize a meeting of the department's business policy teachers. The purpose of the meeting was to determine how the policy course was to be taught.

10:25: Opened the mail. Gave several items to her secretary to distribute. Started revising a research manuscript.

10:36: After checking her schedule, informed sales representatives from two textbook companies that she could see them only after 4:00 P.M.

10:45: Visited with two faculty members who dropped by unexpectedly to discuss problems they were having with graduate assistants. Promised her colleagues that she would discuss their concerns with Dean Crouch, the school's new associate dean for graduate programs.

11:00: As chair, opened the semester's first meeting of the University Research Committee. Committee members disagreed sharply about the university's research role. Tried to steer the discussion so all opinions could be heard.

12:03: Arrived three minutes late for a luncheon with corporate recruiters. Told the recruiters of the department's plans to improve students' communications skills.

The work of managers is important to the success of all types of companies. Because of this, managers hold highly visible positions in their organizations. Chief executive officers (CEOs) of multinational corporations, convenience store managers, product group managers in large firms, construction supervisors, corporate vice presidents, and the president of the United States are all managers. As the chair of her college's management department, Christine Morrison, too, is a manager.

Morrison's Tuesday morning experiences are typical of managerial work, which is varied, fragmented, and difficult to plan and organize. Managing involves continual planning and problem solving, organizing, leading, controlling, and achieving objectives through the work of other people.

The activities listed in the opening case describe only one morning in Christine Morrison's work week. The challenges she faces and the work she completes on other days may be quite different. In addition, the specific tasks of a manager in a college or university department differ from those of people managing in other organizations.

Fortunately, even though their specific tasks vary, all managers share the functions of planning, organizing, leading, and controlling. Because of this, management skills can be learned and applied to varying people, organizations, and events. For example, as one of two co-founders of Seagate Technology, Finis F. Conner was very successful. A few years after leaving Seagate, he was instrumental in founding Conner Peripherals. In just four years, Conner Peripherals surpassed $1 billion in sales. No other publicly reporting startup business has reached this sales milestone as quickly.[1] Thus, it seems that Conner has effectively applied his managerial skills in two different companies. As another example, managers at the Coca-Cola Company used the planning, organizing, leading, and controlling skills they had acquired in other markets to successfully introduce their soft drink products in East Germany as soon as that market opened.[2]

Our study of management begins with a definition of the term. This is followed with a description of the resources managers use and a discussion of management's importance. Managerial skills and levels are explained, followed by an analysis of key management functions and managerial roles and behaviors. The chapter closes with an overview of the text.

In general, *Management & Organization* explores the successful practice of management in business firms. However, since virtually every concept and skill that we examine is also used in managing not-for-profit and charitable organizations, we include examples from such organizations as well.

A DEFINITION OF MANAGEMENT

Management is a complex process. Through management, managers coordinate the work of people with other resources. More formally, **management** is defined as the process of effectively and efficiently using an organization's resources to achieve objectives through the functions of planning, organizing, leading, and controlling. Successful management requires an understanding of how a firm operates. Managers must comprehend the individual components of a firm's activities in order to complete their tasks properly. For example, a manager must understand how the company's products—*goods* or *services*—are produced, financed, and distributed. The management process is shown in Figure 1-1.

Effectiveness and efficiency are especially crucial aspects of management. **Effectiveness** means that the right things are done to provide a product of value. **Efficiency** indicates that resources are used wisely and are not wasted.

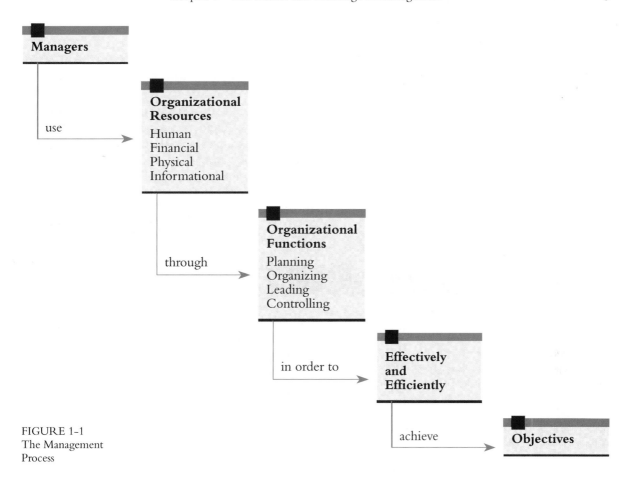

FIGURE 1-1
The Management
Process

The successful company is one that is both effective and efficient. As described in the Organization in Action, Wal-Mart's success suggests that it efficiently offers products that customers want to buy.

ORGANIZATION IN ACTION

At the end of 1990, Wal-Mart, with sales of $32.6 billion, became the nation's largest general merchandise retailer. Historically, this position had been held by Sears, Roebuck and Co. Because of its success, Wal-Mart was prepared to grow rapidly during the 1990s. This growth was to be accomplished primarily by opening stores in the Northeast in the early part of the 1990s.

Wal-Mart's performance suggests that it is both effective and efficient. Some believe that the keys to the company's success are the things that customers do not see, such as its relationships with suppliers and its distribution system. The efficient manner in which it acquires products and then distributes them to stores throughout the chain allows the company to offer products at prices below those of competitors. One analyst believes that Kmart is trying to do the same things that Wal-Mart does. However, Kmart is not as efficient at doing these things.

Sources: Adapted from Pat Baldwin, "Wal-Mart Ranks No. 1 in '90 With $32.6 Billion in Sales," *Dallas Morning News*, February 14, 1991; and Pat Baldwin, "Wal-Mart Not Discounting Future," *Dallas Morning News*, February 15, 1991.

Organizational Resources

The effective manager makes certain that employees work on jobs for which they are well trained and competent. The efficient manager constantly monitors how resources are used in order to minimize waste.[3] The resources available to a manager are human, financial, physical, and informational. Managerial success is determined principally by the degree to which managers coordinate these resources and then use them wisely to offer customers products they want.[4] Achieving this type of success in today's complex and global business environment is challenging. In part, managers must show employees how to welcome and adapt to constant change while helping them make extraordinary contributions.[5]

HUMAN RESOURCES. The one critical resource in all organizations is human resources. **Human resources** are the people through whom and with whom managers work to achieve objectives. The challenge to managers is to motivate each person to work as effectively and efficiently as possible. Managers must also make sure that human resources have the other resources they need to be productive.[6]

The nature of the workforce during the 1990s will be substantially different from the way it was in the past. For example, by the year 2000, as much as 25 percent of the workforce may work at home.[7] By the mid-1990s, only 15 percent of new workers in the U.S. workforce will be white males, while almost 42 percent will be white, U.S.-born females. The other 43 percent will be immigrants and U.S.-born minorities.[8] Dealing with this diversity of human resources in the 1990s and beyond will be a significant challenge to managers. One part of this challenge is to develop career track opportunities that are fair to and equal for all workforce members.[9]

Another challenge may be the integration of different types of leadership styles in organizations. The information presented in the Managers in Action describes a leadership style being used by some female managers. However, the style may also be used successfully by male managers.

ETHICS QUESTION
What ethical responsibilities do managers have to change their firms' practices so they will be consistent with the needs of different kinds of people entering the workforce?

MANAGERS IN ACTION

A new wave of women is now making it to the top of organizations. Instead of adopting male managerial styles, these individuals are drawing from their shared experiences as women to be successful. They are effectively using what traditionally have been thought of as "feminine" characteristics. It has been suggested that these female managers try harder than male managers do to get subordinates to care more about the group or organization than about their own interests. They use personal characteristics—including interpersonal skills, hard work, and personal contact—rather than organizational stature to establish this "interactive leadership" style. They devote much time to encouraging participation, sharing power and information, and enhancing others' self-worth.

Source: Adapted from Judy B. Rosener, "Ways Women Lead," *Harvard Business Review* (June 1991): 119–125.

FINANCIAL RESOURCES. **Financial resources** are all the monetary resources required to support a firm's current and future activities. These resources are used to acquire and maintain the company's human, physical, and informational resources.

For-profit companies acquire financial resources through investments made by stockholders, funds borrowed from banks and other financial institutions, and retained earnings. For governmental agencies, financial resources are provided by a local, state, and/or federal government's taxing authority. Donations serve as the source of financial resources for charitable organizations, churches, and other nonprofit firms.

Because no organization has as many financial resources as it would like, decisions must be made regarding how these limited resources will be used. In the early 1990s, for example, some major corporations (including General Motors, Citicorp, and Goodyear Tire & Rubber) decided to reduce the dividends paid to their stockholders and use the financial resources for other purposes.

PHYSICAL RESOURCES. A third group of resources managers use to accomplish objectives is known as **physical resources**. These include raw materials, land, buildings, furniture and office equipment, computers, machinery (including robots), and physical inventories. Clearly, physical resources are important to a firm's success. However, because a firm with adequate financial resources can buy the best physical equipment, educated human resources may be more important than physical resources.[10]

INFORMATIONAL RESOURCES. **Informational resources** are data that have been analyzed and converted into forms that help managers make effective decisions. To be useful, informational resources must be correct, timely, concise, and comprehensive. Examples of these resources include budgets, sales forecasts, economic forecasts, analyses of in-house training programs, and a host of other documents that help managers make decisions.

Today's complex markets call for skillful use of informational resources that are correct, timely, concise, and comprehensive.

ETHICS QUESTION
Are there limits as to how
managers should use
information to sell their
firms' goods or services? If
so, what are they?

In today's complex global markets, the skilled use of informational resources is necessary for a company's success.[11] For example, a financial institution's ability to sell additional products to current customers is very important. Known as *cross-selling*, this use of informational resources also occurs in other firms. Following the purchase of a washing machine on credit from a large retail store, a customer may receive an offer to purchase a long-term maintenance contract. The store may also encourage the customer to purchase an insurance policy that pays the account in full in the event of the signer's death or disability. Part of American Airlines' success has been attributed to the sophisticated use of a key informational resource—SABRE, the company's reservation system. The company has used this huge centralized computer system to book passenger reservations in a highly efficient manner.[12]

Organizational resources are often closely related. For example, the effective and efficient use of financial resources is influenced by human resources' understanding of international financial markets. Sophisticated computer systems may be needed to convert data into useful information. Human resources can achieve maximum productivity only when they have access to appropriate types of physical resources. The challenge to managers is to recognize the overlap among resources while valuing the importance of each.

Back to the Opening Case

Christine Morrison used various organizational resources on Tuesday morning. Her office, the classroom in which she taught, and the building where she held a meeting are physical resources. Morrison used her personal computer to prepare an examination, work on her research paper, and transmit information via the electronic mail system. She used financial resources to purchase these physical resources. Morrison used informational resources to tell prospective faculty members and recruiters about particular departmental plans.

LEARNING CHECK

Describe the four major organizational resources and offer examples of each.

The Importance of Management

Managers provide direction in all kinds of organizations—business, governmental, educational, religious, and service. Through these efforts, societal, organizational, and individual employees' objectives are achieved. Thus, managerial work is critical to everyone interested in the welfare of individual organizations and a society in general. Effective managers may be one of a developed country's most valuable resources, and they are one of the most needed resources in less developed countries.[13] A nation's standard of living is influenced by the quality of its managers' work. Because of this important responsibility, top-level managers are paid well, typically through stock options and other long-term investments as well as salary. The compensation of top-level executives is discussed in the Managers in Action.

MANAGERS IN ACTION

A survey of executive pay revealed that seven top-level managers were paid at least $10 million in 1989. Michael D. Eisner, CEO of Walt Disney, received $35.41 million. Others receiving large sums were James Wood of A&P ($28.16 million); Martin S. Davis of Paramount ($17.16 million); and Paul B. Fireman of Reebok International ($14.61 million). These figures are certainly large. However, it is perhaps more interesting to note that the average 1989 pay for the CEOs of 200 companies drawn from the largest firms on Fortune's Industrial 500 and Service 500 lists was $2.8 million. This average is dramatic in that the watch for the first $2 million CEO started only in the mid-1980s.

Source: Adapted from Graef S. Crystal, "The Great CEO Pay Sweepstakes," *Fortune* (June 18, 1990): 94–102.

Are top-level executives paid too much? Some people think there is a point beyond which pay for CEOs becomes excessive. Peter Drucker argued that upper limits should be placed on managerial incomes.[14] One analyst suggested that because of inflation and a tendency of executives to change jobs and companies frequently, compensation relationships have an Alice-in-Wonderland quality.[15] Finally, it is possible for upper-level salaries to get out of line if compensation committees fail to develop and enforce strict pay-for-performance guidelines.[16]

ETHICS QUESTION
Is there a limit to the level of compensation CEOs should receive? If so, what is it?

Thus, the pay a company's highest level manager should receive and how that pay should be calculated are controversial issues.[17] What is less controversial is the importance of this position to a company's success. Given the complexity of today's managerial challenges, it is possible that even the highest paid managers are not overpaid. Many top athletes and other entertainers earn much more than top-level managers.

MANAGERIAL SKILLS

Managers need different combinations of skills to manage organizations successfully. It is widely believed that all managers must possess three types of skills—technical, interpersonal, and conceptual—if they are to be effective and efficient.[18] The relative importance of these skills depends on the manager's level within the organization.

Technical Skills

Technical skills are the skills required to complete specialized tasks. The manager of a hospital's diagnostic laboratory uses technical skills to determine the accuracy of a subordinate's work. Data processing managers apply their technical skills when planning the solution of information-based problems. The foreman on a construction job uses technical skills to examine the structural soundness of a building. When consulting with faculty about their courses, Professor Morrison relies on her technical skills. Managerial careers usually begin in positions where technical expertise is required.

Managers usually begin their careers in positions requiring sound technical skills. Here, the foreman of a construction job—who is a first-level manager—goes over plans with the building's architect.

Interpersonal Skills

Interpersonal skills are the abilities needed to work successfully with other people. Managers must be able to understand and respond to others' concerns and needs. They must motivate and encourage employees and be able to deal with diversity in the workforce. Also, it is important for managers to recognize when they have asked too much of their employees and whether too many employees have become "workaholics."[19]

Conceptual Skills

At the highest levels, managers focus on an entire company rather than a single unit. They need **conceptual skills**—those that involve the ability to think in abstract terms—to simplify complex situations and determine a course of action. Conceptual skills are also necessary to determine an organization's mission and to communicate clearly how that mission will be accomplished.[20] Using conceptual skills, managers see relationships among parts of a company that others may not see. In addition, these skills allow managers to identify marketplace opportunities and what to do to take advantage of them quickly. The addition of women's clothing lines in a local men's clothing store is an example of a decision reached through conceptual skills. Conceptual skills were also used by Ford Motor Company managers when they decided to purchase 25 percent of the Mazda Corporation.

Today, it is important for managers to learn how to use their technical, interpersonal, and conceptual skills in global settings. Many companies, such as Procter & Gamble, Colgate Palmolive, and GE, have developed intensive programs to help their younger managers learn global skills. These programs involve cross-cultural training, study of foreign languages, and trips to foreign countries.[21]

MANAGERIAL LEVELS

An important way in which management jobs vary is by organizational level. Managerial work is commonly divided into three levels—top, middle, and first. As shown in Figure 1-2, top-, middle-, and first-level managers use different combinations of managerial skills to accomplish their jobs. Note that conceptual skills are the most critical for top-level managers, while technical skills are the most important for first-level managers. Note, too, that while interpersonal skills are the most critical for middle-level managers, they are also very important for top- and first-level managers. In other words, *all* managers must be able to work successfully with people.

Top-Level Managers

Only a few people in each organization are top-level managers. Chief executive officer, president, and vice president are examples of titles often used for top-level managers. James Preston, CEO of Avon, is a top-level manager, as is Harold Shapiro, the president of Princeton University.

Top-level managers are accountable for an organization's overall performance. They are responsible for the development of a company's mission, its strategies, and its major operating policies. Top-level managers represent their companies in frequent contacts with governmental agencies, executives in other organizations, key suppliers, and important customers. Typically, they work long hours to complete these challenging tasks.[22] The Managers in Action shows that a few successful executives in one particular industry choose to retire at young ages. While the reasons for these retirements vary, pressures of life "at the top" may play an important role in such a decision.

FIGURE 1-2
The Importance of
Managerial Skills by
Managerial Levels

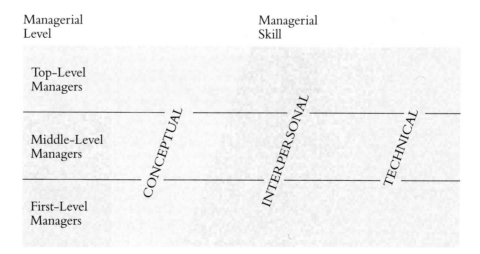

MANAGERS IN ACTION

The computer and telecommunications industries are filled with rapid change and difficult competition. In looking at employment patterns in these industries, one analyst concluded that "nobody works to age 65 anymore." But why are some of these top-level managers either taking long-term sabbaticals (at the age of 37, for example) or retiring at the relatively young age of 55? Their reasons are varied. Some wish to pursue "once-in-a-life-time opportunities" elsewhere. Others, citing even more personal reasons, desire to "put their lives in perspective," "turn down the intensity level," and/or "smell the roses." Sometimes the top-level manager's financial success makes the decision to retire early possible. With good returns from retirement programs and various savings and investments plans, some executives can retire without undue worry about their financial future.

Source: Adapted from Tom Steinert-Threlkeld, "Walking Away From It All," *Dallas Morning News* (February 10, 1991).

Middle-Level Managers

All managers between first-level managers and top-level managers are middle-level managers. The manager of a manufacturing plant, the dean of a business school, and the manager of a hospital nursing unit are examples.

Middle-level managers are responsible for making the visions and strategies of top-level managers fit with the operational realities faced by first-level managers. Because of advances in computer technology, middle-level managers now receive, process, and distribute information much more rapidly than was the case in the past. These advances aid their efforts to integrate the intentions of top-level managers with the day-to-day problems experienced by first-level managers in producing a good or service. Middle-level managers often have a substantial impact on a company's effectiveness and efficiency. For example, these managers could process and distribute information in ways that would create delays in implementing a new strategy.[23]

First-Level Managers

First-level managers supervise the work of all nonmanagerial, or operating-level, employees such as sales representatives, engineers, secretaries, and physical laborers. In addition to *supervisor*, other common titles for first-level managers are *foreman* and *department manager*.

Although their titles vary, first-level managers in different organizations have similar responsibilities. For example, first-level managers in a candy manufacturing plant are responsible for how effectively and efficiently work groups manufacture a particular candy. A professional baseball team's equipment manager is accountable for players' uniforms, team bats and balls, and all other items required to play baseball. The director of a church choir must balance the limited amount of time available from volunteers with the congregation's needs for music. In many organizations, first-level managers are chosen from the ranks of operating-level employees.

The first-level manager's job is likely to change dramatically during the 1990s.[24] For one thing, increasing levels of education and computerization may affect how first-level managers supervise their employees. With greater levels of education, operating-level employees likely will want to be more involved with decisions regarding how their work is to be accomplished. First-level managers will have to respond to this call. On the other hand, some operating-level employees will be much less educated than their counterparts, with poor academic and job-skill training. First-level managers will be challenged to solicit productive work from these relatively unprepared workers. Finally, with access to sophisticated computer technology, first-level managers will have greater opportunities to determine increasingly efficient ways to produce products. The challenge for top- and middle-level managers is to ensure that first-level managers have the support and resources they need to deal with these conditions.

We have seen that top-, middle-, and first-level managers are responsible for different types of activities. However, the important work that must be completed at each managerial level cannot be accomplished without the support of managers at the other two levels. The outcomes of first-level managers' work are influenced significantly by the quality of the informational resources they receive from middle-level managers and by the human, physical, and financial resources provided by top-level managers. Similarly, middle-level managers cannot complete their jobs without high-quality *information* from first-level managers and *direction* from top-level managers. In today's organizations, it is critical that differences among managers be based on strategic factors rather than strictly social distinctions.[25]

LEARNING CHECK

Describe why management is important; the three critical managerial skills; and the differences among top-, middle-, and first-level managers.

WHAT MANAGERS DO

We are now prepared to discuss the managerial job—that is, what managers do—in terms of functions and roles. Each perspective provides a better understanding of the work of a manager.

Functions of Management

Management functions describe a manager's actual work-related activities. The functional view of managerial work is grounded in Henri Fayol's belief that a company's administrative operations are accomplished through the planning, organizing, coordinating, commanding, and controlling functions.[26] (Fayol's work is described in detail in Chapter 2.) The functional view suggests that these functions describe the work managers complete in all types of organizations. In this text, we combine the coordinating and commanding functions to form the leading function. We believe

A manager's activities include the functions of planning, organizing, leading, and controlling

that a manager's activities can be described in terms of planning, organizing, leading, and controlling.

PLANNING. To be successful, organizations must know what they are trying to accomplish, both today and in the future. **Planning** is a process that identifies objectives and the commitments, resources, and actions required for their achievement. Through planning, managers forecast the future and determine courses of action necessary for the firm to be successful in that future. Effective planning involves a range of activities, including understanding the company's present capabilities and the opportunities available to it. Through effective planning, managers select meaningful objectives, make decisions about how resources will be acquired and allocated, select strategies, and establish controls. Planning is the primary managerial function. As such, it influences how managers complete the organizing, leading, and controlling functions.

Planning is necessary in all organizations. For example, a church with a current average weekly attendance of 1,325 worshippers may decide to pursue the objective of having an average weekly attendance of 2000 worshippers by the year 2000. Once it has established this objective, the church must choose plans that will help achieve it. Similarly, top-level managers at General Motors might establish the objective of gaining and then holding 44.5 percent of the domestic automobile market. They must develop plans that show how to use resources efficiently in the pursuit of that objective.

ORGANIZING. **Organizing** is concerned with how work and responsibilities are grouped. When organizing, managers establish authority and responsibility relationships and form work groups. The organizing function also determines the manner in which human, physical, financial, and informational resources are coordinated, thereby establishing the proper balance of resources between and among a firm's divisions.

Different managers have different organizing responsibilities. Top-level managers organize a company's work into major units, divisions, or departments. For example, Rockwell International's work is organized into four major sectors: aerospace, automotive, electronics, and graphics. A middle-level manager for the propulsion and power group in the aerospace sector is responsible for the organization of work, responsibilities, and resource allocations within that unit. As managers of individual work teams in the propulsion and power group, first-level managers are responsible for obtaining, organizing, and using resources efficiently to accomplish their units' objectives.[27]

LEADING. High-quality leadership is becoming increasingly critical to both an organization's and a society's success. In fact, today's companies may be relatively "overmanaged and underled."[28] **Leading** is the process of activating and directing other people's efforts toward accomplishment of organizational and personal objectives. When leading, managers assign tasks, delegate authority and responsibility, ask for cooperation, deal with conflict, use motivation techniques, and develop effective communication channels.

The 1990s may be an era in which managers should lead primarily through inspiration,[29] establishing a vision that is meaningful to all employees. To be effective, a vision must reflect how the organization is unique and inspire employees to become fully involved with its efforts.[30] The focus of the vision will vary from one firm to another. For example, Xerox's vision and leadership practices are grounded in a continuous commitment to increasing levels of product quality.[31] The vision for Eastman Kodak is to be the world's best company in chemical and electronic imaging.[32]

There are other accomplishments that will be associated with successful leadership in the 1990s. Examples include determining ways to help employees cope with change and continuously developing challenging opportunities for young employees.[33] Additionally, managers should recognize that leadership is a bidirectional process. Good leading depends on good following from those being led. Thus, success as a leader requires patience, insight, perseverance, and commitment and dedication from others. Managers have expectations of those they lead while those being led have expectations of their leaders. The Employees in Action describes what followers expect from their leaders.

EMPLOYEES IN ACTION

Based on the results of a survey conducted over a six-year period, two researchers identified characteristics that followers expect from their leaders. Most important, followers want to work for leaders who are honest, competent, forward-looking, and inspiring. Honest leaders are those who have done what they told followers they would do. In addition to having a successful track record, competent leaders challenge, enable, and encourage followers. *Vision*, *personal agenda*, and *dream* are examples of words used by followers to describe what the forward-looking leader possesses. In general, this person has a sense of direction and a concern for the company's future. Finally, the inspiring leader is seen as enthusiastic, energetic, and positive about the future.

Source: Adapted from James M. Kouzes and Barry Z. Posner, "What Followers Expect from Their Leaders," *Management Review* (January 1990): 29–33.

CONTROLLING. **Controlling** ensures that, through effective leading, what has been planned and organized to take place has in fact taken place. When planned objectives are not reached, corrective actions are chosen and implemented. Separate controls are prepared to ensure achievement of all objectives included in various plans. The controlling process consists of six stages: knowledge of strategies and plans, determining a performance standard, measuring actual performance, comparing actual performance with the performance standard, evaluating deviations, and initiating corrective actions. The controlling process and each of these stages are discussed in detail in Chapter 15.

. . . .

Back to the
Opening Case

As a first-level manager, Christine Morrison plans, organizes, leads, and controls. As shown in the description of her Tuesday morning, Morrison, the planner, was involved with plans designed to improve management students' communication skills and to develop internships. As organizer, she scheduled a meeting with the business policy teachers to organize how the course was to be taught. As leader, she talked with prospective faculty, visited with Jack Crawford, and held several meetings. As controller, she arranged to meet with Professor Foster to clarify the department's office hour policy.

. . . .

The relationship between planning and controlling demonstrates the interactions among the four management functions. First, through planning, important objectives are chosen and the actions necessary for their achievement are determined. On a continuous basis, controls (such as a budget, for example) are used to move the organization efficiently along a chosen path. Feedback from different controls is then used to modify original plans. Thus, we see that the management functions can be separated only for the purposes of discussion. In actual practice, they are highly interrelated. The interdependence among the four management functions is shown in Figure 1-3.

FIGURE 1-3
Interrelationships Among
Management Functions

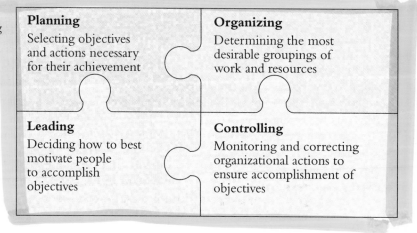

Planning
Selecting objectives
and actions necessary
for their achievement

Organizing
Determining the most
desirable groupings of
work and resources

Leading
Deciding how to best
motivate people
to accomplish
objectives

Controlling
Monitoring and correcting
organizational actions to
ensure accomplishment of
objectives

Clearly, studying the functions of management helps us to understand what managers do and how they do it. Despite some controversy, there is strong evidence that managerial activities can be described as those related to planning, organizing, leading, and controlling.[34] However, viewing management from the perspective of managerial roles, as well as management functions, provides a richer understanding of what managers do.

LEARNING CHECK

Describe a manager's work in terms of the planning, organizing, leading, and controlling functions.

Managerial Roles and Behaviors

A manager's work is sometimes difficult to describe fully in terms of planning, organizing, leading, and controlling. For example, which function are managers fulfilling when they represent their company at the local Lions Club or chair the local United Way campaign? Which function describes managers' discussions with employees about their families' welfare? When examining the impact of proposed legislation with government officials, are managers planning, organizing, leading, or controlling? What function was Professor Morrison involved with when she congratulated Sam Marquez on the acceptance of an article for journal publication?

To better understand managerial work, we can study the observations of those who have actually watched managers work. Henry Mintzberg carefully gathered information about managers and their organizations before starting his research. With this information as background, Mintzberg then observed every minute of managers' workdays over a period of time. He recorded their verbal contacts as well as their incoming and outgoing mail.

BASIC MANAGERIAL ROLES. Based on the results of his study, Mintzberg concluded that managerial work can be described meaningfully by three categories of interrelated roles.[35] He saw the manager's job as a series of roles that leads to accomplishment of objectives. Top-, middle-, and first-level managers engage in all three role categories. The three major categories of roles—interpersonal, informational, and decisional—are shown in Figure 1-4. A total of ten roles included in these categories fully describes the manager's work.

Managers have *interpersonal roles* because of the formal authority attached to their positions; they interact with many different people. In their interpersonal roles, managers develop relationships with other people and groups to receive and transmit information. In their *informational roles*, managers act as "nerve centers" for information and as focal points for communications. Because of their relationships and involvement with information, managers also have *decisional roles*.

ETHICS QUESTION
Because of their interpersonal and informational roles, are managers ethically responsible for decisions made by their firms?

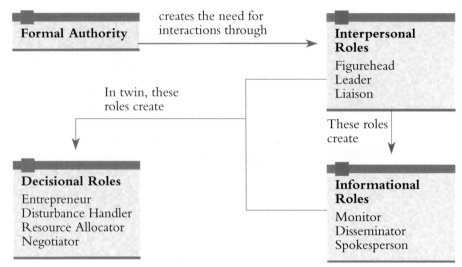

Source: Adapted from Henry Mintzberg, *The Nature of Managerial Work* (New York: Harper and Row, 1973), 54–93.

Interpersonal Roles. Three roles comprise the interpersonal role category. In the *figurehead* role, managers make speeches, give awards to employees, and perform other ceremonial duties. They formally represent their company to people both inside and outside the firm. In the *leader* role, managers motivate, inspire, and set examples through their own behavior. This role is also the one through which managers design jobs and develop authority and responsibility relationships. When dealing with people outside the company, managers engage in their *liaison* role, representing the company's needs to those who can satisfy those needs. Bankers are an example of a group with whom managers interact in this role.

Informational Roles. The first of the three informational roles is the *monitor* role, in which managers watch for valuable data and information. Because of the number and diversity of their interpersonal relationships, managers are uniquely qualified to recognize the relative value of different pieces of information. Through the *disseminator* role, managers route information to various internal and external groups. The *spokesperson* role is related to the figurehead role. When serving as a spokesperson, which they do often during ceremonies, managers make presentations that represent their firms' positions.

Decisional Roles. This category includes four individual roles. As an *entrepreneur*, a manager searches for new opportunities for the firm to pursue and then initiates and authorizes the actions necessary to pursue those opportunities. In the *disturbance handler* role, managers decide how to resolve issues that are preventing the firm from accomplishing its objectives. In the *resource allocator* role, managers approve budgets and, in general, decide how resources will be allocated among competing alternatives. Finally, in the *negotiator* role, managers bargain with employees, suppliers, customers, and other parties important to the firm's success. The objective of these negotiations is to work out agreements that best serve the organization's needs.

BEHAVIORS OF EFFECTIVE GENERAL MANAGERS. John Kotter studied the work-related behaviors of fifteen effective general managers.[36] The results of his study provide us with an expanded understanding of managerial behavior. A **general manager** is responsible for more than a single function, such as marketing, finance, or accounting. Both top- and middle-level managers can be general managers. A firm's size and how it is organized determine who is a general manager. The manager of a large manufacturing plant is a general manager, as is your local community's city manager.

Kotter found that general managers interact and communicate frequently with people inside and outside the firm. He also found that effective general managers work long hours (an average of just under 60 hours per week); spend most of their time with others (up to 90 percent in some instances); engage in short, disjointed conversations with other people; and react often to other people's initiatives.

Agendas and networks are critical to a general manager's effectiveness. An **agenda** is the grouping of the general manager's goals and plans. Examples might include product quality and service, efficient use of resources, innovation programs, and employee development or morale. Because of job complexity, these goals and plans change continuously.

The effective use of networks is linked with the accomplishment of goals and plans. A **network** is a group of people cooperating with one another to achieve organizational and personal goals. Managers use these cooperative relationships to accomplish goals and plans on their agendas.

As our discussion of roles, agendas, and networks shows, managerial behavior is complex and challenging. However, while differences exist, there are remarkable similarities in the work-related behaviors of top-, middle-, and first-level managers.[37] In general, the following comments describe managerial behaviors:

- Managers work at an unrelenting pace. They never catch up.
- Managerial work is characterized by brevity, variety, and fragmentation.
- Managers prefer brief, specific, well-defined activities that are current and nonroutine.
- Managers prefer oral to written communications; that is, they prefer telephone calls and meetings to mail.
- Managers cultivate a vast number of contacts. The intent is to link people inside and outside the firm in ways that contribute to organizational success.
- A great deal of managerial work is initiated by others. It is difficult for managers to control their own schedules and workloads.

ETHICS QUESTION
Is it ethical for managers to form and use networks of people to accomplish their goals and objectives?

LEARNING CHECK   Describe managerial work in terms of roles, agendas, and networks.

к to the
Ɔpening Case

Notice that Professor Morrison's behaviors on Tuesday morning were consistent with those described in this part of the chapter. Her work, which was at an unrelenting pace, was characterized by brevity, variety, and fragmentation. Morrison was involved primarily with verbal conversations (in the form of telephone calls and both scheduled and unscheduled meetings). Notice also that much of her work on that morning was initiated by others.

OUTLINE FOR THE BOOK

The principal purpose of Part I of *Management & Organization* is to introduce you to management. In this first chapter, the definition of management was expanded by studying management functions and managerial roles. The historical foundations of management are examined in Chapter 2. Chapter 3 discusses managerial ethics and corporate social responsibilities and the critical role these play in today's organizations.

The text's contents are presented within the framework of the four management functions. The planning function is the focus of Part II. Because planning involves making decisions, Chapter 4 focuses on the decision-making process. With this information as a background, the fundamentals of planning (Chapter 5) and strategic management and strategic planning (Chapter 6) are then discussed. Today, strategic management and strategic planning play increasingly important roles in a firm's success.

Part III focuses on the organizing function. Chapter 7 discusses how work is divided as well as the various structures used by organizations. Chapter 8 covers authority and power and techniques related to their effective use. The final aspects of the organizing function are treated through analysis of delegation (Chapter 9) and staffing (Chapter 10).

Part IV examines the leading function through discussions of various leadership styles and practices (Chapter 11), techniques used to motivate people toward goal accomplishment (Chapter 12), and the role of effective interpersonal and organizational communications (Chapter 13). The part closes with a discussion of what managers can do to deal with ineffective performances (Chapter 14), an important topic in today's complex work environments.

Controlling, the fourth of the functions, is the focus of Part V. Control principles are discussed in Chapter 15 and then used as a foundation to examine specific control methods and techniques in Chapter 16. Chapter 17 considers the role of operations management in the controlling function. Chapter 18 studies the significance of a firm's management information system to the controlling function.

Part VI addresses the practice of management in special settings. Chapter 19 examines entrepreneurship, while Chapter 20 discusses issues of international management.

Finally, matters related to the development and management of your career and organization culture and change are described in Part VII.

SUMMARY

Managerial work is complex and challenging. Although management differs somewhat across organizations, many similarities exist. Because of these similarities, studying management allows us to gain skills necessary to practice management effectively in organizations of all types.

Management is the process of using organizational resources—human, financial, physical, and informational—to achieve objectives through the functions of planning, organizing, leading, and controlling. In today's environments, it is necessary for firms to be effective (do the right things) and efficient (do things right). Ultimately, managerial effectiveness is determined by managers' ability to use interrelated resources efficiently in the accomplishment of objectives. Effective and efficient management practices are critical to the well-being of individuals, organizations, and societies.

Managerial work involves the use of technical, interpersonal, and conceptual skills. Managers need specialized knowledge of technical skills to produce a good or service. They require interpersonal skills to communicate with and motivate people. They use conceptual skills to determine a firm's mission and objectives and the plans that will ensure their accomplishment.

The technical, interpersonal, and conceptual skills have relative levels of importance for top-, middle-, and first-level managers. Top-level managers, for example, use conceptual skills to determine the course of action for the entire firm. Interpersonal skills are critical to middle-level managers' efforts to integrate the desires of top-level managers with the realities faced by first-level managers. First-level managers use technical skills to help the firm manufacture its goods or services effectively and efficiently.

The work of a manager can be examined from two perspectives: management functions and managerial roles and behaviors. The management functions view suggests that managers engage in planning, organizing, leading, and controlling in order to complete their work.

Henry Mintzberg found that managers complete their work through interpersonal, informational, and decisional roles. Through interpersonal roles, they represent their organizations as figurehead, leader, and liaison official. Because of their unique positions, managers are able to monitor and then disseminate information to appropriate parties and serve as spokespersons in their informational roles. Finally, managers are responsible for making decisions. Their decisional roles include entrepreneur, disturbance handler, resource allocator, and negotiator.

John Kotter's study of the behaviors of effective general managers yielded findings similar to those of Mintzberg. Effective managers form agendas (goals and plans) and use networks (groups of cooperating people) to accomplish tasks. Combining our understanding of managerial roles and behaviors indicates that a manager's work is varied, fragmented, relentless, and grounded in verbal rather than written communications.

KEY TERMS

management	informational resources	first-level managers	general manager
effectiveness	technical skills	management functions	agenda
efficiency	interpersonal skills	planning	network
human resources	conceptual skills	organizing	
financial resources	top-level managers	leading	
physical resources	middle-level managers	controlling	

QUESTIONS FOR DISCUSSION AND REVIEW

1. Describe the four basic organizational resources.
2. Why is the work of managers important to an entire society?
3. Describe the three major skills managers use to be successful.
4. List the three primary levels of management and discuss the managerial skill that is most critical at each level.
5. Describe a manager's work in terms of four management functions.
6. Describe the three categories of major roles managers perform in their work.
7. Discuss some of the behaviors of effective general managers. If you have worked with a manager who displayed these behaviors, describe your reactions.

PROBLEMS FOR ACTION

A. At age 17, Ralph McPherson dropped out of high school. At first, the only jobs he could find were those paying minimum wage. Finally, he accepted an entry-level position at the Perry Company, a diversified company. The unit in which Ralph worked manufactured customized products such as bumpers, grills, and tool boxes for trucks. After five years with this unit, Ralph was promoted to supervisor of the night crew. He was successful in this position, even though he was not fond of being responsible for other people's work. One day, Ray Perry, owner of the company, asked him to become the general manager for the plant. In this position, Ralph would be a middle-level manager. Use the three managerial skills to describe the differences between the skills Ralph has used as a first-level manager and those he would need as a middle-level manager.

B. This chapter described managerial work in terms of levels, functions, and work roles. On the basis of that information, what personal characteristics, interests, and abilities do you think would be ideal for a college sophomore considering a management career?

CONCLUDING CASE

Batavia National Bank's New President

Six months had passed since her appointment to the presidency of Batavia National Bank. In thinking about her experiences as the bank's president, Barbara Ralston concluded that she had encountered few, if any, surprises. After all, Ralston had lived her entire life in the small community (population approximately 14,500) served by the bank. Beginning with the summer months between her junior and senior years in high school, Ralston held various jobs in the bank. Upon completion of her finance degree at a major state university, she returned to the bank. Starting as a credit analyst, she had, at one time or another, worked in all of the bank's departments.

As president, Ralston decided to delegate certain decision-making responsibilities to two senior vice presidents. At first, she had thought this would not be necessary. However, as president, it was hard for her to find the time required to stay current with important trends in the bank's two primary market segments—commercial and consumer lending. One reason for this was her commitment to the local community. Because she believed the bank had an obligation to serve the local community, Ralston readily accepted requests to speak at local Lions and Rotary Clubs and various schools. In addition, she had recently agreed to serve on the boards of several charitable organizations.

Complicating her worklife was a request from the bank's board of directors. Actually, Ralston supported the board's request that a five-year strategic plan be developed. In fact, one of her concerns was that the bank did not have formal plans. She believed that such plans were necessary for the bank to compete more effectively. For example, Ralston felt that the bank's data processing capabilities were unacceptable. Based on her knowledge of what some other banks were doing with information generated through sophisticated computer systems, Ralston felt that Batavia was at a competitive disadvantage. A strategic plan, she thought, would help the bank correct this problem.

To start the planning effort, Ralston appointed a task force. Active members of the local community and several bank employees accepted invitations to serve. She was not certain the original group was the right combination of people. As necessary, she thought, other people would be asked to join the task force.

Ralston was also quite involved with implementing Batavia's new performance appraisal system. Developed by a group of outside consultants, the three-months-old system was the bank's first attempt to

formally appraise employees' performances. Employees were uncertain about how their performances would now be evaluated. Ralston knew that implementing this system would be a challenge.

Although she was extremely busy, Ralston looked forward to the challenges ahead for her and the bank. Sometimes, however, she wondered how much longer she could work at her current pace. She arrived at her desk by 6:30 A.M. and usually did not go home until 7:00 or 7:30 P.M. When she did leave the office, she always carried a briefcase filled with important projects and mail that had not been opened. After spending an hour or so working at home, Ralston felt better prepared to return to her office early the next morning.

1. What managerial skills are the most important for Barbara Ralston to use as president of the Batavia National Bank?
2. Discuss Ralston's work activities in terms of management functions.
3. How do Henry Mintzberg's and John Kotter's studies help in describing Ralston's job as president of Batavia National Bank?

REFERENCES

1. Andrew Kupfer, "America's Fastest-Growing Company," *Fortune* (August 13, 1990): 48–54.

2. Patricia Sellers, "Coke Gets Off Its Can in Europe," *Fortune* (August 13, 1990): 67–74.

3. Patricia Sellers, "What Customers Really Want," *Fortune* (June 4, 1990): 58–68.

4. Fred Luthans, "Successful vs. Effective Real Managers," *Academy of Management Executive* (May 1988): 127–132.

5. Fred G. Steingraber, "Managing in the 1990s," *Business Horizons* (January–February 1990): 50–61.

6. T. J. Rodgers, "No Excuses Management," *Harvard Business Review* (July–August 1990): 84–98.

7. Richard I. Kirkland, "Get Ready for a New World of Work," *Fortune* (February 11, 1991): 139.

8. Mark McLaughlin, "A Change of Mind," *New England Business* (April 1989): 42–53.

9. Felice N. Schwartz, "Management Women and the New Facts of Life," *Harvard Business Review* (January–February 1989): 65–76.

10. Robert B. Reich, "The Real Economy," *The Atlantic* (February 1991): 35–52.

11. James P. Womack, Daniel T. Jones, and Daniel Roos, *The Machine That Changed the World* (New York: Rawson Associates, 1990).

12. Max D. Hopper, "Rattling SABRE: New Ways to Compete on Information," *Harvard Business Review* (May–June 1990): 118–125.

13. Peter F. Drucker, "Management's New Role," *Harvard Business Review* (November–December 1969): 54.

14. Peter F. Drucker, "Management: The Problems of Success," *Academy of Management Executive* (January 1987): 16.

15. Arch Patton, "Why So Many Chief Executives Make Too Much," *Business Week* (October 17, 1983): 24–26.

16. Jaclyn Fierman, "The People Who Set the CEO's Pay," *Fortune* (March 12, 1990): 58–66, and Geoffrey Colvin, "How to Pay the CEO Right," *Fortune* (April 16, 1992): 61–69.

17. Michael C. Jensen and Kevin J. Murphy, "CEO Incentives: It's Not How Much You Pay, But How," *Harvard Business Review* (May–June 1990): 138–153.

18. Robert L. Katz, "Skills of an Effective Administrator," *Harvard Business Review* (September–October 1974): 90–102.

19. R. Roosevelt Thomas, "From Affirmative Action to Affirming Diversity," *Harvard Business Review* (March–April 1990): 107–117; Brian O'Reilly, "Is Your Company Asking Too Much?" *Fortune* (March 12, 1990): 39–46; Walter Kiechel, "Workaholics Anonymous," *Fortune* (August 14, 1989): 117–118.

20. R. Duane Ireland and Michael A. Hitt, "Mission Statements: Importance, Challenge, and Recommendations for Development," *Business Horizons* (May 1992): 34–42.

21. Joann S. Lublin, "Younger Managers Learn Global Skills," *The Wall Street Journal* (March 31, 1992): B1.

22. "How Hard Do Executives Work?" *Fortune* (November 19, 1990): 214.

23. William D. Guth and Ian C. MacMillan, "Strategy Implementation Versus Middle Management Self-Interest," *Strategic Management Journal* (July–August 1986): 313–327.

24. Steven Kerr, Kenneth D. Hill, and Laurie Broedling, "The First-Line Supervisor: Phasing Out or Here to Stay?" *Academy of*

Management Review (January 1986): 103–117.

25. Rosabeth Moss Kanter, "How to Compete," *Harvard Business Review* (July-August 1990): 7–8.

26. Henri Fayol, *General and Industrial Management* (London: Pitman, 1949).

27. This information is drawn from Rockwell International's *1990 Annual Report*.

28. John P. Kotter, "What Leaders Really Do," *Harvard Business Review* (May-June 1990): 103–111.

29. Jay A. Conger, "Inspiring Others: The Language of Leadership," *Academy of Management Executive* (February 1991): 31–45.

30. Abraham Zaleznik, "The Leadership Gap," *Academy of Management Executive* (February 1990): 7–22.

31. David Kearns, "Leadership Through Quality," *Academy of Management Executive* (May 1990): 86–89.

32. This information is drawn from the Eastman Kodak Company's *1989 Annual Report*.

33. Kotter, "What Leaders Really Do."

34. Stephen J. Carroll and Dennis J. Gillen, "Are the Classical Management Functions Useful in Describing Managerial Work?" *Academy of Management Review* (January 1987): 38–51.

35. Henry Mintzberg, *The Nature of Managerial Work* (New York: Harper and Row, 1973); and Henry Mintzberg, "The Manager's Job: Folklore and Fact," *Harvard Business Review* (July-August 1975): 49–61.

36. John P. Kotter, *The General Managers* (New York: The Free Press, 1982).

37. Mintzberg, *The Nature of Managerial Work*.

Chapter 2

The History of Management Thought and Practice

Tracy Gordy was discouraged. Although she was still committed to her job, recent events caused her to question her managerial abilities. While in college, Gordy rarely thought about what she would have to do to be an effective manager. Thinking it was important to acquire an entry-level skill, she chose a computer science major with a minor in business. Managing people, she was certain, would not be difficult.

After graduation, Gordy accepted a job as a systems analyst at a local bank. Eager to learn and do well, she worked long hours and maintained close relationships with her superiors. Gordy's early promotion to a first-level managerial position showed how well she was doing. As a project team leader, she managed nine people.

Gordy quickly discovered that managing people was not easy. She did not know exactly why, but for some reason her people were not working well together. Part of the problem, Gordy thought, might have been the differences among their jobs. Those writing computer programs had relatively structured tasks. Their work seemed somewhat routine and predictable. In contrast, those matching computer users' needs with the bank's computer systems' capabilities faced different challenges with each assignment.

Gordy concluded that she had much to learn about management if she was to be a successful project team leader. She was convinced that the problems facing her were not unique. Surely, she thought, a great deal had been learned about effective management by others who had faced similar problems.

To discuss this matter, Gordy scheduled a meeting with her manager, Dana Akers. Akers had worked at the bank for many years and seemed to manage his people effectively. Gordy was confident that Akers's knowledge about management would be quite helpful.

Gordy's technical skills are important to her success as a first-level manager. However, it is equally important for Gordy to develop her interpersonal skills if she is to be a successful project team leader. Effectively combining her technical and interpersonal skills will help her figure out how to manage people who have different job assignments.

Gordy's belief that she can improve her managerial abilities by studying others' experiences and approaches to work is correct. She will learn that systematic and effective approaches to management have a long history.

This chapter discusses the history of management thought and practice. It presents specific tools, techniques, and concepts developed by effective managers and management scholars. Studying this history reveals how today's managerial tools, techniques, and concepts are grounded in those of yesterday.

Our examination of management history begins with a discussion of why it is important to study this topic. Brief sections then describe the practice of management in the United States before industrialization and the conditions that served as a foundation for the classical approach to management. The chapter examines four major approaches to management practice: the classical, behavioral, quantitative, and contemporary approaches. The major parts of these approaches are shown in Figure 2-1.

FIGURE 2-1
Major Parts of Four
Approaches to
Management Practice

CLASSICAL APPROACH

Scientific Management

Frederick W. Taylor
Henry Gantt
Frank and Lillian Gilbreth

Administrative Management

Henri Fayol
Max Weber

BEHAVIORAL APPROACH

Hawthorne Studies

Human Relations

Douglas McGregor
Abraham Maslow

QUANTITATIVE APPROACH

Management Science

Operations Research

CONTEMPORARY APPROACH

Systems Approach

Contingency Approach

THE IMPORTANCE OF MANAGEMENT HISTORY

Management history is an account of how management has been practiced over different periods of time and in different settings. Some writers
believe that management history is all we have to draw from to learn how to
practice management in the future.[1]

As shown in Figure 2-2, it is important to study management history for
several reasons. One reason is the insights gained through studying the actions of managers in particular circumstances.[2] The managerial practices advocated by Frederick W. Taylor (the father of scientific management) take
on additional meaning when they are considered in light of the conditions
confronting managers and workers during the late 19th and early 20th centuries. Likewise, studying conditions facing today's managers will yield
valuable insights to tomorrow's historians and managers.

FIGURE 2-2
Reasons to Study
Management History

Studying History Helps Managers:

1. Examine managers' actions in terms of conditions faced at a point in time.
2. Avoid repeating previous managerial mistakes.
3. Understand why things are as they are today.
4. Gain some ability to predict future outcomes and conditions.

Studying management history also helps managers avoid repeating mistakes. Lee Iacocca suggested that his decision that the Chrysler Corporation should buy companies in order to compete in businesses other than automobile manufacturing was his "big sin."[3] Future managers who examine this decision in terms of the conditions facing Mr. Iacocca at the time are not likely to make the same mistake. Other benefits of studying management history include gaining a perspective as to why things are as they are and developing the ability to predict. Knowing the results of certain management practices under particular conditions in the past, managers can predict what the outcomes are likely to be if they follow those practices in their own time.

MANAGEMENT PRIOR TO INDUSTRIALIZATION

Management has been practiced successfully for thousands of years. An early example of effective management practices is the building of the pyramids between 5,000 and 525 B.C.. The Great Pyramid of Cheops covered some 13 acres and was made of 2,300,000 stones, each of which weighed an average of two and one-half tons. As many as 100,000 people may have worked up to 20 years to build this pyramid. Management writer Peter Drucker has suggested that those responsible for building the Egyptian pyramids may have been the best managers in history.[4]

A second example of early successful managerial practices appears in the Bible. Exodus 18:13–26 tells the story of how Jethro observed his son-in-law, Moses, listening to his people's problems for an entire day. Jethro then advised Moses that he was doing more than one man should and suggested specific steps to relieve him of his burden. First, he recommended that ordinances and laws be taught to the people. In modern organizations, these guidance techniques are called *policies*, *rules*, and *procedures* (discussed in Chapter 5). Second, Jethro recommended that leaders be selected and assigned "to be rulers of thousands, and rulers of hundreds, and rulers of fifties, and rulers of ten." That is, he recommended delegation of authority. Jethro's third point, that these rulers should administer all routine matters and should "bring to Moses only the important questions," is the basis of the exception principle (discussed in Chapter 9).

There are other examples of early successful managerial practices, including the actions of some managers in Greece, Rome, and the Catholic church.[5] It was not until 1886, however, that a formal call for a systematic approach to management was heard. A **systematic approach to management** is one through which the practice of management is studied and then classified in a logical and orderly manner.

This formal call was issued during a meeting of the American Society of Mechanical Engineers. Henry Towne, the co-founder and president of the Yale and Towne Manufacturing Company, presented a paper titled "The Engineer as Economist." In it he urged engineers to consider the "management of works" to be as important as engineering.[6] Towne suggested that the field of management was as important as the engineering field. He also stated that standards would have to be developed for management to become the systematic and professional field he envisioned.

Towne's paper was the stimulus for the active search for a scientific approach to management. Frederick W. Taylor attended Towne's talk and was one of the first to respond to Towne's call.

In part, Towne's call was a response to what the nature of American business operations was becoming as the 19th century progressed. A range of conditions and events gave rise to the rapid changes occurring on the American business scene.

FOUNDATIONS FOR THE CLASSICAL APPROACH TO MANAGEMENT

Following unprecedented growth in England during the 1700s, the industrial revolution exploded into the United States in the 19th century. The **Industrial Revolution** was the period in which mass production of goods and services, efficient transportation systems, and the substitution of machine power for human power first began to dominate business activities. Free enterprise and the Protestant work ethic provided the philosophical background for the industrial revolution in the United States. The **Protestant work ethic** is a prevailing belief that humans are obligated to use their God-given talents in productive work.[7]

Factory systems also became pervasive during the U.S. Industrial Revolution. A **factory system** is a setting in which many workers join together to perform a variety of organized tasks. The rapid growth of technology, the increased availability of heavy capital equipment, seemingly unlimited natural resources, and the development of the corporation as an accepted business form all contributed to the rapid growth of the factory system.

However, the factory system created a number of managerial problems. Bringing together many workers whose work had to be coordinated carefully was challenging for managers. Many were ill-prepared to cope with masses of workers and the newly formed factories' financial and physical resources. Managers were called on to develop complex organizations for which precedents were few and useful theory was in short supply. The most striking feature of these new organizations was an enormous capacity for productivity. It caused managers to focus primarily on what to do to produce large numbers of goods and services efficiently. The insights offered by the classical approach to management were intended to help managers deal successfully with the challenges created by the rapidly changing business scene.

LEARNING CHECK

Discuss the importance of studying management history and the foundations for the classical approach to management.

THE CLASSICAL APPROACH TO MANAGEMENT

The **classical approach to management** consists of two streams of thought: scientific management and administrative management. The focus of **scientific management** was on the application of scientific methods to increase individual workers' productivity. The key contributor to scientific management was Frederick W. Taylor. An engineer by background, he used scientific analysis and experiments to determine ways to increase workers' outputs. Others who contributed to the scientific management stream of thought were Henry Gantt and Frank and Lillian Gilbreth.

Administrative management was concerned primarily with how organizations should be managed and structured. The French businessman Henri Fayol and the German scholar Max Weber were the main contributors to the administrative management stream of the classical approach. Based on his practical experience, Fayol developed 14 management principles through which managers engaged in planning, organizing, commanding, coordinating, and controlling. Weber suggested that bureaucracy is the best form of organization, one that makes highly efficient management practices possible.

While there are differences, the following three elements are common to the scientific management and administrative management writings:

1. *Concern for productivity.* Classical management thought dealt with efficient production and distribution of goods and services. Some believe that the classical writers' emphasis on production played down the value of individual workers.
2. *A rational view of human nature.* Classical writers were influenced strongly by Adam Smith, who is best known for his capitalistic economic theory and for the assumption that people choose the course of action that best helps them achieve their own self-interests.[8] This view strongly influenced classical thought regarding how managers should motivate workers.
3. *A search for universals.* Classical writers searched continuously for the one best way—for the most efficient work methods, the best management principles, and the ideal organization structure.

The following sections describe scientific management and administrative management in greater detail. As you read these sections, think about Tracy Gordy and her job as a first-level manager.

Scientific Management

The work of Frederick W. Taylor and his followers was the foundation for the search for efficiency in and a systematic way of thinking about management.[9] Taylor believed that inefficiency was the greatest evil of all time.[10] This application of scientific methods to the practice of management paved the way for management to become recognized as a profession.

Frederick W. Taylor is considered the father of scientific management.

ETHICS QUESTION
What are the ethical consequences of job designs that eliminate systematic soldiering but also result in significant layoffs?

FREDERICK W. TAYLOR (1856–1915). Taylor was born in Germantown, Pennsylvania, in 1856. His father was a prosperous lawyer. At an early age, Taylor had an aptitude for mechanics. He even studied croquet to determine how to increase his playing efficiency.[11] Bright and hardworking, Taylor passed Harvard University's entrance examination with honors. However, failing eyesight prevented him from studying there.

When he was 18, Taylor accepted an apprenticeship with the Enterprise Hydraulic Works of Philadelphia. He worked hard and at the end of the four-year apprenticeship, he was earning a significant amount of money for someone in his position ($3 per week). After this, Taylor accepted a common laborer's job at the Midvale Steel Company. He eventually became the chief engineer—his seventh promotion in a six-year period.

Believing in the value of hard work, Taylor was shocked by conditions at Midvale. The quantity of work employees should be producing had not been determined. Workers and managers were always in conflict. Part of the reason for this, Taylor thought, was the lack of clear responsibilities for both groups. He also believed that the workers' output was about one-third of what it could be.

Taylor's Mental Revolution. Taylor saw two main reasons why output at Midvale was low—natural soldiering and systematic soldiering. **Natural soldiering** happened because of the natural instinct to take it easy. In contrast, **systematic soldiering** came from the workers' deliberate efforts to reduce their daily output. One important reason for systematic soldiering was the workers' belief that working faster would cause them to finish their jobs too quickly. The result of this would be large numbers of layoffs. Taylor blamed management for the systematic soldiering problem.[12] In his view, managers were responsible for designing jobs properly and for offering incentives that would cause workers to stop the systematic soldiering practice. After struggling with the problems he saw at Midvale, Taylor decided that a complete "mental revolution" was necessary.[13]

Recall that Taylor heard Henry Towne's paper presented in 1886. Towne's observations were consistent with much of what Taylor thought was necessary for business firms to improve their performances. Taylor's own thoughts, coupled with Towne's, resulted in a belief that business was a system of human cooperation. A business firm would be successful only if managers and workers alike had a common objective. Taylor concluded that his "mental revolution" was required to cause managers and workers to focus on this common objective. He believed that this revolution was the essence of scientific management. The importance of the mental revolution to scientific management is shown in Taylor's comments, in 1912, before a Special Committee of the House of Representatives:

> Now, in its essence, scientific management involves a complete mental revolution on the part of the workingman engaged in any particular establishment or industry—a complete mental revolution on the part of these men as to their duties toward their work, toward their fellow men, and toward their employers. And it involves the equally complete mental revolution on the part of those on the management's side—the foreman,

the superintendent, the owner of the business, the board of directors—a complete mental revolution on their part as to their duties toward their fellow workers in the management, toward their workmen, and toward all of their daily problems. And without this complete mental revolution on both sides scientific management does not exist. That is the essence of scientific management, this great mental revolution.[14]

Taylor also developed four principles of management through which he believed his mental revolution could be carried out. These principles, as shown in Figure 2-3, were the foundation for his scientific experiments at Midvale. Some of these early experiments were carried out to find out how much time was required to finish various job tasks. Taylor's objective was to better understand each step of a production process. With this understanding, he thought he could determine what constituted a full day's work for a **first-class man**—an ambitious individual who was suited for the work he was doing.[15] Through a process known as time study, Taylor recommended work procedures that saved considerable time. **Time study** is the analysis of the amount of time needed to complete a job task. As shown in the Organization in Action, time study is still used today. After reading this description, recall that according to Taylor, a first-class man is one who is ambitious *and* suited for his job.

ORGANIZATION IN ACTION

After graduating from high school, Ron Adams had job interviews with several companies. However, because he wanted to remain in his home town, Ron found that his choices were limited. After much thought, he accepted a job with the local branch of a national financial corporation. He soon learned that he was expected to complete loan applications on the telephone in five minutes or less. After approximately one week of observing that it typically took Ron ten to twelve minutes to finish applications, Kim Yamada, his supervisor, spoke to him. During the conversation, she told

Adams that the corporation's headquarters had used time study to identify all tasks necessary to complete telephone applications. Through careful analysis and structuring of those tasks, managers had concluded that a "solid" worker should complete applications in five minutes or less. Adams remained with the company for another two weeks. During that time, he managed to reduce his processing time to the seven- to eight-minute range. After further discussions with Yamada, he concluded that he was not suited for the job and resigned.

FIGURE 2-3 Frederick Taylor's Four Principles of Management

1. Develop a science for each element of an individual's job. (This approach was to replace the "rule-of-thumb" method.)
2. Select, train, and develop each worker scientifically. (This approach disallowed the previous practice of workers training themselves as best they could.)
3. Cooperate with workers fully and enthusiastically to assure that work is performed in accordance with scientific principles.
4. Divide work and responsibilities equally between managers and workers.

The Pig-Iron Handlers Experiment. In 1898, Taylor worked as a consultant for the Bethlehem Iron Company. It was there that he conducted one of his most famous experiments. His objective was to improve the productivity of workers known as pig-iron handlers. This job required workers to pick up individual pigs of iron, each weighing 92 pounds. The pigs were carried up an inclined plank so they could be placed onto railroad cars. Taylor was taken by the sheer drudgery of the work and felt challenged when told that the workers were slow and incapable of being motivated to work faster. Taylor's analysis indicated that by using proper, less tiring work methods, a first-class worker should be able to load 47 to 48 long tons of pig iron per day. One of the keys to this increased output was to be the use of frequent rest periods. Taylor's anticipated increases in output were impressive in that at the time of his study the average worker was loading twelve and one-half long tons per day.

To put his method into action, Taylor developed a piece-rate pay system. Critical to this experiment was the selection of a worker who placed a high value on money. (Note that this pay system is based on the belief in man's economic rationality, one of the elements common to all of the classical management writings.) The worker Taylor chose as the study of his experiment was a Dutchman he called Schmidt. This worker was earning approximately $1.15 per day at the time of Taylor's experiment. Schmidt accepted Taylor's challenge to use his work methods. By experimenting with carrying positions, rest periods, and other procedures related to the pig-handler's job, he was able to raise his productivity to an average of 48 long tons per day. Because of this additional output, Schmidt's wages increased to $1.85 per day.

A Critique of Taylor's Contributions. Over the years, Taylor worked with other firms such as the Simonds Rolling Machine Company. His work resulted in many contributions to efficiency measures. In general, his methods allowed him to identify the one best way to complete a job and showed the value of selecting the one best worker for each job. Proper training, usually offered together with incentive wage plans, often resulted in significant improvements in individual workers' productivity levels. In fact, improvements of 200 percent or more commonly resulted when Taylor's recommendations were implemented.

Taylor's advocacy of science and the critical role it can play in management practice remains a lesson for today's managers.[16] In addition, his experiments provided methods that, when used effectively, could increase the productivity of individual workers, resulting in increased wealth for them. This was a noteworthy accomplishment because the typical worker during the industrial revolution was relatively uneducated and unskilled.

However, Taylor's efforts had some critics. Because they believed that his methods could result in greater physical demands and increased layoffs, some workers and unions resisted his programs. Furthermore, it was not unheard of for managers and owners to retain virtually all benefits derived through Taylor's methods rather than sharing the gains with workers.

ETHICS QUESTION
Is it ethical for firms to discharge employees who are no longer needed because use of scientific management principles has increased efficiency?

HENRY GANTT (1861–1919).   Henry Gantt worked with Taylor in a variety of jobs at Midvale, Bethlehem Iron, and Simonds. Like Taylor, Gantt sought to increase industrial efficiency through the contributions of individual workers. He believed that managers, like chemists and biologists, should apply scientific analysis to every detail of labor.[17] He thought that managers would always be able to identify ways to increase workers' efficiency in this manner.

One of Gantt's contributions was his chart system of planning and control. Viewed as revolutionary when it was developed, the Gantt chart is still used today.[18] A **Gantt chart** is a graph that shows the relationship between work scheduled and completed and the amount of elapsed time. By using a Gantt chart, managers can visualize the completion stages of various projects such as procurement of materials, manufacturing, and shipping. They can then coordinate related activities, avoid delays, and otherwise make sure that deadlines are met.

Gantt is also known for his incentive systems: bonuses for workers who meet production quotas and for supervisors who train and motivate their workers to meet those quotas. Note that providing managers with direct financial incentives for increasing the productivity of their workers was a clear extension of Taylor's contributions.

FRANK (1868–1924) AND LILLIAN GILBRETH (1878–1972).   This colorful husband-and-wife team is known to many through a book and movie, *Cheaper by the Dozen*, about life with twelve children. Perhaps because of the family's size, the Gilbreths applied their skills to analyzing everyday activities as well as the work environment. For example, they discovered that Frank could save four seconds by buttoning his vest from bottom to top instead of top to bottom.[19]

Frank Gilbreth was well known for his work in the construction industry. It has even been suggested that his efforts "systematized" the industry.[20] He gained his knowledge of this industry through work as a bricklayer. By carefully studying bricklaying, he found ways to reduce the number of motions required to lay exterior bricks from eighteen to four and one-half. Identifying methods to reduce the motions needed to lay interior bricks from eighteen to two was even more impressive. Using Gilbreth's procedures, workers increased the number of bricks laid per day from 1,000 to 2,700.

Combining her work with her husband with rearing a family and going to school, Lillian Gilbreth earned her doctorate in psychology. She was well known for her work on fatigue and other subjects. Her studies reflected a concern for the individual worker's well-being. Although she was not as famous as Frank, Lillian received many honors for her contributions to management and industrial psychology. She was the first woman to receive such acclaim in these traditionally male professions.

Throughout their careers, the Gilbreths focused on motions involved in the performance of job tasks. An important objective of their work was to discover the one best way to complete a job, which fit with Taylor's chief concern. In contrast to Taylor, however, the Gilbreths were equally interested in eliminating worker fatigue. With fewer job-related motions, they reasoned, workers' output and morale would both increase.

Lillian Gilbreth, along with her husband Frank, showed concern for the worker's well-being.

ETHICS QUESTION
Can a manager be ethical and yet unconcerned about worker fatigue?

Back to the
Opening Case

Tracy Gordy should think about the possibility of analyzing her subordinates' jobs scientifically. She might discover, for example, that following a certain procedure to identify users' needs could increase individual workers' efficiency. Gantt charts might also be of value in her efforts to plan and control projects.

A Critique of Scientific Management

Reviewing the times in which these tools and techniques were developed helps us appreciate the importance of scientific management. The standard of living in the nation was low. Very few machines were used to manufacture goods; because of this, companies' operations were highly dependent on labor. The value of first integrating and then coordinating workers' efforts had not been recognized. Through scientific analysis, it became possible to produce much greater quantities of goods. Because of these increases in output, workers' wages increased and the nation's standard of living improved. However, these gains were sometimes achieved at the expense of workers themselves.

LEARNING CHECK

Discuss the contributions to the practice of management made by Frederick Taylor, Henry Gantt, and Frank and Lillian Gilbreth.

Administrative Management

The second stream of thought in the classical approach to management is administrative management. Instead of focusing on the work and management of individual employees, the writers who advocated administrative management studied the work of *all* managers and how organizations should be structured. It is important to recognize that even though they took different perspectives, both the scientific management and administrative management writers were concerned with increasing organizational productivity. The two primary contributors to administrative management theory were Henri Fayol and Max Weber.

HENRI FAYOL (1841–1925). Henri Fayol, a French businessman and engineer, developed the first theory of administration.[21] Fayol's work was completed in France during the time that scientific management theory was being developed in the United States. He approached the study of management from the perspective of top-level administrators.[22]

Fayol was trained as a mining engineer. However, soon after accepting a job with the Commentary-Fourchambault Company in 1860, he realized that successful management required skills for which he had not been trained. Following careful analysis, Fayol concluded that managers had to deal with six essential groups of business activities in order to be successful. These groups are shown in Figure 2-4.

Fayol contended that technical, commercial, financial, security, accounting, and administrative (or managerial) activities were essential in all types of private and public organizations, large or small. One of the important features of his classification system was viewing managerial activities as being distinct from the activities of finance, accounting, and so forth. Beyond this, Fayol believed that the relative importance of these activities varied depending on a manager's position in the management hierarchy. In supervision of operations (or production) workers, for example, technical skills are relatively important. With increasing progression through a management hierarchy, the need for managerial activities increases. These perspectives are the foundation for the differences among managerial tasks discussed in Chapter 1.

Fayol also believed that a firm's size affected the focus of a manager's work. People managing in small firms should have relatively greater technical abilities, while those managing in larger companies require greater levels of what Fayol called *managerial abilities*.

Fayol's 14 principles of management were developed to help managers perform their jobs successfully. A **principle of management** is a statement that provides guidance for the practice of management. Based on his extensive business experiences, Fayol suggested that his principles should be used flexibly. The challenge to managers is in knowing how to use the principles.[23] Gaining this knowledge is difficult and, according to Fayol, it requires intelligence and experience. Fayol's principles[24] are shown in

FIGURE 2-4
Henri Fayol's Essential
Business Activities

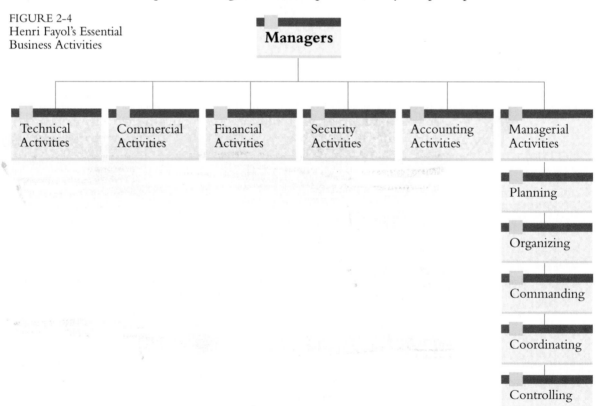

Figure 2-5. He noted that other principles should be added to this list when experience proved their worth.

LEARNING CHECK

Name the two streams of thought of the classical approach to management. Also, name the major contributors to these two schools of thought and describe the nature of their contributions.

FIGURE 2-5
Fayol's 14 Principles of Management

1. **Division of Work.** Increased specialization in individuals' jobs leads to greater efficiency.

2. **Authority.** Managers have a right to give orders and the power required to assure compliance with their orders.

3. **Discipline.** Employees should respect regulations and statements of policy. Clarity and fairness promote this respect.

4. **Unity of Command.** For any job task, an employee should receive orders from only one supervisor.

5. **Unity of Direction.** Each work group or department should operate under one plan and director.

6. **Subordination of Individual Interests to the General Interest.** The interests of society come first, the organization second, the individual and small groups third.

7. **Remuneration.** Workers should be paid wages that are fair and acceptable to both employees and company.

8. **Centralization.** Increasing subordinates' roles in decision-making processes is decentralization, while decreasing their roles is centralization. The challenge to managers is to determine the correct amount of centralization/decentralization for each case.

9. **Scalar Chain (Lines of Authority).** Definite lines make authority relationships clear throughout the organization. Organizational communications should follow this chain.

10. **Order.** Everything has a place and should be in place. Placement of employees should be based on qualifications, allowing each person to have the job for which he or she is best suited.

11. **Equity.** Managers should supervise with kindliness and justice (fairness).

12. **Stability of Tenure of Personnel.** High turnover rates are inefficient. By respecting seniority, managers create a sense of security, retain well-trained employees, and reduce turnover.

13. **Initiative.** Subordinates given opportunities to design and carry out plans will work hard.

14. **Esprit de Corps.** Promoting team spirit builds harmony and creates organizational unity.

Back to the
Opening Case

Recall that Tracy Gordy is managing systems analysts at a bank. Review Fayol's principles of management (see Figure 2-5). Select the principles you believe could help Gordy become a more effective project team leader. As you think about these principles, consider comments you would make to Dana Akers (Gordy's manager) if he were to ask you to support your selections.

Max Weber developed a pure, rational form of organization called bureaucracy.

MAX WEBER (1864–1920). A wealthy German intellectual, Max Weber described what he believed was the ideal or pure form of organization, called a bureaucracy. Weber contended that by using this pure type of organization firms could reach their ultimate level of efficiency. Thus, a **bureaucracy** is an ideal type of organization that is completely rational in its design and impersonal in the way it is implemented.

Weber's bureaucracy was grounded in the principles of order, legitimate authority, and logic.[25] The various parts of rationally structured organizations are designed and coordinated to achieve specific ends. Rationality implies goal-directedness, while impersonality implies objectivity in interpersonal relations. According to Weber, decisions regarding human resources in bureaucracies were to be strictly impartial—based on an employee's technical competence and work demands rather than on a caste system or the personal preferences of decision makers.

The building blocks of organizations are clearly defined offices or positions that are organized into a hierarchy with a fixed chain of command. Weber's ideal bureaucratic organization was designed for efficiency, predictability, and the "reign of rules." To Weber, the rational structuring of organizations was a reaction against the unwarranted influence of political control and the power of people with strong personalities or royalty.

In his writings, Weber attempted to develop a pure form of organization that could be compared with others. He recognized that no form would exactly match his prescriptions. However, he believed that developing an organization that was as consistent as possible with the bureaucratic form would serve both the firm and society well.

LEARNING CHECK

Describe Fayol's principles of management and Weber's bureaucratic organization form. Identify work situations in which these concepts and techniques could be used successfully.

A Critique of Administrative Management

Both Fayol's work and Weber's work have stood the test of time. Even today, managers evaluate conditions to determine the appropriate use of Fayol's management principles. This evaluation process is at the heart of the contingency approach to management, which will be discussed later in this chapter. Although bureaucracy has been justly criticized, it is still used today in many large companies. Thus, administrative management theory remains valid and worthy of consideration.

THE BEHAVIORAL APPROACH TO MANAGEMENT

The **behavioral approach to management** is grounded in the belief that specific attention to workers' needs creates greater satisfaction and productivity. In contrast to the largely technical emphasis of scientific management, a common theme of the behavioral approach is the need to focus on people. This approach assumes that workers are, for the most part, motivated and controlled by social relationships on their jobs. The behavioral approach is traditionally associated with a period from the 1930s through the 1950s. Much earlier, however, some individuals sounded concerns about the human factor in the workplace. One of these was Robert Owen (1771–1858).

Involved in the textile industry in Scotland, Owen criticized fellow managers for failing to understand the human element in the mills. He claimed that showing concern for workers resulted in greater profitability while at the same time reducing the level of workers' misery.[26] Owen also called for establishment of child labor laws and for business firms' involvement in community projects. In assessing the value of his programs, he reported that efforts to keep the human element in good repair often resulted in a 50 percent return on his investment.

Mary Parker Follett (1868–1933) was another forerunner of the behavioral approach. Trained in both political science and philosophy, Follett was obsessed with the importance of groups. Although she wrote during the scientific management era, Follett did not share Taylor's view that organizations should be framed around the work of individuals. In contrast, she argued that groups were the basis on which organizations should be formed. In this setting, Follett proposed, managers were challenged to coordinate and aid the efforts of work groups.[27]

The Hawthorne Studies

The contributions of Owen and Follett were important precursors to the behavioral approach. However, the Hawthorne studies yielded the most significant contributions to the development of this approach.[28]

The purpose of the first study conducted at the Hawthorne plant of Western Electric in Cicero, Illinois, was to determine the effect of changes in lighting on workers' productivity. In this study, workers were divided into an experimental group and a control group. Lighting conditions for the experimental group varied in intensity from 24 to 46 to 70 footcandles. The lighting for the control group remained constant.

As expected, the experimental group's output increased with each increase in light intensity. But unexpectedly, the performance of the control group did not remain constant. In fact, the production of the control group increased at about the same rate as that of the experimental group. Later, the lighting in the experimental group's work area was reduced. This group's output continued to increase, as did that of the control group. A decline in productivity of the experimental group finally did occur, but only when the intensity of light was roughly the same as moonlight. Clearly, the researchers reasoned, something other than illumination caused the changes in productivity.

The relay assembly test room experiment had similar results. In this case, relationships among rest, fatigue, and productivity were examined. Conducted by Elton Mayo and his Harvard colleague, Fritz J. Roethlisberger, these experiments lasted approximately five years. First, normal productivity was established with no formal rest periods and a 48-hour week. Rest periods of varying lengths and frequency were then introduced. Productivity increased as the frequency and length of rest periods increased. Finally, in Period XII of the experiments, the original conditions were reinstated. However, the return to the original conditions did not result in the expected drop in productivity; instead, productivity remained at its usual high level.

Results from the Hawthorne studies yielded valuable insights for managers and researchers alike. Researchers concluded that one reason for the lighting experiments' results was related to the fact that workers received special attention for the first time. These results also pointed to specific guidelines for managerial action, which are presented in Figure 2-6.

The contents of Figure 2-6 may seem to indicate that the researchers only discovered the obvious. Remember, though, that these findings were unique when first reported. Prior to that time, workers were thought to be strictly rational, economic people. As a result of the Hawthorne studies, the social nature of workers was recognized as playing a significant role in an organization's productivity. In addition, managers started to become aware that workers could not be motivated through economic rewards alone.

Although the Hawthorne studies made important contributions, they have been criticized. Some claim that the research was unscientific and that the conclusions did not necessarily follow from the data.[29] In spite of these criticisms, the studies' outcomes were valuable. As discussed in the next section, they also became the foundation for development of the human relations movement.

FIGURE 2-6
Managerial Guidelines
From the Hawthorne
Studies

1. Workers have unique needs, wants, goals, and motives. Managers must treat workers as individuals.
2. Dealing with human problems is complicated and challenging.
3. Personal problems can strongly influence workers' productivity levels.
4. Effective communication with workers is critical to managerial success.

Back to the
Opening Case

Tracy Gordy should think about the insights provided by the Hawthorne studies. Does Gordy understand the influence work groups could have on productivity levels? Has she recognized the degree of teamwork required to complete projects successfully?

The Human Relations Movement

The **human relations movement** was based on the belief that there is an important link among managerial practices, morale, and productivity. Writers contributing to the human relations movement suggested that workers bring various social needs to their jobs. In completing their jobs, workers typically become members of several work groups. Often, these groups provide satisfactions for some of the workers' needs. Satisfied workers, it was argued, would be more productive workers. The challenge for managers was to recognize workers' needs and the powerful influence that work groups and a firm's social context can have on individual and organizational productivity.

A second common theme of the human relations movement was a strong belief in workers' capabilities. Given the proper working environment (or social context in the organization), virtually all workers would be highly productive. Significant amounts of cooperation among workers and managers were critical to achieving high levels of productivity.

Two important contributions to the human relations movement are Douglas McGregor's assumptions about human nature and Abraham Maslow's hierarchy of needs. McGregor's Theory X and Theory Y assumptions are discussed fully in Chapter 12. They are mentioned only briefly here.

Theory X is a set of negative assumptions about people. Managers who hold these assumptions are not optimistic about workers' capabilities or what they can accomplish. They believe that people dislike work, seek to avoid responsibility, are not ambitious, and must be supervised closely. The far more positive Theory Y assumptions are that people do accept responsibility, can exercise self-control, have the capacity to be innovative in their work, and consider work to be as natural as rest or play.[30] McGregor argued that Theory Y assumptions accurately described human nature. It was these assumptions that should guide managerial practice.

Abraham Maslow suggested that humans are motivated by efforts to satisfy a hierarchy of needs.[31] The lowest-level need is the basic physiological need for food, clothing, and shelter. Once satisfied, this need gives way to people's efforts to satisfy the higher-order needs of safety, social and love, esteem, and self-actualization. Maslow also argued that once a need is satisfied it no longer motivates behavior. The challenge to managers is to remove any obstacle preventing workers from satisfying needs that are primary motivators for them at the time. This need hierarchy is examined in greater detail in Chapter 12.

Organizational Behavior

The researchers associated with the Hawthorne studies and the human relations movement made important contributions to the practice of management. In turn, these contributions became the foundation for what is today known as the organizational behavior field. Those working in this field believe that individuals' behaviors are far more complex than suggested by the early contributors to the behavioral approach.

Today, the issues of job stress, motivation, leadership, conflict, and communication, among others, are studied through a combination of perspectives. Organizational behavior theory and practices draw from the fields of psychology, sociology, economics, and anthropology. Building on the contributions of the earlier writers, the work of behavioral scientists today continues to yield important outcomes. These outcomes are a foundation for many of the discussions included in Parts Three and Four of this text.

A Critique of the Behavioral Approach

Recall that many of the major contributors to the classical approach to management were trained as engineers. Because of this, a problem with either a machine or a human being was viewed through an engineer's eyes. If a worker's output fell below established standards, managers believed they faced an engineering problem. An obvious, rational solution to an engineering problem with a worker was to offer the worker more money. After all, no rational being would turn down an opportunity to earn more. The major contribution of the behavioral approach to management was that it convinced managers to reassess this simplistic view of the human element. Managers began to understand the necessity of using interpersonal skills as well as technical skills to be successful.

As is true with the classical approach, however, the behavioral approach did not produce all the information required for managerial effectiveness. As mentioned previously, one key assumption of the human relationists was that a satisfied worker is a more productive worker. However, the results of studies by contemporary organizational behavioral theorists do not provide conclusive support for the position that worker satisfaction is a primary cause of productivity. We also know that consistent, successful motivation of people is far more complicated than Maslow suggested. There are two more approaches to management—the quantitative approach and the contemporary approach—that provide other valuable insights to effective management practices.

LEARNING CHECK   Describe the foundations of the human relations movement. Discuss briefly the assumptions of Theory X and Theory Y and the levels of Maslow's need hierarchy.

THE QUANTITATIVE
APPROACH TO MANAGEMENT

The **quantitative approach to management** is an approach to managerial decision making that is grounded in the scientific method.[32] Today, the quantitative approach is commonly called management science or operations research (OR). In fact, the terms *quantitative approach*, *management science*, and *operations research* are used interchangeably.[33]

The process of management science is interesting. First, the issue to be analyzed is observed. Based on these observations, frameworks and models are developed. By changing the status of variables included in the frameworks and models, managers are able to better understand the issues they choose to examine. Frequently used management science tools and techniques include statistics, linear programming, network analysis, queing theory, decision trees, goal programming, and computer simulations. These tools and techniques can be used when making decisions regarding the control of inventories, selection of plant locations, quality control of products, and a range of other issues. Many of these points will be examined in greater detail in Chapters 16 and 17.

Frederick Taylor's work provided the foundation for the quantitative approach to management. However, the impetus for the modern-day quantitative approach was the formation of operations research teams to solve a range of strategic and tactical problems faced by the Allied forces during World War II. Composed of mathematicians, physicists, engineers, and behavioral scientists, these teams solved common problems through applications of various scientific methods. Examples of the problems considered by the OR teams include the bombing of enemy targets, the effective conduct of antisubmarine warfare, and the efficient movement of troops from one location to another.

Following World War II, two developments stirred the application of quantitative approaches in nonmilitary organizations. First, researchers continued to identify useful applications of quantitative tools and techniques to many different types of problems. Second, the rapid development and distribution of computing power made it possible for greater numbers of organizations to use quantitative approaches. Computers and information systems will be discussed in Chapter 18.

Computer simulations are an important part of the quantitative approach to management. Today, these simulations allow managers to hold some factors constant while others are varied to simulate certain conditions. Doing this allows managers to judge the desirability of alternative outcomes. For example, computers can simulate the effect of a change in the price of a key product on the product's market share. Similarly, competitors' anticipated reactions to a change in product price can be simulated and evaluated. Managers can also use models to forecast the effect of different levels of sales on cash flow.

The quantitative approach to management is of the greatest value in the planning and controlling functions. Often, corporations form OR groups that serve as internal consultants to managers facing problems in other parts of the company. For example, an OR group might help those responsible for corporate planning develop models through which they can understand the meaning of changes in the firm's environment. Similarly, an OR group could help human resources personnel determine the impact on the company of a change in the nation's mandatory retirement age. An OR group could simulate the effect of an increase in the minimum wage law on a firm's ability to make a profit and provide that information to human resources and finance personnel for controlling purposes.

The quantitative approach can be of significant value to managers when they make decisions. However, it is important to remember that the results of quantitative analyses are not decisions. Rather, they are pieces of information that managers must evaluate carefully before reaching a decision. The ultimate effectiveness of the quantitative approach depends on the degree to which this approach is both understood and supported by managers and workers alike.[34]

THE CONTEMPORARY APPROACH TO MANAGEMENT

Each of the three approaches discussed so far has made important contributions to the practice of management. Through the use of scientific analysis, the classical approach helped managers gain some stability in rather chaotic work environments. The behavioral approach introduced managers to the value of recognizing and responding to workers' individual and group needs in structuring work relationships. Through use of the quantitative approach, managers were able to use the results of quantitative analyses to enhance the quality of their decisions.

While they were all valuable, each of these three approaches had a singular focus. The focus of the classical approach was finding the one best way to do a job, to structure an organization, and so forth. The behavioral approach attempted to show managers what to do to increase a worker's morale, motivation, and satisfaction. With the quantitative approach, the focus was on using mathematical techniques to find solutions to difficult organizational problems.

Beginning approximately in the 1960s, it became clear that organizations' problems and challenges were far too complex to be solved through methods based on a singular focus. The systems approach and the contingency approach emerged to help managers deal with these realities. Both of these contemporary perspectives attempt to integrate the findings and contributions of the other major approaches.

The Systems Approach

Although the systems approach is grounded in the work of Ludwig von Bertalanffy, it makes use of contributions from many other disciplines such as psychology and sociology. As a biologist, von Bertalanffy suggested that the survival of any system depends on how well all parts (or subsystems) of that system are functioning.[35] A **system** is a set of interdependent parts that function together to accomplish an objective. Examples of systems include animals, the human body, and organizations. The **systems approach to management** is based on the position that an organization is a collection of parts that are both related to and dependent on one another.

According to systems theory, a human body can function effectively only when all of its parts (e.g., the heart, liver, and kidneys) work together. If one part breaks down, all other parts are affected. A long-distance runner who develops a stress fracture in her left ankle cannot continue training for an upcoming marathon race, regardless of the strength of her heart. An organization that fails to develop an ability to sell its products cannot be successful, regardless of the quality and sophistication of its operations activities.

There are two basic types of systems, closed and open. A **closed system** does not interact with and is not influenced by its environment. An **open system** interacts freely with and is influenced by its environment. An organization's **environment** includes all forces external to the organization that can affect its performance.[36] Examples include government agencies, suppliers, customers, and competitors.

All organizations today are open systems, although the degree to which a company is dependent on parts of its environment varies. It is a significant managerial mistake to assume that a firm is isolated from environmental influences. For example, managers should not be surprised if a string of product failures causes stockholders to sell their stock. Similarly, ministers whose churches fail to address their congregations' needs should anticipate membership losses.

Figure 2-7 represents a view of an organization as an open system. As shown in the figure, organizations receive inputs from their environment in the form of the four key resources—human, financial, physical, and informational—discussed in Chapter 1. Various operations activities are used to transform (or change) these resources into products, such as goods and services, that are valued by the company's environment. Through feedback, the environment indicates what adjustments are needed. **Environmental feedback** is information from the environment regarding the effectiveness of an organization's performance.

The systems approach provides important guidance for managers, since organizations cannot function without successful environmental interac-

FIGURE 2-7 An Open Systems Model

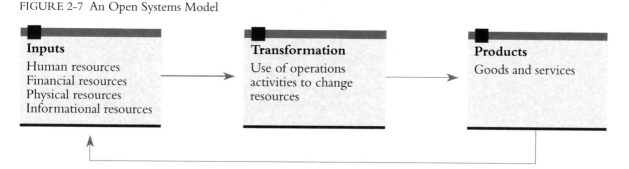

Inputs
Human resources
Financial resources
Physical resources
Informational resources

Transformation
Use of operations
activities to change
resources

Products
Goods and services

Environmental Feedback

tions. They are dependent on their environments to accept their outputs and to provide inputs. Managers must be aware of this reality and monitor their organization's environments continuously.

The systems approach also highlights the interdependencies among all of an organization's internal parts. Because of these interdependencies, managers must be effective coordinators of many activities and events. For example, workers' efforts must be integrated throughout the firm. A marketing group's sales strategy must be coordinated with the firm's purchasing efforts and its operations activities. Market surveys are necessary to track customers' changing wants and needs. This information is vital if the firm is to produce products that customers are willing to purchase.

The Contingency Approach

Grounded in the pioneering work of Burns and Stalker and Lawrence and Lorsch, the **contingency approach to management** suggests that managerial practices depend on all factors influencing a particular situation.[37] The contingency approach builds on the contributions of the scientific management, behavioral, and especially, the systems approaches.

ETHICS QUESTION
Does using the contingency approach require that a manager's ethics change with each situation?

Those supporting the contingency approach believe that there is not one best way to manage in any situation. This position is quite different from that of the classical and behavioral approaches, which argued for universal sets of principles. The contingency approach suggests that other factors, called *situational variables*, affect managerial practices and make it impossible to believe in universal managerial principles. The list of relevant situational variables is seemingly endless. Examples include firm size, differences among resources and operations activities, the manager's assumptions about employee attitudes, and the type of strategy the firm is implementing. The differences between the universal approach and a contingency approach are shown in Figure 2-8.

To account for situational variables, managers develop "if-then" statements (e.g., "if X, then Y"). The advocates of scientific management proposed that *if* greater productivity from individual workers is sought, *then* it is necessary to have a first-class worker complete that job in the "one best way." But, as was discovered, other factors had an effect on the if-then statement and the expected relationship. In the behavioralists' view, workers' social needs affected the if-then statement about how to increase worker productivity levels. Recognizing this, the contingency approach would suggest that social needs are a relevant situational variable in this particular instance. Thus, the desired increase in worker productivity will be achieved only if workers' social needs are considered.

Another example of how the contingency approach could be used concerns a work group's size. A manager might believe, for example, that a work group should never have more than six members. The contingency approach suggests that a decision about the size of the group should be made in light of situational variables. If workers complete a simple task on a repetitive basis, then the size of the group can be larger. Similarly, if the employees are experienced and have a good relationship with their managers,

THE UNIVERSAL APPROACH   **THE CONTINGENCY APPROACH**

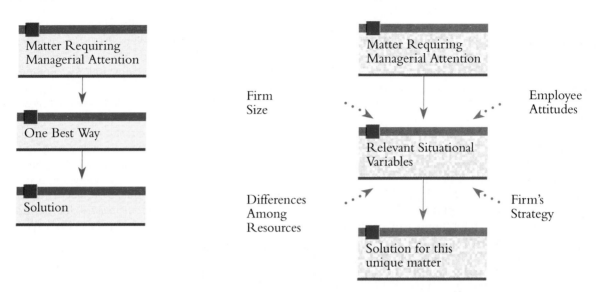

FIGURE 2-8 The Universal and Contingency Approaches

additional support exists for a larger group.

Many of the tools, techniques, and concepts appearing in this book's remaining chapters are presented within a contingency framework. The impact of the contingency approach will be especially apparent in our discussion of the leading function (Chapters 11 through 14). The contingency approach challenges managers to be aware of all relevant situational variables on a case-by-case basis. With this awareness, managers are better prepared to practice the planning, organizing, leading, and controlling functions.

. . . .
Back to the
Opening Case
. . . .

Recall that Tracy Gordy's systems analysts face varying types of tasks. While computer programming can be somewhat routine work, analysts, who must match user needs with computer systems' capabilities, may encounter unique situations with every project. Gordy should be aware of the differences in these job tasks, which suggest the need for situational managerial practices. As a new manager, it will be a challenge for Gordy to recognize all situational factors affecting the management of her nine workers. However, it is her responsibility to accept this challenge and respond to it effectively.
. . . .

LEARNING CHECK
Describe the major perspectives of the quantitative approach and the contemporary approach to management. Recall that the systems and contingency approaches are both part of the contemporary approach.

SUMMARY

Management history holds valuable lessons for managers of today and tomorrow. Studying the practices followed by managers before us helps us avoid mistakes. In addition, examining the conditions managers faced in earlier times enhances our understanding of why particular decisions were made and actions taken.

The industrial revolution was a precursor to development of the classical approach to management practice. Two streams of thought—scientific management and administrative management—formed the basis for the classical approach. These approaches shared a high concern for productivity, a rational view of human nature, and a search for universal principles. However, the precise focus of the two streams was different. Scientific management focused on determining methods through which individual workers' productivity levels could be increased. The administrative management writers discussed ways to practice management and structure organizations more efficiently.

The beginnings of an emphasis on the importance of people in organizations date back to the first half of the 19th century. However, the Hawthorne studies at the Western Electric plant provided the foundation for development of the behavioral approach and the subsequent human relations movement.

The results of the Hawthorne studies convinced managers to recognize and accept the uniqueness of individual workers. Prevailing theories about the human element in the workplace changed with the advent of the behavioral approach. Instead of considering workers to be another type of machine, managers shifted to the belief that a satisfied worker is a more productive worker. They realized that workers were not strictly rational beings who would always respond positively to additional economic rewards. McGregor's Theory X and Theory Y assumptions about human nature and Maslow's hierarchy of needs are examples of perspectives through which managers began to view workers differently from the way they were viewed when the classical approach was predominant.

The quantitative approach to management practice is grounded in the methods of scientific analysis advanced by Frederick W. Taylor and his contemporaries. However, this approach did not emerge until World War II. Commonly called either *management science* or *operations research*, the quantitative approach uses mathematical tools and techniques to assist managers in decision making. The growth and spread of computing capabilities have increased the potential value of the quantitative approach. However, it is important for managers to remember that these tools and techniques only yield *information* for decision-making purposes. It remains management's responsibility to use that information to make effective and efficient decisions.

The contemporary approach includes the systems and contingency approaches. Rather than being totally distinct, these two approaches build on the insights and contributions provided by the classical, behavioral, and quantitative approaches.

The systems approach suggests that each part of an organization is dependent on all other parts of the organization. A company's success is a function of how well these interdependent parts work together in the pursuit of a common objective. Additionally, in the systems approach, managers must recognize that organizations are open systems—systems that freely interact with and are influenced by their environments. An organization's success is a function of the degree to which its interdependent parts work together to accomplish a common purpose that is accepted and supported by its environment.

Founded on previous approaches, the contingency approach suggests that there is no one best way to manage. This perspective takes into account the uniqueness of each situation. Managers consider "if-then" statements and take into account the effects of situational variables (e.g., organization size, differences among individuals, and a firm's technology) on issues confronting them. Today, many managerial practices are based on the contingency approach, recognizing that what works in one situation may not work in another.

KEY TERMS

management history
systematic approach to
    management
industrial revolution
Protestant work ethic
factory system
classical approach to
    management
scientific management

administrative manage-
    ment
natural soldiering
systematic soldiering
first-class man
time study
Gantt chart
principle of management
bureaucracy

behavioral approach to
    management
human relations move-
    ment
quantitative approach to
    management
system
systems approach to
    management

closed system
open system
environment
environmental feedback
contingency approach to
    management

QUESTIONS FOR DISCUSSION AND REVIEW

1. Assume that you are talking to a fellow business student about management history. During this conversation, describe the benefits your friend should derive from studying management history.

2. Describe Frederick W. Taylor's principles of management. Develop arguments for and against the view that the scientific management approach calls for managers to be heartless and unconcerned about their workers.

3. Describe several business situations in which you believe scientific management tools and techniques can be used appropriately.

4. Describe how Henri Fayol's management principles could be applied to a job you have held or a position you occupy in a social organization.

5. How would you describe the characteristics of Max Weber's bureaucracy to a friend who has never taken a business course?

6. Compare and contrast any modern bureaucratic organization with Weber's pure form. What do you think may account for the differences between your description and Weber's ideal organization form?

7. Why do the Hawthorne studies stand out as landmarks in management history? Of what value are these studies' results to your managerial career?

8. As a top-level manager, how would you use the quantitative approach to management?

9. Explain how you would use the systems approach to increase your effectiveness as a manager.

10. How can a manager effectively use the contingency management approach? Why is it sometimes difficult to apply contingency management research in the workplace?

PROBLEMS FOR ACTION

A. An objective of scientific management was to find the one best way to complete a task. Assume that a teacher has mentioned the following in one of your classes: "There is only one way for students to study when taking college courses. During next Monday's class period, I will tell you what that way is." Use materials in this chapter to either support or reject the position that there is only one best way to study when taking college courses.

B. Assume that you are the supervisor of a parking garage that serves a number of establishments located in an active part of your community. You have en-

countered some difficulty in motivating your eight part-time workers. A recent discussion of this matter with the operations manager for the region in which your garage is located was not satisfying. The operations manager told you that it is your challenge to find ways to make work interesting for your people. The view suggested to you was that all workers will be motivated once they have opportunities to be involved with challenging tasks. You are not convinced that the operations manager's perspective is correct. Develop an argument you could present to your superior.

CONCLUDING CASE

Office of Undergraduate Studies

Mary Lynn Latimer was not especially pleased about her husband's acceptance of a job in another community. After all, she had a network of friends with whom she enjoyed various activities such as bowling and bridge. Furthermore, her two children were enrolled in what was thought to be a successful school system. All in all, Latimer thought, moving to a larger community some 1,200 miles from their current home was an unattractive prospect.

Somewhat to her surprise, Latimer found herself settling in quite nicely in the new location. Her husband's job was going even better than they had anticipated. The children were now in the third and sixth grades and seemed to enjoy their new friends and school. Latimer and her husband had made good friends, found a church in which they were comfortable, and appreciated their new town's civic opportunities.

The only negative in Latimer's life was the amount of time on her hands. Unlike the children's previous school, the new school was one where parents were not very involved. Latimer had always participated in school projects, trips, special activities during the Christmas season, and so forth. Frankly, her lack of involvement with the school resulted in a great deal of excess time for Latimer.

After discussions with her husband, Latimer decided to work part time. Her doing so, they concluded, would provide valuable income and allow her to devote some of her energies to activities apart from her children. Following several interviews, Latimer accepted a position as a part-time academic adviser in the business school at the local university.

Latimer adapted to her job quickly. Only four women, in addition to Latimer, worked as academic advisers for the university's business school. Three of the other four women also worked part time. Their supervisor was Dr. Jack Hassell. Because of his confidence in their abilities, Hassell allowed the five women a good deal of freedom in their work. Basically, the women chose their own work hours and designed their work procedures. This latitude was fine with them. They enjoyed each other's company, their frequent discussions, and, in general, all parts of their working relationship.

As Latimer and her co-workers discovered, things changed dramatically when Hassell resigned. His re-

placement, Dr. Tom Leslie, was far more structured than Hassell. An example of this was Leslie's decision regarding the completion of degree plans.

Each business student had to have a degree plan filled out in order to earn a major in the business school. These plans were one of the most important parts of the academic advisers' jobs. Under Hassell's leadership, all five people in the office worked with students to prepare them. Although it was flexible, there was a routine to how the advisers completed degree plans. During a discussion with each student, the adviser learned what degree the student desired to earn. Such a discussion often was quite lengthy. It was a time for the adviser to learn more about the student. Sometimes, after a student left, the women would talk about the student and his or her interests. With knowledge of the chosen major, the adviser then completed a detailed plan of action the student had to follow to earn a degree in that particular field. A standardized form was used for this purpose. Actually completing the form required an adviser to go through certain catalogs, verify that credit would be allowed for any courses a student had taken at another school, and so forth.

Leslie was not pleased with the way degree plans were being completed. After analyzing all tasks involved with completing a degree plan, he was convinced that a more efficient set of procedures could be determined. To discuss this matter, he asked one of the professors from the university's engineering school, Dr. Fred McBride, to observe the office personnel. Leslie wanted McBride to use time study to determine the most efficient way to complete degree plans. After his analysis, McBride told Leslie that, indeed, the office personnel could complete degree plans far more efficiently than was currently the case. He left his recommendations with Leslie and encouraged him to call if he could help in any other way.

Recommendations in hand, Leslie met with the five academic advisers. With considerable energy, he explained how the new procedures would allow them to complete degree plans far more efficiently and quickly. Because the business school's enrollment was increasing rather dramatically, Leslie believed that the additional speed and efficiency would be desirable.

After only two weeks of trying to work with the new degree plan procedures, Leslie found himself with a revolt on his hands. All five academic advisers were irritated and ready to quit if they were forced to continue working with the new procedures. They felt stifled by the new system. Furthermore, they resisted the idea that a degree plan had to be completed within a specified period of time. After discussing this matter with the five advisers, Leslie told them he would talk with them again in the morning.

As he returned to his office, Leslie wondered what had gone wrong. After all, he thought, he was just trying to increase the efficiency of his staff.

1. Describe any characteristics of the process of developing degree plans suggesting that time study might be an appropriate tool to analyze the advisers' work.

2. In your opinion, why did the advisers react so negatively to Leslie's attempts to implement new procedures for completing degree plans? Use materials from this chapter to prepare your response.

3. What specific factors and/or conditions do you believe Leslie should have considered in order to handle this situation more effectively?

REFERENCES

1. W. Jack Duncan, *Great Ideas in Management* (San Francisco: Jossey-Bass, 1989): 2.

2. Alan M. Kantrow, "Why History Matters to Managers," *Harvard Business Review* (January-February, 1986): 81–88.

3. Paul Ingrassia and Bradley A. Stertz, "With Chrysler Ailing, Lee Iacocca Concedes Mistakes in Managing," *The Wall Street Journal* (September 17, 1990): A7–10.

4. Duncan, *Great Ideas in Management*, 3.

5. Daniel A. Wren, *The Evolution of Management Thought* (New York: The Ronald Press, 1972): 19.

6. Henry R. Towne, "The Engineer as an Economist." *Transactions, American Society of Mechanical Engineers*, 1886: 428–432.

7. Wren, *Management Thought*, 27.

8. Adam Smith, *An Inquiry into the Nature and Causes of the Wealth of Nations*, Vol. 1 (London: A. Strahan and T. Cadell, 1973).

9. Wren, *Management Thought*, 109.

10. Duncan, *Great Ideas in Management*, 55.

11. Sudhir Kakar, *Frederick Taylor: A Study in Personality and Innovation* (Cambridge, MA: MIT Press, 1970).

12. Frederick Taylor, *The Principles of Scientific Management* (New York: Harper and Row, 1911).

13. The statement concerning scientific management is based on *Testimony of Frederick W. Taylor at Hearings before the Special Committee of the House of Representatives to Investigate the Taylor and Other Systems of Shop Management Under Authority of House Resolution 90* (January 25, 1912): 1387.

14. Taylor, *Hearings Before the Special Committee of the House of Representatives*, 1387.

15. Wren, *Management Thought*, 122.

16. Louis W. Fry, "The Maligned F. W. Taylor: A Reply to His Many Critics." *Academy of Management Review* (July 1976): 124–139.

17. Henry L. Gantt, *Work, Wages, and Profits* (New York: Engineering Magazine, 1910).

18. Duncan, *Great Ideas in Management*, 55.

19. Frank B. Gilbreth Jr. and E. G. Carey, *Cheaper by the Dozen* (New York: Thomas Y. Crowell, 1948): 3.

20. Wren, *Management Thought*, 160.

21. Wren, *Management Thought*, 209.

22. Henri Fayol, *General and Industrial Management*, translated by Constance Storrs (London: Sir Isaac Pitman and Sons, 1949). The copyright date, 1949, is the date of the English translation. Fayol's "General Principles of Management" first appeared in 1916 in an industrial association bulletin published in France.

23. Wren, *Management Thought*, 217.

24. Fayol, *General and Industrial Management*.

25. A. M. Henderson and Talcott Parsons, eds. and trans., *Max Weber: The Theory of Social and Economic Organization* (New York: The Free Press, 1947).

26. Robert Owen, *A New View of Society*, 1st American ed. from the 3d London ed. (New York: E. Bliss & F. White, 1825): 57.

27. Mary Parker Follett, *The New State: Group Organization the Solution of Popular Government* (New York: Longmans, Green, 1918).

28. Mayo and his co-workers published several books that describe the extensive work completed at Western Electric. Among these are: Elton Mayo, *The Human Problems of an Industrial Civilization*, 2e (Boston: Division of Research, Harvard Business School, 1946); F. J. Roethlisberger and W. J. Dickson, *Management and the Worker* (Cambridge, MA: Harvard University Press, 1939); F. J. Roethlisberger, *Management and Morale*. (Cambridge, MA: Harvard University Press, 1941); and F. J. Roethlisberger, *Man-in-Organization: Essays of F. J. Roethlisberger* (Cambridge, MA: Belknap Press of Harvard University Press, 1968).

29. Wren, *Management Thought*, 370–381.

30. Douglas McGregor, *The Human Side of Enterprise* (New York: McGraw-Hill, 1960): 33–57.

31. Abraham Maslow, "A Theory of Human Motivation," *Psychological Review*, (July 1943): 370–396.

32. David R. Anderson, Dennis J. Sweeny, and Thomas A. Williams, *An Introduction to Management Science: Quantitative Approaches to Decision Making* (St. Paul: West, 1988): 1.

33. Barry Render and Ralph M. Starr, Jr., *Quantitative Analysis for Management*, 3e (Boston: Allyn and Bacon, 1988): 4.

34. Render, *Quantitative Analysis*, 17.

35. Ludwig von Bertalanffy, General Systems Theory: A New Approach to the Unity of Science," *Human Biology* (December 1951): 302–361.

36. Liam Fahey and V. K. Narayanan, *Macroenvironmental Analysis for Strategic Management* (St. Paul: West, 1986): 49–50.

37. Fremont E. Kast and James E. Rosenzweig, *Organization and Management: A Systems Approach*, 3e (New York: McGraw-Hill, 1979).

Chapter 3

Managerial Ethics and Corporate Social Responsibility

Chapter Learning Objectives:

1. Define ethics, managerial ethics, and social responsibility.

2. Describe three views of social responsibility: classical, accountability, and public.

3. Describe three criteria for a firm's values and behavioral standards: legality, common practice, and codes of ethics.

4. Discuss how managerial ethics are influenced by individual, organizational, and environmental factors.

5. Describe several guidelines for ethical management.

OPENING
CASE

BP (British
Petroleum)
America and
Social
Responsibility

The office of James Ross, the CEO for BP America, is located in Cleveland, Ohio. Like many other communities, Cleveland is trying to recover from years of urban decay and a flight of residents to the suburbs. When looking at the area surrounding his office, Ross envisions a place with affordable housing and livable neighborhoods. Because of this vision, Ross's company spent over $20 million for grants and investments in Cleveland over an eight-year period. In part, these funds have helped to build or restore 700 homes and weatherize almost 3,000 other homes.

To support the company's commitments, Ross served as the founding chairman of Neighborhood Progress. Members of this group come from other corporations, the neighborhoods themselves, and various city government offices. The group provides the strategic vision and resources needed to make neighborhood renewal a reality in Cleveland. In discussing these commitments of money and time, Ross says he is "naturally concerned about the needs of the people who live in Cleveland's older neighborhoods and in depressed neighborhoods in other cities in which we operate. The success of our business depends to a great extent on the living standard and support of those communities."

Source: Adapted from "The Philanthropic CEO," appearing in "Private Profit, Public Gain: Corporate Philanthropy in America," *The Atlantic* (September 1990): 7.

Is it "right" or "wrong" for BP America to spend over $20 million to improve Cleveland's inner city neighborhoods? As a CEO, is Ross's decision to use corporate funds in this manner correct or prudent? Is it necessary for firms to make commitments of this type to be considered socially responsible members of their communities? Would you advise Ross to continue allocating BP America's financial and human resources in the manners described in the opening case? Would your advice to Ross change if you were a BP America employee or stockholder?

Answering questions such as these is difficult and challenging. Issues of managerial ethics and corporate social responsibility are almost always controversial. A key reason is that situations involving ethical matters rarely give rise to clear choices. Ethical decisions challenge managers to deal with many points of view and responsibilities. Customers, stockholders, suppliers, employees, and members of the community in which a firm operates are examples of groups who often hold different beliefs about the company's social responsibilities. Furthermore, ethical decisions usually must be made with incomplete and/or unclear information.[1] Complicating this matter even more are the differences in managers' thoughts and feelings about ethical matters. Similarly, some firms are thought to be more moral than others.[2]

Managers at all levels continuously face decision situations requiring moral judgments. Global marketplaces increase both the number and complexity of these situations for today's managers.[3] Competing in countries with widely different business practices and ethical standards creates a complex web of interactions requiring managerial interpretation and action. Without an understanding of their own ethical positions and those of their companies, managers lack the foundation necessary to respond successfully to these challenges.

This chapter evaluates three views of corporate social responsibility. To introduce these views, the chapter first discusses the importance and history of ethics and corporate social responsibility, followed by definitions of these key terms. The chapter also discusses three criteria—legality, common practice, and codes of ethics—that reflect a firm's moral values and standards for ethical behaviors. In addition, the influences of individual, organizational, and environmental factors on managerial ethics are described. The chapter closes with a discussion of several guidelines for ethical management.

These topics are important. In response to society's interests, efforts are currently being made to incorporate the study of ethics into business school curricula.[4] Because you are tomorrow's manager, it is important for you to study ethics today. This chapter's materials challenge you to think about your responses to various ethical situations before you encounter them. Examining these topics will also help you determine the moral values and behavioral standards you want your employer to emphasize.

THE IMPORTANCE AND HISTORY OF ETHICS

The last two decades have seen an increasing awareness of corporate social responsibilities and business ethics. Part of this awareness results from actions of high-profile business people, athletes, and political leaders, among others.[5] Blatant indiscretions on Wall Street, questionable activities in the White House and Congress, and the excessive charges on government contracts are but a few examples of actions that have been brought painfully to the public's attention. Given the events of the 1970s and 1980s, the public interest in ethics and social responsibility may be at an all-time high in the 1990s.[6]

A number of interrelated events serve as the foundation on which the current concern about ethics and corporate social responsibility is grounded. The Civil Rights Act of 1964 was landmark legislation for business ethics. It reflected a growing belief that discrimination against minority groups is morally wrong and dangerous to society. Moreover, the Kennedy and Johnson administrations created high expectations of a new era of social justice, equality of opportunity, removal of urban blight, and even the elimination of poverty. However, regardless of whatever progress may have been made during subsequent administrations, these goals are proving to be highly idealistic. People have become disillusioned, and some have reacted with political activism and expressions of frustration and resentment as evidenced by riots and aggressive demonstrations.

The general unrest of the 1960s, some of which was associated with the Vietnam War, gave rise to the passage of social legislation. This was also a time in which the public's attention became focused on problems such as crime, inflation, environmental pollution, and organizational corruption. During the early part of the 1970s, the Watergate scandal set the mood for investigative news reporting. Some of the nation's most respected corporations admitted to illegal campaign contributions during the late 1970s and early 1980s. Bribes to foreign companies and government officials were exposed.

ETHICS QUESTION
How would you respond
to people who say that
business is an unethical
profession practiced by
unethical people?

In the latter part of the 1980s, there was concern over a significant number of alleged bank embezzlements.[7] In addition, major scandals were reported among Wall Street firms, the Marine Corps tried several of its own for treason, and charges of moral and financial wrongdoings were brought against the founders of the Praise the Lord (PTL) religious organization. Because of such events, ethics became a hot topic for debate at the national level. The view was that the materialism of the 1980s left the nation without values, and society was experiencing a widespread sense of moral disarray.

In the early 1990s, the nation continues to reel from ethical problems, among them the scandals in banks and savings and loan institutions. The bailout for these institutions will cost taxpayers at least $150 billion. Society will feel the effects of illegal and unethical practices in these settings for some time to come. Other ethical issues that are likely to confront managers during the 1990s are electronic monitoring of people's activities, collection and distribution of consumer information and databases, and the practice of drug testing.

The message from these events is clear: Managers must act ethically and corporations must be socially responsible. Businesses of all types, their managers, and their employees are expected to behave in a way that is acceptable to society and conforms to its values. Failing to do this causes firms to lose control of their own destinies. To attain full legitimacy and remain private, corporations must accept the fact that they have a social, or "public," role and function.[8]

In addition to society's explicit expectations, there are other reasons why ethical and socially responsible behavior is important. Although there is some argument, evidence suggests that socially responsible corporations are successful in the long run. The CEO of the Schock Group believes that "just as it is impossible to cook good quality pancakes with bad eggs, it is impossible to achieve successful, long-term business results without strict adherence to high moral principles."[9] While a socially irresponsible firm may be successful in the short term, its actions and orientations are not likely to be profitable in the long term in a highly competitive era.[10]

Another practical reason to support ethical corporate behavior concerns individual workers. Some employees have reported greater levels of job satisfaction when managers stress the importance of ethical behavior. Establishing a clear relationship between ethical actions and success on the job yields even more satisfaction. This relationship is shown as top-level managers reward ethical behavior and punish unethical behavior.[11]

Taking the high road is not always easy. Without support from the top-, middle- and first-level managers often establish behavioral standards on their own. Sometimes this requires managers to report what they believe are unethical practices. Remaining committed to ethical behavior demands managerial courage.[12]

But managers cannot accomplish everything. Individual employees must act ethically at all times, refraining from questionable practices on a daily basis. Examples of questionable practices include taking credit for others' ideas, blaming others for one's own mistakes, trying to "pass the buck" instead of being responsible for one's actions, starting rumors about a co-worker, and trying to find ways to avoid doing legitimate job tasks. Collectively, these types of actions create an environment in which it is virtually impossible for ethical behavior to flourish.

LEARNING CHECK

Describe the importance of managerial ethics and corporate social responsibility. Discuss why studying these topics today will benefit your career tomorrow.

DEFINING ETHICS AND SOCIAL RESPONSIBILITY

ETHICS QUESTION
Have you thought about your ethics? Would you be comfortable describing your ethics to your classmates?

The word *ethics* comes from the Greek root *ethos*, meaning character: guiding beliefs, standards, or ideals of a group, a community, a people. Today, **ethics** refers to the moral values and standards defining desirable conduct. Ethical standards reflect behaviors that promote human welfare in terms of both the individual and society.[13] Some think of ethics as the glue that binds a society together.[14] Terms such as *business ethics*, *corporate ethics*, *medical ethics*, or *legal ethics* are used to indicate the particular area of application. **Managerial ethics** are the moral values and standards that define desirable managerial behaviors.

Social responsibility is concerned with a firm's obligation to pursue long-term goals that will serve its own interests as well as those of society. Social responsibility reflects the moral values and behavioral standards of the entire firm. When dealing with social responsibility issues, managers are aware of both the economic and social outcomes of their firms' actions.

These definitions reflect a tendency to think of social responsibility in terms of firms and of ethics in terms of individual managers and employees. However, this distinction is not meaningful. In the final analysis, decisions are made by people; therefore, individual managers at some level must assume responsibility for every corporate decision. The salesperson lying about the performance characteristics of a competitor's product, the manufacturer marketing a highly flammable article of clothing, and the industrialist dumping pollutants into a stream—all are behaving in an ethically irresponsible manner. When these things happen, the manager's ethics will be in question and the firm will be viewed as socially irresponsible.

The only way a firm can be socially responsible is for its employees to value ethical behavior and act ethically.[15] Long-term ethical behavior is possible only in organizational environments that promote and support such behavior.[16]

VIEWS OF SOCIAL RESPONSIBILITY

Corporations act in a socially responsible manner because of the values various members believe are important. Because of this, a number of views of corporate social responsibility have been developed. Each view implies moral values and behavioral standards thought to be important for both managers and their firms. Three of the most prominent views of corporate social responsibility are discussed in this chapter: the classical view, the accountability view, and the public view (see Figure 3-1).

The Classical View

The **classical view of social responsibility** suggests that firms should concentrate on earning profits and should not be concerned directly with social goals and issues. This perspective dominated business practices during the 19th and early 20th centuries.

The work of the economist Adam Smith is the foundation for the classical perspective. Smith argued that in a capitalistic, free-enterprise economy, an **invisible hand**—the capitalistic competitive system itself—works continually for the public's good.[17] As a firm pursues profits through competition, the economic system forces it to be efficient and produce the highest quality product at the lowest possible price. Competition demands that businesses satisfy customers' needs through their products and deal fairly and honestly with the public. To do otherwise results in a loss of customers to competitors. Competition for labor and the need for a desirable image with society require companies to treat employees fairly. Similarly, competition for jobs encourages employees to work efficiently and productively for their employers.

In summary, the classical view suggests that because of the invisible hand, specific social responsibility philosophies and programs are unnecessary. It is not necessary to establish ethical business or managerial practices beyond the legal rules of the competitive arena. A firm's single social responsibility is to earn profits for its shareholders. Through these efforts, the welfare of all—employees, shareholders, and the general society—are served appropriately and effectively.[18]

ARGUMENTS FOR THE CLASSICAL VIEW. A strong advocate for the classical view is Milton Friedman. This well-known economist believes that managers should engage only in actions intended to maximize shareholders' wealth. He argues that giving resources to social projects without shareholders' explicit consent is wrong. Furthermore, he suggests that managers'

Economist Adam Smith, whose work is the foundation of the classical view of social responsibility, argued that the capitalistic system by its very nature works for the public good.

FIGURE 3-1
Views of Corporate
Social Responsibility

Classical View	**Accountability View**	**Public View**
A firm's social responsibility is to earn profits as permitted by the capitalistic system.	A firm should balance its efforts to achieve both economic and social goals.	A firm should work actively to solve social problems, including poverty, crime, pollution, and unemployment.

ethical responsibility is to make profit-oriented decisions through which the firm engages in open and free competition without deception or fraud.[19] Friedman's position implies that society's needs are served best when the competitive economy is allowed to function with few restrictions.

Back to the
Opening Case

Recall that through James Ross's leadership and support, BP America contributed over $20 million to projects to revitalize parts of Cleveland, Ohio. How would Milton Friedman and other advocates of the classical view see these expenditures? Would they advise that the firm's financial resources continue to be used in this manner? Be prepared to discuss your position.

ARGUMENTS AGAINST THE CLASSICAL VIEW. Some claim that for all its benefits, the actions called for by proponents of the classical view are basically amoral. The impersonality of these actions stifles expressions of values such as love, compassion, concern for the individual, and deep commitment to codes of personal ethics.

Remember that the classical view is based on the invisible hand theory, which suggests that the best outcomes for society as a whole are achieved when individuals pursue their self-interest.[20] Even if the invisible hand serves the public well in the long term, however, many people may suffer in the short term.

Others suggest that, if permitted to operate freely, competition would destroy itself and result in monopoly. As early as the Interstate Commerce Act in 1887, it was obvious that unrestrained trade was not in the public interest. Since that time, the public has expressed a desire to exercise some control over businesses' operations. Antitrust laws encourage competition. Other laws protect parts of society from the freedom of businesses' pursuit of immediate self-interest without concern for the short- and long-term effects of their actions on the environment, consumers, labor, the general economy, and society.

There are arguments opposing these criticisms of the classical view. For example, some believe that capitalism is an open system designed to stimulate initiative and productivity by rewarding individuals on the basis of merit.[21] Refusing to employ members of a minority group, allowing bias to influence promotion decisions, providing an unsafe workplace, or lying to consumers is not consistent with capitalistic beliefs since such actions are not in firms' self-interest. Thus, some argue that the manner in which managers implement the classical view of social responsibility, rather than the view itself, should be criticized.

The Accountability View

The **accountability view** of social responsibility suggests that each firm should pay its own way, be fully accountable for its actions, and treat each group that has an interest in the firm with fairness and consideration. This view is grounded in the position that the capitalistic, free-market economy is virtuous and is the framework within which companies should operate. The view also supports the idea that businesses are chartered by society and should therefore be accountable to it. A business should not only fulfill its responsibilities to its shareholders but also deal fairly with others upon whom its success depends—employees, customers, suppliers, creditors, and the community and larger economy in which the firm operates. Thus, the objective is to achieve a balance between profitability and the accomplishment of social goals. The Sara Lee Corporation appears to be trying to achieve this balance. Its position is that business has a role beyond the generation of profits. By investing their goodwill, time, and money, companies can—and should—serve as catalysts for dealing with social issues.[22]

To implement the accountability view, a firm may encourage its employees to seek out positions through which they can address the needs of their communities.[23] Contributing time and expertise to community projects supports the spirit of this view. The behaviors and standards expected of all employees—managerial and nonmanagerial—often are detailed in codes of ethics that inform employees of the behaviors a firm will and will not tolerate. This information is valuable in that employees can decide whether or not the firm's positions are ones they can support. For their own comfort and productivity, all workers should seek employment in a company with ethical and behavioral standards they can support fully.

ARGUMENTS FOR THE ACCOUNTABILITY VIEW. The important role of the individual's actions is at the heart of the free-market system. Capitalism calls for individuals to accept responsibility for their own welfare and actions. An extension of this philosophy is that firms, too, should be responsible for their actions and should pay their own way. Firms that hold the accountability view are aware of their responsibility to be contributing members to the groups they serve, including society at large.

The American Cancer Society building, located in a blighted area of Long Beach, California, reflects the organization's commitment to improving the environment of the community it serves.

Another argument favoring the accountability view concerns business people's involvement with social projects. Recall that Mr. Ross and other leaders from the Cleveland community volunteered to serve as members of Neighborhood Progress. These individuals' business expertise can be used to solve some of Cleveland's problems. Successful business people have opportunities to give back to local, state, and national communities through use of their time and talents. The Organization in Action describes a company that supports and encourages involvement with local communities. As you read it, think of projects you might choose to be involved with if you worked for Time Warner.

ORGANIZATION IN ACTION

Time Warner's *Social Responsibility Report* spells out the company's philosophies, commitments, and actions regarding many ethical and social responsibility issues. With respect to voluntarism, "Time Warner encourages its employees to volunteer their time to community service. The Volunteer Project Grant program offers funds to support nonprofit organizations to which employees give their time. The annual Andrew Heiskell Community Service Awards are presented to employees who have made exceptional contributions in public service, human rights and equal opportunity."

Source: Used with permission from Time Warner Inc.

ARGUMENTS AGAINST THE ACCOUNTABILITY VIEW. A major argument against the accountability view is that firms should not be concerned with balancing economic and social goals. Their single objective, some argue, is to earn profits for the company's shareholders. It is not their role to serve as a catalyst for solving society's problems.

A related argument against this view is that it is difficult to determine the proper balance between profitability and social goals. Gaining consensus among managers, employees, shareholders, and others as to what constitutes an appropriate balance requires compromise by all parties.

The Public View

The final of the three views extends beyond accountability. The **public view of social responsibility** portrays businesses as partners with government, education, and other institutions in solving society's problems and improving the quality of life for all. The goal of earning profits remains critical, but firms committed to the public view establish genuinely altruistic as well as profit-oriented goals. Firms that share this view work actively to solve social problems such as poverty, unemployment, pollution, inflation, and crime.

The public view holds that because society has given businesses the right to use its scarce resources and has provided an environment favorable to earning profits, business firms are the public's servants. Therefore, the public has a right and an obligation to control businesses for the public good. "Where the public interest . . . is at issue, there is no natural right to be left alone."[24] Thus, firms are no longer viewed as independent beings owned by a few members of the general society. Ethical issues are to be included in analyses of a firm's mission and development of its strategies. (Missions and strategies are discussed fully in Chapters 5 and 6.) Employees are selected, trained, and rewarded in terms of their social as well as economic capabilities and performance.[25]

ETHICS QUESTION
Do you believe that companies have a moral obligation to the society in which they operate? Why or why not?

ARGUMENTS FOR THE PUBLIC VIEW. The primary argument for the public view is that private businesses are approved and promoted by society for the benefit of society. As such, they have a moral obligation to society. Other arguments for this view are more practical. Supporting this view may be one way for businesses to avoid ever-increasing government controls. To the extent that the public view provides solutions to society's problems, businesses' long-term interests are well served by it.

ARGUMENTS AGAINST THE PUBLIC VIEW. Opposing the public view is the argument that the efficiency of businesses and the subsequent benefits to all of society's members are grounded in a limited objective—earning profits. Introducing social goals clashes with the traditional managerial orientation toward efficiency, competitiveness, and profit. It could be said that the traditional contributions of businesses are enough in themselves to justify the role of businesses in society—assuming that they pay their way as advocated by the accountability view.

How do managers react to the public view of social responsibility? As might be expected, some believe businesses should help solve social problems regardless of the causes of those problems, while others do not.

Ben and Jerry's Homemade Inc. is an example of a firm managed by individuals who support the public social responsibility view. The company has been labeled "relentlessly progressive" because of its actions and contributions. Its popsicles are called Peace Pops. It has made donations to

Ben Cohen and Jerry Greenfield, shown here at a public rally, represent a firm that is committed to the public view of social responsibility.

organizations interested in the welfare of the aged and the homeless, among many others.

Even for this firm, however, questions have been raised about its actual orientation to social responsibility. For example, the firm has been criticized for its unclear reaction to the reported lethal link between ice cream and thickening of the arteries.[26] Thus, it is difficult to fully implement the public view of social responsibility. A commitment to this view challenges managers to remain focused on the philosophies and actions appropriate to it.

Selecting a Social Responsibility View

Selecting a firm's social responsibility view is an important activity that should involve many groups. Involving a range of people interested in the company's welfare and performance assures that many valid inputs will be considered. Once chosen, the view reflects the entire firm's moral values and behavioral standards. All policies and actions should be consistent with the view selected.

Conditions sometimes change, affecting a firm's posture toward social responsibility. For example, the cost of providing health coverage for employees is increasing dramatically. To pay for a single appendectomy, the Goodyear Tire & Rubber Company must sell 461 radial tires for passenger cars. Anheuser-Busch must sell 11,627 six-packs of twelve-ounce Budweiser to pay for an appendectomy.[27] These costs have not affected either company's posture toward being socially responsible to its employees. However, the impact of the costs on the firms' financial resources must be considered.

In response to changing consumer interests, the Kentucky Fried Chicken Corp. began adding nonfried items to its menus in the 1990s. These items included broiled chicken and chicken salad sandwiches, among others.[28] These changes in the firm's product offerings may or may not signal movement to a different view of social responsibility. However, such changes in consumer interests encourage a reexamination of the social responsibility view a firm wants to adopt.

The managerial challenge is to select a social responsibility view that fits a firm's resources and dominant values. Selection of a public view by a firm that is barely profitable, for example, is not wise, since implementing a public view requires adequate financial, human, informational, and physical resources. But once an appropriate view is chosen, managers must shape the firm's actions in a way that is consistent with the demands of that view.

Back to the
Opening Case

It is interesting to give some thought to the social responsibility view selected by BP America. What is your opinion? Could it be argued that the firm's commitment of financial and human resources to the active revitalization of Cleveland is consistent with the public social responsibility view? Or, do you believe the firm's actions are more consistent with the accountability view? Be prepared to discuss your opinion.

CRITERIA FOR A FIRM'S VALUES AND BEHAVIORAL STANDARDS

We tend to recall major news events such as the oil spill by the Exxon Valdez when thinking about managerial ethics and corporate social responsibility. However, managers' daily decisions are an equally meaningful reflection of ethics and social responsibility. What may appear to be routine managerial decisions often become the foundation on which major ethical decisions are made. The basis for day-to-day decisions at Johnson & Johnson is described in the Organization in Action.

ORGANIZATION IN ACTION

Ralph Larsen, CEO of Johnson & Johnson, enjoys describing what he witnessed as a J&J trainee in one of the company's baby-shampoo factories. As a trainee, Larsen once attended a meeting during which managers discussed a situation requiring an ethical decision. A large batch of the factory's shampoo was ready for shipment. Although the shampoo was safe, it fell short of satisfying J&J's "no tears" standard. The managers decided that the company should take a loss rather than ship the shampoo.

According to Larsen, this decision is an example of doing what is right. He believes that "if we keep trying to do what's right, at the end of the day . . . the marketplace will reward us." Decisions to do what is right are grounded in the firm's Credo, which stresses honesty, integrity, and putting people before profits. J&J's top-level managers spend considerable time making certain that all employees behave in manners consistent with the Credo. To assure the Credo's usefulness, senior-level executives debate its contents every few years.

Source: Adapted from Brian Dumaine, "Leaders of the Most Admired," *Fortune* (January 29, 1990): 50, 54.

Johnson & Johnson's Credo reflects the firm's posture toward social responsibility issues. It describes the firm's moral values and behavioral standards and provides managers with the direction required to make ethical decisions on a day-to-day basis. Because of the firm's moral values and behavioral standards, J&J's response to the Tylenol tragedy is not surprising.

ETHICS QUESTION
Can you think of anything else Johnson & Johnson could have done to respond ethically to the Tylenol crisis?

Eight people died from poisoned Tylenol capsules in the fall of 1982. The company was convinced that the capsules had been altered in stores, not in a Johnson & Johnson factory. Nonetheless, J&J immediately withdrew Tylenol capsules from shelves around the country, absorbing a $240 million loss in the process. Day-to-day decisions such as the one Mr. Larsen witnessed as a J&J trainee suggest what a firm's response will be to major ethical decision situations such as the Tylenol tragedy.

Different decision criteria reflect different moral values and behavioral standards. Not all organizations use the same decision guideline. Moral values differ among firms, and they are more important in some firms than in others.[29] The managerial challenge is to select a guideline that is consistent with the moral values and behavioral standards held by employees, shareholders, customers, board members, and others involved with the firm. Serious problems develop when people are uncertain of the decision criterion to use when evaluating social responsibility issues. Once selected, a guideline should be used consistently by all employees for all events. Selecting a decision criterion is important in that some firms believe their moral values provide them with a competitive advantage. Johnson & Johnson is an example of such a company.[30]

The sections that follow examine three criteria that express a firm's moral values and behavioral standards (see Figure 3-2). While reading, think about which of these criteria assures consistency between a firm's actions and the demands of the classical, accountability, and public perspectives of corporate social responsibility.

FIGURE 3-2 Criteria for an Organization's Values and Standards

Legality Criterion	**Common Practice Criterion**	**Code of Ethics Criterion**
Obedience to the laws of the land	Pursuit of all practices common among business firms	Development of a formal statement of behaviors expected of all employees

Legality Criterion

The **legality criterion** for behavioral standards suggests that the laws of the land provide all the direction required to make ethical decisions. Adoption of this guideline demonstrates a firm's belief that following a democratic society's laws is all the society can and should expect of corporations. Laws followed in these instances include constitutions, statutes, judicial decrees, and municipal ordinances.[31]

With this criterion, a firm's values and behavioral standards flow from the rules of the state. The firm is more concerned with an action's legality than its morality.[32] Using this guideline to make ethical decisions results in the following reasoning: "If it's legal, do it; if we aren't certain of its legality, check with the lawyers. If they approve, go ahead with it."

The laws of the land do influence corporate behavior. At times, the higher ethical standards called for by new legislation become part of a firm's moral fiber. Furthermore, laws do enforce a basic civility among all of society's members.[33]

The baseline of a society's laws is an important benchmark for making ethical decisions in firms of all types. However, some believe there is a critical difference between ethics and law. Laws reflect a society's feelings about its culture and how people intend to live within that culture. In contrast, ethics, which are concerned with moral values and standards, serve to define what is right and wrong.[34] To understand this subtle difference, consider the following phrase: "There is a difference between the spirit of the law (morality) and the letter of the law (legality)." This subtlety would be unimportant in firms that base their ethical decisions on the legality criterion. In general, the legality criterion causes firms to *react* to social responsibility issues. The moral values and behavioral standards in a firm using this guideline effectively satisfy the basic requirement the firm must fulfill to be sanctioned by society.

Common Practice Criterion

Common practice is another criterion firms use to establish their values and standards. The **common practice criterion** of behavioral standards suggests that failing to engage in certain practices results in a competitive disadvantage. Examples of these practices include bribery, espionage, and paying below-standard wages. Reasons for adopting this guideline include the following: "It's common practice, so why not do it?"; "Everybody else does it, why not us?"; "There's no way anyone will ever find out"; and "We won't get caught, so let's go ahead and do it."[35]

Firms operating in highly competitive markets may be comfortable with this decision guideline. When price competition is fierce, companies may believe they lack the resources required to engage in socially responsible actions beyond the industry's norm. Thus, use of common practice as a decision-making criterion results in what some consider to be practical business behaviors.

However, common practice is not grounded in an absolute value system. Because of this, a firm's moral values and behavioral standards change from one decision situation to another. Unlike the legality criterion, common practice has little value when firms try to formally establish their approach to social responsibility issues. Businesses that use this guideline are often cited for practicing **situational ethics,** an approach in which moral values and behavioral standards change from event to event. Practicing ethics in this manner is inconsistent with society's expectations.

Code of Ethics Criterion

A **code of ethics** is a formal statement of the values and behaviors a firm expects of its employees. As a decision criterion, a code of ethics details actions a firm expects its employees to follow when dealing with ethical decision situations.

A code of ethics is a particularly visible sign of a firm's intended moral values and behavioral standards. Partly because of this visibility, the number of firms with codes of ethics is increasing. In one survey, 75 percent of firms contacted had prepared codes of ethics.[36]

ETHICS QUESTION
Would you prefer to work for a firm that has a Code of Ethics? Why or why not?

Typically, a code of ethics describes a firm's positions with respect to political contributions; use of insider information; illegal payments; bribery and kickbacks; dealing with proprietary information; and the use of corporate assets, gifts, and favors, among other issues.[37] Usually, firms prepare separate written sections to describe their positions in terms of individual issues. *The Colgate-Palmolive Company Code of Conduct*, for example, discusses the firm's values and behavioral expectations in terms of relationships with fellow employees, the company itself, other businesses, consumers, government and the law, society, the environment, and shareholders. Part of this code, as it applies to the company's relationship with other business entities, is presented in the Organization in Action. As you read this information,

ORGANIZATION IN ACTION

OUR RELATIONSHIP WITH BUSINESS ENTITIES

Each of us is responsible for how we are perceived by suppliers and customers. It is essential that we maintain our reputation for honesty and fair dealing with these groups.

We deal ethically with suppliers and customers.

Our aim in conducting our purchasing operations is to assure continuing, reliable sources of supply. Thus, we view our suppliers as partners and expect them to make a reasonable profit. We give all potential suppliers fair and uniform consideration. Factors of race, religion, national origin, sex or friendship play no part in purchasing decisions, which are based on objective criteria such as price and quality or a vendor's reliability and integrity. Needless to say, kickbacks and similar payments or favors are prohibited.

Similarly, we never offer payments or similar inducements to customers to make a sale other than published promotional or other incentive offers. Only gifts without significant value may be given to customers or purchasing agents on traditional gift-giving occasions. We extend no favors to customers on prices, promotional allowances, marketing assistance or the like; we treat all customers the same fair way.

Dealings with customers and suppliers are regulated by the antitrust laws, which are discussed in the section of this manual addressing our legal responsibilities.

We respect the secrets of others.

It is Company policy to respect the trade secrets of others. This is particularly pertinent if you have knowledge of trade secrets of a former employer. If any questions should arise in this area, you should consult legal counsel for your unit or division for guidance.

When outsiders approach you with an invention, discovery or idea, it is important to protect the Company against future infringement or monetary claims, especially in cases where our own efforts or those of our consultants have previously arrived at the same discovery, and we wish to apply our discovery to a new product. Thus do not permit outsiders to reveal any details of their invention, discovery or new idea unless they are suppliers or professionals in the relevant field and have signed a release in the form available from legal counsel for your unit or division or the corporate legal department. If you work for a Colgate company that has a consumer affairs department, you should refer all unsolicited ideas, without review, to it for proper handling and response.

Source: *The Colgate-Palmolive Company Code of Conduct*. Used with permission of the Colgate-Palmolive Company.

consider how this part of the company's code would guide your behavior if you worked for Colgate-Palmolive.

The value of a code of ethics does not lie in the written word. To be effective, employees must endorse the values and behavioral standards included in the code. In its *Code of Conduct*, the Colgate-Palmolive Company states that "the act of producing a written code of conduct must be communicated to and agreed upon by those who are asked to follow them."[38] In addition, a code of ethics must be comprehensive in its design, clear in its presentation, and enforceable.[39]

LEARNING CHECK

Describe three criteria firms use to reflect their intended moral values and behavioral standards. Also discuss your feelings about working under each criterion.

Have you determined how the classical, accountability, and public social responsibility views relate to the legality, common practice, and code of ethics decision criteria for a firm's moral values and behavioral standards? In considering this matter, it is first important to note the inadequacy of the common practice criterion. The ethical and social responsibility challenges facing today's firms are too complex to be approached through situational ethics, and situational ethics tend to result from use of the common practice criterion. Although it is still in use, this decision criterion should be discontinued in favor of one of the other two criteria.

The classical social responsibility view can be held successfully when the legality criterion is used. Carefully and consistently obeying the laws of the land allows businesses to focus on earning profits. The code of ethics criterion is required when firms approach social responsibility from the standpoint of either the accountability or the public view. The managerial challenge is to develop a code of ethics that is consistent with the demands of each view. The code of ethics for firms holding the public view addresses a greater number of issues with greater depth than a code for companies holding the accountability view.

The next sections describe factors that influence managerial ethics. While reading, consider how some of these factors have influenced your views of ethical behavior.

FACTORS INFLUENCING MANAGERIAL ETHICS

A range of factors influences a manager's ethics. Our discussion focuses on three broad categories of factors: individual, organizational, and environmental (see Figure 3-3).

Individual Factors

Values have an effect on individuals' managerial ethics. **Values** are a person's beliefs about proper standards of conduct and desired results.[40] They are

FIGURE 3-3
Factors Influencing
Managerial Ethics

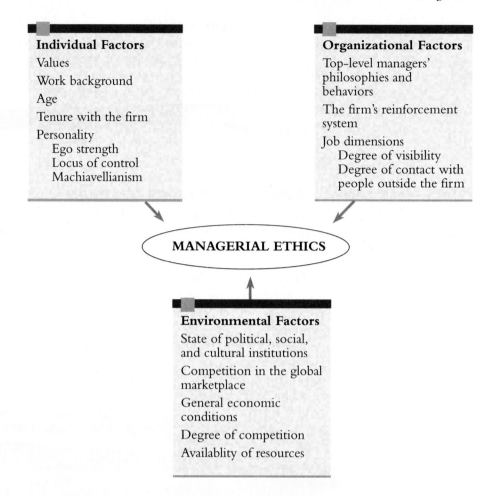

Individual Factors

Values

Work background

Age

Tenure with the firm

Personality
  Ego strength
  Locus of control
  Machiavellianism

Organizational Factors

Top-level managers'
philosophies and
behaviors

The firm's reinforcement
system

Job dimensions
  Degree of visibility
  Degree of contact with
  people outside the firm

MANAGERIAL ETHICS

Environmental Factors

State of political, social,
and cultural institutions

Competition in the global
marketplace

General economic
conditions

Degree of competition

Availablity of resources

shaped by all of life's experiences. Socialization experiences shape people's values in many ways. Deeply religious people, for example, hold a particular set of beliefs that influences their perceptions of proper behaviors. Individuals who believe that education is the pathway to effective performance may have unique viewpoints regarding a company's responsibility for continuously training its employees. People committed to the importance of hard work usually expect others to work as long and hard as they do. Other socialization experiences that influence managerial ethics include work background, age, and tenure with a firm. One study found that, with regard to many ethical issues, people who had spent 10 or more years with a particular company were less tolerant of unethical behavior than those with less experience.[41]

In addition to their socialization experiences, individuals' personalities influence their managerial ethics. Ego strength, locus of control, and Machiavellianism are three personality traits that have important influences on ethics.[42]

Ego strength describes an individual's ability to manage his or her own behavior, particularly in tense situations. People with high ego strength are less impulsive and more determined to follow their convictions than those with low ego strength. If they are committed to a firm's standards, managers with high ego strength can be effective in dealing with value-laden projects.

Locus of control is a measure of an individual's belief about who determines outcomes in his or her life. Those with an **internal locus of control** believe that outcomes are a result of their own actions. Those with an **external locus of control** believe that outcomes are a product of luck, fate, or destiny. Managers with an internal locus of control are likely to accept responsibility for their ethical or unethical behaviors. In contrast, managers with an external locus of control are less likely to accept personal responsibility for the consequences of their ethical or unethical behaviors, preferring to believe that the outcomes were caused by external forces.[43] When possible, managers with an internal locus of control should be responsible for projects when accountability is crucial.

Machiavellianism is a measure of deceitfulness and duplicity. Managers who score high on this measure try to manipulate others for their own personal gain. Of course, the ethics of managers with high scores on the Machiavellianism measure are of serious concern.

Organizational Factors

To a large degree, people imitate behaviors they see taking place around them. Because of this, the impact of managerial philosophies and behaviors on other managers' ethics is significant and pervasive.[44] The most desirable situation is for high-principled behaviors to start with members of a firm's board of directors.[45] The top-level manager who observes board members behaving in highly ethical ways is influenced to behave the same way. Likewise, middle-level managers will imitate the ethical behaviors of top-level managers, while first-level managers will imitate middle-level managers' behaviors.

A second organizational factor influencing managerial ethics is a firm's reinforcement system.[46] Companies must develop performance measures to assess managers' performances in terms of ethical expectations. Rewards must go to those who behave ethically, while punishments must be dispensed to those who behave unethically. Developing such reinforcement systems increases the probability that managers will behave in a consistently ethical manner over the long term.

Several job factors also influence managerial ethics. Highly visible jobs, particularly ones involving personnel with frequent communications with many people, encourage ethical decisions and actions. Jobs that require interactions with people outside the firm have more potential for ethical dilemmas than do jobs completed through contacts only inside the company.[47] Managers who regularly confront ethical and moral dilemmas have numerous opportunities to refine their ability to manage ethically. Purchasing managers, for example, must often deal with offers of gifts, questionable pricing strategies, and so forth.

Environmental Factors

Environmental factors also affect managerial ethics. Because they are outside managers' direct control, these factors are sometimes the most frustrating.

In the view of almost two-thirds of those surveyed, the decay in political, social, and cultural institutions is today's most serious threat to business ethics.[48] This belief challenges managers to become involved with projects and activities that may lead to a reversal of this situation.

Increasing pressures to compete in the global marketplace also affect managerial ethics. Coping with different countries' ethical practices suggests a situational approach to ethics. However, while managers want to achieve competitive success, they should not do so through sacrificing their own or their companies' ethics and standards of behavior.

Other environmental factors influencing managerial ethics include the nation's general economic conditions, the degree of competition facing a firm, and the availability of resources. When economic conditions are poor, the firm is facing severe competition, and they are unable to obtain required resources, managers are challenged to remain committed to ethical business practices.

We have now examined a number of issues of ethics and social responsibility. Our discussions should provide the foundation you need to consider your own views about managerial ethics and corporate social responsibility. We now turn to the principles by which ethical management can be practiced.

LEARNING CHECK   Discuss the three categories of factors that influence the development and practice of managerial ethics.

GUIDELINES FOR ETHICAL MANAGEMENT

You will be challenged to behave ethically in any responsible position you hold. Similarly, society will expect the firms for which you work to be socially responsible. These challenges are important in that some believe successful management and ethical management are synonymous.[49]

For some, it is difficult to practice ethical management; for others, the challenge is not as great. Establishing a strong commitment to the process of ethical management is a critical step. Such a commitment, combined with adherence to the following guidelines, makes maintaining ethical management practices easier.[50]

1. *Behave ethically.* The importance of setting the behavioral standard you expect of employees through your own actions cannot be overemphasized. People tend to imitate behaviors they see repeated consistently. Managers should always act appropriately and ethically. They cannot expect ethical behaviors from employees if they act unethically themselves. Employees should also understand that ethical standards are not negotiable. One person's view of highly ethical managerial behavior is shown in Figure 3-4. Are you comfortable with these behaviors?
2. *Screen carefully and hire the right people.* A firm's ethics are a product of the ethical practices of all those working for the firm. As a result, hiring

FIGURE 3-4
Taking the High Ground

First

Even on little, daily things, quickly take responsibility; take the high ground. Don't let problems fester. Festering problems devolve into bad situations while quickly reacting can save the day and maybe even minimize the cost of your decision.

Second

Pay attention to details. Use these little things to establish an ethical mosaic, your own mosaic.

Third

If you can't change a potentially unethical situation, get out of it. If you operate from an ethical basis, don't perpetuate the lack of ethics.

Fourth

"Never knock the competition," we tell our salesforce and our employees. And it works.

Fifth

It isn't enough to do the legal thing; do the right thing. It feels good. Your staff can sleep at night and so can you. It pays, too—Everybody has more energy for the job.

Sixth

Don't take ethics for granted. Read about it, attend seminars, talk to your bosses, peers, and friends.

Seventh

Finally, never forget that it isn't enough to have a code of ethics; you also need the competence and guts to follow it.

Source: Richard C. Bartlett, President, Mary Kay Cosmetics, Inc.

highly principled people is critical to the firm's ability to be socially responsible and ethical. Although they are controversial, some tests can be administered legally to measure an individual's ethical tendencies. Some companies (e.g., Chemical Bank and Mary Kay Cosmetics) require employees to sign a statement indicating that they understand and are abiding by the firm's ethical standards. Conducting extensive interviews is another method by which an individual's values and behavioral standards can be determined.

3. *Develop a meaningful code of ethics.* The importance of codes of ethics was considered earlier in the chapter. When developed and handed out in an open environment, and when emphasized constantly, a code of ethics influences behaviors in significant ways. The challenge to managers is to make sure that the firm's code is modified over time to ensure its continued usefulness.

4. *Offer ethics training.* Through training sessions, employees can study a firm's code of ethics and evaluate a variety of ethical situations. Often presented in case format, these situations (which can be real or fictitious) should be similar to the ethical dilemmas employees are likely to face in their jobs. Wrestling with difficult questions in these settings

provides opportunities to discuss the firm's behavioral standards.

5. *Do not become isolated.* Ultimately, managers are responsible for the consequences of decisions made within their responsibility areas. Because of this, they must remain in close touch with employees. Failing to communicate with them regularly and in meaningful ways prevents managers from understanding the ethical issues confronting employees.

6. *Create the capability to deal with ethics.* Long-term ethical behavior occurs when such behavior is expected and supported energetically. Over time, firms must find ways to communicate ethical policies and to verify that employees are behaving ethically. Various approaches can be used to make sure these things take place. Xerox, for example, formed an internal audit committee to monitor ethical behaviors. The Norton Company has established an ethics committee among its board of directors. Company newsletters regularly provide an avenue for providing updates about a firm's ethical policies.

ETHICS QUESTION
Do any of the guidelines for ethical management bother you? If so, which one, or ones, and why?

Back to the Opening Case

In the discussion of the opening case, you were asked whether, in your opinion, BP America should continue allocating the firm's financial and human resources to support Cleveland's revitalization. You were also asked what your advice to Ross would be if you were a BP America employee or shareholder. After reading this chapter, what is your response to these questions? What is your recommendation as a member of the general society? What is your advice as an employee? As a shareholder? Be prepared to discuss the chapter materials you referred to in developing your recommendations.

SUMMARY

Today there is significant interest in and concern about managerial ethics and corporate social responsibility. While these topics can be discussed separately, in practice they are interdependent. In the final analysis, corporate social responsibility is evidenced by the ethical practices of individual employees.

Ethics and social responsibility are concerned with value-laden decisions and behaviors. Ethics is concerned with the moral values and standards that define desirable behavior. Individuals' ethics are revealed through their actions in organizations. Social responsibility is concerned with a firm's obligation to pursue long-term goals that will benefit an entire society. Corporate social responsibility defines the desired

moral values and intended behavioral standards of a whole organization.

This chapter examined three views of corporate social responsibility. The classical view emphasizes the importance of the free market as a basis for ethical behavior. This view suggests that the capitalistic system itself works to the benefit of all parts of a society. The accountability view extends beyond the classical view in stating that businesses should be responsible for their own actions. In this view, firms should make an effort to achieve a balance between social and economic goals. Finally, the public view proposes that businesses should contribute unselfishly to solving social problems regardless of who caused them. This view stirs considerable managerial debate. Managers must understand all three views in order to select the most appropriate one for their firm. Then, they must verify that the view has been accepted and ensure its use throughout the firm.

The chapter considered three criteria used for a firm's values and behavioral standards: legality, common practice, and a code of ethics. The legality criterion, often used with the classical view of social responsibility, calls for a firm to abide by the laws of the land. Common practice, by which firms duplicate even the questionable behaviors of their competitors, results in an unacceptable commitment to situational ethics. A code of ethics is a formal statement of the values and behaviors a firm expects of its employees. This guideline is used with both the accountability and public social responsibility views.

Individual, organizational, and environmental factors influence managers' ethics. People's socialization experiences and personalities are the individual fac-

tors discussed in the chapter. Organizational factors include the philosophies and behaviors of a firm's leaders, the firm's reinforcement system, and various other attributes such as the visibility of a manager's job and the number of interactions required with people outside the firm. Managers have relatively little control over environmental conditions. Because of this, their influence can be frustrating. Nonetheless, these external realities do influence managers' ethics.

There are various guidelines available to managers who want to engage in ethical management practices. The chapter discussed six guidelines: behaving ethically, screening carefully and hiring the right people, developing a meaningful code of ethics, offering ethics training for employees, remaining involved with employees about ethical issues they face, and creating a capability to deal with ethics. Following these guidelines helps managers become both ethical and successful.

KEY TERMS

ethics
managerial ethics
social responsibility
classical view of social
  responsibility
invisible hand

accountability view of
  social responsibility
public view of social re-
  sponsibility
legality criterion
common practice crite-

rion
situational ethics
code of ethics
values
ego strength
locus of control

internal locus of control
external locus of control
Machiavellianism

QUESTIONS FOR DISCUSSION AND REVIEW

1. How are the terms *ethics*, *managerial ethics*, and *social responsibility* defined in this chapter?
2. Describe the classical, accountability, and public social responsibility views. Is one of these views more comfortable to you than the other two? If so, why?
3. Discuss the three criteria firms use to act out their desired values and behavioral standards. Have you ever worked for a company that used one or more of these criteria? If so, describe how the criteria

influenced your actions as an employee.
4. The chapter indicates that managerial ethics are influenced by individual, organizational, and environmental factors. Offer examples from each category and describe how they might affect your ethics as a manager.
5. Assume that you have accepted a managerial position. In response to your manager, discuss several principles of ethical management.

PROBLEMS FOR ACTION

A. Allan Garrigues works as a first-level manager for a large mobile home manufacturer. Because of the local economy, the firm has struggled for the last two or three years. In the last several months, Garrigues has observed actions that are against company policy. Some employees, including two or three other first-level managers, borrow company power tools for personal use. Occasionally these tools are stolen, but not necessarily by employees. Garrigues has also noticed that the same people sometimes take home small bolts, screws, and similar items for personal use. Is Garrigues observing unethical behaviors? If so, what should he do about it?

B. Assume that your employees' wages are barely sufficient to allow a standard of living above the poverty level. Most are sewing machine operators. For all practical purposes, these people compete with workers throughout the world. Even though your company is barely profitable, you are concerned about the operators' low wages. These concerns are all the more painful when the media accuse you of running a "sweat shop" and having no compassion for your employees' needs. Are you unethical? Is your firm socially irresponsible? What should you, the manager, do?

CONCLUDING CASE

Yarnell Equipment Corporation

Following extensive interviewing, Michael Woodbury accepted an auditing position with Power, Brown & Tangeman. This was a successful, medium-size accounting firm located in San Antonio. Woodbury's first year was busy. He passed all parts of the CPA examination and worked on a range of projects as a junior member of an audit team. Many hours of overtime were required to complete some of these projects. Because he enjoyed his colleagues, Woodbury did not mind this. He also respected the other members of the firm with whom he worked. It appeared that Power, Brown & Tangeman's employees were hardworking, ethical people. Part of the reason for this, Woodbury believed, was top management's strong endorsement of the American Institute of Certified Public Accountants' ethical code.

During his second year with the firm, Woodbury was assigned to the team auditing the Yarnell Equipment Corporation. A successful company, Yarnell was one of Power, Brown & Tangeman's first major clients. Yarnell's primary business was renovating and then selling oil-field equipment used for drilling, well servicing, and pumping.

Many of Yarnell's customers were outside the United States; in fact, most were in Saudi Arabia. Because of this, Yarnell routinely had large sales expenses. However, one expense—Charles Wheeler's consulting fee of $450,000—caught Woodbury's eye. In comparison to expenses for similar services from other people, this fee seemed extremely high. Woodbury decided to discuss the matter with Sandy Davenport, his immediate supervisor.

To Woodbury's surprise, Davenport was not concerned about the payment. Charles Wheeler, she explained, was an influential person known widely for his contacts with high-level Saudi officials. These contacts enabled him to sell Yarnell's renovated equipment when others could not.

Woodbury did not question Wheeler's value to Yarnell. His concern was the lack of records showing relationships between projects and expenses. Davenport did not share this concern. "Wheeler is a part-time consultant," she noted. "He makes contacts, introduces company sales representatives to the right people, and provides information. He bills Yarnell for his services. They pay him without asking questions because they believe he is worth it. What is the problem here?"

Davenport's explanation did not satisfy Woodbury. Recent publicity about bribes to foreign business and government leaders and kickbacks to company executives sparked too many images of how Wheeler may have spent Yarnell's money. Recognizing it as a bold move, Woodbury made an appointment with Dan Hunt, Yarnell's vice president for sales. It took only a few minutes to realize that Hunt did not want to discuss the matter. "Wheeler is an expensive consultant, but he gets results. He is worth what we pay him and more. Anyway, expenses are high in that part of the world, and that region is critical to us."

Woodbury's concern about the expense item remained. He thought Wheeler should be required to account specifically for his work and expenses. Woodbury's mention of this issue to one of Power, Brown & Tangeman's managing partners was also unsatisfying. He was told emphatically that the firm's partners were aware of this matter and supported Davenport's position.

Davenport was furious when she learned of Woodbury's discussion with a managing partner. "Why can't you accept my judgment on this?" she yelled at Woodbury. "I wouldn't be in charge of this audit if I didn't know my business. You aren't the only one around here with a conscience. Don't get the idea that you have to be the guardian of ethics in this firm. If you can't be a little flexible, you won't make it in the real world. Plus, I never want to hear again that you have gone over my head to a partner."

Davenport's outburst shocked Woodbury. He liked his colleagues and wanted to keep his job. On the other hand, Woodbury wondered, how often would he be expected to keep quiet when his conscience told him to speak out? Was Power, Brown & Tangeman accepting Yarnell's position in order to maintain a long-term relationship with an important client? Would the firm's stance be the same with a smaller client? Was he being foolishly suspicious, overly conscientious, and naive? Under what conditions should he take a strong stand—one that might result in loss of his job or require him to blow the whistle to a regulatory body?

1. What are the ethical issues in this situation?
2. To what extent should Woodbury listen to his own conscience in this matter as opposed to going along with the firm's prevailing view?
3. If Woodbury is not absolutely certain that something unethical or irresponsible is going on, does he have a responsibility to Yarnell Equipment Corporation not to do or say anything that might hurt its relationships with shareholders, customers, and the public?
4. Dan Hunt told Woodbury that, because of the results he gets, Charles Wheeler is actually worth more to Yarnell than he was paid. Does this statement suggest that the ends justify the means? Evaluate.

REFERENCES

1. Kenneth R. Andrews, "Ethics in Practice," *Harvard Business Review* (September–October 1989): 99–104.
2. Paul C. Nystrom, "Differences in Moral Values Between Corporations," *Journal of Business Ethics* (December 1990): 971–979.
3. John Dobson, "The Role of Ethics in Global Corporate Culture," *Journal of Business Ethics* (June 1990): 481–488.
4. David S. Merrill, "Business," *U.S. News & World Report* (March 19, 1990): 52–56.
5. Bruce D. Fisher, "Positive Law as the Ethic of Our Time," *Business Horizons* (September–October 1990): 28–39.
6. Andrews, "Ethics in Practice."
7. "A Wave of Embezzlement Hits Banking," *Business Week* (May 18, 1987): 49.
8. Peter F. Drucker, "Management: The Problems of Success," *Academy of Management Executive* (February 1987): 17.
9. Larry C. Jensen and Steven A. Wygant, "The Developmental Self-Valuing Theory: A Practical Approach for Business Ethics," *Journal of Business Ethics* (March 1990): 215–225.
10. Donald Robin, Michael Giallourakis, Fred R. David, and Thomas E. Moritz, "A Different Look at Codes of Ethics," *Business Horizons* (January–February 1989): 66–73.
11. Scott J. Vitell and D. L. Davis, "The Relationship Between Ethics and Job Satisfaction: An Empirical Investigation," *Journal of Business Ethics* (June 1990): 489–494.

12. W. Edward Stead, Dan L. Worrell, and Jean Garner Stead, "An Integrative Model for Understanding and Managing Ethical Behavior in Business Firms," *Journal of Business Ethics* (March 1990): 233–242.
13. Bernard J. Reilly and Myroslaw J. Kyj, "Ethical Business and the Ethical Person," *Business Horizons* (November–December 1990): 23–27.
14. Dobson, "Ethics in Global Corporate Culture."
15. Jensen, "Developmental Self-Valuing Theory."
16. Reilly and Myroslaw, "Ethical Business and the Ethical Person."
17. Adam Smith, *An Inquiry into the Nature and Causes of the Wealth of Nations* (New York: Modern Library, 1937): 423.
18. R. Eric Reidenbach and Donald P. Robin, "A Conceptual Model of Corporate Moral Development," *Journal of Business Ethics* (April 1991): 273–284.
19. Milton Friedman, *Capitalism and Freedom* (Chicago: University of Chicago Press, 1962).
20. James P. Womack, Daniel T. Jones, and Daniel Roos, *The Machine That Changed the World* (New York: Rawson Associates, 1990).
21. Joseph W. McGuire, "Perfecting Capitalism: An Economic Dilemma," *Business Horizons* (February 1976): 10.
22. Reidenbach and Robin, "Corporate Moral Development."

23. Reidenbach and Robin, "Corporate Moral Development."

24. John K. Galbraith, "On the Economic Image of Corporate Enterprise," in Ralph Nadar and Mark Green (eds.), *Corporate Power in America* (New York: Grossman, 1973): 7.

25. Reidenbach and Robin, "Corporate Moral Development."

26. Daniel Seligman, "Ben & Jerry Save the World," *Fortune* (June 3, 1991): 247–248.

27. "CEOs Seek Help on Health Costs," *Fortune* (June 3, 1991): 12.

28. "And Now, Finger-Lickin' Good for Ya?" *Business Week* (February 18, 1991): 60.

29. Nystrom, "Differences in Moral Values."

30. Rosabeth Moss Kanter, "Values and Economics," *Harvard Business Review* (May-June 1990): 4.

31. Fisher, "Positive Law."

32. Reidenbach and Robin, "Corporate Moral Development."

33. Fisher, "Positive Law."

34. Cecily A. Raiborn and Dinah Payne, "Corporate Codes of Conduct: A Collective Conscience and Continuum," *Journal of Business Ethics* (November 1990): 879–889.

35. Reidenbach and Robin, "Corporate Moral Development."

36. Raiborn and Payne, "Corporate Codes of Conduct."

37. Reidenbach and Robin, "Corporate Moral Development."

38. Colgate-Palmolive Company, *The Colgate-Palmolive Company Code of Conduct:* 9–10.

39. Raiborn and Payne, "Corporate Codes of Conduct."

40. Nystrom, "Differences in Moral Values."

41. James R. Harris, "Ethical Values of Individuals at Different Levels in the Organizational Hierarchy of a Single Firm," *Journal of Business Ethics* (September 1990): 741–750.

42. Stead, Worrell, and Stead, "Managing Ethical Behavior."

43. Linda K. Trevino, "Ethical Decision Making in Organizations: A Person-Situation Interactionist Model," *Academy of Management Review* (July 1986): 601–617.

44. Touche Ross, *Ethics in America: An Opinion Survey*, 1988.

45. Steven Baviara, "Corporate Ethics Should Start in the Boardroom," *Business Horizons* (January-February 1991): 9–12.

46. Stead, Worrell, and Stead, "Managing Ethical Behavior."

47. Stead, Worrell, and Stead, "Managing Ethical Behavior."

48. Touche Ross, *Ethics in America*.

49. Neil F. Brady, "Aesthetic Components of Management Ethics," *Academy of Management Review* (April 1986): 337–344.

50. These materials are drawn from Vernon R. Loucks, Jr., "A CEO Looks at Ethics," *Business Horizons* (March-April 1987): 2–6; and Stead, Worrell, and Stead, "Understanding and Managing Ethical Behavior."

The Management of Taylor Realtors

Located in a community of approximately 175,000 people, Taylor Realtors was the largest realty company in town. Although residential sales had always been the most important part of the firm's business, the company also had a successful commercial sales unit. The firm dominated its market, annually accounting for almost 65 percent of total real estate transactions in the community.

Benton Taylor, the firm's founder and majority owner, started his company after graduating from college. From the first, Taylor seemed to have a knack for matching clients with the property they wanted and could afford. The firm was successful, and Taylor was able to employ other agents. However, because of his beliefs, it took him quite a bit of time to select personnel. He wanted people with interpersonal skills, a strong work ethic, and a sincere commitment to the local community. Taylor thought these qualities were instrumental to his firm's success.

Interviewing for a position with Taylor Realtors was a time-consuming process. Applicants spent hours talking with Taylor on different occasions. Each applicant was also required to spend a day in the field with Sue Mills, the firm's leading sales agent. Mills was the first agent Taylor hired. She was very much like Taylor—hard-working, skilled with people, and involved with the community. Taylor valued Mills's opinions highly. It was well known that getting a job at Taylor Realtors required the enthusiastic endorsement of both Taylor and Mills.

As the firm grew more successful, Taylor spent more of his time with activities outside the real estate business. This was possible largely because Mills took over as the firm's general manager. Essentially, Taylor turned the operations of the company over to Mills. He also sold 49 percent of the business to Mills. She now made all personnel and investment decisions. In addition, she actively managed the 34 agents who worked for Taylor Realtors. To help her with these tasks, Mills appointed Sam Barnett as the manager of residential sales and Jane Huff as the manager of commercial sales. Both Barnett and Huff had been with the firm for a number of years and had solid working relationships with Mills.

With Mills in charge of the firm, Taylor increased his community activities. In some instances, he served as a member of a charity's board of directors. In other cases, he donated time and money directly to help others less fortunate than he. As time passed, Taylor concluded that both he and his firm needed to be even more active in the local community. He decided to discuss this matter with Mills.

"Sue, we continue to have a lot going for us. The company is more profitable than ever and we have great people working for us. But I'm not satisfied. Because of our success, I think we should give more back to the community.

"There are kids out there who, without help, will never have the opportunities they should have. Too many adults in our area have not completed their high school education. And, as in so many other cities, our homeless population continues to grow. Sue, I want Taylor Realtors to do more than we have been doing. I want our people to give more of their time to local charities. I believe in this so deeply that I am even willing to let them take time off from work to do this. I want us to be in the forefront of what is done in this town to make it a better place to live. And I want us to donate more to local charities. Sue, what do you think about all of this?"

After pausing for quite a bit of time, Mills responded in a manner unexpected by Taylor:

"Benton, we have known each other for many years. In fact, if I may be so bold, Taylor Realtors would not be what it is today if it weren't for our work and relationship. Together, we've made this company what it is. But Benton, you have lost touch with what is going on here. I am working harder than ever just to keep this company together. It's rare that I get any time to myself. You know that I don't mind working hard, but this is becoming ridiculous. And, while you may have forgotten it, this is still a tough business. I have to fight harder and harder to manage this company. Instead of being here to help, you are always attending a board meeting or doing something else away from the office.

"While you're helping others, I'm here in the office trying to manage a large, complicated operation. We have people who do not get along very well. Besides this, other companies constantly try to hire our agents. I must spend a lot of time talking with these people, convincing them that staying with us is in their best interest. I also spend a lot of time talking with Sam and Jane about issues that are important to their units' operations. But these discussions are becoming increasingly difficult. I no longer know exactly what your vision and plans are for this company. Sam and Jane want guidance from me, and frankly, I really don't know how to respond to some of their very legitimate concerns. Without frequent input from you, I may not be communicating accurately with them."

After pausing for a few seconds, Mills continued:

"Benton, it isn't that I don't believe in you and what you want to do. I work as hard as anybody, and I am also involved with the community, as are many of our people. But there is a point where it becomes too much. We still have a business to run here. Don't forget, Benton, if we don't earn profits, there won't be anything to give to charities. The competition for residential and commercial listings is keener than it ever has been. We'll be lucky to do as much business this year as we did last year. Without concentrated effort, I think we could lose our edge in the local market.

Frankly, I need more of your time to help me do everything that has to be done. And although you own more of this firm than I do, I am not in favor of donating more to local charities right now. We are already giving more than any company I know. Enough is enough!"

Taylor listened intently to Mills as she talked. After all, he deeply respected and trusted her opinion. Is it possible that she was right? Had he started to spend too much time and too many of the firm's resources on matters of concern to the local community? Was he failing as a manager? Although he didn't have the answers, Taylor knew that Mills had raised issues that the two of them had to resolve. He also knew that how those issues were resolved would affect him and the management of Taylor Realtors.

1. Is Taylor Realtors operating effectively? Is the firm operating efficiently? Use examples from the case to support your positions.
2. Identify the managers mentioned in this case as either top-, middle-, or first-level managers. Discuss the managerial tasks for which each manager is responsible at Taylor Realtors.
3. Using examples from the case to support your position, accept or reject the following statement: The Protestant work ethic is alive and well at Taylor Realtors.
4. Use Maslow's need hierarchy to describe the need(s) you believe Benton Taylor is trying to satisfy.
5. What view of corporate social responsibility does Benton Taylor use in operating his firm? In your opinion, is his view appropriate for Taylor Realtors? Why or why not?
6. Evaluate Benton Taylor in terms of the six guidelines for ethical management presented in Chapter 3.

Part II
Decision Making and Planning

Chapter 4

Managerial Decision Making

Chapter Learning Objectives:

1. Define three terms—decision, risk, and problem—that relate to managerial decision-making processes.

2. Discuss different categories of decisions facing managers.

3. Describe the seven steps of the decision-making process.

4. Explain how certain conditions affect the decision-making process.

5. Discuss guidelines used to increase the effectiveness of managers' decisions.

Located in the downtown part of a community of 125,000 people, Dawson & Gilmore has been a successful retail furniture store for many years. Currently headed by James Dawson, the business was founded in 1947 by James's father and a close friend, Robert Gilmore. The store has always carried a large inventory because doing so has allowed it to command good market shares with different customer groups. Over the years, this approach seemed to work well. Until recently, Dawson & Gilmore was generally recognized as the town's most successful furniture store.

Only 18 months have passed since Lorimar's Furniture Outlet opened in the southwestern part of the community. In that short time, Lorimar's has become very successful. The company carries a fairly small inventory, allowing customers relatively little selection. However, what Lorimar's does carry is comparable to an important part of Dawson & Gilmore's stock. Because of its smaller inventory, many part-time workers, and inexpensive building, Lorimar's prices are considerably lower than Dawson & Gilmore's.

After thinking about the situation, Dawson concluded that his business should be moved to the southwestern part of the community. This was the growth area of the city, a cheaper and smaller building could be used, and the firm would be closer to many of its customers. In his mind, the decision to move was obvious.

Dawson was shocked by his staff's reaction to the idea. Jack Simpson, the firm's sales manager for almost 28 years, claimed that moving to another part of the city was wrong. "Look, James," said Simpson. "Our customers know where we are located. They understand and appreciate how we do business. Moving way out where Lorimar's is and trying to compete with them is not what our customers expect of us." Leslie Tubbs, the firm's controller, supported Simpson's position and added: "James, if you move this firm, you will lose some of your key folks, including me. Most of us have been with Dawson & Gilmore for our entire working lives. We like where we are, enjoy seeing the downtown clientele, and have no desire to change the way things are." Bill Turner, the head of inventory and delivery, said, "James, I think doing what you are thinking about is a big mistake. Why chase what Lorimar's is doing? How do you know they will be as successful tomorrow as they are today? People will get tired of their small inventory and come back to us. Just remain calm. Everything will work out if you leave things the way they are."

Dawson did not know how to react to these comments. He respected his employees; however, he also believed a decision had to be made. As Lorimar's sales increased, Dawson & Gilmore's continued to decline. Dawson was convinced that moving was the right thing to do.

The Dawson & Gilmore incident is typical of complications involved in decision making. James Dawson had one idea about what should be done to solve Dawson & Gilmore's problem. However, three key employees believed that Dawson's solution to the problem was hasty. As owner and manager, Dawson had the right to decide on a course of action without consulting others. However, he recognized that exercising this right would not necessarily result in the best decision. Complex mixtures of personal decision styles, perceptions, and levels of authority create the potential for either successful or unsuccessful decisions in situations such as the one faced by James Dawson.

The importance of decision making is suggested by those who consider it to be the heart of what executives do.[1] Part of this importance may be reflected in the fact that all managers spend a great deal of time making decisions. Top-, middle-, and first-level managers focus on different issues when making decisions, but they all make many decisions. The manager of a local pizza parlor decides whether or not he should offer delivery service in order to compete directly with the national pizza chains. The registrar at a college makes decisions daily concerning the school's registration system. People in managerial positions at churches and synagogues make decisions about how the congregation's needs can best be met. And Jack Simpson, the sales manager at Dawson & Gilmore, makes decisions regarding sales techniques employees should use.

Many managerial decisions go unnoticed. People directly involved with a particular agency, firm, or hospital are typically not aware of every managerial decision. Nonetheless, people's personal and professional lives are affected in significant ways by managerial decisions.[2]

This chapter discusses the types of decisions managers face and the specific steps of the decision-making process. In addition, the chapter describes the impacts of external influences and personal characteristics on the decision-making process. The chapter ends with a set of guidelines you can follow, both as a manager and in your personal life, to improve the quality of your decisions.

As you read the chapter, think of important decisions you have made. Or, if you prefer, think about a problem you currently face that requires a decision. For each topic examined in this chapter, think about how it applied to an important decision you have made. Alternatively, consider how the information could help you make a decision that will solve a problem facing you now.

Back to the Opening Case

Imagine that you are James Dawson. Given the information presented in the opening case, what decision would you make? Would you approach the situation differently? If so, how would your approach differ? As you read the rest of this chapter, you may want to change your responses to these questions.

TYPES OF DECISIONS MANAGERS FACE

Managers make decisions to solve organizational problems. If we were to talk to successful managers, they would probably tell us that an important part of their jobs is making decisions, communicating them to others, and monitoring their implementation.[3] They might also tell us that effectiveness as a decision maker requires time, energy, and a never-ending commitment to improve one's decision-making skills.[4]

A **decision** is the selection of a course of action from two or more alternatives. Today's competitive challenges require managers to accept some degree of risk and to exercise judgment when making decisions. **Risk** is a situation in which the decision maker understands the available options but does not know the probability that each option will occur. A **problem** exists when a standard or an expectation is not met or is exceeded. Becoming aware of and then defining a problem are critical first actions managers should take when making decisions.

No doubt all of us would agree that falling short of expectations is a problem. But performing above expectations may also be a problem. Managers who see employee performances that are consistently above expectation should examine the performance standard itself. Perhaps the expectation should be adjusted to make it more consistent with employees' skill levels and the technology available for their use. Today's managers should study all situations—even those that appear to be positive—to determine whether or not a problem exists. In the next few sections, we examine the different types of decisions managers face.

Managers face many different types of decisions because of their varied managerial responsibilities. In Figure 4-1, the types of decisions that challenge managers are grouped into five categories: personal versus organizational; strategic versus integrative versus operational; structured versus unstructured; intuitive versus analytical; and problem-solving versus opportunistic. The five categories are examined separately in the following sections. However, in reality, any decision may have features of several different decision types. For example, the president of Burger King may make a strategic decision that is based primarily on intuition. Similarly, middle-level managers often are challenged by both structured and unstructured integrative decision situations.

PERSONAL VERSUS ORGANIZATIONAL DECISIONS. Chester I. Barnard, a well-known and successful manager, categorized decisions as either personal or organizational.[5] **Organizational decisions** are those managers make in their official capacities on behalf of their firms. They delegate many of these decisions to subordinates.

Personal decisions pertain to the manager as an individual rather than to the firm. These decisions cannot be delegated, nor should they be subject to the influence of higher-level managers. In some cases, separating personal from organizational decisions is difficult. As the owner and

FIGURE 4-1
Categories of Managerial
Decisions

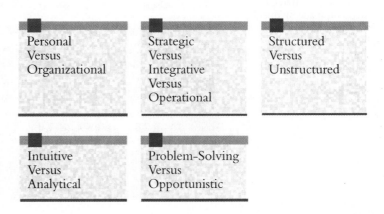

Personal
Versus
Organizational

Strategic
Versus
Integrative
Versus
Operational

Structured
Versus
Unstructured

Intuitive
Versus
Analytical

Problem-Solving
Versus
Opportunistic

manager, it could be difficult for James Dawson to categorize his decisions as purely organizational or purely personal. Illegal actions of Wall Street brokers in the late 1980s represented personal decisions that immediately required managers to make organizational decisions.

Failure to distinguish between personal and organizational decisions sometimes introduces a bias that can harm the firm and individual decision makers. Managers sometimes make decisions that affect their careers and personal fortunes as well as the success of the firms they serve. Because of this, conflicts of interest may surface. An example is the contracts some top-level managers request of their employers for protection in case of a takeover by another firm. Known as "golden parachutes," these contracts usually involve a great deal of money. Incidents could be cited in which such agreements have benefited shareholders as well as corporate executives. However, it is unlikely that top-level managers involved in merger or divestiture decisions always have the objectivity to place shareholder interests above their own.

STRATEGIC VERSUS INTEGRATIVE VERSUS OPERATIONAL DECISIONS. **Strategic decisions** define the direction an organization intends to take. These decisions concern the firm as a whole rather than a single department or division. Decisions to develop a new product line, to increase dividends, to enter a new business area, and to change the manner in which the firm competes are examples of strategic decisions. Strategic decisions usually involve situations that have not been encountered before. The conditions that must be analyzed to make strategic decisions are complex and unclear.[6] Variables outside managerial control, such as actions of competitors and the state of the economy, also influence strategic decisions.

The responsibility for making strategic decisions rests with top-level managers. However, successful strategic decisions result from the input of many managers, nonmanagerial personnel, and others involved with the

Because it is a small business, offering Saturday service to strengthen its competitiveness is an example of a strategic decision made by this dry cleaner.

firm. For example, Wal-Mart's top-level managers, including the CEO, spend at least two days per week visiting stores. The firm believes that the best ideas for the company's operations come from employees and customers.[7] The time spent in the stores allows top-level managers to obtain information required to make strategic decisions. Strategic decisions made in one company are described in the Organization in Action.

ORGANIZATION IN ACTION

With almost $6 billion in sales in 1990, Food Lion Inc. is the fastest growing grocery chain in the United States. The firm's success surprises some analysts because Food Lion's strategy is different from that of its major competitors. Other grocery chains tend to build large stores that carry a wide selection of nonfood items. Their local store managers are allowed to stock items wanted by their particular customer groups. In contrast, Food Lion's stores are relatively small. The focus is strictly on groceries; very few nonfood items are stocked. Responsibility for major decisions is centralized in the home office. The products carried in Food Lion's stores are standardized. Customers buy virtually the same products in Food Lion stores across the country. Even the way products are arranged is almost identical in all of the chain's stores.

Between 1980 and 1990, Food Lion grew from 141 stores to 778. Revenues climbed from $667 million to almost $6 billion. While the average return on equity in the grocery industry was 20.73 percent during this time period, Food Lion's average return on equity was 28.59 percent.

Source: Adapted from Diana Kinde, "Food Fight," *Dallas Morning News* (June 9, 1991): D1 and D3.

The strategic decisions made by Food Lion's top-level managers appear to be successful. However, the success of strategic decisions depends largely on the quality of both integrative and operational decisions.

Integrative decisions integrate top-level managers' strategic decisions with first-level managers' operational decisions. Integrative decisions are made by both top- and middle-level managers. However, the primary responsibility for these decisions rests with middle-level managers. Food Lion's top-level managers decided that the stores' product lines would be standardized for all stores. Middle-level managers then had to integrate that decision with the stocking and shelving realities faced by the first-level managers at each store.

Integrative decisions often require managers to process large amounts of data. Middle-level managers are responsible for analyzing the raw data and converting them into information useful for both top- and first-level managers. Because computers allow rapid analysis of data, some people believed that integrative decisions and decision makers would disappear from the modern-day business scene. Computer technology would allow top- and first-level managers to communicate directly with each other. However, integrative decisions—and middle-level managers—are still critical to organizational success. Management is complex and difficult. Asking top- and first-level managers to make the integrative decisions previously made by middle-level managers is unreasonable.[8] Some researchers examining this issue have concluded that integrative decisions are the most critical to organizational success[9] and that adaptation to today's environments requires strong middle-level managers.[10]

Operational decisions are concerned with a firm's day-to-day operations. First-level managers' decisions are mainly of this type. Carefully following company policies and rules for handling disciplinary problems, grievances, and work assignments are examples of operational decisions.

Operational decisions are products of top-level managers' intended strategic directions and middle-level managers' methods of integrating those directions with the firm's daily operations. Operational decisions are fairly clear and they focus on conditions that are faced frequently. As shown in Figure 4-2, strategic decisions involve a higher level of risk for the firm than do operational decisions. For individual managers, however, there is always a degree of risk associated with decisions. A poorly made operational decision might not be risky for an entire firm, but it could be very costly for the first-level manager who made it.

LEARNING CHECK

Describe the differences between personal and organizational decisions and among strategic, integrative, and operational decisions.

STRUCTURED VERSUS UNSTRUCTURED DECISIONS. A key difference between strategic and operational decisions is the degree of structure involved. Strategic decisions are **unstructured decisions**—decisions that

FIGURE 4-2
Levels of Risk In
Strategic, Integrative, and
Operational Decisions

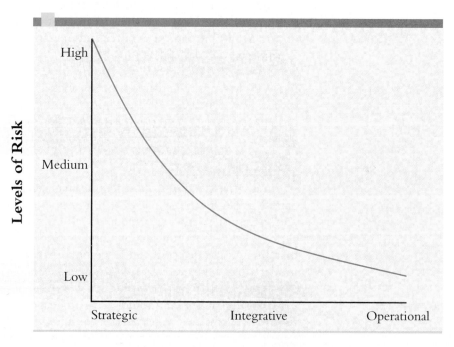

Types of Decision

are relatively free from limitations imposed by prior decisions. These decisions, faced often by top-level managers, have to do with problems for which there is no precise model or formula.[11] A manager evaluating an unexpected proposal to sell one of the company's units faces an unstructured decision.

Structured decisions are those in which prior decisions or company policy limit the manager's latitude in decision making. First-level managers often make highly structured decisions. For example, managers in customer service centers in large retail stores consistently follow company guidelines and procedures when they make decisions regarding the handling of returned merchandise. As customers, we sometimes become upset with the limitations such structured decisions impose on managerial personnel.

Food Lion's approach to the presentation of produce is an interesting example of a structured decision. As first-level managers, store managers follow the plan that was designed at corporate headquarters. Based on the belief that customers like the sameness of the stores, store managers are given very little latitude to design produce displays that are different from those called for by the master plan.

Integrative decisions often have characteristics of both structured and unstructured decisions. Decisions primarily faced by middle-level managers are made with fewer restrictions than operational ones, but with a greater number of restrictions than strategic decisions. Structured and unstructured decisions are also referred to as *programmed* and *nonprogrammed* decisions.[12]

INTUITIVE VERSUS RATIONAL DECISIONS. **Intuitive decisions** are decisions based on instantaneous analysis, personal experiences, and gut feelings. Managers at all levels make intuitive decisions. In these instances, managers gather relatively little information and reach their decisions quickly. Sometimes, when asked why a certain decision was made, a

Each Food Lion store's produce display follows a design planned by corporate headquarters. This is an example of structured decision making on the part of the first-level manager.

manager might respond, "I don't know, exactly. The decision just felt right." This type of decision is reached through intuition.

Intuitive decisions are important for today's decision makers.[13] Top-level managers particularly value intuitive decisions. It has even been said that "the last step to success frequently requires a daring intuitive leap, as many chief executives who control the destinies of America's biggest corporations will reluctantly concede."[14] However, we should recognize that these decisions are often the product of both academic training and work experience. For example, the CEOs of General Electric, H. J. Heinz, Motorola, Honeywell, and Cypress Semiconductor have all earned doctoral degrees.[15]

ETHICS QUESTION
In general, do you think of rational decisions as being more ethical than intuitive ones? Or do you think intuitive decisions are more ethical than rational ones? Why?

Rational decisions are objective, logical, and designed to achieve organizational goals within specified limitations. Managers gather large amounts of information in order to carefully analyze a decision situation. Rational decisions are appropriate when a problem can be defined easily, when people agree on the goal being sought, and when time is not a significant factor.

Recall the discussion of Max Weber's ideal organization form presented in Chapter 2. Weber knew that his bureaucratic form did not exist in reality. Rather, bureaucracy was a basis for theorizing about work and how it could be done in large groups.[16] In this ideal form, all organizational decisions would be well structured and completely rational. The foundation for all decisions would be rules, procedures, and regulations. There is no place for intuitive decisions in Weber's ideal organization form. However, neither organizations nor people are completely rational, and intuitive decisions are made every day in organizations of all types.

Today, managers recognize the importance of both intuitive and rational decisions to managerial effectiveness. All managers should be able to analyze problems rationally and systematically, but they must also be able to respond to situations requiring rapid decisions. The ability to respond rapidly results from the nurturing of intuition and judgment over many years of experience and training.[17]

Back to the Opening Case

James Dawson decided that moving his furniture business to a new location in the southwestern part of the community would allow the store to compete more effectively with Lorimar's. Was this an intuitive decision or a rational decision? Be prepared to justify your answer.

PROBLEM-SOLVING VERSUS OPPORTUNISTIC DECISIONS. **Problem-solving decisions** are made to solve existing or anticipated problems. Managers make decisions to solve problems related to all aspects of a firm's operations. Top-level managers might decide to sell a unit in order to increase profitability. A middle-level personnel manager might decide to conduct a survey to determine workers' feelings about their jobs. A first-level manager working in inventory control might make a decision regarding a problem with the flow of materials to a firm's production processes. A few years ago, top-level managers of Sony Corporation decided to reduce

Conducting a survey of employee attitudes and opinions provides the middle-level manager with information on which to base problem-solving decisions.

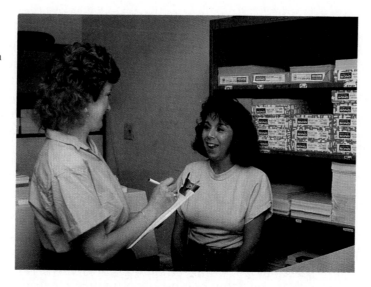

dependence on the electronics market. This decision was intended to reverse a decline in profits. Similarly, Campbell Soup Company's CEO reduced the company's workforce by 15 percent and sold 20 plants worldwide in efforts to stop the decline in the firm's profitability.[18]

Opportunistic decisions are positive actions to take advantage of potential for growth, increased profits, or achievement of some other valued objective. Wal-Mart Stores' decision to open Sam's Wholesale Clubs was designed to result in still more growth for the company. In other firms, decisions to have workers participate in additional job-training seminars are intended to upgrade their skills.

LEARNING CHECK Describe the differences between structured and unstructured decisions, intuitive and rational decisions, and problem-solving and opportunistic decisions.

Opportunistic decisions for both firms and personnel surface quickly.[19] Managers are challenged to respond quickly but appropriately when opportunities arise. As shown in the Organization in Action, what at first appears to be an opportunistic decision situation can have negative consequences.

ORGANIZATION IN ACTION

In 1988, the Clorox Company decided to enter the detergent market. Top-level managers believed that the company's strong base in bleaches such as Clorox, Clorox Fresh Scent, and Liquid Clorox II provided the expertise to develop products for the detergent market. Seeing this as an opportunity to expand sales and profitability, the firm invested approximately $225 million to develop and distribute its detergents. But after just three years, Clorox decided to abandon the detergent business. The principal reason was competition. In one year, Clorox spent $2 million to advertise its detergents. In the same year, Procter & Gamble spent $62 million to advertise only its Tide brands. Furthermore, in another competitive move, Procter & Gamble introduced Tide With Bleach. With massive marketing support, Tide With Bleach quickly gained a 17 percent market share, second only to regular Tide's market share. Not only did it overwhelm Clorox's detergent brand, Tide With Bleach also captured sales from Clorox's bleach products.

Source: Adapted from "A Bright Idea That Clorox Wishes It Never Had," *Business Week* (June 24, 1991): 118–119.

In many ways, Clorox's decision to enter the detergent business is understandable. The company's success was based on products purchased and used with detergents. Developing detergent products and distributing them was a challenge for which the company appeared to be well prepared. However, when examining possible opportunities, companies must carefully evaluate many issues, including competitors' reactions. Procter & Gamble, using its massive resource base, responded aggressively to a new entrant to the detergent market. In hindsight, Clorox executives probably agree that the detergent market was anything but an opportunity.

THE DECISION-MAKING PROCESS

The **decision-making process** is the sequence of steps used to make a decision, that is, to select a particular course of action. The decision-making process can be used to make personal as well as organizational decisions.

Using a decision-making process helps managers approach decisions in a consistent manner so that others understand how problems are identified, examined, and solved in their organization. The managerial decision-making process includes seven steps as shown in Figure 4-3. Each step is important and should be given proper attention. With experience and practice, managers become better decision makers. The seven steps in the decision-making process are discussed in the following sections.

Become Aware of the Problem

To make effective decisions, a manager must recognize that a problem exists. Earlier in this chapter, we defined a problem as failing to meet or exceeding a standard or expectation. The contractor who agrees to complete a family's residence by July 18 has a problem if that expectation cannot be met. If the agreement calls for a $1,000-per-day penalty for noncompletion after July 18, the contractor has a serious problem. If that penalty could lead to bankruptcy, the problem becomes a crisis. The contractor should monitor the situation carefully. By doing so, he may become aware of a condition in May, for example, that could result in a problem. Similarly, a manufacturer who is beginning to incur high costs for repair of products

FIGURE 4-3
The Decision-Making
Process

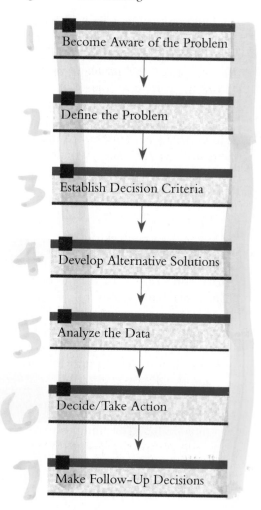

Become Aware of the Problem

Define the Problem

Establish Decision Criteria

Develop Alternative Solutions

Analyze the Data

Decide/Take Action

Make Follow-Up Decisions

still under warranty should be alerted to the possibility that quality control problems are developing. And the manager of a softball team who notices a good deal of friction among players should be aware that, if it continues, the friction could have a negative effect on the team's performance.

To increase their awareness of problems, managers should complete two tasks. First, they should make certain that all employees, both managerial and nonmanagerial, understand the firm's standards or expectations. People must know exactly what is expected of them, and clearly stated and communicated objectives, strategies, policies, procedures, methods, and rules will give them this knowledge. Second, managers should develop early warning systems to alert them when performances fall short. Firms conserve precious resources through early detection and correction, and their employees do not have to continue to work in less than optimal ways.

Define the Problem

Problem awareness and definition are perhaps the most critical steps in the decision-making process. Defining problems poorly results in wasted efforts and resources. To define problems successfully, managers should discover everything they can about the situation at hand. They need to understand how severe the problem is, who is involved, when the problem emerged, the causes of the problem, and what the consequences would be if the problem were not corrected. The problem should be defined clearly in terms of expectations; for example, "Product returns for the correction of defects are running 3 percent of sales rather than the 1 percent expected." How managers define problems is affected by both external influences and personal characteristics, which are described later in this chapter.

Establish Decision Criteria

Decision criteria are the standards of judgment used to evaluate alternatives. When selecting a method to finance a capital expenditure, if the primary concern is growth, the best method may be a public stock offering. But if maintaining control of the company is more important, a bank loan may be more appropriate. In the typical situation, both of these and several other criteria are needed to select the most desirable alternative. Decision criteria should be explicit. Ideally, managers write them down in order of priority before developing alternative solutions.

A second aspect of establishing decision criteria is defining the decision process—determining who will make the final decision, when the final decision will be made, and how many resources will be allocated for determining a solution. Failing to make these decisions can result in wasted time and energy.

Develop Alternative Solutions

Ineffective decision makers often accept the most available solution. They ask, "Will it solve the problem?" rather than, "Is it the best solution available within the guidelines that have been established?" The former results in an accept-reject decision, often preferred for its simplicity. The latter demands a more complex comparison of alternatives. Some managers use the accept-reject approach because of their inability to handle significant amounts of information. Others use it because of habit. However, creating a set of alternatives is a superior method, particularly when considering important and complex decisions.

There are two primary barriers to the creative thinking required to develop alternative solutions. The first is motivational. People who believe they are not creative lack the motivation to attempt creativity. The second is made up of cognitive, emotional, and perceptual predispositions that prevent people from freely associating ideas. A manager who wishes to think creatively must break these perceptual "sets," which are the result of experience, education, prejudices, emotional conflicts, and habit. Creativity requires **divergent thinking**—a risk-taking break with traditional patterns of thinking.

GROUP PARTICIPATION IN CREATIVE THINKING. Many human needs are satisfied through interacting with others. Examples are the needs for acceptance, status, and power. Because these needs can be satisfied through interactions with others, most people are mentally stimulated by groups. Therefore, groups may be formed to reap the benefits of interaction—to engage in creative thinking and make good decisions.

Generally speaking, the diversity within a group enhances the quality of its decisions.[20] However, this diversity must be monitored carefully for maximum effectiveness. For example, diversity that only contributes to interpersonal conflicts is counterproductive, and paralysis may result if diversity prevents agreement on a group's basic goals. Finally, diversity may reduce the quality of a decision if there is serious time pressure.

Several techniques are used to stimulate group creativity. The success of these techniques depends primarily on the following two psychological processes:

1. **Free association:** a process of producing ideas in rapid succession without censorship or control. The original stimulus word or idea is presented by the group leader. The free associations it elicits immediately stimulate a chain reaction of additional ideas.
2. **Social facilitation:** a process in which the productivity of each individual is increased by the stimulation group members provide.

One of the oldest and best-known techniques using social facilitation to stimulate creative thinking is **brainstorming,** developed by Alex F. Osborn. To produce a large number of potential solutions to specific problems, the group leader develops an atmosphere in which free association can occur comfortably. The leader announces the objective and tells participants not to be critical of their own or others' ideas. The leader encourages freewheeling, uninhibited thinking. Occasionally, checklists and suggestions for developing new ideas are distributed. One list, prepared by Osborn, includes the following guidelines: put to other uses, adapt, modify, magnify, minimize, substitute, rearrange, reverse, and combine.[21]

A major criticism of brainstorming is that sometimes only superficial ideas are developed. Also, the time required to conduct sessions and evaluate ideas can be excessive. Nonetheless, it is a valuable group aid to creative thinking, particularly when a specific answer is desired, such as a name for a new product or an advertising slogan.

Another approach to the development of creative alternatives is the nominal group technique. The **nominal group technique** requires group members to generate alternative solutions independently.[22] These noninteracting groups are called **nominal groups.**

Unlike brainstorming, the nominal group technique restricts verbal interactions. Group members work silently and alone to generate possible solutions to a problem. Following a set period of time, they share their ideas in a round-robin fashion. All ideas are recorded on a board for people to see. Once everyone's ideas have been presented, they then openly discuss and evaluate the ideas recorded on the board. During these discussions, the original ideas may be reworked or combined. At this point, the individual group members privately rate the ideas in their order of importance. After consideration of these initial votes, a second private vote is taken. The group's final decision is the result of ranking the alternatives based on the results of the second vote.

Like brainstorming, the nominal group technique has been used successfully in many firms. An advantage of this technique over brainstorming is that it is less inhibiting. Also, the nominal group technique requires each person to generate specific alternatives rather than merely elaborating on those mentioned by others.

IMPROVING INDIVIDUAL CREATIVITY. Individual creativity can be improved through several techniques that help break mindsets. For example, a person may imagine how others—artists, engineers, lawyers, or accountants, for example—might view a problem. Obtaining direct input from others is even better. Learning how others have solved the problem, reading about the subject even if no solutions are offered, and combining elements of different solutions are additional means of breaking the rigid thought patterns that can stifle creativity.[23]

Creativity flourishes when time is available for ideas to incubate. Because of this, it is best to allow time to elapse between periods of work on a problem. To forestall negative thinking (e.g., rejecting ideas because they appear to be unrealistic), solutions should be sought under widely differing assumptions.

Although it is difficult not to, managers should avoid analyzing alternative solutions critically during the creativity phase of the decision-making process. Analytical thinking interferes with the divergent thinking required to be creative. Furthermore, if alternatives are rejected quickly, they cannot be combined with other alternatives to arrive at the best solution.

Analyze the Data

In the data analysis phase, participants in the decision-making process evaluate previously developed alternative solutions. Several mathematical models and techniques are available to help in this evaluation. Two complementary techniques managers often use to help analyze alternative solutions are the payoff matrix and the decision tree.

PAYOFF MATRIX. A **payoff matrix** is a technique used to determine the benefits and costs associated with various alternative decisions. As shown in Figure 4-4, a payoff matrix requires several types of data: the alternatives being evaluated, judgments concerning important states of nature, and probability estimates associated with each state of nature. **States of nature** are uncontrollable influences on decision outcomes. **Probability** is the likelihood that an event will or will not take place. Probability estimates are expressed as percentages. The results of the calculations of a payoff matrix are expected values. The **expected value** of an alternative is the sum of all possible states of nature multiplied by their individual probability estimates.

The use of a payoff matrix can be explained by using Figure 4-4 as an

FIGURE 4-4
A Payoff Matrix

Alternatives	States of Nature			Expected Value
	N1 Recession	N2 Stability	N3 Upturn	
A1: Build new warehouse in another city	($100,000)[1]	$10,000	$230,000	$92,500[2]
A2: Rent local warehouse	($20,000)	$20,000	$150,000	$75,000[3]
A3: Expand present warehouse	($10,000)	$30,000	$160,000	$85,000[4]
Probability	.25	.25	.50	

1. Expected effect on the expected value of alternatives under specific assumptions.
2. EV = -$100,000(.25) + $10,000(.25) + $230,000(.50)
3. EV = -$20,000(.25) + $20,000(.25) + $150,000(.50)
4. EV = -$10,000(.25) + $30,000(.25) + $160,000(.50)

example. In this example, the decision maker is considering three alternatives for coping with a shortage of warehouse space. The firm can build a new warehouse in another city, rent a local warehouse, or expand its present warehouse. The manager believes that three possible general economic conditions—recession, stability, or an upturn–would affect each alternative. As shown in Figure 4-4, the alternative with the highest expected value is the first one.

Based on the decision criterion of expected value alone, the manager's choice would be to build a new warehouse in another city. However, managers consider other factors when selecting alternatives. In the example shown in Figure 4-4, the manager would note that the expected value advantage of the first alternative over the third alternative is only $7,500. It is possible that the third advantage would actually be selected, rather than the first one, in order to avoid a cash flow problem that could occur if a recession were to cause a $100,000 loss.[24] Managers select alternatives by combining the results of a quantitative analysis (the payoff matrix) with other considerations (in this case, the effects of a possible recession). Managers should remember that high-quality expected values are developed only through accurate identification of the states of nature and their respective probability estimates.

DECISION TREE. A **decision tree** is a visual representation of the analysis involved in a payoff matrix. The data included in Figure 4-4 are presented in the form of a decision tree in Figure 4-5. Comparing the two figures shows that the expected values calculated through use of these two techniques are identical. As with the payoff matrix, managers determine states of nature and their estimated probabilities associated with individual alternatives. The visual presentation of expected values in the decision tree allows managers to see the interdependence of events that likely will occur over time. Recognizing interdependence is especially crucial when making complex decisions.

FIGURE 4-5
A Decision Tree

Alternatives	States of Nature	Probabilities	Expected Effect on Net Profit	Expected Value
Build new warehouse in another city	RECESSION	(.25)	($100,000)	
	STABILITY	(.25)	$ 10,000	
	UPTURN	(.50)	$230,000	$92,500[1]
Rent local warehouse	RECESSION	(.25)	($ 20,000)	
	STABILITY	(.25)	$ 20,000	
	UPTURN	(.50)	$150,000	$75,000[2]
Expand present warehouse	RECESSION	(.25)	($ 10,000)	
	STABILITY	(.25)	$ 30,000	
	UPTURN	(.50)	$160,000	$85,000[3]

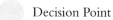

1. EV = .25(-$100,000) + .25($10,000) + .50($230,000)
2. EV = .25(-$20,000) + .25($20,000) + .50($150,000)
3. EV = .25(-$10,000) + .25($30,000) + .50($160,000)

  Decision Point

Decide/Take Action

Selecting the best solution often requires a manager to draw a number of conclusions. This places significant demands on a manager's analytical abilities. But determining the best alternative is not the same as taking action. Committing oneself to a course of action involves accepting risk. This skill is developed through experience with various decision situations.

Make Follow-Up Decisions

The quality of a decision is often determined by how well that decision is implemented, monitored, and adjusted. For example, because of an increase in product demand, a manufacturer's decision to reduce operations capacity by selling excess machinery appeared to have been an error. The decision to sell machines resulted from an erroneous forecast of market demand. However, this decision ultimately resulted in positive outcomes for the firm because the manager decided to purchase more modern machinery to meet the additional demand.

LEARNING CHECK   Describe the seven steps of the decision-making process.

INFLUENCES ON THE DECISION-MAKING PROCESS

Managers cannot make decisions in isolation from realities both inside and outside the firm. In the following sections, we first discuss how conditions in a firm's external environment influence managerial decisions and then consider the effects of individual managers' characteristics on how they make decisions.

External Influences

The effectiveness of managerial decisions is influenced by many external forces. The most obvious are the general nature of the economy and the actions of competitors and suppliers. Governmental laws and regulations also influence decisions. As examples, laws concerning discrimination, employee safety, and labor relations directly influence first- and middle-level managers' decisions. Top-level managers are concerned with factors such as laws, regulations, and court decisions relating to competition, advertising, environmental pollution, and taxation.

All managers learn that to make effective decisions they must influence and at times be influenced by the decisions of financiers, legislators, union officials, government administrators, customers, and others. For example, after many years of court battles, top-level managers at AT&T decided to negotiate with the government for the right to change the nature of AT&T's business. Similarly, following years of resistance to union organizing efforts, J. P. Stevens reluctantly agreed to bargain with a union. Effective managers also make decisions that are consistent with changes in their primary customers' demands for their goods or services. As shown in the Organization in Action, General Dynamics is a company whose decisions are influenced strongly by the federal government's needs.

ORGANIZATION IN ACTION

The federal government's demand for military equipment and arms varies over time. As the nation's number two defense contractor, General Dynamics (GD) makes many of its investment decisions in accordance with the government's needs. By 1995, it is projected that GD's sales to the federal government will be only two-thirds the amount in 1990. Based on this expectation, top-level managers at GD decided to slash employment, capital spending, and research and development expenditures. A problem that might result from these cuts is a dulling of GD's technological capabilities. In addition to making these cuts, the firm decided to use a more selective approach to pursuing defense contracts. In particular, GD decided to concentrate on its part of a $75 billion government contract for the Advanced Tactical Fighter jet program and its selection as the primary contractor on the Seawolf submarine project.

Source: Adapted from "Flight Plans for a Much Altered Future," *Business Week* (May 27, 1991): 74–75.

Personal Characteristics

Regardless of how much managers know about effective decision making, their organizational decisions are influenced by their personal characteristics.[25] With some degree of self-understanding, however, managers may be able to reduce personality-related tendencies that weaken their decisions. In addition, by developing the skills of their subordinates and delegating to them selectively, managers can hold the negative influences of their personalities to a minimum. The five personal attributes of decision makers that are most likely to influence decision quality are impulsiveness, overcautiousness, ego-defensiveness, intelligence, and self-confidence.

IMPULSIVENESS. The vice president for sales of a large appliance dealership must make a proposal to the president and receive written approval before hiring, firing, or disciplining a member of the sales force. Why place such restrictions on this top-level manager? Because previous decisions concerning people often were made impulsively and required adjustment. An **impulsive manager** is one who finds it difficult to delay action and tends to make hasty decisions. The president reasoned that the only alternative to this restriction was to replace this impulsive manager with a more cautious one. The manager's impulsiveness had little apparent effect on his technical decisions because they involved less emotion than did decisions about people.

OVERCAUTIOUSNESS. The tendency to be too cautious—to seek too much information before reaching a decision—may result in decisions that are relatively risk free but are made much too slowly. To some extent, overcautiousness is related to low self-confidence, but it may also be a function of a compelling drive to be thorough. Such a manager will consider all the facts and try to perform with perfection when merely being an effective decision maker would be more appropriate.

ETHICS QUESTION
Is an ego-defensive manager acting unethically? Why or why not?

EGO-DEFENSIVENESS. Decisions are also influenced by ego-defensiveness. In such cases managers feel personally threatened and are consequently motivated more by a desire for self-enhancement than by a desire to make good decisions. A manager's ego-defensiveness tends to become a filter that distorts perception and logic and affects the decision-making process.

INTELLIGENCE. Managers differ significantly in learning speed, fact retention, and other factors that influence decision quality. This is because differences exist in their native ability, experience, general education, and skills development. Some managers have great difficulty handling the abstract reasoning involved in forming multiple assumptions and decision objectives. Others, whose abstract reasoning is superior, may have limited practical judgment or common sense.

SELF-CONFIDENCE. **Self-confidence** is the degree to which managers trust their own judgment and are willing to take calculated risks and confront decision situations boldly.[26] It is a characteristic that can be learned.[27] For example, an individual's self-confidence increases with small successes. Jack Welch, General Electric's CEO, has described the relationship between self-confidence and decision-making effectiveness. In his opinion, self-confidence is required for managers to pick the bets, put the resources behind them, articulate their vision to employees, explain why they said "yes" to this one and "no" to that one, and see reality as it is, not as they want it to be.[28] Similarly, Andrall Pearson, former President of PepsiCo, believes that self-confidence is necessary to make the tough decisions required for organizational success.[29]

Given today's challenges, firms are well advised to make sure that their decision makers have the confidence necessary to make difficult decisions. Managers who make decisions without adequate self-confidence tend to second-guess their actions and those of others. Second-guessing wastes resources and can stifle organizational creativity.

LEARNING CHECK   Discuss five characteristics that influence a manager's decision-making process.

Bounded Rationality

A final factor influencing managers' use of a decision-making process is bounded rationality. **Bounded rationality** means that individuals' limited mental capabilities and emotions, coupled with external influences over which they have little or no control, prevent them from making completely rational decisions.[30] Because bounded rationality is a product of both external influences and a manager's personal characteristics, it is discussed as a separate item.

The concept of bounded rationality suggests that managers' capacity for rationality in decision making is bounded or limited by:

- conflicting and continually changing goals;
- vaguely defined problems;
- limited resources for gathering data and generating alternative solutions;
- human limitations of memory, reasoning, and objectivity; and
- inadequate knowledge of the consequences of alternative courses of action.

Given these boundaries, managers attempt to find merely satisfactory solutions rather than the best possible one. In other words, they try to meet a number of goals satisfactorily rather than maximize profits or meet any other single goal. **Satisficing** occurs when managers make decisions that are satisfactory, or good enough, instead of waiting until the optimum choice is determined to make a decision. Examples of satisficing criteria include choosing an acceptable return on an investment instead of maximizing the return on that investment and taking an acceptable job rather than pursuing the best job. Because of the physical, economic, social, and psychological limits within which managers operate, they must base decisions on the information available to them.

GUIDELINES FOR IMPROVING MANAGERIAL DECISIONS

Managers can improve the quality of their decisions by using the following guidelines, which were derived through analysis of common decision-making errors.

1. Through careful planning, minimize the number of decisions that must be made during times of crisis.
2. Insist that subordinates make all decisions they are capable of making.
3. Seek out opportunities and accept those that are consistent with the firm's objectives.
4. Involve staff specialists actively in decision-making processes.
5. Become aware of biases, mindsets, attitudes, and other personal characteristics that influence decisions.
6. View problems as opportunities to demonstrate problem-solving competence.
7. Make sure that the time spent to identify and solve a problem is consistent with the significance of that problem.
8. Exercise creative talents to generate solutions.
9. Hold back on critical thinking while generating potential solutions.
10. Use quantitative techniques to evaluate alternative solutions.
11. Examine the results of decisions made over time to improve the level of confidence you have in your decision-making capabilities.
12. Recognize that managers make decisions within legitimate and reasonable constraints. Strive for effectiveness rather than perfection in decision making.

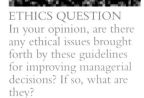

ETHICS QUESTION
In your opinion, are there any ethical issues brought forth by these guidelines for improving managerial decisions? If so, what are they?

People learn to become effective decision makers through trial and error. Because many decisions involve unknowns, some effective decisions will result in undesirable outcomes. Managers who accept this and grow through each experience continue to improve their decision-making abilities. In contrast, managers who never make a wrong decision are being too cautious. Such caution can result in lost opportunities for both the firm and the decision maker.

SUMMARY

A critical aspect of a manager's job is making, communicating, and monitoring decisions. To complete these tasks effectively, managers use a decision-making process. The types of decisions managers make are grouped into five categories: personal versus organizational; strategic versus integrative versus operational; structured versus unstructured; intuitive versus rational; and problem-solving versus opportunistic. Each of these types of decisions is necessary for a firm to be successful.

Managers can improve the quality of their decision making by using the seven steps of the decision-making process. The decision-making process calls for managers to make decisions in a sequential and logical manner. Critical first steps in the process are the recognition and definition of a problem. The effectiveness of any decision-making process depends largely on the accuracy of the problem's definition. Various quantitative techniques, including the payoff matrix and the decision tree, are available to help managers examine the relative values of alternative solutions to problems. The results of these analyses are combined with managerial judgment to select the solution that is to be implemented, monitored, and corrected as necessary.

Managers' decisions, and their use of the decision-making process, are affected by several factors. One is external influences. At a minimum, any decision managers make is affected by the actions of competitors, suppliers, customers, and governmental agencies. Many personal characteristics also influence managerial decisions, including impulsiveness, over-cautiousness, ego-defensiveness, intelligence, and self-confidence.

A final influence on managerial decisions—bounded rationality—was also discussed. Managerial

decisions are rarely as rational as managers like to believe. Because of factors that limit the rationality of decision situations, such as ill-defined problems or conflicting goals, managers typically make decisions that are satisfactory rather than ones that maximize the accomplishment of any single goal.

Decision-making effectiveness is a product of experience. Through trial and error, managers make decisions, observe the results of those decisions, make necessary adjustments, and go on to make still other decisions. A manager who approaches the decision-making process with a commitment to improvement is likely to become an effective decision maker. The guidelines presented in this chapter's final section can help managers make decisions that are effective on both an organizational and a personal level.

KEY TERMS

decision	unstructured decisions	divergent thinking	states of nature
risk	structured decisions	free association	probability
problem	intuitive decisions	social facilitation	expected value
organizational decisions	rational decisions	brainstorming	decision tree
personal decisions	problem-solving decisions	nominal group technique	impulsive manager
strategic decisions	opportunistic decisions	nique	self-confidence
integrative decisions	decision-making process	nominal groups	bounded rationality
operational decisions	decision criteria	payoff matrix	satisficing

QUESTIONS FOR DISCUSSION AND REVIEW

1. Name the five categories of managerial decisions. Describe the differences among the decision types included in each category.

2. Name and discuss the seven steps in the decision-making process. In your opinion, is one of these steps more important than the other six? If so, which one, and why do you believe it is more important?

3. Discuss how external influences and personal characteristics affect managerial decision-making

processes.

4. Assume that you overheard the following comment: "I don't care what you say. As a manager, my decisions will always be totally rational ones." Using the bounded rationality concept, prepare an argument against this perspective.

5. Discuss how you would use the guidelines in the text to improve the quality of your decisions on your first job.

PROBLEMS FOR ACTION

A. Only two months had passed since Diane Palich accepted a job as the director of education for a community center in her town. Believing in the importance of her work, Palich approached her job with a great deal of enthusiasm. She wanted to provide the three people working with her (two full-time employees and one part-time volunteer) with many opportunities to make their own decisions. Palich thought this was appropriate, given the significant amount of work facing the four of them. However, much to her surprise and disappointment, she quickly concluded that her people could neither identify problems nor make decisions. Not being able to identify problems was a mystery to Palich; she thought the center's education programs were full of problems. She knew that she did not have time to tackle all the problems herself. On the other hand, she wondered how much time it would take to help her people gain the skills they needed to use a decision-making process successfully. Using the information presented in this chapter, determine what you believe Palich should do to solve the problem.

B. For six years, Dave Olivarez had served as the director of marketing research for a large consumer products company. Olivarez found his work exciting and challenging because the company took pride in its innovativeness. The firm was working to be a mar-

ket leader in the introduction of new products.

Seven unit directors reported to Olivarez, and each was responsible for research related to particular product categories. Olivarez was pleased with the work of all seven people. However, recently he had become concerned about Ben Seitz's tendency to collect and analyze volumes of data before making a decision. Seitz was recognized throughout the company as a bright, hard-working person, but his desire for perfection seemed to be dominating his projects. Olivarez was fighting harder and harder to get Seitz to make product-introduction decisions based on the results of market surveys. When asked for a decision, Seitz typically responded, "Dave, I am not certain yet about what we should do. Everything is looking pretty good, but I need to test the product with just another one or two customer groups before making a final decision."

Olivarez appreciated Seitz's interest in making the right decision. On the other hand, his company operated in a fast-moving business. The name of the game was to successfully introduce new products on a frequent basis. Based on what you have read in this chapter, what recommendations do you have for Olivarez? How should he deal with this problem? What decision-making realities should he discuss with Seitz?

CONCLUDING CASE

Decisions at FlowerMart

With a degree in accounting, Larry Nickles started his career with a savings and loan association in 1968. While the work was hard, and although he moved his family five times over a period of 16 years, Nickles enjoyed his jobs with different S&Ls. His career progressed nicely, to the point where in 1979 he became the branch manager of the largest S&L in a community of approximately 200,000 people.

As the 1980s approached, Nickles saw many of his friends lose their jobs at banks and S&Ls. Observing the consolidation occurring in the financial industry during the early 1980s, Nickles became a realist. He felt that he, too, could lose his job at any

time. One Friday afternoon in 1985, Nickles finally received the expected news: He was being replaced as a result of a merger of his institution with two others.

At first, Nickles tried to find another job in the financial industry, but jobs were even tighter than he thought. Finally, with personal and family loans, he responded to an opportunity to buy the local FlowerMart unit. Located in the community's most prominent mall, this FlowerMart had never reached its potential. To control costs, Nickles's wife and two daughters worked at FlowerMart. Because Jenny and Jane attended the state university in their home town, working with their parents was convenient.

After a turbulent first six months in which tough decisions had been made, the Nickleses learned to operate their business successfully. To their pleasure, FlowerMart's headquarters provided valuable assistance with purchasing, inventory control procedures, accounting methods, and sales techniques. Coupling this aid with their own hard work helped the Nickles family to develop their unit into one of the Southwest's most profitable FlowerMarts.

After two successful years, the Nickleses bought three additional FlowerMarts in larger communities. All three units were within easy driving distance. After earning their degrees, Jenny managed one of the new units, Jane managed the second one, and one of Jenny's close friends from college managed the third. All three units performed above initial expectations.

After a few years, the situation changed due to Larry's health problems. Although the problems were not extremely serious, Nickles was told that reducing his workload would be to his benefit. This news came at the same time that FlowerMart's headquarters asked him to consider purchasing two additional units. Combining these already successful locations with their current units probably would allow the Nickles family to increase their income substantially. Nickles's wife thought trying to expand, given Larry's health, was foolish:

"Larry, you have worked hard all of your life. Besides, the flower business demands most of my time. And who knows if this business is what our daughters should bank on for their futures? I know what FlowerMart's headquarters says we could become. But let's face it; we have done well for them, too, and they know we are reliable people. I think we should sell the units we have now, take the money for our retirement, and encourage the girls to find other jobs."

Barely five minutes had passed when the phone rang. It was Jenny:

"Hi, Dad. Listen, Jane and I have been talking about the possibility of buying two more units. We know that Mom isn't too happy with things the way they are now. So, we think you should buy the two new units. Then, we want to buy the entire business from you and Mom. We'll pay a fair price so you guys can have the retirement you deserve. Then Jane and I will stay on with the business and continue to grow it. What do you think?"

Nickles told Jenny he would talk the matter over with her mother and get back to her in a couple of days. Nickles did not know what to think. He could see two sides to the situation. His wife was right about one thing: The work had taken a toll on both of them. They were tired and ready to spend more time with each other. And he also had concerns about whether the retail flower business was right for the girls in the long run. On the other hand, if Jenny and Jane wanted to buy the business, should he stop them? After all, part of the business's success was due to their agreement to work for their parents when they were in college. Didn't he and his wife owe something to the girls for their commitment and hard work?

After a few days, Nickles called Jenny:

"Jen, your mother and I don't know what to do. We know that you and Jane want to buy the business. And you know how much we appreciate all the hard work you have given us. But we aren't sure that the debt involved in buying the business and the stresses of running it are the best things for you two. Maybe we should just sell out now, let your mother and me retire, and you two find jobs with fewer headaches. How about if the four of us get together for the weekend to talk this out?"

Although she was disappointed, Jenny agreed to her father's request. They would arrive home on Friday night so the family could visit as long as necessary to consider this important matter.

1. This chapter examines five categories of decision types. Use these categories to define the type of decision facing Larry Nickles and his wife. Justify your answer.
2. Use the decision-making process to analyze Larry Nickles' situation. Be prepared to discuss the decision you think Nickles and his wife should make and why that decision is appropriate.

REFERENCES

1. Herbert A. Simon, *The New Science of Management Decision* (New York: Harper & Row, 1960).

2. W. Jack Duncan, *Great Ideas in Management* (San Francisco: Jossey-Bass, 1989).

3. Herbert A. Simon, "Making Management Decisions: The Role of Intuition and Emotion," *Academy of Management Executive* (February 1987): 57–64.

4. Duncan, *Great Ideas in Management*, 89.

5. Chester I. Barnard, *The Functions of the Executive* (Cambridge, MA: Harvard University Press, 1938).

6. R. Duane Ireland, Michael A. Hitt, and J. Clifton Williams, "Self-Confidence and Decisiveness: Prerequisites for Effective Management in the 1990s," *Business Horizons* (January-Feburary 1992): 36–43.

7. Bill Saporito, "Is Wal-Mart Unstoppable?" *Fortune* (May 6, 1991): 50–59.

8. George Newman, "The Death of Middle Managers," *Across the Board* (April 1991): 10–11.

9. Andre Van Cauwenbergh and Karel Cool, "Strategic Management in a New Framework," *Strategic Management Journal* (July-September 1982): 245–264.

10. Newman, "The Death of Middle Managers."

11. Michael W. McCall and Robert E. Kaplan, *Whatever It Takes: Decision Makers at Work* (Englewood Cliffs, NJ: Prentice-Hall, 1985).

12. Herbert A. Simon, *The New Science of Management Decision*, rev. ed. (Englewood Cliffs, NJ: Prentice-Hall, 1977).

13. Orlando Behling and Norman L. Eckel, "Making Sense Out of Intuition," *Academy of Management Executive* (February 1991): 46–54.

14. Behling and Eckel, "Making Sense Out of Intuition."

15. "Ph.D.s: Another Way to the Top," *Fortune* (June 17, 1991): 8.

16. Duncan, *Great Ideas in Management*, 71.

17. Simon, "Making Management Decisions: The Role of Intuition and Emotion."

18. "Campbell Is Bubbling, But for How Long?" *Business Week* (June 17, 1991): 56–57.

19. Joseph T. Vesey, "The New Competitors: They Think in Terms of 'Speed to Market,'" *Academy of Management Executive* (May 1991): 23–33.

20. Joseph P. Wanous and Margaret A. Youtz, "Solution Diversity and the Quality of Group Decisions," *Academy of Management Journal* (March 1986): 149–159.

21. Alex F. Osborn, *Applied Imagination* (New York: Charles Scribner's Sons, 1953).

22. Andre L. Delbecq, Andrew H. Van de Ven, and David H. Gustafson, *Group Decision Making Techniques in Program Planning* (Glenview, IL: Scott Foresman, 1974).

23. Richard A. Guzzo (ed.), *Improving Group Decision Making in Organizations: Approaches from Theory and Research* (New York: Academic Press, 1982).

24. Kenneth Radford, *Managerial Decision Making* (Reston, VA: Reston Publishing Company, 1975); and David W. Miller and Martin K. Starr, *The Structure of Human Decisions* (Englewood Cliffs, NJ: Prentice-Hall, 1967).

25. Michael Murray, *Decisions: A Comparative Critique* (Marshfield, MA: Pittman Publishing Co., 1986).

26. Ireland, Hitt, and Williams, "Self-Confidence and Decisiveness."

27. Max H. Bazerman, "Impact of Personal Control on Performance: Is Added Control Always Beneficial?" *Journal of Applied Psychology* (August 1982): 472–479.

28. Noel Tichy and Ram Charan, "Speed, Simplicity, Self-Confidence: An Interview with Jack Welch," *Harvard Business Review* (September–October 1989): 112–120.

29. Andrall E. Pearson, "Tough-Minded Ways to Get Innovative," *Harvard Business Review* (May-June 1988): 99–106.

30. James G. March and Herbert A. Simon, *Organizations* (New York: John Wiley & Sons, 1958).

Chapter 5

Fundamentals of Planning

Providence Hospital had long been a part of the local community. Built years ago and located in the downtown part of the city, Providence had grown with the town.

Over the last few years, however, things began to change. Providence no longer had the capital it needed to purchase sophisticated medical equipment. Physicians expressed concerns about Providence's facilities and the quality of its nursing staff. The result of these realities was a serious decline in the hospital's financial performance.

Mike Duncan, the chief administrator, thought he knew the main cause of Providence's problems. Approximately eight years ago, a new hospital had been built in the area where the community was growing. The area in which Providence was located continued to decay as the business community moved to shopping malls and other locations. An increasing percentage of Providence's patients were unemployed. Moreover, the hospital's operating costs continued to rise at a rapid rate.

Recently, Duncan had spent considerable time talking with Ellie Squires, the chair of the board of directors, about the hospital's deteriorating condition. Squires and Duncan concluded that bold action had to be taken to reverse what had become a dangerous trend.

Squires called a meeting of the board of directors. Duncan described the hospital's decaying financial position and other operations-related issues. In response to Duncan's presentation, Bob Shellenberg offered the following comments:

"Although this is only my third meeting as a board member, I must say that I am taken aback by the hospital's situation. How did Providence get into such shape? Hasn't the board been providing the direction required for plans to be developed? Aren't Mr. Duncan and his staff making decisions that are consistent with the actions detailed in the plans?"

Absolute silence greeted Shellenberg's comments. Board members stared at one another until Squires finally started to talk. "Well, Bob, to be perfectly honest, we have never had the time to plan. It seems that taking care of daily problems is all Mike and his staff have time for." A few other people then supported Squires's position. However, none of these comments satisfied Shellenberg. "Look," he said. "If Providence is to straighten this mess out, we simply must plan for both the short run and the long run. I am no expert, but I think I know how to get us started." After a lengthy discussion of Shellenberg's ideas, the board agreed that it must start planning if Providence was to become successful again.

Shellenberg is correct. The quality of Providence's planning efforts will be critical to its recovery. Successful organizations carefully design and execute various types of plans.

The importance of planning in large organizations—both profit and nonprofit—is not usually questioned. For small organizations, however, some believe that planning is too expensive or unnecessary. Many small companies and agencies have fewer resources for planning than larger firms, and the broad range of tasks completed by managers in small firms can cause them to lose sight of the importance of planning. However, planning is critical to success in both large and small firms of all types. Managers must find a way to devote sufficient time to the planning function.

This chapter presents a broad overview of the fundamentals of planning. The chapter begins with a definition of planning and a discussion of its benefits. This is followed by a description of how planning helps firms adapt to their environments and develop competitive advantages. The chapter then considers different methods organizations use to formulate and implement plans. The final section discusses conditions that cause managers to resist planning. The contents of this chapter serve as the foundation for the discussion of a special type of planning—strategic planning—in Chapter 6.

A DEFINITION OF PLANNING

In Chapter 1, **planning** was defined as a process that identifies objectives and the commitments, resources, and actions required for their achievement. Planning is concerned with ends (what is to be accomplished) as well as means (how those objectives are to be accomplished). Missions, objectives, strategies, and plans are documents in which ends and means are specified. When planning, managers make decisions in light of conditions they believe the firm will face in the future. Thus, planning is sometimes thought of as anticipatory decision making.

Formal planning, the type discussed here and in Chapter 6, becomes increasingly effective when managers and employees accept it as a way of life.[1] Those who accept the value of ongoing planning activities constantly think about what they should be doing in the present to assure the firm's future success.[2]

A firm's success is an indication of the degree to which its products (goods or services) satisfy customers' desires.[3] Achieving success is especially difficult in the 1990s because consumers are careful with their money and will buy only what they really want. For example, executives at Kraft General Foods Corporation believe that customers seek "TNCVV" (taste, nutrition, convenience, value, and variety) in all their purchases of food products.[4] Through planning that is linked with the firm's purpose, Kraft will determine how to go about developing products that satisfy the TNCVV criterion.

Kraft General Foods Corporation offers consumers a large array of food products to satisfy their desire for taste, nutrition, convenience, value, and variety.

Because of its critical role, planning is a primary managerial function. Effective planning is the framework in which the organizing, leading, and controlling functions are activated. The interrelationships between planning and each of the other functions are shown in Figure 5-1.

DOES PLANNING MAKE A DIFFERENCE?

To be successful, a firm must use logical processes to determine how to use its resources in the most effective and efficient manner. As we will see in the following sections, planning has a positive effect on firms and their employees. First, we will consider the relationship between planning and financial performance. Then we will discuss the benefits of planning as well as specific outcomes that are achieved through planning.

Planning and Financial Performance

Evidence shows that, over time, the financial performance of firms that plan exceeds the performance of those that do not plan.[5] One study, for example, showed that companies that use planning systems combining a long-term perspective with a customer-oriented focus provided superior returns to shareholders.[6] In general, firms that formally plan earn higher returns on their investments and higher profits than do nonplanning firms.[7]

FIGURE 5-1
Planning as a Primary
Function

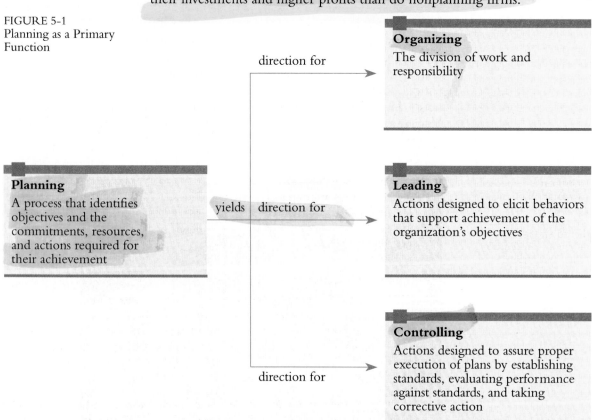

Although the evidence is in favor of planning, formal planning is not necessarily required for improved financial performance in every case. For one thing, managers sometimes make significant decisions informally and intuitively, outside formal planning processes. In spite of these exceptions, however, there is little reason to question the value of formal planning in today's firms.[8]

Additional Benefits of Planning

The value of formal planning is not measured strictly by financial performance indicators such as return on investment. In this section, we discuss planning-related benefits that are both economic and noneconomic in nature. In some instances, these benefits result from the actual process of planning. The experiences people have when planning often are as valuable as the plans that are developed.[9] Having opportunities to discuss the firm's goals and objectives and how it intends to accomplish them can yield valuable insights. Employees may learn things about operational realities facing the firm that they did not know before.

A COORDINATED SENSE OF DIRECTION. Planning allows managers and others in a firm to come together to decide what the firm wants to accomplish in both the short term and long term. From this they develop a coordinated sense of direction—a sense that they have the same objectives and priorities. First-level managers can be confident that middle-level managers have carefully integrated operations planning with top-level managers' goals for the entire firm. Without such consensus, conflicts can develop that waste valuable resources and reduce the probability of success.

MANAGERIAL PERSPECTIVE. Formal planning requires that all managers, but especially top-level managers, think of the organization as a whole rather than as a series of independent parts. To plan effectively, managers must understand the interrelationships among all parts of a firm. For example, decisions regarding how a firm's activities are to be financed affect how goods can be produced. Similarly, people working in the operations and marketing functions must integrate their actions carefully to make sure that the goods produced will satisfy customers' needs.

Thus, when planning, managers must keep in mind how decisions made for one part of the firm's activities will affect other parts. They must also analyze individual aspects of the firm in order to use the company's resources in the most effective manner. Participating with managers in the discussions required to reach these important decisions provides valuable insights to other employees. And, devoting thought to how a firm's parts could be integrated more effectively can help an individual develop the perspective of a manager.

IMPROVED CONTROL. From the first-level manager to a company's president, a major managerial responsibility is maintaining control.

Basically, controlling is concerned with establishing clear standards or expectations, devising methods to recognize when standards have not been met, and taking corrective actions. The controlling function is discussed in detail in Chapters 15 and 16.

Objectives established during planning processes are an important part of controlling. Keeping these objectives in mind, managers at all levels can recognize when actions called for in the planning process are not being implemented. Action can then be taken to ensure that the firm's activities will lead to achievement of objectives. When they participate in the development of organizational controls, managers and their workers tend to be more accepting of the behavioral restrictions those controls sometimes demand.

IMPROVED IMAGE. In today's competitive environment, image sometimes plays an important role in a firm's success. Businesses may decide to spend a lot of money to present a consistent image to customers. Its advertising illustrates that the image sought by General Motors for its Cadillacs is different from the image it seeks for Corvettes. Similarly, the image of the Mercedes-Benz differs from the image of the Hyundai Excel. If a company decides to develop and emphasize a particular image, it is important for managers and nonmanagerial personnel to know and understand that image. In helping to determine the desired image, personnel sometimes see the company's products—and the image they present—as extensions of themselves. Accepting the company's image as part of their own sometimes motivates people to take more pride in their work and the goods or services they produce. The Organization in Action describes the image sought by a particular Sears store.

ETHICS QUESTION
From an ethical standpoint, how much time should managers devote to developing a company's image?

ORGANIZATION IN ACTION

The Sears store located in Mexico City's wealthy Polanco neighborhood is one of 41 Sears stores in Mexico. However, this unit is unlike any Sears store in the United States. Merchandise is the latest in fashion and comes from well-known designers such as Estée Lauder, Giorgio, Givenchy, and Nina Ricci. Customers walk on shiny marble floors and look at products displayed in polished glass cases.

Thurmon A. Williams, president of Sears Roebuck de Mexico SA, notes that "our reputation here, in almost every category, is as a more upscale store." Williams intends for this Sears store to be positioned as "one of Mexico's premier retailers, in image and sales."

Source: As reported in Wilma Randle, "Bucking the Trend," *Dallas Morning News* (July 22, 1991): D1 and D4.

To date, Sears's home office in Chicago continues to provide the resources necessary for the Mexico City store to project the image of an upscale merchandiser. The image the company seeks in this one particular store has evolved through and been supported by the firm's planning efforts.

General motors uses advertising to project different images for its Cadillac and Corvette automobiles.

THE COSTS OF INADEQUATE PLANNING

Firms that plan inadequately face two problems. In Chapter 1, we discussed the differences between effectiveness and efficiency. Recall that effectiveness is doing the right things while efficiency is doing things the right way and not wasting limited resources. Proper planning leads firms to produce goods or services desired by customers. (This is being effective by doing the right thing.)

Proper planning also leads organizations to determine how to use their human, financial, physical, and informational resources prudently. (This is being efficient by doing things the right way.) Without the forward-looking thinking that results from planning efforts, firms can lose touch with their customers' desires and fail to identify ways to become more efficient. For example, without planning, a firm might not recognize how using sophisticated management information systems could conserve other resources. Today, being either ineffective or inefficient almost guarantees a firm's failure.

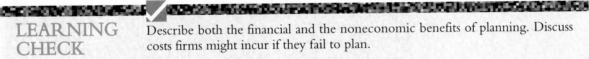

LEARNING CHECK   Describe both the financial and the noneconomic benefits of planning. Discuss costs firms might incur if they fail to plan.

PLANNING AND ADAPTING TO THE ENVIRONMENT

To survive and succeed, organizations must find ways to adapt to conditions in their environment. Effective planning helps them do so. The **environment** is a set of forces or groups outside an organization that influences its performance.[10] **Environmental adaptation** is an ongoing process through which a firm matches its resources and capabilities with marketplace opportunities. This process calls for managers to constantly shape human, financial, physical, and informational resources in ways that lead to the development of products that will satisfy customers' needs.

The matches between capabilities and opportunities are subject to constraints facing the firm from competitors, suppliers, and various regulatory agencies. Firms face different constraints over time. For example, Snapper (a lawn mower manufacturer) now faces severe competition from private-label mowers sold by discounters such as Wal-Mart. This competitive pressure, the firm's weakened financial position, and continued competition from the Toro Co., the nation's number one lawn mower manufacturer, limit the actions Snapper can take in the marketplace.[11] In general, managers must recognize the different kinds of competition a firm may encounter and learn how to cope with the demands of each type. They must also understand clearly what their firm requires from suppliers in order to produce its products effectively and efficiently. Solid and mutually supportive relationships between a firm and its suppliers often improve its performance.

A complex process, environmental adaptation poses three problems: entrepreneurial, engineering, and administrative (see Figure 5-2).[12] For discussion purposes, these problems are treated separately. However, in ongoing firms they are evaluated simultaneously.

FIGURE 5-2
Three Environmental
Adaptation Problems

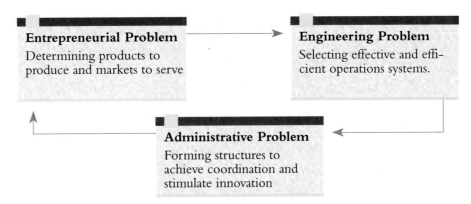

Entrepreneurial Problem
Determining products to
produce and markets to serve

Engineering Problem
Selecting effective and efficient operations systems.

Administrative Problem
Forming structures to
achieve coordination and
stimulate innovation

Source: Adapted from Raymond E. Miles and Charles C. Snow, *Organizational Strategy, Structure, and Process* (New York: McGraw-Hill, 1978): 24.

The Entrepreneurial Problem

The **entrepreneurial problem** is concerned with determining the products to be produced by a firm and the particular markets in which these will be offered. To solve this problem, managers evaluate the firm's resources, examine opportunities and constraints in the general business environment, and identify a product the firm can produce and sell successfully. A firm may decide that it can produce paint effectively and efficiently. But will it target the residential or industrial paint market? Similarly, a firm that decides to offer consulting services must select target markets—for example, manufacturing firms rather than energy companies. Without clear specification of the products to be produced and markets to be served, firms often waste their resources.

For ongoing businesses, solutions to the entrepreneurial problem are constrained by previous decisions. For example, the decision by General Motors' original owners that the company would manufacture transportation products constrains the corporation's managers today, although the company has diversified somewhat from its original business. However, it is very difficult for a firm, especially a large one, to abandon its original product market and enter other markets.

Back to the
Opening Case

Providence Hospital faces a serious situation. As a member of the board, how do you think this organization should answer the entrepreneurial problem?

The Engineering Problem

The **engineering problem** is concerned with developing and using operations systems through which a firm's products can be produced effectively and efficiently. To solve this problem, managers choose production technologies and the information, communication, and control linkages necessary for the operations systems to be used successfully.

Executives at Daimler–Benz, the manufacturer of the Mercedes-Benz automobile, long ago chose a solution to the engineering problem. The company's manufacturing system calls for "elegant engineering solutions to simple problems."[13] This system can be complex and expensive, and it does not permit the mass production of automobiles. In considering this matter, the company's chairman noted: "We continually study our position and we always come to the conclusion that we should stay away from mass production . . . . Besides, we have a culture of engineering . . . that would make it difficult."[14] As suggested by this example, Daimler–Benz's solution to the engineering problem is consistent with the decision to serve the upper ends of the automobile market.

The Administrative Problem

The last of the three problems presented by the environmental adaptation challenge is the administrative problem. The **administrative problem** requires a firm to form internal systems and structures to coordinate its engineering response with its entrepreneurial problem. Simultaneously, these systems and structures allow the flexibility needed to anticipate and deal with constantly changing environmental conditions. The objective of the internal systems and structures is to create stability within the firm. In coordinating its engineering response to the external environment, the firm seeks to develop its capacity to innovate. To be successful, businesses must be both internally stable and externally focused. Administrative configurations are changed in response to modifications in a firm's answers to either the entrepreneurial or the engineering problem. The manner in which one manager has solved the administrative problem is described in the Manager in Action.

MANAGER IN ACTION

John B. McCoy, chairman of Banc One, has been cited as a person who knows how to manage a bank profitably during troubled times. Banc One has concentrated on the individual consumer and on a particular segment of the commercial market. Its commercial clients are small and medium-size firms. Loans to these customers range from $300,000 to $6 million. The returns to Banc One on these loans are approximately two to three times the returns from loans to large commercial customers.

McCoy is committed to the practice of carefully acquiring other firms. He looks for small retail banks with good franchises. The banks must be ones whose profitability he believes can be improved quickly. The administrative structure McCoy has developed calls for back-office tasks such as data processing to be centralized. However, individual bank presidents, who McCoy believes know their own markets best, retain full responsibility for loan approval and decisions about pricing their institutions' goods and services.

Source: Rahul Jacob, "Banking's Best Acquirer," *Business Week* (July 29, 1991): 106.

McCoy's answer to the administrative problem is to both centralize and decentralize Banc One's operations. Functions permitting economies of scale, such as data processing, are centralized. This provides a degree of stability throughout Banc One's facilities. To be innovative and responsive to customers, McCoy's administrative structure calls for decentralization of decision-making authority to the local level.

A firm's answers to its entrepreneurial, engineering, and administrative problems should result in a competitive advantage. This is discussed in the next section.

LEARNING CHECK

Discuss the environmental adaptation process. As part of this discussion, define the entrepreneurial, engineering, and administrative problems.

PLANNING AND A COMPETITIVE ADVANTAGE

Businesses must develop a competitive advantage to be successful in the short term and the long term.[15] A **competitive advantage** occurs when a firm selects markets in which it can excel or in which its unique capabilities provide an edge over competitors.[16] Effective planning permits the development of a competitive advantage.

A competitive advantage is formed through application of a firm's financial, strategic, technological, or organizational capabilities.[17] To excel in a competitive environment, firms use their financial resources, their strategic positioning in the marketplace, their technological skills, and/or their ability to manage people effectively (the organizational capability).

Sometimes, however, a competitive advantage is defined in different terms. To determine what causes marketplace success, the General Electric Corporation asked 24 firms the following simple question: "What's the secret of your success?" The answers GE received were strikingly similar. First, the companies noted that they focus on how departments work together to move a product from idea to marketplace rather than concentrating on the performance of individual departments. In addition, these companies treated their suppliers as partners, introduced new products more rapidly than competitors, and managed their inventories in such a way that they had to use little of their working capital to pay for inventory costs.[18] These findings suggest how firms can develop a competitive advantage.

A particular firm's competitive advantage often is reflected in its answer to any of the three environmental adaptation problems. Daimler-Benz may have a competitive advantage because of the manner in which its automobiles are engineered and manufactured. Banc One may have a competitive advantage because of the administrative systems and structures developed by its chairman. Similarly, Foster's Family Donuts may have a competitive

ETHICS QUESTION
In your opinion, is it ethical for companies to discuss the type of information that was requested by this one company?

advantage because of its answer to the entrepreneurial and engineering problems. Through Warren Foster's innovation, his company can produce a doughnut that can sit sterilized and shrink-wrapped at room temperature for up to ten days. An industry analyst said of Foster's invention that "in terms of time saved and freshness of product, it's just revolutionary."[19]

Managers must realize that virtually all competitive advantages are imitated over time; few, if any, last forever. Other banks can learn how to imitate the particular way Banc One has decentralized its operations to solve its administrative problem. Daimler-Benz's engineering techniques can be duplicated. And, once Foster's patent expires, others will be able to duplicate the production technique of his doughnut.

Faced with imitation, firms constantly work to upgrade or change their competitive advantage. As soon as one advantage is developed, they must seek out the next. The process of continually upgrading or developing a new competitive advantage is critical to success in today's businesses.[20] Through effective planning, firms can constantly identify new competitive advantages that will last for a period of time.

TYPES OF PLANS

Business success requires many organized and integrated actions by a wide range of people. Managers use different categories of plans to cope with challenges. In the following sections, we discuss three categories of plans: strategic, tactical, and operational. As shown in Figure 5-3, there are differences among these plans in terms of time frame, scope, and the level of manager primarily responsible for their formation and execution. Although different managers have different primary planning responsibilities, planning efforts must be integrated carefully across all managerial levels if a firm is to achieve success.

Strategic Plans

Strategic plans reflect corporate-wide objectives and the business, or businesses, in which the firm intends to compete. These plans are focused on

FIGURE 5-3
Differences Among
Three Categories of
Plans

Type of Plan	Time Frame	Scope	Primary Responsibility
Strategic	Long-term	Broad	Top-level managers
Tactical	Medium-term	Intermediate	Middle-level managers
Operational	Short-term	Narrow	First-level managers

the long term (five years or longer) and are broad in scope. The primary responsibility for strategic plans rests with top-level managers.

Annual reports provide excellent insights into the strategic plans being implemented by particular companies. The Quaker Oats Company, for example, is developing strategic plans to achieve its long-term objective. This objective is to develop a worldwide portfolio of grocery products that will result in competitive success during the 1990s and beyond. According to the firm's CEO, Quaker is now focused solely on high-margin, high-growth grocery products. The company offers a wide selection to consumers, including several ready-to-eat and hot cereals, a variety of offerings under the Aunt Jemima trademark, Celeste frozen pizzas and other corn-based items, pet foods such as Gravy Train and Cycle, Gatorade, and Van Camp's beans.[21]

Tactical Plans

Tactical plans detail the actions necessary for a firm (or a unit within a large, diversified company) to compete in its chosen business area. Middle-level managers bear the primary responsibility for formation and execution of tactical plans. These plans are based on marketplace realities. Conditions can change rapidly in competitive arenas. Because of this, tactical plans have a medium-range time frame (usually one to five years) and an intermediate scope. The scope of tactical plans is broader than that of operational plans, but not as broad as that of strategic plans. It is through tactical plans that managers determine how to integrate a firm's available resources effectively and efficiently.

Hasbro Inc. is the world's largest and most consistently successful toy company. Many companies competing in this industry strive to constantly introduce new products. Often, these products are immensely popular, but for only a short period of time. Hasbro has chosen to compete differently in this volatile industry. G.I. Joe is an example of how it does this. This product was introduced decades ago. During the latter part of the 1980s, it appeared that children were beginning to lose interest in it. To update G.I. Joe's image, the company eliminated his combat fatigues, replacing them with spacesuits and jetpacks. These changes resulted in a substantial increase in the sales of a product that is much older than most toys offered by competing firms.[22]

Hasbro's commitment to these competitive tactics is reflected by the CEO's intention for the company to earn 70 percent of its revenues from staple products. Managers are challenged to develop tactical plans that will allow Hasbro to remain successful in its chosen business area. The firm's middle-level managers concentrate on effective integration of manufacturing strategies with marketing strategies. Manufacturing the same goods over time allows the firm to continuously seek ways to lower its manufacturing costs. With relatively predictable sales, retailers are willing to devote shelf space to Hasbro's goods. The methods of achieving the objectives of lower manufacturing costs and solid relationships with retailers are detailed in tactical plans.

Operational Plans

Operational plans guide a firm's day-to-day actions. These plans specify what is to be done, who will do it, and when it will be done.[23] Operational plans have a short time frame (one year or less) and a narrow scope. The contents of operational plans limit the behaviors of both managerial and nonmanagerial personnel. Often, the focus of these plans is on operational efficiency—how the firm can produce its product more efficiently in order to achieve its objectives.

First-level managers are primarily responsible for the development and execution of operational plans. However, middle-level managers often supervise them in this process in order to verify that what they are doing is consistent with the strategic plans designed by top-level managers.

Recall the focus suggested by the Quaker Oats Company's strategic plans. To develop its worldwide grocery product portfolio, the firm must also successfully formulate and implement both tactical and operational plans. Commenting on issues related to operational plans, the CEO noted that Quaker has "a company-wide commitment to reduce costs and improve efficiency and has implemented programs to integrate better asset management and improve the way in which it goes to market with its products."[24] The details of these operationally based programs will be specified in the firm's operational plans. As shown in Figure 5-4, companies usually develop two types of operational plans: standing plans and single-use plans.

ETHICS QUESTION
When implementing policies, do managers have opportunities to reveal their ethics?

STANDING PLANS. **Standing plans** help managers deal with recurring planning issues. Policies, procedures, methods, and rules are the most common examples of standing plans. These plans help firms establish orderly ways of accomplishing work on a daily and continuous basis.

Policies are general statements (preferably written) that mirror an organization's objectives and describe the limits within which managerial decisions fall. Today, for example, many retail establishments have a policy of guaranteeing their customers' total satisfaction. In each firm, such a policy is accompanied by a set of actions to be taken in response to each dissatisfied customer. Effective policies provide a degree of consistency in dealing with varied situations that helps firms achieve their objectives.

Procedures define the standard sequence for completing a task, such as filling an order, paying a bill, or maintaining the proper inventory level. **Methods,** closely related to procedures but often more detailed, may specify exact arm and hand movements as well as the standard time required for each movement. **Rules** are plans that limit individuals' discretion severely in

FIGURE 5-4
Types of Operational
Plans

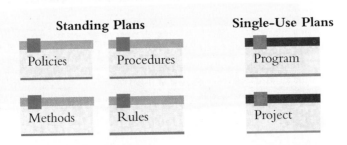

certain areas (much more so than policies) but do not specify time sequences (as do procedures and methods). A rule is an unequivocal statement: "Always wear goggles while grinding"; "No smoking in this area"; "All shipments must be quality inspected and approved before being accepted"; "All quarter-pound hamburgers must be a certain precooked weight." Rules are to be obeyed. If frequent exceptions are necessary, the rule should be eliminated or modified.

SINGLE-USE PLANS. **Single-use plans** deal with planning situations that are expected to occur only once. Programs and projects are single-use plans. A **program** is a plan in which activities required to achieve a broader objective are specified. The program includes information regarding goals being sought, actions to achieve the goals, people to be involved with the program, and anticipated costs. Recall that Banc One acquires other financial institutions. When it does this, it must develop a program to describe how the acquired firm's operations will be integrated into Banc One's existing structure.

   A **project** is a single-use plan that describes actions necessary to achieve a specific objective. Examples of projects include the construction of a new manufacturing facility, development of a new product, and identification of a new market for an existing product. The manager of a local restaurant might ask people to prepare a plan evaluating the possibility of adding an item to the firm's menu.

Back to the Opening Case

What types of plans should be developed at Providence Hospital? Justify your viewpoint with materials included in the chapter.

Developing and implementing strategic, tactical, and operational plans require the efforts of many people. Top-, middle-, and first-level managers all play critical roles in the formation and use of these plans. The following sections discuss the various groups that firms use to help them prepare these plans.

Businesses ensure that work is accomplished in a safe and orderly way by establishing rules for the workplace. Rules are unequivocal and must be obeyed.

PLANNING GROUPS

Ultimately, top-level managers are responsible for developing and implementing all organizational plans. As we have noted, planning requires major decisions about where a company is going and how it intends to get there. Because of the breadth and depth of analysis and synthesis required to make these critical choices, top-level managers may decide to use various groups to assist in the preparation of plans.

Five groups can contribute to the preparation of strategic, tactical, and operational plans. In virtually all large firms and in many medium-sized and small ones as well, more than one planning group is formed. Over time, different groups are used to develop and implement different plans. For example, one of the planning groups discussed in this section is outside consultants. On some occasions, consultants may be used to help with strategic plans. At other times, middle-level managers may seek their services to help form tactical plans. Effective managers recognize situations in which each planning group can be used to maximum benefit.

Board of Directors

ETHICS QUESTION
Does an ethical issue surface if almost all members of a board of directors are employees of the firm?

A **board of directors** is a group of people elected by stockholders to make sure the firm is managed well. In many firms, and certainly in large, publicly traded companies, the board of directors has members from both inside and outside the firm. A firm's top-level officials, such as the chief executive officer and the chief operating officer, are examples of employees who might serve on the board. Outside directors often are successful executives from other companies, physicians, lawyers, or prominent community leaders.

A board of directors' planning responsibilities are grounded in strategic issues. From a legal perspective, a board is required to direct a firm's affairs, but not to manage the company. As such, the board is concerned about strategic plans but is less involved with either tactical or operational plans. Typically, a board of directors has the following planning-related responsibilities:

- evaluating and approving the firm's philosophy, mission, objectives, and strategies;
- supervising the company's resource allocations, methods of capitalization, and other financial matters;
- evaluating diversifications, mergers, acquisitions, and divestments;
- establishing the chief executive officer's compensation;

- appraising management's performance;
- ensuring that the organization is developing management talent;
- providing for an orderly succession to the chief executive officer's position.[25]

. . . .

**Back to the
Opening Case**

Questions posed by Bob Shellenberg suggest that the members of the Providence board of directors had not been completing their jobs successfully. Using the information in the case and the planning responsibilities generally assigned to a board of directors, accept or reject the following position: "The members of the Providence board of directors were discharging their planning responsibilities in an effective manner." Be prepared to provide evidence to support your opinion.

. . . .

ETHICS QUESTION
Given today's legal environment, would you want to know something about a person's ethics before appointing that person to a board of directors?

Today's legal environment, which holds board members liable for their corporation's actions, has reduced the number of qualified individuals willing to serve on boards. This is a serious matter. Competing successfully in dynamic domestic and international markets requires strong, competent, and motivated board members. Some believe that for such people to be willing to serve on boards, two things must change. First, the legal opportunities for shareholders to file frivolous lawsuits must be eliminated. Second, the incentives for board members must change so they are more willing to spend the time required to discharge their duties effectively. Paying board members with stock rather than cash may create the type of commitment required.[26] A few individuals' reactions to the realities of serving on boards of directors in today's business world are described in the Managers in Action.

MANAGERS IN ACTION

The Federal Deposit Insurance Corp. (FDIC) filed a civil suit against former officers and members of the board of directors of Republic Bank and First Republic Bank. Executives serving currently on other companies' boards were asked whether the FDIC's civil suit would affect their decision if they were asked to serve on a bank's board.

A well-known finance professor stated that in his opinion the FDIC's action would definitely affect people's decisions to serve on boards. The professor noted that he would serve on a bank board again only if he knew and respected the institution's management team. Similarly, the executive director of the Center for Nonprofit Management commented that people would now be far more cautious about accepting offers to join a board. In contrast, the chairman and president of one company stated that the FDIC's suit would not keep him from serving on a bank's board. In explaining his position, he suggested that one must always be alert while serving on a board: "It's not just an honor. It's a responsibility."

Source: "Executive Survey: Risks of Board Membership," *Dallas Morning News* (August 6, 1991): D1 and D7.

Another issue concerning boards of directors today is the cost of insurance. Called director's and officer's insurance (D&O), this coverage can be prohibitively expensive. Corporations that cannot or simply refuse to purchase D&O policies may lose their board members and/or top-level managers. For example, eight of ten directors of the Armada Corporation resigned when the firm refused to pay significantly higher D&O costs. The firm was also left without a chairman and chief executive officer. The Continental Steel Corporation found itself in a similar situation. Six of this firm's outside directors resigned simultaneously when the company dropped its D&O insurance.[27]

Planning Professionals

Since 1970, many large organizations have employed professional planners. The size of a professional planning group ranges from two to over 50 people. Typically, professional planners collect and analyze data. Based on their analyses, they generate and evaluate alternatives, which are in turn considered by managers and/or members of other planning groups. Because of their involvement with the development of all types of plans, professional planners are in unique positions to offer advice regarding the integration of various activities. Such integration is especially critical in large organizations or in companies operating in many different business areas.[28]

The effectiveness of professional planners has been questioned. This concern is grounded in the typical professional planner's background. In the past, planners were often people who had not been involved directly with the production of a firm's products. Although they were well educated and talented, these individuals tended to be young and relatively inexperienced. Seasoned first- and middle-level managers sometimes doubted that people who had not been on the firing line knew much about how a firm should operate.

Today, however, the emphasis of the professional planner's work is being sharpened. In many firms, the responsibility for developing and implementing plans now rests with managers. Because they are closer to the work of producing, selling, and distributing a firm's good or service, some believe that these managers have planning-related insights that others (including professional planners) simply cannot possess. In these cases, planners concentrate on responding to managers' requests to gather and analyze various types of data or information. Thus, the data being gathered and analyzed by professional planners today are initially chosen in consultation with planning managers. Through this type of work, professional planners become a valuable resource to top-, middle-, and first-level managers. Critical to these efforts is the planners' ability to interact effectively with the managers they serve.

Will professional planners continue to play an important role in firms? Almost certainly the answer to this question is "yes." Environments are becoming more complex, difficult, and ambiguous. Because of this, firms find it more and more challenging to determine effective solutions to their entrepreneurial, engineering, and administrative problems. The challenge for top-level managers is to develop organizational pathways through which professional planners can apply their skills to enhance the quality of a firm's planning efforts.

Task Forces

A task force is a group of managers to whom a specific planning task has been assigned. Each task is to be completed within a certain period of time. Typically, these managers are drawn from top-, middle-, and first-level positions. As shown in Figure 5-5, they come from different parts of the company. While working on a specific planning assignment, task force members continue to fulfill many of their regular jobs' requirements. When the planning task is completed, the temporary task force is disbanded.

Task forces have several advantages. One is the high energy level and concentration managers can devote to assignments that are time bound. Furthermore, because only members with the expertise required to examine a particular issue are assigned to a task force, the group can develop creative, yet effective solutions to problems.

Planning Coalitions

Informal networks develop in organizations. Composed of managers from all levels, these networks are products of how people in a firm interact with

FIGURE 5-5
Composition of a Task
Force

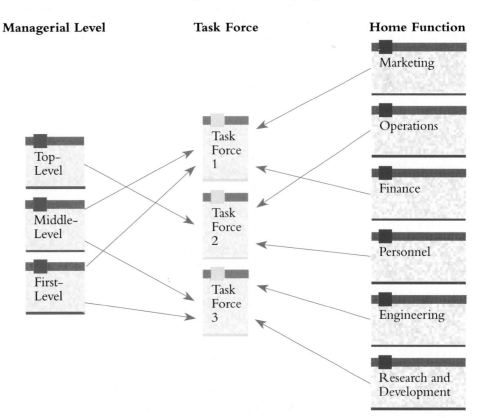

each other and with members of other firms to complete their work. Planning issues often are negotiated within the network, or coalition. Resolution of conflicts arising from managers' desires to gain additional resources for their own areas and yet avoid injury to the ability of the firm as a whole to be successful is critical to the negotiation process. Results from these informal negotiations often are articulated in other planning forums (for example, during meetings with professional planners or a task force).

The idea that informal coalitions influence planning activities is consistent with findings reported by Henry Mintzberg and John Kotter. As discussed in Chapter 1, these researchers discovered that managers' jobs require extensive interactions with peers, subordinates, superiors, and people outside the organization. Through these interactions, information-based relationships evolve that are used to develop and implement plans. Negotiations within informal coalitions often yield effective and efficient solutions to complex problems. These coalitions have dominant roles in government and other nonprofit organizations. In a college setting, for example, it would not be uncommon for several department heads to form a coalition to negotiate solutions that are in turn submitted to a dean for approval and implementation.

Outside Consultants

When planning expertise does not exist within a firm, outside consultants can play a vital role in planning activities. Consultants can bring objective inputs to a firm's planning efforts. In addition, because they have not been intimately involved with a firm on a daily basis, consultants can sometimes define problems more effectively than can the firm's managers.[29] To be effective, an outside consultant must have the ability to involve key people in the planning process. Without such involvement, personnel are denied an opportunity to learn how the planning process should be developed and used in a company.

RESISTANCE TO PLANNING

Planning can be threatening for some managers. Occasionally, it is threatening enough to cause managers to resist efforts to establish formal planning procedures. **Resistance to planning** is a set of behaviors through which managers resist accepting the outputs of planning, neglect to emphasize planning, and pose threats to the continuation of planning. Resistance to planning has been reported as one of the most significant influences on the effectiveness of companies' planning systems.[30] Therefore, it should not be underestimated.

Managers should be aware of the fears that can cause resistance to planning. These fears include the following:

- Will the planning system reduce my stature and power within the organization?

- Will I be able to meet the performance standards included in formal plans?
- How much of my decision-making freedom will be lost?
- Will formal planning disrupt the existing culture and management styles?
- Do I have the skills necessary to help others learn how to conduct planning?[31]

ETHICS QUESTION
Is it ethical for managers to resist the establishment of formal planning processes?

Resistance among middle- and first-level managers often revolves around the fact that formal planning usually produces more stringent accountability. Managers who have not previously been held accountable for results are often threatened by the change.

Formal planning can even restrict the freedoms of upper-level officials, including chief executive officers. Because of this, CEOs, too, sometimes resist planning efforts. For these individuals, resistance to planning is evidenced when a firm continues to operate without the guidance provided by strategic, tactical, and operational plans.

Back to the
Opening Case

In your opinion, how high is the probability that managers at Providence Hospital will resist efforts to plan? Be prepared to justify your position with information included in the chapter.

The probability of resistance to planning underscores the importance of preparation. Resistance may be reduced by educating managers about planning's benefits as well as the nature of and probable reasons for resistance to it. Managers who are keenly involved with planning processes likely will tell other managers how planning can benefit the firm and each of them as managers. Knowing the organizational and personal benefits of planning can reduce or eliminate a tendency to resist it.

LEARNING CHECK

Describe fears that cause managers to resist planning.

SUMMARY

Effective planning allows managers to make decisions today so their organizations will be successful now and in the future. Planning is concerned with both ends, the objectives to be accomplished, and means, what is to be done to accomplish these objectives. Strong evidence supports the value of planning in both large and small firms. Over time, organizational experiences suggest that planning increases a firm's financial performance. In general, firms that plan earn higher returns on their investments and higher profits than those that do not plan.

The process of planning yields noneconomic

benefits as well as economic benefits. Many of these result from the planning process itself. Simply taking opportunities to discuss a firm's future and what must be done to realize that future yields benefits that are difficult to quantify. Nonetheless, the following benefits are known to accrue to firms through planning:

- a coordinated sense of direction among managers, gained through acceptance of a prioritized set of objectives;
- a managerial perspective, acquired through viewing the firm as an entity rather than as a collection of discrete parts;
- improved control of operations through the acceptance of carefully integrated actions called for by plans; and
- development of an image in the marketplace that allows a firm to meaningfully and consistently distinguish its product from competitors' offerings.

Firms that do not plan, or that plan poorly, run the risk of becoming ineffective, inefficient, or both. Effective firms are doing the right things while efficient firms are doing things right. Successful planning efforts reduce the probability that a firm will be ineffective or inefficient.

To achieve long-term success, organizations must adapt to conditions in their environment. Environmental adaptation is a process through which a firm matches its resource capabilities with marketplace opportunities. Constraints facing a firm—including competitors' and suppliers' actions and policies and procedures of governmental agencies—affect the environmental adaptation process. Three problems are considered when dealing with the environmental adaptation challenge: the entrepreneurial problem, the engineering problem, and the administrative problem.

The entrepreneurial problem is concerned with determining the products a firm intends to produce and the markets in which they will be sold. The engineering problem calls for managers to select operating systems through which products can be produced effectively and efficiently. When addressing the administrative problem, managers select internal systems and structures that will coordinate the firm's response to the engineering problem with the requirements suggested by the firm's answer to the entrepreneurial problem. It is important that the solution to the administrative problem allow the firm to have both the stability necessary for day-to-day functioning and the flexibility to innovate in response to environmental changes.

Responses to the entrepreneurial, engineering,

and administrative problems should result in a competitive advantage. Defined as a condition that results from a company's selection of markets in which it can excel or in which its unique skills provide an edge over competitors, a competitive advantage is necessary for a firm to be successful in both the short term and the long term. Planning helps a firm develop a competitive advantage through application of one or more of its financial, strategic, technological, or organizational capabilities. Because competitive advantages are imitated by other firms over time, managers are challenged to help a firm develop new advantages on an ongoing basis.

The complexity of today's environment requires firms to develop and implement three types of plans: strategic, tactical, and operational. Strategic plans are concerned with determining corporate-wide objectives and the business in which the firm intends to compete. Tactical plans involve the competitive details necessary for a firm to compete successfully in its chosen business. Based on the mandates of the first two types of plans, operational plans are designed to guide a firm's day-to-day actions. Through effective organizational planning processes, the actions called for by the three types of plans are carefully integrated. Operational plans focus on organizational efficiency. To develop operational plans, many specific actions must be detailed. This type of detail is presented through standing plans and single-use plans.

Successful planning is a product of many people's efforts. Planning groups aid these individuals in their work. Among the most popular of these groups are boards of directors, planning professionals, task forces, planning coalitions, and outside consultants. In many companies, and certainly in large ones, several groups are used to prepare various plans.

Some planning groups consist primarily of top-level managers, perhaps with support from planning professionals or consultants. However, a much broader representation is preferable. Middle-level and first-level managers, as well as nonmanagerial employees and key parties from outside the organization (important customers, for example), should also be involved in planning efforts. Planning effectiveness tends to be increased through active participation of many people in the development and implementation of strategic, tactical, and operational plans.

Sometimes managers resist the development and implementation of organizational plans. Such resistance may surface for several reasons. Among them are concerns about potential losses in stature within the firm that could result from situations called for by plans and a fear that the managers may lack skills required to participate successfully in the development of plans. Managers should be prepared to minimize the effects of any resistance to planning that may surface. Involving people actively in planning and discussing various benefits that will accrue to the firm and its people help to reduce resistance.

KEY TERMS

planning
environment
environmental adaptation
entrepreneurial problem
engineering problem

administrative problem
competitive advantage
strategic plans
tactical plans
operational plans
standing plans

policies
procedures
methods
rules
single-use plans
program

project
board of directors
resistance to planning

QUESTIONS FOR DISCUSSION AND REVIEW

1. What is planning and what are the benefits of effective planning?
2. What are the entrepreneurial, engineering, and administrative problems facing managers when dealing with the environmental adaptation challenge? Is one of these problems more challenging than the other two? Which one and why?
3. What is a competitive advantage and what does a firm do to develop one? Does a single competitive advantage last over the life of a firm? Why or why not?
4. Describe the differences among strategic, tactical, and operational plans. Which management level has primary responsibility for each type of plan?
5. What groups are involved with the development and implementation of strategic, tactical, and operational plans? Why might many firms, and especially large ones, decide to use more than one planning group?
6. What are some of the issues that might cause managers to resist efforts to develop organizational plans? Describe a situation in which you, as a manager, might resist planning efforts.

PROBLEMS FOR ACTION

A. Recently, Betty Mason became the general sales manager for a large automobile dealership located in the Northeast. Although the company's owners were generally pleased with the dealership's performance, they thought things could be improved.

After examining the situation for roughly five weeks, Mason decided that a key problem was the loose manner in which the dealership operated. Everyone was friendly and busy, but seemed to work without much guidance or direction. Somewhat to her surprise, responses to her suggestion that the company develop different kinds of plans were not enthusiastic. In particular, Sam Melendez, the manager of new car sales, was especially opposed to any

planning activities. Discuss why Melendez might resist Mason's suggestion regarding planning.

B. Assume that you have been employed as a consultant by the owner of Harlon and Associates, a men's clothing store. This store is located in a city with a population of approximately 100,000. The lines carried in the store are rather expensive. Two other stores appear to be Harlon and Associates' major competitors. Harlon has asked that you assist him in developing a tactical plan. Given your knowledge of planning fundamentals, what specific activities would you recommend to Harlon to develop a tactical plan for his business?

CONCLUDING CASE

Planning At Lorillard University

Edwin Knowles recently assumed the presidency of Lorillard University. This was not an easy decision to reach. The other members of his family were quite happy in Maryland. Moving to the Southwest was a major adjustment, both in terms of climate and, more importantly, with respect to the nature of Knowles's job.

Knowles had always worked in state-supported universities. He had been successful in his career. In a period of 16 years, he progressed from being chairman of a psychology department to being president of a major state university. Unlike his previous school, Lorillard was an older, well-established private university. The school was well known throughout most of the country, but especially in the Southwest. Lorillard was a comprehensive university. It had six schools: arts and sciences, business administration, engineering, education, law, and medicine. The university's endowment was growing, but at a lower rate than that experienced in the last decade.

Knowles recognized that he was accepting quite a challenge in assuming the presidency of Lorillard. In the last 18 months, the university had endured two major scandals. The first one involved serious recruiting violations in the football and basketball programs. After an extended time period, the university accepted the National Collegiate Athletic Association (NCAA) sanctions. These sanctions included a reduction of 25 scholarships that could be offered for each of the next three years and the condition that the university's teams could not appear on television or compete for the conference championship for three years.

The second scandal concerned widespread allegations of cheating in the business administration and law schools. Several "cheating rings" had been discovered and eliminated during the last academic year. Approximately 30 students were suspended from the university permanently. Another 50 or so received suspensions ranging from one semester to two years.

Both scandals had major impacts on the school's student body, alumni, faculty, administrators, and board members. Students currently pursuing degrees claimed that ineffective security procedures made it easy for students to gain copies of tests in advance. Worse, students claimed that some faculty members did not monitor examinations aggressively, allowing students to scan others' exams and even to read notes placed at their feet. Powerful alumni groups suggested that contributions to the university's endowment fund would be reduced sharply if Lorillard could not correct the current problems and prevent others from surfacing. Representatives of the university's influential faculty senate argued that the university's admission standards had been reduced to an unacceptable level. They suggested that this resulted in enrollment of students with questionable ethics and abilities.

In addition, the faculty and many administrators believed that far too much emphasis had been placed on the football and basketball programs. It seemed that the only acceptable outcome was competing for the national championship in each sport every year. Added to this full set of concerns was the general feeling among upper-level administrators that Knowles's predecessor had developed an ineffective organizational structure. The university's board of directors was disturbed by the image created by these scandals. In the board's view, the problems had to be corrected immediately. The person to whom the board would look for direction in these matters was the new president, Edwin Knowles.

Knowles was fully aware of the university's problems and various groups' expectations. When interviewing for the position, he met with representatives from student, alumni, faculty, and administrative groups. Before accepting the presidency at Lorillard, Knowles devoted considerable thought to how he would deal with the school's problems. His primary conclusion was that through effective planning the university could address its current difficulties and chart a successful course for the future. Now that he was on the job, Knowles was prepared to initiate the type of planning efforts he believed were critical to Lorillard's health and effectiveness.

1. What are the entrepreneurial, engineering, and administrative problems facing Lorillard University?

2. Based on information in the case, does Lorillard

currently have a competitive advantage? Justify your position with points from the case.

3. Given its current situation, which planning group (or groups) would be best used at Lorillard?

REFERENCES

1. George A. Steiner, *Strategic Planning: What Every Manager Must Know* (New York: The Free Press, 1979).

2. Steiner, *Strategic Planning*, 13–15.

3. Thomas A. Stewart, "GE Keeps Those Ideas Coming," *Fortune* (August 12, 1991): 41–49.

4. Patricia Sellers, "Winning Over the New Consumer," *Fortune* (July 29, 1991): 113–124.

5. Lawrence C. Rhyne, "The Relationship of Strategic Planning to Financial Performance," *Strategic Management Journal* (September-October 1986): 423–436.

6. Rhyne, "Strategic Planning."

7. John A. Pearce, K. Keith Robbins, and Richard B. Robinson, "The Impact of Grand Strategy and Planning Formality on Financial Performance," *Strategic Management Journal* (March-April 1987): 125–134.

8. Deepak K. Sinha, "The Contribution of Formal Planning to Decisions," *Strategic Management Journal* (October 1990): 479–492.

9. V. Ramanujam and N. Venkatraman, "Planning System Characteristics and Planning Effectiveness," *Strategic Management Journal* (September- October 1987): 453–468.

10. Liam Fahey and V. K. Narayanan, *Macroenvironmental Analysis for Strategic Management* (St. Paul: West Publishing Co., 1986): 49–50.

11. "Fuqua Runs into a Patch of Tall Weeds," *Business Week* (August 5, 1991): 52.

12. Raymond E. Miles and Charles C. Snow, *Organizational Strategy, Structure, and Process* (New York: McGraw-Hill, 1978): 13–30.

13. Alex Taylor, "BMW and Mercedes," *Fortune* (August 12, 1991): 56–63.

14. Taylor, "BMW and Mercedes," 56.

15. Michael E. Porter, *The Competitive Advantage of Nations* (New York: The Free Press, 1990): 33.

16. Henry Mintzberg and James Brian Quinn, *The Strategy Process: Concepts, Contexts, Cases*, 2e (Englewood Cliffs, NJ: Prentice-Hall, 1991).

17. Dave Ulrich and Dale Lake, "Organizational Capability: Creating Competitive Advantage," *Academy of Management Executive* (February 1991): 77–92.

18. Stewart, "GE Keeps Those Ideas Coming," 45.

19. "Warren Foster Revolutionizes the Doughnut," *Fortune* (July 29, 1991): 14.

20. Porter, *Competitive Advantage*.

21. Quaker Oats Company, "1990: Addressing Current Issues," *1990 Annual Report*.

22. Keith H. Hammonds, "Has-Beens Have Been Very Good to Hasbro," *Business Week* (August 5, 1991): 76–77.

23. Stephanie Marrus, *Building the Strategic Plan: Find, Analyze and Present the Right Information* (New York: Ronald Press, 1984): 4–6.

24. Quaker Oats, "1990: Addressing Current Issues."

25. Lloyd L. Byars, *Strategic Management: Formulation and Implementation*, 3e (New York: HarperCollins, 1991): 168.

26. William A. Sahlman, "Why Sane People Shouldn't Serve on Public Boards," *Harvard Business Review* (May-June 1990): 28–36.

27. Roswell B. Perkins, "Avoiding Director Liability," *Harvard Business Review* (May-June 1986): 8–14.

28. James M. Higgins and Julian W. Vincze, *Strategic Management: Text and Cases*, 4e (Chicago: Dryden, 1989): 55–56.

29. D. Ray Bagby and R. Duane Ireland, "Consultants and Small Manufacturing Firms: Some Preliminary Insights," *Consultation* (Winter 1989): 267– 283.

30. Ramanujam and Venkatraman, "Planning Effectiveness."

31. Gerry Johnson and Kevan Scholes, *Exploring Corporate Strategy* (Englewood Cliffs, NJ: Prentice-Hall, 1984): 316.

Chapter 6

Chapter
Learning
Objectives:

1. Discuss the
importance of
strategic planning.

2. Describe the
relationship between
strategic planning
and strategic
management.

3. Detail activities
involved with each
part of strategic
management.

4. Describe the use of
forecasting
techniques in
strategic planning.

5. Discuss the use of
management by
objectives in strategic
management.

6. Summarize the
misuses of strategic
planning and
strategic
management.

Strategic Planning and Strategic Management

For the past three years, sales at Webster's Maintenance Services have almost doubled. The firm specializes in providing complete building maintenance services to commercial clients. Webster's is located in a major metropolitan area that has significant growth in its business community.

Jack Webster, the firm's owner, was a bit surprised by his company's success. Basically, he thought, the firm seemed to have been in the right place at the right time. When the company first opened its doors, it was the second firm in the city to focus on commercial clients. Recently, however, Webster became convinced that continued growth would happen only if his firm started to plan what it was doing. With this conviction, Webster hired a local consultant to help the firm learn how to conduct strategic planning.

At first, both managers and workers seemed to accept the need for strategic planning and worked well with the consultant. After a few months, the consultant recommended a set of actions to develop a strategic planning process at Webster's. The consultant also suggested that the firm implement an overall cost leadership strategy. Several reasons for this recommendation were given. Among these were Webster's large share of the commercial building market, its ability to buy cleaning products at lower prices than its competitors, and its sophisticated scheduling system. The scheduling system kept overtime costs low. Webster accepted the consultant's suggestions and began to implement the strategy.

Almost immediately, Webster ran into trouble. From cleaning crew supervisors to the general manager, he heard complaint after complaint. A statement from one of the top crew supervisors captured the essence of the managers' concerns:

"I don't have time for all this planning stuff. It looks to me as though planning is just another word for getting more out of people who are already overworked and underpaid. I have always tried to schedule my workers carefully to avoid overtime and to get the most out of the supplies. But now I have to fill out a form to justify even an hour of overtime. And trust me, none of my people will ever throw out a bottle of cleaning solution until the last drop is gone! If you ask me, I think the boss wasted a lot of money on this 'strategic planning.'"

Effective strategic planning and strategic management are critical to a firm's survival and success. Many of the mistakes made by companies can be attributed to ineffective strategic planning and management.[1] Effective strategic planning and management require leadership, direction, and visibility from top-level managers.[2] When formulated and implemented effectively, strategic management improves a firm's performance.

For these reasons, Jack Webster, the owner and highest-level manager in Webster's Maintenance Services, is right to use some of his firm's resources to learn how to conduct strategic planning. Given Webster's large share of the commercial market, its relatively low supply costs, and its sophisticated scheduling system, a cost leadership strategy seems appropriate. (Cost leadership is one type of strategy we will discuss later in this chapter.) But something went wrong. Webster's employees were resisting either the use of strategic planning or the way it was being implemented.

Using the materials presented in Chapter 5 as a foundation, this chapter focuses in detail on strategic planning and strategic management. The discussion begins with a description of strategic planning's growing importance and the relationship between strategic planning and management.

Following this is a detailed analysis of the individual parts of strategic management. The chapter closes with discussions of how strategic planning and management are sometimes used improperly and a general critique of these important activities.

THE IMPORTANCE OF STRATEGIC PLANNING

Today's firms—small and large, for-profit and not-for-profit—recognize the need for effective strategic planning. A key reason for this increased attention is the complex environment facing managers and their firms.

When environmental conditions were relatively stable, managers could safely assume that what worked well in the past would work well in the future. Under rather predictable conditions, involving a large number of people in planning activities was not vital. But today, the situation is strikingly different. Environmental changes are often both frequent and major in scope. In addition, competition is more intense and markets more global. To deal with these realities, firms must gather and carefully analyze inputs from everyone involved with their activities. At the least, input should be sought from customers, suppliers, financial analysts, and most, if not all employees. With this information, firms can identify environmental opportunities and determine how to take best advantage of them more effectively and efficiently.

Back to the Opening Case

Notice that Jack Webster apparently did not seek input from anyone before hiring a strategic planning consultant. Although it was not specified in the case, it also seems that the consultant did not contact others in the process of preparing a strategic planning system. Would you have predicted trouble for Jack Webster based on how strategic planning was introduced at Webster's Maintenance Services? What is your opinion about how he approached the matter of strategic planning for his firm?

STRATEGIC MANAGEMENT AND STRATEGIC PLANNING

Strategic management is a six-step process through which a firm determines actions it will take and how those actions will be implemented and evaluated. As shown in Figure 6-1, strategic planning is the first five steps in the strategic management process. **Strategic planning** is the process used to evaluate opportunities and risks and determine strengths and weaknesses in order to define a firm's mission, establish its long-term objectives, and formulate its strategies. Strategic planning is the link between a firm and its environment. It ensures that the firm's outputs and activities are consistent with the conditions in its environment. Strategic planning also helps a firm integrate its activities. *Integration* means that activities required for establishing and achieving objectives are done in a coordinated manner.[3] Thus, the

STRATEGIC MANAGEMENT

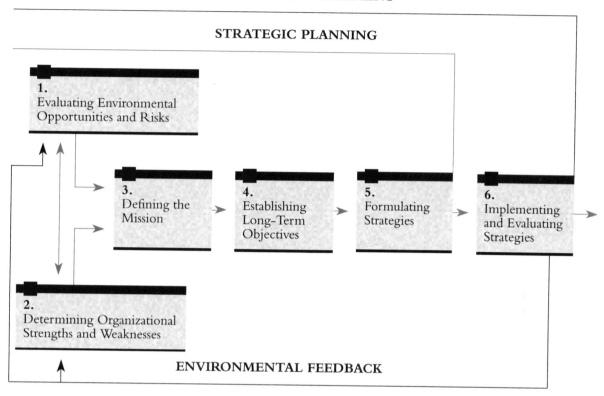

FIGURE 6-1 Strategic Management and Strategic Planning

focus of strategic planning is relating current actions to desired future states.[4]

Important as it is, strategic planning alone does not assure a firm's success. It is in the final stage of the strategic management process that decisions are made regarding how to implement and evaluate the firm's mission, objectives, and strategies. The finest strategies are of little value if they are implemented poorly.

Note that each part of strategic planning and management often requires a significant investment of time and energy. For example, at one college, 5 members of the board of directors, 10 faculty members, 7 administrators, and an outside consultant met for a minimum of 8 hours per week over a 14-week period. The result of their efforts was a set of assumptions about the college's future environment and a written mission statement.[5] On a larger scale, it took 3 years and the participation of over 5,000 people to develop General Electric's corporate values. (Corporate values strongly influence all aspects of strategic planning and management.) Jack Welch, GE's chairman and CEO, observed that they "sweated over every word" in writing the company's value statement.[6]

As these examples show, effective strategic planning and management are time- and resource-intensive activities. Nonetheless, because of their importance, failure to use resources for these activities may result in serious competitive deficiencies.

COMPONENTS OF STRATEGIC MANAGEMENT

As shown in Figure 6-1, strategic planning and strategic management are sequential processes. Before a mission can be identified, a firm's opportunities, risks, strengths, and weaknesses must be known. Likewise, the firm cannot establish long-term objectives without knowledge of its mission. And, of course, a firm cannot implement strategies until they have been carefully defined. These strategic planning and management steps are discussed in the following sections.

Step 1: Evaluating Environmental Opportunities and Risks

ETHICS QUESTION
In terms of ethics, are managers more responsible to some stakeholders than to others?

The first step of strategic planning calls for managers to evaluate the opportunities and risks in their firm's environment. As mentioned in Chapter 2, organizations are open systems. Their survival and effectiveness depend ultimately upon successful exchanges with stakeholders. **Stakeholders** are individuals or groups who influence the development and achievement of a firm's mission, long-term objectives, and strategies. They include customers; suppliers of raw materials, labor, and capital equipment; competitors; financial sources; and regulatory agencies, including government agencies and trade associations.[7]

Firms compete with one another for the services and support of various stakeholders. Wal-Mart, Sears, and Kmart, for example, compete with one another for customers through pricing strategies, depth and breadth of product lines, and a range of customer services. Similarly, these firms try to obtain the most favorable relationships with suppliers of products for their stores. And, not surprisingly, they all seek the most desirable terms when obtaining money from financial institutions.

A firm's external environment contains both opportunities and risks because of competition and rapidly changing market conditions. In Chapter 2, we defined a firm's environment as all the forces external to the firm that have an ability to affect its performance.[8] These environmental forces can be grouped into three categories. The first, the *remote environment*, includes economic, social, political, technological, and ecological factors beyond the control of any single firm.

The second category, the *industry environment*, includes characteristics of the particular industry in which a firm competes: the power of buyers and suppliers, degree of rivalry among firms, availability of substitute products, and strength of barriers to entry in the industry. In combination, these characteristics determine an industry's profit potential.

The third category, the *operating environment*, includes factors and conditions such as profiles of a firm's competitors, customers, and suppliers that have a direct impact on its competitive position.[9] Managers focus most of their attention on the second and third categories of environmental forces when evaluating opportunities and risks.

Environmental opportunities are conditions in a firm's external environment that might aid in the accomplishment of its objectives. Examples include identification of additional uses for the firm's current products by current customers, expansion of current markets by selling existing products to new customer groups, and acquisition of another company.

The decision to establish a franchise of the I Can't Believe It's Yogurt company in Mexico is an example of taking an opportunity to sell existing products to a new customer group. With an initial investment of $1.5 million, the firm decided to open 40 company-owned outlets in Mexico City and 100 franchised locations throughout Mexico, with special emphasis on tourist areas. The units in Mexico feature the same design and quality as the U.S.-based stores.[10] Changes in political structures throughout the world during the 1990s will pave the way for a fascinating array of opportunities for many other firms that are prepared to marshal and use their resources wisely.

Environmental risks are conditions in a firm's external environment that might prevent it from accomplishing its objectives. Consumer and political demands for protection of the natural environment are seen by some managers as a significant risk. Many believe that the 1990s will continue to be known as the "decade of the environment" and that their firms must respond to society's demands for more appropriate environmental concerns if they are to be successful. These managers feel challenged to reconcile society's ecological goals with other equally demanding goals.[11]

Firms must consider many issues when evaluating opportunities and risks. These include current product mix, anticipated actions of competitors, prospects of entering a new market, problems with suppliers, and probable impacts of new laws. These issues are especially important since international competitors and world economic conditions are increasingly affecting business success.

Situations that appear to be risks can be changed into opportunities by enterprising people. For example, Small World Animal Grahams look like the familiar Animal Cracker. However, this new product is strictly for the environmentally aware consumer of the 1990s. The crackers are shaped in the form of 10 endangered species, including a gorilla and a tiger. They are free of preservatives, low in fat and sodium, and 100 percent organic. The

External demands for protection of the natural environment have prompted this consumer products company to respond with more ecologically sound packaging.

Biodegradable packaging
With concern for our environment, this package has been designed without the use of internal foam protection support. All material used in its construction is biodegradable. Recycled paper is used whenever available.

RENEWABLE RESOURCE · RECYCLABLE · BIODEGRADABLE

Thomson Consumer Electronics, Inc.
P.O. Box 1976, Indianapolis, Indiana 46206
Made in Malaysia

package is made of recycled materials, and each box contains a card with tips on protecting an endangered species.[12]

Small World Animal Grahams may prove to be successful in the marketplace while responding to society's concern for the world's environment. Another example of how a large, well-known company has tried to turn an apparent risk into an opportunity is described in the Organization in Action.

ORGANIZATION IN ACTION

California is the first state to mandate zero-emission vehicles (ZEVs). By 1998, two percent of the cars a manufacturer sells in California must be ZEVs. This number will rise to ten percent by 2003. Because about two million cars are sold annually in California, the government has essentially created a market for 200,000 cars by 2003.

General Motors decided that the market for ZEVs is an opportunity worth pursuing. It knew it needed an electric car with both good acceleration and a long range—a difficult technological challenge. To support this decision, the firm has designed the Impact.

The preproduction model of the Impact is a two-seat, 2,200-pound fiber glass car. It can reach 60 miles an hour in eight seconds, has a top speed of 100 miles an hour, and can travel 120 miles before the batteries must be recharged. These impressive numbers are made possible because of aerodynamics and tires. The Impact's coefficient of drag is a mere 0.19, compared to 0.34 for the typical 1991 automobile. Innovative Goodyear tires used on the Impact also contribute to its performance. These special radial tires have 55 percent less rolling resistance than conventional radials. (A great deal of an engine's output goes toward overcoming the rolling resistance of tires.) The car's impressive initial performance is a product of its low coefficient of drag and the reduced rolling resistance of its tires.

Sources: "The Greening of Detroit," *Business Week* (April 8, 1991): 54–60; and Mike Knepper, "New Life for a Pipe Dream," *American Way* (August 15, 1991): 30–32.

General Motors's efforts with the Impact show how a firm can change an apparent environmental risk into an opportunity. GM did not want to risk losing its share of the California automobile market by failing to meet the state's ZEV legislation. Thus, the company decided to view the possible loss of new car sales in California as an opportunity to establish a front-running position in the race to produce less polluting cars.

In a similar manner, the Honda Motor Company began developing a so-called "lean-burn" technology in 1984. This effort was founded on the belief that the future held significant opportunities for companies that could manufacture highly efficient engines without sacrificing power. Through lean-burn technology, engineers attempt to boost fuel efficiency by raising an engine's air-to-fuel ratio above typical standards.

In September 1991, Honda introduced the 1992 Civic VX. This car is powered by an engine that gets 48 miles per gallon in the city and 55 miles per gallon on the highway. Interestingly, although it is very efficient, the engine has the same power as its less fuel-efficient predecessor.[13] Honda's systematic, dynamic thinking and decision making result from effective strategic planning and management.

FORECASTING. Successful forecasting is critical to a firm's efforts to evaluate environmental opportunities and risks. **Forecasts** are predictions of future events. They help a firm identify actions to take today in anticipation of tomorrow's opportunities and risks. High-quality forecasting greatly improves the effectiveness of strategic planning and management efforts. The Organization in Action describes changes one firm made because of forecasted changes in environmental conditions.

ORGANIZATION IN ACTION

Bausch & Lomb is the world's leading maker of contact lenses. However, the long-term forecast for this product is not as positive as company executives would like. In particular, the size of a key customer group—women between the ages of 18 and 25—fell during the early 1980s. Compounding this situation was a warning issued by the Food and Drug Administration in 1986 that cited problems associated with improper use of extended-wear lenses. This warning reduced demand for contact lenses further.

The demand for Bausch & Lomb's laboratory and industrial instruments (such as microscopes and computer-aided drafting equipment) is highly cyclical in nature. In light of forecasts suggesting that neither the contact lens nor instrument markets would change substantially in the future, the company decided to restructure its operations. It set about a carefully designed acquisition program and now sells high-end, brand-name products for the eyes, ears, and mouth. Typically, these products are recommended by health-care professionals. The company also expanded its foreign operations significantly, and it streamlined the process through which it designs its products to satisfy the demands of customers in particular countries. To date, results from these efforts have been positive.

Source: James S. Hirsch, "Bausch & Lomb Shifts Focus from Eyes," *The Wall Street Journal* (February 27, 1990): A1.

As Bausch & Lomb's experiences indicate, effective forecasting can provide information needed to evaluate a firm's opportunities and risks. Forecasts showed that remaining overly dependent on contact lenses presented a risk for Bausch & Lomb. However, the company also determined that opportunities existed if it expanded its offerings to include products designed to take care of "all problems above the neck." An understanding of opportunities and risks, combined with knowledge of the firm's strengths and weaknesses, provided the information required to complete the remaining stages of the strategic planning and management processes.

It is important to use a forecasting technique that is consistent with a firm's needs at a particular time. Many issues should be considered before selecting a forecasting technique (or techniques). These include availability of data, technical sophistication required to use the technique, amount of detail required from the forecast, and how accurate the forecast must be.[14] Forecasting techniques fall into two groups: qualitative (or judgment) methods and quantitative methods.

Qualitative Methods. If precise historical data are not available, managers' judgments must provide the basis for developing forecasts. Often, these subjective judgments are based on both facts and intuition. (Recall Chapter 1's discussion of how managerial intuition can be critical to effective decision-making processes.) Experience tends to improve a manager's judgment and ability to forecast events.

In many cases, the manager will seek information and opinions from other knowledgeable people to forecast future events. Because these opinions come from several people, the forecast is less risky than one made by a single person. One technique is called the *sales force composite,* which relies on the combined expert judgments of field sales personnel. Sales representatives are polled about their customers' expected purchases for the next time period. Another technique is the *jury of opinion.* In most cases, this uses the average opinion of managers from various company divisions and departments. However, if the forecast concerns some new technology, the jury of opinion may include experts from outside the firm.

Two strengths of qualitative forecasting are that it is inexpensive and the forecasts can be prepared relatively quickly. A weakness of this method is the possibility of bias. Generally the accuracy of forecasts improves as the forecaster becomes more experienced.

ETHICS QUESTION
Is it ethical for managers to use forecasting techniques that they know are subject to their own biases?

Quantitative Methods. **Time series analysis** examines past data for trends and uses them to forecast what would happen in the future if a particular trend were to continue. Trend analysis develops a mathematical equation from past performance and uses the equation to project into the future. Because it is based on the assumption that past trends will continue in the future, time series analysis is most useful in stable environments.

Time series analysis is often used to forecast future sales volume and revenue. For example, it might be used to predict the next quarter's sales based on five years' worth of quarterly sales data. Time series analysis can also be used to predict other outcomes, including employee turnover and absenteeism rates.

There are two interrelated strengths of time series forecasting methods. First, now that most companies have extensive data readily available on computer files, very little time is required to develop forecasts with time series analysis. Second, these forecasts can be updated quickly and without major expense. A weakness of time series methods is the assumption that what has happened in the past will continue into the future.

Like time series analysis, causal modeling is used to forecast future events in mathematical terms. However, there is one important difference between the two quantitative techniques. Time series analysis assumes that past events will predict the future without considering why those past events occurred. **Causal models** analyze the causes of past events and use them to predict future events. For example, while time series analysis forecasts future sales based on past sales, causal models forecast future sales by looking at factors that cause sales to increase or decrease. Factors such as advertising expenditure, price of the product, competitors' prices, and the unemployment rate might be included. *Regression analysis* develops a mathematical equation that describes the relationship of one or more causal variables to a variable that is dependent on the causal variable. Another causal modeling technique is an *econometric model,* which uses a set of regression equations to simulate the interaction between economic conditions and a firm's activities. An example would be to predict changes in home sales as a result of changes in the tax laws.

A strength of causal models is the ease with which additional relationships can be examined. This allows managers to update forecasts as relevant data become available. A weakness is the time required to build some models and the sophistication needed to interpret their results. When managers need to use econometric models to make forecasts, they may hire a consulting firm that specializes in constructing these models.

Step 2: Determining Organizational Strengths and Weaknesses

Organizational strengths are internal conditions that help a firm attain its objectives. The variety of conditions in which a firm can develop strengths is virtually endless. An efficient distribution channel, a strong financial position, high-quality managers and personnel, and an excellent marketing program are examples of strengths. Managers need to recognize their company's internal strengths so they can support them. Managers at the Southwestern Bell Corporation believe that "for any company to succeed, it must have a clear understanding of its strengths and a commitment to doing the job better than its competitors."[15]

Management can identify a firm's distinctive competence by examining organizational strengths. A **distinctive competence** is a strength that allows a firm to perform especially well compared to competitors.[16] For example, Wal-Mart's distribution system is thought to be superior to those of its competitors. The Intel Corporation's culture has been mentioned as a strength that is unique to that firm. The delivery system used by the Domino's Pizza company has long been the basis for its success.

Domino's has identified its delivery system as its distinctive competence in the pizza industry.

To gain a competitive advantage, managers must work to match their firm's distinctive competence with an opportunity in the external market environment. This matching process also allows companies to maximize their strengths while minimizing their weaknesses.[17]

Organizational weaknesses are internal conditions that make it difficult to achieve objectives. There are many internal conditions that could be organizational weaknesses. Poorly trained employees, ineffective advertising campaigns, and an inadequate cash position are examples. Managers must identify weaknesses, determine their impact on the firm, and allocate resources to correct the most serious problems.

Step 3: Defining the Mission

The environments in which firms operate today are dynamic and complex. Because of this, it is important for them to focus their efforts. They must not pursue activities for which they do not have the necessary distinctive competencies. Mission statements provide the boundaries within which companies focus their activities. In at least one study, the highest-performing companies were those that had prepared written mission statements and distributed them to stakeholders.[18]

A **mission** is the unique purpose that sets a business apart from other firms of its type and identifies the scope of its operations in product and market terms.[19] Grounded in external opportunities and internal strengths, or distinctive competencies, a mission statement reflects a firm's character and the contributions it intends to make in terms of products offered and markets served. Often, mission statements reflect a firm's philosophy (basic beliefs, values, aspirations, and priorities), self-concept (including competitive strengths), and desired public image.[20] An effective mission statement establishes a firm's individuality, is exciting and inspiring, and is relevant to all its stakeholders.[21]

Figure 6-2 presents the mission statements of three diverse organizations. The Shell Oil Company is a large, for-profit corporation, the Great Plains Vo-Tech is part of a state educational program, and the Internal Revenue Service (IRS) is a federal agency familiar to all of us. Even though the fundamental characters of these organizations differ, it is important for each to develop a mission statement.

Mission statements are not changed frequently, but they are sometimes modified as a result of changes in a firm's opportunities, risks, strengths, and weaknesses. For example, Xerox Corporation redefined its mission from being a producer of copiers to being a supplier of automated office systems.

Step 4: Establishing Long-Term Objectives

Long-term objectives are concrete goals that ensure achievement of a firm's mission. As shown in Figure 6-3, long-term objectives are more specific than mission statements. Effective long-term objectives are:

1. *Specific.* They should be expressed in action terms, with clear directions about what is to be done.

ETHICS QUESTION
Is there a correct ethical response when one of a company's weaknesses is a poorly trained workforce? If so, describe that response.

ETHICS QUESTION
Describe why you might know something about a firm's commitment to social responsibility by reading its mission statement.

SHELL OIL COMPANY

Our Mission

Our mission is to excel in our three principal businesses—exploration and production, refining and marketing, and chemical, with operations primarily in the United States.

We are committed to being the best in our inudstry—as measured by financial performance; health, safety, and environmental performance; product quality; and customer service. We intend to accomplish this while adhering to high ethical standards and being a responsible citizen of the communities where we live and work.

We are dedicated to satisfying our customers and continuously improving performance. We will pursue these fundamental values with discipline and intensity and measure progress by tangible business results. This is our commitment to excellence and quality, and it requires the effective involvement of every member of the Shell team.

GREAT PLAINS VO-TECH

Mission Statement

Our mission is to provide vocational-technical education programs and support services to secondary and postsecondary students who seek to develop the knowledge, skills, and attitudes necessary for successful employment.

INTERNAL REVENUE SERVICE

Mission

The purpose of the IRS is to collect the proper amount of tax revenues at the least cost to the public, and in a manner that warrants the highest degree of public confidence in our integrity, efficiency, and fairness. To achieve that purpose, we will:

Encourage and achieve the highest possible degree of voluntary compliance in accordance with the tax law and regulations;

Advise the public of their rights and responsibilities;

Determine the extent of compliance and the causes of noncompliance;

Do all things needed for the proper administration and enforcement of the tax laws;

Continually search for and implement new, more efficient, and effective ways of accomplishing our Mission.

2. *Measurable.* Results to be achieved should be specified in measurable terms (preferably quantitative in nature). With measurable results, it is easy to determine whether or not an objective has been reached.
3. *Achievable.* Long-term objectives should be realistic. It must be possible to achieve objectives as they are stated.
4. *Written.* Each long-term objective should be committed to writing. Written objectives are valued more highly and are more likely to be achieved than those that are merely spoken.

FIGURE 6-3
An Example of a Mission
Statement and Long-
Term Objectives

MISSION STATEMENT

To produce and market programs of management development of the highest quality.

LONG-TERM OBJECTIVES (PARTIAL LIST)

Market Share

To increase our share of the national management seminar market for materials 5 percent within five years.

Product Quality

To upgrade each program substantially each year until we are considered a leading publisher of superior-quality materials nationally.

Profitability

To achieve an annual return on sales of 10 percent after covering growth costs and above-average salaries to partners and employees.

Control of Organizational Growth

To contract out all possible writing, art, typesetting, printing, and binding in order to minimize expansion of human resources and facilities.

5. *Comprehensive.* Long-term objectives should be established for all major areas that play a role in the achievement of a firm's mission.
6. *Coordinated.* Individual and group objectives should be coordinated so they are consistent with and contribute to achievement of the objectives of other individuals and groups and of the firm as a whole.
7. *Prioritized.* To provide guidelines for the allocation of resources and the resolution of conflicts, long-term objectives should be ranked in their order of importance.
8. *Time bound.* Target dates should be set for the achievement of each long-term objective and for each contributing short-term objective.
9. *Flexible.* Long-term objectives should be developed in a manner that allows modification if conditions change.
10. *Accepted.* Effective long-term objectives should be accepted by all involved parties. Otherwise, people will not develop the commitment required to pursue an objective until it is accomplished.

Long-term objectives help to define a firm's mission in more detail. The unique purpose of the IRS, as shown by its mission statement, becomes more concrete through development of long-term objectives that define specific measures to ensure that it is able to "determine the extent of compliance and the causes of noncompliance." Similarly, the Shell Oil Company is committed to being the best in its industry as measured by financial performance (among other outcomes). Given this mission, the company must select the financial indexes it will use to determine the progress being made toward its objective.

Once they have developed long-term objectives, firms must formulate strategies. Types of strategies are described in the next few sections.

LEARNING CHECK   Describe the first four components of strategic planning: evaluating environmental opportunities and risks, determining organizational strengths and weaknesses, defining the mission, and establishing long-term objectives.

Step 5: Formulating Strategies

A **strategy** is made up of the decisions and resource allocations a firm makes to accomplish its mission and long-term objectives. According to founder Bill Gates, Microsoft's primary long-term objective is to create the standard for the industry in which the firm competes.[22] To achieve this long-term objective, Microsoft must formulate and implement strategies that reflect a series of decisions and resource allocations.

A very small firm with only a single product offered to one customer group can develop a single strategy or plan to specify everything the firm should do. However, most private companies and public agencies require several strategies to direct their activities successfully. Our discussion of this important topic describes the differences among corporate-level, business-level, and functional-level strategies. The issues addressed at each of these levels are shown in Figure 6-4.

FIGURE 6-4
Three Strategy Levels

DIVERSIFIED BUSINESS FIRMS

Corporate-Level Strategy
Selection of businesses
Management of business units
Allocation of resources

Business-Level Strategy
Means of competing within individual business units' product markets
Positioning within competitive markets

Functional-Level Strategy
Achievement of fit among functional strategies
Development of actions consistent with business- and corporate-level strategies

SINGLE-BUSINESS FIRMS

Corporate-Level Strategy
Selection of a single business
Means of competition within chosen product market

Functional-Level Strategy
Achievement of fit among functional strategies
Development of actions consistent with corporate-level strategy

Diversified firms compete in two or more businesses. Many large firms such as General Electric and the Dow Chemical Company can be classified as diversified. For these firms, **corporate-level strategy** is concerned with three primary questions: What businesses should the company be in? How should corporate headquarters manage the businesses? How should resources be allocated among them?[23]

Because the diversified firm is involved in a range of businesses, managers must determine the relative attractiveness of each. Typically, the most attractive businesses are those earning the largest profits. However, managers also examine other issues. For example, certain business units may use the same raw materials to manufacture their products. Buying the shared raw materials in bulk can reduce the firm's overall costs. Likewise, large firms often use certain business units as training grounds for managers. These units may be attractive because of the opportunities they provide to promising managerial talent. Linking information of this type with the firm's mission and long-term objectives helps managers determine how to manage and allocate resources to the various businesses.

Two primary types of diversification strategies are formulated at the corporate level. Through **related diversification,** a firm undertakes a new activity that shares some characteristic with its current products or markets. Acquisition of the Miller Brewing Company by Philip Morris is an example of related diversification. The two companies sell consumer products whose success depends on effective marketing. Philip Morris's marketing skill helps Miller Brewing position its products more effectively in the marketplace. **Unrelated diversification** occurs when a firm undertakes a new activity that has nothing in common with its current products or markets. The acquisition of Marathon oil by USX (then U.S. Steel) moved the firm into an area completely different from the steel business. Managers study their firm's human, financial, physical, and informational resources before deciding to pursue either related or unrelated diversification strategies.

As shown in Figure 6-4, corporate-level strategy involves different questions for **single-business firms**—firms that compete in a single business or product market. For them, corporate-level strategy focuses on two questions: Should the firm remain in its current business? How should it compete within its single business or product market?

Recall that diversified firms are involved with two or more businesses. Typically, each of these is known as a *strategic business unit (SBU)*. SBUs may be, for example, the schools or colleges of a university, the major automobile divisions of the Ford Motor Company, or the various parts of the diversified Anheuser-Busch Companies. (Divisions in this corporation include the Metal Container Corporation, Busch Agricultural Resources, Inc., St. Louis Refrigerator Car Company, and the Busch Creative Services Corporation. A strategy must be formulated for each SBU in the diversified firm. The **business-level strategy** focuses on the question: How should we compete in each of our businesses?

According to Michael Porter, a well-known professor of strategic management, there are three strategies firms can use to compete in the marketplace: overall cost leadership, differentiation, and focus. Thus, as shown in Figure 6-4, business-level strategies in the diversified firm and corporate-level strategies in the single-business firm are the same. The three strategy choices for the single-business firm and for each of the SBUs in the diversified firm are overall cost leadership, differentiation, and focus.

The **overall cost leadership strategy** is one by which a firm works to provide a product with features acceptable to customers at the lowest competitive price.[24] Dollar General is an example of a firm that follows an overall cost leadership strategy. Started in 1939, the chain's name derives from the fact that originally no product sold for more than a dollar. In the early 1990s, all products sold in the chain's 1,500 stores were priced under $25 (less than $2.50 in 1939 dollars). The average item recently sold for about $5.29.[25]

Over time, the overall cost leadership strategy can be successful only if a firm can continuously reduce its costs. This is necessary in order to continue offering a lower price than those charged by competing firms. Customers are willing to purchase a cost leader's products as long as those products have features that are close to those of competitors' products. These features could include product quality, service after the sale, innovative design, and so forth. For example, customers are willing to purchase Dollar General's clothing items as long as they are similar in durability and style to clothes available in other stores.

Back to the Opening Case

The consultant hired by Jack Webster suggested that the firm implement a cost leadership strategy. Because of Webster's large share of the commercial maintenance market, its ability to buy cleaning products at lower prices than those paid by competitors, and its sophisticated scheduling system, the consultant concluded that it could offer clients the lowest price. Notice that to continue implementing this strategy successfully, the company must remain focused on driving its costs even lower over time. If it fails to accomplish this objective, the firm could lose its ability to compete successfully.

As reflected in its advertising, Circuit City has formulated an overall cost leadership strategy to accomplish its mission and objectives.

A **differentiation strategy** is one whereby the firm provides a product to customers that is differentiated in some way from others in the market. That is, the product has features that customers value and perceive as being unique.[26] Such features could include good design, high-quality technology, responsive customer service, and so forth. For example, customers value Mercedes-Benz automobiles because of their reliability and prestige. Likewise, Ralph Lauren has differentiated his products in terms of status and quality. To use this strategy successfully, firms must be able to identify features that are valued highly by particular customers and enhance those features on an ongoing basis.

When implementing this strategy, firms must continually differentiate their products from those of competitors. Mercedes-Benz, for example, constantly looks for ways to manufacture its automobiles in a manner superior to techniques used by competing firms. For his clothing lines, Ralph Lauren must manufacture products that provide customers with unique value in terms of features that are important to them. Customers buying differentiated products are willing to pay for the features they value highly. However, the prices of these products must not be too much above the prices of competing firms' offerings.

With the overall cost leadership and differentiation strategies, firms attempt to gain a competitive advantage in many parts of an industry. With the **focus strategy**, on the other hand, a firm focuses on a narrow segment of an industry—a particular customer group, part of the product line, or geographic area—to the exclusion of other segments. This strategy is based on the premise that by doing so the firm is better able to serve its customers than competitors who compete on an industrywide basis. As a result, the firm attempts to achieve either cost leadership or differentiation in a narrow segment of an industry.[27] This strategy is selected when a company lacks the resources or the desire to compete successfully in more than one industry segment. To be successful with this strategy, a firm must be able to identify the industry segment in which customers have unique needs that can be served by the firm's distinctive competencies. Because of their resource constraints, the focus strategy is often the most viable option for small business firms.

According to Michael Porter, Laker Airways is a classic example of the focus strategy. At first, this company's strategy was to provide no-frills service in the North American market. The industry segment targeted by the firm was the highly price-sensitive North American traveler. After a period of initial success, Laker added frills, new routes, and new services. These expansions blurred the company's mission and image, and eventually, Laker Airways went bankrupt.[28] The challenge to managers adopting the focus strategy is to verify that the firm's efforts remain targeted strictly to the particular industry segment in which it originally decided to concentrate its efforts.

Functional-level strategies are used in both diversified and single-business firms. They are formulated to specify actions required to successfully implement business- and corporate-level strategies. Examples of functions include marketing, production/operations, finance, and administration.[29] The focus at this strategy level is to achieve a good fit. A firm's entire set of functional strategies should be consistent with one another. In addition, they should support the firm's intention to compete on the basis of overall cost leadership, differentiation, or focus.[30]

Functional-level strategies are based on the issues that are unique to each function. For example, to develop a strategy for the production/operations function, managers would consider scope of operations, functions performed, type of operations, operations control, manufacturing costs, and labor issues.[31] In all instances, functional-level strategies should be formed with a strategic focus. The difference between an operational and a strategic focus can be explained as follows. With an operational focus, the question managers ask is "How can we manufacture products more efficiently than in the past?" With a strategic focus, the question becomes "How can products be manufactured in order to beat the competition?"[32]

Step 6: Implementing and Evaluating Strategies

No matter how appropriate it is, no strategy can be successful until it is implemented properly and its results are evaluated carefully. Sometimes managers neglect the implementation process, believing that the value of the firm's mission, long-term objectives, and strategies will be fully accepted by all. But effective implementation comes about only through deliberate actions. Managers must see to it that relationships are developed between and among departments to ensure that strategies are implemented in an integrated and coordinated manner. The leadership styles, motivation techniques, reward systems, and communication practices used must be consistent with the company's strategies and the abilities of its personnel. (These topics will be discussed in Parts 3 and 4 of this book. For now, it is sufficient to note that successful strategy implementation and evaluation are made possible by the careful design and use of appropriate tools and techniques.)

LEARNING CHECK	Discuss the types of strategies firms can formulate and issues related to the implementation and evaluation of those strategies.

MANAGEMENT BY OBJECTIVES. **Management by objectives (MBO)** is a technique used to determine the activities employees will complete to implement strategies. It is a managerial process through which managers and employees identify the goals the employees are held accountable for achieving. The primary purpose of MBO is to (a) provide employees with goals to accomplish, (b) permit them to help determine what the goals will be, and (c) foster evaluation of the results achieved compared to the goals.[33] When MBO is used in strategy implementation and evaluation processes, employees are held accountable for the accomplishment of goals related to particular strategies.

The essence of MBO is goal setting at every level of management and throughout the ranks of nonmanagerial employees. A high degree of employee involvement in goal setting strengthens the relationship between individual and organizational goals. Since it takes many different forms, defining, describing, and evaluating MBO is challenging. In some MBO programs, a manager assigns each employee's goals. In most cases, employees set their own goals, subject to the approval of their managers. Although the process varies among organizations, the three major steps in MBO are goal setting, implementation and review, and performance appraisal.[34] (See Figure 6-5.)

Goal Setting. In this initial step, managers and their employees (often lower-level managers) identify the employees' job responsibilities and determine priorities among them. To integrate an employee's actions with the needs of the firm, both the manager and the employee must have a clear understanding of the firm's mission, long-term objectives, and strategies.

Once they have determined prioritized responsibilities, the two parties set realistic, yet challenging goals and milestones. (*Milestones* are used to measure the degree to which goals are being reached at various times.) Then the manager and employee should detail and accept specific courses of actions (or plans) that will lead to accomplishment of the goals.

These discussions require significant give and take. In practice, such interactions may be difficult. Some people find it difficult to engage in open exchanges in which accountability for performance is examined. In addition, some rigidity is built into the process itself. Managers cannot allow their employees to concentrate on goals that fail to contribute to effective

FIGURE 6–5
The MBO Process

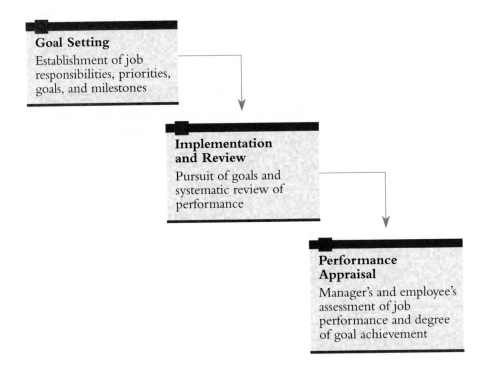

Goal Setting
Establishment of job responsibilities, priorities, goals, and milestones

Implementation and Review
Pursuit of goals and systematic review of performance

Performance Appraisal
Manager's and employee's assessment of job performance and degree of goal achievement

implementation of the firm's strategies. Because of this, during the goal-setting step, managers should clearly specify the parameters within which acceptable goals must fall.

Implementation and Review. The implementation step is the actual accomplishment of agreed-upon goals. Managers interact with employees frequently to verify that goals are being reached. In particular, a manager should not allow a milestone date to pass without ensuring that the employee has in fact reached that milestone.

It may be necessary to change some of an employee's goals during the implementation stage. For one thing, environmental conditions may develop that require the employee to reexamine job priorities. This could surface as a result of technological change or a major competitor's aggressive pricing tactics. A second factor indicating the need to adjust goals is related to the employee. For example, an employee may master job skills more rapidly than was expected during the goal-setting stage. In this case, goals should be adjusted in order to challenge the employee to perform at a level of maximum effectiveness and efficiency.

Performance Appraisal. In the final step of the MBO process, the manager and the employee compare the employee's achievements to agreed-upon goals. The results of this comparison can be used to identify areas of training needed by the employee and to determine future job assignments and compensation.

A criticism often leveled at traditional performance appraisals is that they tend to focus on personality characteristics and other qualities that may not be related to an individual's effectiveness. With the MBO process, appraisals are more objective, since actual achievements are evaluated against previously set goals. The more effectively the goals are achieved, the higher the employee's performance evaluation. By allowing for any unexpected influences on productivity or sales, such as depressed markets, strikes, and extraordinarily good luck, managers can evaluate employees' achievements objectively.

Looking at results to determine effectiveness is a useful approach. Yet, when used alone, this approach is inadequate because the manner in which results are achieved can be vitally important. Actions that have a negative impact on the efforts of others to implement relevant strategies and plans are just as damaging as an individual's failure to reach performance-related goals. Increased attention is also being placed on ethics as an important consideration in comparing and evaluating different individuals' job performance.

LEARNING CHECK   Describe each of the three major steps in the MBO process.

A CRITIQUE OF MBO. There are many reasons why MBO processes should be successful. MBO is a relatively objective way of measuring employees' performances; the process provides concrete feedback to employees; specific, yet challenging goals are established between a manager and an employee; and customized evaluations are given to each employee.[35] But after more than three decades of experience with and research on MBO, the results are mixed. Many companies that have tried some form of MBO have discarded it—enough to create skepticism about the process. On the other hand, some MBO programs have produced positive results in both productivity and satisfaction.

MBO is similar to other managerial tools. If used correctly, it can be beneficial. The MBO process can be an integral part of strategy implementation efforts if the following conditions are met:

1. Managers (especially top-level managers) are committed to the process.
2. The process has been designed carefully and appropriately for the conditions facing a firm at a particular time.
3. People using the process focus on performance rather than personalities.
4. All managers accept the view that the process can be of value to every single manager and to the firm as a whole.[36]

GUIDELINES FOR AN EFFECTIVE MBO PROCESS. Certainly managers starting MBO processes can learn from mistakes made by other firms. However, the unique characteristics of each firm must be taken into consideration. Figure 6-6 contains 11 guidelines for developing an effective MBO process.

MISUSES OF STRATEGIC PLANNING AND STRATEGIC MANAGEMENT

All managerial and nonmanagerial activities should increase a firm's value. Strategic planning and management, too, must add to a firm's value if their practice is to be continued. Use of these processes should enable a firm to capture additional returns from its activities.[37] This chapter and the previous one have shown that the value of strategic planning and strategic management has generally been established. Nonetheless, there are both business writers and practicing managers who question the worth of these practices.

Research has been conducted to examine this important issue. In one study, information was gathered from a broad sample of SBU heads, corporate planning directors, and chief executive officers engaged in strategic planning and management activities in diversified firms. In addition, 14 seminars were held with these executives in order to identify problems and potential remedies more clearly. Analysis of the data suggested that the executives had experienced the following six common problems:

FIGURE 6–6
Guidelines for an
Effective MBO Process

1. Verify that participants understand the MBO process and know how they can benefit from it before starting the program.
2. Tailor MBO to the organization. Avoid generic programs.
3. Avoid excessive paperwork. Keep it simple.
4. Allow individuals to set their own goals where the firm's overall leadership style permits. Avoid assigning goals authoritatively to persons who value personal autonomy and responsibility.
5. Verfiy that a person who is held responsible for results has access to the resources required to achieve them (e.g., authority, money, materials, human resources, technology).
6. Provide for team effort where the success of one individual is dependent on the productivity of others over whom he or she has no authority.
7. Do not place too heavy an emphasis on results. Otherwise, people may be considered only as a means to an end.
8. Allow participants the freedom to determine the means for achieving their goals insofar as possible.
9. Establish effective controls and feedback systems to track the progress of subordinates, but avoid excessively close supervision.
10. Provide for changing goals as conditions change. Be adaptable enough to change any aspect of an MBO process that proves to be unworkable.
11. Verify that results of using MBO are integrated with and supportive of other implementation activities.

1. poor preparation of line managers for participation in strategic planning;
2. faulty definition of SBUs;
3. vaguely formulated goals;
4. inadequate information bases for action planning;
5. badly handled reviews of SBU plans; and
6. inadequate linkage of strategic planning with other control systems.[38]

One interpretation of these six common problems is that there is nothing wrong with formal strategic planning and management processes. In fact, it is possible that these common problems could be solved through careful planning prior to the actual implementation and evaluation of formulated strategies and plans. Careful planning calls for:

- line managers to be given the training necessary to be active participants in these important processes;
- SBUs to be defined correctly;
- goals to be defined with a reasonable degree of precision;
- action plans to be developed in greater detail;
- strategies and plans to be evaluated and integrated carefully; and
- control systems to be established carefully.[39]

Thus, as is the case with all tools and techniques available to managers, strategic management and planning must be used correctly if they are to contribute to the accomplishment of a firm's mission and objectives.

Back to the
Opening Case

It is certainly possible that Jack Webster's actions did not contribute to the effectiveness of strategic planning in his firm. The text listed problems executives have encountered with strategic planning and management. Notice that some of these problems could apply to Webster's Maintenance Services. In your opinion, which of these problems apply in this instance?

A CRITIQUE OF STRATEGIC PLANNING AND MANAGEMENT

Strategic planning and strategic management are based on both theory and practical managerial experience. Their relationship with organizational success is well established. Strategic management is uniquely suited for providing managers with a broad perspective. With this perspective, managers develop meaningful assumptions regarding issues that are critical to a firm's success. Although strategic planning and management are not perfect managerial tools, when understood and used properly they can help firms survive the challenges of today's global and competitive markets.

SUMMARY

Strategic management and strategic planning are critical to the success of all types of organizations. Through strategic planning, a firm determines its environmental opportunities and risks, internal strengths and weaknesses, mission, long-term objectives, and strategies. Strategic management includes all phases of strategic planning plus the very important implementation and evaluation step.

When evaluating environmental opportunities and risks, managers identify conditions in the firm's external environment that may either aid accomplishment of objectives (an opportunity) or prevent it (a risk). An important aspect of evaluating opportunities and risks is the effective use of qualitative and quantitative forecasting techniques.

Assessing organizational strengths and weaknesses involves determining conditions inside the firm that help in the achievement of objectives (a strength) or hinder it (a weakness). Through this process, a firm identifies its distinctive competencies. A distinctive competence is a strength that makes it possible for a firm to compete especially well compared to competitors. The mission statement specifies a firm's unique purpose—what it is that makes the firm different from others. In establishing long-term objectives, managers set concrete outcomes that contribute to achievement of the firm's mission. Once a mission and objectives are established, strategies can be formulated. A strategy is the pattern of decisions and resource allocations made in order to accomplish a firm's long-term objectives and mission.

Specific strategies are formulated in both the single-business firm (where corporate- and functional-level strategies are formed) and the diversified firm (where corporate-, business-, and functional-level strategies are formed). Corporate-level strategy is concerned with determining the businesses in which a firm intends to compete and how to manage those businesses and allocate resources among them. Business-level strategies specify how a firm will compete within a particular business or product market area. The focus of functional-level strategies is on activities required to coordinate actions across all functional areas such as marketing, purchasing, and so forth. The implementation and evaluation step is designed to identify deviations from planned outcomes and to initiate appropriate corrective actions.

As a part of the implementation and evaluation step of strategic management, MBO is intended to ensure that employees' goals are consistent with the actions required to implement various strategies. MBO emphasizes the importance of goals rather than activities or bureaucratic controls as guides to employee behavior. The MBO process includes three major steps: goal setting, implementation and review, and performance appraisal. In the goal-setting step, managers and employees agree on goals for which the employees are held accountable. During the implementation and review step, employees complete milestones necessary to accomplish their goals. Managers and employees review achievements to verify that agreed-upon goals will be reached. The final step—performance appraisal—measures and examines actual performances. Outcomes from the appraisal are used to determine the employees' training needs, future job assignments, and compensation packages.

Strategic management and planning are managerial tools. As such, they are subject to misuse. Recent evidence suggests that problems encountered in some firms have been caused by a misuse of these tools rather than by the tools themselves. The managerial challenge is to understand strategic planning and management and to use them effectively and efficiently.

KEY TERMS

strategic management
strategic planning
stakeholders
environmental opportunities
environmental risks
forecasts
time series analysis

causal models
organizational strengths
distinctive competence
organizational weaknesses
mission
long-term objectives
strategy

diversified firms
corporate-level strategy
related diversification
unrelated diversification
single-business firms
business-level strategy
overall cost leadership strategy

differentiation strategy
focus strategy
functional-level strategies
management by objectives (MBO)

QUESTIONS FOR DISCUSSION AND REVIEW

1. Discuss why strategic planning is important in today's organizations. Do you believe strategic planning's importance will grow over the next 10 years? Why or why not?
2. What are the differences between strategic planning and strategic management? Are these differences important to those attempting to be effective managers?
3. Fully describe the six steps of the strategic management process. Do you believe any one of these steps is more important than the others? Why or why not?
4. What forecasting methods are used in strategic planning? Describe the conditions calling for the use of each method.
5. How can management by objectives be used in strategic management?
6. Have strategic planning and strategic management been used improperly? If so, what has caused this to occur?

PROBLEMS FOR ACTION

A. Assume that you have been selected as the new general manager of a small company, Astin's Book Publishers. Your employer, the Disch Corporation, recently acquired Astin's. The primary objective you have been asked to achieve is to maximize Astin's cash flow to the Disch Corporation so that the corporation can finance additional acquisitions. As a strong advocate of strategic planning, you have decided to involve all of Astin's managers in strategic planning and individual goal setting.

Plan your strategic planning process. Given that strategic planning has not been conducted previously by Astin's, what should you do in order to develop an effective strategic planning process?

B. Assume that you recently purchased a small sandwich shop near your school's campus. Using the information in this chapter about the components of strategic planning, develop a mission statement and a set of long-term objectives for the sandwich shop. Be as realistic as possible with this assignment. Develop your long-term objectives in terms of the categories included in Figure 6-3.

CONCLUDING CASE

Developing Vanguard's Mission Statement

As chair of Vanguard's board of trustees, Sharon Perry believed that certain events had to occur for the school to continue growing and developing. As a small private college preparatory school, Vanguard had served the community well in its first 15 years. But changing events suggested that the school would have to sharpen its focus and use its resources wisely to be successful in the future. Perry believed that a mission statement would be of significant value to those involved with and concerned about the school. Admittedly, a statement of purpose had been prepared when the school was established. However, this statement had been written quickly and with the participation of only a few people. Besides, Perry thought, the school's situation was quite different now from what it was 15 years ago. In Perry's opinion, the statement of purpose no longer provided the direction required for the school to be successful.

Perry knew many successful business people in the local community. While downtown to visit with one of her firm's clients, she stopped in to see Jim Freeman, the managing partner of a large law firm. The firm had offices in three locations and had been identified recently as the second largest law firm in the state.

Perry knew that Freeman's firm had formed a mission statement during the last year. That experience, she thought, could help her decide how to proceed with developing a mission statement for Vanguard:

"Jim, I think you would agree that over all, Vanguard has been pretty successful. But, in my opinion, the school is at a point where it could wander a bit if it isn't careful. A new headmaster just joined us, we continue to have more people than ever applying for admission to the school, and our finances are still not what they should be. Basically, I just don't believe that we know exactly where we are going or how to get there. Wouldn't a mission statement help us deal with these matters?"

"Well, Sharon," he replied, "I do think that mission statements help a great deal. As you know, we just prepared one for our firm. But let me forewarn you. Based on my experiences, you can expect people to resist your idea. In our firm, even the partners said that mission statements were much to-do about nothing. I imagine that the same story will unfold at Vanguard."

"I can't imagine that, Jim," said Sharon. "But I will let you know what happens. I am going to propose the need for a mission statement during one of our upcoming board meetings." After this, the conversation turned to other issues.

To her surprise, Perry discovered the accuracy of Freeman's prediction. Her suggestion of the need for a mission statement was met with what at best could be called a lukewarm response. Some argued that the school's statement of purpose was sufficient. Others said that no one ever read a mission statement and that preparing one would be wasted time and effort. A few board members even suggested that mission statements were an academic exercise and as such were not practical.

Although she was discouraged, Perry decided that she would continue to push for development of a mission statement. What, she wondered, could she do to convince the board of the need for a mission statement?

1. In your opinion, is Sharon Perry correct in her assumption about the potential value of a mission statement?
2. As a consultant, what steps would you recommend that Perry adopt in order for the Vanguard board of trustees to support the idea of developing a mission statement?
3. In addition to a mission statement, are there other activities that should be completed to help Vanguard in its efforts to be successful? If so, what are they?

Source: Adapted, with permission, from R. Duane Ireland and Michael A. Hitt, "Mission Statements: Importance, Challenge, and Recommendations for Development," *Business Horizons* (May-June 1992): 34–42.

REFERENCES

1. David M. Reid, "Operationalizing Strategic Planning," *Strategic Management Journal* (November-December 1989): 553–567.

2. Kenneth A. Andrews, *The Concept of Corporate Strategy*, 3e (Homewood, IL: Richard D. Irwin, 1987): 115–116.

3. Peter Lorange, *Implementation of Strategic Planning* (Englewood Cliffs, NJ: Prentice-Hall, 1982): 93.

4. George A. Steiner, *Strategic Planning: What Every Manager Must Know* (New York: The Free Press, 1979): 13–15.

5. Comment from a reviewer of this text, Professor Philip C. Grant of Husson College, Bangor, ME.

6. Noel Tichy and Ram Charan, "Speed, Simplicity, Self-Confidence: An Interview with Jack Welch," *Harvard Business Review* (September-October 1989): 112–121.

7. James D. Thompson, *Organizations in Action* (New York: McGraw-Hill, 1967): 27–28.

8. Liam Fahey and V. K. Narayanan, *Macroenvironmental Analysis for Strategic Management* (St. Paul: West, 1986): 49–50.

9. John A. Pearce, II and Richard B. Robinson, Jr., *Formulation, Implementation, and Control of Competitive Strategy*, 4e (Homewood, IL: Richard D. Irwin, 1991): 76–116.

10. Richard Alm, "Helping Them See the Lite," *Dallas Morning News* (September 2, 1991): 2D and 4D.

11. James E. Post, "Managing As If the Earth Mattered," *Business Horizons* (July-August 1991): 32–38.

12. Faye Rice, "Eco-Correct Crackers," *Fortune* (September 9, 1991): 156.

13. "55 Miles Per Gallon: How Honda Did It," *Business Week* (September 23, 1991): 82–83.

14. David M. Georgoff and Robert G. Murdick, "Manager's Guide to Forecasting," *Harvard Business Review* (January-February 1986): 112 and 119.

15. Southwestern Bell Corporation, *1990 Annual Report*, 4.

16. Andrews, *The Concept of Corporate Strategy*, 47.

17. Andrews, *The Concept of Corporate Strategy*, 49.

18. John A. Pearce and Fred David, "Corporate Mission Statements: The Bottom Line," *Academy of Management Executive* (May 1987): 109–116.

19. Pearce, II and Robinson, Jr., *Competitive Strategy*, 13.

20. Pearce and David, "Corporate Mission Statements," 110.

21. Russell L. Ackoff, *Management in Small Doses* (New York: John Wiley & Sons, 1986): 38–42.

22. "Jobs and Gates Together," *Fortune* (August 26, 1991): 50–54.

23. Michael E. Porter, "From Competitive Advantage to Corporate Strategy," *Harvard Business Review* (May-June 1987): 43–59.

24. Michael E. Porter, *Competitive Strategy* (New York: The Free Press, 1980): 35–37.

25. "Dollar General," *Fortune* (August 26, 1991): 98.

26. Porter, *Competitive Strategy*, 36–40.

27. Porter, *Competitive Strategy*, 38–40.

28. Michael E. Porter, *Competitive Advantage* (New York: The Free Press, 1985): 17.

29. Kenneth J. Hatten and Mary Louise Hatten, *Strategic Management: Analysis and Action* (Englewood Cliffs, NJ: Prentice-Hall, 1987): 3.

30. John R. Berthold, "The Failure of Strategic Planning," *Stanford Business School Magazine* (Summer 1987): 16–19.

31. Hatten and Hatten, *Strategic Management*, 17.

32. Elizabeth A. Haas, "Breakthrough Manufacturing," *Harvard Business Review* (March-April 1987): 75–81.

33. W. Jack Duncan, *Great Ideas in Management* (San Francisco: Jossey-Bass, 1989): 124.

34. Richard E. Kopelman, *Managing Productivity in Organizations* (New York: McGraw-Hill, 1986): 72.

35. Kopelman, *Managing Productivity*, 73.

36. Max D. Richards, *Setting Strategic Goals and Objectives*, 2e (St. Paul: West, 1986): 123–124.

37. Hatten and Hatten, *Strategic Management*, 3.

38. Daniel H. Gray, "Uses and Misuses of Strategic Planning," *Harvard Business Review* (January-February 1986): 89–97.

39. Gray, "Uses and Misuses,'" 89–97.

Planning for Growth at Raymond's Interiors

Upon graduation from a well-respected interior design institute, Mario Barron accepted a job with Raymond's Interiors. Raymond's was a successful medium-size company. The owner, Raymond McCutchen, had been in the interior design business for over thirty years. His firm catered to people interested in custom drapes, wallpapers, and carpets. Although it was known to be expensive, Raymond's had an excellent reputation. The staff was respected for its creative flair and innovativeness. Customers were pleased to tell friends that their home's interior design work had been handled by Raymond's.

Barron admired McCutchen's design skills. Because of this, he spent considerable time listening to McCutchen talk with customers. Barron was impressed with his boss's ability to quickly recognize a customer's style and color preferences. Armed with that knowledge, it was then a simple matter for McCutchen to select drapes, wallpapers, and carpet that would satisfy each customer's unique desires.

Observing McCutchen was helpful to Barron. Within three years, he became the firm's top salesperson. More importantly, a number of customers had started to request his services when they entered the store. Barron knew that building a dedicated clientele was important to his (and the firm's) success.

During Barron's fifth year at Raymond's, McCutchen approached him with an interesting offer:

"Mario, I am almost 65 years old. This business has been good to me, but I'm ready to relax and travel to places I've never seen. My wife keeps telling me that if we don't start traveling soon it will be too late. If I'm honest with myself, I have to admit she may be right about that.

"I've watched you carefully since you joined my studio. You're good, Mario. You treat customers with respect, understand their needs, and put together interior packages they like. I think you could take this business and make it even more successful than it is today. Mario, how would you like to buy Raymond's from me?"

Barron was surprised by McCutchen's comments. While he thought McCutchen would retire some day, he did not anticipate that it would be this soon. After all, McCutchen appeared to be in excellent health. In a way, Barron had always thought that McCutchen lived for his business.

Barron's response to McCutchen was honest and enthusiastic. "Raymond, I love this business and what you have done with it. This is a great place with super employees and tremendous clients. I would be honored to work out a deal with you. I don't know that I can ever do as well as you have, but I want to try." The conversation then closed, with the men agreeing they would complete the sales transaction as soon as possible. Because of their strong personal relationship, Barron and McCutchen completed the transfer of the business quickly.

As the new owner of Raymond's, Barron discovered challenges he had not known existed. Being responsible for all decisions related to the firm's inventory was more difficult than he had imagined. Ordering the right quantities at the right prices was a skill Barron knew he had to refine. Also, scheduling installation of customers' purchases was proving to be difficult. It seemed that they all had to have their work done yesterday. Finally, dealing with the firm's 22 employees was more troublesome than he had anticipated. Each employee always wanted more of Barron's time. He was willing to talk with his people, but the demands for his time seemed to exceed the supply. Sometimes, while trying to fall asleep, Barron wondered how in the world McCutchen had handled everything as well as he did.

Over all, however, Barron appeared to be coping reasonably well with his challenges. In a relatively short time, Raymond's sales volume started to grow. A key reason for this was Barron's decision to develop working relationships with several of the largest builders in the area. He had always thought this would be a good thing to do, but McCutchen had never responded positively to the idea. By offering deep discounts and guarantees of satisfaction, Barron was able to secure the builders' business for the installation of drapes, wallpapers, and carpets in the homes they built. This relationship proved successful. People saw Raymond's designs as they looked at the builders' homes, and their positive impressions were passed on to their friends. As a result many contracted with Raymond's to custom design drapes, wallpapers, and carpets for their homes.

Although everything seemed to be going well, Barron was unsettled. Somehow, he knew that more direction was needed if the firm was to become even more successful. One day, he talked about this matter with Linda Simpson. A member of the business faculty at a local university, Simpson was one of Barron's customers. Over lunch, Barron sought Simpson's advice:

"Linda, my store is doing better than I thought it would. But it all seems so unorganized. We have more than enough business right now, but what would we do if the local economy were to go south?

"Or how would Raymond's compete if another design studio entered our market? There are already three of us competing for business. I'm afraid another studio would make it pretty tough for all of us. Besides this, I'm beginning to wonder why clients choose one studio over another. It seems to me that we all offer essentially the same things. And what can I do to make my employees take more responsibility for their actions? It seems that I have to make all the decisions. Sometimes I just want people to make their own decisions and accept responsibility for them. What do you think about all of this? Is there anything I can do?"

Simpson answered quickly:

"Well, Mario, there are many steps you can take to deal with the issues you mentioned. Basically, I think you need to plan carefully for Raymond's future. Doing this means that you must develop and examine quite a bit of information. And after you look at all of that information, you may have to make some difficult decisions. But planning carefully is the only way I know for any firm to ensure its future success."

Without hesitation, Mario responded: "That sounds great, Linda. Can you get me started in the right direction?" Linda offered the response Barron wanted to hear: "I'll be glad to help you, Mario. Give me a couple of days to put some materials together. When I'm ready, I'll come by your shop so we can talk and get started. This will take quite a bit of your time, but I think you'll be very pleased with the results."

1. Use the concept of bounded rationality to describe Barron's situation as the owner of Raymond's.
2. Does Raymond's Interiors have a distinctive competence? If so, what is it? Use materials in the case to support your position.
3. What type of strategy should Raymond's Interiors implement? Support your answer with case materials.
4. Describe the recommendations you believe Linda Simpson will present to Mario Barron. What response would you anticipate from Barron to these recommendations? Why?

Part III

Organizing

Chapter 7

Job Design and Organization Structure

Mary Alvarez established a catering service several years ago, working out of her kitchen. She began by making a sales pitch to friends and acquaintances who were giving special-occasion parties at home. Alvarez prepared both generic and ethnic foods, suiting the demands of her clientele. Word spread quickly that "Mary provides fabulous food in large quantities at low prices."

Unexpectedly, Alvarez began receiving requests from local businesses to cater parties and other functions. Within six months, Alvarez Catering had moved from her home to rented quarters at the site of a former restaurant. Alvarez purchased a minivan and hired three full-time employees plus six part-timers. Within three years, her sales volume had increased by 500 percent and her staff had grown to eleven full-time and nine part-time employees.

Alvarez assigned each worker a job title such as "sauce maker," "salad chef," "meat cook," "baker," and "kitchen helper." She was responsible for coordinating the employees' work and for selling. Sales consisted mostly of responding to orders and helping customers plan appropriate banquets.

Driving home from work one evening, Alvarez thought, "Business is great so far. But things are too helter-skelter. I notice a lot of people bumping into each other in the kitchen. It bothers me also that my people don't have enough pride in their work. It's probably time to organize my company better. An organization chart sounds so stiff for an outfit my size, yet I've got to do something."

Dividing up work and creating an appropriate structure are essential to running a successful business—even a small one. People have a natural tendency to want order and direction. Alvarez must take action because her company's efforts have become too "helter-skelter." Unless management brings order and direction to the activities of team members through an organization structure, the result can be low productivity, indecision, and even chaos. The **organization structure** is arrangement of people and tasks to accomplish organizational goals. It helps specify who reports to whom and who does what.

To explain how work is divided in an organization, this chapter begins with a discussion of the design of jobs and work groups, followed by a description of organization structure. We then specify how the best structure is chosen and describe the various types of organization structures.

JOB DESIGN

The starting point in understanding how work is divided is to examine **job design,** the way tasks and work are divided to form an entire job. The three basic considerations in job design—job specialization, task dimensions, and job descriptions—are discussed in the following sections.

Job Specialization

The most important step in designing a job is to decide on the degree of specialization involved. **Job specialization** is the degree to which a worker performs only a limited number of tasks. Examples of specialized jobs include investment banker, systems analyst, and municipal bond specialist. Job specialization has long been heralded as the key to the advancement of civilization.[1] Without it there would be no architects, no equipment designers, no computer programmers.

The most important advantage of job specialization is that it allows employees to develop expertise at all occupational levels. Expertise leads to increased productivity because employees carry out their tasks more efficiently. Task specialization at lower job levels increases productivity because employees can learn specialized tasks quickly. For instance, unskilled workers can learn to assemble high-tech products such as compact-disk players. Managers who have to worry about shortages of highly skilled workers can rely on job specialization to help overcome the problem. Since workers can be taught minute aspects of jobs quickly, they do not need to have a broad range of skills. For example, an employee can learn to run one specific piece of software without being a computer expert.

Job specialization also has some disadvantages. Specialization makes coordination difficult when several employees perform several minor tasks on one job. One person has to be responsible for combining these small tasks into the total job. Specialization can also lead to boredom and frustration, even at high job levels. As one technical writer stated, "After five years of writing service manuals for clothes washers and refrigerators, I'm ready to do anything else. I would even operate a food vending cart downtown."

Task Dimensions

When jobs are designed systematically, they are analyzed by defining their various dimensions. The dimensions of a job must be specified in order to

ETHICS QUESTION
What ethical issues are involved when management encourages job specialization even though it often leads to boredom and frustration?

Through job specialization, these employees have developed expertise and a high degree of productivity in assembling circuit boards.

perform an analysis of it. A standard method of specifying task dimensions is the job characteristics model, which was developed originally to assist in employee motivation. The **job characteristics model** is a method of job design that focuses on the tasks and interpersonal dimensions of a job.[2] The model identifies the following five key job characteristics, which are said to improve employee motivation, satisfaction, and performance:

1. *Skill variety*: the degree to which the job requires the worker to perform many skills successfullly.
2. *Task identity*: the degree to which the task must be done from beginning to end with a tangible and visible outcome.
3. *Task significance*: the degree to which the job has a heavy impact on other people, either in the immediate organization or in the external environment.
4. *Autonomy*: the degree to which the job involves substantial freedom, independence, and discretion in scheduling and in determining the procedures involved in its implementation.
5. *Feedback*: the degree to which the job provides direction for and information about job performance.

The characteristics of variety, identity, and significance contribute to the *meaningfulness* of the job. Autonomy leads to feelings of *responsibility*, and feedback contributes to *knowledge of results*. When a job includes all of these characteristics to a large degree, it is said to have high motivating potential. The job characteristics model combines these five characteristics into a single index that reflects the overall potential of a job to trigger high internal motivation. The index, called the Motivation Potential Score (MPS), is computed as follows:

$$MPS = \frac{\text{Skill variety} + \text{Task identity} + \text{Task significance}}{3} \times \text{Autonomy} \times \text{Feedback}$$

Numerical values for each of the five job characteristics are obtained from jobholders' answers to the Job Diagnostic Survey, a written questionnaire. The MPS has been shown to relate to high motivation, productivity, satisfaction, and attendance.[3] In a recently reported study, the jobs of 526 bank tellers were redesigned by following the job characteristics model. For example, feedback was enhanced by using an automated system to inform tellers immediately when they made an error and to allow them to monitor the pace of their own work. As a result of the improved work design, the tellers' job satisfaction increased temporarily. Although their job performance showed no change after 6 months, it showed significant improvements after 24 and 48 months.[4]

After the degree of specialization has been determined and the various task dimensions have been rated in terms of the degree to which they are present in a job, the job can be described. A **job description** is a written statement outlining the key responsibilities of the job along with the activities required to perform the job effectively. It explains in detail what the jobholder is supposed to do. High-level jobs such as company president have less detailed job descriptions than lower-level jobs. Job (or position) descriptions are based on the information gathered from people who hold the positions and their managers. A sample job description is presented in Figure 7-1.

Job descriptions serve several important purposes. For one thing, managers can use them to evaluate how well group members are doing their jobs. Job descriptions also present a concise overview of anticipated job responsibilities for use in recruiting, and they can be used to set boundaries of the job for current jobholders.

Work Schedules

A discussion of different work schedules is relevant here because working hours are part of the design of a job. To attract and retain workers and sometimes to increase productivity, many companies allow some employees to follow nontraditional work schedules. Modified work schedules include flexible working hours, a compressed work week, job sharing, and working at home. A major reason for the popularity of modified work schedules is demographic changes in society. Modified work schedules help attract and retain employees in an era of labor shortages in some job categories. The growing number of dual-career and single-parent families also contributes to the attractiveness of modified work schedules.

FLEXIBLE WORKING HOURS. Perhaps the most popular modified work schedule is **flexible working hours,** a method whereby employees have flexibility in choosing their own hours. Flexible working hours (also referred to as *flextime*) are used more often in offices than in factories, mills, construction sites, stores, or restaurants. The major reason is that the system works best when employees do not depend on each other to accomplish their work. Flexible working hours are also poorly suited to positions in which people have to interact across time zones. An example would be an international investment banker.

FIGURE 7-1
Sample Job Description

Buyer, under direction of purchasing agent,
1. Obtains materials from suppliers at the lowest cost consistent with considerations of quality, reliability of source, and urgency of need.
2. Studies market trends, interviews vendors, and recommends sources of materials.
3. Analyzes quotations received, selects or recommends suppliers, and schedules deliveries.
4. Supervises preparation of orders and follows up to expedite delivery and shipment.
5. Obtains certifications of delivery and conducts checks against orders.
6. Checks and approves payment of invoices for orders placed.
7. Develops and maintains necessary records and files for efficient operations.

Source: Adapted from ECS, A Wyatt Data Services Company, *1990/91 Professional and Scientific Personnel Compensation Questionnaire.*

A sample flexible working schedule is shown in Figure 7-2. A core work period is typically from 10:00 A.M. to 3:30 P.M. Employees are free to choose which hours they wish to work between 7:00 A.M. and 10:00 A.M., and between 3:30 P.M. and 6:30 P.M. Time-recording machines may be used to monitor whether employees have put in their required hours for the week.

Flexible working schedules create some problems. Managers must either be present for the entire band of working hours or arrange tasks so that some employees can function well without direct supervision. The problems are usually outweighed by the high satisfaction of employees who can work full time yet still accommodate family and outside interests. Another advantage of flexible working hours is that they allow employees to avoid lengthy rush-hour commutes.

ETHICS QUESTION
In what way are flexible working hours related to the social responsibility of business?

COMPRESSED WORK WEEK. A **compressed work week** is a full-time schedule that allows 40 hours of work to be accomplished in fewer than five days. The usual arrangement is to work four 10-hour days, which allows most employees to take off Saturdays and Sundays. Important exceptions include police workers, hospital employees, and computer operators. A compressed work week, as with any other work schedule, must conform to law. Especially relevant is the Fair Labor Standards Act, which requires overtime pay for nonexempt employees who work beyond 40 hours. Some union contracts require time-and-one-half pay for work beyond eight hours in one day.

Compressed work weeks are popular with employees who prefer long weekends and with those who hold two jobs, but there are potential problems associated with them. For one thing, many employees find it both exhausting and inconvenient to work for 10 consecutive hours. Even when employees are strongly in favor of the compressed work week, employers may discover significant problems. An executive from a company that discontinued its compressed work week program offered this explanation:

> "The employees loved the program, but we stopped it for a good reason. Under the usual eight-hour schedule, many of our best employees would stay a couple of hours to get their work done. We would usually be getting about 46 hours per week productivity from these conscientious employees. Under the 4-40 program, nobody would stay past ten hours. We lost all our casual overtime."[5]

FIGURE 7-2
Typical Flexible Working
Hours Schedule

A.M.	LUNCH (One Half Hour or One Hour)		P.M.
Flextime	Core Time		Flextime
7:00	10:00	3:30	6:30

Sample Schedules: Early schedule, 7:00–3:30
                              Standard schedule, 9:00–5:30
                              Late schedule, 10:00–6:30

TELECOMMUTING PROGRAMS. Another deviation from the traditional work schedule is **telecommuting,** an arrangement in which employees perform their regular work duties from home or at another location. The term *telecommuting* implies that workers commute to work by electronic means such as telephone and computer. (Telecommuting programs are also referred to as *work-at-home programs*.) Approximately 26.6 million Americans conduct job-related work at home, with 10 million of them operating their own businesses. Over 500 large U.S. corporations have formal work-at-home programs, with over 900,000 employees participating.[6] Many small businesses also allow selected employees the opportunity to perform some of their work at home.

Telecommuting can work well with self-reliant, self-starting, and self-disciplined employees who also have relevant work experience. In fact, since work-at-home employees usually request such an arrangement, they are likely to experience a high degree of job satisfaction. Employees derive many benefits from working at home, including easier management of personal life, lowered commuting and clothing costs, less office politics, and fewer distractions from co-workers. Companies, in turn, may benefit from smaller office space requirements, reduced absenteeism and turnover, and access to a wider labor pool.

Moreover, of major significance to managers, productivity is likely to increase when work is moved into the employee's home. Where direct measurements have been possible, they have indicated that productivity increases average about 50 percent in such situations.[7] For example, a market research firm in New York moved certain work projects into the home in order to tap a wider labor market and save office space. Data-entry productivity increased 30 percent over when the projects were conducted in the office.[8]

Telecommuting programs also have disadvantages to both employees and employers. Telecommuters themselves complain of losing visibility, being

Telecommuting offers several advantages to experienced workers who have the self-reliance and self-discipline to work at home.

isolated from co-workers, and always being on call to work. Many telecommuters also find that more distractions exist in the home than in the office. Children, neighbors, and telephone calls are leading distracters from work that requires concentration. Employers may find that it is difficult to build loyalty among telecommuters and that it is difficult to keep these employees fully occupied at all times. In addition, creativity may suffer because work-at-home employees do not spark each others' thinking.

Work-at-home programs are likely to be the most effective when the assigned work has measurable outputs. Suitable work includes data entry, computer programming, report writing and editing, and piecework in general.

JOB SHARING. **Job sharing** is a modified work schedule in which two people share the same job, both usually working half time. The job sharers organize their time according to their needs by dividing up days or the work week, for example. If the job is complex, the sharers will have to spend some overlapping time discussing it. The Center for the Advancement of Work and Family maintains that job sharing can be of benefit to some employees who must juggle work and family obligations.[9] Employers benefit from job sharing because employees are likely to stay more productive for four hours than for eight hours. Also, if one employee quits, the remaining employee can teach the job to a new job sharer.

Job sharing has several disadvantages to both employees and employer. For one thing, a person who can only make a half-time commitment to the firm is unlikely to be promoted. Also, the firm may have difficulty evaluating, supervising, and rewarding job sharers. For example, should both receive identical raises and performance evaluations?

WORK GROUP DESIGN

Jobs can be designed for groups as well as individuals. To improve productivity, some employers have formed **work teams** (or **production work teams**). These are small groups of individuals who work somewhat independently to complete a large task. Members of these groups have the authority to create the processes and procedures needed to handle their internal work. In extreme situations, they might even be given the authority to negotiate with vendors for supplies and to recruit new members. Work teams usually have the responsibility to handle internal problems such as establishing work schedules and disciplining members.

Team members act as generalists rather than as specialists, because they are required to perform many different tasks. For example, if a work team assembled an automobile, each member would perform various functions. Work teams are also referred to as *semiautonomous work groups*, which reflects their self-governing nature.

Work teams stand in contrast to assembly-line operations. In an assembly line, individuals perform highly specialized tasks and have limited decision-making authority. Work teams, on the other hand, are designed to offer team members skill variety, task identity, task significance, autonomy, and feedback—precisely the dimensions featured in the job characteristics model. A work team is thus a form of group job enrichment—a more responsible and interesting way of organizing work described in detail in Chapter 12.

Work teams have been consistently effective in both factory and office settings.[10] One example is the Hillerich & Bradsby Co., manufacturer of Louisville Slugger baseball bats and other sports equipment. The company shifted to work teams of eight to ten employees and eliminated the jobs of supervisors. At the same time, it incorporated other sweeping changes such as a no-layoff policy and improved inventory control procedures. Productivity and quality improvements stemming from these changes include the following:

- In the past, it took two weeks to deliver a baseball bat to a professional player, while now it takes an average of two days.
- Unsatisfied customers used to return about 25 percent of the company's PowerBilt golf clubs. Now fewer than 3 percent are returned.
- Union grievances at the Jeffersonville, Indiana, plant used to average about 100 per year. Now only one or two are filed annually.[11]

Although work teams are somewhat self-governing, they still report to a middle-level manager who oversees the operation of several teams. It is the manager's job to ensure that the various work teams are pursuing organizational goals adequately. The Organization in Action provides additional insights into work teams.

ORGANIZATION IN ACTION

Aid Association for Lutherans (AAL) is an insurance company run by a fraternal society. One day, the entire insurance staff of 500 clerks, technicians, and managers loaded their personal belongings onto office chairs and bade farewell to working with their former co-workers. All 500 workers then rolled their chairs down the halls to their new work areas. Within two hours, AAL's home office employees had converted from the department structure typical of insurance companies into all-purpose teams that required little supervision.

AAL switched to teamwork primarily to process insurance cases more rapidly and to provide better service to its field agents and policyholders. All life insurance cases were previously handled by one unit, health insurance by another, and support services by a third. These divisions often resulted in some cases' being bounced from one section to another, with embarrassing delays.

Under the new system, the insurance department is divided into five groups, each serving a group of agents from a certain geographic area. Each group is composed of three or four teams of 20 to 30 employees. A team carries out all of the 167 tasks formerly divided among the three units, and team members are cross-trained to learn skills that used to be the responsibility of only one unit. Field agents in each district deal solely with one team and develop close working relationships with its members.

The abrupt switch from a traditional way of working to working on teams elicited mixed feelings among employees: "There was uncertainty and a lot of broken friendships when we moved to the new system, and personally I feel more tension," said one worker. Yet most employees now like the team approach because it allows them to manage themselves. For example, although team members have little direct contact with a supervisor, they have extensive contact with the agents they serve.

The work team structure has already been responsible for a 20 percent increase in productivity and a reduction of as much as 75 percent in case-processing time. Team members put up banners to signify their team's excellence and hold spontaneous parties when they achieve production and quality goals.

Source: As reported in "Work Teams Can Rev Up Paper-Pushers, Too," *Business Week* (November 28, 1988): 64–72; and "Sharpening Minds for a Competitive Edge," *Business Week* (December 17, 1990): 72–78.

LEARNING CHECK

Describe the design of jobs for individuals and for work groups, including a discussion of alternative work schedules.

Back to the Opening Case

Mary Alvarez explains to you that she wants her employees to take more pride in their work and to identify more with the banquets they are helping to prepare. How would the work team structure help Alvarez achieve her goals?

CONTINGENCY FACTORS IN ORGANIZATION DESIGN

In following sections, we will describe the various types of organization structures—the arrangement of people and tasks to achieve organizational goals. One major type of structure is bureaucratic—a rational, systematic, and precise form of organization. In a bureaucracy, rules, regulations, and techniques of control are defined clearly. Another major type of structure is the **organic organization structure**—one that is loose and flexible and therefore highly adaptable to change. Which organization structure is best depends on factors such as strategy and goals, technology, size, financial condition, and environmental uncertainty.

Strategy and Goals

In an effective firm, managers design an organization structure that has the best chance of helping the firm achieve its objectives. For example, assume that a business machine company establishes the goal of serving the needs of small businesses and individuals who want to operate business equipment in their homes. The company would choose a structure that creates a geographically dispersed marketing organization, giving them maximum access to small customers. Radio Shack computer stores are an example of such a structure.

Technology

The dominant technology of a firm influences its choice of organization structure. High-technology firms such as aerospace companies make extensive use of organic structures. Low-technology firms such as lumber mills and refuse-collection companies, on the other hand, rely more on bureaucratic structures. The relationship between technology and structure is so complex that it has been the subject of extensive research and theorizing. Examples are discusssed in the following sections.

THE PIONEERING STUDIES OF JOAN WOODWARD. Two decades ago, Joan Woodward studied 100 British firms. She identified differences among them in terms of organization structure, operating processes, and profitability. The firms were categorized into the following three groups on the basis of their manufacturing processes:

1. Firms using *small-unit or small-batch production technology*. These firms made one-of-a-kind items or produced a small number of units to meet customer specification.
2. Firms using *assembly-line technology* for large-batch and mass production.
3. Firms using *process-production technology* to produce liquids, gases, and crystalline substances.

Woodward found a significant pattern among the most successful firms in each category. The unit and small-batch firms and the process-production firms used the organic structure, while the successful mass-production firms used bureaucratic structures.[12] This finding fits the belief of many managers that the bureaucratic structure is well suited to large-scale, repetitive production.

Since Woodward's research, many other studies have investigated the relationship between technology and organization structure. Quite often, these investigations have failed to find a simple relationship. Some researchers have found that the size of the organization must be taken into account in understanding the relationship between technology and structure. Technology has its biggest impact in small, production-oriented units, but at the highest level of the organization the dominant technology has very little influence on structure.[13] This finding makes sense, because technology exerts the most influence on the actual production of goods and services.

An attempt was made recently to further clarify the contingency factors that influence the relationship between technology and structure. The investigators analyzed the results of three decades of research and were able to draw three conclusions. First, they found that the routineness of an operation is related to centralization of authority (top executives holding most of the power) in the organization. In addition, they found that routineness is positively related to formalization (the extent of rules and regulations) in the organization. Finally, they concluded that routineness is not related to the degree of specialization of tasks in the organization.

The researchers described contingency factors that help to explain these results. They found that routineness and formalization are more positively associated among less professionalized organizations drawn from one industrial sector. An *industrial sector* refers to either service or manufacturing.[14] To illustrate, routine technology might be associated with many rules and regulations in a firm that manufacturers metal tubing.

CHARLES PERROW AND KNOWLEDGE TECHNOLOGY. Much of the research just cited referred to manufacturing technology and is therefore limited to one segment of work. However, Charles Perrow classified technology in a broader way by examining knowledge technology.[15] (Knowledge technology refers to how problems are analyzed.) He classified this technology along two primary dimensions: (1) the number of exceptional cases found in the work and (2) the type of search process people use to analyze the exceptional cases. The first dimension is called **task variability,** while the second is called **problem analyzability** (see Figure 7-3).

According to Perrow, one primary category is technology with few exceptions and problems that lend themselves to analysis. This category includes routine technologies such as the manufacture of screws and bolts or chocolate bars (cell 4). The other primary category is technology characterized by many exceptions and problems that are difficult to analyze. As seen in cell 2, this category includes nonroutine technologies such as the aerospace industry.

One of the secondary categories is technology with few exceptions and problems that are not easy to analyze. An example would be a craft industry, as shown in cell 1, such as a manufacturer of industrial pumps. The other secondary category is technology with many exceptions and problems that are easy to analyze. An engineering firm making heavy machinery fits this category, as shown in cell 3.

Perrow's model implies that a change in technology will prompt some change in organization structure. If the technology becomes very routine, the structure can be more standardized. For example, a tax preparation firm that developed a software program that would process most of its clients' tax forms might then shift to a bureaucratic structure. However, if a firm's technology became less routine, it would be necessary to move toward a nonbureaucratic, more adaptable structure.

FIGURE 7-3
Perrow's Classification of
Technological Variance
in Industry

TASK VARIABILITY		Analyzable	Difficult to Analyze
Many Exceptions		Engineering 3	Nonroutine 2
Few Exceptions		Routine 4	Craft Industries 1

PROBLEM ANALYZABILITY

This heavy equipment manufacturer fits into Charles Perrow's category of technology with many exceptions and problems that are easy to analyze.

Size

An organization's size also influences its structure. As an organization grows and matures, it inevitably needs centralized controls and some degree of formalization. Yet when the firm becomes very large, it is necessary to develop smaller, more flexible organizational units, such as tasks forces. These units help the firm remain adaptive.

Many people believe that all large organizations are bureaucracies and all small organizations have organic structures. In reality, many small firms are controlled tightly by one person who centralizes authority by making all significant decisions. Conversely, very large firms such as Avon (cosmetics) and Century 21 (real estate) are decentralized.

Financial Condition

Size influences structure, and the financial condition of a firm influences both size and structure. At present, many large business organizations have moved toward a flatter structure in order to trim costs. Chase Manhattan Bank, for example, reduced its workforce by 12 percent in response to declining earnings.[16] Many middle-level management positions were eliminated in the process.

Environmental Uncertainty

The research of Paul R. Lawrence and Jay W. Lorsch has provided valuable insights into the relationship between environmental uncertainty and choice of organization structure. They studied ten firms in three industries to investigate the relationship between environmental differences and the most appropriate organization structure.[17] Lawrence and Lorsch concentrated on two opposing dimensions of structure: differentiation and integration. **Differentiation** refers to the degree to which managers and specialists think and act differently, particularly with respect to goals and values. **Integration** is collaboration, or pulling together, among managers and specialists to achieve a common purpose.

An effective balance between differentiation and integration helps organizations adapt to their external environments. For instance, the financial services division of Ford Motor Company may require an organization structure that is different from the one required by its truck-making division, because these two groups face different challenges in the external environment. An effective balance between differentiation and integration can therefore improve the firm's financial performance.

Before we draw conclusions about the relationship between differentiation versus integration and the effective structure, both ideas require elaboration. The extent of differentiation can be measured along the following four dimensions:

1. *Formality of structure.* A highly formal structure places high reliance on rules and procedures, and organization members are supervised closely. An informal structure is the opposite.
2. *Goal orientation.* Concerns about sales, production, and conducting research may vary in different subunits.
3. *Time orientation.* Some groups focus on long-term goals, while others focus on short-term goals and feedback cycles.
4. *Interpersonal orientation.* Contact with other organization members is characterized by concern for task accomplishment versus concern for effective interpersonal relationships.

When managers and specialists differentiate themselves highly, integration becomes more difficult. Some integrating devices can be used to help coordinate differentiated subsystems (units). One of these is *the management hierarchy itself.* The organization can appoint a common superior for the subunits whose efforts require coordination. For instance, if marketing and engineering need to coordinate their efforts, they both can report to the same vice president.

A second integrating device is *liaison individuals.* Staff specialists are sometimes assigned to work with two different functions to enhance communication and coordination between them. Many large organizations, for example, have created a position for a person who acts as interface between information systems and user groups. This person is knowledgeable about computer science but also understands the viewpoint of one or more user groups.

Finally, *committees and cross-functional teams* are key integrating mechanisms because they foster coordination and cooperation among people from different units. Cross-functional teams are small groups of individuals from different functions such as finance, materials handling, and human resources. They function as task forces to solve problems—such as cost cutting or mergers and acquisitions—that cut across disciplines.

Lawrence and Lorsch discovered that the successful organization differentiates itself to deal with the environment. If a firm faces a dynamic or uncertain environment (such as the market for high-fashion women's clothing), it needs a highly differentiated structure. Conversely, a less differentiated organization structure is better suited to dealing with more certain (stable) environments. An example is the market for leading candy bars, which has proved to be both recession proof and resistant to competition.

SPAN OF CONTROL

Span of control refers to the number of employees reporting to one manager. Spans are wider in flat organizations than in tall organizations. A **flat organization structure** is one that has relatively few layers of management, whereas a **tall organization structure** is one that has many layers of management. Figure 7-4 shows the contrast between a tall and a flat structure. Wide spans of control are currently favored by executives and management advisers. Jack Welch, the CEO of General Electric, has offered this analysis:[18]

> "Remember the theory that a manager should have no more than 6 or 7 direct reports? I say the right number is closer to 10 or 15. This way you have no choice but to let people flex their muscles, let them grow and mature. With 10 or 15 reports, a leader can focus on the big important issues, not on minutiae."

FIGURE 7-4 Contrast Between a Tall and a Flat Organization Structure

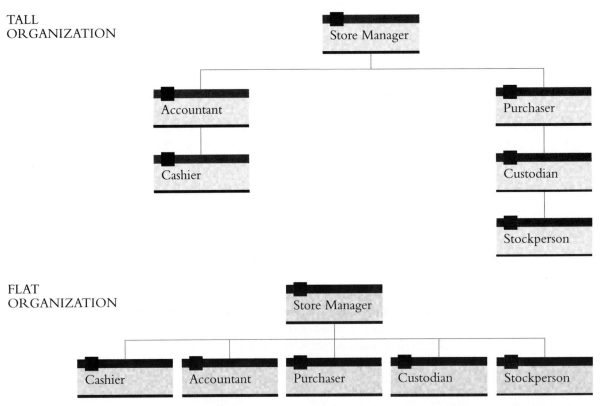

TALL ORGANIZATION

FLAT ORGANIZATION

Although the trend is toward wider spans, there is an upper limit to the number of employees a manager can supervise effectively. Contingency factors for deciding on an appropriate span of control include the following:

1. *Capabilities of the manager.* A highly capable manager can supervise more employees than one who is less well trained, experienced, and knowledgeable.
2. *Capabilities of group members.* Capable employees consume less time in performing their jobs than do their less capable counterparts. A narrower span of control is needed to manage less capable group members effectively.
3. *Similarity of work activities supervised.* When employees are performing similar work, the manager can effectively handle a wider span of control.
4. *Amount of nonsupervisory activity in the manager's job.* The more analytical work the manager must perform, the less time there is available for dealing directly with employees. When a manager's nonsupervisory tasks are limited, a wider span of control is possible.
5. *Degree of environmental uncertainty.* Managers working in firms confronted by volatile and complex environments have a larger number of activities to perform. As a result, they can effectively manage only a smaller number of people.[19]

ETHICS QUESTION
What ethical issues are involved in encouraging very wide spans of control throughout the organization?

THE BUREAUCRATIC ORGANIZATION STRUCTURE

The roots of the term *bureaucracy* shed light on the nature of this type of structure. *Bureau* refers to the rule book, while *cratic* means the source of power. *Bureaucratic* therefore means that following the rule book is the operating way of doing things. Figure 7-5 depicts the basic concept of the bureaucratic form of organization.

FIGURE 7-5
The Bureaucratic Form of Organization

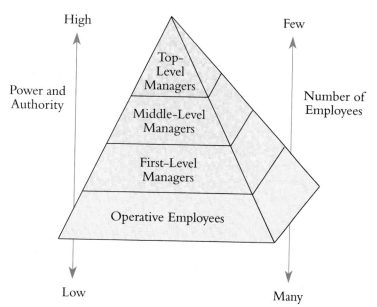

The major characteristics of the ideal bureaucracy as formulated by Max Weber are as follows:[20]

- Rules and procedures control organizational activities.
- There is a high degree of differentiation among organizational functions.
- The organization of offices is determined by hierarchy. Each unit reports to a higher unit, and no unit is free floating.
- There is a heavy emphasis on rules and norms to regulate behavior.
- Interpersonal relationships are characterized by impersonality. Favors are not granted to individuals based on the likes or dislikes of managers.
- Promotion and selection are based on job competence.
- All administrative actions are recorded in writing.

The ideal organization just described is called a **machine bureaucracy** because it standardizes work processes. It is best suited to large organizations whose work is largely performed by production, technical, and support workers. In contrast, a **professional bureaucracy** standardizes skills for coordination and is composed of a core of highly trained professionals.

Professional bureaucracies include organizations such as accounting firms, consulting firms, hospitals, and universities. Because it is difficult to regulate the work of professionals performing complex work, the professional bureaucracy decentralizes decision making and is less formal than a machine bureaucracy. The professional bureaucracy is relatively flat, with a great deal of differentiation across units.[21]

The Contribution of Bureaucracy

Bureaucratic forms of organization have persisted because, used properly, they make possible large-scale accomplishments that cannot be achieved by small groups of people working independently. The military is a prime example of bureaucracy on a large scale. The contribution of bureaucracy has been aptly expressed by Elliot Jacques:

> "Thirty-five years of research have convinced me that managerial hierarchy (or bureaucracy) is the most efficient, the hardiest, and in fact the most natural structure ever devised for large corporations. Properly structured, hierarchy can release energy and creativity, rationalize productivity, and actually improve morale."[22]

Hierarchical organizations exist, according to Jacques, because tasks occur in lower and higher degrees of complexity. In general, less complex tasks are performed at lower levels. A hierarchy is also important because people at top of the organization work with longer time perspectives than people at the bottom. The CEO may be working on projects with a 20-year perspective, for example, while the inventory stocker has a one-day perspective.

The hierarchical form of organization called bureaucracy emerged from necessity. It is the only form of organization that enables a firm to employ large numbers of people and still hold them clearly accountable for their results.[23]

Problems Associated with Bureaucracy

Organizations that rely heavily on formal controls to direct people some-times suppress initiative and decision making in the middle and first levels of management. Too many controls and too much review of decisions can also lower productivity, as illustrated by the Organization in Action.

ORGANIZATION IN ACTION

The Tennessee Valley Authority set up an em-ployee suggestion program to encourage cost-sav-ing ideas. TVA received nearly 1,000 suggestions over a period of 10 months that collectively saved about $580,000. Ten percent of that saving was paid to employees as suggestion awards.

However, the program cost more to adminis-ter than it saved: TVA spent $700,000 on it, in-cluding $514,000 in staff expenses. "The idea of the program was good, but what we ended up with was a bureaucratic, convulted system that took so long to review suggestions that it proved to be ineffective," said Sue Wallace, acting director of TVA's human resources department.

Source: Adapted from "It Cost Too Much to Save Money," Associated Press (August 27, 1988).

Another problem with bureaucracies is that they sometimes expand in size even if their workload does not increase. One reason is that a blind commitment to following rules and a proliferation of useful rules create the need for more workers to develop and enforce these rules. Thus bureaucra-cies sometimes allocate too many resources to their own self-preservation and maintenance.[24]

The current trend, however, is for top-level managers in larger firms to eliminate positions that are not needed. Managers at all levels must be pre-pared to defend why each position is necessary. Small businesses have rarely had the luxury of needless expansion, except for holding on to a few mar-ginally productive relatives!

LEARNING CHECK   Describe contingency factors in choosing an organization structure, the concept of span of control, and the nature of bureaucracy.

DEPARTMENTALIZATION

In a bureaucracy or any other form of organization, work must be subdi-vided into logical groups. **Departmentalization** is the grouping of work or individuals into manageable units. When an organization grows beyond several people, some form of grouping becomes inevitable. Even in a typical two-person business organization, one person is often responsible for sales and the other for production.

As organizations grow, they must be departmentalized to cope with increasing complexities. Over a period of years, certain well-recognized and accepted forms of departmentalization have been developed. Small organizations typically operate with one type of organization structure, while large organizations may rely on several types of groupings to accomplish their objectives. The most appropriate form is chosen for each subsystem or unit. The two major forms of departmentalization, functional and product/market, are described in the following sections.

Functional Departmentalization

Functional departmentalization is grouping people according to their expertise. Bureaucracies are almost always organized into functional departments. The departments most often found in small manufacturing firms, where functional departmentalization is especially appropriate, are production, finance, marketing, and engineering. Within a given department, the work may be further subdivided. For instance, finance may include subunits for accounts receivable, accounts payable, and payroll. A restaurant may departmentalize as dining room, banquet sales, cooking, baking, and dishwashing.

The names of functional departments vary widely with the nature of the business. The production department of a manufacturing firm may be called *production* or *manufacturing*, for example, whereas airlines use the word *operations* for their production function (the transportation of passengers and goods). The concept of functional departmentalization is illustrated in Figure 7-6.

ADVANTAGES OF FUNCTIONAL DEPARTMENTALIZATION. The advantages of this traditional form of organization are virtually the same as those of the bureaucracy. Functional departmentalization works particularly well when a firm has to process large batches of work on a recurring basis

FIGURE 7-6 Functional Departmentalization at Village Green Book

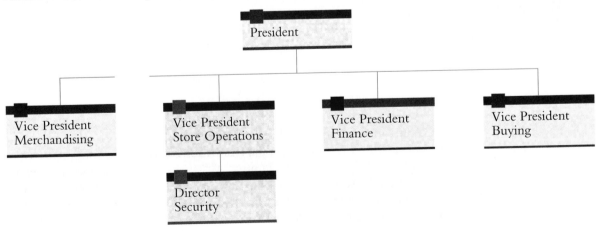

and when the work requires the expertise of specialists. It is the structure of choice for smaller businesses with a limited line of products, because it makes efficient use of specialization. In addition to being a logical and time-proven method, functional departmentalization helps ensure that the power and prestige of the basic activities of the firm will be defended by top-level management. The vice president in charge of quality assurance, for example, will heavily promote the importance of quality.

DISADVANTAGES OF FUNCTIONAL DEPARTMENTALIZATION. The problems encountered by a functional organization are similar to the problems of bureaucracy. Often, they are partially due to the firm's large size and complexity. The delay of decision making is an example: A problem may have to be passed up the chain of command through many layers of management before a decision is finally reached. Poor coordination is another problem stemming from the functional grouping since no one individual, except the CEO or division head, has complete responsibility for costs and profits. Functional departmentalization is also poorly suited to dealing with too much complexity and change.

The functional form of organization can breed narrow viewpoints, or tunnel vision. Members of specific departments often develop the false belief that their discipline and viewpoint is right and those of other departments are wrong. The banquet sales manager may say, "If we don't spend money on advertising, we will have no need for chefs." The chef may say, "If we put more money into quality food, people will flock to our restaurant. Spending money on advertising is fluff."

Product/Market Departmentalization

Companies with diversified product lines frequently create departments based on the products they produce or the markets they serve. This arrangement is known as *product/market departmentalization*. When certain individual products provided by an organization are so important that they function almost as independent companies, product departmentalization is imperative. An example of this is the baby products division of a pharmaceutical firm. The three subtypes of product/market departmentalization—product, customer, and territorial—are discussed in the following sections.

PRODUCT DEPARTMENTALIZATION. Product departmentalization is also referred to as *divisional structure* because an entire division may be devoted to making a given product or related family of products. For example, Procter & Gamble has a different division for each of its major types of consumer products. Another example of a company with product divisions is USX corporation. Its divisions are oriented around major products such as oil or steel, or major divisions such as its diversified companies. A simplified version of the USX product departmentalization is shown in Figure 7-7.

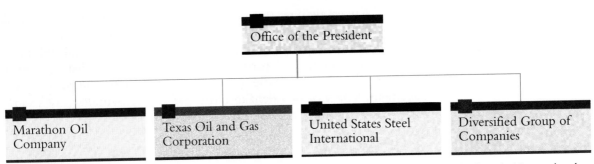

Note: The term *office of the president* means that several key executives work closely with the president in making decisions, rather than one person functioning independently as the president.

FIGURE 7-7 Product Departmentalization at USX

CUSTOMER DEPARTMENTALIZATION. A grouping of this type is an organization structure based on customer needs. Aerospace companies, for example, often organize according to commercial versus government products. The concept of customer departmentalization is illustrated in Figure 7-8.

FIGURE 7-8 Customer Departmentalization in a Computer Training Company

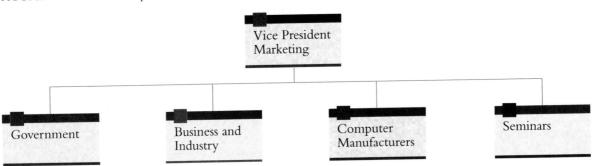

TERRITORIAL DEPARTMENTALIZATION. Organization by territory is the grouping of subunits according to the geographic area served. In this structure, those responsible for all the activities of a firm in a given geographic area report to one manager. Service organizations make extensive use of territorial departmentalization. For example, large insurance and financial services firms organize territorially, and so do the Internal Revenue Service and the U.S. Postal Service. Territorial departmentalization is used frequently to supplement functional groupings. For example, a corporate headquarters might departmentalize by function while the field forces are organized by territory. Marketing divisions often use territorial departmentalization to divide the sales force into geographic areas. Figure 7-9 illustrates this extension of the functional structure.

ADVANTAGES OF PRODUCT/MARKET DEPARTMENTALIZATION. The overriding advantage of organizing by product, customer, or territory is that it gives major attention to enhancing that product's growth or pro-

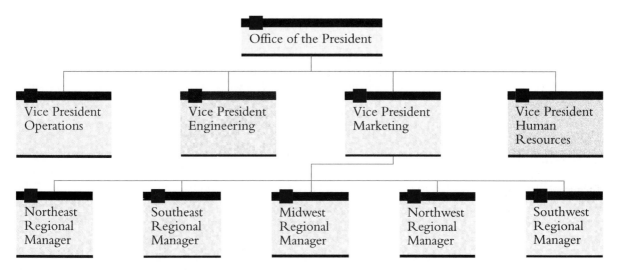

FIGURE 7-9 Territorial Departmentalization as a Supplement to Functional Departmentalization

viding good service to the customer. For example, the catalog division of Eddie Bauer (an outdoor clothing and sportswear firm) concentrates on mail-order customers, while the retail division concentrates on mall shoppers. The divisions sell the same merchandise, but through different channels requiring a different organization structure. As a result, both mail-order and store customers are well served. Customer departmentalization is also helpful in developing customer loyalty. Finally, product/marketing departmentalization helps train general managers, because many decisions are made at the local level.

DISADVANTAGES OF PRODUCT/MARKETING DEPARTMENTAL-IZATION. Organizing by product, customer, or territory presents the same problems as any other form of decentralization. It can be expensive because of duplication of effort, and top-level management may find it difficult to control the separate organization units. Chase Manhattan and Shearson-Lehman are examples of organizations that have recently consolidated many branches in order to trim costs.

ORGANIC ORGANIZATIONAL STRUCTURES

Bureaucracy is still the basic structure used by the vast majority of private and public organizations, yet it rarely exists in its pure form without being supplemented by some type of organic structure. As Rosabeth Moss Kanter contends, "Managerial work is undergoing such enormous and rapid change that many managers are reinventing their profession as they go. With little precedent to guide them, they are watching hierarchy fade away and the clear distinctions of title, task, department, and even corporation blur."[25]

The organic structure takes several forms, all designed to make bureaucracy more adaptable to change and able to move more swiftly. The following sections describe three varieties of the organic structure: flat organization structures, matrix organization structures, and adhocratic units.

Flat Organization

ETHICS QUESTION
What are some of the ethical issues involved when management creates flat organization structures wherever possible?

As stated earlier, the flat organization structure is one that has relatively few layers of management. Its relevance to modern organizations has been championed by Peter Drucker, who predicted several years ago that "the typical large business 20 years hence will have fewer than half the levels of management of its counterpart today, and no more than a third the managers."[26] A flat structure is nonbureaucratic for two reasons: First, few managers in this form of organization are available to review the decisions of other people, and second, because the chain of command is shorter, there is less concern about authority differences between people.

By 1992 most large organizations had moved toward flatter structures. For example, during the 1980s General Electric went through a major delayering and streamlining in all of its businesses. Similarly, IBM eliminated over 5,000 middle-level manager and staff positions by transferring these people into customer-contact jobs. The reasoning behind this move was to both increase sales and speed up decision making. GE achieved a more rapid increase in profitability from these moves than did IBM.[27] Small and medium-size businesses have held on to their traditionally flat structures, which are usually imposed on them by economic necessity.

Matrix Organization Structure

Traditional organizations can be slow to respond to change. A frequently used antidote to this problem is the **matrix organization,** which consists of a project structure superimposed on a functional structure. The word *matrix* refers to the fact that something is contained in something else, similar to a grid with numbers in the cells (See Figure 7-10). The distinguishing feature of the matrix organization is the responsibility of the manager in charge (typically a project or program manager) to achieve results through employees who also report directly to another manager or have dual reporting responsibilities. For example, a person assigned to a project in a matrix structure might report to both the project manager and the manager in his or her regular department.

A major purpose of the matrix organization is to allow the firm to take advantage of new opportunities and solve special problems. Instead of developing a new organization containing functional departments, the firm leaves the original organization intact. The project or program managers within the matrix structure have access to the resources of the functional departments.

A unique way of using the matrix is not as an organization structure but as a reminder to develop a flexible point of view. As one senior executive

FIGURE 7-10
The Matrix Organization
Structure

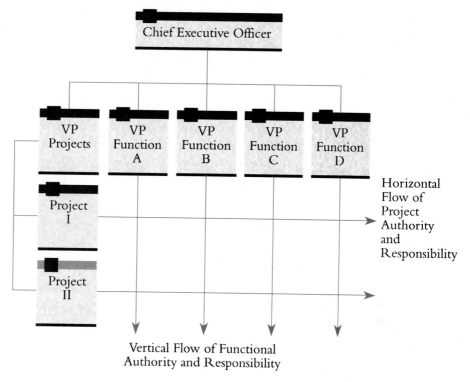

noted, "the challenge is not so much to build a matrix structure as it is to create a matrix in the mind of our managers." In practice, this would mean that managers would build a matrix of flexible perspectives and relationships within their minds. Furthermore, they would make the judgments and the trade-offs needed to move the organization toward attaining a shared strategic objective.[28]

ADVANTAGES OF THE MATRIX STRUCTURE. The matrix structure is effective for implementing important projects that demand intense, sustained attention for a limited time. It has been used, for example, to build a prototype for a new airline reservation system. Matrix organizations encourage the use of a firm's human resources and facilities for the immediate achievement of an objective without requiring the development of a new organization. As we have already implied, matrix organizations can respond readily to external change. For example, a matrix structure may be used to meet customer demands for an advanced computer without disrupting the manufacturing and marketing of existing computers. Compaq Computers uses a matrix structure to launch many of its new products.

In addition, the matrix structure provides an excellent ground for developing managers who understand all parts of a firm's operations. Instead of managing one function, a project manager's duties might span such functions as marketing, research and engineering, manufacturing, and finance.

DISADVANTAGES OF THE MATRIX STRUCTURE. The matrix structure often creates problems because people assigned to projects within the

matrix have two managers, a project manager and their functional manager. One research report concluded that matrix organizations have proved unworkable, particularly in international settings. Dual reporting can lead to conflict and confusion, and information becomes log-jammed as an outpouring of committees and reports bogs down some organizations. Overlapping responsibilities can produce turf battles and a loss of accountability. Separated by the barriers of distance, language, culture, and different time zones, international managers could not overcome the confusion created by matrix structures.[29]

Despite these disadvantages, however, a project manager in a matrix structure should not regard the assignment as being doomed to failure. The challenge for the manager is to use a high level of interpersonal skill (e.g., the ability to resolve conflict) as well as technical skill to get things accomplished.

. . . .

Back to the Opening Case

Mary Alvarez wants to find a suitable organization structure for her catering service. She is now using a functional structure, which makes sense because she hires specialists such as cooks and bakers. To help create more pride, Alvarez might assign people to special projects, so that they operate much like work teams. Major banquets could become the projects. If business expanded dramatically, a matrix structure could be established to manage the banquets as if they were projects.

. . . .

Adhocratic Organizational Units

Adhocratic organizational units are small, organic structures of a temporary nature. They include task forces, projects, ad hoc (temporary) committees, and so-called "skunk works." Work teams (discussed earlier in this chapter) are not bureaucratic, but since they are relatively permanent they are not adhocratic. A matrix organization is not considered adhocratic because it is closely aligned with a bureaucratic structure and it usually has a relatively long duration.

The members of adhocratic units must work together cooperatively to achieve a common goal. People assigned to these units tend to deemphasize their regular rank and job titles, instead assuming a co-equal role with other members of their units. The following sections describe skunk works and task forces.

SKUNK WORKS. Several large firms, including Hewlett-Packard and 3M, allow selected employees to operate out of **skunk works,** a secret place to conceive new products. The term derives from the fact that something secret is thought to be going on in these off-site locations. The rationale supporting skunk works is that people will think more creatively when working in a small organizational unit, freed from most bureaucratic restraints. Skunk work employees are given latitude in pursuing new products. Examples of major products conceived in skunk works include jet fighter technology (Lockheed), the IBM family of personal computers, and a giant-screen video monitor (General Electric). When a product becomes a major success, it is moved out of the skunk works and may become the basis for a new company division.

ETHICS QUESTION
How ethical is it to put managers "on the spot" in front of their own supervisors during a work-out session?

TASK FORCES. A task force is a problem-solving group of a temporary nature, usually working against a deadline. Task forces are used for such purposes as developing a recycling or energy conservation program, investigating charges of sexual harassment, and developing a new product. The Organization in Action describes a variation of the task force developed by General Electric that involves a large group of people solving problems in a compressed time period.

ORGANIZATION IN ACTION

Work-outs at General Electric are much like a town meeting. A group of 40 to 100 people selected by management from different functions and ranks meet at a conference site. Informality in dress is the rule. The three-day session begins with a talk by the manager, who establishes a tentative agenda. Typical agenda items deal with eliminating unnecessary meetings, forms, approvals or other administrative chores. After establishing the agenda, the manager leaves.

An outside facilitator helps the group break up into five or six teams to tackle the agenda. For a day and a half, the groups engage in problem solving, listing complaints, proposing the merits of different solutions, and preparing presentations for the final day.

On the third day, the manager returns to sit at the front of the room. Senior executives often drop by to watch as spokespersons for the teams make their proposals. Managers can make one of three responses: agree on the spot, say no, or ask for more information.

Work-out groups put a great deal of pressure on managers. In one session, for example, a manager had to respond to 108 proposals. He had about one minute to respond to each, and his own supervisor was present. According to estimates, the work-out proposals from that meeting would save plant services $200,000 in the upcoming year.

Source: Adapted from Thomas A. Stewart, "GE Keeps Those Ideas Coming," *Fortune* (August 12, 1991): 42–43.

SUMMARY

Establishing a job design at the individual and group level and choosing an organization structure are part of the task of subdividing work. The degree to which a job is specialized is a key aspect of its design. Job specialization allows employees to develop expertise, but it can lead to coordination problems and worker frustration.

Task dimensions are useful in analyzing a job. Five such dimensions stemming from the job characteristics model are skill variety, task identity, task significance, autonomy, and feedback. Task dimensions contribute to the formation of a job description, a written statement of the key features of a job.

Another important aspect of job design is to provide alternatives to traditional work schedules. This includes allowing employees some say in choosing their working hours. Four of these alternatives are flexible working hours, the compressed work week, job sharing, and telecommuting (working at home).

Self-managing work teams are an important advance in work group design. These work teams are small groups of individuals who work somewhat independently to perform a large task. The groups have the authority to create the processes and procedures needed to handle their work. Team members are generalists, rather than specialists.

Choice of the best organization structure depends on the firm's strategy and goals, technology, size, and the degree of environmental uncertainty. One major factor in choosing the best structure is the fact that the bureaucratic structure is well suited for mass production and routine technology. In contrast, small-batch production and process production are better suited to an organic structure.

The concept of differentiation versus integration also influences which structure is best for a particular firm. Differentiation is the degree to which employees think and act differently, while integration is the collaboration of employees to achieve a common purpose. A differentiated structure is required when a firm faces an uncertain environment. A less differentiated structure is better suited for dealing with more certain (stable) environments.

Span of control (the number of direct subordinates a manager has) is a major consequence of the tallness or flatness of an organization. Contingency factors in choosing the most effective span include the capabilities of the manager and the group members and the similarity among work activities supervised.

A bureaucracy is a rational, systematic, and precise form of organization. In it, rules, regulations, and techniques of control are defined precisely. Properly used, bureaucracy allows for large-scale accomplishments not achievable by small groups of people working independently. Problems associated with bureaucracy include suppression of initiative, overuse of controls, and growth for its own sake.

Departmentalization is the grouping of work or individuals into manageable units. The two basic forms of departmentalization are functional and product/market (subdivided into product, customer, and territory). The functional organization has both the advantages and disadvantages of a bureaucracy. The product/market organization gives major attention to a customer or market. It can be expensive because of duplication of effort, and it is difficult to control.

Bureaucratic structures are commonly supplemented by organic, or highly adaptable and flexible, organizational units. Three versions of the organic structure are flat structures, matrix structures, and adhocratic organizational units. A flat structure has relatively few layers, which speeds up decision making. A matrix structure consists of a project structure superimposed on a functional structure. The matrix manager must achieve results through employees who are also responsible to another manager. Matrix organizations respond quickly and are flexible, but they create problems of uncertain authority and power. Skunk works (specialized units for new product development) and task forces are widely used adhocratic organizational units.

KEY TERMS

organization structure	job sharing	integration	departmentalization
job design	work teams (or production work teams)	span of control	matrix organization
job specialization		flat organization structure	adhocratic organizational units
job characteristics model	organic organization structure	tall organization structure	skunk works
job description	task variability	machine bureaucracy	
flexible working hours	problem analyzability	professional bureaucracy	
compressed work week	differentiation		
telecommuting			

QUESTIONS FOR DISCUSSION AND REVIEW

1. How can you determine whether or not a job is specialized? Explain your reasoning.
2. In our society, do specialists or generalists tend to command the biggest incomes? Support your answer.
3. What use can managers make of job descriptions?
4. Rate each of the alternative work schedules in terms of how much they require having self-reliant and responsible employees.
5. Would you accept a work-at-home position after completing your current school program? Why or why not?
6. One manufacturing company after another is converting to teams. How would you explain the surge in popularity of this form of work group design?
7. Is Pizza Hut a bureaucracy? Explain your reasoning.
8. Describe an organization in which it would be proper to use more than one basis for departmentalization.
9. Assume that, as a manager, you were given the latitude to choose the number of subordinates reporting directly to you. How would you arrive at the proper number?
10. Explain whether work teams should be classified as adhocratic organizational units.

PROBLEMS FOR ACTION

A. Your employer decides to establish a new subsidiary located 500 miles from corporate headquarters. Your assignment is to establish an organization structure for this new subsidiary. Describe what information you will need in order to establish an effective structure.

B. Assume that your manager has said to you, "Our company is suffering from poor coordination. The right hand doesn't know what the left hand is doing. We're paying for this problem in wasted motion and customer dissatisfaction. I'm particularly concerned about the poor cooperation between manufacturing and marketing." Make a concrete proposal to remedy these problems.

CONCLUDING CASE

The Unresponsive Supermarket Chain

Grocery World, Inc., is a locally owned chain of 10 supermarkets that has operated for over 60 years. In recent years, statewide and national chains have gained an increasing share of the grocery business in the city. On the retirement of the previous president, Daniele Labassi was chosen as the new president. She had worked previously as the operations manager of a competitive supermarket chain.

During a recent staff meeting, Libassi had a surprise announcement. She informed the supermarket managers that the chain was long overdue for a change in organization structure. Libassi stated:

"After two years of working here, I've decided that Grocery World is not responsive enough. We cannot compete successfully in today's rapidly changing food shopper's environment. We are too conventional in the way we do business and the way we are organized. I want to confer with you before I make any changes, but my general thinking is that our

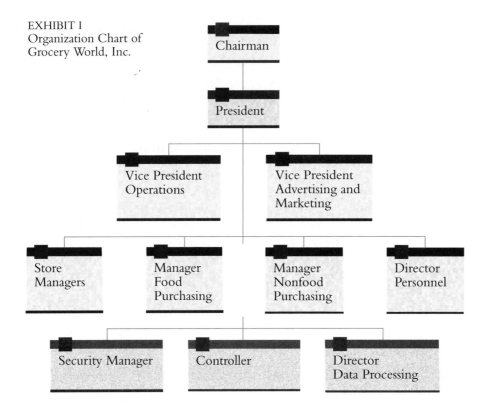

EXHIBIT I
Organization Chart of
Grocery World, Inc.

organization structure slows us down. Look at this chart I've placed on the overhead projector."

(Libassi pointed to the organization chart shown in Exhibit 1.)

"Notice that I've presented an overview of the organization structure of our supermarket chain. Our policy manual presents more details. I would like you to think about a revised structure that will help us take better advantage of opportunities such as garden stores, freestanding specialty stores in nearby locations, fast food restaurants, and theme restaurants.

"We have a fine advertising and marketing department, but our marketing efforts rarely lead us into new markets. Instead, we aim at increasing our market share of something we already do well. Sometimes our marketing strategy is so bland that all it amounts to is lowering the price on food.

"Cost must be considered when we design a new structure. As you know, the retail food business runs on very slim profit margins. Therefore we cannot justify lavish expenditures. Let's all take some time

to sketch out a revised structure for our supermarket chain."

The vice president of store operations responded:

"Are you sure you're not expecting too much from changing the organization structure? No matter how much we switch around the boxes on the chart, we are still dealing with conventional thinking. Some of us are hesitant to change something that has gone so well for us. Our chain is looking very good in comparison to the many supermarkets that have failed recently. We all recall the deep-discounter that moved right next to one of our best locations and failed within a year."

1. Draw a revised organization chart for Grocery World that will help the supermarket be more responsive to new opportunities.
2. Explain why the structure you proposed should help the supermarket be more responsive.
3. What is your opinion of the operation manager's belief that you can only expect so much from an organization structure?

REFERENCES

1. James A. F. Stoner and R. Edward Freeman, *Management*, 4e (Englewood Cliffs, NJ: Prentice Hall, 1989): 262.

2. J. Richard Hackman and Jon L. Pierce, "Conditions Under Which Employees Respond Positively to Enriched Work," *Journal of Applied Psychology* (August 1976): 395–403.

3. J. Richard Hackman and Greg R. Oldham, *Work Redesign* (Reading, MA: Addison-Wesley, 1977): 81.

4. Ricky W. Griffin, "Effects of Work Redesign on Employee Perceptions, Attitudes, and Behaviors: A Long-Term Investigation," *Academy of Management Journal* (June 1991): 425–435.

5. Researched by Don Buffum, Rochester Institute of Technology, 1990.

6. Andrew J. DuBrin, "Comparison of the Job Satisfaction and Productivity of Telecommuters versus In-House Employees: A Research Note on Work in Progress," *Psychological Reports* (68), 1991: 1223–1234; Dori Sera Bailey and Jill Foley, "Pacific Bell Works Long Distance," *HRMagazine* (August 1990): 50–53.

7. Donald C. Bacon, "Look Who's Working at Home," *Nation's Business* (October 1989): 21.

8. DuBrin, "Job Satisfaction and Productivity," 1231.

9. Renee Magid, *The Work and Family Challenge*, Management Briefing (New York: American Management Association, 1990): 43–44.

10. "Sharpening Minds for a Competitive Edge," *Business Week* (December 17, 1990): 72–78; "The Payoff from Teamwork," *Business Week* (July 10, 1989): 56–62.

11. Ursula Thomas, "Bat Maker Adjusts Timing to Beat Rivals," Gannett News Service (April 13, 1991).

12. Joan Woodward, *Industrial Organization: Theory and Practice* (London: Oxford University Press, 1965): 65–80.

13. Research synthesized by Richard M. Hodgetts, *Management* (Orlando, FL: Academic Press, 1985): 184.

14. C. Chet Miller, William H. Glick, Yau-De Wang, and George P. Huber, "Understanding Technology-Structure Relationships: Theory Development and Meta-Analytic Theory Testing," *Academy of Management Journal* (June 1991): 370–399.

15. Charles Perrow, "A Framework for the Comparative Analysis of Organizations," *American Sociological Review* (April 1967): 194–208.

16. "Agony at Chase Manhattan," *Business Week* (October 8, 1990): 2.

17. Paul R. Lawrence and Jay W. Lorsch, "Differentiation and Integration in Complex Organizations," *Administrative Science Quarterly* (June 1967): 1–47.

18. Noel Tichy and Ram Charan, "Speed, Simplicity, Self-Confidence: An Interview with Jack Welch," *Harvard Business Review* (September-October 1989): 114.

19. David D. Van Fleet, "Span of Management Research and Issues," *Academy of Management Journal* (September 1983): 546–552.

20. Max Weber, *The Theory of Social and Economic Organization*, translated by A. Henderson and T. Parson (New York: Free Press, 1947).

21. Henry Mintzberg, *Structure in Fives: Designing Effective Organizations* (Englewood Cliffs, NJ: Prentice-Hall, 1983): 189–214.

22. Elliot Jacques, "In Praise of Hierarchy," *Harvard Business Review* (January-February 1990): 127.

23. Jacques, "In Praise of Hierarchy," 127.

24. Ralph P. Hummel, *The Bureaucratic Experience*, 3e (New York: St. Martin's Press, 1987).

25. Rosabeth Moss Kanter, "The New Managerial World," *Harvard Business Review* (November-December 1989): 85.

26. Peter F. Drucker, "The Coming of the New Organization," *Harvard Business Review* (January-February 1988): 45.

27. "IBM: As Markets and Technology Change, Can Big Blue Remake Its Culture?" *Business Week* (June 17, 1991): 25–32; Thomas A. Stewart, "GE Keeps Those Ideas Coming," *Fortune* (August 12, 1991): 41.

28. Christopher A. Bartlett and Sumantra Ghosal, "Matrix Management: Not a Structure, a Frame of Mind," *Harvard Business Review* (July-August 1990): 145.

29. Bartlett and Ghosal, "Matrix Management," 139.

Chapter 8

Authority and Power in Organizations

OPENING
CASE

Semco S/A
(Brazil)

Ricardo Semler is the president of Semco S/A, Brazil's largest marine and food-processing machinery manufacturer. Semco was close to financial disaster in 1980, but today it is one of Brazil's fastest-growing corporations. Semco recently showed a profit margin of 10 percent on sales of $37 million. Management associations, labor unions, and the media have frequently described Semco as the best employer in Brazil. Jobs are no longer advertised; instead, word of mouth attracts up to 300 applications for every position.

Managing a firm in Brazil is difficult, Semler says, because of a paternalistic system that keeps outsiders from gaining power. He attributes the turnaround in his firm to treating its 800 employees like responsible adults. The majority of employees, including production workers, set their own working hours. All employees have access to the company books, and most vote on many major corporate decisions. Every employee is paid by the month. More than 150 members of management set their own salaries and bonuses.

A company president's turning over so much power and authority to employees is a sign of the times. Executives in all types of organizations are attempting to make effective use of authority, and some, like Semler, are willing to experiment. The major purpose of this chapter is to provide the basis for understanding the nature of authority and power in organizations. Among the key topics it explores are the sources of authority and power, the use of politics to acquire power, and the different types of authority. As you study this chapter, keep in mind that the major purpose of granting authority and power to employees is to achieve organizational objectives.

Source: As reported in Ricardo Semler, "Managing Without Managers," *Harvard Business Review* (September–October 1989): 76.

AUTHORITY IN ORGANIZATIONS

Effective use of power and authority differentiates the successful manager from the unsuccessful one. For example, a manager who uses authority to abuse people will soon lose key employees. A more successful manager will use authority in a constructive way, to set challenging goals, for example. To use both power and authority effectively, it is important to understand the difference between them.

The Meaning of Authority and Power

Authority is the *right* inherent in a managerial position to make decisions that guide the actions of others. **Power** is the *ability* to influence decisions and control resources. The amount of power associated with managerial authority varies substantially. Some of this variation stems from the amount of authority granted by the firm. An executive with line authority can make major decisions such as whether or not to buy another company. Staff authority, on the other hand, is primarily advisory. Much of its power stems from technical knowledge and persuasion. For example, a business forecaster (a staff position) might be able to persuade top-level management that buying a particular company is a good idea.

Authority and power are linked to **responsibility,** the obligation to perform. Managers use authority and power to carry out the responsibilities delegated to them from people higher in the firm. The topic of responsibility is described more fully in Chapter 9, which deals with delegation and decentralization.

Sources of Authority

Authority in firms flows in two directions: from the top down and from the bottom up, as shown in Figure 8-1. The "top-down" theory is the classical theory of authority, while the "bottom-up" theory is the acceptance view. Both views of the source of authority in organizations have merit.

THE CLASSICAL VIEW OF AUTHORITY. According to the **classical view of authority**, an organization derives its authority from its stakeholders. In turn, the organization grants its managers formal authority to carry out specific responsibilities. In countries that allow private ownership, the top-down flow of authority follows the pattern shown in Figure 8-2.

The classical view of authority means that if people abide by the Constitution they accept the right of others to own private property, to operate a business, and to administer a governmental agency or an educational institution. It also means that employees accept the authority of those above

FIGURE 8-1 Two Views of Authority

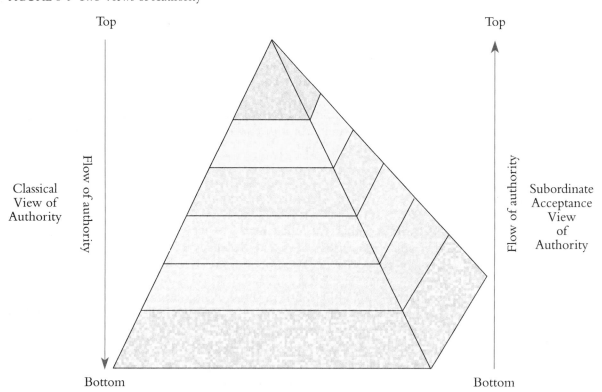

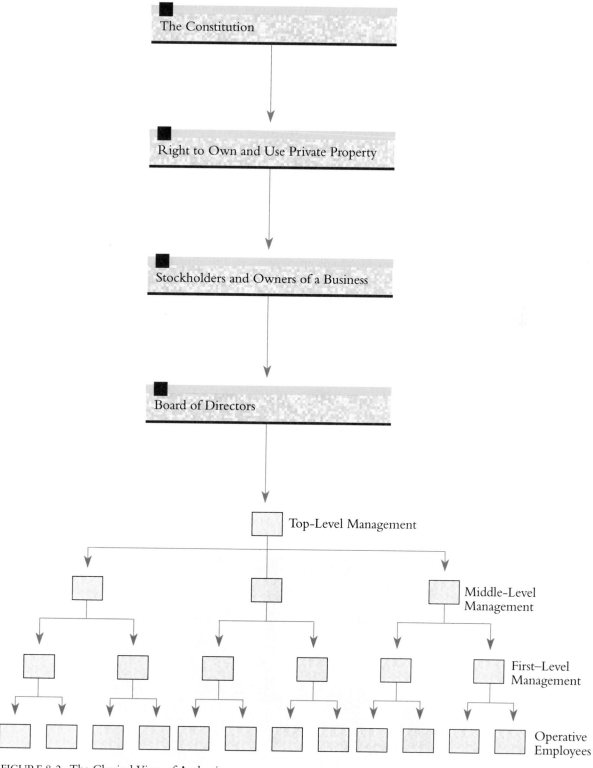

FIGURE 8-2   The Classical View of Authority

them in the hierarchy and therefore have an obligation to follow directives. If every employee behaved in accordance with the classical view of authority, there would be few problems in administering orders and discipline would be unnecessary.

THE ACCEPTANCE VIEW OF AUTHORITY. The **acceptance view of authority** contends that authority stems from below. This view helps explain why orders from above are not always followed. Those who receive the orders decide whether or not to comply. If they perceive an order as being legitimate, they will comply; if not, they will ignore or disobey the order. Authority thus flows upward in a limited sense because a manager can only issue directives that team members will follow. An example is the administrative assistant who refuses to visit a bank to arrange a personal loan for a superior.

ETHICS QUESTION
How ethical is it for managers to push employees to the limits of the employees' zones of indifference?

The area in which employees will permit managers to exercise formal authority is the **zone of indifference.** Employees are indifferent to (do not mind following) orders within this zone, but they generally reject attempts to exercise authority outside the zone. Frequently, the employee defines the zone of indifference. Arranging a personal loan for the superior was outside the zone of indifference for the employee just mentioned.

Effective managers need adequate amounts of authority from both above and below. Managers who are perceived as having clout (a high degree of formal authority) will have an easier time achieving results than those who are not perceived this way. In addition, effective managers work within their employees' zones of indifference. Managers with good leadership skills who are well respected find that employees are willing to grant them a wider zone than managers with less personal influence.

Managers who have good leadership skills and are well respected by their employees have a wider zone for giving orders.

SOURCES OF POWER

Managers must have power in order to influence people to complete tasks. Unfortunately, power can also be used for less lofty ideals, such as arranging extraordinary severance payments for oneself or sexually harassing employees. Sources of power can be categorized in many ways, and there are different ways of exercising power. In the following sections we discuss five sources of power.

Position Power

The power of a manager's position stems from three sources: legitimate power, coercive power, and reward power.[1] **Legitimate power** is based on the manager's formal position within the organizational hierarchy. A government agency head, for example, has much more position power than a unit supervisor in the same agency. Managers can enhance their position power by formulating policies and procedures. For example, if a manager establishes a procedure whereby he or she must approve all purchases over $500, the manager is in a position to exercise a great deal of authority in deciding which purchases will be made.

Coercive power is controlling others through fear of punishment or the threat of punishment. Typical organizational punishments include bypassing an employee for promotion and terminating employment. The threat of lawsuit by an employee who is treated unjustly serves as a constraint on coercive power.

Reward power is controlling others through rewards or the promise of rewards. Examples of this are the promotions, challenging assignments, and recognition given to employees by managers.

The effectiveness of coercive power and reward power depends on the perceptions and needs of subordinates. For coercive power to be effective, the employee must fear punishment and care about being a member of the firm.

Personal Power

Managers also derive power from two separate personal characteristics: knowledge and personality. **Expert power** is the ability to influence others because of one's specialized knowledge, skills, or abilities. An example of a manager with personal power is Tina Floyd, the owner of Doctor's Corner Professional Services Inc., a placement firm. Floyd teaches her 14 employees the basics of placing medical employees.[2] She has expert power because she knows the essential details of running a medical placement firm and her employees respect her knowledge. For expertise to be an effective source of power, employees must respect that expertise. A more general example is the substantial power of the only person in a firm who knows how to maintain the personal computer network.

Referent (charismatic) power is the ability to influence others that stems from the manager's desirable personal traits and characteristics. It is based on the desire of group members to be led by or identified with an inspiring person. A recent study concluded that charisma has three components: expert power, referent power, and job involvement.[3] In order to be charismatic, the manager must have a high level of expertise and be well liked. In addition, the manager must help employees get involved in their jobs by such means as providing them with challenging work. (The "being liked" aspect of charisma is highly subjective. Even the most beloved organizational and political leaders are disliked by some of their subordinates and constituents.) The Manager in Action describes a charismatic executive who exerts expert and referent power.

MANAGER IN ACTION

While she was president of Calvin Klein Cosmetics Corporation, Robin Burns rejected a number of job offers from Estée Lauder, Inc. When Calvin Klein was acquired by another company, Burns decided to leave. She got back in touch with Estée Lauder, and at age 37 was hired as president of the USA division. As head of a $600 million business, Burns has one of the most responsible and powerful jobs in the industry. Many people who have worked with her describe her as an extraordinary executive who inspires others. A co-op student reported, "Robin Burns has a magnetism that can't be beat. Most of the people in my merchandising group thought it was a privilege to work for her."

Burns faces the challenge of breathing new life into Estée Lauder. The firm's sales growth has been hurt by a general weakness in the department store industry. Burns has keen intuition about the marketplace. At Calvin Klein, she introduced four breakthrough fragrances: Obsession and Eternity, a pair each for men and women. Her strategy is to move away from Lauder's mature image to cultivate a younger, "hipper" customer. Some say she is moving Estée Lauder closer to her own image.

Source: As reported in "Executives to Watch," *The 1990 Business Week 1000*, (April 13, 1990): 120; employee interviews.

Power from Providing Resources

Another way of understanding the sources of power is through the **resource dependence perspective.** According to this perspective, the organization requires a continuing flow of human resources, money, customers, technological inputs, and material to continue to function. Subunits or individuals within the organization who can provide these key resources derive power from this ability.[4]

An important consequence of the resource dependence perspective is that when managers start losing their power to control resources, their power declines. A case in point is Donald Trump. When his vast holdings were generating a positive cash flow and his image was one of extraordinary power, he found many willing investors. The name *Trump* on a property escalated its value. As his cash flow position worsened, however, Trump found it difficult to find investment groups willing to buy his properties at or near the asking price.[5]

Control of the Decision Premise

People who can place constraints on decisions acquire power. An important part of constraining a decision is to control its premises. A **decision premise** is the basic values and objectives followed in making the decision. As Jeffrey Pfeffer has explained, two elements are involved in making any choice. First are the presumed goals or objectives to be served by the decision, and second are the constraints on the decision that must be satisfied by the choice that is made. Such constraints may be physical, financial, social, or political.[6] An executive might state, for example, "It is acceptable to purchase another firm providing the acquisition is projected to yield a profit by the second year [a financial constraint]. Also, the purchased firm should not be a competitor of a major customer [a political constraint]."

Organizational policies and procedures and the organization chart determine to a large extent who has the power to control decisions. Yet decision makers can interpret those policies and procedures in such a way that they exert greater control over the decision premises.

Centrality

The final source of power is **centrality,** or closeness to power. According to this perspective, the closer a person is to power, the greater the power that person exerts. Likewise, the higher a unit reports in a firm's hierarchy, the more power it possesses. In practice, this means that a department reporting to the president has more power than a department reporting to a vice president. It also means that working for a highly influential subunit gives a person more power, even at the same reporting level. In most organizations, for example, a marketing manager exerts more influence than the materials management manager. For these reasons, some people have proposed a globe-shaped organization chart, as shown in Figure 8- 3.

LEARNING CHECK   Explain the difference between authority and power, and describe the sources of organization power.

Back to the Opening Case   Part of Ricardo Semler's strategy of giving more power to employees was to give them more control over resources and decisions. You will recall that most employees at Semco vote on major corporate decisions. Also, more than 150 managers set their own salaries and bonuses.

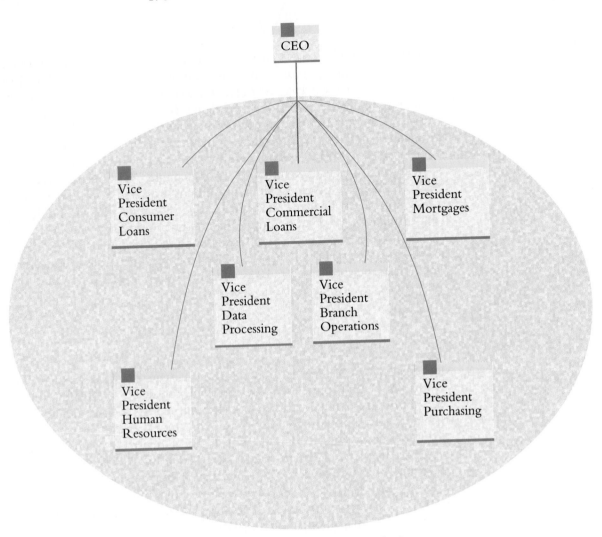

Note: The shorter the distance to the CEO, the greater the power of an organizational unit.

FIGURE 8-3 Organization Chart of Bank Depicting Relative Power of Units

ORGANIZATIONAL POLITICS: THE QUEST FOR POWER

Authority and power are closely linked to political behavior, or organizational politics. Politics is the study of power in action, and people engage in organizational politics to acquire personal power and position power. Political behavior is often thought to be devious and motivated by self-interest.[7] However, sometimes managers need to make effective use of political tactics in order to achieve their objectives.

As defined here, **organizational politics** is an influence process in which an individual or group attempts to gain advantage by using informal tactics in addition to merit. Therefore, political tactics are used in addition to, but not as a substitute for, job competence. The advantage sought is typ-

ETHICS QUESTION
How does one know whether or not a method of acquiring power is ethical?

ically to gain power, as in the classical meaning of politics, but organizational politics can also be used for purposes of gaining acceptance and approval or avoiding hard work. For example, some employees will strive for the approval of their superiors in order to avoid uncomfortable and physically taxing assignments.

Importance of and Reasons for Organizational Politics

Few experienced managers or staff specialists would dispute the importance of using political power sensibly and ethically. A manager who ignored organizational politics would not be able to get much accomplished. One study of 337 men and women reported that both sexes use politically toned influence tactics such as exchanging favors.[8] Because so many workers use these tactics, we can assume that they are important.

Research conducted by Fred Luthans and his associates supports the idea that managers who get promoted rapidly rely on organizational politics to achieve their purposes. They studied the work behaviors of 300 managers from all levels and all types of organizations including the industrial, retail, service, and public sectors.

The primary method of study was direct observation of the behavior of managers, supplemented by interviews and questionnaires. The researchers defined managerial success in terms of how high the managers had risen in the hierarchy relative to their years of experience. In contrast, they defined managerial effectiveness in terms of the quantity and quality of the managers' work and the performance, satisfaction, and commitment of their group members.

Luthans and his associates found that the successful managers gave more attention to networking than did the less successful managers (those who were promoted less frequently). Networking in this context referred to the systematic use of personal contacts to advance one's career. The specific behaviors associated with networking were interacting with outsiders, socializing, and politicking. An equally important finding was that effective managers relied less on networking but spent more time communicating.[9] The results of this study suggest, therefore, that politicking is more helpful in getting promoted than in accomplishing valid results.

The most fundamental reason for organizational politics is the political nature of organizations. Coalitions of interests and demands arise both within and outside organizations. Similarly, organizations can be viewed as loose structures of interests and demands in competition with each other for attention and resources. The interaction among different coalitions results in an undercurrent of political tactics (e.g., one group trying to promote itself and discredit another).

Another contributor to political activity is the pyramidal shape of organizations. The people at the top of the organization hold most of the power, while people at each successive level down the hierarchy hold less and less power (see Figure 8-1). The amount of power that can be distributed in a hierarchy is limited. Power-oriented managers sometimes cope with the limited amount of power available by expanding their sphere of

Networking is an avenue to promotion, but effective managers spend more time communicating.

influence sideways. For example, the director of the food stamp program in a government agency might attempt to gain control over the housing assistance program, which is at the same organizational level.

Organizational politics is also fostered by the need for power. Executives have much stronger power needs than other people and are thus propelled toward frequent political behavior. Because executives are responsible for controlling resources, their inner desire to do so helps them in their jobs. The power need that triggers political behavior is often a quest for personalized power—making an impact on others, aggressiveness, and conquest. Or the need may be for socialized power—exercising power for the good of others.[10] An executive who builds an organization to help children who have cancer might exemplify socialized power.

Finally, a devious reason for the existence of politicking is **Machiavellianism,** a tendency to manipulate others for personal gain. One study found that people who scored very high on a politics questionnaire also scored high on a test of Machiavellianism.[11]

ETHICS QUESTION
To what extent is Machiavellianism really just part of the free-enterprise system?

Control of Organizational Politics

Too much negative political behavior is detrimental to a firm. One consequence is that when political factors far outweigh merit, competent employees may become unhappy and quit. Another problem is that politicking takes time away from tasks that could contribute more directly to achieving the firm's goals.

The most comprehensive antidote to improper, excessive, and unethical organizational politics is to rely on objective measures of performance. This is true because people have less need to behave politically when their contributions can be measured directly. With management by objectives (discussed in Chapter 6), the results a person attains should be much more important than the impression the person creates (a political factor). However, even MBO is not immune from politics. Sometimes the goals set are designed to impress key people in the organization. As such, they may not be the most important goals for getting work accomplished.

Meshing individual and organizational objectives would be the ideal method of controlling excessive political behavior. If their objectives, needs, and interests can be met through their jobs, employees will tend to engage in behavior that fosters the growth, longevity, and productivity of the firm. Another approach to controlling politics in a firm is for top-level managers to minimize their own political behaviors (e.g., showing favoritism). By so doing, executives can create a positive model for other employees.

Finally, organizational politics can be curtailed by threatening to discuss questionable information in a public forum. If one employee engages in backstabbing of another, the manager might ask him or her to repeat this anecdote in a staff meeting. It has been said that sunlight is the best disinfectant to deviousness.

LEARNING CHECK

Discuss the meaning of organizational politics, the reason for its existence, and how to control its overuse.

EMPOWERMENT OF EMPLOYEES

Distributing decision-making power throughout an organization is seen as the key to gaining the competitive edge in today's markets.[12] Nevertheless, in some situations a highly centralized bureaucracy is still the key to success, as described in Chapter 7. Employees experience a greater sense of self-efficacy (effectiveness) and ownership in their jobs when they share power. **Empowerment** is a manager's process of sharing power with subordinates, thereby enhancing their feelings of self-efficacy.[13]

Sharing power with subordinates encourages them to feel better about themselves and perform at a higher level. However, for power sharing to be effective, the employees must be competent and interested in assuming more responsibility. Otherwise the work will not get accomplished. Many of the techniques to accomplish empowerment are described in this text, among them participative management, goal setting, quality circles, and feedback.

A model of the empowerment process is shown in Figure 8-4. According to this model, managers must do certain things to empower employees. They must remove conditions that keep employees powerless, such as authoritarian supervision or a job over which they have little control. An

Sharing power with
subordinates results in
increased motivation and
better performance.

FIGURE 8-4 Five Stages in the Process of Empowerment

Stage 1	**Stage 2**	**Stage 3**	**Stage 4**	**Stage 5**
Conditions leading to a psychological state of power-lessness	**The use of managerial strategies and techniques**	**To provide self-efficacy information to subordinates using four sources**	**Results in empowering experience of subordinate**	**Leading to behavioral effects**
Organizational factors	Participative management	Enactive attainment	Strengthening of effort—performance expectancy or belief in personal efficacy	Initiation/ persistence of behavior to accomplish task objectives
Supervision	Goal setting	Vicarious experience		
Reward system	Feedback system	Verbal persuasion		
Nature of job	Modeling	Emotional arousal		
	Contingent/ competence-based reward			
	Job enrichment			

and

Remove
conditions
listed under
Stage 1

Source: Jay A. Conger and Rabindra N. Kanungo, "The Empowerment Process: Integrating Theory and Practice," *Academy of Management Review* (July 1988): 475.

example of a person in a low-control job would be a manager who cannot shut off interruptions even to prepare budgets or to plan. Employees must also receive information that increases their feelings of self-efficacy. When they are empowered, they will take the initiative to solve problems and strive hard to reach objectives. The Manager in Action illustrates the importance of empowerment in one of the world's best-known multinational corporations.

MANAGER IN ACTION

IBM is working hard to compete successfully in Europe, but U.S. and Japanese competitors are eroding some of the company's formerly wide profit margins. To hold on to the winning edge, IBM Europe Chairman David E. McKinney is making a sweeping reorganization of IBM's business practices within his sphere of influence. He is also building alliances with European companies to compete favorably with the Japanese.

Part of the new thrust is to trim $28 billion in costs while learning to be more responsive to customer demands. McKinney is also moving IBM Europe away from thinking in terms of one country at a time. With Europe becoming one giant market, he wants his managers in each country to "think big" also. Managers from each country are assuming pan-European duties for each product line and marketing speciality. For example, IBM Germany is responsible for mainframe computers, while IBM Britain takes responsibility for finance marketing.

McKinney's goals are to save money, respond more rapidly to market changes, and get national units to cooperate rather than compete with each other. Many local managers will now have more freedom to act as they see fit. "People do better when they're empowered to act on their own," says McKinney.

Source: As reported in "IBM Europe Starts Swinging Back," *Business Week* (May 6, 1991): 52.

ETHICS QUESTION
How ethical is it for management to attempt to empower employees who are not looking for additional responsibility?

To empower people, firms must provide them with the tools and confidence they need to exercise authority. A human resource consultant recommends that managers teach employees to ask the following four questions whenever they are unsure of how to act in a situation:

1. Is it good for the customer?
2. Is it good for the organization?
3. Is it in agreement with our philosophy and values?
4. Is it good for me?

If the answer is "yes" to all four questions, the employees should be given the authority to make the decision. Managers should also remind them that it is easier to ask forgiveness than permission.[14]

Back to the Opening Case

Ricardo Semler, the CEO of Semco S/A, empowered employees in order to overcome financial disaster in his firm. To Semler, empowerment translates into "treating employees like responsible adults." For example, the majority of employees set their own working hours and vote on many major corporate decisions.

LINE AND STAFF RELATIONSHIPS

The preceding discussion emphasized relationships between managers and subordinates. Another, equally important, relationship is that between line authority and staff authority. These two types of authority reflect the differences between line organizations and staff organizations. This section discusses the nature of line and staff authority, functional authority, and problems between line and staff.

Line Authority

The concept of line authority deals with the relationship between a manager and an employee. As a superior-subordinate relationship, **line authority** is the right of a manager to allocate resources and assign tasks to employees. Line authority is a command authority. For example, a marketing manager has the right to direct a marketing department employee to develop a marketing plan for a new product.

Line authority is a command relationship extending from the top of an organization to the lowest level. A **chain of command** is the steps by which authority flows downward in the organization; it specifies who reports to whom. As a link in the chain of command, a manager has the authority to direct the work of subordinates, yet the manager also reports to a superior.

A **line organization function** is one that contributes directly to the creation and distribution of goods. The departments of the firm that edited and marketed this book are part of the publisher's line organization.

The key to distinguishing between line and staff is not by function, however. Instead, it is the degree to which the function contributes directly to the achievement of organization objectives. In manufacturing organizations, operations and marketing are regarded as line functions, while purchasing is usually classified as a staff function. In a department store, on the other hand, the purchasing function is a vital part of the line organization; it provides the goods to sell to customers. Most firms regard finance as a staff function, but for a finance company the departments in charge of acquisition and management of capital are part of the line organization.

Staff Authority

Modern organizations are composed of both line and staff groups. In their dealings with other units, staff managers have **staff authority**—authority of an advisory or service nature that lacks the right of command. Staff specialists and managers offer advice and provide service to line managers and specialists. In complex organizations, some staff groups also advise and serve other staff groups. For example, an information systems specialist might help the human resources department develop a human resources information system.

Staff employees perform one of two somewhat different sets of activities. Executives often hire personal staff members to ease their workloads. In contrast, specialized staff workers **(staff specialists),** such as corporate attorneys, human resource trainers, and business forecasters, provide expertise that is not ordinarily possessed by managers. These professionals are still a vital part of many firms, even if there are not as many of them as in the past.

Large numbers of staff groups are much more likely to be found in large than in small firms. Small firms may employ contract or temporary workers when needed. A trend in larger firms has been to reduce the ratio of staff workers to line workers. Thus, many people who once worked in staff activities have been transferred to customer-contact line positions.

Functional Authority

Managers and staff professionals (or specialists), as well as other employees, can exert authority outside their own units or chains of command. For example, the vice president of quality assurance can pressure any employee to uphold quality because the vice president is exercising authority with regard to the function of quality. Thus, **functional authority** is the right to influence the activity of other employees or units outside one's chain of command.

Functional authority can go in any direction. Employees can exercise functional authority over others at the same level. Lower-level employees can exercise functional authority over their superiors. The security officer can tell the CEO, "You cannot go beyond my desk unless you present your security badge." It is helpful to specify in writing the nature of all functional authority relationships. Failure to do so is frequently a source of organizational conflict. However, it is seldom practical to draw all the lines of functional authority on the organization chart; the chart would become too confusing. Functional authority is exercised most frequently by staff managers and line managers.

THE FUNCTIONAL AUTHORITY OF THE STAFF MANAGER. Staff managers can exercise functional authority in two ways. First, they may have functional authority over their counterparts at lower organization levels. Second, a particular functional specialty may be separated from the line manager's job and then assigned to an appropriate staff specialist. For example, an operations vice president might be responsible for cultural diversity training within his or her command. Because this activity is so specialized, the vice president will probably assign it to a training department.

Figure 8-5 shows the exercise of functional authority. Observe that the manager of each staff function reports functionally to the staff counterpart at the next higher level. The functional relationship is indicated by a dotted line. In large firms, this next higher level may be a geographic division, with the managers at the divisional level reporting to their counterparts on the corporate staff.

Functional authority need not exist only between successive levels in a firm. Sometimes a high-level unit will exert functional authority over a unit several levels away. As firms have become less concerned about violating

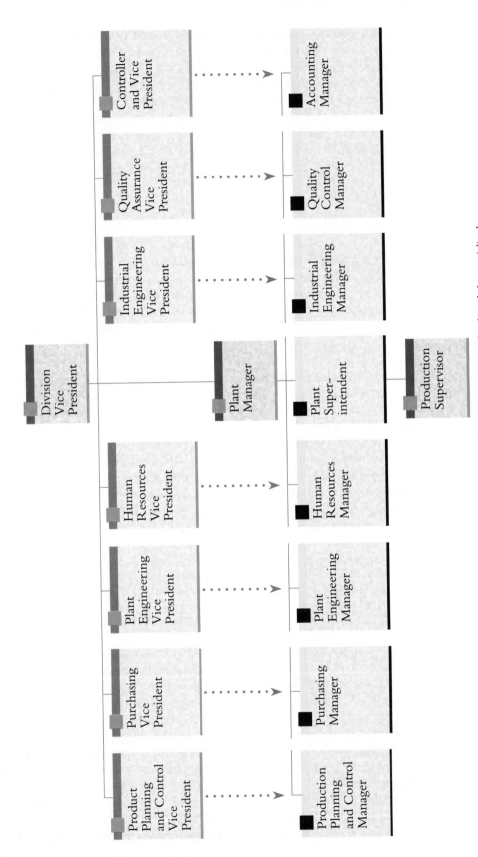

Arrows show flow of functional authority. Staff department managers report functionally to the next higher level, and the specialized portions of the production supervisor's job are assigned to the appropriate staff specialist.

FIGURE 8-5 The Exercise of Functional Authority

206

chains of command ("going through proper channels"), the authority to influence remote units has become more important.

THE FUNCTIONAL AUTHORITY OF THE LINE MANAGER. Functional authority is usually thought of in relation to staff managers. However, line managers can exercise functional authority when they have valid reasons for controlling some method or process of another operating department. For instance, the vice president of manufacturing might be given the authority to prevent marketing executives from accepting orders the firm cannot fulfill.

Product departmentalization lends itself naturally to the exercise of functional authority over product division managers. The product manager exercises control over all divisional operating functions that directly affect the well-being of the product. Yet the firm may want to ensure that corporate policy is followed properly in the divisions. As a result, the corporate executives may be given functional authority. For example, the vice president of finance would oversee the division product managers to ensure that division credit policies were consistent with corporate policies.

Problems in Line-Staff Relationships

Line departments and line employees are frequently in conflict with staff departments and staff employees. The fact that two authorities exist within a single organization is the reason for this conflict. Line authority has the right to command and staff authority has the right to advise. Line and staff groups also serve different functions. The line function pursues organizational objectives directly, while the staff function pursues them by helping the line.

An example will help explain the nature of line-versus-staff conflict. A staff group generates a recycling program it thinks everyone in the firm should follow. With general backing from top-level management, this group decides to conduct recycling seminars on company time. Several line groups object, stating that the staff group has no right to take employees away from ordinary activities. In turn, the staff group complains to top-level management that the line groups are not cooperating in reaching an important organizational goal.

LINE RESPONSIBILITY VERSUS STAFF RESPONSIBILITY. When only line positions exist in an organization, line managers are constrained only by their own superiors. When staff positions are introduced, more constraints appear: Line managers are expected to consult with staff. Line managers frequently view consultations with staff as an infringement on their authority to manage. Their resulting resentment toward staff is expressed through such statements as "Staff does not operate in the real world" and "Consultation means delay."

The authority of the functional staff to monitor line personnel creates the most pressure on line and staff relationships. For example, the president of a subsidiary company is responsible for the profits of that subsidiary, but, through its functional authority, the corporate industrial relations staff negotiates the labor agreements for all subsidiary companies. As a result, two of the major cost factors, wages and work rules, are determined by a corporate staff specialist who does not report to the subsidiary's president. This can lead to resentment and frustration.

THE IMPORTANCE OF FUNCTION. The major cause of conflict between line and staff concerns the relative importance of each function. Staff's infringement on the line manager's authority is the major cause of line-versus-staff conflict as perceived by line personnel. The main source of conflict as perceived by staff personnel is the fact that they are thought to be of secondary importance.

Differences in career perspectives also contribute to the conflict over the importance of function. Staff personnel are employed because of their specialized knowledge. Because they are ambitious, it is only natural that they advance by what seems the most logical avenue: advancing their ideas.

The suggestions of staff personnel are sometimes rejected by line managers. Staff are told that the line manager has the authority to decide and that they can only advise. To staff workers, the interpretation that the line manager makes the decisions is a distortion of reality. In their view, line managers would not be able to make sound decisions without input from the staff. For example, before a bank offered a new product or service to customers (a line decision), market researchers (staff personnel) might inform top-level managers what new product or service would be in demand.

Currently, line functions have regained much of the power that had shifted to staff departments during the previous two decades. A notable example of this shift occurred with the staff specialty of strategic planning. From the mid-1970s to the mid-1980s, strategic planners exerted considerable influence on the strategic planning of line managers. Much of this activity took place in departments with titles such as "Corporate Planning." Strategic planning is still a highly regarded organizational function. However, line management has taken back more direct responsibility for formulating and implementing strategic plans. Planning specialists are now playing more of an advisory role, and much of their activity has been placed into operating units.

As modern organizations become flatter and less concerned about hierarchy, the distinctions between line and staff will continue to blur. As a result, many of the conflicts between line and staff will diminish.

LEARNING CHECK   Describe the difference between line and staff and explain why they are often in conflict.

SUMMARY

Authority is the right to make decisions that guide the actions of others. Power is the ability to mobilize resources, energy, and information on behalf of a preferred objective or strategy. Authority in organizations stems from the top down (the classical view) and from the bottom up (the acceptance view). Subordinates generally comply with orders that lie within their zones of indifference. Authority and power are linked to responsibility, the obligation to perform.

Position power stems from three main sources: legitimate power (that granted by the organization), coercive power (the ability to punish), and reward power (the ability to dispense rewards). Personal power stems from two sources: expert power (specialized knowledge) and referent, or charismatic, power.

According to the resource dependence perspective, people and groups who provide key resources acquire power. Controlling the premises of decisions is another source of power. The person who determines the constraints of a decision, and its basic values and objectives, thus has power.

Organizational politics is an influence process in which an individual or group attempts to gain power and other advantages by using informal tactics in addition to merit. The appropriate use of political tactics contributes to managerial effectiveness. Dysfunctional organizational politics can be controlled through objective performance measurement and the meshing of individual and organizational objectives.

Empowerment is the process of a manager's sharing power with subordinates. The process enhances the subordinates' feelings of self-efficacy and increases their motivation. To be empowered, people must be provided with the tools and confidence that enable them to exercise authority.

Line authority is exerted over activities that are directly related to the primary objectives or outputs of the organization. Staff authority is advisory or service-related in nature, yet some staff specialists exert considerable power on the basis of their expertise. The two types of staff are personal staff (such as an administrative assistant) and staff specialists (such as an information systems specialist). Functional authority is the right to monitor activities of both line and staff groups outside of one's chain of command.

Line and staff groups enter into conflict for many reasons, including disputes over how much authority each possesses and the importance of each function. Currently, line functions are regaining some of the power that had shifted to staff departments previously.

KEY TERMS

authority	zone of indifference	resource dependence	line authority
power	legitimate power	perspective	chain of command
responsibility	coercive power	decision premise	line organization func-
classical view of author-	reward power	centrality	tion
ity	expert power	organizational politics	staff authority
acceptance view of au-	referent (charismatic)	Machiavellianism	staff specialists
thority	power	empowerment	functional authority

QUESTIONS FOR DISCUSSION AND REVIEW

1. Where do managers get their authority?
2. How does the acceptance view of authority between the instructor and students operate in a classroom?
3. From what do managers and specialists derive their organizational power?
4. When first entering a full-time professional job, what sources of power does a person possess?
5. What can managers do to increase the amount of charismatic power they possess?

6. What ethical issues might be associated with the use of organizational politics?
7. How do managers know whether they possess line or staff authority?
8. What line authority does a staff manager exercise?

9. Give a specific example of how the president of a small firm might exercise functional authority.
10. Why are line workers and staff workers often antagonistic toward each other?

PROBLEMS FOR ACTION

A. You are the assistant to the operations manager of a telephone company. The CEO says to you one day, "I've just read an exciting book about empowering employees. It sounds like a great idea for making our firm more productive. Maybe we can reduce customer complaints and increase profit margins. I want you to develop a plan for empowering our employees. Let me know what help you'll need to get the job done.'" Sketch out your plan for an employee empowerment program in your firm.
B. You are working as a human resource specialist for

a regional bank with 10 branches. The CEO of the bank is concerned that the organization has become far too political and gives you this assignment: First, measure the inclination of bank employees to engage in organizational politics. Second, make recommendations for improving the conditions that might be breeding political behavior. Third, suggest how the bank might decrease the amount of political behavior that does exist. Outline how you would take care of the first part of the assignment, and summarize your thoughts on the second and third parts.

CONCLUDING CASE

Who Has the Right to Tell Whom What to Do?

Gordon Dean, the customer service manager at First National Bank, was sorting through his paper and electronic mail one day. He came across an E-mail message from the human resources department announcing a new training program, "Total Quality Management." The purpose of the program, as explained by human resources director Sheryl Anderson, was to upgrade quality in every aspect of the bank's activities. This would include dealing with both external and internal customers. (An internal customer, Anderson explained, is any other person in the bank who uses your input.)

The quality improvement program was based on the one developed by Xerox Corporation. It included the following components:

I. Concepts of Quality (a description of key concepts about quality, including the language of quality and the cost of quality).
II. Quality Improvement Process (a description of problem solving, planning for quality, organizing for quality, and monitoring for quality).

Dean recalled participating in a planning session about the quality-improvement program, but he was not aware until this moment that the program had reached implementation. Anderson noted that all recipients of her electronic message should enroll immediately. She provided a list of dates for the training sessions.

As Dean deleted the file from his computer in-basket, he thought to himself: "If I did everything the human resources department wanted me to do, I would have very little time to manage the customer service department. Besides that, customer service is already at the forefront of quality."

One week later, Dean received another electronic message from the human resources department. It was labeled "Second Notice." This time Dean responded, "Sorry, our workload in customer service is too heavy now to attend a training program."

Three days later, Dean was visited by his boss, who explained to him: "I've been getting some complaints from the human resources department about you. They say you won't cooperate with them about the quality-improvement program. Sheryl Anderson wants me to talk to you about the program."

Dean replied,

I resent those comments from the human resources department. Sheryl is complaining because I won't buy into her quality-improvement program right now. I'm not saying her training program isn't worthwhile. It's just that as a manager in this bank, I have the right to choose how to budget my time.

I don't like the heavy-handed tactics Sheryl is using to force me to cooperate. Are the line departments here to please staff departments? Who has the right to tell whom to do what?

1. What types of line versus staff conflict does this case illustrate?
2. In what way is Anderson attempting to use a political tactic to get Dean to send his staff to the quality-improvement training program?
3. What type of authority and power should Anderson have used to obtain compliance from Dean (and presumably other managers)?

REFERENCES

1. Timothy R. Hinkin and Chester A. Schriesheim, "Power and Influence: The View from Below," *Personnel* (May 1988): 47–50. The original formulation is from John R. P. French and Bertram Raven, "The Basis of Social Power," in Darwin Cartwright and Alvin Zander, eds., *Group Dynamics: Research and Theory* (Evanston, IL: Row, Peterson and Company, 1962): 607–623.

2. Jenny C. McCune, "Persistence Pays Off," *Success* (November 1990): 25.

3. Jane A. Halpert, "The Dimensionality of Charisma," *Journal of Business and Psychology* (Summer 1990): 399–410.

4. Jeffrey Pfeffer, *Managing with Power* (Boston: Harvard Business School Publications, 1990).

5. "Welcome to the Nineties, Donald," *Business Week* (May 14, 1990): 119.

6. Jeffrey Pfeffer, *Power in Organizations*, (Marshfield, MA: Pitman Publishing, 1981): 115–116.

7. Barbara Gray and Sonny R. Ariss, "Politics and Strategic Change Across Organizational Life Cycles," *Academy of Management Review* (October 1985): 707.

8. Andrew J. DuBrin, "Career Maturity, Organizational Rank, and Political Behavior Tendencies: A Correlational Analysis of Organizational Politics and Career Experience," *Psychological Reports* (1988): 531–537; DuBrin, "Sex Differences in Endorsement of Influence Tactics and Political Behavior Tendencies," *Journal of Business and Psychology* (Fall 1989): 3–14.

9. Fred Luthans, "Successful vs. Effective Real Managers," *Academy of Management Executive* (May 1988): 127–132.

10. David C. McClelland, *Power: The Inner Experience* (New York: John Wiley & Sons, 1976): 258.

11. Gerald Biberman, "Personality and Characteristic Work Attitudes of Persons with High, Moderate, and Low Political Tendencies," *Psychological Reports* (1985): 1303–1310.

12. Barbara Woller, "Giving Workers a Voice Improves Production, Says Work Institute," Gannett News Service (September 12, 1990).

13. Jay A. Conger and Rabindra N. Kanungo, "The Empowerment Process: Integrating Theory and Practice," *Academy of Management Review* (July 1988): 473–474; Kenneth W. Thomas and Betty A. Velthouse, "Cognitive Elements of Empowerment: An 'Interpretive' Model of Intrinsic Task Motivation," *The Academy of Management Review* (October 1990): 666–681.

14. Wolf J. Rinke, "Empowering Your Team Members," *Supervisory Management* (April 1989): 24.

Chapter 9

Delegation and Decentralization of Authority

OPENING
CASE

The Girl Scouts'
Super Executive,

Several years ago, Frances Hesselbein retired as the executive director of the Girl Scouts of America. Her accomplishments have become legendary. Before she took over, Girl Scout membership had declined for eight consecutive years, but Hesselbein turned the organization into an efficient, innovative, customer-driven enterprise. By rejuvenating an institution that was in danger of losing its relevance to modern society, Hesselbein has become a key figure in management. Managers in other companies study videotapes that showcase Hesselbein and her ideas.

Business students at Harvard have also been exposed to her thinking through case histories and personal appearances. A faculty member noted that "Frances displays a clarity of purpose and a management strategy and direction that very few for-profit CEOs visiting this campus have shown."

Hesselbein sharpened the Girl Scouts' focus by installing a common planning system for 350 independently run regional councils. Each council plotted new goals and initiatives. Hesselbein modified the top-down management system when she dealt with such contemporary issues as teen pregnancy, drug use, and child abuse. She developed a series of monographs on each controversial topic that gave latitude to the autonomous councils to decide what to do. Another cornerstone of her management style was to encourage field workers in the regional councils to try new ideas, and she cleared the way for ideas and change to move upward.

Source: As reported in John A. Byrne, "Profiting from the Nonprofits," *Business Week* (March 26, 1990): 66–74. :

Hesselbein believes that granting field units the authority to make decisions helps solve important problems. Successful collective effort depends on **delegation**—the shifting of authority from superior to subordinate. Organization growth and success cannot be achieved without delegation or decentralization. **Decentralization** is the extent to which executives delegate authority to lower organizational units.

This chapter discusses the nature of delegation of authority and its behavioral aspects. In the "more work, fewer people" environment of today, delegation is important for managers.[1] We emphasize decentralization of authority because of its contemporary relevance and examine it in terms of its advantages and disadvantages. Contingency factors for decentralization and delegation of authority are considered later in the chapter, as well as the role of teamwork in delegation and decentralization.

DELEGATION OF AUTHORITY

Delegation of authority is a process of transferring authority from superior to subordinate. Figure 9-1 presents a broad overview of what a manager must do in order to delegate authority successfully. The figure is also an outline of our discussion of delegation.

The Process of Delegation

Delegation of authority proceeds in three steps: assigning tasks to be performed, granting authority, and creating an obligation. For delegation to be

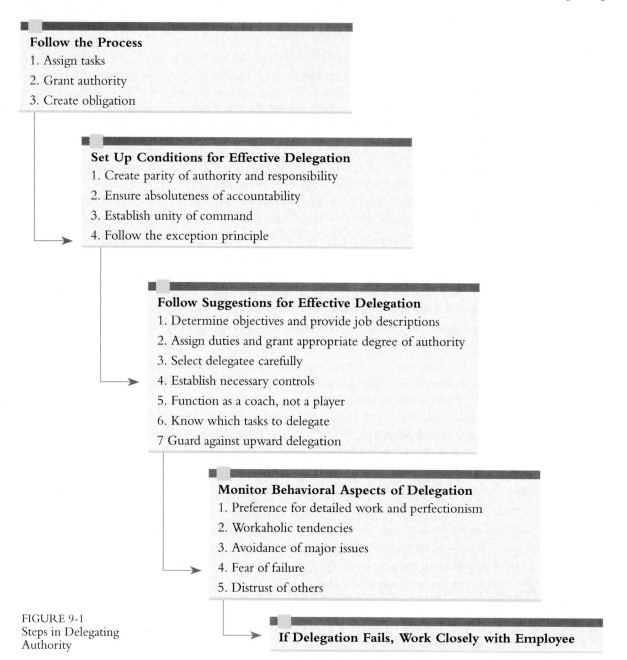

Follow the Process
1. Assign tasks
2. Grant authority
3. Create obligation

Set Up Conditions for Effective Delegation
1. Create parity of authority and responsibility
2. Ensure absoluteness of accountability
3. Establish unity of command
4. Follow the exception principle

Follow Suggestions for Effective Delegation
1. Determine objectives and provide job descriptions
2. Assign duties and grant appropriate degree of authority
3. Select delegatee carefully
4. Establish necessary controls
5. Function as a coach, not a player
6. Know which tasks to delegate
7 Guard against upward delegation

Monitor Behavioral Aspects of Delegation
1. Preference for detailed work and perfectionism
2. Workaholic tendencies
3. Avoidance of major issues
4. Fear of failure
5. Distrust of others

If Delegation Fails, Work Closely with Employee

FIGURE 9-1
Steps in Delegating
Authority

successful, all three of these steps must take place. Delegation is therefore sometimes referred to as a three-legged stool. If a manager does not clarify even one of these elements, delegation may fail.

ASSIGNING TASKS OR DUTIES. Employees may be assigned tasks, or duties, in two ways. First, the tasks can be described in terms of activities consistent with the employee's job description and position title. For example, a manager assigned to analyze a competitive product might be told to conduct a focus group of people using the product in question. Second, tasks can be described in terms of the results the manager intends to achieve. In this case, the manager would have been told to present an analysis of the strengths and weaknesses of the product.

Whether the assignment of tasks is by activities or results, managers must communicate their expectations clearly and subordinates must listen carefully. Managers can give competent and responsible employees fairly general guidelines about what needs to be accomplished, but less competent and responsible employees need more specific guidelines. While the latter approach does not leave much room for initiative, it does increase the probability that an employee will accomplish the task successfully.

It is also important for managers not to "dump assignments"—hand them over to team members at the last moment and without much explanation. An example of this would be a manager saying, "Terry, I forgot until just now about a meeting I was supposed to attend this afternoon. You attend, and tell me what happens."[2]

ETHICS QUESTION
What are the ethical issues involved in granting a team member the responsibility to accomplish a task but not granting sufficient authority?

GRANTING AUTHORITY. The person to whom the task is delegated should also receive the authority to act for the delegator. In the illustration discussed previously, the manager had the authority to allocate funds for conducting the focus groups. Without such authority, the manager could not complete the task. The delegator must be in the position to grant authority to others.

Research conducted with 44 managers and 198 claims adjusters offers some insights into the question of when a manager is most likely to delegate authority. Delegation took place most often when (1) the manager perceived the subordinate to be capable, responsible, and trustworthy; (2) the manager faced a heavy workload; and (3) the manager faced a decision of less than major consequence. In other words, the supervisor delegated less when faced with a major decision.[3]

When assigning a task, the manager must communicate clearly and the employee must listen carefully.

CREATING RESPONSIBILITY. When an employee accepts a task and the authority necessary to carry out the task, he or she incurs an obligation. **Responsibility** is the obligation to perform the assigned work and to use the granted authority properly. The person who accepts responsibility must provide tangible evidence that the task was accomplished.

Conditions for Effective Delegation

Although the delegation process appears straightforward, it is not easy to delegate effectively. Several classical principles of delegation are still relevant today. The conditions under which delegation is likely to be effective—parity of authority and responsibility, absoluteness of accountability, unity of command, and the exception principle—are discussed in the following sections.

PARITY OF AUTHORITY AND RESPONSIBILITY. For delegation to be effective, the authority granted to a person must be sufficient to carry out the assigned responsibility. This condition is referred to as **parity of authority and responsibility.** When managers have too little authority, they have to consult their superiors before making even minor decisions. For example, the grounds manager at a hospital was delegated the responsibility of purchasing a new riding mower. He found the appropriate mower at a favorable price but could not complete the purchase until his supervisor approved the brand. Note that the grounds manager had not exceeded his approved level of expenditure, but he still could not act independently. The grounds manager's situation is not unusual. In practice, the principle of parity of authority and responsibility is violated frequently, and managers are expected to accomplish objectives without enough support from the firm. Budget limitations often create this problem. For example, one college assigned the placement director the responsibility of developing new sources of job leads for students but did not give her sufficient funds to travel to employers.

ABSOLUTENESS OF ACCOUNTABILITY. While a manager might assign duties and grant authority to subordinates, accountability to the manager's superior can neither be transferred nor delegated. Each person who delegates or redelegates is accountable to an immediate superior for the results. This is known as **absoluteness of accountability.** Assume, for instance, that a benefits manager has delegated to a benefits specialist the task of sending out a mailing about a change in the retirement plan. If the assistant fails to get the mailing out, the benefits manager is responsible for the error. The manager is also accountable to his or her superior for not getting the assignment completed on time.

UNITY OF COMMAND. A classic management principle, **unity of command,** states that each subordinate receives assigned duties and delegated authority from one superior only and is accountable only to that superior.

Projects, task forces, and matrix organizations are examples of successful violations of the unity of command principle. Unity of command does not exist in these structures because each project, task force, or matrix member has two superiors: the project or task force leader and the functional manager. Furthermore, some employees belong to several projects or task forces simultaneously. One reason these violations of unity of command are often successful is because modern managers have learned to accept dual reporting relationships as inevitable.

THE EXCEPTION PRINCIPLE. Another condition for effective delegation is the **exception principle.** Under this principle, the manager gets involved in the details of a group member's work only when a problem exists. After delegating a task, the manager does not get involved unless it appears that the task will not be accomplished on time. For example, noting that a delegated assignment is way behind schedule, a manager might discover that several of the people involved have given the assignment low priority. The manager might then schedule a meeting with these employees to try and resolve the problem.

Suggestions for Successful Delegation

In this section, we offer practical suggestions for successful delegation. Following them will enable a person to apply the conditions for effective delegation. Ideally, all of these suggestions should be met, but in reality, not all of them can be followed in all circumstances.

DETERMINE OBJECTIVES AND PROVIDE JOB DESCRIPTIONS. Before delegating authority, managers must determine objectives, understand them, and state them clearly. As a first step, it is necessary to determine the objectives expected to be accomplished as the result of a specific work assignment. For instance, a manager might say to a group member, "Once you have removed the toxins from the work area, we should be able to pass government health regulations."

Job descriptions are closely related to objectives, and they are powerful devices for aiding delegation. Those which specify recurring responsibilities reduce the manager's need to constantly communicate delegated assignments. A manager can handle wider spans of control when job descriptions decrease the need to haggle over delegated responsibilities.

ASSIGN RESPONSIBILITY AND DELEGATE PROPER AUTHORITY. Managers must determine all the duties that must be performed to complete the task at hand and then assign the whole job or a meaningful portion of it. Managers sometimes assign only the minor or routine details of a job and retain the key aspects for themselves—a very limited form of delegation.

Defining the whole job at the start of a project helps to establish the degree of authority needed to ensure parity of responsibility and authority.

Also, employee motivation is likely to increase when assignments encompass the entire job, because such responsibility creates job enrichment.

ETHICS QUESTION
How ethical is it for a manager to delegate responsibility to an unprepared team member and then reprimand him or her for not properly carrying out the assignment?

SELECT THE DELEGATEE CAREFULLY. Select the **delegatee**—the person to carry out the delegated assignment—in light of what is expected. Certain skills and knowledge are required to complete the delegated assignment successfully. The best candidate for the assignment is the person who is willing to accept full responsibility for the results.

ESTABLISH THE NECESSARY CONTROLS. Delegating authority does not mean abdicating responsibility. Instead, the delegator retains the right to recall delegated authority and remains responsible for tasks assigned to others. The delegator must therefore establish and exercise control (or use checkpoints) to make sure that obligations are met. For proper control, the manager must have clear channels of communication with employees to allow for full exchange of information. Controls also imply that corrective action will be taken if needed.

RECOGNIZE THAT THE MANAGER IS A COACH, NOT A PLAYER. To delegate successfully, managers must understand their true role. They must derive more satisfaction from coaching than from playing. Many people are promoted to managerial positions partially because they have good technical skills. To be an effective manager, however, the former technician must now derive satisfaction from watching other people perform delegated technical tasks. Moreover, according to the Fair Labor Standards Act, a manager must spend at least 50 percent of the time managing. As one management writer observed, "The future of our firms rests on the ability of managers to get work done through others—in short, to delegate successfully."[4]

KNOW WHICH TASKS TO DELEGATE. Managers should exercise discretion in delegating important work assignments. For example, it is unwise to delegate tasks that involve confidential information.[5] Suppose an employee were receiving treatment for a drug-abuse problem. It would be ill-advised to delegate to a co-worker the task of checking on this troubled employee. Matters involving department budgets or human resources problems ordinarily should not be delegated. Problems calling for the unique technical expertise of the manager should also be handled by the manager.

Laws such as the Federal Privacy Act and the Federal Freedom of Information Act also influence which tasks can be delegated. These laws restrict employees from handling confidential information about co-workers. In addition, most firms restrict a husband and wife from reporting to each other. Because the loyalty partners feel toward their spouses may be greater than their loyalty to the company, a manager cannot delegate to a spouse tasks involving confidential information.

It is crucial for managers to delegate some challenging and interesting tasks as well as the more routine ones. A manager who does otherwise runs the risk of being accused of delegating only "dirty work."

Guarding Against Upward Delegation

ETHICS QUESTION
Is a subordinate who engages in upward delegation behaving in an ethical and responsible manner?

Subordinates sometimes add to their manager's workload through **upward delegation,** the process of assigning part of one's job to a superior. Upward delegation is not simply asking the supervisor to do something that is part of his or her job, such as recommending a person for a special assignment. It most often occurs when an employee asks a manager for assistance in solving a problem. The manager then takes ownership of the problem and goes into great detail about how to solve it.[6]

The general antidote to upward delegation is to encourage subordinates to solve their own problems. At the same time, managers must assure them that they will not be penalized for making an occasional mistake.[7]

Back to the Opening Case

We can infer from Frances Hesselbein's accomplishments that she is able to delegate comfortably. A cornerstone of her management style as executive director of the Girl Scouts was to encourage field workers to try new ideas. To accomplish this, Hesselbein delegated assignments that required innovation.

Behavioral Aspects of Delegation

The major problems in delegation stem from the personality of the delegator. Managers who are poor delegators are reluctant to delegate for a number of different reasons that are linked closely to the personal characteristics and traits described in the next few pages.

PREFERENCE FOR DETAILED WORK AND PERFECTIONISM. Some types of occupational training may reinforce the personality traits of concern for detail and perfectionism. Examples include training in the fields of accounting, computer science, and engineering. All three of these fields require meticulous attention to detail because even one error can lead to a serious problem. When individuals with a preference for details are promoted to managerial positions, they often get involved in more details than the job requires. The tendency of these managers to enjoy detailed work may prevent them from delegating because they prefer to keep for themselves problems involving details.

When a passion for details evolves into perfectionism, delegation is further hampered. Perfectionists are uncomfortable with delegation because it takes out of their hands control over how the job is carried out. A human relations consultant observed, "As managers, perfectionists are often terrible decision-makers who constantly second-guess themselves and everyone else. They keep changing their minds, reviewing, revising, revamping."[8]

Although a bias for detail may hamper delegation, many effective executives are familiar with technical and operating details. As Thomas Peters concluded about effective leaders in all types of organizations:

"These leaders seem to know, indeed revel in knowing, every detail of their operation. Their only mischievous tendency is one-upping subordinates with their knowledge of detail. The less effective leaders espouse a 'big picture' view, and literally pride themselves in not knowing the details of a new system or piece of equipment."[9]

Although Peters is prone to exaggeration and dramatization, his major point is a good one. Effective executives are often conversant with many important technical details of their operations.

WORKAHOLISM. **Workaholism** is an addiction to work. To a workaholic, work is a source of pleasure, while nonwork activities such as family life and recreation are a source of discomfort. Nevertheless, workaholics are not all miserable, driven souls trapped in a vicious cycle of achievement and begetting more work until they drop from exhaustion. Many people at the top of their fields are workaholics, and so are many successful people moving ahead. Workaholics are more likely to be successful in fields such as financial deal-making and entrepreneurship than as traditional managers.

Many workaholics are doing exactly what they love—work—and they cannot seem to get enough of it. They are intense, energetic, competitive, and driven. For the workaholic, each day begins with a burst of enthusiasm, because she or he can accomplish more work.[10]

ETHICS QUESTION
What ethical issues might be involved in encouraging workaholics to work as much as they would like?

Despite the success of many workaholics, some of them are poor managers who set a poor example for others who want to get ahead and be team players. Workaholics are often notoriously poor delegators. A workaholic manager would be more likely to take home an extra chore than to delegate it to a subordinate. Also, workaholic managers are often unwilling to delegate work because of their belief that they can do it better than anyone else.[11]

AVOIDANCE OF MAJOR ISSUES. Attention to detail sometimes offers a degree of security and comfort that is not possible when one's attention is directed toward the major problem at hand. Crucial problems produce anxiety. For example, a marketing manager might personally review each sales representative's expense report and then tally the amount spent on telephone calls in order to avoid the real problem of increasing the number of new customers. Managers who preoccupy themselves with busywork are performing work that should be delegated.

FEAR OF FAILURE. Delegation also may be limited by a fear of failure that stems from personal insecurity. For some, the fear may be real and imminent. They may realize that one more mistake can cost them their job or a promotion. For others, even though failure may not be near, there is the constant fear of what might happen if they did fail. Whether failure is imminent or imagined, managers like this delegate only sparingly. They worry that if anyone else were given the assignment it would be handled poorly.

DISTRUST OF OTHERS. A fifth reason for not delegating authority may be the result of a false distrust of the motives of others. **False distrust** refers to a manager's erroneous belief that subordinates are trying to displace or discredit him or her. The manager may refuse to delegate authority to team members as a means of countering their supposed threat. As a result, collective effort is weakened.

Consequences of Ineffective Delegation

Whatever the reason for ineffective delegation, the results are similar. A manager who refuses to delegate and let subordinates carry projects through to their normal completion sacrifices valuable training experiences. At the extreme, team members will never develop their expertise because the opportunity to learn through experience is denied them. Moreover, valuable expertise is wasted as the manager tries to take over too much work that should be done by others.

Refusal to delegate also has the effect of stifling initiative, suggestions, and new ideas. The team member wonders, "Why should I say anything? I'm not allowed to do anything important around here anyway." A manager's refusal to delegate may cause employees who are eager to develop and accept more responsibility to leave the firm because their needs for accomplishment and achievement are frustrated.

Handling the Problems of Failed Delegation

Assume that a manager has followed the suggestions for delegation as presented so far, yet the team member is still having problems getting the assignment completed. The worst thing the manager can do is take the assignment away. The most productive action is to work with the employee until she or he learns how to perform the delegated task properly. Taking over the job denies team members the opportunity to straighten things out and redeem themselves. A business professor has offered the following specific suggestions for handling failed delegation:[12]

1. *Speak to the employee before taking action.* Have a private meeting with the worker to review performance standards and explain why the delegated work is not acceptable. Be specific about what aspects of the work are unacceptable. Ask for employee suggestions for correcting the problem, and offer assistance of your own.
2. *Get closure on the conference.* End the meeting with a clear understanding of which parts of the delegated work will be retained by the employee and which might be taken back. Agree on performance standards and timetables for progress reviews.
3. *Monitor performance and offer praise as warranted.* Performance problems of any type require frequent review. Give praise for improvement and sterner warnings for continued poor, or worse, performance. (See Chapter 14 for more details.)
4. *Delegate additional parts of the job as performance improves.* Any tasks taken back in step one can be redelegated if the team member performs better. A piecemeal reassignment may work the best, so the employee can integrate tasks back into the job gradually.

When an employee's performance is unsatisfactory, the manager should hold a private meeting with that employee to explain why the work is unacceptable and offer advice and assistance.

LEARNING CHECK

Describe the process of delegation, including the steps in the process, how to be an effective delegator, and the personal characteristics of a manager that can hamper effective delegation.

DECENTRALIZATION OF AUTHORITY

Delegation transfers authority from superior to subordinate, while decentralization is the extent to which authority is delegated to organizational units.[13] Decentralization is a relative concept, at the opposite end of the continuum from centralization. A firm is never either completely centralized or completely decentralized. Complete centralization of authority would require one person to make all the decisions, while with complete decentralization there would be no central authority. In either extreme, there is no organization.

An example of a highly centralized firm is Domino's Pizza. The company headquarters makes all the major decisions about matters such as menu, quality, decor, and policy regarding speed of delivery. An example of a highly decentralized firm is Laura Ashley, a worldwide chain of British stores with quaint storefronts that features women's wear and fabrics. Laura Ashley, the founder, grants her store operators considerable leeway in merchandising.

Decentralization must not be confused with departmentalization or geographic dispersion. Departmentalization is the grouping of work and people into manageable units. However, the mere creation of separate departmental units does not constitute decentralization. The vice president of marketing who appoints five marketing managers, each in charge of a different product, is further departmentalizing the marketing function along product lines. However, the marketing function has not necessarily been decentralized, because the new marketing managers may not have been granted additional decision-making authority.

The division of one large insurance claims processing unit into six widely separated smaller units illustrates geographic dispersion (or geographic decentralization), yet the units may not be decentralized. However, if the claims managers can now make more decisions on their own, the claims function has been decentralized. Figure 9-2 outlines important differences between decentralization of authority and decentralization by geography.

The degree of decentralization is described by four characteristics of decisions made at lower organization levels, as illustrated in Figure 9-3.[14]

The greater the frequency of important decisions made at lower levels of a firm the greater the degree of decentralization in that company. In contrast, most important decisions in centralized firms are made by a small group of centralized administrators.

Significance is measured in terms of the impact of a decision on the welfare of the firm. The greater the significance of decisions made at lower levels, the more decentralized the firm is. A highly significant decision made by a **field unit** (a segment of the firm located away from headquarters) would be for that unit to acquire a company on its own. Similarly, the broader the scope of decisions made at lower levels of a firm, the greater the degree of decentralization. The breadth of decision making is determined by the number of functions affected by a decision. Thus, in one store a manager might make only decisions that directly affect merchandise displays, whereas in a more decentralized situation managers would do much of their own buying.

FIGURE 9-2
Decentralization by
Authority and
Geography

By Geography	By Control	Number of Locations	Number of Headquarters
Centralized	Centralization =	One	One
Decentralized	Centralization =	Many	One
Centralized	Decentralization =	One	Many
Decentralizad	Decentralization =	Many	Many

FIGURE 9-3
Contrast Between
Centralized and
Decentralized Firms

	Centralized Firm	Decentralized Firm
Frequency of decisions at lower levels	Few	Many
Significance and breadth of decisions at lower levels	Minor	Major
Extent of control of decisions at lower levels	Major	Minor
Approval of decisions after they are made	Rare	Frequent

The extent of control over the decisions made at lower levels of a firm is an important measure of the degree of decentralization. For example, decisions are frequently classified in terms of dollars involved, with dollar limitations placed on decisions that may be made without prior approval. A firm that permits a regional sales manager to approve customer credit up to $10,000 is much more decentralized, other things being equal, than one that permits the sales manager to approve only $2,000 credit.

More centralization exists when approval is required before a decision is made, and more decentralization exists when a superior is notified after the decision is made. When a higher authority is not even informed, decentralization is even greater. The number of approvals required before a manager can finalize a decision is also an index of the degree of decentralization. Generally, the fewer the number of people who must be contacted for approval, the greater the degree of decentralization.

The question of whether to move an organization further toward or away from centralization is a major issue facing top-level managers. The Organization in Action illustrates how top-level managers in one firm thought decentralization might improve business results.

ORGANIZATION IN ACTION

Compaq Computer Corp. faced growing competition, poor sales, and a $70 million loss in one quarter. Part of its top-level management's comeback plan was to expand distribution, cut prices, and lay off 12 percent of the company's 12,000 workers. Even more revolutionary was the idea of splitting the company into two decentralized units. One unit would develop and market large computer systems such as network servers, and the other would handle mainstream PCs.

Prior to this move, Compaq had been heavily centralized and divided into functions such as marketing, manufacturing, and development. A consensus-style procedure for decision making was in operation that tended to be too slow for the rapidly changing computer market. The new, decentralized structure has smaller, separate units with their own engineering and marketing departments. Since each business has its own cost structure, the price of a low-end personal computer will not have to contribute toward research funds for expensive computer systems.

Source: Facts as reported in Mark Ivey, "Can Rod Canion Stop Compaq's Erosion?" *Business Week* (November 4, 1991): 134, 136.

THE CENTRALIZATION-VERSUS-DECENTRALIZATION ISSUE

Any firm with multiple locations or multiple layers of management faces the issue of how much to centralize or decentralize. This issue can often be resolved by examining the advantages of both centralization and decentralization and then deciding which is the most relevant in a given situation. The advantages are summarized here, and the disadvantages of each can be inferred from the advantages of the other. For instance, one advantage of centralization is that it decreases duplication of effort. Therefore a corresponding disadvantage of decentralization is that it increases duplication of effort.

Advantages of Centralization

The arguments for centralization center on the following five important advantages.

1. *Top-level managers have greater control over the enterprise.* The issue of control sums up the major argument for centralization.[15] Centralization makes it possible for top-level managers to know precisely what is going on at all times, especially in this era of computerized controls. An effective computer network can encourage more decentralization of branches and at more remote locations while at the same time maintaining centralized control due to improved information flow. Several of the other advantages of centralization are variations of the theme of better control.

2. *There is strong leadership at the top.* If relatively few highly capable and competent top-level managers are available, centralization allows the firm to make the best use of them. Also, highly competent executives often prefer the power and responsibility associated with a headquarters position.

3. *Decisions are more consistent.* Because major decisions are made at the top, employees, clients, and customers will receive similar handling when faced with similar issues. Many arguments are prevented by such centralization of policy. When a decision is made centrally, the policy stemming from that decision often leads to consistent handling of problems. Assume, for example, that the company decides to implement a total quality management (TQM) program. Many decisions made at lower levels will now be oriented toward enhancing customer satisfaction. (See Chapters 17 and 22 for more details.)

4. *A balanced perspective is maintained.* Top-level managers at company headquarters are able to view the objectives of the subunits in relation to the strategic objectives of the firm as a whole. This perspective often leads to better decisions in terms of the long-range interests of the firm.

5. *Duplication and overlap are minimized.* Duplication of equipment and other resources is costly. Many firms prefer to staff a large, centralized computer facility and let the field units share the hardware and software. The alternative would be to purchase a large number of smaller computers and ancillary equipment. Similarly, purchasing is often centralized in order to economize by making bulk purchases at a discount.

Advantages of Decentralization

The arguments for decentralization also center around five major points, as follows:

1. *Decentralization fits in with the spirit of the times.* A dominant theme today is less tolerance for hierarchy and more power, autonomy, and entrepreneurial spirit at lower organizational levels. Decentralization is therefore appropriate for the times. Among the reasons for this are an increasingly competitive climate for business and a need to penetrate global markets. With decentralization, more key decisions are made by managers who have greater knowledge of the customer. A need also exists for more involvement of employees at all levels. Employees want to feel responsible for and involved with what they are doing.[16]

2. *Decisions can be made more rapidly.* The people closest to a problem generally have better information about the problem and valid ideas for taking care of it. Therefore, it makes sense for the manager at the decentralized location to make the decision without having to first check with a higher-ranking official.

3. *Professional managers can be developed.* Handling responsibility is the primary method for improving managerial skills, and a decentralized operation grants lower-ranking managers considerable responsibility. When the vast majority of critical decisions are made at the top of a firm, managers in field units get little training in handling significant responsibility. An official from a research and advisory firm noted that "in the upper echelons [executive suite] the opportunities are really exciting. While before each company had only one CEO, in a decentralized company there's a chance for 50 or even more people to be CEOs of their own, smaller businesses. It leads to a lot more innovation."[17]

4. *Employee identification can be created.* Most decentralized firms create field units that are small enough for employees to understand and identify with. This accounts for the high job satisfaction frequently found among branch managers. One branch manager put it this way: "In Duluth, Minnesota, we are Mutual of Omaha."

5. *Corporate cultures can be melded.* When one firm acquires another firm, the two corporate cultures may clash, resulting in low morale and low productivity. It has been estimated that three-fourths of all mergers fail to meet financial expectations. The human side of buying and selling companies, especially when the culture fit is poor, is a leading factor behind so many failures. However, if the acquired firm is granted autonomy, the two corporate cultures can co-exist in harmony. Several Japanese banks have used this approach in recent years in their acquisition of American and Canadian banks.[18]

LEARNING CHECK   Describe what decentralization is and is not, and list the advantages of centralization and decentralization.

CONTINGENCY FACTORS IN DELEGATION AND DECENTRALIZATION

Contingency factors influence the extent to which a firm should be decentralized or authority delegated. Not every one of these factors need be analyzed in every decision about decentralization or delegation, but they are all of potential importance in some situations. Each of the contingency factors described next is related to issues of both delegation of authority and centralization versus decentralization.

Size of Organization

Delegation of authority is imperative in large companies. Decentralization of decision making to managers of lower-level subunits is also characteristic of large firms since some decentralization must take place in order for a firm to expand. As a firm reaches a certain size, a high degree of centralization becomes too cumbersome, and so many layers of management may have been created that selective pruning is necessary.

Characteristics of Delegatees and Delegators

The capabilities, talents, and motivations of the manager and employees influence the feasibility of delegation and decentralization. As the president of a candy company said, "With a team like mine, I can leave for a week and everything is handled properly." Large-scale decentralization depends on having employees who are capable of assuming responsibility and who have the appropriate technical skills.

Geographic Dispersion of Subunits

The greater the degree of geographic dispersion, the more essential it is for both decentralization and delegation to be practiced extensively. The underlying reason is that as a firm's units become more dispersed geographically, it becomes more difficult for central office staff to understand local conditions. For example, strict adherence to a 45-minute lunch break for managers would be almost impossible to implement in most large cities.

Level of Technology

As tasks become more complex and dependent on advanced technology, it becomes increasingly important to grant more authority to technical experts. Typically the people in the decentralized units (such as a research laboratory) have more technical knowledge than do centralized administrators. Furthermore, among professional employees, the subordinate often possesses the more advanced technical knowledge. It is therefore necessary and prudent for the superior to delegate authority over technical matters.

Time Frame of the Decision

When decisions have to be made quickly, subordinates should have the authority to make those decisions. Similarly, when decisions have to be made rapidly by subunits of a firm, those subunits should have considerable deci-sion-making authority. Bringing a tentative decision back to headquarters for approval could create a delay that would result in a missed opportunity. (This issue can also be approached from another perspective: The most managerial time is saved when managers make decisions without consulting anybody else.)

Significance of the Decision

A standard criterion for deciding whether or not to delegate is the signifi-cance of the decision as expressed in terms of money or impact on the firm. A decision regarding a $10 million building expansion is less likely to be delegated than a decision to purchase new furniture for one office. The sig-nificance criterion also applies to centralization versus decentralization. Major strategic decisions such as those relating to mergers and acquisitions are almost always made at the highest centers of authority.

Subordinate Acceptance of the Decision

When employee acceptance of a decision is critical, delegation and decen-tralization are strongly indicated. This is especially true when employees play an important role in implementing the decision. A negative example of this would be local credit managers who are handed new credit procedures from above. If the local managers believe the new credit procedures are un-workable, they will tend to avoid implementing them.

Degree of Conformity and Coordination Required

When work flow requires the coordination and integration of a large num-ber of subunits, centralized decision making becomes more important. An example would be following safety procedures in the manufacture of phar-maceuticals. A central planning and control unit would be best equipped to handle this requirement. In more independent tasks such as selling, there is less need for centralization.

INTEGRATING TEAMWORK WITH CENTRALIZATION AND DECENTRALIZATION

Conventional approaches to organization design focus on the issues of cen-tralization versus decentralization. Explicit thought is rarely given to how teamwork or cooperation can also be built into the structure. A new con-cept developed by management consultant Robert W. Keidel addresses this problem. The **organization design triangle** is an organization struc-ture that includes cooperation (or teamwork) as well as centralization and decentralization.[19] Figure 9-4 illustrates this structure.

A triangular design includes both centralization and decentralization. In addition, teamwork is built into the design. Thus, organization is a function of three variables: autonomy (decentralization), control (centralization), and cooperation (teamwork). Conventional organizational structures do not include mechanisms for cooperation.

The organization design triangle has important implications both for designing organizations and for balancing centralization versus decentralization. One implication is that every organization, and every organizational unit, must blend the three factors of autonomy, control, and cooperation. A major reason why no two organizations are identical is that each one is a different blend of these three factors. Sales and research and development (R&D) groups favor autonomy because they rely on individual effort. These groups would therefore favor a decentralized structure. Operations and process engineering have historically favored control because of their need for uniform procedures. They have therefore tended toward a centralized structure.

A second important implication of the organization design triangle is that autonomy, control, and cooperation represent trade-offs. This is because the factors are somewhat mutually exclusive. For example, if you want people to act independently (autonomy), they are not likely to engage in much cooperation (teamwork). Businesses must assign priorities in order to balance these trade-offs. If a firm wants its field units to be autonomous, it

ETHICS QUESTION
How ethical is it to centralize operations in order to exert greater control over employees?

FIGURE 9-4
The Organizational
Design Triangle

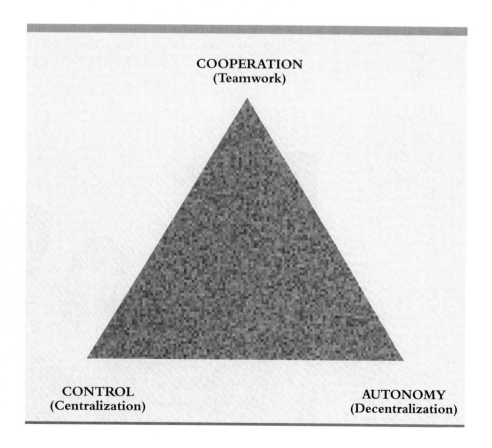

must sacrifice some control. The trade-off of autonomy versus control also helps explain the field-versus-headquarters dilemma. Field representatives are in touch with local customers, but they lack the "big picture" perspective of headquarters staff. If a high degree of teamwork is desired, the firm cannot grant too much autonomy. This is because people who pursue their own interests are not very good team players. They are more concerned about their own than group accomplishments.

Firms can balance cooperation, control, and autonomy. In fact, some companies achieve a near-symmetrical balance between two of the three design variables. The most familiar example is the large, divisionalized corporation. In it, the advantages of decentralization (through divisional autonomy) are blended with those of centralization (through corporate policy setting). Teamwork is also achieved because employees identify with field units and pursue corporate objectives.

Work teams (as described in Chapter 7) blend control and cooperation. In a work team, top-down control is maintained, but it is melded with high levels of cooperation within the units. Work teams are also characterized by good cooperation among various units. For example, a team leader might work directly with the human resources department to obtain assistance in recruiting and training.

Back to the
Opening Case

To revitalize the Girls Scouts of America, Frances Hesselbein carefully blended centralization, decentralization, and cooperation. A common planning system was installed (centralization), but the 350 autonomous councils plotted their own goals. Under Hesselbein's leadership, a spirit of teamwork pervaded the Girl Scout organization.

Work teams blend two variables of the organization design triangle: cooperation and control.

SUMMARY

Delegation of authority permits the transfer of authority from superior to subordinate. Without delegation an organization cannot grow. Delegation proceeds in three steps: assignment of tasks, granting of authority, and creation of an obligation. Four conditions must be met for the process of delegation to be effective: (1) authority must be commensurate with responsibility; (2) accountability must be absolute (cannot be transferred); (3) unity of command must exist; and (4) the exception principle must be practiced.

Delegation can be improved by following these suggestions: (1) determine objectives and provide job descriptions; (2) assign duties and grant commensurate authority; (3) select the delegatee carefully; (4) establish necessary controls; (5) recognize that the manager is a coach and not a player; (6) know which tasks to delegate; and (7) guard against upward delegation.

The major problems in delegation often result from the personality traits and behaviors of the delegator. Among these are a delegator's preference for detailed work, workaholism, avoidance of major issues, fear of failure, and distrust of others. The consequences of limited delegation include the sacrifice of valuable training experience and the curtailment of suggestions and new ideas.

Decentralization is the delegation of decision-making authority to managers of lower-ranking organizational units. Another type of decentralization is geographic dispersion. The degree of decentralization depends on four factors: frequency of decisions, breadth of the decisions, the control exerted over the decisions, and whether approval precedes or follows decisions.

Centralization and decentralization both have advantages and disadvantages. The key advantage of centralization is improved control, while decentralization leads to employee autonomy and empowerment.

The choice of a movement toward or away from centralization depends on a wide range of contingency factors. When a firm reaches a certain size, a high degree of centralization becomes cumbersome. Centralization is favored if top-level managers are highly competent and experienced and lower-level managers are less competent and experienced. Extensive decentralization and delegation are essential when subunits are widely dispersed.

As tasks become more complex and dependent on advanced technology, delegation of authority to technical experts is necessary. When decisions must be made quickly, subordinates and subunits should have the authority to make those decisions. The significance of a decision in terms of money or impact on the firm is a standard criterion for determining whether or not to delegate or to decentralize or centralize. When acceptance of the decision is critical, delegation and decentralization are strongly indicated. When the work flow requires the coordination and integration of a large number of subunits, centralized decision making becomes more important.

Conventional approaches to organization design focus on the issues of centralization versus decentralization. In contrast, the organization design triangle is a structure that includes cooperation as well as centralization and decentralization. The triangle implies that every firm must blend autonomy, control, and cooperation. However, the three factors represent trade-offs. For example, the greater the control, the less the autonomy.

KEY TERMS

delegation	responsibility	exception principle	false distrust
decentralization	absoluteness of account-	delegatee	field unit
responsibility	ability	upward delegation	organization design tri-
parity of authority and	unity of command	workaholism	angle

QUESTIONS FOR DISCUSSION AND REVIEW

1. Describe the delegation process. Explain why you think you would or would not be an effective delegator.
2. Under what circumstances is delegation likely to be effective?
3. Think about your present manager or the last person you worked for in any capacity. Is (or was) that person an effective delegator? Support your conclusion.
4. What impact does a "mean and lean" operating philosophy have on delegation?
5. Identify and explain four behavioral aspects of delegation.
6. Would you hire a known workaholic for a key position within your firm? Why or why not?
7. Identify several ways in which a manager's job in a decentralized firm is different from a manager's job in a centralized firm.
8. State three advantages of centralization and decentralization.
9. Visualize a major automobile dealership that you have visited. To what extent do you think dealerships are decentralized organization subunits? Explain.
10. How do top-level managers know when to centralize operations?
11. Of what practical use is the organization design triangle?

PROBLEMS FOR ACTION

A. Assume that you have accepted a position as a manager and your span of control is 11 people. To professionalize your approach to management, you want to be an effective delegator. Develop a handy checklist of the types of tasks you should delegate.

B. You receive a telephone call from a small-company president. She explains to you that her company manufactures a line of smoke detectors, fire extinguishers, and fire-proofing chemicals. She employs 65 people, and her firm is divided into several departments: manufacturing, engineering, marketing and sales, finance, and administration (purchasing, human resources, and the like). The president tells you, "I need your help. My company is doing well and is poised to expand, but I don't know whether we should become more centralized or more decentralized. I will pay you and give you a few of our products if you will find me some answers." Please take on this assignment and explain in detail how you will study the problem and reach your conclusions.

CONCLUDING CASE

Revamping the IBM Culture

John F. Akers, chairman of IBM, decided several years ago that the sales improvements and cost-cutting measures taking place in his company were not good enough. In his evaluation, the measures taken were only temporary fixes. IBM therefore needed a major overhaul. On January 28, 1988, a reorganization of IBM was announced that Akers described as the most significant restructuring of the company in 30 years.

Akers was frustrated for many years by what he perceived to be a slow-moving headquarters bureaucracy. His response was to delegate responsibility to a half-dozen general managers. With IBM's product lines and markets expanding continuously, Akers made this comment: "There's no way that one small set of managers at the top should think they are close enough to the action to make the decisions in all these areas." He handed the relatively young managers more power and asked them to bring an entrepreneurial spirit to their lines of business.

A major reason for wanting to improve the

efficiency of IBM was that the company was being forced to compete on all fronts at once: minicomputers, PCs, software, and systems integration consulting. Even in the mainframe business, the company was facing worthy rivals, including Japanese computer manufacturers. Some analysts believe that IBM began to lose some of its competitive edge in the 1970s. For example, it has been charged that IBM salespeople lost sight of the problems customers wanted solved. Instead, they concentrated more on just selling machines.

Improving products was the primary goal of the reorganization. Akers formed five autonomous product groups and pushed much of the decision making down to general managers in these units. He hoped that these moves would overcome some of the delays in decision making that had slowed product introductions. In the new structure, general managers in personal computer systems, midrange systems, mainframes, and communications are given latitude to develop the products they need for their particular markets. The fifth new unit will be responsible for delivering state-of-the-art building-block technology such as memory chips.

Another part of the reorganization was to transfer thousands of employees from other positions into sales and customer service. Despite all these changes, one year later some Wall Street analysts maintained that IBM's cost structure had become bloated. Furthermore, they contended that the company's domestic sales force had not been deployed efficiently. "They don't know what to do, so they're throwing money at the problem," said one analyst.

By late 1991, IBM was still struggling to regain its domination of the computer market. At that time a *Business Week* writer felt that IBM still faced the toughest technological and management job in business. Wall Street analysts have recently reduced their estimates of future IBM earnings. Operating profit margins for 1991 were predicted to fall below 20 percent. A decade ago, the IBM operating profit margin was 35 percent.

Late in 1991, IBM announced the most radical restructuring in its history. A plan was drawn to spin off all of IBM's divisions into decentralized units and give them considerable autonomy. Each division will be like a subsidiary and have the authority to develop its own marketing strategies, set wages, and release its income statement to the public. Akers again stated his determination to free IBM from its stifling bureaucracy.

Shortly after the reorganization was announced, IBM revealed plans to eliminate as many as 9,000 of its 85,000 jobs in the United States. Employees targeted for layoffs were given six months to choose between relocation to another facility or a severance package.

1. To what extent do you think the reorganization at IBM will achieve (or has achieved) its aims of making IBM less bureaucratic and improving its products? (Current media sources may be helpful in answering this question.)
2. How can an executive justify tampering with the structure of a corporation that has been so successful for so many years?
3. What were Akers's specific attempts at decentralization?

Source: As reported in "Big Changes at Big Blue," *Business Week* (February 15, 1988); "On the Street Big Blue Is Blah," *Business Week* (May 29, 1989); "IBM: As Markets and Technology Change, Can Big Blue Remake Its Culture?" *Business Week* (June 17, 1991): 24–32; and "IBM Tells Workers Which Jobs Are Cut," Gannett News Service (April 12, 1992).

REFERENCES

1. Stephen S. McIntosh, "Buying Time by Delegating," *HRMagazine* (October 1991): 48.
2. "When Delegating, Don't Dump," *Communication Briefings* (Vol. VIII, No. IX, 1990): 8.
3. Carrie R. Leana, "Predictors and Consequences of Delegation," *Academy of Management Journal* (December 1986): 754–774; Leana, "Power Relinquishment Versus Power Sharing: Theoretical Clarification and Empirical Comparison of Delegation and Participation," *Journal of Applied Psychology* (May 1987): 228–233.
4. Suzanne Savary, "Ineffective Delegation: Symptom or Problem?" *Supervisory Management* (June 1985): 28.
5. William R. Tracey, "Deft Delegation: Multiplying Your Effectiveness," *Personnel* (February 1988): 38.
6. William S. Birnbaum, "Delegating: What? How? And to Whom?" *Executive Management Forum* (December 1990): 2.
7. William G. Callarman and William W. McCartney, "Reversing Reverse Delegation," *Management Solutions* (July 1988): 12.
8. Judith Segal, "The Perils of Perfectionism," *Personnel* (October 1990): 22.
9. Thomas J. Peters, "Good Leaders Share Same Stellar Traits," syndicated column (December 7, 1986).
10. John W. Hodge, "Workaholic Organizations May Not Work," *HRMagazine* (March 1991): 6–8.
11. Ruth Haas, "Workaholics: Good News—Bad News," *Human Resources Forum* (July 1990): 1.
12. Joseph T. Straub, "Delegation Dilemma: What Should You

Do If It Doesn't Work?" *Supervisory Management* (August 1989): 7–10.

13. Vijay Govindarajan, "Decentralization, Strategy, and Effectiveness of Strategic Business Units in Multibusiness Organizations," *Academy of Management Review* (October 1986): 844.

14. The classic reference on this topic is Ernest Dale, *Planning and Developing the Company Organization Structure*, Research Report No. 20, (New York: American Management Association, 1952).

15. Robert Kreitner, *Management*, 5e (Boston: Houghton Mifflin, 1992): 291.

16. Marlene C. Piturro, "Decentralization: Rebuilding the Corporation," *Management Review* (August 1988): 32.

17. *Ibid*.

18. Mitchell Lew Marks, "Merger Management HR's Way," *HRMagazine* (May 1991): 61.

19. This entire section is based on Robert W. Keidel, "Triangular Design: A New Organizational Geometry," *"Academy of Management Executive* (November 1990): 21–37.

Chapter 10

Staffing and Human Resources Management

Jerry Snyder, a bank human resources manager, was having lunch with the president, Anne Dixon. Said Snyder:

"I want to talk to you about something important. People have been talking about Workforce 2000 for several years. I read an article implying that human resources professionals are moving too slowly. According to one survey, there is already a varied workforce in corporate America. At one-third of the companies in the United States, approximately 15 percent of the employees are members of minority groups. Besides that, at three-quarters of the companies, at least one-third of the employees are female, and at about one-eighth of the companies, over half the workforce is over age 40.

"I'm the bank's internal consultant on management of human resources. I think we should be doing something to deal with the new workforce."

"To my knowledge, we are already very progressive,"' said Dixon.

"I'm not faulting the bank. I just think at a level beyond affirmative action. The future is here; let's deal with it positively and creatively. I'll get back to you in several weeks with a master plan for managing the Workforce 2000. Right now I don't know exactly what we should be doing."

Jerry Snyder makes a couple of important points. Human resources (or personnel) professionals have a major responsibility in helping their organizations manage employees properly. This includes helping companies do a better job of managing the modern workforce. One reason why the human resources function is growing in importance is that people are the primary source of productivity. Another reason is that employee training (a human resources management activity) helps improve the quality of goods and services.

Human resources management is heavily involved with the staffing function. **Staffing** is the process of ensuring that the firm has qualified employees to meet its objective. It is thus the lifeblood of any firm. Staffing requires considerable short- and long-range planning and attention to detail, as well as a thorough knowledge of human resources management techniques.

Staffing includes the varied activities shown in Figure 10-1. The dotted lines in this model indicate that the results of performance appraisal can be used to evaluate the other aspects of staffing. For instance, performance appraisals may show that people are being selected for a particular job without having sufficient skills. In the first part of this chapter, we describe the four major components of the staffing model: human resources planning, equal employment opportunity legislation, pay and benefits, and recruitment. This is followed by discussions of personnel selection, placement and orientation, training and development, and performance appraisal.

HUMAN RESOURCES PLANNING

Staffing often begins with **human resources planning**—anticipating and providing for the movement of people into, within, and out of a firm. The planning activity anticipates future needs and selects employees who will

FIGURE 10-1 The Organizational Staffing Model

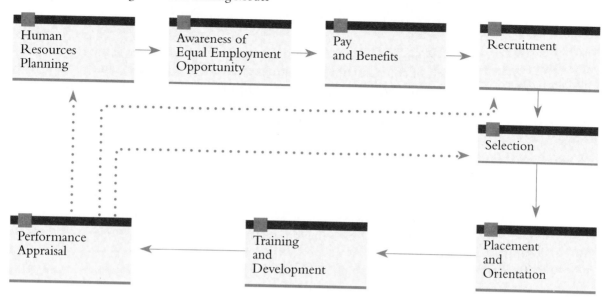

meet those needs. **Replacement tables** are an important human resources planning technique. They specify the number of people to be moved if a key employee retires or is removed. Although human resources planning emphasizes the future, it also solves immediate problems such as recruiting.[1]

Human resources planning should be an integral part of a firm's strategies and plans. Assume, for example, that the firm's strategy calls for decentralization. Emphasis would then be placed on planning to hire and train a greater number of managers for the future, because more managers are required in a decentralized organization. Human resources planning generally involves the following steps:

1. Analyzing a firm's present pool of talent in light of current and future needs and organizational goals.
2. Anticipating vacancies because of promotions, transfers, dismissals, layoffs, deaths, retirements, and parental or maternity leaves. The effect a promotion will have on all lower and higher positions within a particular career path must also be predicted. This step also includes assessing the potential for promotion from within the firm and need for outside recruitment.
3. Forecasting personnel needs because of normal growth, planned expansion, acquisitions, and other predictable changes.
4. Planning for long-term succession into critical positions and for emergency replacement as needed.
5. Forecasting business and economic trends and their effects on human resources needs.

Human resources planning often produces considerable quantitative data. These data become part of the **human resources information system (HRIS),** a formal system for providing managers with information about employees.

EQUAL EMPLOYMENT OPPORTUNITY AND STAFFING

In staffing, managers should abide by the letter and spirit of the law in all aspects of compensation, recruitment, selection, placement, and performance appraisal. **Equal employment opportunity** is a legal requirement that provides protection against all forms of employment discrimination. Managers must be familiar with equal employment opportunity laws to avoid practicing intended or unintended job discrimination.

U.S. Equal Employment Opportunity Legislation

Federal, state, or provincial legislation influences every stage of organizational staffing. The following sections describe the most relevant pieces of legislation.

CIVIL RIGHTS ACT OF 1964 (TITLE VII). This act prohibits employer and union discrimination based on race, color, religion, gender, and national origin. (Laws concerning discrimination on the basis of age and disability were added later.) The Equal Employment Opportunity Commission (EEOC) was established to administer this act.

AGE DISCRIMINATION ACT OF 1967 AND AMENDMENTS. This act prohibits discrimination based on age of recruits, applicants, or employees between the ages of 40 and 70. With a few exceptions, the amendments prohibit employers from requiring employees to retire before age 70 solely because of age, and a 1986 amendment did away with the mandatory retirement age.

VOCATIONAL REHABILITATION ACT OF 1973. Discrimination against people with physical or mental disabilities is prohibited by this law. Employers are required to make accommodations so that people with physical disabilities can perform jobs.

ETHICS QUESTION
A chief executive officer suggested relocating to an area where people with mental disabilities were less likely to apply for jobs. What ethical issues are raised by his behavior?

AMERICANS WITH DISABILITIES ACT (ADA) OF 1990. Extending the 1973 Vocational Rehabilitation Act, the ADA has redefined disabilities and discrimination. This act applies to all employers, including privately owned businesses and local governments. It prohibits them from discriminating against employees or job applicants with disabilities when making employment decisions. Employers must provide "reasonable accommodation" to these people, but the accommodations do not have to be made if they impose "undue hardship" on the firm.

The ADA defines *disability* as a physical or mental impairment that substantially limits an individual's major life activities. Among the impairments included are sight and hearing deficiencies, cancer, epilepsy, emotional disturbances, and extremely low mental ability.

The Civil Rights Act of 1991

This law extends civil rights by overturning a series of U.S. Supreme Court rulings on job bias complaints. For the first time, women, religious minorities, and people with disabilities are allowed to sue for damages in cases of employment discrimination. However, the law sets maximum awards for compensatory and punitive damages. It also prohibits all racial discrimination in contractual relationships.

Canadian Human Rights Programs

Canadian programs follow the model of equal employment opportunity programs in the United States. The enforcement phase of these programs began in the late 1970s. The Canadian programs emphasize training to improve the employment opportunities of minorities.

ETHICS QUESTION
How does Digital's "Valuing Differences" program conform to the meaning of social responsibility?

In summary, discrimination may occur in seven major areas: age, physical and mental disabilities, national origin, race, color, religion, and sex. Discrimination on the basis of marital status is usually included under sex discrimination. Several lower court rulings have suggested that unequal treatment of any candidate on the basis of any factor not related to job performance is discriminatory. Among these factors are weight, height, physical appearance, sexual orientation, and baldness. The Organization in Action illustrates how a company can exceed the minimum requirements of equal employment opportunity.

ORGANIZATION IN ACTION

Digital Equipment Corporation wanted to move beyond the minimum requirements for equal employment opportunity to become a company in which every employee could reach his or her potential. Digital therefore decided to explicitly value the differences among people. The program to achieve this purpose, "Valuing Differences," has two components. First, core groups are used to help employees recognize their stereotypes and false assumptions. Core group leaders encourage discussion and self-development. Thousands of Digital employees have also attended a training program, "Understanding the Dynamics of Diversity."

Second, a number of senior managers are assigned to groups that highlight the importance of cultural diversity. These senior managers encourage younger managers to strive for employee diversity. The groups also sponsor celebrations of racial, gender, and ethnic differences such as Hispanic Heritage Week and Black History Month.

Source: As reported in R. Roosevelt Thomas, Jr., "From Affirmative Action to Affirming Diversity," *Harvard Business Review* (March-April 1990): 111.

PAY AND BENEFITS

A firm must offer appropriate pay and benefits in order to recruit people. In addition, it must pay employees justly and offer them competitive benefits to encourage them to remain with the firm. Yet, if employees are overpaid, the firm will become noncompetitive. Many firms move their manufacturing arms to geographical areas where wages are lower for this very reason. Compensation (which includes both pay and benefits) is a key part of running a company. One estimate is that pay and benefits account for about 75 percent of total production costs.[2] Another is that compensation often equals 50 percent of the cash flow of a firm.[3] The proportion of money allocated to compensation is higher in service organizations than in manufacturing companies. Our discussion of pay and benefits centers around determinants of compensation levels, current trends in pay, and employee benefits.

Determinants of Compensation Levels

Many factors influence compensation decisions. So far, compensation theory has not provided a reliable answer to what a person is worth.[4] We therefore use procedures that best calculate a particular person's worth in performing a particular job in a particular firm. Both internal and external methods are used in setting compensation levels.

POINT-FACTOR JOB EVALUATION. A widely used internal method of establishing compensation levels is **point-factor job evaluation.** This is a systematic method of measuring the financial worth of a job. Most compensation plans include four or five factors that differ substantially in their weight or value (capacity for earning points): education, experience, job complexity, interpersonal skills, and physical demands. These factors reflect the major job demands of the firm. A job evaluation committee decides on both the factors and their relative importance.

Job evaluation begins with a written job description. Individual jobs are then measured according to how much of each factor they contain. Points are assigned for each factor (e.g., 100 points for job complexity), and a total point score is produced for each job. The point score is then converted into a salary level. Each job ends up with a score, such as 420 points for a department store manager.

A disadvantage of this method is that employees working under a job evaluation system tend to follow their job descriptions too tightly. This may limit their potential contribution to the firm. Many small and medium-size businesses do not use job evaluations. Alternatives to the job evaluation system include paying people for skills they possess or relying on market factors.[5] Under a **pay-for-knowledge system,** management calculates starting pay based on the knowledge and skill level required for a given job. Subsequent increases depend on the worker's mastering additional blocks of knowledge as set forth by the firm.

EXTERNAL FACTORS. Many factors outside the firm also influence pay levels. Two important external factors for managerial and professional jobs are supply and demand and wage surveys. The supply and demand factor dictates that the fewer the number of qualified people available to perform a particular job, the more these people will be paid. Similarly, the larger the number of qualified people available to perform a particular job, the less these people will be paid.

Management often establishes pay rates on the basis of results of wage surveys conducted by trade associations, trade magazines, and state employment agencies. The results of these surveys can help a firm prevent costly overpayments to employees or turnover due to underpayments.

Current Trends in Pay

Compensation responds to changes in the environment. One dominant trend is to use pay and benefits to motivate employees to achieve high performance, thereby increasing their productivity. Three examples of this practice are variable pay, gainsharing, and entrepreneurial pay. Another current trend is to strive for pay equity by paying comparable wages for comparable work.

VARIABLE PAY (PAY FOR PERFORMANCE). Compensation is most likely to motivate employees when they are paid for performance. **Variable pay** is an incentive plan that intentionally pays good performers more money than poor performers. Employees receive higher raises, bonuses, or prizes for excelling on a variety of quantitative indexes such as units shipped per hour. Traditionally, variable pay has been referred to as *merit pay*. Whatever the specific plan, employees receive a base level of pay along with a bonus related to performance.

Many companies have shifted to variable pay plans because these plans fit the modern organization better than traditional systems did. Based on his study of 46 companies in the United States and Canada, a researcher concluded, "Whatever changes these companies make, it all adds up to the same thing: fewer managerial levels, fewer job classifications and more emphasis on teamwork and employee decision making."[6] The traditional pay systems did not fit these new working arrangements. For example, employees accustomed to sticking closely to their job descriptions wanted additional pay when they went beyond their assigned duties. To make the new workplace work, most of these organizations moved to variable pay.

Variable pay plans also have a downside. One problem is that these plans may be stressful to workers, because pay-for-performance is often given instead of a permanent salary increase. Another concern is that variable pay plans sometimes encourage an unhealthy degree of competition among employees. The Concluding Case at the end of this chapter illustrates what can go wrong with variable pay.

GAINSHARING. Individual incentive systems sometimes lead to intense competition and poor cooperation among employees. An antidote to this problem, while still retaining the pay-for-performance principle, is **gainsharing.** It is a profit-sharing plan that calculates the contribution of specific

ETHICS QUESTION
Assume that a company
with a gainsharing
program made no profits
this year and therefore is
granting no year-end
bonuses. Is the company
behaving in a socially
responsible manner?

groups or departments. When employees make labor-saving suggestions that increase productivity, they share in the gains by receiving a bonus. An important side effect is that employee involvement in productivity improvement boosts morale.[7]

The most successful gainsharing programs combine individual piece-work, company profit sharing, and some team incentives. A widely publicized team incentive program has been in operation at Lincoln Electric for many years. Employees have earned bonuses from 88 to 115 percent of base salary.[8]

ENTREPRENEURIAL PAY. Entrepreneurs typically want to earn money for their efforts. A select number of employees are given a chance to satisfy this motive through **entrepreneurial pay**—a plan in which people who help found a new corporate venture share in its profits. Most entrepreneurial pay plans pay the participants in the venture a base salary equivalent to their former salary levels. The balance of their compensation (such as bonuses, perks, or profit sharing) is put at risk—pegged to the profitability of the new venture. Payouts may occur several times as the venture grows.

AT&T is one company that has initiated a venture development process accompanied by entrepreneurial pay. In the most extreme form, venture participants can contribute a percentage of their salary to help capitalize the project. The payoff is up to eight times their investment in the venture.[9]

COMPARABLE WORTH. **Comparable worth** is a compensation plan in which the firm grants equal pay for jobs that it judges to be of comparable value. This plan uses job evaluation to help reduce pay inequities related primarily to gender. As a result, one form of job discrimination is eliminated. Proponents of the comparable worth method note that, without it, clerical workers, nurses, and librarians receive relatively low pay. The reason is that most of these positions are filled by women.[10]

The major argument against the comparable worth method is that it ignores market factors in determining wages. Comparable worth can also lead to inequities and layoffs. One community equated the pay of school bus drivers to that of airline pilots because both are responsible for the lives of their passengers. This community showed no apparent concern for supply and demand, training, or talent.

Ontario, Canada, broke ground by putting into law comparable worth standards for business as well as government. Despite pay equity provisions in Canadian law, a substantial gap still existed between the pay of men and that of women. To correct these inequities, the Pay Equity Act of 1987 was passed. Its key provisions are as follows:

1. Defining male and female job classes. (Most firms are using the point system of job evaluation to value each job class.)
2. Setting standards by which the job classes are defined.
3. Mandating pay equality between classes of comparable worth in both the private and public sectors.
4. Creating two permanent government agencies to ensure the law's enforcement.

Companies in Ontario are working hard to comply with the Pay Equity Act. One example is the T. Eaton Company, a retailer with 15,000 employees in the province. Eaton's compensation manager noted that the new job analyses will result in equity adjustments costing several million dollars annually.[11]

Employee Benefits

An **employee benefit** is anything of value given to workers, in addition to their base salary, as a condition of their employment. As such it is part of compensation. Benefits are crucial today because they help firms stay competitive in attracting and retaining valuable employees. The appropriate benefits package is also necessary to provide for Workforce 2000.[12] For example, working parents value company-sponsored child-care facilities.

Among the benefits most frequently provided are health and life insurance coverage and pension and retirement plans. Employee benefits cost employers an average of 35 percent of cash salaries. The fastest-growing trend in benefits is the **flexible benefit package,** which tailors benefits to the preferences of individual employees. Flexible benefit packages generally provide employees with one category of fixed benefits such as a minimum level of medical and disability insurance. In addition, it offers a second, flexible category, with a menu of benefits from which employees choose according to their needs and preferences. For instance, an employee might choose to have less vacation time and more dental insurance.

Another benefit plan that is rapidly being adopted is **parental leave**— time off for new parents with continuing benefits and the promise of a job when they return. A typical plan would offer a parent up to 18 weeks' leave after a birth or adoption. However, the parent does not receive salary while on leave, and only one parent in the family can claim the benefit. Many companies have extended parental leave to *family leave*, to grant employees

Corporate child-care centers are becoming an increasingly important employee benefit for working parents.

time off to take care of elderly parents. A representative list of employee benefits is shown in Figure 10-2.

The cost of benefits, particularly medical insurance, continues to escalate. Many employers now require employees to contribute a larger share of the cost of medical benefits than they did in the past. One area in which benefits are expanding, however, is child care. Some companies are forming joint ventures to provide child-care services. The rationale is that a shortage of high-quality child care lowers employee productivity.[13] A summary of these joint ventures is presented in Figure 10-3.

RECRUITMENT

After a firm has established staffing needs and compensation levels, the next step is to recruit job candidates. **Recruitment** is the process of finding and attracting people who are capable of and interested in filling job vacancies. The recruiter matches the supply of jobs available with the demands of job seekers.

Contingent Workers and Recruiting

Recruitment includes searching for full-time employees, part-time employees, and temporary workers, referred to as **contingent workers.** These are people who perform work for a firm but are not members of its permanent workforce. Some are temporary workers; others are part-timers (including job sharers), employees of subcontractors, and people who do piecework at home. Contingent workers account for one-fifth of the U.S. workforce, the

FIGURE 10-2
Employee Benefits

Frequently Offered and Sometimes Legally Mandated	Less Frequently Offered
Social Security	Parental leave
Workers' compensation	Child-care centers
Unemployment compensation	Paid travel time to work
Paid vacations	Telecommuting
Paid sick leave	Stress management programs
Medical and hospitalization insurance	Employee credit unions
Relocation payment	Orthodontia payments
Term life insurance	Cash payments for unused vacation
Flexible working hours	and sick time
Group life insurance	Stock ownership
Dental insurance	Legal insurance
Retirement pensions	Carpooling services
Tuition assistance	Preretirement planning
Employee training	Outplacement counseling
Personal time off	Payment of adoption fees
Paid maternity leave	Discount purchasing program
Company cafeteria	Payroll deduction IRA
Holiday parties	Assistance in finding affordable housing

FIGURE 10-3
Corporate Collaboration
in Child Care

Companies	Location	Purpose
IBM, American Express, Allstate, Duke Power, and University Research Park, developer	Charlotte, NC	Built $2-million child-care center that exceeds state standards.
IBM and Travelers	Dallas-Fort Worth	A $375,000 program to recruit and train family day-care providers. Also funds efforts by child-care centers to gain accreditation.
Eastman Kodak, Xerox, Bausch & Lomb, Blue Cross/Blue Shield, and others	Rochester, NY	Training and low-cost group health insurance for child-care workers.
IBM and Burroughs Wellcome	Research Triangle Park, NC	Staff training, facilities, equipment, and accreditation help for child-care centers; recruiting and training family day-care providers.
Time Warner, Colgate-Palmolive, and 13 other companies and professional firms	New York City and suburbs	Referral and subsidized in-home care for sick children and emergency child care.
Honeywell, First Bank System, 3M, and 12 other companies	Minneapolis area	Referral and subsidized in-home care for sick children.
IBM and a PepsiCo unit	Katonah, NY	Consolidate, relocate, and expand a child-care center.

Source: Sue Shellenbarger, "Companies Team Up to Improve Quality of Their Employees' Child-Care Choices," *The Wall Street Journal* (October 17, 1991): B1. Reprinted by permission of *The Wall Street Journal* © 1991 Dow Jones & Company, Inc. All Rights Reserved Worldwide.

highest proportion of them in retailing. These workers receive few benefits.

Temporary workers (or "temps") are such an important part of today's workforce that some companies have developed in-house pools of them. Instead of using temporary agencies, these companies negotiate directly with pools of temps who work for them almost exclusively. Frequently hired temporary workers become prime candidates for full-time positions since the temporary work they perform provides an excellent sample of their capabilities.[14]

Recruitment has a big influence on employee turnover and retention. When job candidates are given a realistic job preview, they are less likely to quit when they encounter job frustration.[15] A **realistic job preview** is a frank discussion of all aspects of the job, both positive and negative.

Recruiting Sources

The term *recruitment* brings forth images of newspaper advertisements and campus recruiters, yet about 85 percent of all jobs are filled by word of mouth. Being aware of recruiting sources can help a manager find suitable job candidates. Job seekers can also use this information in conducting their job campaigns.

There are three categories of recruiting sources. The first is present employees. A standard recruiting method is to post job openings so that current employees may apply. Another way to recruit current employees is for managers to recommend them for transfer or promotion. A human resources information system helps identify current employees with the right skills.

The second recruitment category is referrals by present employees. If a firm is already established, present employees can be the primary recruiting source. Satisfied employees may be willing to nominate relatives, friends, acquaintances, and neighbors for job openings.

The third category is external sources. The best known external recruiting source is recruiting advertisements. A study conducted with life insurance agents found that classified ads attracted higher-quality applicants than did employment agencies or placement offices.[16] Other external sources for higher-level jobs include placement offices and employment agencies.

Executive search firms are an additional recruiting source, for high-level positions. Search firms charge a fee and expenses to conduct an industry-wide search for the right person for a job. Colleges and universities sometimes hire search firms to find a new president or dean. However, a job seeker has little to gain by contacting a search firm; these firms work for the employing organization.

LEARNING CHECK

Explain the basics of staffing and summarize the four steps in the organizational staffing model: human resources planning, awareness of equal employment opportunity legislation, pay and benefits, and recruitment.

Students check the job bulletin board at their college placement office. A service such as this is an external recruiting source used by many firms.

HUMAN RESOURCES SELECTION

Human resources selection follows recruitment. It has two major components: preparing job specifications and using selection techniques such as interviews.

Preparing Job (or Person) Specifications

Job (or person) specifications describe the personal characteristics required for a particular job. Specifications for a job might include ranking in the top half of one's class, good computer skills, leadership potential, and high motivation. Ideally, job specifications are based on evidence that the presence of certain qualifications is related to job success. The specifications are developed by line managers working with human resources specialists. Job specifications increase objectivity in the selection decision and reduce the likelihood that irrelevant criteria and personal bias will influence judgment.

Some companies include in job specifications a fit between the characteristics of the candidate and the characteristics of the organization. Many firms, including high- and low-technology firms, from both the United States and Japan, look for an organization-person fit. This fit is used to build organizational cultures that rely on self-motivated, committed people for their success. Sun Microsystems, for example, goes to great lengths to find people with the right fit. Job candidates at all levels are brought in as many as five times for interviews with up to 20 interviewers.[17]

Selection Techniques

Human resources selection is made up of a series of steps, or hurdles, as depicted in Figure 10-4. A candidate can be ruled out at any step of the selection process. Displaying functional illiteracy on the application form, for example, would be a disqualifying factor. In each step of the selection process, the firm matches the performance capabilities of the individual with the job specifications and decides whether or not to keep considering the candidate. The discussion that follows mirrors the sequence of steps in the selection process.

PRELIMINARY SCREENING INTERVIEW. A member of the firm's human resources department conducts a brief screening interview, in person or by telephone, early in the recruitment or selection process. The interviewer asks the candidate background information. One goal is to find people who seem to qualify for the job. People are often disqualified by their answers to a few *knockout* questions. A knockout question is one that, answered in a certain way, disqualifies the applicant from further consideration. For example, "Are you willing to work weekends and holidays?" is a vital question for a prospective store manager. During the screening

FIGURE 10-4
The Selection Process

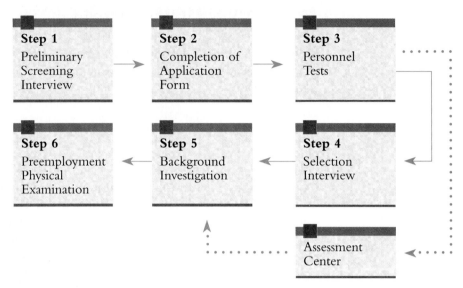

NOTE:
The hiring decision is based on composite information from more than one step, and the applicant can be rejected at any step. An assessment center can be used instead of personnel tests (step 3) and as a supplement to the selection interview (step 4).

interview, the interviewer also looks for disqualifying behavior. An example is rudeness shown by an applicant seeking a customer service position.

Applicants who pass the screening interview then complete a job application form. (Sometimes the written application precedes the screening interview.) A job résumé may be used instead of a preliminary application form.

JOB APPLICATION FORMS. A completed application provides information about a person's schooling, job experience, citizenship status, special abilities, and other pertinent factors. Applicants sign the form to show that they agree with the stated conditions of employment. Because it is against the law in many cases, few firms ask about personal facts (See Figure 10-5). Applicants can voluntarily submit a photo or offer information about factors such as age or gender.

In addition to providing information for record keeping, the application form provides some information that may be related to job performance. How the applicant completes the form might indicate his or her ability to organize thoughts on paper. A form completed in a disorganized fashion (e.g., with many cross-outs or excessive writing in the margins) could suggest poor work habits. Job history often provides a good indicator of the type of work suited to an applicant's talents. A record of the person's past accomplishments is the best predictor of future performance.

PERSONNEL TESTS. Wide varieties of tests are available to measure mental ability, special aptitudes, creativity, and personality characteristics. Tests from reputable publishers are developed scientifically and evaluated

FIGURE 10-5
Topics Avoided in Job
Application Forms

Race
Religion
Gender
Pregnancy
Number of children
Ages of children
Marital status
Worker compensation claims in previous positions
Child-care plans (could be gender related)
Height or weight (could be ethnic or gender related)
Physical or mental disability
Age
Criminal record
Union affiliations

Source: Compiled from facts in Loretta D. Foxman and Walter L. Polsky, "Select the Right Application Form," *Personnel Journal* (October 1989): 28–29.

extensively for reliability and validity. *Reliability* refers to the consistency or stability with which a test measures a human characteristic. *Validity* refers to a test's ability to measure what it claims to measure—in this case, predicting job performance. In the following sections, we look at the legal requirements of testing and at integrity testing.

Legal Requirements. Personnel tests have been attacked by the government and private groups because they sometimes discriminate against minorities. As a result, it has become necessary for firms to subject personnel tests to extensive validation procedures. Generally the process involves demonstrating that people who score well on the test or group of tests subsequently display good job performance. (To illustrate, people who score high on a test of assertiveness should perform better in a sales job than those with low scores on the test.) Also, test questions and topics should be clearly related to job performance. For example, questions about mechanical ability should be asked only if mechanical ability is a requirement of the job.

Personnel tests and other selection devices can contribute to job discrimination against protected-class members in two ways. (A protected class is a group the government believes to have been discriminated against in the past.) Under **disparate treatment,** protected-class members receive unequal treatment or are evaluated by different standards. An example would be requiring higher test scores for Asians than Caucasians. **Disparate impact** occurs when a protected class is adversely affected by an employment standard that is applied equally. For example, an achievement test might contain several questions about calculus. African-Americans in a given geographic location might do poorly on those questions because most of them did not take a course in calculus. The EEOC offers suggestions for detecting disparate impact. When the selection rate for any protected group is less than four-fifths the rate of the group with the highest selection rate, disparate impact may be occurring.[18] Assume that 70 percent of Asians pass an employment test, for example, and they are the group with the highest selection rate. At least 56 percent of other groups should pass the same test to show that disparate impact is not a factor.

Integrity Testing. An **integrity (or honesty) test** is a preemployment test designed to measure the extent of a person's integrity as it relates to job behavior. These tests are used frequently in workplaces such as retail stores, banks, and warehouses, where employees have access to cash or merchandise.

Paper-and-pencil tests of honesty typically ask questions about a job applicant's attitudes toward theft and other forms of dishonesty. One frequent area of inquiry is punitiveness of attitudes toward theft. (For example, Should a person be fired for taking home $10 worth of merchandise without authorization?) Another approach to integrity testing is to measure general personality traits such as a tendency toward deviant behavior on the job.[19]

Lie-detector or polygraph tests are the best-known forms of honesty testing. A **polygraph** is an instrument that measures physiological indicators of emotion including blood pressure, heartbeat, breathing rate, and decreases in skin temperature. The examiner begins by asking the candidate neutral questions to establish a normal rate of emotional response. The balance of the examination measures the candidate's response to controversial questions. Lying is supposed to trigger increased emotional response.

Integrity testing is highly controversial. The Employee Polygraph Protection Act of 1988 generally prohibits employers from conducting polygraph examinations of all job applicants and most employees. Exemptions include government employees, and employers with national defense or nuclear-power-related contracts. The legal future of paper-and-pencil integrity tests may also be in jeopardy.[20] Many psychologists contend that polygraphs have not been validated. However, there is some evidence suggesting that both forms of honesty testing do help employers screen out dishonest employees.[21]

THE SELECTION INTERVIEW. The interview is the most widely used employee selection technique. Although researchers disagree, recent evidence shows that interviews have at least moderate validity.[22] For example, assume that smiling is required for a customer service job. The propensity to smile is easier to measure in an interview than through other selection devices. Interviews are also valuable opportunities to exchange information with job candidates. A carefully planned and structured selection interview will often predict future job performance accurately.

Interview structure is the degree to which interview questions and formats are formalized. Experienced employment interviewers typically use a structured form but also ask additional questions geared to the interview at hand. For instance, if an interviewee appeared particularly ill at ease, the interviewer might ask, "What kind of problems have you experienced when working under pressure?" The following are some typical instructions and questions used in evaluating candidates for managerial and professional jobs:

- Tell me anything about yourself you think I may need to know.
- What are your strengths—the things about you that will help you perform well in the job under consideration?
- What have been your most important job accomplishments?

Skilled interviewers use questions as points of departure. They follow up these questions with probes. A **probe** is an additional question suggested by the interviewee's response (such as the ill-at-ease incident just mentioned). Probes are designed to uncover detailed information needed for the selection decision.

ASSESSMENT CENTERS. An **assessment center** is a place for evaluating job candidates and a process that relies heavily on simulated job experiences. Many large firms have their own assessment centers. The centers are used to aid in making selection decisions about both external job applicants and internal candidates for promotion. Smaller firms have access to assessment centers established to process candidates from several firms simultaneously. The sources of evaluation in an assessment center include interviews, written biographies, and personnel tests in addition to job simulations.

The situational tests used in assessment centers provide trained observers with a sample of behavior that simulates behavior that would occur in the work situation. Participants are rated on such factors as administrative ability, leadership skill, communication skills, and decisiveness. Two frequently used situational tests are the in-basket exercise and the leaderless group discussion. The in-basket exercise requires the candidate to answer a manager's correspondence and decide how to handle specific problems. A typical leaderless group discussion requires candidates to engage in group problem solving (e.g., to handle a sudden product recall). Because no leader is appointed, the exercise gives participants a chance to display leadership skill.

One of the advantages of assessment centers is that they predict behavior from performance on simulated job tasks. This eliminates the possibility of error that exists when behavior is predicted from tests and interviews. Another advantage is that the assessment center method has a much greater appearance of validity than traditional tests. A potential disadvantage of this method is that it is accused of perpetuating stereotypes of how an effective manager should behave. For example, articulate and well-mannered people tend to be rated highly.

BACKGROUND INVESTIGATION. Information obtained from a candidate's résumé, application form, and selection interview must be verified. The background investigation thus includes reference checks, but it can also be used to clarify judgments about the candidate. Assume, for example, that the interviewer is concerned about the apparent abrasiveness of a candidate for a job dealing with clients. The interviewer might say to a reference, "We've been interviewing Billy Joe Anderson for a position as an accident investigator. What was your experience with Anderson in his handling of people?" The background investigation might also include contracting for the services of a firm that specializes in investigating such matters as drug abuse, criminal record, and amount of indebtedness.

It is difficult to obtain written reference information because of many libel suits against former employers who gave damaging references.[23] For this reason, the reference check is becoming a process to verify that a candidate did work for a particular employer for a specified period of time.

PREEMPLOYMENT PHYSICAL EXAMINATION. The preemployment physical examination has gained importance because of concerns about hiring drug abusers or AIDS victims and about insurance costs. The Federal Drug-Free Workplace Act of 1988 has increased the importance of drug testing. Under the Act, federal contractors who receive more than $25,000 in government business must certify that they will maintain a drug-free workplace. Nevertheless, drug testing remains highly controversial. Particular concerns are invasion of privacy and the fact that drug testing can be inaccurate. The physical examination is an important part of the organizational staffing process for several other reasons, including the following:

- To provide some assurance that the job applicant will be a productive member of the firm. For example, a person with a lower back problem may accumulate a poor attendance record.
- To provide some assurance that the applicant is physically fit for placement in a particular job. A person who suffers from frequent fainting spells would represent a poor risk as a company pilot.
- To provide a basis of comparison against which later physical examinations can be compared. This is an especially important matter in settling disability claims.
- To screen out drug abusers whose addiction may create problems such as lowered productivity, lost time from work, and misappropriation of funds in order to pay for drugs. A clinical laboratory reported that evidence of drug use was found in 11 percent of 1.9 million workers tested in a recent year.[24]
- To provide additional data for making sound placement decisions. One example is using the physical examination to assess properly both the assets and the limitations of an applicant with physical disabilities.

At this point in the selection process, the firm has collected considerable information about each candidate. One method of integrating all this information is to prepare a job specification grid that is used throughout the process. Candidates receive a rating or score on each specification at every step in selection. For example, Juanita Sanchez is being evaluated as a management trainee candidate for The Limited. She is assigned a "leadership potential" grade at each selection phase as follows: preliminary screening interview, A; completion of application form, B; personnel tests, B; and so forth. Next, Sanchez can be compared to other candidates with respect to leadership potential.

PLACEMENT AND ORIENTATION

The candidate who has passed through the recruitment and selection phases of staffing successfully is now ready to be placed in the right job. For example, if a firm hires three management trainees, it will try to achieve a good fit between each trainee's capabilities and his or her initial job assignment.

Orientation involves such activities as showing new employees around, explaining rules and regulations to them, and giving them employee handbooks. Proper orientation helps prevent problems such as rule violations due to lack of knowledge. It is also useful in helping new workers develop the attitudes that are important in providing good customer service.[25]

TRAINING AND DEVELOPMENT

The training and development of employees begin at orientation and may continue throughout their employment. **Training** is any method of increasing the level or range of employee skills in order to improve current job performance. While an increasing amount of technical training is now computer assisted, training for human relations skills, including customer service, is more likely to involve interaction with a live trainer. **Development** refers to increasing the capabilities of employees in order to improve their future job performance. Special emphasis is placed on interpersonal and decision-making skills.

Training and development programs are important because of rapid technological change and intense foreign competition. Companies also use training programs to help cope with workplace illiteracy and employees' limited mathematics skills. Furthermore, a training and development executive reports, "It is well documented that productivity gains from workplace learning exceed the gain from capital investment by more than 2 to 1."[26] Not all researchers and managers share this executive's enthusiasm, however.

Framework for Training and Development

Improving the skills of employees at any level should proceed in a systematic manner that allows for correction and renewal. As shown in Figure 10-6,

Much on-the-job technical training is now assisted by computers, but learning human relations skills requires interpersonal contact.

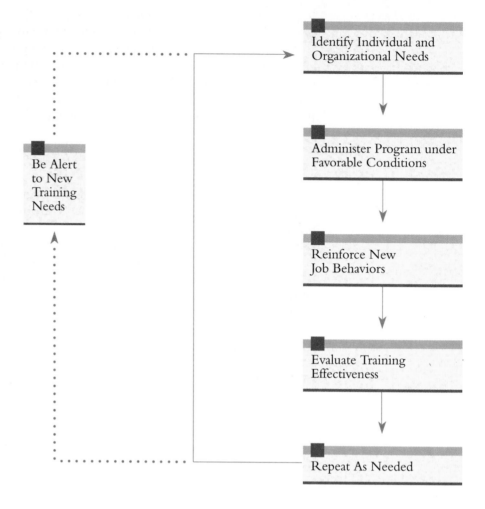

FIGURE 10-6
Framework for Training
and Development

Identify Individual and
Organizational Needs

Administer Program under
Favorable Conditions

Reinforce New
Job Behaviors

Evaluate Training
Effectiveness

Repeat As Needed

Be Alert
to New
Training
Needs

the framework for training and development is as follows:

1. *Identify individual and organizational needs.* It is important to identify needs for improvement prior to starting any training or development program. Such information can be obtained from the results of performance appraisals, surveys of managers, or analyses of job requirements, or from human resources forecasting.

2. *Administer the program under favorable conditions.* The program must be technically sound, and the participants must have the capacity and willingness to acquire new knowledge and skills. It also helps when top-level management values training.

3. *Reinforce new job behaviors.* If new skills are not practiced and rewarded, they will be forgotten. For instance, if a manager learns new control techniques and then is rebuffed when these are applied on the job, the newly learned techniques will be forgotten quickly.

4. *Evaluate training effectiveness.* It is important to evaluate whether or not the training accomplished its goals. Critical outputs from training include changes in productivity, quality, and customer service. Employee reaction to the training is also important.

5. *Repeat as needed.* A common failing of most training and development programs is that they are "one-shot affairs." A person attends the program and perhaps tries out the new skills. After a while, she or he returns to the old techniques and skills. Refresher or follow-up programs each year or two help organizations cope with this problem.

6. *Be alert to new training needs.* As employees learn new skills, it often creates a need to develop additional skills. For example, a manager might attend a training program on achieving zero defects. Despite the value of these concepts, the manager might meet resistance in applying them. The manager would then want to attend a seminar on overcoming resistance to change.

Management Development and Training

Training and development for managers take many different forms. **Management development** is any planned attempt to improve the effectiveness of present or future managers. We can classify management development programs as being related to acquiring cognitive (mental) knowledge and skills versus interpersonal skills. Figure 10-7 gives a sampling of management development programs that are classified in this manner. The Organization in Action provides an example of a leadership development program that is widely used with managers. Many people also pay for this type of development themselves.

FIGURE 10-7
A Sampling of
Management
Development Programs

Emphasis on Acquisition of Knowledge and Cognitive Skills

Financial management for nonfinancial managers
Total quality management
Quality circles for the service organization
Developing a quality circle in any organization
Forecasting techniques for marketing managers
Essentials of international management
Zero-base budgeting
Matrix management
Project management
Planning and control techniques
Just-in-time inventory control
Spreadsheet analysis for managers

Emphasis on the Development of Interpersonal Skills

Developing leadership style
Assertiveness training for managers
Conflict resolution
Coaching and counseling employees
Prevention and control of sexual harassment
Negotiating skills for managers
Wilderness training
Diversity awareness training

Federal Express Corporation has been committed to developing employee leadership potential since the company was founded. One program used for this purpose is the "wilderness experience," an intensive program of outdoor activities. The experience helps people gain confidence in their ability to make decisions quickly in a stressful environment. Participants learn to overcome their fears and self-imposed arbitrary limits. Their increased self-esteem enables them to take more responsibility for their personal and professional lives.

One wilderness experience is the "zip line," a rope with a T-bar on a pulley. Each participant, with safety harness attached, must jump off a cliff and slide 500 feet to the ground on the other side of the river. "Jumping off a cliff can be terrifying," says Roy Yamahiro, vice president of human resources development. "But the purpose of this activity is to confront reluctance to take the risk. It helps participants build confidence in their ability to handle any situation." Because the participants are dependent on each other for their safety, the program also helps build teamwork.

Source: Based on facts in William H. Wagel, "An Unorthodox Approach to Leadership Development," *Personnel* (July 1986): 4–5; Rick Gladstone, "Executives Take Their Insecurities Outdoors," Associated Press (September 25, 1988); Outward Bound, 1991 revised course schedule.

PERFORMANCE APPRAISAL

Up to this point in the staffing model, employees have been recruited, selected, and trained. The next step is to evaluate performance. A **performance appraisal** is a formal system for measuring, evaluating, and reviewing performance. Appraisals are a useful device for discovering whether or not the previous steps in the staffing model have been effective. For this text, information about performance appraisal is organized into four parts: the purposes of appraisals; types of appraisals; potential forms of bias in appraisals; and characteristics of a legally and scientifically sound appraisal system.

Purposes of an Appraisal System

The general purpose of performance appraisal is to improve the control of human resources. An effective appraisal system helps identify problems and possible solutions to them. We can summarize the specific purposes of performance appraisal in five key points. First, performance appraisal should lead directly to increased productivity.[27] An effective performance appraisal helps focus attention on the results employees are trying to achieve. It can help identify factors within the work system that interfere with employee productivity. For example, the employee might be working with obsolete or cumbersome software.

Second, the appraisal program helps managers make decisions about pay. They use the results of the appraisal to determine both salary increases and bonus payments. Third, performance appraisals help determine an employee's suitability for promotion. Employees who demonstrate leadership and administrative skills are considered promotable to managerial positions.

Fourth, appraisals assist employees in career development, because their results can serve as a basis for coaching and counseling. During an appraisal session, a manager might coach an employee on how to overcome a performance problem. Finally, performance appraisal results are used in human resources research. For example, most selection methods are validated by using performance appraisal evaluation ratings as a measure of success.

Types of Performance Appraisal

Numerous appraisal methods have been developed, and hundreds of articles and books have been written on the topic. The methods vary in the degree to which their results are based on objective data. All types of appraisal methods have their own advantages and disadvantages.

A RESULTS-ORIENTED SYSTEM. Chapter 5 described a form of appraisal that evaluates results (management by objectives). With MBO, employees receive high evaluations to the extent that they achieve their work and personal-improvement goals. Results-oriented systems help reduce some of the subjectivity involved in judging the performance of others.

EVALUATION OF TRAITS AND PERSONAL CHARACTERISTICS. The majority of performance appraisal methods evaluate employees on specific traits and characteristics related to performance. They also rate employees on such overall factors as quantity and quality of work produced. A representative example of the measurement of a trait (in this instance, creativity) within a performance appraisal is shown in Figure 10-8.

Evaluation of traits and characteristics can lend itself to subjective judgments and false stereotypes, but when used judiciously, trait evaluation has merit. Any manager would be willing to staff a department with employees who are dependable, well motivated, and trustworthy. In addition, the trait approach draws managers away from an overemphasis on results associated with excessive job stress, abundant paperwork, and a tight control system.[28]

GLOBAL ESSAY. The **global essay** is an overall summary of an employee's performance for the period under consideration. Managers use this method

FIGURE 10-8
Example of Trait
Evaluation Within a
Performance Appraisal

CREATIVITY is a talent for having new ideas, for finding new and better ways of doing things, and for being imaginative.

_____ Rarely has a new idea.

_____ Occasionally comes up with a new idea.

_____ Has a reasonable number of new ideas.

_____ Frequently suggests new ways of doing things.

_____ Continually seeks new and better ways of doing things.

by itself or as a supplement to the results and trait approaches. Although this method is easily biased, it forces managers to think of specific aspects of performance. The flavor of the global essay can be captured by the following first paragraph from the evaluation of a construction project supervisor by his project manager. (The "we" means that a vice president also provided input for the appraisal.)

> "Our overall evaluation of your performance is that you achieved about average results for a supervisor of your experience. We are impressed by the fact that you finished the condominium project on time. It is also noteworthy that you were usually fully staffed. However, we believe your performance as a project supervisor needs improvement. You continue to be late in submitting your weekly status reports. You also do not place enough emphasis on safety training."

SELF-APPRAISALS. Under a typical self-appraisal system, employees are asked to analyze their core job duties. The employees write down how well they handled these duties during the appraisal period. Key dimensions of self-appraisal for a supervisor might be cost control, planning, training, delegating, and decision making. Each of these general responsibilities is associated with a more specific set of duties. For example, under training, a supervisor might state, "I showed four employees how to use our voice mail system."

To assist in the self-appraisal, the supervisor might solicit the input of a few peers and subordinates, asking, "What do you think most people in our group would report if asked how well I am delegating?" Next, the supervisor would bring the self-evaluation to his or her superior for further input.[29] The superior can use this information in preparing the performance appraisal required by the company.

Self-appraisals have merit because they actively involve employees in monitoring their own performance. Yet because so many people operate from self-interest, the method cannot substitute for appraisals by superiors.[30]

Potential Errors in Performance Appraisals

Traditional appraisal methods are subject to many errors. *Constant error* refers to the tendency of raters to use only a portion of the scale in rating people. (Rarely does anybody receive a "totally unacceptable" rating.) Some raters are too lenient, some too strict, and some tend toward rating most people in the middle. The *halo effect* literally means that raters sometimes assign people a "halo" because of one outstanding trait. A high (or low) rating on one trait leads automatically to high (or low) ratings on other traits. Recent evidence suggests that quite often the halo effect is warranted and leads to more accurate ratings.[31] This is true because many aspects of performance are truly related to one another.

Recency of events refers to the tendency of evaluators to be more influenced by recent than by old behaviors. Recognizing this evaluation error, some employees will show a burst of good performance just before a scheduled performance review. The term *errors of variable standards* refers to the fact that different organizational units have different standards of good performance. For example, it might be more difficult to be rated outstanding in new product development than in maintenance.

Bias and prejudice can also inflate or deflate ratings. The bias can relate to any demographic or personal factor. One manager was accused by her superior of never giving a man with a good physique a low performance rating.

Organizations can avoid or lessen many of these rating errors by training the people who conduct appraisals. It is also important to have more than one person make an appraisal.

Legally and Scientifically Defensible Appraisal Systems

To satisfy legal requirements, an appraisal system must have the same reliability and validity that are found in a selection device such as a personnel test. Suggestions have been developed for building an appraisal system that satisfies both legal requirements and scientific requirements, which center around having statistical proof that the test is valid. Legal and scientific requirements are similar because both strive for objectivity and accuracy. Key recommendations and suggestions include the following:

1. Appraisal of job performance must be based on an analysis of job requirements as reflected in performance standards. These performance standards must be communicated to and understood by employees.
2. The courts are more likely to sustain appraisal systems that emphasize work behaviors rather than personal traits. It is difficult to defend measuring job performance in terms of personal appearance or subjective traits such as "dependability."
3. The dimensions of job performance rated should be clearly defined and specific rather than ill defined and general. It is better to rate "quality of work" than "pride in work."
4. The appraisal forms should require both subjective and objective information and should include space for additional comments. Subjective information relates to managerial impressions of performance. Objective information relates to tangible results achieved by the employee.
5. Appraisal systems must be validated (correlated with job performance) and of known reliability.
6. An appeal mechanism must be provided if an employee disagrees with a manager's appraisal.
7. Appraisal systems should be kept current by updating job descriptions to ensure that performance is being measured against current expectations.
8. Appraisals should be written, documented, and filed. Furthermore, human resources decisions (such as promotions and salary increases) should be consistent with the appraisals given to employees.
9. Performance appraisal systems should support equal employment opportunity. An employer has little cause for legal concern unless the

performance appraisal system has a disproportionately negative impact on a protected class.[32]

Back to the
Opening Case

Jerry Snyder wanted his employer to work effectively with Workforce 2000, which has already arrived. Snyder should proceed with modern human resources programs as described in this chapter. He should especially hire a diverse group of workers, provide benefits that fit the modern workforce, and conduct diversity awareness programs.

SUMMARY

Staffing ensures that the organization has qualified human resources to meet its objectives. Staffing consists of human resources planning, awareness of equal employment opportunity, pay and benefits, recruitment, selection, placement and orientation, training and development, and performance appraisal. Human resources planning should be linked closely to a firm's strategies and plans.

A firm must consider equal employment opportunity legislation at every step of staffing. The most far-reaching act is the Civil Rights Act of 1964 (Title VII), which established the Equal Employment Opportunity Commission to enforce the law. The seven major areas subject to discrimination are race, color, religion, gender, national origin, age, and disability.

Pay and benefits (compensation) are key aspects of staffing. Pay levels are determined internally by job evaluation. Key external factors include supply and demand and wage surveys. Current trends in pay include an emphasis on variable pay, gainsharing, entrepreneurial pay, team incentives, and comparable worth.

Recruiting is carried out for both full-time employees and contingent workers. Recruiting sources include classified advertisements, present employees, referrals by present employees, and a variety of external sources.

Human resources selection in the staffing model presented in the chapter includes the preliminary screening interview, the application form, personnel (or psychological) tests, the selection interview, the background investigation, and the physical examination. Integrity testing is often included in personnel testing, while drug testing is included in the physical examination. The assessment center method is a comprehensive selection method featuring job simulations.

Job specifications (the personal characteristics and capabilities required for a particular job) should be drawn up before selection methods are put into use with applicants. It is legally necessary to validate personnel tests and other selection techniques to help minimize bias. Validation involves proving that people who score well on the tests will perform well in the job. Placement and orientation help get employees on the right track in performing well in appropriate jobs. Training and development programs help sharpen job skills and improve productivity.

Performance appraisal systems can be used for a variety of purposes including productivity improvement, salary administration, and career development. Some performance appraisal systems include inputs from self-appraisals. Appraisals are subject to various sources of error, and appraisal systems must be scientifically designed to satisfy equal employment opportunity requirements.

KEY TERMS

staffing

human resources planning

replacement tables

human resources information system (HRIS)

equal employment opportunity

point-factor job evaluation

pay-for-knowledge system

variable pay

gainsharing

entrepreneurial pay

comparable worth

employee benefit

flexible benefit package

parental leave

recruitment

contingent workers

realistic job preview

executive search firms

job (or person) specifications

disparate treatment

disparate impact

integrity (honesty) test

polygraph

interview structure

probe

assessment center

training

development

management development

performance appraisal

global essay

QUESTIONS FOR DISCUSSION AND REVIEW

1. What are the components of the organizational staffing model?
2. How does performance appraisal relate to other aspects of the organizational staffing model?
3. How is Workforce 2000 likely to affect your career?
4. Which aspects of human resources planning do you think require quantitative and computer skills?
5. How would an employer know the appropriate starting salary to offer a particular individual?
6. How do you explain the fact that the highest-ranking executive in a company sometime earns

1,000 times more than the lowest-paid full-time employee?

7. Why do you think most job applicants are more apprehensive about psychological tests than selection interviews?
8. Why are placement, orientation, and training considered to be part of organizational staffing?
9. What is your opinion of the value of an executive's sliding down a "zip line"? In what way might it be a form of job discrimination?
10. Are taking this course and reading this text part of your management development? Explain your reasoning.

PROBLEMS FOR ACTION

A. You are placed on a company task force to recruit and select 25 investment banker trainees for your firm. (An investment banker helps companies raise capital and buy and sell other companies.) Describe (1) how you would develop the job specifications for this position and (2) the recruiting and selection techniques you would use.

B. Assume that you work for a chain of department

stores as an assistant to the vice president of store operations. She informs you that the major problem facing the retailer is the rudeness and discourtesy of sales associates (sales clerks). Your superior gives you the assignment of sketching out a training program to deal with this problem. Present your plan in approximately 150 words.

CONCLUDING CASE

Variable Pay at Du Pont

Workers in Du Pont's fibers division tied their pay raises to profits under a special incentive plan. As a result, they were hoping for a big payout around the holidays. But, in the first year of the new plan, the division fell short of its $725 million annual profit goal. So the department's 20,000 employees, who had as much as 4 percent of their pay at risk, did not receive year-end bonuses.

Du Pont decided to scrap the innovative three-year plan in its second year because several employees had cried foul. Division employees have since been returned to a traditional pay plan. James F. Kearns, the fibers division head, said that employees weren't ready for a pay-at-risk program: "It was fine when they were getting more back than they put in, which was the case last year. But when they found out they were not going to get back as much as they invested, some employees said: 'No, this is not fair.'"

The pay incentive plan was mandatory for nonunion employees at the division's 10 nationwide plants. Four of the five plants that have unions also agreed to participate. Here's how the plan worked. Employees this year "gambled" as much as 4 percent of their annual pay that the division would reach its $725 million goal. Last year it was as much as 2 percent on a $670 million goal. An employee with an annual salary of $30,000 this year could have reached a one-time payout of as much as $1,200 if the goal had been met. The worker's regular salary, however, would not be touched if the goal was not met. Last year, that same employee with the same salary earned an extra $600 because the goal was met. The company awarded an additional small bonus because the target was exceeded.

The Du Pont program was designed to give employees a stake in the division's profits to help improve the fibers business. But the fibers business, which represents nearly a quarter of Du Pont's profits, has been hurt by a rise in foreign competition and raw materials costs.

The plan had an additional provision. Employees also could have received half of what was at risk if the division achieved 80 percent of this year's profit goals, or $580 million. Such lofty profits did not materialize.

1. In what way was the Du Pont incentive program a variable pay program?
2. Did the company move too quickly in scrapping the program?
3. How might the Du Pont incentive program been modified to lower the risk of it's failing?

Source: Theresa Humphrey, "Du Pont's Incentive-pay Experiment Falls Flat," Associated Press (December 3, 1990).

REFERENCES

1. Randall S. Schuler and James W. Walker, "Human Resources Strategy: Focusing on Issues and Actions," *Organizational Dynamics* (Summer 1990): 4–19.

2. John Charles Pool and Ross M. Laroe, "Inflation Fears Are Greatly Exaggerated," Rochester *Democrat and Chronicle* (May 23, 1988): 11D.

3. John M. Ivancevich and William F. Glueck, *Foundations of Personnel/Human Resource Management*, 3e (Plano, TX: Business Publications, 1986): 326.

4. Edward J. Giblin, Geoffrey A. Wiegman, and Frank Sanfilippo, "Bringing Pay Up to Date," *Personnel* (November 1990): 17.

5. Edward E. Lawler, III, "What's Wrong with Point-Factor Job Evaluation?" *Personnel* (January 1987): 44.

6. Stuart Feldman, "Another Day, Another Dollar Needs Another Look," *Personnel* (January 1991): 9.

7. Prescott Behn, "An Answer to the Japanese Challenge," *HRMagazine* (August 1990): 77–78.

8. David P. Swinehart, "A Guide to More Productive Team Incentive Programs," *Personnel Journal* (July 1986): 112.

9. Rosabeth Moss Kanter, "From Status to Contribution: Some Organizational Implications of the Changing Basis for Pay," *Personnel* (January 1987): 22.

10. Kenneth A. Kovach and Peter E. Millspaugh, "Comparable Worth: Canada Legislates Pay Equity," *Academy of Management Executive* (May 1990): 93.

11. Kovach and Millspaugh, "Comparable Worth," 96–97.

12. Julie A. Cohen, "Managing Tomorrow's Workforce Today," *Managment Review* (January 1991): 17.

13. Sue Shellenbarger, "Companies Team Up to Improve Quality of Their Employees' Child-Care Choices," *The Wall Street Journal* (October 17, 1991): B1.

14. Sharon E. Barnes, "Looking for a Temporary Solution?" *Human Resources Forum* (August 1990): 1.

15. John P. Wanous, "Installing a Realistic Job Preview: Ten

Tough Choices," *Personnel Psychology* (Spring 1989): 117★–134.

16. Jean Powell Kirnan, John A. Farley, and Kurt F. Geisinger, "The Relationship Between Recruiting Source, Applicant Quality, and Hire Performance: An Analysis by Sex, Ethnicity, and Age," *Personnel Psychology* (Summer 1989): 307.

17. David E. Bowen, Gerald E. Ledford, Jr., and Barry R. Nathan, "Hiring for the Organization, Not the Job," *Academy of Management Executive* (November 1991): 35.

18. *Federal Register* (August 25, 1978): 38290–38315.

19. Paul R. Sackett, Laura R. Burris, and Christine Callahan, "Integrity Testing for Personnel Selection: An Update," *Personnel Psychology* (Autumn 1989): 493; Sackett and Michael M. Harris, "Honesty Testing for Personnel Selection: A Review and Critique," *Personnel Psychology* (Summer 1984): 223.

20. Larry Reynolds, "Truth or Consequences," *Personnel* (January 1991): 5.

21. Sackett, "Integrity Testing," 520.

22. Michael M. Harris, "Reconsidering the Employment Interview: A Review of Recent Literature and Suggestions for Future Research," *Personnel Psychology* (Winter 1989): 691.

23. Art Durity, "Time for a Reference Check-Up," *Personnel* (December 1990): 1.

24. Erich Smith, "Fewer Workers Test Positive for Drug Use," Associated Press (February 13, 1991).

25. Stephen B. Wehrenberg, "Skill and Motivation Divide Training and Orientation," *Personnel Journal* (May 1989): 111.

26. Elizabeth M. Fowler, "Companies Stress Training at All Levels for the 1990s," *The New York Times* (December 31, 1990).

27. David A. Waldman and Ron S. Kenett, "Improve Performance by Appraisal," *HRMagazine* (July 1990): 66–69.

28. James L. Gibson, John M. Ivancevich, and James H. Donnelly, Jr., *Organizations: Behavior, Structure, Process*, 6e (Plano, TX: Business Publications, 1988): 607–608.

29. John W. Lawrie, "Your Performance: Appraise It Yourself!" *Personnel* (January 1989): 21–23.

30. David J. Nigrelle, "Reverse Performance Review: A Good Idea That Doesn't Really Work," *Human Resources Forum* (January 1991): 1, 3.

31. Barry R. Nathan and Nancy Tippins, "The Consequences of Halo 'Error' in Performance Ratings: A Field Study of the Moderating Effect of Halo on Test Validation Results," *Journal of Applied Psychology* (June 1990): 290.

32. Charles Lee, "Smoothing Out Appraisal Systems," *HRMagazine* (March 1990): 72–76; Wayne F. Cascio and H. John Bernardin, "Implications of Performance Appraisal Litigation for Personnel Decisions," *Personnel Psychology* (Summer 1981): 211–212.

COMPREHENSIVE CASE
FOR PART III

The World's Largest Temporary Workforce

At the U.S. Census Bureau, a workforce of 565,000 "temps" came and went in a few short months during the 1990 census. They carried out data collection and processing functions for the census. About 300,000 of them worked during the peak time in the spring of 1990. This scenario will be repeated in the year 2000. Mandated by the Constitution, statistical data collection by the Census Bureau has many important consequences. Among them are assigning the number of members of Congress for each state, legislative redistricting, government funding, and community planning.

In the past, census data were collected by federal marshals who collected information from their local offices. Years later, temporary workers (enumerators) visited each home in the country and recorded vital statistics. Although the census is now highly automated, the enumerator has not disappeared. For the 1990 census, enumerators gathered addresses of people living in remote areas. With the help of satellite photos, they tracked down buildings block by block. The Census Bureau used this information to produce 106 million address labels for the project's mass mailing. The remainder of country's residence addresses were compiled from mailing lists with the help of the U.S. Postal Service.

After census questionnaires are distributed, the results must be retrieved and tabulated. Three retrieval methods are used. Almost 90 million housing units are covered by asking the occupants to mail back the census forms. In rural areas, enumerators drop off the census forms and request that the residents complete them and mail them back. People living in the most remote areas receive their forms by mail, but enumerators retrieve them personally. During their visits, the enumerators gather additional information.

All completed forms wind up at one of seven processing offices located around the country. During the peak of the 1990 census processing, each office had 1,500 employees and operated 16 hours per day. Each office is equipped with advanced computing equipment, high-speed cameras, and microfilm units. This technology is not able to solve all of the Bureau's problems, however. Keypunching is still required to enter written responses. Also, many employees are needed to track forms, maintain computer equipment, ensure quality control, and provide telephone assistance.

At the Census Bureau, a core staff of 70 manages the transition from processing one census to the next, which occurs every 10 years. An additional 150 census workers are reassigned from other jobs about 2 years out of 10 to work on the census. The remainder of the staff in the processing offices are hired from the local community. Eighty percent of positions in the processing offices are filled on an as-needed basis. The Bureau relies on training to get the temporary workers in the processing offices up and running.

Staffing for the Training Process

For the 1990 census, an on-site staff of four trainers was hired at each of the seven processing offices to "train the trainers." During several days of intense activity, the headquarters staff led the trainers through a dry run of actual census conditions. The headquarters staff had to envision the many possible job duties of census workers and develop specialized training packages for different job categories. The training program developed by the Bureau comprises the following five areas:

1. *Management and supervisory training.* Staffers are given an overview of census operations and procedures along with skill sessions in interpersonal relations, team building and problem solving.
2. *Employee orientation.* All new processing office employees are provided with general information about Census Bureau operations and procedures. They are also shown how to complete appointment papers, and they take an oath to uphold the confidentiality of census data. The Bureau presents three videotapes on such topics as the history of the census and quality assurance.
3. *Processing and administration training procedures.* The Bureau uses three types of training formats—classroom, on-the-job training, and videotapes—to explain core job duties.

4. *Technical training.* The Census Bureau staff and some equipment vendors instruct computer workers on the technical aspects of their job.
5. *Self-study.* Each office has resource material in book, computer, and video formats covering subjects such as supervising or operating minicomputers.

For each census, the Bureau trains approximately 500,000 people in the field offices. Aside from the enumerators, these include clerks, keyers, and problem solvers. The last group helps citizens complete forms over the telephone. All this training follows a "cascading-down" plan of instruction. For example, district office managers are trained at central locations, and they return to their field offices to train supervisors. The supervisors then train crew leaders.

Quality Assurance

Census Bureau management has several strategies to maintain high quality. One challenge it faces is that temporaries are paid little more than the minimum wage. Management attempts to motivate these workers by offering them useful work experience in fields such as data entry and interviewing. Every employee's work is checked routinely. Field supervisors often reinterview occupants to verify information. When they discover errors, the supervisors give feedback and counseling to the clerks who made them. After discovering a second set of errors the supervisors provide retraining. A third set of errors leads to a job change or dismissal.

Training Problems

Bureau management has identified some training problems. They are concerned that the training department receives less than 1 percent of the overall budget for the census. Scheduling of large numbers of people requires extraordinary coordination, and half a million people must be trained only a short time prior to the operation. Producing accurate software training packages has proved to be a difficult task. For the 1990 census, every software package underwent extensive content changes up to the last minute before it was shipped.

Employee turnover has always been a major problem in completing the census. All employees are hired on a temporary basis. They receive no benefits, and they are subjected to being laid off and rehired as the work flow changes. Employment lasts from six weeks to two years. The Bureau usually recruits and trains 20 percent more workers than it requires to get the job done.

Unfavorable Reaction to the Census

Despite the efforts of the Census Bureau to do a high-quality job, some citizens are displeased with its output. An advocate for the poor in New York City made this comment:

"The census is a ripoff. Hundreds of thousands of people aren't counted because they don't live anywhere in particular. They roam the streets and sleep in doorways. Thousands of other people aren't counted because they want to hide their identity. Suppose you know the law says only four people can live in an apartment. You're going to be afraid to tell the census taker that nine people live in your little apartment with only one bathroom. And some of the census takers are afraid to go into the neighborhoods where people are not being counted.

"Not counting all these people in the census hurts the poor. It means that New York doesn't get nearly the government support it should. It also minimizes the problem of how many people are homeless and starving."

1. What suggestions do you have for improving the training program for temporary census workers?
2. What personal characteristics and qualities should the Census Bureau look for in hiring enumerators?
3. How adequate is the organization structure chosen by the Census Bureau?
4. How could census workers be trained to do a better job of counting the urban poor (assuming there is a problem)?
5. To what extent is the Census Bureau a bureaucracy?
6. What suggestions can you offer for reducing the turnover of temporary workers at the Bureau?
7. What suggestions do you have for doing a better job with Census 2000?

Source: Information about the Census Bureau is from facts reported in Catherine Burt and Joan March, "Census '90: How to Train and Manage 500,000 Temps," *Management Review* (April 1990): 40–45. The interview comments were gathered from a direct source.

Part IV
Leading

Chapter 11

Leadership and Teamwork

OPENING
CASE

An Industrialist
Loosens the
Reins

Since its origins in 1947, the Lucky-Goldstar Group has diversified rapidly into a range of products from shampoo to solar power systems. During the firm's expansion, the founding Koo family made all the major decisions. Ultimately the management group became too large for the Koo family to manage effectively. When worldwide annual sales reached $25 billion, both quality and innovation suffered.

As Lucky-Goldstar lost business to competitors, critics blamed the authoritarian style of Chairman Koo Cha-Kyung. One top-level manager explained, "Nobody had the guts to tell him to get out of the daily management and let the professionals run the business."

At the recommendation of consultants, Koo is attempting to increase innovation in his company. His method is to grant more decision-making authority to front-line managers. He has also created three special executive committees. Their job is to develop Lucky-Goldstar's strategy, along with budgeting and human resources policies. A senior Goldstar top-level manager said, "We are becoming more efficient in management and quicker in decision making."

Koo's lessening of control is also aimed at increasing the quality of the Goldstar line of consumer electronics. Newly empowered managers are making their products (such as VCRs) more user friendly. They are also investing more in high-technology products.

Goldstar management has learned to take the new decision-making style seriously. The company fired three top-level managers because they were not allowing authority to be pushed downward.

Source: As reported in Laxmi Nakarmi, "At Lucky-Goldstar the Koos Loosen the Reins," *Business Week* (February 18, 1991): 72–73.

Chairman Koo's shift has implications for leadership in many settings. A manager who exerts the right approach to leadership can have a profound impact on the well-being of the group. Leadership has always been a topic of major importance to scholars and practitioners, and current interest is intense as organizations struggle to survive in a competitive world.

Leadership is no longer just the domain of a company president or a few top-level managers. In today's world, take-charge ability is important at all levels of management. Employees who are in direct contact with customers and clients often require stronger leadership than top-level workers, because entry-level workers often lack experience, direction, and a strong work ethic. Furthermore, the current emphasis on work teams means that first-level managers have to provide leadership to foster teamwork.

ETHICS QUESTION
What ethical responsibilities does a leader have in setting a vision for the firm?

Leadership involves influencing others to achieve specific objectives in specific situations. Although leadership is a major function of management, it is not the same thing as management. In the view of John Kotter, management copes with complexity, which requires preserving order and consistency. Leadership, in comparison, copes with change in a competitive, rapidly changing world. Effective leaders deal with change by formulating a vision of the future and setting a direction for that vision.[1]

Leadership and management can also be differentiated by their outcomes. Management produces a degree of predictability and order. It has the potential of consistently producing key results expected by various stakeholders, such as delivering products to customers on time. Leadership produces change, such as Koo's efforts in enhancing product quality.[2]

Although leadership is considered a separate function within management, it is important for carrying out the other functions. Effective leadership skills help managers do a better job of planning, organizing, and controlling.

The discussion of leadership in this chapter centers around three topics of relevance for managers: leadership traits and behaviors, styles of leadership, and the leader's role in enhancing teamwork and quality. Most of what we say here has relevance for all three levels of managers, unless otherwise noted.

TRAITS, CHARACTERISTICS, AND BEHAVIORS OF EFFECTIVE LEADERS

A logical approach to understanding leadership is to study the traits, characteristics, and behaviors of effective leaders. For many years scholars downplayed the study of leadership characteristics, but recently an interest in the inner qualities of leaders has reawakened. The traits of leaders are related closely to the degree to which others perceive these people to be leaders. For example, a person who exudes self-confidence would generally be perceived by others as having leadership qualities. Recent evidence confirms the fact that effective leaders are different from other people. Their differences relate to the traits and characteristics described in the following sections.[3] The current interest in leadership traits is also reflected in a demand for leaders with vision and charisma.

Hundreds of traits and personal characteristics of leaders have been studied at one time or another. Furthermore, most people with work experience have an opinion about the traits, characteristics, and behaviors that are required for effective leadership. The following sections discuss several leadership qualities that are supported by research evidence or careful observation. They are grouped under the categories of cognitive skills, personality traits and characteristics, and relationships with subordinates.

Cognitive Skills

An effective leader must have appropriate **cognitive skills,** or mental abilities and knowledge. Three cognitive skills are particularly important: problem-solving ability, insight into people and situations, and technical and professional competence.

PROBLEM-SOLVING ABILITY. A current theory of leadership supports what has been long known: Managerial leaders possess an effective problem-solving ability or intelligence. According to the **cognitive resource theory,** intelligent and competent leaders make effective plans, decisions, and strategies.[4] They anticipate problems before they occur and persevere until the problems are solved. In the process, they demonstrate imagination, creativity, and a willingness to experiment with unproven methods and approaches.

Leadership positions in today's firms place a continuously increasing demand on problem-solving ability. An example is the leadership approach of Paul H. O'Neill, CEO of ALCOA. Although he has vastly decentralized his company, he remains its chief strategist. For example, he has worked out the details for setting up joint ventures with foreign partners.[5]

INSIGHT INTO PEOPLE AND SITUATIONS. An effective leader has the ability to read people and situations. Insight into people is essential when assigning work to subordinates and choosing among job candidates. Insight into situations enables a leader to choose the appropriate leadership style for the task at hand.

TECHNICAL AND PROFESSIONAL COMPETENCE. Some people argue that a person who has the right leadership characteristics and skills can lead various types of groups. Perhaps this is true in top-level leadership situations, such as when a former army general becomes a company president and then a secretary of state. In lesser leadership positions, however, it is difficult for a leader to establish rapport with subordinates when the leader does not understand the technical details of their work. Group members must respect the leader's technical skills. At a minimum, a leader who manages specialists must not be readily bluffed by their technical arguments.

Personality Traits and Characteristics

Although they are difficult to measure accurately, personality traits and characteristics have an important influence on leadership effectiveness. Which traits and characteristics are the most relevant varies with the situation. For example, enthusiasm may be more important for a sales manager than for an inventory control manager. The sales manager's enthusiasm may be needed to help sales representatives cope with rejection by customers.

ETHICS QUESTION
What ethical responsibilities does a firm have to appoint people with pleasant dispositions to leadership positions?

The relevance of leadership traits was illustrated by a study conducted in a contracting firm. The traits studied were Type A behavior (impatient, demanding, and hostile) and negative affectivity (an unpleasant disposition). First-level managers who possessed these characteristics had lower-performing units, and their employees experienced more symptoms of poor health.[6]

The following sections describe personality traits and characteristics associated with leadership effectiveness.

SELF-CONFIDENCE. A realistic degree of self-confidence enhances leadership effectiveness. A leader who is self-confident without being overbearing instills confidence among subordinates. In one study, interviews conducted with 60 top-level managers revealed that they believed in themselves but were not cocky or self-worshipers.[7] The concept of self-confidence is useful in studying leadership because it illustrates the relationship between traits and behavior. A manager who is inwardly self-confident will behave confidently and will be perceived as acting cool under pressure.

POWER MOTIVE. Effective top-level managers have a strong need to control resources. Leaders with strong power motives have three dominant characteristics. First, they act with vigor and determination to exert their power. Second, they invest much time in thinking about ways to alter the behavior and thinking of others. Third, they care about their personal standing with those around them.[8] This high need for power is important because it means that the leader is interested in influencing others. Both the power motive and the achievement motive (described next) will be reintroduced in Chapter 12.

NEED FOR ACHIEVEMENT. The need for achievement refers to a strong desire to accomplish things for their own sake. When a person with a strong drive for achievement is placed in a leadership position, he or she will often exhibit a leadership style characterized by a strong sense of time urgency. In turn, this strong sense of time urgency can be a positive force for innovation.[9] Entrepreneurial leaders have a strong need for achievement.

SENSE OF HUMOR. The right amount of humor contributes to leadership effectiveness because it relieves tension and boredom and defuses hostility. If people can be made to see the humor in a situation, some of their anger will dissipate. In one company, several sales representatives did not get the technical support promised by the home office to help them negotiate with prospective customers. When an official from the home office finally met with these representatives, he congratulated them and explained that they had just completed the first phase of a training program called "Self-Reliance for Field Personnel." The Managers in Action illustrates the use of humor in dealing with group members and running a business.

ENTHUSIASM. Enthusiasm is desirable in most leadership situations. Employees respond positively to enthusiasm, partially because they perceive its expression as a reward for doing things right. Enthusiasm is also desirable because it helps build good relationships with group members. A leader may express enthusiasm verbally ("Way to go, Erika!") or nonverbally through gestures, handshakes, or touching.

ASSERTIVENESS. Leaders, along with other professionals, must be forthright in expressing their demands, opinions, feelings, and attitudes. Assertiveness helps leaders perform many tasks and achieve goals. Among them are confronting group members about their mistakes, demanding higher performance from employees, and making legitimate demands on higher management. In contrast, leaders who express their demands in an overly pushy, obnoxious, and abrasive manner are termed *aggressive*. Also in contrast to assertive leaders are passive individuals who suppress their own ideas, attitudes, feelings, and thoughts as if they were likely to be perceived as controversial.

MANAGERS IN ACTION

Why does a golfer wear two pairs of socks? In case he or she gets a hole in one.

Telling jokes like this one, Michael Pasternak and Allen Sullivan have created Socks Galore. The company is chain of 62 stores in 34 states with an $18 million annual sales volume. Pasternak was formerly an education professor at Vanderbilt University, and Sullivan was one of his graduate students. The two call themselves the Sock Docs. Their freewheeling business tactics include attending sales meetings in clown suits and performing skits. Socks Galore are sold with the instruction "TGIF," or toes go in first.

When the company was purchased by Sara Lee, a company spokeswoman said, "Their management style and personalities were certainly an attractive part of the acquisition." Pasternak and Sullivan emphasize producing high-quality socks even though they cost up to twice as much. Another aspect of quality control is that they train their own salespeople at the "Sock Doc College" in Franklin, Tennessee.

Source: As reported in Phil West, " 'Sock Docs' Operate Footwear Empire with Offbeat Humor," Associated Press (October 9, 1990).

Relationships with Subordinates (Leadership Behaviors)

Some traits of effective leaders are linked closely to behaviors involving relationships with team members. Several of the most important of these traits are described next.

INTERPERSONAL SKILLS. As described in Chapter 1, one of the key managerial skills is the ability to work effectively with others. Frequently the person chosen for a managerial position is not the highest producer in the team. Instead, this person is an ample producer who gets along well with co-workers.

LEADING BY EXAMPLE. A simple but effective way of influencing team members is to **lead by example,** or by acting as a positive model. Among the behaviors effective leaders set an example for are integrity and honesty, concern for quality, good teamwork, and careful work habits.

SENSITIVITY AND TACT. Being sensitive to team members' feelings and using tact help build morale. In contrast, being insensitive may block a manager's career, preventing him or her from exercising leadership at a higher organizational level. Insensitivity to others, which is characterized by an abrasive, intimidating, bullying style, is a critical flaw. In one instance, when top-level managers perceived such behavior in an aspiring middle-level manager, they made the judgment that this insensitive person was not promotable.[10] Another important aspect of leadership sensitivity is responding to cultural diversity by, for example, not asking an employee to work on a religious holiday that is significant to him or her.

SUPPORTIVENESS. Providing emotional support to team members contributes to leadership effectiveness. By giving encouragement and praise, a leader usually increases morale and often increases productivity. Supportive behavior typically stems from personal characteristics such as empathy, warmth, and flexibility.

MAINTAINING HIGH EXPECTATIONS. Holding high expectations for team members often raises their levels of performance. This is known as the *Pygmalion effect*. It works because people develop more self-confidence when they recognize that their superiors have confidence in them. Increased confidence leads in turn to increased performance. Although the Pygmalion effect does not always work, it has been documented recently. Twenty-nine platoons in the Israeli defense forces were randomly assigned to either a "Pygmalion group" or a group that was treated as usual. Leaders of the Pygmalion platoon were told that their troops had, on average, unusually high command potential. The Pygmalion platoon outscored the other platoons on such measures as job knowledge, physical fitness, and target shooting.[11] In short, the self-fulfilling prophecy came true.

Limitations to the Trait Approach

The trait approach to understanding and predicting leadership effectiveness has merit, but it also has limitations. One problem is that the desirable amount of the trait or characteristic is not indicated. A second problem is that traits are defined imprecisely and they overlap. A third problem is that the trait approach does not specify how leadership requirements may vary from one situation to another.

Finally, the trait approach fails to show how a person who lacks a certain desirable trait or behavior may succeed because of a compensating quality. For instance, an insensitive top-level manager who has extraordinary ability to make financial deals may still be an effective leader.

LEARNING CHECK   Describe leadership from the standpoint of the key traits, characteristics, and behaviors of successful leaders.

STYLES OF LEADERSHIP

Effective leaders are relatively consistent in the way they attempt to influence the behavior of team members. The manager who makes all the major decisions in one situation is not likely to share decision making in another. Likewise, the manager who is considerate in one situation is not likely to be insensitive in another. **Leadership style** is the relatively consistent pattern of behavior that characterizes a leader. Much of the consistency occurs because a leadership style is based somewhat on an individual's personality.

Despite this consistency, some managers can modify their style as the situation requires.

The behavior of most managers is too complex to be described by a single style. In this chapter, we study three approaches to categorizing leadership style: the leadership continuum, the Leadership Grid,® and the transformational and charismatic leader.

The Leadership Continuum

The classical method of classifying leadership styles is to arrange leadership behavior along a continuum of the amount of authority exerted by the leader. Although this approach originated almost 50 years ago, most new approaches to leadership style are rooted in it. As shown in Figure 11-1, the leadership continuum begins with the autocratic style, passes through the participative style, and ends with the free-rein style.

AUTOCRATIC STYLE. An **autocratic leader** maintains most of the authority in a group by issuing orders and telling group members what to do without consulting them. To the autocrat (or authoritarian), the basis for leadership is formal authority. Autocratic leaders may have a few favorite subordinates, but they usually regard close interpersonal relationships with group members as unnecessary.

The autocratic style of leadership is generally not favored by modern firms, but it works well in some situations. One example is a high-accident work area where the employees are not particularly knowledgeable about the potential risks. Also, managers who are typically more laid back will sometimes become autocratic when faced with a crisis. When Daewoo (the South Korean conglomerate) faced major financial troubles, Chairman Kim dramatically changed his leadership style. Kim switched from a hands-off manager to one who took decisive control of operations. His methods included writing personal letters to managers, expressing dissatisfaction with their "poor performance and easygoing manner," and retiring many others.[12]

PARTICIPATIVE STYLE. A **participative leader** is one who shares decision-making authority with group members. This makes it possible to share

FIGURE 11-1
The Leadership
Continuum

AMOUNT OF AUTHORITY HELD BY THE LEADER

Autocratic Style   Participative Style   Free-Rein Style

• Consultative   • Consensus   • Democratic

AMOUNT OF AUTHORITY HELD BY GROUP MEMBERS

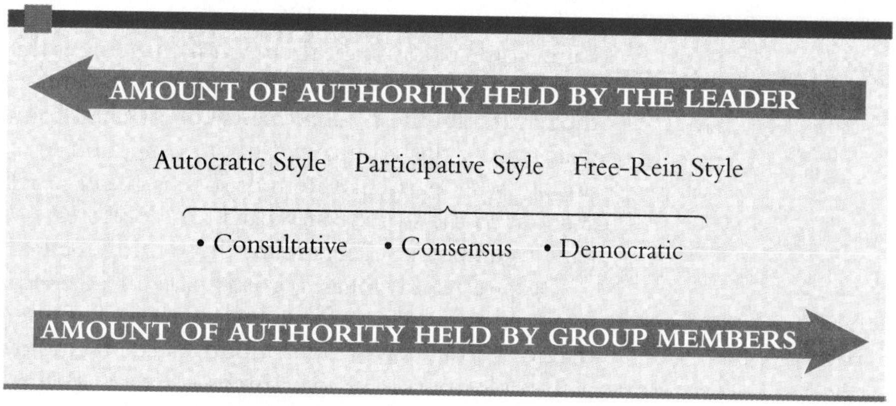

A consultative leader discusses an issue with group members before making his decision.

leadership and empowerment in a group. Participative leadership occupies enough space on the leadership continuum to warrant dividing it into three subtypes: consultative, consensus, and democratic. A **consultative leader** solicits opinions from the group before making a decision, yet does not feel obliged to accept the group's thinking. A standard way to practice consultative leadership would be for the leader to call a group meeting to discuss an issue before making a decision.

A **consensus leader** encourages group discussion about an issue and then makes a decision that reflects the consensus (general agreement) of group members. Consensus leaders thus turn over more authority to the group than do consultative leaders. The consensus leadership style results in long delays in decision making, because every party involved provides input. However, consensus often leads to commitment to the decision.

A **democratic leader** confers final authority on the group. This leader functions as a collector of opinions and takes a vote before making a decision. Democratic leaders turn over so much authority to the group that they are sometimes classified as free-rein leaders (one extreme on the continuum).

In recent years, the shift to employee participation and empowerment has become a dominant theme in management thought and practice. A case in point is Levi Strauss, a company that has endured despite tough times in the apparel business. Chairman Robert Haas commented, "Basically, as the chairman of this company, I can't go out and sew a better seam. I can't figure out what particular item or style is going to sell next year. I can't sell the account to the store. But what I can do is create a climate within the company to empower others to do those things better."[13]

Despite its advantages, participative leadership does create some problems. Many managers feel a loss of power because of it. Another problem is that for participative leadership to succeed, employees must want to participate and must have worthwhile input. Before practicing participative

ETHICS QUESTION
Why might empowerment of employees be considered a socially responsible act?

leadership it is advisable to provide firm guidelines as to what is to be accomplished.

FREE-REIN STYLE.   A **free-rein leader** turns over almost all authority to group members and does as little leading as possible. Such leaders make few attempts to increase productivity or to coach their employees. At their best, free-rein leaders define company constraints and act as resource people. Should anybody have a question, the free-rein leader is available for consultation.

At times the free-rein leader is simply an abdicator of responsibility who cares little for achieving productivity goals or developing people. At other times, however, the free-rein style is appropriate and leads to high productivity. This is especially true in leadership situations in which the manager directs the work of highly skilled and reliable employees. These individuals may not require technical direction or encouragement, but in the long run, even the most self-sufficient employees require some feedback and recognition in order to sustain high performance.

Leadership Grid Styles

The **Leadership Grid** (formerly called the *Managerial Grid*) is a framework for classifying leadership styles that examines a leader's concern for task accomplishment and people simultaneously. The Grid has been updated several times and has been tested with millions of managers throughout the world. It is also a comprehensive system of leadership training and organization development.[14]

As shown in Figure 11-2, the Leadership Grid describes leadership style in terms of concerns for production and people. The concerns reflect attitudes rather than actual behavior. Concern for production includes results, the bottom line, performance, profits, and mission. Concern for people includes group members and colleagues. Each of these concerns (or dimensions) exists in varying degrees along a continuum from 1 (low) to 9 (high). These dimensions are independent. A manager's standing on one concern does not influence his or her standing on any other. For example, a leader can show high concern for both people and production.

GRID STYLES.   The styles shown in Figure 11-2 represent the most important style differences among leaders, although 81 potential styles exist.

- Style 9,1, shown in the lower right corner of the Grid, is a maximum concern for production combined with a minimum concern for people. A leader with this orientation concentrates on maximizing production by exercising formal authority and power and dictating what people should do. Autocratic leaders are typically 9,1.
- Style 1,9, shown in the top left corner, is a minimum concern for production coupled with a maximum concern for people. Leaders with this orientation place primary emphasis on good feelings among co-workers and group members even at the expense of accomplishing work.

FIGURE 11-2 The Leadership Grid® Figure

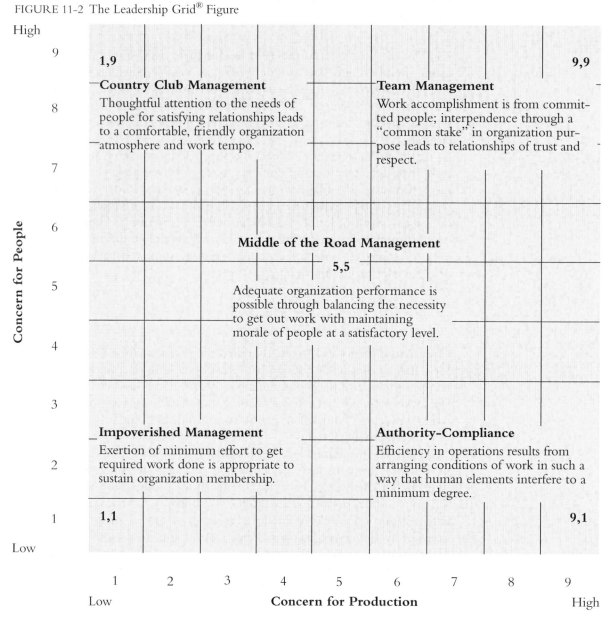

High

9   **1,9**   **9,9**

    Country Club Management   **Team Management**
8   Thoughtful attention to the needs of   Work accomplishment is from commit-
    people for satisfying relationships leads ted people; interpendence through a
    to a comfortable, friendly organization   "common stake" in organization pur-
    atmosphere and work tempo.   pose leads to relationships of trust and
                                              respect.
7

6   **Middle of the Road Management**

                                              5,5
5
                               Adequate organization performance is
                               possible through balancing the necessity
                               to get out work with maintaining
4   morale of people at a satisfactory level.

3

    Impoverished Management   **Authority-Compliance**
2   Exertion of minimum effort to get   Efficiency in operations results from
    required work done is appropriate to   arranging conditions of work in such a
    sustain organization membership.   way that human elements interfere to a
                                            minimum degree.
1   **1,1**   **9,1**

Low

    1   2   3   4   5   6   7   8   9

    Low   **Concern for Production**   High

Concern for People (vertical axis label)

Source: The Leadership Grid® Figure from *Leadership Dilemmas—Grid Solutions,* by Robert R. Blake and Anne Adams McCanse. Houston: Gulf Publishing Company, p. 29. Copyright © 1991, by Scientific Methods, Inc. Reproduced by permission of the owners.

ETHICS QUESTION
Why might a 1,1 leader on
the Leadership Grid be
considered unethical?

- Style 1,1, shown in the lower left corner, is a minimum concern for both production and people. The 1,1 manager does only the minimum required to stay with the firm. Free-rein leaders who are abdicating responsibility are 1,1 managers.
- Style 5,5, shown in the center, is the orientation of the "middle-of-the-roader," who does the job but avoids making waves and who conforms to the status quo. These managers "go along to get along."

- Style 9,9, shown in the upper right corner, integrates concerns for production and people. This is a goal-directed, team approach that seeks to gain optimum results through participation, involvement, and commitment. Consultative and consensus subtypes of participative managers are typically 9,9 leaders.

Although a manager's Grid style may be consistent over a range of situations, managers may revert to a backup Grid style when the dominant style does not fit the situation. A manager's backup style will surface when the manager is under pressure, tension, or intense conflict with others. An example of shifting to the backup style would be when an employee performs poorly despite the manager's 9,9 style and the manager shifts to a 9,1 tactic of threats and punishments.[15]

ONE BEST STYLE. The Leadership Grid philosophy contends that a 9,9 style is almost always best, because it leads to such positive consequences as high productivity, satisfaction, and creativity. The 9,9 style is said to be almost universally applicable, because it is based on the belief that conflict should be confronted and resolved rather than suppressed or subjected to ineffective compromises.

The 9,9 style has a built-in flexibility, rather than a "one size fits all" philosophy. With it, the manager evaluates the situation and then uses principles of human behavior to handle problems.

Back to the
Opening Case

In Grid terminology, Koo Cha-Kyung used mostly a 9,1 leadership style. In order to increase innovation at Lucky-Goldstar, Koo shifted toward a 9,9 leadership style. Part of this shift in leadership style was to grant more decision-making authority to front-line managers.

The Transformational and Charismatic Style of Leader

Considerable attention is currently being paid to a style of leader who goes beyond merely conducting transactions with people. The **transformational leader** is one who helps organizations and people make positive changes in the way they do things. This type of leader exerts a higher level of influence than does a transactional leader, thereby motivating people to do more than expected. Transformational leadership is seen as the key to revitalizing large business corporations. A transformational leader can develop new visions for a firm and mobilize employees to accept and work toward attaining these visions. To bring about these changes, the transformational leader revamps the organizational culture.

HOW TRANSFORMATIONS TAKE PLACE. Transformations take place in one or more of the following four ways:

1. By raising people's level of consciousness about the importance and value of designated rewards and the ways to achieve them.

2. By getting people to transcend their self-interests for the sake of the work group and the firm.
3. By raising people's focus on minor satisfactions to a quest for self-fulfillment.
4. By altering or expanding group members' needs on Maslow's hierarchy of needs.[16]

James Kinnear's role in the revitalization of Texaco several years ago is an example of transformational leadership. Over a four-year period, CEO Kinnear brought Texaco back from the brink of disaster. The company had paid out $11 billion in a damage award to Getty Oil, faced bankruptcy, and fought a takeover fight. In addition, it had an inefficient bureaucracy and a poor oil exploration record. Kinnear reshaped virtually all of Texaco's operations and transformed the company into an innovative and growing force in the industry.[17]

HOW CHARISMA TIES IN WITH TRANSFORMATIONAL LEADERSHIP. Transformational leaders have **charisma**—the ability to lead others based on personal charm, magnetism, inspiration, and emotion. The study of charisma is important because organizations are in search of inspiring leaders. Following are some significant characteristics of charismatic leaders.[18]

First, charismatic leaders have vision. They offer a vision (or goal) of where the organization is headed and how it can get there (a plan). A vision is more than a forecast. It describes an ideal version of the future of an organization or an organizational unit. As described in Chapter 1, organizational progress depends on the top-level manager's having this sense of vision. A sense of vision also inspires employees to perform well. Visionary leadership may be most appropriate at the top levels of a firm, but it also applies to organizational units. For example, the head of a branch may choose to inspire the employees under his or her command to become the best branch in the firm.

Second, charismatic leaders are masterful communicators. They formulate believable dreams and portray their vision of the future as the only path to follow. They use metaphors to inspire people. An example is one of Mary Kay Ash's (of Mary Kay Cosmetics) favorites: "Bumble bees are not supposed to be able to fly because they have such heavy bodies and small wings. But they do fly. You, too, can achieve your goals even if other people say you can't."

Third, charismatic leaders inspire trust. They inspire such confidence that subordinates are willing to risk their careers to pursue their chiefs' vision. To strengthen the perception that they are leaders, they take the initiative to get recognition for their accomplishments. They toot their own horns without feeling embarrassed.

Fourth, charismatic leaders help group members feel capable. They build feelings of competence among group members. One technique they use is to let their people achieve success on relatively easy projects. They praise their people and then give them more demanding assignments.

Finally, charismatic leaders have energy and an action-oriented leadership style. They exude energy, serving as a model for getting things done well and on time. In Grid language, they are 9,9 leaders.

Mary Kay Ash, of Mary Kay Cosmetics, a well-known charismatic leader who inspires her employees through colorful communication.

Few people are born with or develop the type of magnetic personality that makes it easy to be charismatic. Nevertheless, managers can learn to act charismatically. They can develop a vision statement for whatever small part of an organization they run. They can become more emotionally expressive by letting their feelings be known. They can strengthen their communication skills and use colorful metaphors. They can give ample recognition and verbal praise to people working for them. Most important, they can empower the people who work for them to get them involved in the vision. The Manager in Action describes a leader who is charismatic and visionary.

MANAGER IN ACTION

Yvonne Scruggs-Leftwich had a distinguished record of public service. She had held such key positions as commissioner of the New York State Division of Housing and deputy mayor of Philadelphia. After leaving public service, she joined the glamorous world of investment banking. However, Scruggs-Leftwich was concerned that she wasn't helping people directly as an investment banker, and she wanted to create a business to serve the people. Her novel idea was to build the country's first "nondepository bank," to be located in her hometown of Buffalo. Customers could cash checks, purchase money orders, wire money, and pay bills in cash. Scruggs-Leftwich would then transfer the funds to the utilities.

When she decided to staff the bank's offices with people from the community, her friends scoffed. "I was accused of having made a classic bad business decision," she said. "When you divert energies and resources to training, it means that you have to work a lot harder." But she felt that she owed the communities these precious jobs.

After the Buffalo center became profitable, she opened two more centers. Soon each of these locations was serving around 45,000 people each month. Scruggs-Leftwich believes her vision of a bank for low-income people has positioned her for the 1990s. "These are meat-and-potatoes times," says the entrepreneur.

Source: As reported in Don Wallace and Michael Maren, "Artists of the Impossible," *Success* (January-February 1991): 30.

FIEDLER'S CONTINGENCY THEORY OF LEADERSHIP

According to **contingency leadership,** the best style of leadership depends on factors relating to group members and the work setting. Similarly, managerial effectiveness depends on a match between leadership style and the situation. The best developed contingency theory is **Fiedler's contingency theory of leadership.** His model specifies the conditions under which leaders should use task-motivated and relationship-motivated styles. A starting point in Fiedler's approach is to analyze the amount of control the leader has in a particular situation.[19]

Situational Control (or Favorableness)

Situational control is the degree to which the leader can control and influence the outcomes of group effort. Fiedler's measurements of situational control (or favorableness of the situation to the leader) are based on three factors. Listed in order of importance, they are:

1. *Leader-member relations*—the extent to which group members accept and support their leader.
2. *Task structure*—the extent to which the leader knows exactly what to do and how well and in what detail the tasks to be completed are defined.
3. *Position power*—the extent to which the organization provides the leader with the means of rewarding and punishing group members and with appropriate formal authority to get the job done.

A leader would therefore have good control over a situation in which she or he (1) was well liked by group members, (2) had a specific task for them to accomplish, and (3) was given substantial formal authority by the organization.

Leadership Effectiveness

Numerous studies have investigated the relationship among leadership style, situational control by the leader, and leadership effectiveness. Figure 11-3 summarizes the major findings of these studies with over 800 groups in various settings. The task-motivated style (high concern for production) generally produces the best results when the leader has very high or very low control of the situation. The relationship-motivated style (high concern for people) is best when the situation is under moderate or intermediate control. Fiedler has also added an intermediate style of leadership, called *socio-independent leadership,* that falls midway between relationship-motivated and task-motivated. Socio-independent leaders tend to perform the best when their control is high.

What is the rationale behind these findings? When the leader is in a highly favorable situation, the group is prepared to complete its task and therefore appreciates a task-motivated style. Working from a base of mutual

FIGURE 11-3
Summary of Findings
from Fiedler's
Contingency Theory of
Leadership

Task-motivated and socio-independent leaders perform best when they have the most control (highly favorable).	Relationship-motivated leaders perform best when they have moderate control (moderately favorable).	Task-motivated leaders perform best when they have low control (highly unfavorable).
High	*Moderate*	*Low*

AMOUNT OF SITUATIONAL CONTROL BY LEADER

a. Leader-member relations are good. b. Task is well structured. c. Leader has high position power.	A combination of favorable and unfavorable factors.	a. Leader-member relations are poor. b. Task is poorly structured. c. Leader has low position power.

trust and clarity about job duties and rewards, the leader can focus on task accomplishment. Likewise, when the situation is unfavorable and the leader has little control, the leader must take forceful charge of the situation. A task-oriented style therefore works well in this situation.

In situations of moderate control or favorability, the leader faces ambiguity and leader-member relationships are strained. A relationship-motivated style works well because the leader must get close to group members to reduce anxiety, conflict, and uncertainty. The reason why socio-independent leaders perform the best with high control has not yet been determined.

IMPLICATIONS. A major implication of Fiedler's theory is that managers should modify situations to match their style. Task-motivated leaders would want to make a situation more favorable or less favorable. To make the situation more favorable for exercising control, the leader might take steps such as smoothing out relationships with group members, better defining the task to increase task structure, and obtaining more formal authority. A relationship-motivated leader who wanted to create a situation of intermediate favorability might create ambiguity by giving out vague instructions.

LEARNING CHECK

Describe several approaches to classifying leadership styles and explain how Fiedler's contingency theory of leadership relates to leadership style.

THE LEADER'S ROLE IN BUILDING TEAMWORK

As emphasized throughout this text, teamwork is an important requirement in the modern organization. A key role for the leader is therefore to encourage teamwork. One of the explanations of leadership described in this chapter, the Leadership Grid, emphasizes the importance of becoming a group manager. This section describes more specific leadership attitudes and techniques that can foster teamwork. The Manager in Action illustrates the emphasis organizational leaders place on building teamwork.

MANAGER IN ACTION

Project manager Danielle Roget believes that if a team's first experience is successful, the members have a good chance of working well together and being successful on future projects. The challenge she faces regularly is to get a new group off to a good start. Her solution is to host a spaghetti dinner. When Roget assembles a new team, she invites all the members over to her home for dinner. After the guests have met and talked briefly, Roget announces that she hasn't had time to prepare dinner. She suggests that the group visit the supermar-

ket and purchase what is needed to cook a spaghetti dinner.

Roget participates but does not direct. The group is able to purchase what is needed, assign tasks, and prepare dinner, thereby experiencing its first success as a team. Group members also build interpersonal relationships in an informal setting before the formal work project begins. Roget says, "My method may sound a little hokey, but it works."

Source: Based on facts reported in Tom De Marco and Timothy Lister, *Peopleware: Productive Projects and Teams* (New York: Dorset House Publishing Co., 1990).

To encourage teamwork, the most effective step the leader can take is to set a good example. If the leader is a good team player, group members will follow. It is important for the group leader to set an example of candor and honesty. One consultant observed, "I've never known a synergistic group that wasn't consistently candid."[20] (In a synergistic group, the group output exceeds what would be expected from the group members working independently.) Candor and honesty are also important because honesty is the most important leadership quality group members expect from top-level managers.[21]

The group leader should also cultivate the attitude that working together effectively is an expected standard of conduct, or **norm.** An obvious but often overlooked method of building teamwork is to encourage cooperation rather than intense competition within the group. One way would be for the leader to praise employees for having collaborated on joint projects. The best-known method to encourage teamwork is to rally the support of the group against a real or imagined threat from the outside. Beating the competition makes the most sense when the competition is outside your own firm.

Minor problems between the leader and group members often fester into major problems. These major problems, in turn, adversely affect team spirit and productivity. In order to resolve little problems, the group leader should keep open channels of communication with the group. Good teamwork also includes emotional support to group members. Such support can take the form of verbal encouragement for ideas expressed, listening to an employee's personal problems, or even providing help with a work problem.

Teamwork on the athletic field is enhanced by group symbols such as uniforms and nicknames (Wildcats, Orangemen, Lady Volunteers, and so forth). Symbols are also a potentially effective team builder on the job. Company jackets, caps, T-shirts, mugs, and business cards can be modified to symbolize a work group.

It is important for leaders to avoid the common mistake of creating in-groups and out-groups within the work unit. The group members who are "in" may cooperate with each other, but the "outs" will probably not cooperate with the "ins." This type of favoritism tends to breed dissension instead of teamwork.[22]

Finally, a key strategy for encouraging teamwork is to reward the group as a whole when a reward is deserved. A popular form of incentive is to reward good group performance with an organization-paid banquet. Scheduling the banquet on a weekend and inviting spouses and guests is an even bigger morale booster. This is important because teamwork depends on high morale.

THE LEADER'S ROLE IN ENCOURAGING QUALITY

Total quality management(TQM) is a management system for improving performance throughout the firm by maximizing customer satisfaction. It has become a dominant theme in many private and public organizations. TQM involves paying careful attention to every detail of the work process in order to achieve high quality. Much of this text describes ideas and techniques that foster quality. Total quality management is described in Chapter 17, dealing with operations, and in Chapter 22 as a key aspect of organizational culture. According to leading quality experts, approximately 90 percent of quality problems are the fault of management.[23] Managers must provide the right commitment, tools, procedures, and rewards for achieving quality. This section describes seven actions by the leader that will promote quality within the work group.[24]

First, the leader can discuss the importance of quality. Awareness of the importance of quality begins with frequent discussions in which the group is asked what quality means to them. A useful discussion method is to hold rap sessions in which everybody has a chance to participate. At this point the manager should act as a facilitator but not impose an opinion on the group.

Second, the leader can close the quality credibility gap. Most firms talk about quality, but few follow through rigorously with their plans. An effective leadership technique is to close the **quality credibility gap**—the difference between the message employees hear and the actual follow-through. A survey conducted by the American Society for Quality Control revealed an average gap of 19 points. To close the credibility gap, a manager can do such things as audit quality and use the performance appraisal to comment on quality of work.

Third, the leader should listen to employees. A key ingredient of a successful quality enhancement effort is to create an atmosphere in which the manager listens to employees. The rap sessions mentioned previously and management by walking around (MBWA) should become standard practice. Managers should listen for suggestions about even minor aspects of quality. Many of the improved features in the 1991 Chrysler Corporation minivans resulted from listening to employee (and customer) suggestions. Among them was a small drawer placed above the radio.

Fourth, the leader should encourage group members to focus on the customer. Since quality centers on customer satisfaction, group members should think of the customer as they conduct their work. The "customer" can be internal or external. Anyone who uses the output of a team's work becomes a customer or client. For example, according to the concept of *next operation as customer (NOAC)*, the manufacturing department becomes the engineering department's customer. One management briefing on quality states that "no longer can engineering slap a design together and throw it over the wall, like a ticking time bomb, for manufacturing to catch." Manufacturing, as engineering's customer, measures and grades engineering's performance.

Fifth, the leader should set quality goals and measure achievements. The leader can be influential in encouraging the group to set goals regarding quality. Particularly useful are goals that strive for small, steady steps, not unrealistic leaps in improvement. Following the control model, goal attainment must be measured. Without specific measurements, quality remains too abstract to result in improved performance.

Sixth, the leader can initiate a formal quality program. Formal programs for quality improvement typically have to be approved by top-level management, but they can be suggested by a leader anywhere in the firm. A program developed at Motorola is **Six Sigma,** a quality standard whereby

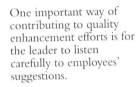

ETHICS QUESTION
What ethical issues are raised by meeting customer needs even when the customer is misinformed about what is best for him or her?

One important way of contributing to quality enhancement efforts is for the leader to listen carefully to employees' suggestions.

errors occur only once in 3.4 million opportunities. (The Six Sigma means that the percentage of errors is six standard deviations away from the mean.) In comparison, the quality of most manufacturing processes is plus or minus three sigma, which translates into 66,810 defects per million opportunities for error. A leader can illustrate Six Sigma with statements such as, "Under Three Sigma, we would have at least 20,000 wrong drug prescriptions each year nationwide. Under Six Sigma, we would have one wrong drug prescription in 25 years."

Finally, the leader can conduct five-minute quality updates. To keep quality awareness in the forefront of employees' minds, the leader should begin work unit meetings with a five-minute quality update. Tom Peters has recommended that each agenda item begin with a brief discussion of its quality implications.[25] For example, assume that the topic for discussion is employee recruitment. This could be related to how the selection of high-caliber employees leads to the production of high-quality goods and services.

A SYNTHESIS OF LEADERSHIP APPROACHES AND THEORIES

Although the explanations of leadership presented in this chapter may seem to compete with one another, they all have some merit. Taken together, they help us understand leadership. Figure 11-4 presents a capsule summary of the various approaches to leadership described here. No single explanation is so comprehensive as to make other approaches superfluous. For instance, the Leadership Grid might help us identify a 9,9 leader, but it would still be important to know whether that leader had a sense of vision.

No one best theory or explanation of leadership yet exists, but a state-of-the-art approach to leadership would consider the following factors:

1. Leadership effectiveness results from the combined influences of the inner qualities and behaviors of the leader, leadership styles, and a responsiveness to contingency factors.

FIGURE 11-4 Key Perspectives of Various Explanations of Leadership

Explanation	Key Variables	Key Outputs
Trait approach	Inner qualities and subordinate relationships of leaders	Leadership effectiveness
Leadership continuum	Amount of authority exercised by leader	Productivity, satisfaction
Leadership Grid	Relative concern for people and production	Productivity, morale
Transformational leader	Leader's ability to create profound change	Organizational change
Fiedler's theory	Leadership style and amount of control over situation	Group effectiveness

2. Leadership style generally centers around the relative amount of emphasis placed on the task to be accomplished versus the emphasis placed on people.

3. No matter what the leader's style, his or her effectiveness also depends on having an effective combination of traits and characteristics. Nevertheless, a style or a set of personal characteristics only leads to effectiveness when it is appropriate to the situation.

4. Providing a sense of vision to the group is important in all but the most mundane and stable operations. Even leaders who are unable to develop full charisma should develop a vision statement.

5. Leaders in virtually every organizational setting should encourage a commitment to quality among group members. Encouraging teamwork is also important, except in those rare instances in which a manager is supervising people who are working independently of one another, such as tax accountants.

6. An important goal for all leaders is to develop **superleadership,** or getting group members to be self-directing. A superleader leads others to lead themselves by acting as a teacher and coach, not a director. This type of leader also helps people to think positively about themselves and minimize negative thinking.[26] The motivational strategies described in Chapter 12 and the coaching techniques in Chapter 14 can help managers become superleaders.

In choosing the appropriate style to match a situation, leaders should consider the following factors as a starting point:

1. Technically competent and well-motivated employees require less guidance and control than do their less competent and poorly motivated counterparts. Competent and well-motivated employees respond well to participative management, while their opposites may respond better to autocratic management.

2. When time is critical and the situation is favorable to the leader (e.g., when the leader has good relationships with the group), a task-oriented approach may contribute to goal attainment.

3. When group members are facing ambiguity, heavy work demands, and heavy job stress, a relationship-oriented leadership style may lead to increased morale and productivity.

4. Whichever leadership style a manager chooses, the manager should emphasize quality. Ordinarily, quality is included in the meaning of productivity. Nevertheless, group members must be reminded that true productivity includes quality.

Back to the Opening Case

Chairman Koo, with the help of consultants, decided to change his leadership style from authoritarian to participative. Instead of making major decisions by himself he has granted more authority to front-line managers. His new leadership style appears to border on democratic.

SUMMARY

Leadership is the process of influencing others to achieve objectives in specific situations without the use of unduly coercive techniques. Leadership produces change. Management, in contrast, produces a degree of predictability and order.

Certain traits, characteristics, and behaviors contribute to leadership effectiveness in a wide variety of situations. These fall into the general categories of cognitive skills, personality traits and characteristics, and relationships with subordinates. Although the trait approach has its critics, it still is necessary for a full understanding of leadership. The current interest in leaders who are charismatic and visionary supports the trait approach to leadership.

Leaders generally influence others in a relatively consistent pattern of behavior referred to as *leadership style*. The classical method of classifying leadership styles arranges leadership behavior along a continuum of authority exerted by the leader. The three major styles, or points on the continuum, are autocratic, participative (including consultative, consensus, and democratic), and free-rein.

The Leadership Grid describes a manager's leadership style along the dimensions of concern for production and concern for people. Each of these concerns exists in varying degrees along a continuum from Level 1 (low) to Level 9 (high).

The transformational leader is a charismatic person who helps bring about profound changes in people and the organization. In the process, this style of leader revamps the organizational culture. Charismatic leaders are known to have vision, be masterful communicators, and inspire trust. They also help group members feel capable, and they are action oriented.

Fiedler's contingency theory specifies the conditions under which leaders need to use task-motivated and relationship-motivated styles. A key concept in the model is situational control or favorableness. A leader has the most control when leader-member relations are good, the task is well structured, and the leader's position power is strong. In situations of high control and low control, the task-motivated style is most effective. In situations of intermediate favorableness, the relationship-motivated style is better.

Leaders enhance teamwork through setting a good example, being candid and honest, and encouraging cooperation. Other techniques include giving emotional support to group members and avoiding the creation of in-groups versus out-groups.

Another key leadership role is to encourage quality. Techniques to enhance quality include discussing its importance, listening to employee suggestions, focusing on the customer, and initiating a formal quality program.

KEY TERMS

cognitive skills	participative leader	transformational leader	norm
cognitive resource theory	consultative leader	charisma	total quality management (TQM)
lead by example	consensus leader	contingency leadership	quality credibility gap
leadership style	democratic leader	Fiedler's contingency theory of leadership	Six Sigma
autocratic leader	free-rein leader	Leadership Grid	situational control	superleadership

QUESTIONS FOR DISCUSSION AND REVIEW

1. What is the difference between power and leadership?
2. Explain how somebody can be a leader without occupying a managerial position.
3. How might a person develop some of the traits, characteristics, and behaviors necessary to be an effective leader?
4. If a sense of humor is important for leadership,

should a manager memorize a bunch of good jokes?

5. How might you be able to use the Pygmalion effect to enhance your own performance?

6. Where does the head of your country fit on the leadership continuum? Justify your answer.

7. A manager says to you, "My philosophy is to never make waves and to never submit an idea that might bomb." Where would this person most likely fit on the Leadership Grid?

8. In what way does the discussion of the transformational leadership style fit the trait approach to leadership?

9. Using Fiedler's theory, which style of leadership is recommended for (a) a bank president and (b) a Little League coach?

10. What really is so important about teamwork?

11. How might a leader set a good example of concern for quality?

PROBLEMS FOR ACTION

A. Assume that you are managing a task force of financial analysts whose assignment is to evaluate whether or not the company should purchase a particular insurance company. You report directly to the president. All the task force members are well paid and satisfied with their general working conditions. Following Fiedler's theory, select the appropriate leadership style to use in this situation.

B. Assume that you are newly hired as a manager in a large company. For your first assignment, you are asked to manage a new department called "Recycling and Energy Conservation." The mission of this department is to find ways to save the company money and protect the environment. Your staff consists of six people with some appropriate technical skills who have never worked together before. They are mostly workers who have received poor performance evaluations in the past, and they are not known for their cooperativeness. Map out a plan for transforming this group of strangers into a smooth-working team.

CONCLUDING CASE

· · · · · · · · · · · · · · · · ·

The CEO of Chaparral Steel

Gordon Forward, the CEO of Chaparral Steel in Midlothian, Texas, says that people and machines are his strategic weapons. Manage them well, he points out, and almost any business can be profitable. His company has been one of the most successful of the small-scale "mini mills." Chaparral's main business involves melting down scrap metal and turning it into high-grade steel for automobile and construction companies. In one year, for example, while several other mini mills failed, Chapparal sold 1.1 million tons of steel for $297.2 million in sales and $8.9 million in profits. Chapparal has been described as the "mouse that roared." The company is growing, but it has yet to fall into the elite category of *Business Week's* 1000 most valuable companies.

The mild-mannered Forward wears thick glasses and looks more like a researcher than a revolutionary. His background fits the image. He holds a Ph.D.

from the Massachusetts Institute of Technology (MIT) in thermodynamics and spent many years in the research and development divisions of Canadian steel mills. Forward observes that his steel mill experiences taught him two valuable lessons. First, the bureaucratic form of organization hinders the flow of new technology from R&D departments to the floor of steel mills. Second, the traditional adversarial relationship between management and labor lowers productivity.

When Forward joined the start-up group of Chaparral as vice president of operations in 1973, he promised himself to apply what he had learned. To compete with low-priced foreign steel mills, he broke the barriers separating managers and workers and pushed for extensive automation. His ideas took hold rapidly within the company. Since Chaparral began production in 1975, Forward and his staff have traveled throughout the world in search of the most efficient machines and equipment. To ensure that procedures reflect the state of the art, Forward sends employees of all levels on paid leaves to study other mills. Several years ago, the company sent a group of electricians to Sweden to study the use of electric furnaces. It has been estimated that Chaparral spends one-tenth of its annual income on finding new technology.

Chaparral is an industry leader in productivity. Many larger companies in the steel industry require at least seven hours to produce one ton of steel. Chaparral, a nonunion firm, requires only 1.7 hours. A clearly stated management philosophy underlies these productivity figures. Forward believes in boosting the egos of his workers. He says that when an operative employee is treated with the same respect as a vice president, productivity will increase. Consequently the company has removed symbolic distinctions between management and labor. Chaparral has no reserved parking spots for top-level managers. Managers and line workers wear the same color hard hats. Every employee, from the CEO to an office assistant, receives the same health benefits.

Many larger firms such as USX are following Chaparral's lead by instituting nonbureaucratic structures within their larger structures. Forward is not worried by these developments. Chaparral is a few steps ahead of its competitors and intends to hold on to its lead. One industry expert says, "Looking at Chaparral is like seeing the future of steel."

1. Classify Forward's leadership style according to an explanation of leadership presented in this chapter. Explain the basis for your answers.
2. Identify several of Forward's leadership traits, characteristics, and behaviors. Explain the basis for your answers.
3. What does this case tell you about the relationship between bureaucracy and leadership style?

Source: As reported in Mark B. Rowan, "Five Who Broke the Rules," *Success* (December 1986): 31–32; updated with information in *The 1991 Business Week 1000* (April 1991): 189; "Conversation with Gordon Forward," *Organizational Dynamics* (Summer 1991): 63–72.

REFERENCES

1. John P. Kotter, "What Leaders Really Do," *Harvard Business Review* (May–June 1990): 103–111.
2. John P. Kotter, *A Force for Change: How Leadership Differs from Management* (New York: The Free Press, 1990).
3. Robert G. Lord and Associates, "A Meta-Analysis of the Relationship Between Personality Traits and Leadership Perceptors: An Application of Validity Generalization Procedures," *Journal of Applied Psychology* (August 1986): 402–410; Shelley A. Kirkpatrick and Edwin A. Locke, "Leadership: Do Traits Matter?" *Academy of Management Executive* (May 1991): 48–60.
4. Fred E. Fiedler and Joseph E. Garcia, *New Approaches to Effective Leadership: Cognitive Resources and Organizational Performance* (New York: John Wiley & Sons, 1987).
5. Michael Schroeder, "The Recasting of ALCOA," *Business Week* (September 9, 1991): 62.
6. Daniel C. Ganster, "Unhealthy Leader Dispositions, Work Group Strain and Performance," *Academy of Management Best Papers Proceedings 1990* (San Francisco: Academy of Management, 1990).
7. Warren Bennis and Burt Nanus, "The Leading Edge," *Success* (April 1985): 58.
8. David C. McClelland and Richard Boyatzis, "Leadership Motive Pattern and Long-Term Success in Management," *Journal of Applied Psychology* (December 1982): 737.
9. Martin L. Maher and Douglas A. Klieber, "The Graying of Achievment Motivation," *American Psychologist* (July 1981): 787–793.
10. Morgan W. McCall, Jr., and Michael M. Lombardo, "What Makes a Top Executive?" *Psychology Today* (February 1983): 28.
11. Dov Eden, "Pygmalion Without Interpersonal Contrast Effects: Whose Groups Gain from Raising Manager Expectations?" *Journal of Applied Psychology* (August 1990): 394–398.
12. Laxmi Nakarmi, "At Daewoo, a 'Revolution' at the Top" *Business Week* (February 18, 1991): 68–69.
13. John Ince, "At Levi's, Comfortable Employees Work Harder," *Gannett News Service* (April 16, 1989).
14. Robert R. Blake and Anne Adams McCanse, *Leadership Dilemmas—Grid Solutions* (Houston, TX: Grid Publishing Company, 1991).
15. Robert R. Blake and Jane S. Mouton, *The Managerial Grid III: The Key to Leadership Excellence* (Houston, TX: Grid Publishing Company, 1985): 15.
16. John J. Hater and Bernard M. Bass, "Superiors' Evaluation and Subordinates' Perceptions of Transformational and Transactional Leadership," *Journal of Applied Psychology* (November 1988): 695; Bass, *Leadership and Performance Beyond Expectations* (New York: The Free Press, 1985).
17. "Texaco: From Takeover Bait to Dynamo," *Business Week* (July 22, 1991): 50.
18. Jay A. Conger, *The Charismatic Leader: Beyond the Mystique of Exceptional Leadership* (San Francisco: Jossey-Bass, 1989); Conger, Rabindra N. Kanungo, and Associates, *Charismatic Leadership: The Elusive Factor in Organizational Effectiveness* (San Francisco: Jossey-Bass, 1988).
19. Fred E. Fiedler, Martin M. Chemers, and Linda Mahar, *Improving Leadership Effectiveness: The Leader Match Concept*, 2e (New York: John Wiley & Sons, 1984).

20. Robert E. Lefton, "The Eight Barriers to Teamwork," *Personnel Journal* (January 1988): 18.

21. James M. Kouzes and Barry Z. Posner, "The Credibility Factor: What Followers Expect from Their Leaders," *Management Review* (January 1990): 29–33.

22. Dave Day, "Beating the In Group-Out Group Problem," *Supervisory Management* (August 1989): 17–21.

23. Keki R. Bhote, *Next Operation as Customer (NOAC)*, American Management Association Briefing (New York: American Management Association, 1991): 52.

24. Eberhard E. Scheuing, "How to Build a Quality-Conscious Team," *Supervisory Management* (January 1990): 6; "Quality Is As Quality Does," *Personnel* (January 1991): 16; Keki R. Bhote, "America's Quality Health Diagnosis: Strong Heart, Weak Head," *Management Review* (May 1989): 34–38.

25. Tom Peters, "Quality Starts with Zealous Supervisor," syndicated column (November 8, 1987).

26. Charles C. Manz and Henry P. Sims, Jr., "SuperLeadership: Beyond the Myth of Heroic Leadership," *Organizational Dynamics* (Spring 1991): 18–35; Charles C. Manz and Chris P. Neck, "Inner Leadership: Creating Productive Thought Patterns," *The Executive* (August 1991): 87–95.

Chapter 12

Motivation and Productivity

Days Inn of America has an intensive program of hiring senior citizens, people with physical disabilities, and people who are homeless. These employees are hired as reservation sales agents who answer calls to telephone 800-numbers. The recruitment policy was prompted by business savvy rather than altruism. The human resources vice president of the Atlanta-based hotel-motel chain declares, "The program is not a social experiment. We did it because of a void. We had positions that were difficult to fill and saw using homeless people as an opportunity. They had potential. We made a commitment to do this to meet the business needs of the organization."

The homeless employees are recruited primarily from Atlanta shelters for battered women. Most of these women have few or no job skills, and they lack previous office experience. To remedy this, Days Inn offers classroom instruction and on-the-job training. The workers receive coaching as long as necessary, as judged by their supervisors. The process consumes eight hours a day for up to six weeks.

The task of helping people who were formerly homeless is not always easy. The first three people hired into the program quickly failed. According to the vice president, "They not only lacked basic skills, they lacked everything else required to be responsible. We can't impact 20 years of upbringing. But if the basic skills, desires and intentions are there, we can provide the opportunity, training and support required to help them turn around their lives."

Source: Based on information in Dorri Jacobs, "Wanted: Jobs for a Homeless Workforce," *Management Review* (May 1990): 40–41; and Bill Stack, "Jobs Available: Homeless and Seniors Encouraged to Apply," *Management Review* (August 1989): 13–15.

ETHICS QUESTION
Would top-level
management of Days Inn
be acting in a socially
responsible manner if it
held homeless employees
to lower performance
standards?

Days Inn cannot achieve its important work of helping people who are homeless unless these employees are properly motivated. With proper motivation, they will take an important step toward earning their own keep. If it is not cost effective to hire and train people who are homeless, Days Inn will be forced to abandon the program. In fact, *any* type of employee must be properly motivated if high productivity is to be achieved. **Motivation** (in a work setting) is the process by which behavior is mobilized and sustained in the interest of achieving organizational goals. Despite this straightforward definition, motivation is complex and encompasses a broad range of behaviors. Employee motivation cannot be adequately understood without relating the concept of motivation to attempts on the part of leaders to motivate people. In this chapter, therefore, we look at motivation from the standpoint of the individual and discuss methods used to increase employee motivation.

MOTIVATION, PERFORMANCE, AND PRODUCTIVITY

Trying hard to reach a goal, or being motivated, does not inevitably lead to desired performance, nor does it inevitably lead to high productivity. Many ambitious, hard-working individuals fail to achieve their job and career goals. The basic explanation of the relationship between motivation and performance is that Performance = Ability × Motivation. You need the right skills to achieve what you want to accomplish. For example, if the homeless people at Days Inn would not, or could not, learn to use the computer, their responsibilities would be limited. Similarly, to become an effective manager, a person needs many of the abilities and skills mentioned throughout this text.

Many other factors, including economic and technological ones, also influence performance and productivity. For instance, a securities sales representative's performance may decrease suddenly because of a plunge in the stock market despite the representative's attempts to generate business. Likewise, many plants have been forced to close because of low productivity stemming from obsolete equipment rather than from a poorly motivated workforce.

Four factors cause individual performance, only one of which is motivation. To perform well, a person must (1) understand the expectations of the job; (2) have the required abilities; (3) be motivated to do what is required; and (4) work in an environment that allows the intention to be translated into performance.[1] The last point implies that there are sometimes political reasons why an individual's best efforts will be resisted. For example, the new work method an employee worked hard to develop might conflict with a particular manager's solution to the problem.

A GENERAL MOTIVATIONAL MODEL

An important purpose of behavior is to satisfy needs such as the need for recognition from others. As shown in Figure 12-1, the presence of an active need (such as recognition) is expressed as an inner state of craving or imbalance. The individual engages in actions, or goal-directed behaviors to satisfy this craving or correct the imbalance. These actions might include attending classes or working longer, with the hope of being promoted.

If behavior leads to a successful outcome, two things happen: Tension is reduced and an inner state of satisfaction or equilibrium is achieved. If this state is not achieved, however, tension continues and motivation persists to discover another means of restoring the equilibrium. For instance, the manager who fails to receive a promotion may continue efforts to reach that

FIGURE 12-1 A General Motivational Model Based on Need Satisfaction

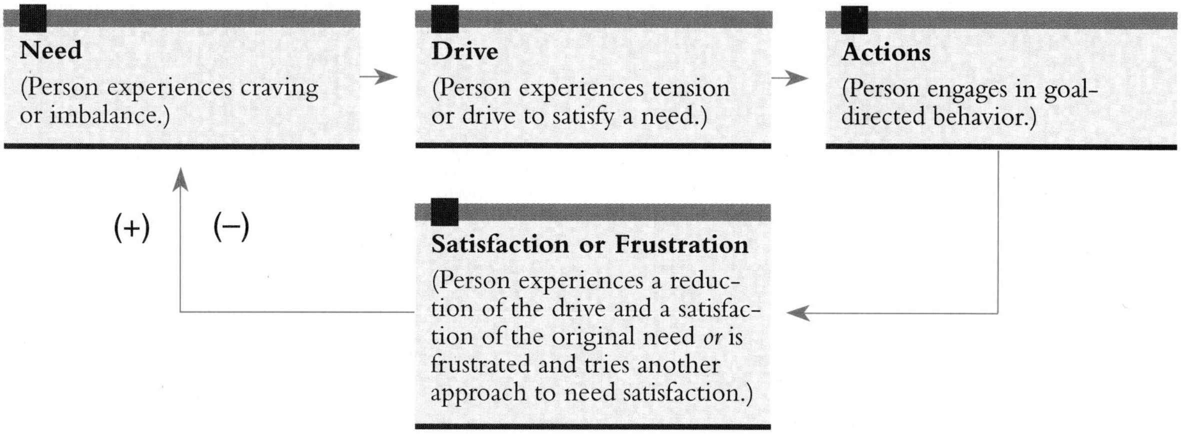

Need
(Person experiences craving or imbalance.)

Drive
(Person experiences tension or drive to satisfy a need.)

Actions
(Person engages in goal-directed behavior.)

(+)   (−)

Satisfaction or Frustration
(Person experiences a reduction of the drive and a satisfaction of the original need *or* is frustrated and tries another approach to need satisfaction.)

+ Positive outcomes lead to a repeat of the successful behavior.
− Negative outcomes imply blockage and tend to result in behavioral adjustments to improve the person's success rate.

goal, or the manager may seek to satisfy the same need by running for membership on the city council.

If a person's actions lead to positive outcomes, she or he will repeat those successful behaviors. On the other hand, behavior that leads to negative outcomes will usually not be repeated. Instead, the person will likely change tactics to improve his or her success rate.

Although the general model shown in Figure 12-1 is accurate, it is an oversimplification. For one thing, it does not specify the conditions under which incentives will be motivators, nor does it specify why one person will exert more effort than another. The discussions of motivation presented in the balance of this chapter help explain such issues.

MOTIVATION THROUGH NEED SATISFACTION

Understanding of need theories helps managers to be effective leaders. These theories are also important because they are incorporated into other explanations of work motivation such as expectancy theory. Four explanations of motivation through need satisfaction are reviewed in the following sections: Maslow's need hierarchy, Herzberg's two-factor theory of motivation, McClelland's acquired needs theory, and the needs for recognition and autonomy.

Maslow's Need Hierarchy

Maslow's need hierarchy arranges human needs into a pyramid-shaped model with basic physiological needs at the bottom and the need for self-actualization at the top. (See Figure 12-2.) Before higher-level needs are

FIGURE 12-2
Maslow's Need
Hierarchy

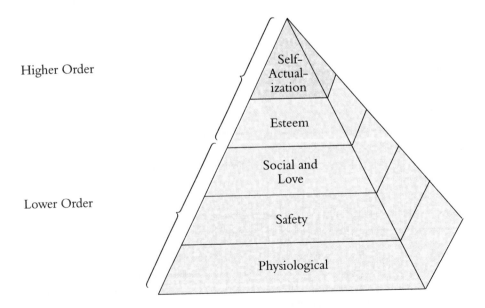

Higher Order

Lower Order

Self-Actualization

Esteem

Social and Love

Safety

Physiological

activated, certain lower-level needs must be satisfied. The central concept in Maslow's theory is that needs fall into five groups or classes: physiological needs, safety needs, social and love needs, esteem needs, and self-actualization needs.[2]

PHYSIOLOGICAL NEEDS. These are basic bodily needs such as the need for water, air, food, rest, and sleep. Most normal working conditions in manufacturing and service firms allow for the satisfaction of these needs.

SAFETY NEEDS. These include needs for security and freedom from environmental threat. Many employees who work at dangerous jobs, such as loggers and miners, would be motivated by the chance to have safer working conditions. Sexual harassment is an example of frustration of the safety need for security, because the harassed person is subjected to an environmental threat.

SOCIAL AND LOVE NEEDS. These include needs for love, belonging to a group, and affiliation with people. Managers can contribute to the satisfaction of such needs by promoting teamwork and encouraging social interaction in matters concerning work problems.

ESTEEM NEEDS. These include needs for self-respect based on genuine achievement and respect from others, prestige, recognition, and appreciation. Occupations with high status satisfy esteem needs. Managers can satisfy the esteem needs of employees by praising their work and giving them the opportunity for recognition.

SELF-ACTUALIZATION NEEDS. These are the needs for self-fulfillment and personal development and the need to grow to one's fullest potential. Self-actualized people are those who have become what they are capable of becoming. Managers can help employees move toward self-actualization by giving them challenging assignments, including the chance to do creative work.

A key principle of the need hierarchy is that as needs at a given level are gratified they lose their strength. The next level of need is then activated. A satisfied need ceases to be a motivator. For instance, once employees can pay for the necessities of life, they ordinarily seek opportunities for satisfying social relationships. Next, they strive to enhance their self-esteem. Many successful executives leave corporate life late in their careers in order to pursue activities that will move them further toward self-actualization. David Kearns, the former CEO of Xerox Corporation, left Xerox in his late 50s to accept a position in government to help upgrade secondary-school education.

MANAGERIAL IMPLICATIONS. Maslow's need hierarchy has several implications. Because a satisfied need is not a motivator, managers must discover their employees' unsatisfied needs when making a motivational appeal. The needs for belonging and acceptance become poor motivators once they have been satisfied and once esteem needs have started to emerge. A less obvious implication is that satisfaction at the self-fulfillment level does not reduce the potency of that need. Instead, the highest-level needs take on new forms. An example is a successful product designer looking for another product to design. Thus, the need for self-actualization always provides a basis for motivation.

EVALUATION. Maslow's theory endures partly because it is such a sensible and useful explanation of job behavior. Suppose, for example, a worker is hungry and tired. Until that worker gets food and rest, he or she will pay very little attention to thoughts about getting promoted or learning a new skill. The need hierarchy has stimulated many managers and leaders to take an optimistic view of employees. Another reason for its appeal is that it is convenient to classify needs into higher and lower orders. Despite these contributions, however, additional explanations of motivation are needed to supplement Maslow's theory.

Herzberg's Two-Factor Theory of Work Motivation

On the basis of research and interviews with 200 engineers and accountants, Frederick Herzberg developed an explanation of job satisfaction that evolved into a theory of job motivation.[3] The **two-factor theory of motivation** divides job elements into two types: Motivators, or satisfiers, can motivate and satisfy workers, and dissatisfiers, or hygiene factors, can only prevent dissatisfaction. Herzberg's theory is also called the *motivator-hygiene theory*. Motivators relate to higher-order needs, while hygiene factors relate to lower-order needs.

KEY POINTS IN THE THEORY. The motivational elements are the intrinsic, or job content, factors that make a job exciting. Intrinsic factors include achievement, recognition, advancement, responsibility, the work itself, and growth possibilities. The extrinsic, or job context, factors are hygienic; they are health producing and desirable, but not motivational. Examples of extrinsic factors are pay, status, job security, working conditions, and quality of supervision. As described in Chapter 10, linking pay to performance can serve as a potent motivator. Herzberg believed that motivation increases when pay combines with a motivator such as challenging work.

Herzberg considered only the presence of intrinsic factors to be motivational. For example, challenging work will motivate many people to exert increased effort. If intrinsic factors such as challenging work are not present, the result is neutral rather than negative, and the employee will feel bland rather than angry or unhappy.

Although the presence of extrinsic factors is not motivational, their absence can cause dissatisfaction. For example, a police captain reported that when officers were assigned old patrol cars, they complained frequently.

However, when assigned brand new patrol cars, they did not express much appreciation. Nor did they increase their productivity (as measured by the number of citations issued).

EVALUATION. The two-factor theory has made two important, lasting contributions to work motivation. First, it has helped managers realize that money is not always the primary motivator. Second, it has spurred much of the interest in redesigning jobs to make them more intrinsically satisfying. The discussion of job enrichment that appears later in this chapter includes more information on the two-factor theory.

Although the two-factor theory has received considerable support, it has also been criticized.[4] Above all, the two-factor theory deemphasizes individual differences. It does not account for the fact that hygiene factors such as good benefits and company management satisfy and motivate many people. Moreover, many workers show no particular interest in such motivators as opportunity for growth and advancement. They work primarily so they can pay their bills and enjoy their time with family and friends.

McClelland's Acquired Needs Theory

Many other needs influence job behavior in addition to those mentioned specifically in the need hierarchy. David C. McClelland and his associates have provided a useful explanation of several of these needs.[5] They have proposed a theory of motivation based on the premise that people acquire or learn certain needs from their culture. When a need is strong enough, it prompts a person to engage in work activities to satisfy it. Three of these acquired needs are achievement, power, and affiliation. The first two were described briefly in Chapter 11 as characteristics of effective leaders.

THE NEED FOR ACHIEVEMENT. The **need for achievement** is the desire to accomplish something difficult for its own sake. People with a strong need for achievement frequently think of how to do a job better. They are also concerned with how to accomplish something unusual or important and how to progress in their careers. Workers with a high need for achievement are interested in monetary rewards primarily as feedback about how well they are achieving. Individuals with a high need for achievement seek responsibility. They also set realistic yet moderately difficult goals, take calculated risks, and desire feedback on performance. Entrepreneurs are strongly achievement motivated, and so are fast-track managers in large companies. In general, those who enjoy building activities and programs from scratch have a strong need for achievement. Complete the questionnaire in Figure 12-3 to obtain a tentative measure of your own achievement need.

ETHICS QUESTION
To what extent is it ethical for a person to look upon work as a place for satisfying power needs?

THE NEED FOR POWER. The **need for power** is the desire to control other people, to influence their behavior, and to be responsible for them. Managers with a high need for power like to control resources (such as

FIGURE 12-3
How Strong Is Your
Achievement Motive?

Answer the following questions Yes or No to compare your traits to those of people with a strong achievement motive (or need).

_____ 1. I easily put work out of my mind when off the job.

_____ 2. I very much enjoy gambling and football pools, lotteries, races, etc.

_____ 3. I dislike seeing things, such as food, fuel, and so forth, wasted.

_____ 4. I give a good deal of respect to people in positions superior to mine.

_____ 5. I prefer working with a congenial but somewhat incompetent partner to working with one who is difficult but highly competent.

_____ 6. I frequently do things today rather than put them off until tommorrow.

_____ 7. I have strong interest in the lives of successful people.

_____ 8. I spend money without too much planning for the future.

Explanation

Give yourself one point for each correct answer.

1. No. Whether you judge it as good or bad, strivers have a strong sense of involvement and continue to dwell on work problems long after quitting time.

2. No. Those with high aspirations rarely engage in the magical thinking that success comes through outside forces.

3. Yes. Achievers abhor waste in any form and they try to avoid unnecessary motions.

4. Yes. Those with a strong need for achievement take on successful role models. If a person does not respect successful role models, he or she probably has a self-defeating attitude.

5. No. Most achievement-motivated people don't agree with this type of partner arrangement. They're willing to sacrifice congeniality for a partner who helps them make it to the top.

6. Yes. Achievers usually have a strong sense of urgency. They keep ahead of their work by finishing assignments on time.

7. Yes. (See No. 4 above.)

8. No. Most achievers are good planners. They use money in the same manner as they use their personal resources.

Score

7–8 points: Your achievement motive is high; you think and act like a striver. 4–6 points: Your achievement motive is equal to that of most people. 0–3 points: You are a low achiever.
If your score was low, remember that achievement is a relative term and we have largely been discussing success in the workplace. You may find that your sense of success lies elsewhere.

Source: Reprinted and adapted with permission from Salvatore Didato, "High Achievers Are Self-Confident, Welcome Responsibility," Syndicated column, April 4, 1987.

money and real estate) in addition to people. A person with a strong need for power spends time thinking about influencing and controlling others and about gaining a position of authority and status. Executives who have buildings named after themselves or buy professional athletic teams have strong power needs. The need for power is the primary motivator of successful managers.[6]

THE NEED FOR AFFILIATION. The **need for affiliation** is the desire to establish and maintain friendly and warm relationships with others. People so motivated care about restoring disrupted relationships and soothing hurt feelings. They also want to engage in work that permits close companionship. Successful leaders have low affiliation needs,[7] but managers with an extremely low need for affiliation may not show adequate concern for the needs of others.

EVALUATION. The acquired needs theory has made an important contribution in identifying needs related to managerial performance. However, the theory is not a complete explanation of work motivation, it focuses on just several key needs. The following section describes two other needs of major importance in understanding motivation in organizations.

The Needs for Recognition and Autonomy

One useful way of motivating workers is to give them a chance to satisfy their needs for recognition and autonomy. The need for recognition is more universal than the need for autonomy.

THE NEED FOR RECOGNITION. The **need for recognition** is the desire for attention, praise, and approval for personal accomplishments. Recognizing employees for work well done exerts a powerful influence on their productivity. Researchers have also discovered that once sales representatives are recognized, their desire for additional recognition becomes insatiable.[8] Among the formal methods of satisfying recognition needs is giving service

Giving awards for outstanding performance is an effective way to motivate employees by satisfying their need for recognition.

awards, recognition pins, and jewelry for outstanding achievement. Managers can also give recognition for good performance and high productivity informally through announcements that a particular employee has done an outstanding job, handshakes, and complimentary memos in the employee's file.

THE NEED FOR AUTONOMY.   The **need for autonomy** is a desire for freedom, independence, and control over one's destiny. Accordingly, people with a high need for autonomy may prefer to be self-employed. Those working for a large organization may gravitate toward positions such as field representative or manager of a field unit. Autonomy can often be gained through power, but true autonomy is difficult to find through association with an organization, despite the power of the position. As one supposedly independent business person remarked, "Now that I'm self-employed, I have the freedom to work 70 hours per week any time I choose."

LEARNING CHECK

Demonstrate your understanding of how human needs influence motivation in organizations. You should be able to summarize three need theories.

MOTIVATION THROUGH JOB ENRICHMENT

Job enrichment refers to making a job more motivational and satisfying by adding variety and responsibility. It is a direct application of Herzberg's two-factor theory. An important aim in designing jobs that are intrinsically interesting, satisfying, and motivating is to increase productivity. Our discussion of job enrichment encompasses characteristics of an enriched job, implementation of job enrichment, and limitations of job enrichment. The job characteristics model of job enrichment was described in Chapter 7, as was job enrichment in the form of work teams.

Characteristics of an Enriched Job

Based on the work of Herzberg, we can consider nine job characteristics as major contributors to enrichment. Seven of these characteristics relate directly to client relationships, because performing work for a client or user is a key factor in influencing one's motivation and satisfaction. Two other characteristics—skill variety and vertical job loading—also are important contributors to an enriched job.[9]

CLIENT RELATIONSHIPS.   Directly serving a client makes a job seem more responsible. Herzberg noted that too often the "customer" is either a bureaucratic regulation or a supervisor. Because of this, the individual evaluates the job by such factors as how well the supervisor is pleased or procedures are maintained. It is more satisfying and motivational for employees to deal directly with end users such as employees from another department.

FEEDBACK. This dimension involves the degree to which employees know how well they are performing on a regular basis. Feedback from the client focuses on the quality of the work itself. Therefore, it is preferable for employees to receive feedback from managers that mixes evaluation of the person's characteristics with evaluation of the work.

SELF-SCHEDULING. Closely related to autonomy, this dimension refers to an employee's authority to decide, within reason, when to accomplish work. For example, a computer operator might have the authority to say to clients, "You will have this back in four or five days."

DIRECT COMMUNICATION AUTHORITY. Another contributor to job enrichment is to have the authority to communicate information directly to the people who use the information. For instance, an airplane service technician might tell the pilot directly that a tire requires replacement.

PERSONAL ACCOUNTABILITY. A job that is high in personal accountability is one in which the client directly judges how well the employee is performing and can voice complaints to the employee. As Herzberg noted, "Personal accountability to the client is attempted by decals and stamps with the name and phone numbers of the workers, but the most useful results come from the client close enough to provide immediate feedback."[10]

CONTROL OVER RESOURCES. A job that scores high on this characteristic allows the worker to allocate some of the resources necessary to accomplish the job. Improving control over resources includes holding the employee accountable for tools and material. Thus, the manager delegates this responsibility to the employee.

NEW LEARNING AND UNIQUE EXPERIENCES. This characteristic refers to the opportunity for growth that comes from acquiring new knowledge and skills on the job. Respect for one's job stems directly from the opportunity to learn from it regularly. A sales representative for a business forms company had this to say about the new learning aspects of her job: "My boss says I'm the most motivated sales rep who ever worked for her. The reason is simple. I learn something new every time I find a new customer. Some people think that selling business forms is straightforward stuff. But it isn't. We are problem solvers who have to teach customers how they can make efficient use of business forms. Each customer represents a new learning experience."

SKILL VARIETY. This characteristic reflects the degree to which the job requires the person to engage in different activities and use many skills, abilities, and talents. Skill variety is also called *job enlargement*. Most managerial positions score high on skill variety, sometimes to a point where there is too much variety.

VERTICAL JOB LOADING. **Vertical job loading** is pushing responsibility down from the manager to the employee, as shown in Figure 12-4. The process allows the employee to be accountable to a client, the next worker in the work flow, or a customer. Accountability allows the employee to develop new skills and provides a base for seeking additional technical support from both the supervisor and support groups.

Implementation of Job Enrichment

It is the responsibility of managers to implement job enrichment programs. In doing so, they must keep in mind certain considerations. First, they must ask themselves and others whether or not their employees need or want more responsibility, variety, and growth. Employee participation and consultation are appropriate ways to gather ideas for setting up job enrichment programs. After such a program has begun, the manager should interview employees to find out whether their feelings about their jobs have changed. If their feelings have not changed, the changes in job design have not gone far enough. Managers should be prepared to shift many supervisory tasks over to group members as part of job enrichment since the emphasis in job enrichment is on performing tasks at a higher level.[11] Managers should recognize that job enrichment can be conducted with groups as well as individuals.

The Organization in Action describes an approach to job enrichment that combines both job enrichment in general and the job characteristics model.

FIGURE 12-4
Vertical Job Loading

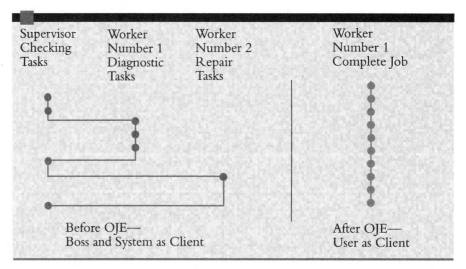

Source: Frederick Herzberg. "Motivation and Innovation: Who Are Workers Serving?" Copyright © 1979 by the Regents of the University of California. Reprinted from *California Management Review*, Vol. XXII, No. 2, Winter, 1979, p. 66 by permission of the Regents.

ORGANIZATION IN ACTION

Guided by a job design specialist, the 110 employees of the letters-of-credit department of the First National Bank of Chicago studied their jobs. These people concluded that their paperwork assembly line was antiquated, expensive, and slow. Segmented tasks kept the bank employees from comprehending the overall meaning of their work. It also frustrated the efforts of managers to decrease turnaround time and improve work quality. A study of the problem revealed that about 80 percent of the staff were dissatisfied with their jobs. The 20 percent who were satisfied were all professionals (managers and technicians). The nonprofessionals were in some stage of the assembly line.

Over a six-month period, employees redesigned their work, combining separate tasks into complete jobs to be performed by broadly trained professionals. They eliminated traditional job specialties and created a new, more responsible, higher-paying job classification: documentary products professional. Employees then went through training programs that upgraded their skills and allowed them to perform the restructured work at salaries averaging 20 percent higher. Job redesign was achieved through involvement of the entire staff. In addition to creating the new job, the employees also established work goals such as improving profits by $2 million the first year, increasing job satisfaction, and improving turnaround time.

Source: As reported in F. K. Plous, Jr., "Redesigning Work," *Personnel Administrator* (March 1987): 99.

Limitations to Job Enrichment

Despite its major contributions, job enrichment has limitations. Some forms of job enrichment place too much emphasis on the importance employees attach to client contact. In reality, some employees probably do not care who they deal with, so long as their working conditions are comfortable and the job pays well. Another problem is that not all jobs can be made intrinsically satisfying without curtailing productivity. Job enrichment ignores the fact that many employees prefer routine work that enables them to daydream or socialize with co-workers. Only certain employees are likely to make their work a central life interest. They are people whose higher needs are active, who are older, who prefer self-control to external control, and who have a strong work ethic.[12]

Finally, although it usually does improve job satisfaction and often leads to enhanced work quality, job enrichment may not always lead to increases in productivity. A firm might therefore incur expensive changes in job redesign without receiving a suitable return on its investment.

Back to the
Opening Case

Supervisors at Days Inn faced the challenge of motivating homeless people to become productive employees. So far, the company is pleased with their productivity. If this new group of employees made serious mistakes, the hotel would lose considerable business. The most basic motivational technique used by the company was to give them the opportunity to satisfy previously frustrated physiological, safety, and social needs. Working as reservation sales agents also offered homeless people a form of job enrichment based on extensive client contact.

MOTIVATION THROUGH GOAL SETTING

Goal setting is a basic process that is directly or indirectly part of all major theories of work motivation. Goal setting is accepted widely by managers as a means to improve and sustain performance. Goals (desired outcomes of an action) relate to motivation in another important way because goals and needs are closely associated. A person's needs influence which goals he or she will pursue. For example, the manager who has a strong need for power pursues the goal of receiving promotions. In the next sections, we discuss the basics of goal theory and some supporting research evidence.

Goal-Setting Theory

The core of goal-setting theory, as developed by Edwin A. Locke and Gary P. Latham, is based on 300 studies. The starting premise is that a person's goals regulate his or her actions: An individual who is committed to a goal will keep trying to reach that goal. Goals affect not only the level of effort a person will exert and his or her level of performance, but also the choice of behaviors. For example, a person pursuing a difficult goal will often search for efficient and powerful methods to achieve that goal.

The regulation of motivation by goal setting is the best-demonstrated principle of human behavior. This conclusion is based on both research and managerial practice. The following are key propositions of goal theory developed by Locke and Latham and various researchers:[13]

1. Difficult goals result in higher performance levels than do easy ones.
2. Specific goals get better results than do generalized, "do-your-best" goals.
3. Goals enhance performance by increasing effort and persistence, directing attention, and improving the tactics chosen to reach the goals.
4. Feedback on performance improves the effectiveness of goal setting.
5. Participation in goal setting improves performance only when it leads to clarified goals, difficult goals, and goal acceptance.
6. Goal setting improves performance when people believe that their performance will be evaluated against goals.
7. When goals are set for both individuals and the work group, their impact multiplies.

Research Findings on Organizational Goal Setting

ETHICS QUESTION
What ethical obligation does management have to set goals that are in the best interests of employees?

Substantial research has been conducted to evaluate goal theory. The results of dozens of these studies have been combined through **meta-analysis**, a term that refers to a family of techniques used to combine research evidence from many studies.[14] Consistent evidence has supported the idea that difficult and specific goals improve individual and group performance.

Meta-analysis was applied to 70 investigations of the impact of management by objectives on productivity. (To review, MBO includes goal setting, participation, and feedback on performance.) Among the many measures of productivity included were waste reduction, quality, sales-to-visit ratio, and foster-care placement. Of the 70 studies, 68 showed productivity gains, while only 2 showed losses. Interestingly, when top-level management commitment was high, the average gain in productivity was 56 percent. When commitment was low, the average productivity gain was only 6 percent.[15]

Goal-setting theory has received consistent research support, so managers need to be aware of the value of goal setting on the job. Goal setting is a key factor contributing to productivity increases in such programs as performance appraisal and quality improvement. The Organization in Action illustrates a successful application of goal setting.

ORGANIZATION IN ACTION

Top-level management at People's Natural Gas Company (PNG) decided to overhaul the company's system of evaluating and rewarding performance. Interviews with executives revealed that employees did not see a link between performance appraisals and company or individual performance. An even more important issue was brought up during the interviews. It was uncertain whether employees understood their own performance goals and were achieving them. Because the utility was facing a more competitive market, aggressive productivity efforts and improved customer service were necessary.

Follow-up interviews with 600 employees revealed the same problem. A lack of clarity about performance goals resulted in a lack of focus on results. PNG developed a new performance management system that would focus on results, objectives, and the behavioral skills needed to achieve these results. For example, how a customer service representative handles a customer was deemed as important as the number of transactions with customers. The company also attempted to relate employee performance to the business plan. (For example, part of the business plan includes enhancing customer satisfaction.)

PNG instituted a new four-point performance appraisal rating scale: (1) unsatisfactory, (2) approaches expectations, (3) meets expectations, and (4) far exceeds expectations. The rating scale was designed to be descriptive, and it focused on describing performance against expectations. (An expectation in this system functions as a goal, such as a manager's expectation of "reducing voluntary turnover in my unit by 25 percent this year.")

Top-level managers at PNG are pleased with the contribution of the new performance management system to productivity. After the first year of implementation, 14.5 percent of the employees were rated "far exceeds performance." About one-half of this select group was made up of nonexempt (not managerial or professional) employees. The employees were pleased with the system too. A survey indicated a range of 84 percent to 95 percent favorable responses to the new performance management system.

Source: Based on Kathleen A. Guinn and Roberta J. Corona, "Putting a Price on Performance," *Personnel Journal* (May 1991): 72–75

MOTIVATION THROUGH EXPECTANCY THEORY

According to **expectancy theory**, work motivation results from deliberate choices to engage in certain activities in order to achieve worthwhile outcomes. People will be well motivated if they believe that effort will lead to good performance and good performance will lead to preferred outcomes. The basic version of expectancy theory shown in Figure 12-5 is of use to managers and professionals.[16] Components of this model are described next, followed by an explanation of how motivation is calculated and an evaluation of expectancy theory.

Expectancy, Instrumentality, and Valence

The key components of expectancy theory are expectancy, instrumentality, and valence. Each one of these components exists in each situation involving motivation. This occurs because each act of motivated behavior serves several ends. Assume that an advertising copywriter develops a good advertising campaign. The copywriter may achieve such outcomes as a pay increase, higher status, and the opportunity to make a client presentation. An **expectancy** is a person's subjective estimate of the probability that a given level of performance will occur. The effort-to-performance ($E \rightarrow P$) expectancy refers to the individual's subjective hunch about the chances that increased effort will lead to the desired performance. In the copywriter example, the expected performance is creating the advertising slogan. If a person does not believe that he or she has the skill to accomplish an assigned task, that person might not even try to perform the task.

An **instrumentality** is the individual's estimate of the probability that performance will lead to certain outcomes. The ($P \rightarrow O$) instrumentality refers to the person's subjective evaluation of the chances that good performance will lead to certain outcomes. For the copywriter, outcomes include a pay raise and making a client presentation. In formulating the instrumentality, the employee seeks a subjective answer to the question "If I do perform well, will the organization really make good on its promises to me?" Expectancies and instrumentalities range from 0.00 to 1.00, because both are probabilities.

Valence refers to the value a person places on a particular outcome. People attach positive valences to rewards and negative valences to punishments. The copywriter might place a high positive valence on making a presentation to a client and assign a negative valence to having his or her work insulted by the manager or client. The maximum value of a positive valence is +100, while the maximum value of a negative valence is −100. Neutral outcomes (indifference) carry a valence of zero. (Most versions of

FIGURE 12-5 A Basic Version of Expectancy Theory

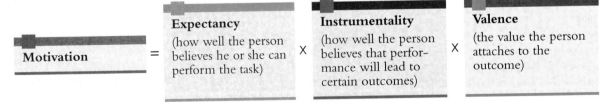

| Motivation | = | Expectancy (how well the person believes he or she can perform the task) | X | Instrumentality (how well the person believes that performance will lead to certain outcomes) | X | Valence (the value the person attaches to the outcome) |

expectancy theory limit the range of valences from −1.00 to +1.00. However, such a limited range fails to capture the intensity of highly preferred or feared outcomes.) The numerical values of valences are unknown in most situations, yet it is reasonable to assume that people attach values of "good," "bad," and "neutral" to potential outcomes derived from their efforts.

The Calculation of Motivation

In expectancy theory, motivation, M, $= (E \rightarrow P) \times (P \rightarrow O) \times V$, valence. The potential of an expected outcome to increase motivation can be high only if the expectancies, instrumentalities, and valences are high. And since anything multiplied by zero is zero, a zero value for $(E \rightarrow P)$, $(P \rightarrow O)$, or V will reduce motivation to zero. Suppose an employee places a maximum value on receiving a raise ($V = 100$). The employee is confident that she or he can perform the task required ($E \rightarrow P = 0.85$). And the employee is even more confident that the firm will come through with the raise if she or he performs well ($P \rightarrow O = 0.90$). Note that the values of 0.85 and 0.90 are subjective estimates, not true calculations. The employee's motivation is consequently $(100)(0.85)(0.90) = 76.5$ (above average on a scale of −100 to +100).

A note of caution: The simple formula just presented does not tell the entire story, because each task involves many expectancies, instrumentalities, and valences. Desirable and undesirable outcomes may cancel one another, resulting in a zero valence and therefore producing zero motivation force. For example, a person might not strive for a promotion because its positive valences (such as more money and status) are neutralized by its negative valences. An example would be having to relocate and leave friends behind.

Evaluation and Illustrative Research

Expectancy theory has much to offer practicing managers. Aspects of the theory have been integrated into leadership training, the design of reward programs, and employee participation programs. The research evidence in support of expectancy theory continues to be positive, and supervisors exposed to expectancy theory have been positive about its application. These people see expectancy theory as a powerful diagnostic tool in determining the motivational level of employees.[17]

One study calculated the motivational scores of 703 unionized construction workers, using the equation described earlier. The researchers found a strong positive relationship between the motivational scores and the levels of effort reported by these workers. They also found that the workers' motivation scores were related to the job satisfaction they reported and that the highest instrumentalities were associated with intrinsic factors such as challenging work.[18] This means that workers are more confident of receiving internal than external rewards when they perform as expected.

MOTIVATION THROUGH ORGANIZATIONAL BEHAVIOR MODIFICATION

ETHICS QUESTION
Can management rightfully be accused of manipulating people when using OB Mod to motivate employees?

The motivational approaches discussed so far emphasize inner states such as needs, satisfactions, expectancies, and valences. In contrast, **organizational behavior modification (OB Mod)** is a system of changing behavior by controlling rewards and punishments. This distinction does not mean that OB Mod contradicts all other theories. To use expectancy theory, for example, managers must offer employees appealing rewards. OB Mod is based on reinforcement theory or behaviorism. Using reinforcement theory, managers are not concerned with the inner states of employees. Instead, they attempt to structure the environment to bring forth constructive effort (motivated behavior) from employees. OB Mod has become the most widely used formal method of motivating employees today. Its principles are incorporated into pay-for-performance programs. The following sections discuss some of the strategies, applications, methods, and implications of behavior modification.

OB Mod Strategies and Schedules

OB Mod is a field of study by itself, but for the purposes of this text we will examine four cornerstone strategies. The first is *positive reinforcement*, which means increasing the probability that behavior will be repeated by rewarding people for making the desired response. The reward is received *contingent upon* making the right response. In other words, a bonus is paid for *good* performance, not just *any* performance.

The second OB Mod strategy is *negative reinforcement (or avoidance motivation)*—rewarding people by taking away an uncomfortable consequence of their behavior. An employee who performs well, for example, is rewarded

This employee is being rewarded for good performance, a cornerstone OB Mod strategy. Positive reinforcement often includes a monetary award along with social recognition.

by being able to avoid an assignment he or she dislikes. There is an important distinction between negative reinforcement and punishment. Negative reinforcement is *not* punishment; it is rewarding a person by removing discomfort.

The third strategy is *punishment*—the presentation of an undesirable consequence, or the removal of a desirable consequence, because of unacceptable behavior. A manager can punish a team member by suspending him or her for violating company policy or by taking away the employee's company car.

The fourth cornerstone strategy of OB Mod is *extinction*—decreasing the frequency of undesirable behavior by removing the desirable consequence of such behavior. Because the person is ignored, she or he is discouraged. For example, an effective method of getting a person to stop asking redundant questions is to ignore that person.

OB Mod strategies, particularly positive reinforcement and punishment, are administered according to schedules. Positive reinforcement is used more frequently than punishment in OB Mod programs. Punishment is usually part of employee discipline, however, and it therefore has an important role in the workplace.[19] Under a *continuous reinforcement schedule*, every instance of the right response is rewarded. For example, store associates might receive 25 cents each time they sell a pair of socks to accompany a pair of shoes. They are not rewarded just for asking "How about a pair of socks?". The desired behavior here is completing the sale.

Under an *intermittent reinforcement schedule*, the employee is rewarded sometimes, rather than every time the right response is made. The more unpredictable the payoff, the higher the motivation will be for many types of behaviors. If a manager praises a team member each time a report arrives on time, the praise will become routine. Slot machines and roulette wheels are designed with intermittent reinforcement schedules, which is what makes them so enticing.

OB Mod Applications

There are many applications of OB Mod in the workplace. A representative example of a large-scale OB Mod program took place in a labor-intensive firm. The general purpose of the program was to achieve productivity and quality improvement in 11 product areas. The five implementation steps in this program were as follows:

1. *Identify the critical performance behavior.* The critical (or desired) behavior must be observable and measurable, and it usually affects both quality and quantity of performance. It could be something as simple as "Completes the paperwork before sending part to the next department."

2. *Measure the behavior identified in the first step.* If the company is not collecting data on quality and quantity, a measurement scheme must be established. An example is tallying the percentage of parts rejected because of poor quality.

3. *Analyze the behavior.* An essential ingredient of OB Mod is called the *A-B-C (antecedent-behavior-consequence) analysis.* The antecedents set the occasion for the behavior to occur, such as a customer making an inquiry. The behavior is what the worker does, and consequences are the outcomes that now maintain the behavior, such as having a part accepted by another department.

4. *Intervene to accelerate the desirable performance behaviors and decelerate the undesirable ones.* The major intervention strategy is to give employees feedback on the critical performance-related behavior. Employees also receive positive reinforcement for progress and goal attainment. The program strives for immediate, objective, accurate, and positive feedback.

5. *Evaluate the intervention to ensure that performance is indeed improving.* This evaluation makes use of the data that were gathered in the second step and should be as rigorous as possible.

The results of this OB Mod program were substantial, as found in similar studies. Dramatic improvement took place in all product areas. The results included a 64 percent quality improvement in one product and a 52 percent productivity increase in another.[20]

The Organization in Action describes a company that pioneered in offering substantial rewards for outstanding performance.

ORGANIZATION IN ACTION

The Lincoln Electric Co., of Cleveland, Ohio, has driven General Electric, Westinghouse, and several Japanese companies from its niche despite being a smaller company. Lincoln manufactures arc-welding machinery and electric motors. Its product pricing is not especially low, nor is the company protected by patents. Instead, company management claims to achieve its edge through a fired-up workforce and entrepreneurial management ideas.

Workers are paid only for what they produce, and they repair defective work on their own time. Labor unions do not represent the workers, and no one receives paid holidays. Seniority is ignored in promotions, and overtime is mandatory. To encourage innovation, Lincoln uses piecework rates. Should a worker improve his or her productivity rate, the company does not recalculate the rate. The average production worker at Lincoln earns $45,000 per year. A particularly hard-working and imaginative production employee earned close to $100,000 one year. Nonproduction jobs are compensated according to a bonus system that approximates 50 percent of pay.

A merit rating system rewards individual initiative, quality, and teamwork. About 12 percent of sales goes to the work bonus pool. However, employees who do not meet performance standards earn below-average pay.

Source: Gene Epstein, "Inspire Your Team: The Merit System Earned a Worker $97,000," *Success* (October 1989): 12.

Evaluation of OB Mod

OB Mod has produced many tangible increases in productivity, yet it has been criticized widely on philosophical and scientific grounds. Critics have said that behavior modification is manipulative and dehumanizing—that it promotes dependence rather than self-determination and maturity. Another concern is that OB Mod is only for simple jobs, ignoring the fact that workers at all levels appreciate rewards for accomplishment.

MOTIVATION THROUGH SELF-DETERMINATION THEORY

Critics of organizational behavior modification contend that workers should be motivated by the joy of work. Herzberg's two-factor theory is also based on this assumption. One alternative to OB Mod is **self-determination theory**, the idea that people are motivated when they have a choice in initiating and regulating their actions.

The Rationale for Self-Determination Theory

Self-determination theory and intrinsic motivation, the idea that work itself is rewarding, are closely related. According to self-determination theory, workers are active agents rather than passive reactors to environmental forces. Two factors influence the perception of intrinsic motivation. Certain characteristics of a task, such as challenge and autonomy, promote intrinsic motivation because they allow for satisfaction of the needs for competence and self-determination. Workers' perceptions of why they perform a task also can affect intrinsic motivation. Such motivation is likely to increase when people perceive that they perform tasks for themselves rather than for an external reward.

Intrinsic motivation is based on an employee's need for competence and self-determination. This worker's sense of accomplishment in performing job tasks is a powerful motivator.

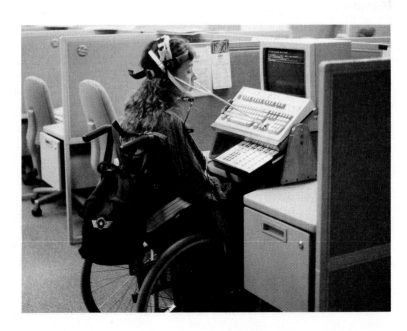

When an individual performs a task to achieve an external reward such as money or recognition, a shift occurs. The individual believes that the external reward caused the behavior, and money or recognition is now controlling his or her actions. The worker no longer perceives that he or she is self-determining, and as a result intrinsic motivation may decrease.[21]

Problems Associated with Extrinsic Rewards

Self-determination theory is based on the fact that rewards have some disadvantages. Extrinsic rewards can sometimes lower a person's job performance and be demotivating, particularly when a creative task is involved. The appeal of extrinsic rewards can also cause people to:

- focus narrowly on a task;
- rush through a job to get a reward;
- regard the task as a drudgery that must be suffered to receive the reward; and
- see themselves as less free and less self-determining.[22]

Despite these problems, a firm should not abandon financial bonuses and other forms of positive reinforcement. Even the people who enjoy their work intensely still want recognition from management. Also, people who love their work, such as successful novelists, entertainers, and athletes, demand huge fees. The sensible solution is for firms to balance extrinsic and intrinsic rewards.

MOTIVATION THROUGH ORGANIZATIONAL CULTURE

The methods described so far aim to motivate people individually or in small groups. A strategic way of enhancing motivation is to establish an organizational culture that encourages hard work and the pursuit of goals. **Organizational culture** is a system of shared values and beliefs that actively influence the behavior of organization members. (Chapter 22 provides more details about organizational culture.) The right organizational culture can inspire employees to be productive, whereas the wrong culture can lead to low productivity. It takes a long time to develop a culture that fosters strong motivation and productivity.

A firm that fosters strong motivation has several important cultural characteristics. For one thing, it rewards excellence by substantially rewarding top performers. Outstanding performers receive large raises and promotions, while poor performers do not get promoted, receive few raises, and may even be terminated. The firm also provides an atmosphere that rewards creative thought by giving tangible rewards to innovators. It imposes few penalties on people whose creative ideas fail, because such penalties discourage innovation.

Employees harbor a pervasive belief that the firm is a winner. If employees perceive that they belong to a winning team, they will be highly motivated.

Proud companies such as Ben & Jerry's Homemade and the Hewlett-Packard Company capitalize on this aspect organizational culture.

Finally, a firm that fosters motivation has a spirit of helpfulness that encourages employees to believe that they can overcome setbacks. Employees believe that when they face job hurdles the company will help them.[23]

LEARNING CHECK   Describe the basics of job enrichment, goal-setting theory, expectancy theory, and self-determination theory. Also explain how organizational culture contributes to motivation.

OVERVIEW OF SUGGESTIONS FOR MOTIVATING EMPLOYEES

Many practical suggestions for employee motivation stem directly from research on and theory about motivation and leadership.[24] As you study the suggestions presented here, observe the link between leadership and motivation. Most motivational methods require leadership skill and good judgment.

1. *Select motivated employees.* Because the source of motivation is within the individual, outstanding organizations try to hire employees who are well motivated in the first place. For example, conscientiousness relates to good job performance in all the occupational groups that have been studied.[25]

2. *Pay careful attention to individual differences in choosing rewards.* It is the manager's task to identify high valence outcomes of specific employees. Among these might be pay, additional vacation time, challenging assignments, recognition, or simply a few words of appreciation. Valences often can be identified by a direct discussion with employees about their preferences.

3. *Use positive reinforcement more than punishment.* At times, punishment is necessary. Yet it can produce such negative side effects as anxiety and retaliation against the firm, including making costly mistakes intentionally.

4. *Choose appropriate rewards.* For maximum results, managers should choose a combination of intrinsic and extrinsic, individual and group rewards. Intrinsic rewards are ideal because the employee's work becomes self-motivating. However, virtually no employee will be content with intrinsic rewards alone. Tangible rewards such as above-average salary increases are important. Financial incentives are the most effective when pay is a burning issue, such as with people in financial difficulty or those who crave luxuries.

5. *Provide feedback on performance.* Team members need to know what they are doing wrong as well as what they are doing right. Managers should give criticism privately in order to minimize negative side effects.

6. *Make rewards contingent on successful job performance.* Average performance is encouraged when all forms of accomplishment receive the same reward. Rewards should be linked to levels of accomplishment.

7. *Make the links between performance and rewards explicit.* For instance, a manager might tell a health and safety specialist what percentage of decreases in job-related illnesses would lead to an outstanding performance appraisal.

8. *Be aware of the motivational power of interesting work, appreciation of work, and the feeling of "being in on things."* Surveys have shown that employees strongly value these motivators. A manager should therefore make interesting assignments, give appropriate credit, and encourage participative decision making. Recognizing employee contributions is especially important because it raises personal and professional self-esteem, leading to higher motivation.

9. *See to it that rewards follow as soon as possible after the desirable behavior has taken place.* Even if a full reward, such as a new assignment, cannot be given immediately, the manager should mention immediately that the reward will be forthcoming.

10. *Empower team members.* When employees feel more important, they work more productively and have higher job satisfaction.

11. *Capitalize on the Pygmalion effect.* Managers who do an outstanding job of motivating employees believe in their team members. This confidence becomes a self-fulfilling prophecy.

12. *Use training and encouragement to enhance employee motivation.* Sometimes team members do not believe strongly that effort leads to good performance. They may require some encouragement and training to believe that they are capable of achieving performance standards. Similarly, the manager needs to see to it that factors beyond the employee's control, such as paperwork delays, do not affect performance adversely.

SUMMARY

Motivation is the process by which behavior is mobilized and sustained in the interest of meeting individual needs and achieving organizational objectives. Motivation contributes to performance, but ability and other factors are also critical. An important purpose of behavior is to satisfy needs such as the need for recognition. An active need is expressed as an inner state of craving or imbalance, and the individual seeks to satisfy the craving or rectify the imbalance.

Through his need hierarchy, Maslow contended that human needs fall into five groups: physiological, safety, social and love, esteem, and self-actualization. As needs on one level are gratified, they lose their strength and the next level of needs is activated. Herzberg's widely quoted two-factor theory divides job elements into motivation and satisfiers versus maintenance factors or dissatisfiers. According to Herzberg, motivational factors are the intrinsic or job content factors (such as achievement and recognition) that make a job rewarding. Maintenance factors are the extrinsic aspects of the job (such as working conditions and benefits). Dissatisfaction stems from substandard extrinsic factors.

McClelland's acquired need theory explains that certain needs that people strive to satisfy are acquired from the culture. His research centers around three needs of particular significance in understanding entrepreneurs and managers: achievement, power, and affiliation. (Ambitious people have strong needs for achievement and power but relatively low needs for affiliation.) The needs for recognition and autonomy are also important for motivation in organizations.

Job enrichment is an application of the two-factor theory. It revolves around the idea that a responsible, challenging job is motivational. Many of the characteristics of an enriched job relate to dealing directly with the client or use of the worker's product or service. Skill variety and vertical job loading are also important.

Goal setting plays an important part in all major theories of motivation. The regulation of motivation by goal setting is the best-demonstrated principle of human behavior. Goal-setting theory includes the following ideas: goals regulate actions; difficult and specific goals result in high performance; specific goals are better than general goals; goals increase effort and persistence; feedback is important; and the combination of individual and group goals is very effective.

Expectancy theory is based on the idea that work motivation results from deliberate choices to engage in certain activities in order to achieve worthwhile outcomes. The three most important components of expectancy theory are effort-to-performance expectancies, instrumentalities, and valence. Managers should take all three components into account to mo-

tivate people.

OB Mod is a system of motivation based on reinforcement theory. It centers on the idea that behavior followed by positive consequences is often repeated. In contrast, behavior followed by negative consequences tends not to be repeated. OB Mod programs have improved performance impressively.

An alternative to behavior modification is self-determination theory. It contends that people are motivated when they have a choice in initiating and regulating their actions and that the presence of external rewards makes people feel that the rewards are controlling their behavior.

A strategic method of increasing motivation is to establish an organizational culture that encourages hard work. This can be done by such means as granting big rewards to top performers, encouraging innovation, and cultivating a pervasive belief that the organization is a winner.

Many practical suggestions for employee motivation stem directly from research on and theory about motivation and leadership. Twelve of these suggestions are presented in the chapter, including the suggestions to select highly motivated job candidates and choose rewards based on individual differences.

KEY TERMS

motivation
Maslow's need hierarchy
two-factor theory of
  motivation
need for achievement
need for power

need for affiliation
need for recognition
need for autonomy
job enrichment
vertical job loading
meta-analysis

expectancy theory
expectancy
instrumentality
valence
organizational behavior
  modification (OB

Mod)
self-determination the-
  ory
organizational culture

QUESTIONS FOR DISCUSSION AND REVIEW

1. Explain why motivation alone will not bring about performance and productivity.
2. Use the general model of motivation to explain how a manager can use a worker's need for affiliation as a motivational tool.
3. How does Maslow's need hierarchy explain why an executive might leave a high-paying job to work as a remedial reading teacher for adults?
4. How would you know if a particular person had strong needs for power, achievement, or affilia-

tion?
5. How might a manager use the two-factor theory of motivation to increase the effort expended by a data-entry technician?
6. How does setting difficult goals tie in with the need for achievement?
7. How can a manager strengthen the expectancies of group members?
8. How might organizational behavior modification be used with higher-level workers such as man-

agers and professionals?

9. Assume that one of the leading researchers in self-determination theory received the Distinguished Scientist Award from the American Psychological Association. How would this award affect the research psychologist's motivation, based on the psychologist's own theory?

10. What characteristics of an organizational culture might demotivate individual workers?

11. Why do some people show such low work motivation?

PROBLEMS FOR ACTION

A. Your superior, an executive from a chain of instant auto service centers, returns from a workshop on expectancy theory. She is sold on the idea and asks you to set up a motivational program based on expectancy theory that will spur service technicians toward high performance. Summarize the steps you will take to accomplish this assignment.

B. Use OB Mod to develop a store associate (cashier) motivation program designed to improve the quality of customer service in a retail chain such as Kmart or Wal-Mart. Keep in mind that the program should be cost effective and that its value to the company should be demonstrated.

CONCLUDING CASE

Motivation at the Hyatt

John Allegretti joined the Hyatt Regency Chicago as a switchboard operator and assistant housekeeping manager. He disliked the prospect of waiting a long time to become a hotel manager. This 23-year-old preferred a more challenging job that also would help the environment. After months of conducting a job search, Allegretti landed his ideal job back at the Hyatt. Vice President Don DePorter wanted to retain Allegretti, so he invited him to head a project to reduce waste at the huge hotel. Allegretti did the job so well that the Hyatt authorized him to develop and operate a new waste-consulting company, International ReCycleCo. Its clients include several large Hyatt hotels along with other companies. Allegretti can sometimes be found working until 2:00 A.M.

Hyatt has actively searched for ways to keep its managerial employees excited about their work. A major reason is that in the 1960s it took as little as three years to be promoted to hotel manager within the chain, whereas aspiring managers today may have to wait eight years or longer to run even a small hotel.

To keep staffers enthusiastic and their ideas forthcoming, Hyatt uses such techniques as employee rap sessions and anonymous employee critiques of managers. The major motivation program, however, follows the model of ReCycleCo. Employees with novel ideas outside of the hotel field are being helped to establish freestanding companies. Among these new ventures have been party caterers, retirement apartment complexes, and sporting-equipment rental shops. The Hyatt employees who help develop the ideas are typically assigned to manage them. Hyatt grants them money to start the ventures, but the employees do not receive an equity stake.

Regency Productions by Hyatt is another business stemming from an idea contributed by a staff member. The firm provides catering and entertainment for groups such as the National Football League. James E. Jones, the director of sales development, noticed that professional party planners were receiving large fees for many services Hyatt could perform. The sports contacts Jones had developed gave him a large potential customer base. After Jones presented Hyatt senior executives with a business plan, the company invested $780,000 in the new business. The new business has made a promising start.

Hyatt senior executives are regularly bombarded with ideas from employees who appear to lack the business or technical skills to launch a new venture.

Top-level management, however, is willing to take risks. The president of Hyatt says, "It's always better to have a race horse you have to rein in than a donkey that you have to whip."

1. Identify specific aspects of a motivation theory or theories that support the idea of motivating employees by allowing them to start a new business for the parent company.

2. What do you think are the limitations of motivating people by allowing them to run a new venture?

3. What do you think are the motivational impacts of employee rap sessions and anonymous critiques of the boss?

4. Which of the practical suggestions for employee motivation are being used by Hyatt senior executives.

Source: As reported in James E. Ellis, "Feeling Stuck at Hyatt? Create a New Business," *Business Week* (December 10, 1990): 195.

REFERENCES

1. Terence R. Mitchell, "Motivation: New Directions for Theory, Research, and Practice," *Academy of Management Review* (January 1982): 82.

2. Abraham H. Maslow, "A Theory of Human Motivation," *Psychological Review* (July 1943): 370–396; Maslow, *Motivation and Personality* (New York: Harper and Row, 1954): Chapter 5.

3. Frederick Herzberg, Bernard Mausner, and Barbara Snyderman, *The Motivation to Work*, 2e (New York: John Wiley & Sons, 1959); Herzberg, *Work and the Nature of Man* (Cleveland: World Publishing, 1966).

4. John B. Miner, *Theories of Organizational Behavior* (Hinsdale, IL: The Dryden Press, 1980): 81–99.

5. David C. McClelland, "Business Drive and National Achievement," *Harvard Business Review* (July-August 1962): 99–112; L. Allen Slade, "Repeated Task Difficulty Choices as a Function of Achievement Motivation," *Academy of Management Best Paper Proceedings 1988* (Anaheim, CA: Academy of Management): 221–225.

6. David C. McClelland and David H. Burnham, "Power Is the Great Motivator," *Harvard Business Review* (March-April 1976): 159–166; Edwin T. Cornelius III and Frank B. Lane, "The Power Motive and Managerial Success in a Professionally Oriented Service Industry Organization," *Journal of Applied Psychology* (February 1984): 32–39.

7. David C. McClelland and Richard E. Boyatzis, "Leadership Motive Pattern and Long-Term Success in Management," *Journal of Applied Psychology* (December 1982): 737.

8. David J. Cherrington and B. Jackson Wixom, Jr., "Recognition Is Still a Top Motivator," *Personnel Administrator* (May 1983): 87.

9. Frederick Herzberg, "Motivation and Innovation: Who Are Workers Serving?" *California Management Review* (Winter 1979): 60; J. Barton Cunningham and Ted Eberle, "A Guide to Job Enrichment and Redesign," *Personnel* (February 1990): 56–61.

10. Herzberg, "Motivation and Innovation," 62.

11. Cunningham and Eberle, "A Guide to Job Enrichment and Redesign," 59–60.

12. Antone Alber and Melvin Blumberg, "Team vs. Individual Approaches to Job Enrichment," *Personnel* (January-February 1981): 66–71.

13. Edwin A. Locke and Gary P. Latham, *A Theory of Goal Setting & Task Performance* (Englewood Cliffs, NJ: Prentice Hall, 1990): 27–62.

14. Mark E. Tubbs, "Goal Setting: A Meta-Analytic Examination of Empirical Evidence," *Journal of Applied Psychology* (August 1986): 474–475.

15. Robert Rodgers and John E. Hunter, "Impact of Management by Objectives on Organizational Productivity," *Journal of Applied Psychology* (April 1991): 322–336.

16. Derived from Victor H. Vroom, *Work and Motivation* (New York: John Wiley & Sons, 1964); Lynn E. Miller and Joseph E. Grush, "Improving Predictions in Expectancy Theory Research: Effects of Personality, Expectancies, and Norms," *Academy of Management Journal* (March 1988): 107–122.

17. Walter P. Newsom, "Motivate, Now!" *Personnel Journal* (February 1990): 51.

18. Research cited in Robert Albanese, *Management Update* (Fall 1988).

19. Paul J. Champagne and Bruce R. McAfee, *Motivating Structures for Performance and Productivity: A Guide to Human Resource Development* (Westport, CT: Quorum Books, 1989).

20. Fred Luthans, Walter S. Maciag, and Stuart A. Rosenkrantz, "OB Mod: Meeting the Productivity Challenge with Human Resources Management," *Personnel* (March-April 1983): 28–36.

21. Edward L. Deci and Richard M. Ryan, *Intrinsic Motivation and Self-Determination in Human Behavior* (New York: Plenum Publishing, 1985); Deci, James P. Connell, and Richard M. Ryan, "Self-Determination in a Work Organization," *Journal of Applied Psychology* (August 1989): 580.

22. Alfie Kohn, "Incentives Can Be Bad for Business," *Inc.* (January 1988).

23. Michael Cavanagh, "In Search of Motivation," *Personnel Journal* (March 1984): 81; Kenneth M. Dawson and Sheryl N. Dawson, "How to Motivate Your Employees," *HRMagazine* (April 1990): 78–80.

24. Raymond A. Katzell and Donna E. Thompson, "Work Motivation," *American Psychologist* (February 1990): 144–153; Dawson and Dawson, "How to Motivate Your Employees," 78–80; Kenneth A. Kovach, "What Motivates Employees? Workers and Supervisors Give Different Answers," *Business Horizons* (September-October 1987): 58–65.

25. Murray R. Barrick and Michael K. Mount, "The Big Five Personality Dimensions and Job Performance: A Meta-Analysis," *Personnel Psychology* (Spring 1991): 1–26.

Chapter 13

Interpersonal and Organizational Communication

Chapter Learning Objectives:

1. Specify the steps in the communication process.

2. Identify the major forms of organizational communication.

3. Identify and give examples of the four directions of interpersonal communication in organizations.

4. Explain how nonverbal communication can be used to enhance communication.

5. Explain the nature of the grapevine and how it can serve to management's advantage.

6. Summarize the causes of communication breakdowns.

7. Explain how to improve the sending and receiving of messages.

8. Explain ways to overcome potential cross-cultural communication problems.

At Fisher Body Fleetwood, a manufacturer of car bodies, feedback was almost nonexistent. Plant performance reflected the limited feedback. Body repair costs were 30 percent higher than at comparable plants, and interdepartmental relations were confrontational at best and injurious at worst.

The plant manager and his staff made a commitment to improve quality and developed quality-improvement goals. Some improvements were achieved in the first five weeks, although quality levels were not yet acceptable. Managers reinforced all improvements and improvement efforts in a timely and specific manner with statements such as: "Way to go, Mark. I see we've gone from an average of 7.2 nonconformances per body to an average of 6.9. I appreciate the effort that's gone into that improvement. Keep up the good work. We're making good progress toward our target of averaging less than 3 by the end of the quarter."

Within 45 days, the performance feedback training and implementation started having a significant effect on quality levels. More important, these results were maintained and improved as the plant became more involved with quality improvement. Two years after the principles of feedback and reinforcement were introduced, the plant achieved significant results. Body repair costs fell by 32.8 percent, scrap costs per body fell by 68.7 percent, and the plant's quality index improved by 18.9 percent. A consultant to Fisher Body believed that much of the performance improvement could be attributed to the feedback given employees. This feedback was part of a program of positive reinforcement.

Source: Thomas K. Connellan, "Interpersonal Feedback," *Quality Progress* (June 1991): 22.

This case history illustrates one of many ways in which communication is important for managers (in addition to being linked to motivation). Communication is also important because of the time invested in communicating and the consequences of communication problems. Estimates are that the average worker spends about 20 percent of his or her time communicating.

Communication refers to sending and receiving messages, including ideas, emotions, and thoughts. **Organizational communication** is a formal method of sending messages in the workplace by such means as memos, bulletin boards, newsletters, and suggestion systems. Communication pathways such as the organization chart can also be classified as part of organizational communication. **Interpersonal communication** is sending and receiving messages between and among people through informal methods such as talking, writing, and body language. These two types of communication overlap. For example, formal communications are often sent between two people via electronic mail.

In this chapter, we begin our study of communication by presenting a model of the process. This is followed by a description of various types of organizational and interpersonal communications and an examination of communication problems. Finally, we summarize the means for improving the sending and receiving of messages and spotlight ways of dealing with cross-cultural communication barriers.

PROCESS MODEL OF COMMUNICATION

Interpersonal and organizational communication takes place through a series of steps, as illustrated in Figure 13-1. For true communication to take

FIGURE 13-1
The Communication
Process

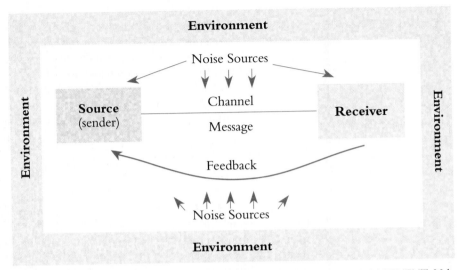

Source: Reprinted with permission of Macmillan Publishing Company from *MANAGEMENT: Making Organizations Perform* by H.R. Smith, A. Carroll, H. Watson, and A. Kefalas. Copyright © 1980 by Macmillan Publishing Company.

place, six components must be present: a communication source or sender, a message, a channel, a receiver, feedback, and the environment. To help explain the communication process, assume that a production manager at Fisher Body wants to inform a supervisor that quality in his department slipped last month.

Source (Sender)

Every communication event begins with a person or thing (such as an electronic paging device) transmitting a message. The source of a communication event is usually a person trying to send a spoken, written, or nonverbal message to another person or persons. The perceived authority and expertise of the sender are important factors in influencing how much attention the message will receive. For example, employees are more likely to pay attention to a message sent by the vice president of finance than to one sent by the bookkeeping supervisor.

Message

The heart of a communication event is the **message,** a purpose or idea to be conveyed. Many factors influence how a message is received, among them clarity, the alertness of the receiver, the complexity and length of the message, and how the information is organized. The production manager's message will most likely get across if he says directly, "I need to talk to you about last month's below-average quality figures."

Channel (Medium)

Several communication channels, or media, are usually available for sending messages in organizations. Typically messages are written, spoken, or a combination of the two. Some kind of nonverbal cue such as a smile or hand gesture accompanies most spoken messages. The most practical method for sending an important message is to use both written and spoken channels, and appropriate nonverbal messages should accompany spoken communications. If a person asks for additional money in a budget, for example, the words should be reinforced with such actions as gesturing and speaking in an emphatic tone. In the production manager's case, he has chosen to drop by the supervisor's office and deliver his message in a serious tone.

Receiver

A communication can only be complete when another party receives the message and understands it properly. In the example being examined, the supervisor is the receiver. There are many filters that can prevent a message from being received as intended by the sender. **Selective perception** is one major filter that people use to distort messages according to their needs. It is an unconscious process by which only selected aspects of a given message are received and processed. Selective perception is why people so often do not hear the full message when it contains negative news. If the supervisor is worried that his job is at stake, he might get defensive when he hears the production manager's message.

Formal written messages such as memos are an important channel for organizational communication. The communication is complete when the receiver understands it.

Feedback

Messages sent back from the receiver to the sender are referred to as **feedback**. Without feedback it is difficult to know whether a message has been received and understood. The feedback step also includes the reaction of the receiver. If the receiver takes action as intended by the sender, the message has been received satisfactorily. The production manager will know his message got across if the supervisor says, "Okay, when would you like to review last month's production figures?" Effective interpersonal communication therefore involves an exchange of messages between two people. In other words, the two communicators take turns being receivers and senders. (Keep in mind that communication can also take place between computers.)

Environment

A full understanding of communication requires knowledge of the environment in which messages are transmitted and received. The organizational culture is one key environmental factor that influences communication. In some cultures, the organization permits and promotes a free and open exchange of ideas and information among its members.[1] It is easier to transmit controversial messages when trust and respect are high than it is when they are low.

Noise

It is important to consider the pervasive influence of noise and other distractions on all components of the communication process. In this context, **noise** is anything that disrupts communication, including the attitudes and emotions of the receiver. For example, job stress often results in a loss of concentration that interferes with receiving messages. Other "noises" include fear, ambivalence, and strong advocacy for an opposing position. The whir of machinery and the chatting of co-workers taking a work break are among the many examples of noise on the job.

ORGANIZATIONAL COMMUNICATION

Organizational communication includes formal messages sent to and from employees by such means as publications, bulletin boards, meetings, suggestion systems, and complaint programs.

Publications and Memos

A survey of business firms showed that 87 percent have some kind of written (or visual) source of company information. The most frequent types are newsletters, newspapers, and magazines. Others include daily news bulletins, annual reports, and paycheck-envelope stuffers.[2] Written memos and electronic messages are also part of organizational communication. The Organization in Action describes a program to achieve two-way communication with employees. The results were more successful than most typical attempts at improved communication.

ORGANIZATION IN ACTION

"What's Happening" is a program developed at Polaroid Corp. by plant manager Harvey Greenberg. He noticed something wrong with monthly meetings between supervisors and workers. Hourly workers complained that the meetings were a waste of time, and supervisors wondered what information to communicate. The meetings began to improve when a secretary assembled a packet of information for the supervisors.

Greenberg took further steps to strengthen the meetings. He required each member of the management team to add something to the packet and asked the managers to review their input with the supervisors each month. The meetings still fell flat until the format was revised further. Middle-level managers and all other salaried employees were now invited to attend, and the packet of information was distributed several days before the meeting. At each meeting Greenberg would say, "Now I want to hear what you think." He also would ask people to bring items for discussion at the next meeting.

Under the new format, supervisors began to engage in constructive dialogue with Greenberg. For example, a supervisor explained why it was difficult to enlist applicants for a basic skill program. She said, "Look, it's difficult to tell someone you know he or she has a reading problem, let alone get that person to sign up." In response, the human resources department developed a workshop to help supervisors deal with such problems.

Source: As reported in Ruth G. Newman, "Polaroid Develops a Communication System—But Not Instantly," *Management Review* (January 1990): 34–38.

Bulletin Boards

ETHICS QUESTION
To what extent is management behaving in a socially responsible manner when it screens the information employees place on a company bulletin board?

Bulletin boards are the most popular form of basic employee communication.[3] Companies use them to post job openings, changes in policies and procedures, legally required notices involving equal employment opportunity, and wage and salary information. Bulletin boards also can be used for informal personal communications such as for-sale items, birth and death announcements, and other noncompany notices. Employers must often set limits to the use of bulletin boards to prevent items of no value or with anticompany content from being posted. Electronic bulletin boards are often used to display permanent messages such as smoking regulations at periodic intervals.

Meetings

Meetings are another standard component of organizational communications. Meetings to communicate information from top-level management downward are held at regular intervals or as the need arises. The most

Meetings are often held to build consensus, in addition to communicating information from top-level management downward.

frequent topics discussed are benefits and policies, the state of the firm, procedures, finances, and the budget. Less frequent topics are strategic planning, new product lines, industry programs, and general information about the firm.[4]

In addition to providing information, meetings can serve the important purpose of building **consensus**—a state of harmony, general agreement, or majority opinion with a reasonable amount of disagreement still present. When consensus is achieved, each member of the group is willing to go along with the plan because it is logical and feasible. To build consensus, the leader should:

1. Encourage participants to clarify and build on one another's ideas and be sure that everyone's ideas are heard.
2. Avoid heated arguments in favor of one person's position, especially his or her own.
3. Strive for win-win solutions or plans instead of such methods as majority vote or coin flipping. Win-win means that all participants feel that their interests have been reasonably satisfied by the agreed-upon plans.[5]

Suggestion Systems

A **suggestion system** is a written method of receiving and processing employee suggestions for job-related improvements and cost savings. Specific suggestions relate to such matters as improved methods of production, safety improvements, and ways of handling employee problems. A committee passes judgment on the merits of each suggestion and often assigns a reward to each acceptable suggestion.

Many awards are small, such as $25 or $50, but some may reach as high as $50,000. At McDonnell Douglas Astronautics Company (MDAC), St. Louis, the rewards range from $25 to $25,000 cash or $50 to $30,000 in U.S. Savings Bonds. The size of a reward is based on the anticipated savings to the company. MDAC saved $4 million from employee-submitted recommendations in one year. Suggestions typically reveal technical and process problems.[6]

Although some suggestion systems are productive, many others waste time and money. The review committee frequently gives a minimum award to everyone to encourage more suggestions and to avoid hurting feelings. In one company, a $25 award was made for a suggestion to install an umbrella rack in the office entrance. (In this way, people would waste less time looking for a place to rest their umbrellas.)

Complaint Programs

A **complaint program** is a formal vehicle for listening to the concerns and problems of employees and customers. At times, however, employees use the complaint program to get even with people they dislike. Processing complaints systematically helps the organization by reducing conflict. Reasons for complaint processing include (a) identifying individual or system-wide problems, (b) diagnosing problems and finding solutions to problems, and (c) providing feedback to the parties who initiated the complaint.[7] Firms using a formal method of processing complaints include Northrop, Florida Power and Light, McDonald's, and Kmart.

Use of a corporate ombudsman is related to a complaint program. An **ombudsman** is a neutral person designated by the firm to help employees process complaints. This person has the right to speak to anybody at any level in the company. Unlike an arbitrator, the ombudsman does not have the power to decide, but she or he can bring a problem to the attention of higher-level management. In the words of one corporate ombudsman, "My job is to help employees fight their way through an impenetrable bureaucracy."

LEARNING CHECK   Explain the process model of communication and identify typical components of an employee communication system.

INTERPERSONAL COMMUNICATION

Organizational communication aims primarily at disseminating information. Interpersonal communication is used to disseminate information and to convey feelings, attitudes, needs, and motives. The aspects of interpersonal communication discussed here are communication directions, communication networks, nonverbal communication, and the grapevine.

Communication Directions

Organizational communication systems are geared primarily to act as conduits for downward and upward communication. In contrast, interpersonal communication also takes place horizontally and diagonally. The four communication directions are illustrated in Figure 13-2.

DOWNWARD COMMUNICATION. **Downward communication** is the passing of messages from higher to lower levels in an organization. The importance of keeping employees informed is widely known, yet a lack of downward communication is still a widespread problem. One key reason is that many managers feel they are too busy to communicate. Another is that many believe they are already good communicators.[8]

Most downward interpersonal communication takes place from immediate superior to subordinate. However, higher-level managers sometimes speak and write directly to people at lower levels. Too much flexibility in this can create problems of its own. A loan officer in a bank made this comment: "When the president wants a loan approved for a friend, he speaks to me directly. My boss gets ticked off, but if I don't comply with the president, I could get in bigger trouble." (Such a procedure, of course, leads to conflict and confusion.)

One problem with downward communication through several levels is that the message may lose some of its original meaning and motivating power. A message is likely to be much more forceful when it is delivered by its originator.

UPWARD COMMUNICATION. **Upward communication** is the passing of messages from lower-level to higher-level organization members. People assume that leader-team member communication operates as a two-way system, permitting a free flow of information upward as well as downward. However, businesses frequently have faulty upward-communication

FIGURE 13-2 The Four Directions of Communication in Organizations

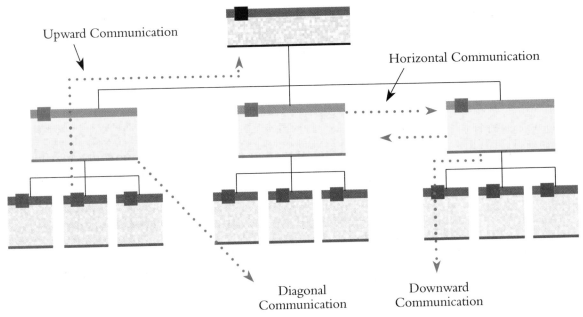

networks. Many upward networks are distrusted, and therefore unused, by employees.[9] A survey of 32,000 people from 26 firms pointed to the need for improved upward communication. The researchers observed:

> "What are the people telling us about employee communication? The loudest and clearest message is that they want human presence. They want to see and talk to leaders. They want a supervisor who shares information and listens. They want small group meetings so they can talk about their concerns and their ideas. And they want upward communication that can cut through bureaucratic formalities and status."[10]

To improve upward communication many managers initiate an open-door policy, allowing employees to drop in without an appointment to discuss concerns. Along the same lines, several companies have implemented an Operation Speakeasy program. In this new forum, a group of employees meets once a month with several top-level managers. The employees represent their departments by posing their concerns and questions. (E.g., "How can we continue to meet our goals of increased quality if we keep having to lay off people and cut expenses?") A one-month maximum limit is set for answering questions. Many are answered on the spot.[11]

HORIZONTAL COMMUNICATION. **Horizontal (or lateral) communication** is the sending and receiving of messages among people at the same organizational level. It is information sharing among people in the workplace. People sometimes write memos to co-workers, but the most frequent means of horizontal communication are telephone calls, face-to-face conversations, and informal meetings conducted in hallways and work-break areas.

According to one survey, approximately 60 percent of employees in a variety of organizations believe that lateral communication is inadequate. At the same time, communication among co-workers is seen as more effective than communication among departments. One method of improving horizontal communication is to establish lateral teams throughout the firm. These teams work on shared goals, engage in joint problem solving, explore new opportunities, and coordinate special projects.[12] **Lateral teams** are thus task forces or committees composed of people from different organizational units.

DIAGONAL COMMUNICATION. **Diagonal communication** is the sending and receiving of messages down or up the organization through different units and to people at different job levels. As an example, Maria, the head of advertising, sends a message to Luke, a middle-level manager in the purchasing department. She states that she wants to purchase a new computer printer if enough money is left in the budget. Luke, in turn, writes a memo to Gil, a budget analyst in the finance department, to request a current statement of the balance in Maria's budget. When Gil responds to Luke and Luke gets back to Maria, the diagonal communication cycle is complete. Networking is aided by diagonal communication.

The organizational structure also affects the flow of communications. In multilayered organizations, communications must pass through many channels and are thus subject to delay. Flatter organizational structures (those with fewer layers) allow for more rapid communication of messages because fewer people act as filters. If management makes proper use of electronic mail, communication can be swift even in a multilayered organization.

Communication Networks

Closely related to communication directions are **communication networks.** These are the linkages that connect people and groups for sending and receiving information. Five of these networks have been studied extensively in laboratory experiments (see Figure 13-3). The major difference among them is the amount of centralization in each. Among the major consequences related to centralization are the speed and accuracy of problem solving and the frequency of communication.[13]

In the *circle network*, communication may be initiated on either side of a group member. A restriction is that people can only communicate with adjacent group members. Problem solving is slow in a circle network, and people send many messages.

The *chain* is a version of the circle network except that it has a missing link. Because fewer messages can be sent, this communication system is more efficient. However, satisfaction with the communication process decreases because communication becomes more centralized.

In a *Y network*, individuals can communicate only with people one step above or below them. The two people in the tails of the Y are on the same organizational level, but they do not communicate directly with each other. The Y network saves time, but some group members feel that they are excluded from receiving potentially valuable information.

In the *wheel network*, one person sits in the communication hub and all messages are sent through that person. Assume that one or more group members have strong leadership skills. The communication advantage held

FIGURE 13-3
Five Basic
Communication
Networks

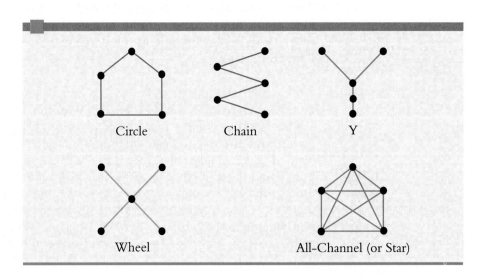

Circle   Chain   Y

Wheel   All-Channel (or Star)

by the person at the hub still gives him or her decision-making power. Groups using the wheel network organize more quickly and solve problems more accurately than groups using other networks.

The *all-channel (or star) network* allows each member to communicate directly with any other person. Although the communication patterns in a star network are confusing, many people enjoy the abundant interaction.

Research on networks indicates that the communication pathways affect productivity and satisfaction. A wheel network appears to be the best in a task-oriented environment, and the most likely to promote generation of new ideas. On the other hand, it lowers satisfaction. Creativity is fostered in a circle because group members can build on each other's ideas. A star network enhances satisfaction, but it may be inefficient because so much time is consumed with all the cross-communications.

The Grapevine

The **grapevine** is the major informal communication pathway in an organization. As the name suggests, the grapevine is entwined throughout the organization with branches going in all directions. Messages transmitted across the grapevine are much more likely to be part of interpersonal rather than organizational communication.

THE NATURE OF THE GRAPEVINE. Two characteristics of communication over the grapevine are especially important. First, the grapevine is often a rapid form of communication. Information travels rapidly because the grapevine reflects the interests and personal concerns of its members. Examples include news about an impending merger or layoff, an increase in profit sharing, or gossip about top-level managers. Second, the information sent is frequently distorted.[14]

Keith Davis, who has studied the grapevine extensively, has uncovered four separate grapevine patterns. First is the *single strand*, a chain network in which each person tells the other. Second is the *gossip* pattern, a wheel network in which one person tells all. Third is the *probability* pattern, in which each person tells others randomly. Fourth is the *cluster*, in which some employees tell selected others.[15] The last two patterns are modified star networks.

ETHICS QUESTION
What ethical issues are involved when management uses the grapevine to gauge employee reaction to a proprosed program or plan?

MANAGEMENT'S USE OF THE GRAPEVINE. Grapevines can create major problems for managers. They can breed employee resentment, embarrass managers, distort messages, and spread damaging rumors.[16] Despite these problems, a company can sometimes make positive use of the grapevine. For example, it can use the grapevine to measure the reaction of employees to an announcement before transmitting it through formal channels. If the reaction is bad, management can sometimes modify its plans. For example, top-level managers might want to see how seriously morale would be affected by announcing a two-day vacation without pay for all employees. They would feed the idea into the grapevine, and reactions to the plan could be gauged by the types of rumors created.

Nonverbal Communication

A substantial amount of interpersonal communication occurs through **nonverbal communication,** the transmission of messages by means other than words. The general purpose of nonverbal communication is to express the feeling behind a message. Assume that a sales representative stands tall when saying "Our payroll processing service is devoid of bugs and glitches." The representative's posture reveals confidence in making this pitch. The same message delivered in a slouched position with one hand over the mouth would communicate a feeling of limited confidence.

CATEGORIES OF NONVERBAL COMMUNICATION. The study of nonverbal communication is as complicated as the study of language because it incorporates such a wide range of behavior. Nevertheless, nonverbal communication can be divided into the following eight categories:[17]

1. *Environment.* This is the physical setting in which the message takes place, such as a person's office or desk or the restaurant chosen for a business meeting.
2. *Body placement.* This refers to the placement of one's body relative to that of another person. Facing a person in a casual, relaxed style indicates acceptance. Moving closer to another person is also a general indicator of acceptance. Yet moving too close may be perceived as a violation of personal space, and the message sender will be rejected.
3. *Posture.* This is the positioning or attitude of the body, including standing straight and opening the arms or legs to express confidence.
4. *Hand gestures.* These include movement of the hands, such as frequent movements to express approval and palms spread outward to indicate perplexity.
5. *Facial expressions and movement.* The particular look on a person's face and movement of the person's head provide reliable cues as to approval, disapproval, or disbelief.
6. *Voice tone.* Aspects of the voice such as pitch, volume, quality, and speech rate may communicate confidence, nervousness, and enthusiasm.
7. *Clothing, dress, and appearance.* The image a person conveys communicates such messages as "I feel powerful," and "I think this meeting is very important." For example, wearing one's best business attire to a performance appraisal interview would communicate the idea that "I think this meeting is very important."
8. *Mirroring.* This refers to building rapport with another person by imitating his or her voice tone, breathing rate, body movement, and language. Mirroring relies 10 percent on verbal means, 60 percent on voice tone, and 30 percent on body physiology. The technique is thus 90 percent nonverbal. A specific application of mirroring is to conform to the other person's posture, eye movements, and hand movements. The person feels more relaxed with you as a result of your imitation.[18]

MANAGERIAL APPLICATIONS OF NONVERBAL COMMUNICA-
TION. Managers would be well advised to pay more attention to the messages they send and receive. A starting point is for them to become more
conscious of their own facial expressions and those of other people. They
can listen more carefully to vocal inflections, look closer to see what other
people's eyes show about their true feelings, and pay attention to what they
wear to transmit the desired messages about themselves.[19] By paying close
attention to nonverbal communication, managers can improve communication and consequently improve productivity.

Keep in mind, however, that many nonverbal signals are ambiguous. For
example, a smile usually indicates agreement and warmth, but at times it
can indicate nervousness.

LEARNING CHECK

Describe the key aspects of interpersonal communication, including communication directions, communication networks, the grapevine, and nonverbal communication.

CONTRIBUTORS TO COMMUNICATION BREAKDOWNS

In addition to understanding the nature of the communication process, it is
important to understand why communication may not proceed as planned.
Communication problems are ever present in the workplace. For example, a
roofing company installed a roof on the wrong house in Toronto because
the term *Road* was used instead of *Way* in the address. This section describes
the types of messages most likely to be misinterpreted and key contributors
to communication breakdowns.

Characteristics of Readily Distorted Messages

A readily distorted message is complex, emotionally toned, or in conflict
with the mental set of the receiver. Often the distorted message results from
a combination of these three conditions. For instance, a manager might inform his or her department that payroll envelopes will be printed with the
company's new logo. Because this message is simple, emotionally neutral,
and does not clash with their mental set, it will probably be received accurately by most employees.

However, assume that the same manager announces that in the future,
payroll envelopes will be disbanded, direct deposit will replace paychecks,
and the payday cycle will be changed. The message is complex because it
has several elements, and it is emotionally toned because it deals with
money. Mental sets are disturbed because so many employees cling rigidly
to the idea of a weekly paycheck and budget their expenses accordingly.
Under these circumstances, an employee might start the rumor that the

company is modifying the pay system in order to hold on to employees' money longer.

Communication Barriers

As shown in Figure 13-1, any form of noise can prevent messages from being received as intended. We have already noted the pervasive effect of selective perception in blocking the accurate reception of messages. Eight other key communication barriers (or contributors to breakdowns) are described next. One reason why several of these barriers may appear to overlap is that most contain an element of selective perception.

DIFFERENT FRAMES OF REFERENCE. People perceive words and concepts differently depending on their **frame of reference,** a perspective and vantage point based on past experience. A typical example of the frame of reference problem took place in a financial service company that was instituting a quality-circle program to improve productivity. The vice president of operations announced the program with great enthusiasm only to find that the message was received in a distorted, negative fashion. The problem was that the vice president perceived productivity improvement as a vehicle to ensuring increased profits and survival. Lower-ranking employees, however, perceived productivity improvement as a way of maintaining output while laying off workers.

SEMANTIC PROBLEMS. Many communication problems are created by **semantics,** the varying meanings people attach to words. The symbols (both words and nonverbal behavior) used in communication can take on different meanings for different people. Consequently, it is possible for a person to misinterpret the intended meaning of the sender. An example of a semantic problem took place at a budget meeting.

After the meeting had run for two and one-half hours, the vice president chairing the meeting announced, "Let's break." All six participants in the room left. Five of them visited the water fountain, the restroom, or both. Dennis Gabe, the sixth member, left the premises to take care of some off-site business. The next day, the vice president met Gabe in the office and said, "I must say I didn't appreciate your running away from the meeting without giving us notice. Aren't you interested in our new budget?"

Gabe innocently replied, "When you said 'Let's break,' I thought you meant that we should break up the meeting. It seemed to me that we had already reviewed the agenda items." The vice president retorted, "When I say 'Let's break,' I mean take a brief break. Keep that in mind for the next time."

TIME PRESSURES. Time pressures can create communication barriers. The busy manager does not have time to see all group members or talk with them as fully as desired. Likewise, busy group members have neither the time nor the inclination to report every detail of every problem to their managers. As a result, a few important details may not be communicated.

VALUE JUDGMENTS. Making value judgments prior to receiving an entire message interferes with the communication of its intended meaning. A **value judgment** is an overall opinion of something based on a quick perception of its merit. When value judgments are made too hastily, the receiver hears only the part of the message that he or she wishes to hear. For example, a manager might begin to read an announcement about a child-care center to be sponsored by the company. The manager might make a quick value judgment that this program "is just another human resources program to keep people happy." By so doing, the manager will block out the information that child-care facilities often increase productivity by reducing absenteeism and turnover.

FILTERING OF NEGATIVE INFORMATION. A formidable upward-communication barrier is **filtering,** the coloring and altering of information to make it more acceptable to the receiver. Many managers and individual workers filter information to avoid displeasing their superiors. A case in point took place at a small software development company.

Several software engineers told their managers that they would leave the company if the president continued his tyrannical, insensitive attitude toward their efforts. The middle-level managers hesitated to pass along this information for fear of irritating the president. After five engineers quit simultaneously, the president was informed of the nature of the problem. After an initial burst of anger, the president said he would become more tolerant.

Filtering is most likely to take place when top-level management has a history of punishing the bearer of bad news. Another contributor to filtering is the political motivation of employees who color information in order to avoid being associated with bad news.

CREDIBILITY OF THE SENDER. The more trustworthy the source or sender of a message, the greater the probability that the message will get through clearly. In contrast, when the sender of the message has low credibility, many of the messages will be ignored. Sam Walton, the colorful chairman of Wal-Mart stores, was a positive example of source credibility. As described by a Wal-Mart manager, "We believe whatever Mr. Sam tells us. He's always been a straight shooter."

Today, low source credibility has become a widespread problem in business and government. Unfortunately, many truthful and important messages may be ignored because of the low reputation of the sender.

Blocked Downward Communication

Denying, as well as lying, can block communication. A communication barrier is erected when top-level management decides to withhold information from employees. Senior executives, for example, may wish to keep secret information about an impending layoff or the closing of a facility, reasoning that the disclosure of such information could interfere with the ordinary conduct of business. However, research and experience show that hiding the truth from employees is counterproductive. Rumors and anxiety increase in the absence of honest communication, and loyalty decreases as employees feel that they are being betrayed.[20] Thus, management's fear of honesty makes a bad situation worse. Communication worsens as employees worry about what relevant information will be hidden next.

Depersonalized Electronic Communication

High-technology devices have both aided communication in organizations and created the challenge of dealing with depersonalization. These devices include electronic mail, voice mail, fax machines, videotapes, and teleconferencing.

Electronic communication devices have one problem in common. They do not give a full sense of **social presence,** the feeling that a live person is present. Instead of communicating with another person face to face, or even over a conventional telephone, the user of an electronic mail system is forced to interact with a video display terminal (VDT). Because these devices do not provide a social presence, frustrations with voice mail and telephone answering machines are mounting. Likewise, a videotape is one-way communication, and even teleconferencing lacks the warmth of person-to-person interaction.

When senders cannot observe the nonverbal behavior of receivers and do not project nonverbal cues, they may not convey the true meaning of their messages. Even though information is exchanged by means of electronic channels, subtle aspects of communication are lost. The implication for management is that top-level information should not be communicated through a system of information processing. Top-level meetings hinge on nuances much more than on routine exchanges.

Despite these problems, advances in electronic communications continue to create new forms of communicating with a potential for productivity improvement. The Organization in Action provides details about electronic meetings.

ORGANIZATION IN ACTION

Recently, about 30 executives from the Greyhound Financial Corp. sat in a meeting and interacted with each other. Yet no one was shouted down and no one was intimidated into silence. Furthermore, each executive's comments were given equal weight. The Greyhound managers were interacting via personal computers programmed to let them offer their opinions anonymously and simultaneously. The electronic meeting enabled them to formulate a new corporate mission statement in less than two hours. "It would have taken forever in a conventional meeting, assuming it could have been done at all," said Greyhound's president.

The electronic meeting used by Greyhound was developed by Professor Jay F. Nunamaker with assistance from IBM. Such meetings typically begin with a leader posing a question or problem. Participants then spend about one hour keyboarding their suggestions. The computer searches the comments for common themes and categorizes them. A discussion is held next, either orally or electronically, about the results of the computer sort. Participants can then rank the ideas, comment on them, or vote on their implementation.

Electronic meetings have been generally well received, but some participants with poor keyboarding skills complain that they lose their train of thought as they hunt and peck.

Source: Claudia H. Deutsch, "IBM, Professor Market Concept of Electronic Meetings," *The New York Times* (October 22, 1990).

Communication Overload

Electronic communication has contributed to the problem of too much information being disseminated throughout most business firms. **Communication (or information) overload,** occurs when people are so overloaded with information that they cannot respond effectively to messages. As a result, they experience job stress. Managers and staff specialists alike are exposed to such a significant amount of printed and spoken information that their capacity to absorb it is taxed. The human mind is capable of processing only a limited quantity of information at a time. As implied in Chapter 4, information overload limits the rationality of managerial decisions.

Constructive steps can be taken to prevent and treat the problem of information overload. The most important strategy is to decrease the amount of information reaching a person. Progress along these lines has been made in the financial services industry. Since brokerage firms sell hundreds of products and services, including stocks, bonds, money-market funds, and retirement plans, each financial consultant is inundated with information. To get around the problem, management provides brokers with concise summaries of new products and services. Managers and other professionals must be selective in deciding how much information to absorb.

LEARNING CHECK   Describe why communication breakdowns occur.

IMPROVING INTERPERSONAL AND ORGANIZATIONAL COMMUNICATION

Businesses are now trying to improve all modes of communication: spoken, written, and nonverbal. One reason is that successful firms are characterized by an abundance of straightforward communication.[21] The following sections provide an overview of tactics and strategies for improving the sending and receiving of messages. In addition, they describe methods of overcoming problems in cross-cultural communication.

Improving the Sending of Messages

Improving the ways in which messages are sent will help overcome communication barriers. Managers can use the following suggestions for overcoming communication breakdowns to send their messages more effectively.

1. *Clarify ideas before communicating.* Many communications fail because of inadequate planning and lack of understanding of the true nature of the message to be communicated. To plan effectively, managers must consider the goals and attitudes of those who will receive the message and those who will be affected by it.

2. *Motivate the receiver.* The recipient of the message often has to be motivated to attend to the message. This is best accomplished by appealing to the receiver's interests or needs. In sending messages to higher-level management, therefore, it is important to frame a message in terms of how it contributes to productivity, quality, earning money, or saving money.

3. *Talk or write in specifics.* As Ken Blanchard has observed, being specific means conveying directions that are precise and clear about what is to be accomplished. It also describes the behavior of people instead of just labeling them.[22] "Reduce errors to 4 percent," is much more specific than "Be thorough."

4. *Frontload the writing.* Key ideas should appear at the beginning of a memo, paragraph, or sentence—a process referred to as **frontload writing.** Consider, for example, the difference in impact between these titles: (a) "Subject: Statistical Data Due Dates," and (b) "Subject: Due Dates for Statistical Data." A communications consultant says that the phrase *statistical data* is not the critical information in the title. It does not hook the reader by answering the question "What do I have to do?". Because the phrase *due date* is urgent, it should be frontloaded.[23]

5. *Minimize the use of junk words.* Phrases such as "like," "you know," "you know what I mean," and "he goes," (to mean "he says") detract from communication effectiveness. An effective way to cut down the use of these extraneous words is to tape record one's own side of a telephone conversation and then play it back. Once an individual hears how these words detract from speech effectiveness, he or she can monitor his or her own speech for improvement.[24]

6. *Use plain English.* The aim of the plain English movement is to make documents and forms readable and understandable. The payoff from using plain English is impressive. For example, an easy billing form saves the Southern California Gas Company $252,000 each year by reducing customer inquiries. Approaches to using plain English include (a) finding the simplest way to say what needs to be said; (b) replacing the legal vocabulary with common, everyday words; (c) using headings for documents longer than three pages; and (d) using short sentences.[25] Despite the merits of plain English, message senders should avoid insulting receivers by talking or writing down to them.

7. *Use bias-free language.* Biased terms often make the recipient of a message defensive, thus serving as a communication barrier. The use of biased words may also be interpreted as a subtle form of job discrimination. For example, the term *physically disabled* (or *physically challenged*) is bias-free, but *handicapped* is biased; *engineer* is bias-free, but *woman engineer* is biased; *nurse* is bias-free, but *male nurse* is biased; *accountant's perspective* is bias-free, but *bean counter's viewpoint* is biased.

It is difficult to entirely avoid offending people because our culture is so diverse. Terms have such a variety of meanings and implications that it is difficult not to say something that somebody will interpret as politically incorrect. Another problem is that a term that is perceived as neutral at one time may become biased at another time. For example, many people of Spanish origin now prefer "Latino" to "Hispanic." The solution is to use neutral terms to describe groups of people whenever feasible.

8. *Communicate feelings behind the facts.* The facts in a message should be accompanied by the appropriate feelings. Feelings add power and conviction to the message. The sender of the message should explain his or her personal feelings and encourage the receiver to do the same. For example, a manager who is disappointed with the quality of housekeeping in a department might say, "The office looks terrible, and I'm very disappointed with the attention you have paid to housekeeping. How do you feel about my criticism?" A less effective approach would be to simply criticize the poor housekeeping without mentioning the feelings; for example: "The office looks terrible." A message without feeling may not be taken seriously.

9. *Be aware of nonverbal behavior.* A speaker's tone of voice, expression, and apparent receptiveness to the responses of others all have an impact on the receiver. These subtle nonverbal aspects of communication often affect the listener's reaction to a message even more than the content of the communication. When sending messages to others, it is important to keep in mind all the aspects of nonverbal behavior previously described.

10. *Support words with actions.* Organizations, as well as individuals, must support their words with actions to remain credible and to avoid sending mixed messages.[26] For instance, if top-level management espouses quality in speeches, it is important not to frown on painstaking attention to detail in the office or factory.

11. *Obtain feedback.* The best efforts at communication may be wasted if feedback on how well the message came across is not received. Asking questions, encouraging the receiver to express reactions, following up on contacts, and subsequently reviewing performance are ways of providing feedback. Every important communication should include feedback to ensure thorough understanding and appropriate action. Managers should actively solicit feedback on such matters as clarity of instructions, work problems, and employee attitudes. Frequent visits to the work site by the manager also encourage feedback.

12. *Use personalized employee communications.* The human resources departments in many large companies are now communicating to employees

Speaking personally to employees regarding the specifics of their benefits is an effective means of improving communication in a firm. Here, a representative of the human resources department discusses the employee's retirement program with her.

in personalized terms about their benefits and retirement programs. A personal message specifies how the addressee would specifically benefit from a particular program. (The alternative approach is to write about employees in general and have each employee complete his or her personal application.) Several companies that have used this approach have found that the number of volunteers for early retirement has far exceeded expectations.[27] In short, the personalized message communicated effectively.

13. *Lighten up.* Communications consultant Roger Ailes has offered the following suggestion: "The only advice some of my clients need can be summed up in two words: 'Lighten up!' It's ironic, but your career can depend on whether you get serious about taking yourself less seriously."[28] The message here is that a humorous touch can enhance a person's effectiveness as a communicator.

Back to the
Opening Case

Fisher Body Fleetwood wanted to improve product quality. A key component of the company's quality-improvement program was to provide accurate and timely feedback to employees about how well they were performing. Improved feedback led to improved communication, which in turn led to better quality and improved business results.

Improving Listening

Listening is a basic part of communication. Managers must be good listeners because so much of their work involves gathering information from others. For example, middle-level managers must integrate information they receive from many sources and report the information to top-level managers. Careful listening helps reduce the need to rewrite letters, reschedule appointments, and reship orders. Listening also can lead to positive outcomes such as increased sales. The experience of David-Edward, a maker of high-quality upholstered furniture, is relevant. The company president brought together groups of 12 prominent designers at various locations in the country and asked them about their furniture requirements and about industry trends in general. Sales increased approximately 35 percent as a result of actions taken based on these formal listening sessions.[29]

Improved listening begins with an appreciation of the difference between listening and hearing. **Hearing** is the physical reception of sound, whereas **listening** is the mental translation of sound into meaningful communications. Following are some key suggestions for improving listening:

1. *Concentrate on meaning.* Instead of trying to listen to each word, try to catch the essence of what is said. Stay focused on the speaker. Two leading causes of listening failures are daydreaming and distractions.

2. *Get involved in what is said.* Merge your thoughts and prior information about the subject with what is being said. Think about additional facts that support or refute the sender's comments.

3. *Listen to the full story.* Avoid arriving at a conclusion before hearing the speaker present the complete story. Many people reach a verdict about a controversial topic in the first few moments of conversation. They then listen for confirming evidence.[30]

4. *Recognize emotions.* Listening to facts alone is not fully effective listening. Instead, put yourself in the position of the other person by recognizing feelings as well as facts. Pinpoint the meaning of the feelings behind the statements being made, rather than the meaning of the words being said. Look for signs of eagerness, hesitancy, anger, tension, or despair. Watch for evasions, the words left unsaid, or areas of discussion that the speaker consistently avoids.

5. *Restate the sender's position.* As a test of your understanding, provide feedback by restating the person's statement from his or her point of view. Suppose, for example, that your superior opposes your taking a part-time job in addition to your regular responsibilities. You might say, "You are concerned that my part-time work will divert some of my energies from my full-time position. I understand your point of view, but I would like to explain my position more fully."

6. *Evaluate yourself by the 50/50 rule.* According to this rule, it is best if you do not speak more than 50 percent of the time. As you and the other person engage in conversation, observe the second hand on a watch or clock. (Do not do this too often, or you will lose concentration.) If your analysis shows that you are speaking more than half the time consistently, you are not listening enough.[31]

7. *Summarize what you have heard.* Conversations, presentations, and speeches are not as well organized as written words. Rather than daydream while a person is delivering a message, periodically do a quick mental summary of what is being said. Summarizing helps you capture the gist of the message.

Overcoming Cross-Cultural Communication Barriers

The modern workforce has become more culturally diverse in two major ways. More subgroups from within our own culture have been assimilated into the workforce, and there is increasing interaction with people from other countries. Because of this, businesses face the challenge of preventing and overcoming communication barriers created by differences in language and customs. Cultural differences within a diverse country such as the United States can be as pronounced as the differences between two countries. Sensitivity to cultural differences goes a long way toward overcoming these potential communication barriers, but in addition, there are six specific tactics and strategies that communicators should keep in mind.

1. *Modify Your Language as Appropriate.* Reflect on the struggle you may have had in attempting to converse in a second language. To enhance your communication effectiveness with a person who is not fluent in your language, simplify, clarify, and specify.[32] Speak deliberately and slowly, and minimize jargon and idioms. For example, saying "There is bad chemistry between you and your boss" may be puzzling to someone raised in a non-English-speaking culture. A written note is a helpful supplement to oral communication about a key topic, because most people read a second language better than they speak it.

2. *Be Alert to Cultural Differences in Customs and Behavior.* To minimize communication barriers with people from other cultures, recognize that many subtle job-related differences in customs and behavior may exist. For example, Asians typically feel uncomfortable when asked to brag about themselves in the presence of others. To them, calling excessive attention to oneself, particularly at the expense of another person, is both rude and unprofessional.[33] Therefore, during a job interview, a worker raised in Vietnam might recoil when asked to list his or her accomplishments and strengths. Figure 13-4 presents a sampling of cross-cultural differences in customs and behavior that relate to communication.

3. *Be Sensitive to Differences in Body Language.* All cultures use nonverbal language, but the specific cues differ from one culture to another. To receive messages accurately when working with people from diverse cultures, one must be sensitive to these differences. An important example is eye gaze. In North America and Europe, looking directly into another person's eyes, in moderation, is a sign of self-confidence. In many Asian cultures it is not proper to look a superior in the eyes too frequently. Another significant cross-cultural difference is the use of physical closeness and touching. Latin Americans and Southern Europeans are more likely to stand very close to or touch a work associate than are North Americans.[34] Thus, if a Mexican touches an American it does not necessarily mean that a deal is about to be struck.

4. *Be Understanding of Phonetic Differences.* A person's inability to pronounce a sound from another language should not be interpreted as poor comprehension. In truth, even those who are fluent in another language may have difficulty with certain sounds. For example, Ger-

FIGURE 13-4
Cross-cultural
Differences in
Communication

- Members of Asian and some Middle-Eastern cultures consider direct eye contact rude.

- Japanese people rarely use the word "no." When they say "Yes" ("hai"), it only acknowledges that they have heard what was said.

- When Japanese people say "We'll consider it," they probably mean "No."

- British people understate their feelings. If an English person says "Your report does raise a few questions," the real meaning is probably "Your report is atrocious."

- People from the United States, Great Britain, Scandinavia, and Northern Europe require more personal space than people from Southern Europe, the Caribbean, and India.

- People from Latin America are very conscious of rank, and they expect the manager to be the voice of authority. Consequently Latin Americans may be hesitant to make suggestions to a superior.

- Americans are eager to get down to business quickly and will therefore spend less time than people from other cultures in building a relationship when conducting business.

- Americans value time much more than people from other cultures. They are therefore more likely than people from other cultures to appear perturbed when a person shows up late for a meeting.

- To an American, "Table the motion" means put that agenda item away for a while. To a British person, "Table the motion" means put the agenda item up for discussion now. (Many other idioms also lead to confusion when used with other cultures.)

Source: Gleaned from many sources, including Rose Knotts and Sandra J. Hartman, "Communication Skills in Cross-Cultural Situations," *Supervisory Management* (March 1991): 12; and Sandra Thierderman, "Overcoming Cultural and Language Barriers," *Personnel Journal* (December 1988): 34–40.

mans and Hungarians have extreme difficulty pronouncing the English *W* sound, and Japanese struggle with the English *L* and *R* sounds.[35] Likewise, people whose native language is English have difficulty pronouncing the French *R* (which is similar to a cat purr).

5. *Be Open About Any Concerns and Confusions.* A skillful way of overcoming cross-cultural communication barriers is to be open and honest about concerns and confusions.[36] If a person from another culture consistently avoids looking at you during conversation, you might say, "I'm having a problem. I want to communicate effectively with you, but I don't know how to interpret your looking away from me. Could you explain what it means?" Or if a person consistently stands too close, you might say, "Sometimes I may appear a little uptight when you get close to me in conversation. It's just part of my cultural upbringing. I need more personal space than you give me."

6. *Know the Audience.* As with any other attempt at overcoming communication barriers, you should try to learn the basic values, attitudes, preferences, customs, and peculiarities of the receiver of your message. You can then frame your message in such a way as to increase the chances that the receiver will understand it.

SUMMARY

Organizational (or formal) communication refers to the dissemination of messages in the workplace. Interpersonal (or informal) communication refers to face-to-face communication. A general model of the communication process has six components: sender, message, channel, receiver, feedback, and environment. Both noise and psychological barriers can interfere with the receiving of messages.

Organizational communication includes such channels as publications and memos, bulletin boards, meetings, suggestion systems, and complaint programs. Interpersonal communication in organizations can proceed in four directions: downward, upward, horizontally, and diagonally.

Communication networks are the linkages connecting people and groups for sending and receiving information. Five key networks are the circle, chain, Y, wheel, and star.

The grapevine is the major informal communication pathway in an organization. Communication through the grapevine is rapid, and the information transmitted is often distorted. Managers can sometimes use the grapevine to advantage by transmitting information they may not want to transmit formally.

A substantial amount of interpersonal communication occurs through nonverbal communication—the transmission of messages by means other than words. The major purpose of nonverbal communication is to express the feeling behind a message. Nonverbal communication includes environment; body placement; posture; hand gestures; facial expression and movement; voice tone; and clothing, dress, and appearance. Building rapport by mirroring another person's actions or language is another aspect of nonverbal communication.

Communication breakdowns occur frequently, particularly when the communications are complex or emotionally toned or clash with the mental set of the receiver. Factors contributing to communication breakdowns include different frames of reference, semantic problems, selective perception, time pressures, value judgments, filtering of negative information, and low credibility of the sender.

Additional communication barriers are created by blocked communication (withholding information from employees), depersonalized electronic communication, and communication overload.

Suggestions for improving the sending of messages include clarifying ideas before communicating, motivating the receiver, and communicating the feelings behind the facts. A key point in improving listening is to recognize the distinction between hearing (the reception of sound) and true listening (the mental translation of sound into meaningful communication).

Differences in language and customs create more communication barriers. To overcome these barriers, communicators should modify their language as appropriate and be alert to cultural differences in customs and behavior. They should also be sensitive to differences in body language, understand phonetic differences, and express their concerns and confusions.

KEY TERMS

organizational communication
interpersonal communication
message
selective perception
feedback
noise
consensus

suggestion system
complaint program
ombudsman
downward communication
upward communication
horizontal (or lateral) communication
lateral teams

diagonal communication
communication networks
grapevine
nonverbal communication
frame of reference
semantics
value judgment

filtering
social presence
communication (or information) overload
frontload writing
hearing
listening

QUESTIONS FOR DISCUSSION AND REVIEW

1. Why is communication referred to as the "basic process by which managers get their jobs done"?
2. Summarize the steps in the communication process. Which one of these steps are you now best able to perform? Explain your reasoning.
3. Give two examples of organizational communication from your school or employer.
4. How can an organization benefit from good upward communication?
5. Provide an example of a problem that diagonal communication could handle efficiently.
6. What is the true meaning of the phrase "I heard it through the grapevine"?
7. Why do you think most communication problems are not solved even though most executives are aware that such problems exist?
8. Explain how selective perception could prevent a company from doing a good job of improving product quality.
9. How does office automation contribute to communication problems?
10. What differences in language have you noticed among subgroups in your country? For example, do people from one geographic region use unique expressions?

PROBLEMS FOR ACTION

A. Use the communication process model shown in Figure 13–1 to develop a set of basic guidelines managers can use in delivering controversial messages to team members. Prepare your guidelines in the form of a brief report to managers.

B. You have been assigned to manage a department of 15 employees. English is a second language for five of these workers, and you speak only English. Develop a plan for overcoming communication barriers that might stem from these language differences.

CONCLUDING CASE

Rumors at the Date Book Company

John Cotter is a senior book bindery operator for the Date Book Company located in New York City. He was talking to Hanna Garfield, a sales representative for McCain Book Binding Equipment. Garfield told Cotter that the brother of the Date Book Company's owner (Larry Calumet) was buying equipment from competitors and setting up a bookbinding plant in nearby New Jersey. After Garfield left, Cotter went to talk to Dan Guarino, one of the other operators.

"Hanna Garfield from McCain just told me that Larry Calumet's brother is setting up a bookbinding plant in New Jersey. You know how Calumet is always complaining about the union. My hunch is that as soon as the plant is up and running, our work will be shifted over to the nonunion plant. We will all be out looking for jobs. Let's call a meeting of all the operators tomorrow after work at the union meeting hall."

Cotter was the first to speak at the meeting with the 22 other operators. With anger in his voice, he said, "We have all worked hard for the Date Book Company. Now our owner is setting up a nonunion bindery to cut labor costs. We will all be out of jobs in six months. There's little we can do about it. I suggest we all start looking for new jobs. We should also teach Mr. Calumet a good lesson by ruining as much product as possible before they shut us down."

Three weeks later, plant superintendent Peter Reynolds walked into the office of the owner, Larry Calumet. Reynolds said, "Larry, I just don't know what's going on. I just had to reject another large batch of date books because of bindery error. We have had more spoiled product in the last two weeks than we had all last year. Besides that, two very experienced operators just quit without explanation. We now not only have to worry about your brother opening a business to compete against us, but also have to find a solution to our quality problems."

Calumet responded, "Why didn't you tell me about the spoilage problem before today? I think I know what's going on. Two weeks ago Arnie, the head maintenance technician, told me about a rumor running through the plant. The story was that I was building the new plant with my brother to shut down our bindery. Supposedly, my motive was

Case researched by Cliff Grinell, Rochester Institute of Technology.

to save money by hiring nonunion labor.

"I figured the rumor would run its course. Besides, I thought those overpaid bindery operators needed a good scare. I had no idea they would start ruining the product and quitting their jobs. I hope it's not too late to repair the damage."

1. What communication problems are illustrated by this case?
2. What could Larry Calumet have done to prevent this problem?
3. What should Larry Calumet do now?

REFERENCES

1. Corwin P. King, "Crummy Communication Climate (and How to Create It)," *Management Solutions* (July 1986):30–31.
2. Paul L. Blocklyn, "Employee Communications," *Personnel* (May 1987): 62.
3. Blocklyn, "Employee Communications," 62–63.
4. Blocklyn, "Employee Communications," 63.
5. Francis X. Mahoney, "Team Development: Part 4: Work Meetings," *Personnel* (March-April 1982): 52–53.
6. George G. Rich, "Revamped Communication System Saves MDAC Millions of Dollars Annually," *Personnel Journal* (January 1987): 32.
7. James T. Zigenfuss, Jr., "Corporate Complaint Programs Make Gains from Gripes," *Personnel Journal* (April 1987): 40.
8. Len Sandler, "Rules for Management Communication," *Personnel Journal* (September 1988): 40.
9. Alan Zaremba, "The Upward Network", *Personnel Journal* (March 1989): 34.
10. Roy Foltz and Roger D'Aprix, "Survey Shows Communication Problems," *Personnel Administrator* (February 1983): 8.
11. Joyce S. Anderson, "Blueprint for Real Open-Door Communication," *Personnel Journal* (May 1989): 32.
12. Valorie A. McClelland and Richard E. Wilmot,"Improve Lateral Communication," *Personnel Journal* (August 1990): 32, 38.
13. The research reported here is synthesized in James L. Bowditch and Anthony F. Buono, *A Primer on Organizational Behavior*, 2e (New York: John Wiley & Sons, 1990): 117–118.
14. Alan Zaremba, "Working with the Organizational Grapevine," *Personnel Journal* (July 1988): 38.
15. Keith Davis and John W. Newstrom, *Human Behavior at Work: Organizational Behavior*, 8e (New York: McGraw-Hill, 1989).
16. Walter St. John, "In-House Communication Guidelines," *Personnel Journal* (November 1981): 877.
17. Michael Argyle, *Bodily Communication*, 2e (Madison, CT: International Universities Press, 1990); Andrew J. DuBrin, *Contemporary Applied Management: Behavioral Science Techniques for Managers and Professionals*, 3e (Homewood, IL: Richard D. Irwin, 1989), 96–111.
18. "Instant Rapport," *Executive Strategies* (October 3, 1989): 6.
19. Thomas I. Sheppard, "Silent Signals," *Supervisory Management* (March 1986): 33.
20. Dave Francis, *Unblocking Organizational Communication* (Brookfield, VT: Gower Publishing Company, 1987).
21. Robert A. Dilenschneider, *A Briefing for Leaders: Communication as the Ultimate Exercise of Power* (New York: HarperBusiness, 1991).
22. Ken Blanchard, "New Communication Skills, New Roles in the '90s," *Supervisory Management* (July 1991): 1.
23. Sherry Sweetham, "How to Organize Your Thoughts for Better Communication," *Personnel* (March 1986): 39.
24. "Ridding Your Speech of Junk Words," *Success* (May 1985): 16.
25. "Plain English Pays," *Research Institute Personal Report for the Executive* (December 1, 1986): 2–3; Robert W. Goddard, "Use Language Effectively", *Personnel Journal* (April 1989): 34.
26. Valorie McClelland, "Communication: Mixed Signals Breed Mistrust," *Personnel Journal* (March 1987): 24.
27. George E. L. Barbee, "Communicating with a Personal Touch," *Personnel Journal* (October 1989): 38–45.
28. Roger Ailes,"Lighten Up!" *Success* (April 1990): 14.
29. Thomas Peters, "Listening Is So Easy, Yet Often Ignored," syndicated column (September 29, 1985).
30. Points 1, 3, 4, and 7 are from "Sharpen Listening Skills," *Personal Report for the Executive* (April 1, 1987): 7.
31. Theodore Kurtz, "Dynamic Listening: Unlocking Your Communication Potential," *Supervisory Management* (September 1990): 7.
32. James B. Stull,"Giving Feedback to Foreign-Born Employees," *Management Solutions* (July 1988): 45.
33. Sandra Thierderman, "Overcoming Cultural and Language Barriers," *Personnel Journal* (December 1988): 34.
34. C. Barnum and N. Wolniansky, "Taking Cues from Bodly Language," *Management Review* (June 1989): 59–60.
35. Thierderman, "Overcoming Cultural and Language Barriers," 34–35.
36. Bob Abramms-Mezoff and Diane Johns, "Managing a Culturally Diverse Workforce," *Supervisory Management* (February 1989): 37–38.

Chapter 14

Management of Ineffective Performance

· ·

OPENING
CASE
· · · · · · · · · · · · · ·
Substance Abuse
at a Distribution
Center

As he was reviewing a report, the director of industrial relations at Tri-Valley Growers picked up his ringing telephone. The caller identified herself only as a forklift driver at a large company distribution center. She explained, "Many of my co-workers are either drunk or on drugs. There are people using and selling drugs on the job. I'm frightened, and I don't want to work with them any longer. You, the industrial relations chief, have a responsibility to stop this craziness. If you don't I'm going to find another job."

This phone call caught top-level management's attention. The company had rules prohibiting the possession and use of drugs and alcohol on the job, but management did not actively prevent workers from engaging in those activities. The words of the forklift operator, "You have a responsibility to stop it," stayed in the director's mind.

Source: Adapted from Edward J. Miller, "Investing in a Drug-free Workplace," *HRMagazine* (May 1991): 48.

· ·

The industrial relations executive is wondering how to handle alcoholism and drug abuse in the workplace. Substance abuse is but one of many factors that contribute to ineffective performance. Ineffective performance lowers productivity, and dealing with ineffective performance creates some problems of its own. Because poor performers consume an inordinate amount of a manager's time, they can lower managerial productivity. Managing poor performance also lowers satisfaction, because it is an inherently unpleasant task for all concerned: managers, staff specialists, and poor performers themselves. Nevertheless, learning how to manage ineffective performance effectively is an important aspect of leadership and management.

This chapter examines the causes of ineffective performance and presents a general model for managing it. Corrective discipline—a general-purpose strategy for managing ineffective performers—is then highlighted. This is followed by a description of employee assistance programs. These programs help employees overcome personal problems that adversely affect job performance. The chapter closes with a discussion of terminating employees whose performance remains substandard despite help from the firm.

Ineffective performers are found at all levels of management, as well as among professional, technical, and operative employees. Yet some of the problems discussed in this chapter are more applicable to employees at some job levels than at others. For example, entry-level employees are more likely to have problems of low work motivation and limited intelligence, while managers are more likely to wander away from the work area to take care of personal business or take extended lunch breaks. Also, some assistance programs are used more often with top-level managers than with lower-ranking employees. An example is that companies will pay for a consultant to counsel with an executive about work problems, whereas it would rarely offer such assistance to a technician.

FACTORS CONTRIBUTING TO POOR PERFORMANCE

Managers blame employees for most instances of substandard performance.[1] But in truth, numerous factors relating to the person and the person's envi-

ETHICS QUESTION
What obligation does management have to rehabilitate, rather than simply fire, ineffective performers?

ronment can contribute to this problem. The term *contribute to* is more accurate than the term *cause* when explaining ineffective performance because most instances of poor performance result from a combination of individual and situational factors. For instance, an employee with an abrasive personality might perform adequately for years as a materials handling specialist. The specialist is able to get by because the manager accepts the abrasiveness. Then a new manager is appointed who clashes with the employee, thus intensifying the employee's abrasiveness. The employee soon is labeled as an "oddball" who is ineffective because of an inability to get along with people. Thus, the combination of this abrasive personality with the not-very-compassionate manager may lead to poor performance.

Factors contributing to poor performance can be classified as either individual or organizational (or environmental). Organizational factors include those related to the job, the manager, the work group, and the firm as a whole. The following sections summarize the major factors contributing to poor performance. These factors can serve as a checklist for managers to use in thinking through why an employee is performing ineffectively in a given situation. Each contributing factor does not require a separate type of remedial action by the manager or firm. Instead, one course of action can be used in dealing with performance problems created by a variety of underlying factors. For example, counseling programs might be used to help overcome such problems as work stress, job burnout, absenteeism and tardiness, and family and personal problems.

Individual Factors

The following is a list of individual factors that can contribute to poor performance.

1. *Insufficient intellectual ability.* The employee lacks sufficient mental ability or other intellectual skills such as oral and written communication skills, needed to deal with the complexities of the job. Many companies today have found it necessary to offer reading and mathematical literacy programs to employees.[2]

2. *Insufficient job knowledge.* The employee lacks adequate knowledge of how to perform the job due to inadequate job training or experience.

3. *Low work motivation or work ethic.* The employee puts forth a low level of effort, is not interested in the job, and has poor personal work standards. Some employees believe that the company owes them a good job without thinking through what they owe the company.

4. *Work stress.* The employee's internal equilibrium is disturbed by one or more factors in the work setting, including excessive work demands, heavy conflict, job insecurity, and conflicting demands.[3]

5. *Job burnout.* The employee becomes emotionally, physically, and mentally exhausted as a consequence of long-term stress. The employee also becomes cynical, apathetic, and bored.[4]

6. *Obsolescence.* The manager or specialist who was effective in the past becomes ineffective because of technical deficiencies in his or her own field or inadequate interpersonal skills.

7. *Physical limitations.* The employee may have insufficient physical

strength, coordination, vision, or hearing for the demands of the job. AIDS has become a physical limitation of special concern because employees with AIDS are regarded legally as having a disability.[5]

8. *Alcoholism or drug addiction.* The employee lacks concentration and makes errors in judgment, misses work, and creates morale problems because of the adverse effects of alcohol or drugs. Alcohol and drug abuse in the workplace amounts to $41.7 billion annually in terms of lower productivity and treatment costs.[6]

9. *Cigarette addiction.* The employee is fatigued, wastes time searching for cigarettes and lighting them, burns and stains company property, and creates morale problems because of cigarette addiction. Other employees may complain about the smoker's cigarette breaks outside the building.[7]

10. *Emotional illness and personality disorder.* The employee experiences inner conflicts and engages in counterproductive behaviors. This condition could include delusional thinking, disruptive anxiety, depression, excessive euphoria, lying, cheating, stealing, abrasiveness, and compulsive gambling.

11. *Difficult person.* Although the employee is not emotionally ill, he or she is often annoying and counterproductive because of stubbornness, craving for attention, and unpredictability.[8]

12. *Family and personal problems.* The employee is unable to pay proper attention to the job because of a preoccupation with family crises, fights, the break-up of a key relationship, the misfortune of a loved one, or severe financial problems.[9]

13. *Absenteeism and tardiness.* The employee loses time from work for a variety of reasons (other than alcoholism), including job dissatisfaction, job stress, drug abuse, or family problems. The average cost of sick leave per employee averages around $400 per year.[10]

14. *Co-worker romance.* Two romantically involved employees (including a manager and a group member) may become so preoccupied with each other that they divert time and energy from their regular job responsibilities. Such behavior often disrupts the work of others.[11]

Organizational Factors

The major organizational (or environmental) factors contributing to poor job performance are as follows:

1. *Ergonomic problems.* The employee develops neckache, backache, and eyestrain from working at a VDT for long periods, indicating a poor fit between the human requirements of the job and the machinery. A special category of ergonomic problems is *repetitive motion disorder.* The worker becomes less productive or incapacitated because of overuse of the wrist, hands, and fingers in jobs such as data-entry specialist or butcher in a meat or poultry processing plant.[12]

2. *Inadequate communication.* The manager does not clearly communicate the job expectations or does not provide candid feedback about perfor-

Ergonomic problems cause physical discomfort and contribute to poor performance. This employee is especially at risk for developing eyestrain and repetitive motions disorder from performing keyboarding tasks at a workstation that does not meet the requirements of the job.

mance deficiencies. For example, the manager does not review the job description with the employee carefully. As a result, the employee increases his or her unproductive behavior.

3. *Counterproductive work group influences.* Group pressures or ostracism make it difficult for the employee to engage in cooperative effort. In order to achieve group acceptance, the employee follows the model of the "goof-offs."

4. *Overly permissive organizational culture.* The firm has a history of not imposing sanctions on employees who perform poorly. When the situation demands better performance, many employees may not respond to the new challenge.

5. *Counterproductive work environment and organizational support.* The employee does not have the proper tools, support, budget, or authority to accomplish the job.

6. *Inappropriate leadership style.* The manager's leadership style does not fit employee requirements. An example is when an inexperienced employee does not receive close enough supervision and thus learns key job tasks incorrectly.

7. *A "sick" building.* Contaminants in the workplace may create such symptoms as headache, eye irritation, and lethargy, thereby lowering productivity. Sick (or tight) buildings are created when airborne pollutants are trapped inside and continuously circulated. Such contaminants include fibers from new furniture, cigarette smoke, fumes from cleaning chemicals, and fungus spores.[13]

ETHICS QUESTION
Should the company be obliged to cure a "sick" building even if the cost of the cure would eliminate profits for the year?

Managers can compensate for factors that might ordinarily contribute to poor performance by placing employees properly. For instance, people with low mental ability can be superior performers if they are placed in a repetitive, well-defined job. The Organization in Action illustrates this point.

ORGANIZATION IN ACTION

Twenty-two-year-old Gary Hemminghaus has realized his dream of working at McDonald's in his home town of Florissant, Missouri. Hemminghaus, who has Down's syndrome, learned restaurant job skills through the McJobs training program. Since 1981, more than 9,000 people with mental and physical challenges, age 16 and older, have been part of this six- to eight-week program.

The McJobs program is implemented from corporate headquarters down through individual restaurants. Regional personnel managers, job coaches, store managers, assistant managers, and crew members also help implement it. The McJobs program now includes 22 states and 47 restaurants, and it is growing. (McDonald's receives about $800 in state funds for each person trained.) McJobs graduates an average of 900 individuals with disabilities annually.

More than 90 percent of the people who begin training graduate and later become McDonald's crew members, although certain graduates need additional training to achieve satisfactory performance in food service operations. Experience with the program has pointed toward ways of increasing the chances that employees with mental disabilities will succeed. For example, McJobs employees now train in the stores in which they will be working. Before this approach was implemented, trainees often became confused when they moved out of the training site into a restaurant with different coworkers and equipment.

McDonald's makes certain that each of these employees is able and willing to assume the responsibilities of his or her job. The program provides job opportunities to a special segment of the workforce, but it is not charity.

Source: As reported in Jennifer J. Laabs, "The Golden Arches Provide Golden Opportunities," *Personnel Journal* (July 1991): 52–57.

MODEL FOR THE MANAGEMENT OF INEFFECTIVE PERFORMANCE

The model for managing ineffective performance is presented in Figure 14-1. It is a control model based on a synthesis of ideas gathered from managerial practice and research. The manager defines effective or acceptable performance, then detects any deviation from acceptable performance, diagnoses the cause of the problem, and takes corrective action. Although this can be difficult, it is an important management activity. Details of the model are described in the next several pages.

The model applies to all levels of employees from mailroom assistant to CEO. However, some remedial activities and interventions are not equally appropriate at all levels. In general, the more complex, time-consuming, and costly programs are better suited for higher-ranking employees. Assume, for example, that a vice president of mergers and acquisitions becomes involved in many personal disputes with others in the office. The company might send this executive to a management psychologist. An office assistant with the same problem might at best be sent to a half-day seminar on human relations.

A model such as this works best in an organizational culture that emphasizes performance. The culture must also value taking corrective action when performance suffers. The following sections describe how the model works step by step.

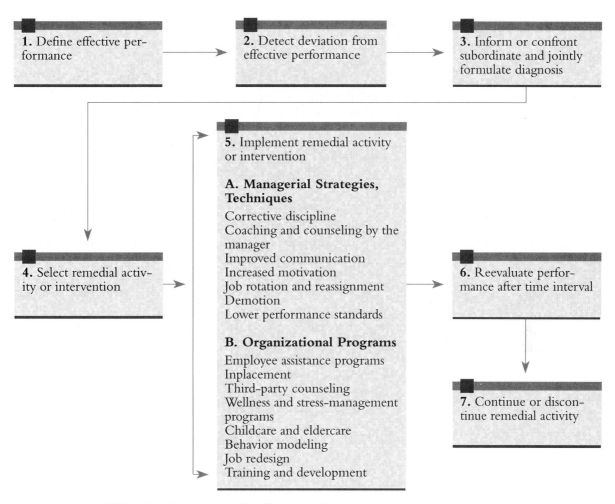

FIGURE 14-1 Model for the Management of Ineffective Performance

Step 1: Define Effective Performance

To improve substandard performance, a manager must define standards clearly. Job descriptions and work goals are two widely used methods for specifying performance standards. These standards should be explained carefully during hiring and then again during training.

Step 2: Detect Deviation from Effective Performance

A manager who is alert to what is happening in his or her unit can detect performance problems readily. Symptoms of potential performance problems include increased complaints from customers or clients and budget overruns. Complaints from co-workers about the poor performer, late reports, a high number of errors, employee lethargy, and low concentration are also significant. Frequent absenteeism and tardiness on Mondays are important symptoms of a personal problem such as alcoholism, drug abuse, or being physically abused.

Step 3: Inform or Confront Subordinate and Jointly Formulate Diagnosis

After detecting a problem, the manager must bring it to the attention of the poor performer. Current opinion recommends that the confrontation be straightforward and clear cut, rather than sandwiched between statements of praise.[14] Such a confrontation can take place during a performance appraisal or at any other time. Most managers dislike confronting group members because of the defensive or hostile reaction they may elicit. Managers also recognize how uncomfortable they would feel if confronted about their own mistakes.

The manager should focus on the ineffective behavior itself, not on the individual. People usually become defensive and hostile when their traits or personal characteristics are under attack. A manager should therefore avoid confronting an employee in this manner: "You have become a sloppy loan officer recently." A statement that focuses on behavior is less likely to cause defensiveness, for example: "The percentage of defaulted loans you have placed lately is falling below standard."

The manager may have a good idea of the reason behind ineffective performance. Nevertheless, it is important to determine a tentative diagnosis together with the problem performer. An employee who helps formulate the diagnosis will be more likely to commit to making constructive changes. Careful listening, as described in Chapter 13, is an important part of making the right diagnosis. The list of factors contributing to poor performance presented earlier can be used as a diagnostic aid in pinpointing the reason or combination of reasons for substandard performance.

Step 4: Select Remedial Activity or Intervention

Working together, the manager and ineffective performer can choose a logical plan for dealing with the problem. At times it may be advisable to enlist the help of a human resources specialist. In some instances, the ineffective performer will have a distorted perception of the problem. In this case the judgment of the manager, sometimes in conjunction with the human resources specialist, should be given priority. The importance of the task that is being performed poorly helps determine how much time should be invested in overcoming the problem.

The remedial activity or intervention will work only if the employee wants to be a productive member of the firm. The employee's willingness to change can often be evaluated during the confrontation stage. For example, if the employee is emotionally bland and detached about the performance problem, it is doubtful that she or he really cares about improving.

Step 5: Implement Remedial Activity or Intervention

The methods of bringing about improved performance can be divided into (a) managerial strategies and techniques and (b) organizational programs.

MANAGERIAL STRATEGIES AND TECHNIQUES. The methods described here are methods that managers can usually carry out themselves, with their own resources. A company program is not required.

Corrective Discipline. The most important technique for dealing with ineffective performance is corrective discipline. Instead of merely informing the employee to "shape up or ship out," the manager gives assistance in correcting the problem. Because this technique is so important in managing ineffective performance, it receives separate attention later in the chapter.

Coaching and Counseling by the Manager. The technique of coaching and counseling by the manager is a standard approach to improving performance. In fact, some consider good coaching the essential feature of managing people.[15] The effective coach patiently guides people toward improved performance. As a counselor, the manager does not judge the employee harshly or fully diagnose the problem. Instead, the manager encourages the team member to make some self-discoveries.

Effective coaching and counseling are often important in implementing the control model. Together, they constitute a complex management skill that requires considerable practice. The following are a few suggestions that can be applied to coaching and counseling employees at any level:

1. *Establish a comfortable atmosphere.* The person being counseled should be made to feel as much at ease as possible.
2. *Provide specific feedback.* Pinpoint areas of concern rather than speaking in generalities. For example the superior could say, "You are the only manager in my group who is not yet using the electronic mail system."
3. *Encourage employee involvement.* As Herb Meyer, a specialist in performance appraisal, has noted, "Effective organizations are moving away from the control-oriented approach toward an involvement-oriented

An effective manager acts as coach and counselor to guide the employee toward better performance.

climate designed to elicit commitment on the part of employees at all levels."[16]

4. *Give emotional support.* By being helpful and constructive, the manager provides much-needed emotional support to employees whose performance requires improvement.

5. *Reflect content or meaning.* A good way of reflecting meaning is to rephrase and summarize concisely what the employee is saying. For example, a substandard performer might go on at length about the piling up of his or her responsibilities. The manager might respond, "You are falling behind because the workload is so heavy." Feeling understood, the employee might be willing to examine the problem more carefully.

6. *Give some constructive advice.* Too much advice-giving can interfere with two-way communication, but some advice can lead to improved performance. The manager should assist the employee in answering the question "What can I do about this problem?"

7. *Gain a commitment to change.* The manager should receive a commitment from the employee to carry through with the proposed solution to the performance problem. Otherwise, the employee might tend to continue aimlessly as before.

Improved Communication. Many performance problems stem from inadequate communication about job responsibilities. An obvious remedy is for the manager to increase the amount of two-way communication about job responsibilities with the employee. Included in this communication would be a thorough description of the job. The manager must also listen to questions from employees, respond fully and clearly, and encourage feedback from the employees.

Increased Motivation. Increasing an employee's motivational level may lead to improved performance. Behavior modification is well suited to dealing with motivational problems of ineffective performance. The manager gives the employee positive reinforcement in the form of encouragement whenever the employee makes progress toward reaching acceptable performance. Conversely, if the employee makes no progress or slips further, the manager may have to administer some form of punishment. Chapter 12 provided detailed suggestions for increasing motivation.

Job Rotation and Reassignment. If the diagnosis suggests that ineffective performance results from staleness or burnout, rotating to a different job of comparable responsibility may prove helpful. Reassignment to a different type of job will lead to improved performance if the ineffective performer is better qualified for the new position. However, the manager must consider organizational constraints before choosing job rotation as an antidote to ineffective performance. One reason is that few managers welcome poor performers into their departments. Another is that an employee who is reassigned after performing poorly might interpret the reassignment as a reward for poor performance.

Demotion. A person who is performing in a substandard manner may have been effective in a previous position of lesser responsibility. Demotion may therefore help the employee become successful again. The potential damage to a person's ego when demoted, however, may create some performance problems of its own. A person with an inflexible personality may sulk instead of capitalizing on the situation. In this instance, the performance of the demoted person may have to be reviewed frequently.

Lowered Performance Standards. Ineffective or substandard performance sometimes results from setting unrealistically high performance standards. If these standards are lowered to a more realistic level, the employee can then achieve satisfactory performance. Unrealistically high performance standards occur most frequently when they are established for the first time. Examples would be when a firm establishes sales quotas for a new product or asks a division general manager to achieve a profit level that is unrealistic.

ORGANIZATIONAL PROGRAMS. Many organizations have formal programs to help manage ineffective performance. The increasing popularity of these programs suggests that they are cost effective. Eight such programs, described here, are particularly representative of interventions designed to remedy as well as prevent substandard performance.

Employee Assistance Programs. The basic thrust of an employee assistance program is to help troubled employees receive professional help for problems that adversely affect performance. Employee assistance programs are the most widely used formal method for managing ineffective performance. They are covered later in the chapter.

Third-Party Counseling. Through **third-party counseling,** an outside consultant helps a manager and team member resolve a problem. Counseling of this type is usually reserved for top-level managers. The consultant diagnoses the problem, counsels the poor performer, and makes recommendations to other managers. The third party may be able to examine the problem more objectively than the superior and subordinate can themselves. Counseling of this type will only work if the manager who has a performance problem is motivated to change.

Inplacement. Another approach to helping executives overcome interpersonal problems that interfere with performance is **inplacement.** An outside consultant works with the troubled executive, the executive's manager, and the human resources specialist to develop and implement an action plan for improvement. Inplacement includes considerable performance counseling and coaching. Throughout the process, which typically lasts three months, the executive receives frequent feedback on performance.[17]

ETHICS QUESTION
What ethical issues would be raised if employees were told that "the company president wants 100 percent participation in the wellness program"?

Wellness and Stress-Management Programs. Wellness programs encourage employees to stay physically and mentally healthy. By being in shape,

The company fitness program offers employees a healthy and enjoyable way to manage stress.

employees may prevent health problems that interfere with job performance or lead to absenteeism. A key feature of most wellness programs is a stress-management program that shows employees how to manage both work and personal stress. The dual purpose of such programs is to prevent people from succumbing to stress disorders and to treat people who are currently facing too much stress. These programs teach people beneficial physical exercises, how to relax, and how to monitor internal stress signals.[18]

Both large and small companies offer wellness and fitness programs. Research conducted in several settings has shown that absenteeism was reduced by 0.5 to 1.5 days per year after the introduction of corporate fitness programs. Coors, for example, has estimated that its wellness program saves the company almost $2 million annually by decreasing medical costs and increasing productivity.[19] Wellness programs often result in a large enough decrease in workers' compensation taxes to pay for the programs. The Organization in Action describes impressive results from a corporate stress program.

ORGANIZATION IN ACTION

Two years ago, the customer service department at Ortho Diagnostics suffered from the worst absenteeism rate in the company. One year after the introduction of a comprehensive stress-reduction program, absenteeism had dropped 60 percent. To lower stress and absenteeism, the manager of customer service developed a three-point program.

First, the manager determined whether employees were in the right job. Some customer service representatives preferred to move to less pressure-filled jobs. One-half of the representatives with absenteeism problems transferred to another department.

Second, the manager replaced workstations with ones that adhered to principles of ergonomics. One representative had already undergone surgery for carpal tunnel syndrome (a common disorder that affects a key nerve in the hand and is caused by repetitive motions).

Third, the manager initiated an ongoing stress-reduction program. Employees are now encouraged to participate in an on-site health facility. In some cases attendance is mandatory, as explained by the customer service manager: "Attendance at the facility can be required as part of your performance review if we think it could be a help with handling your job. If you've had attendance problems because of illness, you could also be ordered to attend."

Source: Adapted with permission from *Customer Service Newsletter* (Silver Spring, MD: Customer Service Institute, 1992).

Child-Care and Elder-Care Programs. Employee concerns about taking proper care of children and elderly parents during work hours can lead to poor concentration and absenteeism. Therefore, organizational programs that make it easier for employees to care for children and elderly parents can sometimes improve productivity and reduce absenteeism. However, as with any program aimed at improving employee welfare, there are some potential drawbacks. The need for child-care and elder-care programs may encourage firms to give hiring preference to applicants who do not have elderly parents or children.

Behavior Modeling. **Behavior modeling** is the process of acquiring skills by imitating people who perform the skills correctly. Modeling is a useful way to teach skills such as interviewing, making sales presentations, resolving conflicts, and terminating employees. Specific modeling modules can be built for most skills that involve interaction with people. Behavior modeling typically includes the following six stages:

1. Presentation of the concept.
2. Step-by-step demonstration on cassette or film of actions the person can take to handle the situation.
3. Rehearsal of skills in a supportive environment.
4. Supportive feedback from peers and modeling specialists.
5. Commitment to transfer the newly learned skills to the actual job situation.
6. Follow-up to evaluate any problems encountered and to suggest ways to overcome them.[20]

Job Redesign. Ineffective performance can stem from faulty job design, as in an excessively repetitive job or one in which failure is almost inevitable. One example of inevitable failure took place in a design support group in an aerospace company. The company authorized project leaders and certain levels of engineers to give assignments directly to the designers. As a result, the designers were beset with conflicting priorities and forced to make difficult-to-keep promises. Both problems lowered their performance. The company decided to redesign the job so that the project heads and engineers would have to make their requests through the department manager, who would attach priorities to the assignments.

Training and Development. A standard antidote to performance problems is to ask the ineffective performer to attend a training or development program focusing on the person's area of deficiency. One current trend is for employees with high rates of absenteeism to participate in **attendance training.** Such training is based on behavior modification and teaches the employee to regulate his or her attendance. It includes setting attendance goals, writing a contract with oneself, and administering self-chosen rewards and punishments. An experiment with attendance training conducted with state government employees showed good results.[21]

Step 6: Reevaluate Performance After Time Interval

The remedial activities and interventions just described do not lead to improved performance automatically. The manager must therefore reevaluate the poor performer at least once. Meetings about performance provide an opportunity to encourage employee progress or to discuss problems encountered in trying to improve performance.

Step 7: Continue or Discontinue Remedial Activity

If the performance reappraisal suggests that performance is still unsatisfactory, the remedial activity should be continued. For example, an overly tense and agitated employee should continue to attend a stress-management program. Employees who do not respond to help offered by the firm should be subject to disciplinary procedures. Businesses do not have the resources to invest in substandard performers who show no promise of improvement.

LEARNING CHECK

Identify some of the many causes of substandard job performance and describe the model for dealing with these problems constructively.

CORRECTIVE DISCIPLINE

Corrective discipline is a positive method of improving poor performance that gives employees a chance to correct their behavior before the firm applies punishment. The manager tells the employee that his or her behavior is unacceptable and that corrections must be made if the employee wants to stay with the firm. A key feature of corrective discipline is that the employee and the manager share the responsibility for solving the performance problem. Discipline is usually thought of in relation to lower-ranking employees. Some companies, however, have developed discipline policies for managers and professionals that are based on corrective discipline. For example, Textron gives poorly performing salaried employees up to three documented discussions. The firm then terminates employees who do not improve. Human resources specialists are involved in reviewing and making recommendations about the appropriateness of the discipline and the fairness of the write-ups.[22]

Stages in Corrective Discipline

Corrective discipline comprises six stages or components that flow in an orderly manner. Several of these stages are similar to those in the model for the management of ineffective performance.

1. *Identification of the problem.* Poor performance must be identified in specific behavioral terms. Managers should avoid generalities about the individual's attitude and should not use labels such as "lazy" or "incompetent." It is preferable to say something of this nature: "Major purchases are being made without getting bids from more than one supplier. This is in clear violation of company policy." Managers must carefully document all instances of the need for discipline.
2. *Early intervention by the manager.* The manager should begin to work with the poor performer as soon as the problem appears. Work should begin preferably no later than the second occurrence of the problem.
3. *Clear expectations.* The employee should know exactly what is expected in terms of improvement. In the previous example, the manager should say, "From now on, every purchase of more than $3,000 must be preceded by a bid from two or more suppliers." The clearer the expectations, the less opportunity for ambiguity and confusion.
4. *Feedback.* Shortly after the disciplinary session, the manager should inform the employee orally or in writing of how well the employee is meeting expectations. Documentation of progress is important, particularly if the employee does not improve and eventually has to be terminated.
5. *Positive reinforcement.* The manager should reward the employee for all improvements to help sustain the good performance. Everyday reinforcers such as praise, a handshake, or a favorable note placed in the employee's personnel file are usually adequate. Each small step toward the goal should be rewarded.
6. *Follow-Up.* The manager should continue to observe the employee's progress and discuss with the employee how well he or she is progressing. When the employee begins to perform satisfactorily, the issue should be dropped. To be fully rehabilitated, the employee must feel that his or her behavior is no longer being singled out for scrutiny.

Corrective Versus Summary and Progressive Discipline

Corrective discipline is a positive approach to discipline. It stands in contrast to two negative types of discipline; summary and progressive. The use of corrective discipline to deal with ineffective performance does not mean that a manager should never fire an employee without attempting to correct the employee's behavior. Under certain circumstances it is necessary to administer **summary discipline,** the immediate discharge of an employee because of a serious offense such as stealing, sabotage, selling illegal drugs on company premises, embezzlement, and extortion.

Progressive discipline is a system of making escalated penalties known to employees in advance and imposing them with increasing severity for repeated infractions. The sequence of penalties typically proceeds in this order: first, an oral warning; second, a written warning; third, disciplinary layoff or suspension; and finally, discharge. Progressive discipline does not involve as much counseling and coaching as corrective discipline, but it does recognize the importance of giving poor performers a second chance. Progressive discipline is widely used and accepted despite its emphasis on the negative. However, concern about the negative tone to progressive discipline has led to the use of corrective discipline.

. . . .

Back to the
Opening Case

. . . .

After thinking through the consequences of the alleged drug and alcohol use on company premises, the director of industrial relations thought that administering employee discipline was the answer. However, he then asked himself, "Who are we going to discipline? Without proper documentation you cannot discipline anyone."

. . . .

EMPLOYEE ASSISTANCE PROGRAMS (EAPS)

Many firms have a formal system of giving a second chance to employees whose personal problems interfere with their work performance. An **employee assistance program (EAP)** is a formal organizational unit designed to help employees deal with personal problems that affect job performance. Alcoholism and drug addiction are the two leading reasons for referral to an EAP, followed by financial, family, and physical problems and disputes with co-workers and supervisors. EAPs have become standard practice in most large and medium-size firms, and many small firms also offer such assistance. Some EAPs have recently expanded their services by including a wellness program.[23]

The key aim of an employee assistance program is to restore a troubled employee to satisfactory performance. This aim is significant because personal problems lower job performance in a number of ways, including increased absenteeism and tardiness, poor decision making, equipment damage, safety violations, and lower morale among co-workers.[24] Our description of EAPs centers around their general format, the manager's role in an EAP, and the effectiveness of these programs.

General Format

Employee assistance programs vary in format, but there are four basic versions. The most frequent arrangement is to refer employees with distracting personal problems to an outside agency that offers direct assistance. A second format is the in-house EAP, and a third is an intermediate internal/external arrangement. For instance, in-house drug and alcohol counseling might be provided, but financial and family problems might be referred to outside agencies such as credit counselors or mental health practitioners in private practice. The fourth arrangement is for the company to contract with a firm that provides employee assistance to many employers. Figure 14-2 presents an advertisement for such an outside firm and also provides useful details about an EAP.

The EAP coordinator is the contact for the employee who has been referred to the program either by a manager or through self-referral. After completing initial interviews about the nature of the program, the program coordinator refers the employee to the in-house facility or an external agency. An important role of the coordinator is to track and report on the overall impact of the EAP in terms of absenteeism, tardiness, accidents, and other areas of organizational performance that can be affected by employee problems.

The next step is for a diagnostic and referral agency to evaluate the employee's problem and determine which treatment or rehabilitation action is indicated. (Internal as well as external units make these recommendations.) The agency then sends the employee to the appropriate resource. Smaller companies are more likely than larger companies to refer an employee to an external EAP such as that described in Figure 14-2.

An essential feature of EAPs is their confidentiality. Brochures, notices, and articles in company newspapers all state that the program is highly confidential and that records remain in EAP files only. Details of an employee's problem or treatment program are not reported back to management. However, if an EAP specialist thinks that an employee is homicidal, suicidal, or a potential saboteur, these confidences will be broken. A business is aware of which people it refers to an EAP, but most EAPs do not reveal the names of self-referrals.

Manager's Role in an Employee Assistance Program

The manager's role in the EAP usually begins with a training program that includes a behavioral checklist to use in detecting signs or symptoms of significant employee problems. A representative checklist of this nature is shown in Figure 14-3. After learning about how the EAP works, managers refer employees to it as needed. Supervisors and other managers initiate most of the referrals because they are in a position to monitor and evaluate employee performance continuously. When a notable downturn in performance becomes evident, the employee's superior must decide whether or not referral to the EAP is appropriate.

Although the manager is expected to diagnose whether the problem might be individual or organizational, managers should not make specific psychological or medical diagnoses. Managers are also cautioned not to attempt to counsel employees about personal problems.

18% OF YOUR PEOPLE RELY ON THESE MANAGEMENT TOOLS.

One in six American workers is dependent upon drugs or alcohol—or both.

Your company suffers from this problem. It shows up in decreased productivity, absenteeism, accidents, shoddy work, equipment damage, employee disputes, and spiraling health care and insurance costs.

People who are chemically dependent will <u>always</u> put drugs or alcohol before work.

The Occupational Health Services Employee Assistance Plan provides the <u>professional help</u> you need to put troubled employees back on track—without delay.

OHS serves American business 24 hours a day, 365 days a year. OHS has a nationwide network of licensed professional counselors experienced in dealing with drugs, alcohol, and a range of other personal problems which impact job performance—problems like marital, relationship, and divorce issues; financial and credit difficulties; legal conflicts; stress and emotional issues; and concerns related to parenting, as well as child and elder care.

While drugs and alcohol may be the most dramatic, <u>any</u> of these issues can and do affect your bottom line. The OHS EAP Plan assists you and your employees in effectively addressing them all—professionally and confidentially.

<u>Here's the best part:</u> The cost of an OHS Employee Assistance Plan is surprisingly low—especially when compared to other types of benefit plans and coverages. The return on investment can more than offset the cost.

For 17 years, OHS has helped enlightened companies overcome drug, alcohol, and other personal and behavioral problems that affect productivity.

Why wait? Start improving the performance of your workforce today. Just give us a call.

CALL 1-800-EAP-PLAN
(that's 1-800-327-7526, nationwide)

OHS
The Complete Employee Assistance Plan
187 Fortieth Street Way, Oakland, California 94611

FIGURE 14-2 Advertisement for an Employee Assistance Program

FIGURE 14-3
Symptoms of Serious
Employee Problems

Behavioral

1. Patterns of excessive absenteeism on Monday, Friday, and days before and after holidays.
2. Unexcused and frequent absences.
3. Tardiness and early departure.
4. Altercations with co-workers.
5. Negligence that causes injuries to other employees.
6. Poor judgment and bad decisions.
7. Unusual on-the-job accidents.
8. Increased spoilage and breaking of equipment through negligence.
9. Involvements with the law, such as wage garnishments.
10. Deteriorating personal appearance.
11. Impaired psychomotor skills, such as poor eye-hand coordination.
12. Prolonged and serious lethargy.

Physiological and Emotional

1. Dilated pupils.
2. Facial pallor.
3. Disorientation and forgetfulness.
4. Unexplainable states of apathy or elation.
5. Frequent agitated look.

When an employee elects to ignore the manager's initial referral and performance continues to decline, the matter is handled through normal disciplinary means. However, the manager should persist in providing advance warning and continue to encourage voluntary participation. Encouraging voluntary participation is important, because many employees feel that they are pressured into enrolling into the EAP as an alternative to harsh discipline.

The manager's role does not end with the employee's referral to a company-sponsored program. Instead, the manager continues to monitor the employee's work performance and takes disciplinary action if improvement is not forthcoming.

Evaluation of EAP Effectiveness

Over all, EAPs have proved to be effective from both a humanitarian and a financial standpoint. One estimate is that the recovery rate from drug abuse is three times as high for EAP clients as for the general public.[25] One executive stated, "We did a study indicating that for every $1 invested in our drug program, we got $7 back in reduced benefits usage and absenteeism."[26] Some of the return on investment from EAPs also stems from the improved job performance of employees who are treated successfully.

Despite these good overall results, not every EAP is cost effective, and some of these programs are misused by managers who refer any substandard performer. Another concern about EAPs is that many managerial and professional employees fear attending them. Although these programs are confidential, some workers believe that they will be labeled as "problem employees" if they request assistance.

Back to the
Opening Case

Management hired an investigative firm to determine the extent of the alleged alcohol and drug abuse problem at Tri-Valley Growers. The investigators uncovered offenders, including three employees who sold drugs to operatives. These three were discharged, arrested, and convicted. Tri-Valley Growers then established a drug-free workplace program at an annual cost of $500,000. The program included testing of applicants and employees who appeared to be "under the influence," undercover surveillance, and a volunteer employee assistance program.

LEARNING CHECK

Describe two key methods of helping substandard performers: corrective discipline and employee assistance programs.

TERMINATION AND OUTPLACEMENT

When ineffective performance has not been improved by such measures as corrective discipline and referral to an EAP, two closely related alternatives remain. One is to terminate the employee outright; the other is to fire the employee but also offer assistance in finding a new position.

Termination

ETHICS QUESTION
What social responsibility does management have to keep ineffective performers on the payroll?

Firing an employee has been described as "the most unpleasant moment in workaday capitalism."[27] Yet at times termination of employment can benefit both the firm and the individual. In general, every feasible alternative, such as retraining and counseling, should be attempted before dismissal, as diagrammed in Figure 14-4.

THE CASE FOR FIRING. If done with sensitivity, tact, and a concern for human welfare, firing can have positive consequences. The key arguments for firing substandard performers can be summarized as follows. First, the shock of being fired may be therapeutic. After being fired, the employee may realize that he or she must improve in order to earn a living. Second, department morale may spurt. Effective co-workers may be happy to know that all employees must carry a fair workload in order to remain employed. Third, fired employees often wind up finding a job for which they are better suited and often improve their occupational status. Career counseling firms consistently report that as many as two-thirds of fired managers ultimately find better jobs.[28]

Moreover, firing a poor performer usually creates a job opening for a more deserving and better qualified employee. Getting rid of so-called "dead wood" thus creates new opportunities in an era when new opportunities do not abound. Finally, firing a substandard performer may increase

FIGURE 14-4
Framework for Deciding
Whether to Terminate or
Provide Additional
Counseling to an
Employee

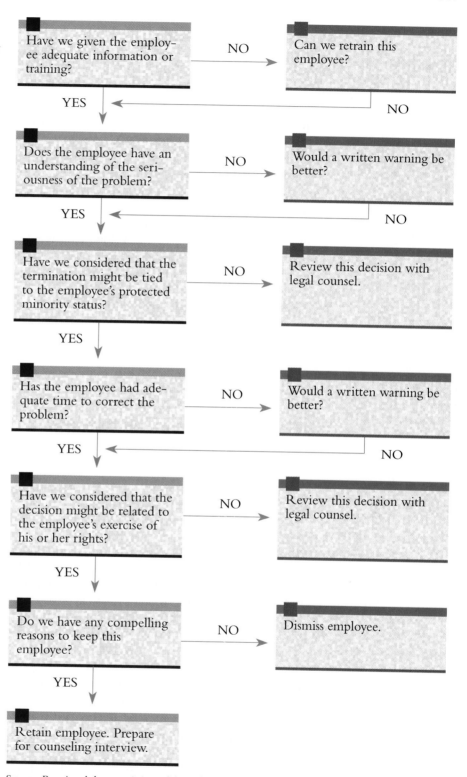

the productivity of employees who are not fired. Such an act conveys the message that the firm sets high limits of acceptable performance. When poor performers are not replaced, department productivity increases because fewer workers are now accomplishing the same amount of work.

THE CASE AGAINST FIRING. As one would suspect, firing employees also has notable disadvantages. These are summarized as follows. First, firing may be considered an admission of error in the selection, training, and management of human resources. If the substandard performer had been selected and trained properly, the dismissal would not have been necessary.

Second, if an employee is wrongfully discharged, the result can be costly litigation. In the early years of such litigation, only highly paid executives sued, but currently one-half of such suits are brought by nonmanagerial employees. In addition to suing for being terminated, some workers have filed and won libel suits against their former superiors for comments that damaged their reputations. To make firings fairer, some companies have initiated employee complaint committees to review firings. Such committees help curtail wrongful discharge suits.[29]

Third, firing may lead to job stress for co-workers of the fired employee. They may become fearful and anxious because they fear the same thing may happen to them. And finally, firing too many employees may lead to a poor reputation for the firm that can interfere with future recruiting of high-caliber employees. Security-conscious people avoid applying for work at firms with a reputation for firing employees readily. Although the employer may be fully justified in firing certain employees, the dismissed employees may not see it this way. They may bad-mouth the employer in the community.

Outplacement

Standard practice today is for employers to help dismissed employees find new positions through a formal program called outplacement. **Outplacement** is a method of helping terminated employees find new employment through professional career counseling and other assistance. Termination may come about because of poor performance, layoffs, or redundancy in positions created by a merger or acquisition.

The primary aim of outplacement should be to provide a compassionate transition for employees who no longer fit into the corporate picture for whatever reasons.[30] The emphasis in outplacement counseling is on conducting a job campaign and providing emotional support to the job seeker. This includes counseling sessions and granting the terminated worker the use of office space while job hunting.

Emotional support may be necessary because unemployment can be a major life trauma to a manager or skilled professional employees. This is particularly true for a person who is not independently wealthy and whose identity is partly linked to the job. A recent study of outplaced executives concluded that the emotional fallout from job loss may be greater for women than for men. The researchers observed that women have a greater sense of loss, while men tend to deny the emotional side of losing a job.[31]

All levels of employees, from office and operations workers to top-level managers, use outplacement services. Nevertheless, normally only high-level managers receive the full range of assistance. A new trend in outplacement is to include assistance in financial planning. One reason for this is that departing employees often face a long period of unemployment.[32]

Outplacement counseling firms provide individual assistance, small- and large-group programs, and mass-layoff seminars. These firms generally report a high success rate in helping people find new employment.

Despite the help outplacement offers, it does raise some ethical and moral questions. Through polished job-finding techniques, many ineffective performers are placed in positions for which they are underqualified. As a result, they soon become poor performers in their new environment and receive another serious career setback. It seems more advisable to encourage outplaced employees to work through their problems before embarking upon another negative career experience. Another concern is that most outplacement firms do not provide job leads. Instead, job seekers use their own resources—something they would have done without outplacement.

SUMMARY

Ineffective performance lowers productivity, and ineffective performers consume an inordinate amount of managers' time. A large number of individual and organizational factors contribute to ineffective performance. Individual factors are related to intelligence, motivation, stress and burnout, currency of skills, physical limitations and addictions, and personal problems. Organizational factors include those related to the job, the manager, the work group, and the company as a whole. These factors serve as a checklist to use in thinking through why ineffective performance exists in a particular situation.

The conceptual approach and a general procedure for managing ineffective performance are summarized in the model presented in Figure 14-1. The model applies to ineffective performance at any job level and consists of seven stages: (1) definition of effective or acceptable performance; (2) detection of deviation from acceptable performance; (3) confrontation of the subordinate and joint formulation of diagnosis; (4) selection of a remedial activity or an intervention; (5) implementation of the activity or intervention; (6) reevaluation of performance after a time interval; and (7) continuation or halting of the remedial activity or intervention.

A major managerial strategy for dealing with inef-

fective performance is corrective discipline. It consists of six stages: (1) early intervention in the problem by the manager; (2) identification of the problem; (3) establishment of clear expectations; (4) feedback to the employee about how well expectations are being met; (5) positive reinforcement for progress toward the goal of improved performance; and (6) follow-up on progress.

The most widely used formal method for managing ineffective performance is the employee assistance program (EAP). Its key aim is to restore a troubled employee to satisfactory performance. An EAP deals with a wide range of personal problems, with the treatment taking place at an outside agency or an in-house facility. Supervisors and other managers play a key role in referring employees to the EAP, although self-referrals are also allowed.

Sometimes such measures as corrective discipline, other managerial intervention strategies, and formal organizational programs fail to improve ineffective performance. Termination may therefore be necessary. Many firms soften the blow of being fired or laid off by using outplacement counseling services. Such services may be valuable, but they are said to over-market many employees and offer few job leads.

KEY TERMS

third-party counseling   attendance training   progressive discipline   outplacement
inplacement   corrective discipline   employee assistance pro-
behavior modeling   summary discipline   gram (EAP)

QUESTIONS FOR DISCUSSION AND REVIEW

1. What similarities do you see between managing ineffective performance and managing performance in general?

2. Give an illustration from your own experience of how an individual factor contributed to ineffective performance.

3. Give an illustration from your own experience of how an organizational factor contributed to ineffective performance.

4. How does a manager know when an ineffective performer is worth salvaging?

5. What should a manager do when a problem employee flatly rejects the manager's diagnosis of his or her problem even in the light of conclusive evidence for the diagnosis?

6. What similarities do you see between corrective

discipline and the model for the management of ineffective performance?

7. Some employees will pay for personal counseling themselves rather than visit the organization's EAP. Why might these employees be reluctant to visit the EAP?

8. If a person is fired from one job, what should that person tell future prospective employers?

9. Outplacement counselors have noted that many terminated executives either attempt or commit suicide. Why would people take a job loss so seriously?

10. What contribution does an outplacement firm make if it does not furnish the job seeker with leads?

PROBLEMS FOR ACTION

A. Assume that you have been appointed by your employer to prepare a briefing paper to help managers understand some of the reasons for ineffective performance by some newcomers to the workforce. Your company is a chain of high-fashion clothing stores. Select from the list of factors presented in the chapter those that you think would be helpful in explaining the problems of these people. When you mention a contributing factor, explain how it applies to inexperienced workers. For example: "Counterproductive work group influences—new workers become confused when their co-workers tell them not to work so

hard."

B. Ashley Braun is a restaurant manager whose heavy gambling and credit-card debts have placed her in deep financial trouble. She faces frequent hounding from her creditors. Because of this, Ashley is having trouble concentrating on her scheduling of workers and has been making frequent errors. Take her case through the Model for the Management of Ineffective Performance shown in Figure 14-1. Comment on each step and select an appropriate remedial activity or intervention.

CONCLUDING CASE

Rudeness on the Floor

"Can you direct me toward the shoe-care center? You know, the polish, the shoe trees, and the shoe laces?" asked the customer.

"Nope, I can't help you," answered the store sales associate. "I just started working here last week. I ain't that familiar with all the stuff. Just look around yourself."

"Hard to believe. You are not familiar with the merchandise or even with proper grammar. You don't belong on the sales floor," said the customer in a loud, angry tone. Before leaving the store, the customer demanded to see the manager, Bill Payton. During the 10-minute interview with Payton, the customer reviewed her brief encounter with the sales associate. Payton pleaded with the customer to forgive the matter this once. He assured the customer of courteous treatment in the future.

The next day, Payton telephoned the corporate training director, Lisa Valone, to schedule a meeting about the issue of courtesy to customers. Payton and Valone met the next day.

"I hope that what I'm going to tell you will not make me appear weak as a store manager," Payton began, "but I suspect that the other branches are having the same problem. Some of our sales associates are so rude that they are driving our customers to use catalog shopping services."

"Tell me more about the problem," said Valone. "I need some specifics."

"As the store manager, I receive a lot of customer complaints. To verify these complaints, I asked my wife and children to shop in my store. After shopping they would tell me what kind of treatment they received from the sales associates. They didn't bring back horror stories, but some of their observations were along the lines of those made by our other customers."

Payton continued, "Many customers contend that our sales associates just ignore them. They carry on conversations with co-workers while the customer is trying to check out or ask for help. I've also received a few complaints about gum chewing. Another problem I've noticed is that some of our employees never look customers in the eye or smile at them."

"What have you done so far about the problem?" asked Valone.

"Sometimes I talk to our employees about the problem. I've even brought a few of the ruder ones into my office for a little discussion about courtesy."

"What do your employees say about the problem?" asked Valone.

"Most of them claim that it's the customers' fault. The customers show them very little respect. My sales associates say that some of the customers treat them like servants. There's also the problem of customers taking out their hostility on our sales associates."

"What would you like me to do about this problem?" asked Valone.

"Fix it," replied Payton. "You're the corporate training director."

1. Whose responsibility is it to fix this problem?
2. How thorough has Payton been in his attempts to deal with the problem of rudeness toward customers?
3. Develop a realistic plan to deal with the problems revealed in this case.

REFERENCES

1. Karen A. Brown and Terence R. Mitchell, "Influence of Task Interdependence and Number of Poor Performers on Diagnoses and Causes of Poor Performance," *Academy of Management Journal* (June 1986): 423.

2. Lynne F. McGee, "Teaching Basic Skills to Workers," *Personnel Administrator* (August 1989): 42–47.

3. Debra L. Nelson and Charlotte Sutton, "Chronic Work Stress and Coping: A Longitudinal Study and Suggested New Directions," *Academy of Management Journal* (December 1990): 859–869.

4. Patti Watts, "Are Your Employees Burnout-Proof?" *Personnel* (September 1990): 12–14.

5. Art Durity, "The AIDS Epidemic," *Personnel* (April 1991): 1.

6. "Is Business Bungling Its Battle with Booze?" *Business Week* (March 25, 1991): 77.

7. Michael R. Manning, Joyce S. Osland, and Asbjorn Osland, "Work-Related Consequences of Smoking Cessation," *Academy of Management Journal* (September 1989): 606–621.

8. Donald D. Weiss, "How to Handle Difficult People," *Management Solutions* (February 1988): 33–38.

9. Stanley D. Nollen, "The Work-Family Dilemma: How HR Managers Can Help," *Personnel* (May 1989): 25–30.

10. "Paid Sick Leave Produces Substantial Costs for Employers," *Ideas & Trends in Personnel* (January 9, 1991): 1.

11. "Should You Risk an On-the-Job Romance?" *Working Smart* (February 11, 1991): 1.

12. "Video Display Terminal Radiation: The Controversy Explored," *Healthy Buildings International Magazine* (March–April 1991): 2–3; Dan Huntley, "Key Injuries Hurt Companies," *HRMagazine* (June 1990): 72–75.

13. "Gas Sensors to Control Indoor Pollution," *Healthy Buildings International* (March–April 1991): 8–9.

14. John Veiga, "Face Your Problem Subordinates Now!" *Academy of Management Executive* (May 1988): 148.

15. Roger D. Evered and James C. Selman, "Coaching and the Art of Management," *Organizational Dynamics* (Autumn 1989): 16–32.

16. Herbert H. Meyer, "A Solution to the Performance Appraisal Feedback Enigma," *Academy of Management Executive* (February 1991): 75.

17. Kenneth Dawson and Sheryl Dawson, "Inplacement: Maximizing Employee Performance," *Management Review* (April 1989): 39–43.

18. Loren E. Falkenberg, "Employee Fitness Programs: Their Impact on Employees and the Organization," *Academy of Management Review* (July 1987): 511–522.

19. Cynthia M. Pavett and Gary G. Whitney, "Exercise Makes Employees Work Better," *HRMagazine* (December 1990): 84; Shari Caudron, "The Wellness Payoff," *Personnel Journal* (July 1990): 55–60.

20. Lester R. Bittel and Jackson E. Ramsey, "What to Do about Misfit Supervisors," *Management Review* (March 1983): 43.

21. Gary P. Latham and Colette A. Frayne, "Self-Management Training for Increasing Job Attendance: A Follow-Up and a Replication," *Journal of Applied Psychology* (June 1989): 411.

22. Martin Levy, "Discipline for Professional Employees," *Personnel Journal* (December 1990): 27–28.

23. Thomas L. Moore, "Build Wellness from an EAP Base," *Personnel Journal* (June 1991): 104–109.

24. Steven H. Appelbaum and Barbara T. Shapiro, "The ABCs of EAPs," *Personnel* (July 1989): 40.

25. Howard W. French, "Employee Drug Abuse Programs Spawn a New Industry," *The New York Times* (March 27, 1987).

26. John Hoerr, "The Drug Wars Will Be Won with Treatment, Not Tests," *Business Week* (October 13, 1986): 114–119.

27. Walter Kiechel, III, "How to Fire Someone," *Fortune* (March 1986): 166–167.

28. Richard Hoban, "The Outplacement Option: Everybody Wins!" *Personnel Administrator* (June 1987): 184–193.

29. James G. Frierson, "How to Fire Without Getting Burned," *Personnel* (September 1990): 48.

30. "Outplacement Counseling Services," *Research Institute Personal Report for the Executive* (January 21, 1986): 5.

31. Stanlee Phelps and Marguerite Mason, "When Women Are Fired," *Personnel Journal* (August 1991): 64.

32. Gilbert Zoghlin, "Financial Planning Takes Lead as Outplacement Service," *Personnel* (May 1991): 14.

No-Excuses Management at Cypress Semiconductor

Cypress Semiconductor Corporation is a highly publicized, yet comparatively small, manufacturer of computer chips. The company has 1,400 employees and current annual sales of approximately $300 million. Its large competitors—Advanced Micro Devices, Intel, Motorola, National Semiconductor, and Texas Instruments—have combined annual revenues of $24 billion.

Top-level management at Cypress shrugs off its giant competitors because the company is a niche player. Cypress specializes in a fast memory chip labeled as static random-access memory, or SRAM. Yet as its sales volume and product lines continue to expand, Cypress may attract competition from U.S. and Japanese rivals.

Much of the attention Cypress has attracted can be attributed to its articulate and outspoken founder and CEO, T. J. Rodgers. His many credits include a Ph.D. in electrical engineering from Stanford University, several articles published by the *Harvard Business Review*, and dozens of stories about him in business magazines and newspapers.

Rodgers describes most chip manufacturers as dinosaurs who whine for political protection from Japanese rivals rather than innovating and investing. He contends that mediocre management, not unfair competition by Japanese companies, has created most of the problems faced by U.S. chip manufacturers. Some people describe "T. J." as a genius-like entrepreneur, while others call him a publicity-grabbing braggart.

Rodgers maintains that for Cypress to succeed in the long run the company must do at least four things better than the competition:

1. Hire exceptional people and retain them.
2. Encourage every employee to establish and attain challenging goals.
3. Allocate human resources, capital, and operating expenses so as to maximize productivity.
4. Reward the workforce in ways that encourage superior performance rather than demotivate superior performers.

Knowledge of the Business

Another important part of Rodgers's operating philosophy is that top-level management cannot manage effectively without a thorough mastery of the details of its business. Rodgers says that no CEO can claim to be in charge of the organization unless, within 15 minutes, he or she can answer questions such as the following: What are the company's revenues per employee? How do these figures compare with the competition? What is the average outgoing quality level in each product line? How many orders are delinquent? Which of the company's top 20 managers are outstanding performers, which are low performers, and why? What are the yields, costs, and cycle times at every manufacturing operation? What explains the company's stock market valuation relative to the competition? To help himself acquire such knowledge, Rodgers typically works 13 hours per day. He schedules meetings from 8:00 A.M. to 5:00 P.M. or 7:00 P.M. four days per week.

Cypress has achieved considerable financial success. During 1991, for example, its revenues climbed 31 percent. In comparison, the growth of the U.S. semiconductor industry in general was 5 percent. Even during tough economic times, the company's gross profit margins have been around 60 percent and pretax earnings have been above 20 percent. Only the chip maker Intel can rival these figures.

The Hiring Book

Rodgers has developed hiring procedures that he believes contribute greatly to the success of the firm. He requires managers throughout the company to follow scrupulously the recruiting and selection system he has developed. No manager can bring in a new employee without submitting a "hiring book," which documents the hiring process and provides comprehensive results of interviews and reference checks. Until the company reached 400 employees, Rodgers read every one of those books before the company extended a job offer. He now shares the task with six other senior managers. When the system is followed, the job candidate is hired. When the system has not been followed, a job offer is denied.

A Cypress vice president once submitted a hiring book that violated the key rule of not offering large raises to job candidates. The manager offered this explanation: "At my old company we had to give big raises to convince people to sign on." Rodgers retorted, "We've hired 1,400 people with this system. Is there any reason we can't hire number 1,401 the same way?" The vice president resubmitted the hiring book two weeks later with the same above-policy raise. To emphasize his point, Rodgers cut the book in half and mailed it back to the vice president.

Rodgers insists that managers do their own recruiting rather than rely on much assistance from the human resources department. Human resources professionals occasionally suggest candidates, but they play no role in evaluating them. New employees do not meet anyone in human resources until they report to work and fill out the necessary employment forms. Rodgers estimates that it takes 10 prescreening telephone interviews to find one candidate strong enough to qualify for the formal evaluation process. About 25 percent of the candidates who go through the evaluation receive an offer. About 85 percent of those candidates accept the offer.

Rodgers explains that his company does not bid for talent. New hires can receive up to an 8 percent increase over what they were receiving previously. Rodgers believes that people with great talent join Cypress because they want to win, not for a large salary increase. Nevertheless, people who join the company receive stock options and the highest percentage raises in the industry.

Killer Software

Some observers attribute much of the company's success to Rodgers's aggressive management style. He runs Cypress with an engineer's precision. Rodgers has designed software to help manage everything from detecting minor production glitches to holding people to deadlines and following procedures. Every Wednesday, Rodgers scans printouts on the status of key projects, noting the names of managers who are five weeks or more overdue on attaining goals. A tardy manager will usually receive a handwritten note from a pad inscribed "From the Desk of God."

A major component of the Cypress performance measurement system is "killer software." Assume, for example, that a manager has ordered a product from an outside supplier. The order does not arrive on time, but no one has provided senior management with an explanation. A computer program then shuts down all the computer systems in purchasing. To get the systems back up, the offending manager has to contact the supplier, obtain a new delivery date, and report the news back to the Cypress chief financial officer.

Rodgers believes that the benefits gained from increased productivity outweigh the costs of an occasional shutdown. After a shutdown, employees say, "What happened, and how can we make sure it never happens again?" The Cypress system of electronic bloodhounds has now been copied by a number of other companies.

Perpetual Entrepreneurship

Rodgers claims that Cypress will never become a huge, unwieldy company. Instead, it will become a collection of small entrepreneurial units. As the company expands into new businesses, Rodgers converts new product lines or manufacturing plants into separate companies. Each company has its own president, a board of directors (including Rodgers), and funding from the parent company. The manufacturing subsidiaries sell their products back to Cypress to be resold by its centralized sales force. The presidents of the Cypress subsidiaries can eventually sell their stock back to the parent company, or they can sell it to investors or on the open market.

Company functional groups also follow an entrepreneurial mold. Virtually every internal company function is set up as its own profit-and-loss center. For example, a company print shop might sell its services to a technical group that produces user manuals. If the print shop charges too much, the technical group will find another supplier. Rodgers claims, "Free money is one of the biggest problems of a large company. We've gotten rid of socialism in the organization."

Rodgers in Action

Some people who work for or have worked for Rodgers claim that he is heavy handed. A former division president, Narpat Bhandari, notes that his every decision was undermined by Rodgers. He claims that he needed approval from the CEO even to buy a pen. The chief financial officer at Cypress recalls several instances of Rodgers pounding on the desk in front of him demanding the almost impossible. Rodgers has also been known to criticize his managers severely in front of others.

Rodgers's former secretary, and now his girlfriend, recalls how he once demanded that she find software to convert hand-drawn cards into slides. She worked around the clock for five days to find appropriate software, learn its use, and then make the slides. In an exhausted and tearful state, the secretary said she could not complete the project on time. Rodgers responded that he needed a secretary, not a crybaby. She did complete the job after the confrontation.

Rodgers frequently belittles his adversaries, often stating that everyone else is an idiot. The CEO of one of his rival companies, Sematech, says Rodgers is more talk than action.

Looking toward the future, some industry observers doubt that small and nimble companies can survive in the semiconductor business of the future. Yet others think that as Cypress grows in stature and U.S. competitiveness becomes an even bigger issue, the world will continue to listen to Rodgers.

1. How would you describe the management style of T. J. Rodgers?

2. How suitable is Rodgers's attention to detail for a top-level manager?

3. How would you like to work directly for T. J. Rodgers?

4. What possible negative consequences do you see resulting from the recruitment and selection system at Cypress?

5. What motivational approaches does Rodgers use?

6. What do you see as the advantages and disadvantages of "killer software"?

7. How effective is Rodgers as a role model for employees in the current business climate?

8. What recommendations do you have for T. J. Rodgers as a manager and a leader?

Source: Based on Richard Brandt, "The Bad Boy of Silicon Valley," *Business Week* (December 9, 1991): 64–70; Richard Brandt, "Here Comes the Attack of the Killer Software," *Business Week* (December 9, 1991): 70; and T. J. Rodgers, "No Excuses Management," *Harvard Business Review* (July-August 1990): 84–98.

Part V
Controlling

Chapter 15

Principles of Control

OPENING
CASE

Inventory
Control at
Carini's
Clothiers

"Roger, I want to talk with you about something that happened the other day. I think what I have to say is important. Essentially, what I want to talk about concerns how we are running this store."

"This is what happened. Khalil Mathur came in last Wednesday to look at suits. He is one of my better customers, one who followed me to your store. An avid jogger who owns his own insurance agency, Mathur is a successful businessman. He enjoys his clothes and believes it is important to wear sharp-looking, up-to-date suits. Mathur takes a size 37 long, and I had only one suit to show him. Obviously, this was disappointing. Roger, I am going to lose customers if I can't show them a decent selection. Can't we carry more suits in our inventory?"

Roger Carini, who had been listening carefully to Bob Johnson's comments, thought seriously before responding. "Bob, I understand what you are saying. It is important for us to be able to show several suits to each customer. And, because of your success with my store, I want to respond properly to your concerns. But Bob, a key part of this store's success is a commitment to controlling costs. And remember, it's becoming increasingly expensive for us just to keep the doors open. With the economy suffering, our business simply is not what it used to be. You know how expensive suits have become. We can't afford to have five, six, or seven suits in every size category. Reducing our inventory is one way we can control costs. Besides, a 37 long is not a common size. In my opinion, we should carry the largest number of suits in the most popular sizes. Why don't you show Khalil Mathur swatches of material so he can special-order the suit he wants?"

"Roger, I understand your viewpoint," said Bob. "It *is* important for us to control our costs. And, for some customers, special-ordering suits may be the way to go. But other customers, such as Khalil Mathur, want to try on several suits and make their purchase right away. They don't want to look at a small piece of material and then wait six weeks or more before seeing the product. I think we need to compromise on this. Can't we increase our inventory enough to carry two or three suits in every size?"

"I don't know, Bob. I'll think about what you have said. It isn't that I disagree with you. It's just that we must control our costs better than we have been if we are going to survive in this tough clothing market. Let's talk about it again in a few days."

Controlling—following planning, organizing, and leading—is the fourth of the four classical management functions. **Controlling** is a six-stage process designed to ensure that a firm's strategies and plans will be put into effect successfully. It has long been recognized as an important part of effective managerial practice.[1] In the opening case, inventory control had become an issue between the owner and his key salesperson. Roger Carini's decision about how to control his store's inventory costs will affect the firm's competitiveness and its profitability.

Controls, such as the inventory controls used at Carini's Clothiers, imply the existence of standards of judgment. Today, these standards are often developed in terms of the manufacture of high-quality products and delivery of appropriate service to customers.[2] All businesses must offer high-quality products and superior service to succeed in a global business environment. Some experts believe that the banks that survived the troubles in the early 1990s did so in part because they provided superior service to their customers.[3]

Managers often argue that effective controls are based on objective measures. But even the most sophisticated objective controls, including those using computer-based information systems and budgets, can be inadequate if employees do not understand the information they provide and/or are not committed to acting on that information.[4] Thus, successful controls are ones that have been developed properly and are understood fully and accepted by those affected by them.

. . . .

Back to the Opening Case

The inventory controls at Carini's Clothiers may not be working effectively. The conversation with Bob Johnson suggests that Carini had not explained the firm's approach to controlling its inventory to all employees, including Johnson. Without full knowledge of how the firm controls its inventory, Johnson lacked the information he needed to deal effectively with his customers.

. . . .

This chapter describes the principles of the controlling function. It opens with a brief description of the nature of controlling, followed by a comprehensive discussion of each of the six stages of the controlling process. The chapter also examines several subtopics, including descriptions of key result areas for which performance standards should be established and methods used to establish those standards. **Key result areas** are parts of a firm's operation that are especially critical to its success. The characteristics of effective controls are described in the chapter's final section. Using all of these materials as a foundation, we will examine specific controlling methods and techniques in Chapter 16.

THE NATURE OF CONTROLLING

Today's complex organizations often face difficult conditions in their external environments. In addition, coordinating the work of many individuals and groups is quite challenging. Because of this, firms do not always function smoothly. When they do not achieve the results they intended, they must change their actions. Such changes are necessary to maintain a company's health and to ensure accomplishment of its mission, objectives, strategies, and plans.[5] The systems and techniques necessary to bring about change are developed and implemented through the controlling function.

It is important to realize that some managers rely too heavily on the controlling function.[6] This is because controls allow managers to reduce the amount of variation in individuals' work. With less variation, the conditions managers face become more predictable. Thus, the tendency to rely too extensively on controls is understandable.

However, success in today's global marketplaces requires the creative energies of a firm's entire workforce. The use of too many controls prevents employees from using their innovative talents. First-, middle-, and top-level managers should use only controls that are appropriate to the conditions they face. For example, mature, experienced employees require fewer controls than do those who are just beginning to develop their work skills. Generally speaking, managers should use the controlling function to set the

ETHICS QUESTION
Is developing controls that are appropriate for individual employees an ethical challenge for today's managers? Why or why not?

parameters within which employees are encouraged to use their innovative abilities in pursuit of the firm's mission.[7]

Who Controls?

The answer to this question depends on the particular firm, but, as shown in Figure 15-1, it is safe to say that in the most effectively controlled companies, many people do. Finance controllers, all levels of managers, corporate planners, quality control analysts, and, potentially, every employee in the firm contribute significantly to the controlling process. At the highest level, members of the board of directors are responsible for controlling the entire firm's actions and accomplishments.[8] The board of directors' responsibilities are especially critical with respect to the proper use of the firm's assets.

The traditional controlling model was designed to establish order in the workplace and allow managers to exercise direct control over employees. A more commonly accepted model of controlling today recognizes that employees respond best and most creatively "not when they are tightly controlled by management, placed in narrowly defined jobs, and treated like an unwelcome necessity, but, instead, when they are given broader responsibilities, encouraged to contribute, and helped to take satisfaction in their work."[9] Thus, effective controls establish boundaries within which employees can engage in meaningful and productive work.

FIGURE 15-1 Parties Involved with Controlling

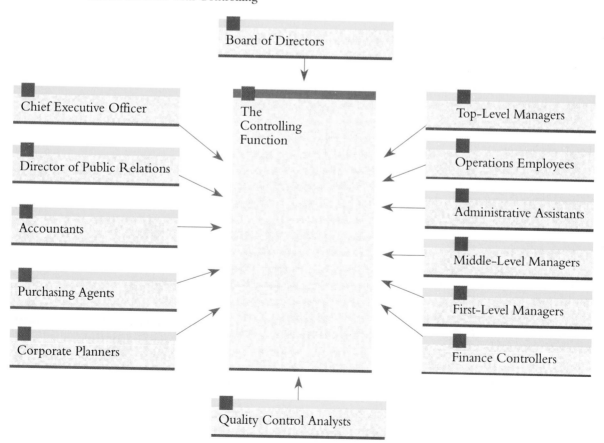

Roger Carini has not involved all employees in decisions about controls to be used
in his firm. If Bob Johnson had been a party to decisions regarding control of the
store's inventory costs, he might have supported Carini's decisions about how many
suits should be in the store's inventory.

A company gains commitment from all of its employees when it establishes controls at three organizational levels (see Figure 15-2). **Operational
control** is concerned with activities related to the production of a company's goods or the provision of its services. An example is recording daily
sales figures in order to measure an individual's or group's performance.
Generally, first-level managers are responsible for operational control. The
controls they develop must be consistent with the guidelines and controls
developed by middle- and top-level managers.

Tactical control concerns how well a firm's actions are being received
in the marketplace. Middle-level managers monitor competitor, supplier,
and customer reactions to the firm's market-related activities. Conducting
feedback sessions to evaluate the relationship between a firm and one of its
suppliers is an example of tactical control. Tactical controls must be consistent with guidelines set by top-level managers and supportive of controls established by first-level managers.

Through **strategic control**, top-level managers examine the accuracy
of their assumptions about general economic conditions and the actions of
the firm's competitors. Comparing a firm's financial performance with that
of competitors is an example of strategic control. In addition, top-level
managers attempt to predict future environmental conditions that may call
for adjustments in the firm's strategy or plans. Through effective integration
of these three levels of control, all employees can have meaningful opportunities to participate in the development of controls.[10]

FIGURE 15-2
Levels of Control

Operational Control
Concerned with activities
required to produce a
firm's product

Tactical Control
Concerned with the marketplace success of a firm's product

Strategic Control
Concerned with how effectively
top-level managers have been
able to align their firm with
environmental conditions facing
the firm

As a part of the strategic control process, top-level managers study reports on the firm's financial performance and use the information to adjust strategies and plans.

THE CONTROLLING PROCESS

As stated earlier, controlling is a six-stage process (see Figure 15-3). The planning and controlling functions are closely related. Firms develop the controls necessary to implement their strategies and plans as they formulate those strategies and plans. They activate the controls when they implement the strategies and plans. The use of controls may generate reports indicating the need to adjust a strategy or a plan. For example, performance results showing that a firm's objective of increasing its sales volume by 3 percent over the previous year's volume is not being reached may suggest the need to adjust particular strategies or plans.

FIGURE 15-3 The Controlling Process

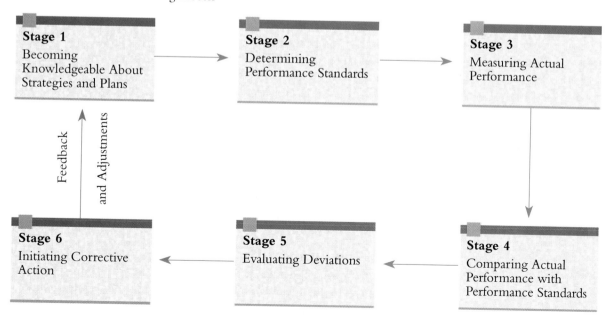

Managers follow a particular set of actions to establish effective controls. These actions, grouped into six stages, are discussed in the following sections.

Stage 1: Becoming Knowledgeable About Strategies and Plans

Controlling is effective only when it is based on actions specified by a firm's strategies and plans. (Recall from Chapter 6 that strategies and plans are formulated in light of a firm's mission and its long-term objectives.) Thus, the controls required to implement a differentiation strategy differ from those necessary to implement an overall cost leadership strategy. Managers must develop controlling methods and techniques that are consistent with their firms' intended accomplishments.

The actions of two well-known firms illustrate the importance of knowledge of strategies to an effective controlling process. Cargill, Inc., is a large, privately held firm with over $13.5 billion in assets. In the early 1990s, it was the nation's largest grain merchandiser, second largest beef packer, and eighth largest steel company. However, disagreements among the firm's owners, coupled with increasingly intense competition from foreign grain merchandisers, caused Cargill's top-level managers to conclude that strategic changes were necessary. To regain its growth and profitability, the firm chose to break with its traditional wholesaling roots in order to enter higher-margin retail markets. In particular, Cargill decided to sell brand-name consumer products such as poultry and corn oil.[11]

This decision was a major change in Cargill's strategy and plans. To implement strategy changes successfully, managers must develop appropriate operational, tactical, and strategic controls. The performance standards for a consumer products company are different from those for a wholesaler. Likewise, the service expectations of the final consumer are different from those of a wholesaler. The unique characteristics of each market demand unique controls.

Philip Morris's decision to change the organization of its food division also called for changes in controls. Built primarily through acquisitions, the food division includes many well-known brands such as Miracle Whip, Velveeta, Post, Jell-O, Oscar Mayer, Birds-Eye, and Maxwell House. Because this unit accounts for about one-half of the company's sales volume, restructuring was important. According to company spokespersons, the changes were made primarily to increase efficiency and to control the unit's costs.[12] This required different performance standards and, in general, different controls.

ETHICS QUESTION
Are there any ethical issues involved with the development of performance standards? If so, what are those issues?

Stage 2: Determining Performance Standards

A **performance standard** is a level of performance established to serve as a model, criterion, or expectation. The unit of measurement in which the standard is expressed changes from one situation to another. But whether it is expressed as units assembled, pages word-processed, or dollars of sales, a standard always serves as a performance expectation.

SCOPE OF PERFORMANCE STANDARDS. Regardless of size, all companies should establish formal objectives and performance standards for each of several key result areas.[13] The following items are examples of such areas:

- Profitability
- Market share
- Productivity
- Product leadership
- Human resources development
- Employee attitudes
- Social responsibility
- Balance between short-term and long-term objectives.

Profitability. A commonly used measure of profitability is **return on investment (ROI)**—a company's net income before taxes divided by net worth. Profitability may also be expressed in terms of total revenue or rate of return (using the ratio of profit to sales). ROI allows comparison of a firm's current performance with its past accomplishments and with the level of performance expected in the current time period. In a diversified firm, managers can compare the ROIs of different divisions side by side to determine which parts of the firm are providing the greatest returns. Results of these comparisons suggest how corporate resources should be allocated in the future.

Describing profits in terms of total revenue is a measure of the effectiveness of sales efforts over a period of time. Standards of profitability should reflect the importance of controlling costs and expanding volume, as well as the use of informational, physical, and financial resources.

Market Share. **Market share,** the percentage of total sales volume captured by a firm's product, measures the extent to which the firm's customers have accepted its products. Performance standards intended to measure a firm's market position should be expressed in terms of the total available market or as compared to competitors' market position. A firm that increases its market share by 2 to 3 percent per year may believe it is quite successful. However, if a major competitor is increasing its share by 4 to 5 percent per year, the firm's performance is not as desirable as it believes. During 1990, for example, although Domino's Pizza increased its share of the pizza market, the increase was substantially less than that recorded by Pizza Hut, the firm's chief rival. After considering these results, Thomas Monaghan, Domino's CEO, decided that the theme of his firm's strategy would be a back-to-basics focus on the delivery of pizza.[14]

Many studies have demonstrated the importance of market share. These studies have found that as a product increases its share of a market, the probability that the firm will earn a higher ROI with that product also increases.[15] Thus, generally speaking, firms want their products to have the largest share of their markets. In some companies, market share is an absolute standard of performance. At General Electric, for example, a product is eliminated if it does not hold either the largest or second largest share of its market.[16]

Productivity. Productivity measures are usually associated with a firm's production function. However, productivity standards should be established for administrative and sales functions as well as for the operations function. Typically, **productivity** is expressed as the relationship between total output—measured by dollar volume or units produced—and units of input. For example, labor productivity is the number of worker-hours required to produce a unit of product.

Product Leadership. Performance standards for profitability, market share, and productivity can be expressed in relatively objective, quantitative terms. In contrast, some other areas of achievement are measured through qualitative criteria. **Product leadership** is an estimate of the degree to which a firm's products are thought to set the standard for others to try to match. A firm's product leadership position is difficult to express quantitatively. Nevertheless, an estimate is required if the firm's objective is to become or remain a leader in its field. A simple quantitative measure—such as the number of new products or services the firm has introduced within a certain time period—is not sufficient by itself. The firm should also use a qualitative measure to assess its leadership within the industry.

The significance of new goods or services a firm introduces to the marketplace is one qualitative measure of product leadership. The firm should compare the standards of quality and performance for its products to those of competitors. While such comparisons are helpful, managers often discover that in the final analysis they must make value judgments to determine whether or not the firm is reaching its product leadership objective.

LEARNING CHECK

Describe the first four key result areas for which managers should establish performance standards.

Human Resources Development. In today's competitive environments, managers constantly seek to upgrade their employees' skills. This requires the allocation of additional resources to training and development programs.[17] Both qualitative and quantitative standards are used to measure the effectiveness of these programs. Skill development programs are usually the result of long-range planning and are intended to satisfy both short- and long-term needs. Thus, it is sometimes difficult to fully assess their success on an annual basis. However, annual reporting of the results of training and development programs can help a firm establish a baseline from which trends can be determined.

Companies should include the number of employees involved in formal developmental programs and the success of those who received training

compared to those who did not in their annual reports of human resources development. The Organization in Action describes a training and development program used at Motorola.

ORGANIZATION IN ACTION

Until recently, Motorola had a $7 million training budget. Now this budget includes an annual investment of $120 million in education. At the center of the firm's education efforts is the Motorola Training and Education Center (MTEC). MTEC is the company's approach to coping successfully with the challenges of the global markets in which it competes. Changes in the world's competitive markets have forced Motorola to alter its managerial approaches and the quality of its products. To address the training needs resulting from these changes, MTEC originally had two goals: to expand the firm's participative management program and to help improve product quality tenfold in five years.

Today, Motorola requires its manufacturing employees to have three capabilities: (1) communication and computation skills at the seventh-grade level (soon to be raised to the ninth-grade level); (2) individual and team-based problem-solving skills; and (3) acceptance of the company's definition of work and the work week. For those who lack them, the skills are provided through the firm's training programs. Having the third capability means that employees accept the need to use whatever amount of time is required to ship perfect product to each customer. This definition sometimes results in work weeks of 50 or even 60 hours. According to Motorola officials, the firm needs people who are willing to work to accomplish challenging quality and output goals instead of working against a time clock.

Source: Adapted from William Wiggenhorn, "Motorola U: When Training Becomes an Education," *Harvard Business Review* (July-August 1990): 71–83.

The three capabilities Motorola expects of all manufacturing employees serve as quantitative performance standards to measure the effectiveness of the firm's training and development programs. Included in these quantitative standards are qualitative standards. For example, determining how well participative management programs have been used requires a qualitative analysis of how openly and actively people share in the management of their units. Combining the quantitative and qualitative performance standards provides a complete and meaningful measurement of the company's efforts to develop its human resources.

Employee Attitudes. There is some question as to whether or not there is a positive relationship between employee attitudes and the achievement of corporate objectives. However, there is little doubt that employee attitudes affect a firm's long-term success. Attitudes may be measured by analyzing labor turnover, absenteeism, grievances, and safety records. These factors can be measured quantitatively and objectively; the difficulty lies in selecting an acceptable performance standard. Year-to-year figures and comparisons among different units in a company or within an industry can be used to measure results against performance standards.

ETHICS QUESTION
Is a firm without performance standards in terms of social responsibility less ethical than the firm that has developed such standards? Why or why not?

Social Responsibility. Measuring the degree to which a firm has achieved social responsibility objectives is challenging. These valuations are made in terms of the view of social responsibility accepted by the firm's managers. As discussed in Chapter 3, managers (as decision makers for their firms) adopt a classical, accountability, or public social responsibility view. Whichever view they have adopted, managers should identify performance standards that are consistent with it. Quantitative measures can be used as standards for the classical view. At the other extreme, more qualitative measures must be selected to evaluate performance in terms of the public social responsibility view. Both quantitative and qualitative measures can be used as standards for the accountability view.

Balance Between Short-Term and Long-Term Objectives. Both short- and long-term objectives are required to fully measure a firm's performance. In recent years, many U.S. companies have been criticized severely for emphasizing short-term profits at the expense of long-term profitability. Today, managers must devote their energies to actions that will ensure survival in the short term *and* profitability in the long term.[18] Matching a firm's internal strengths with its external opportunities, as discussed in Chapter 5, helps to accomplish both short- and long-term objectives.

LEARNING CHECK

Name and describe the second four key result areas for which managers establish performance standards.

ESTABLISHING PERFORMANCE STANDARDS. In today's firms, managers commonly use three methods to establish performance standards. One method relies on statistical data from sources within and outside the organization; a second appraises results in light of managerial experience and judgment; and a third uses engineered standards.

Statistical Standards. **Statistical standards** are performance standards based on an analysis of data from past experience. The data may be drawn from a company's internal records or from industry records if they are available. The particular statistic selected as the performance standard may be an average or it may be a stated amount above or below a midpoint. A restaurant manager, for example, may use the average amount of time required to serve customers during one month as the performance standard for the next several months. The scheduled-maintenance programs recommended by automobile manufacturers are based on statistical standards. Examining volumes of data over time indicates to these manufacturers that, on average, a particular automobile should have its oil changed at a particular interval.

ETHICS QUESTION
What ethical challenges do managers face when they use their own judgment to establish performance standards?

Standards Set by Managerial Judgment. In certain instances, performances are appraised primarily in terms of a manager's judgment. **Managerial judgment standards** are essentially value judgments, but they can be as realistic and useful as statistical or engineered standards. In the absence of established standards, all managers are expected to rate their employees' outputs in terms of what they, as managers, believe to be satisfactory. Without formal attitude surveys, for example, managers may rate employees' attitudes in terms of the qualities they believe enhance productivity. In making these assessments, managers are establishing their own performance standards.

Engineered Standards. **Engineered standards** are performance standards based on objective, quantitative analyses of specific work situations. They may be developed to measure machine output or an individual's output. Machine output standards reflect the production capacity of a piece of equipment and are determined by mechanical design factors. Machine capacity figures represent the optimum output of the equipment during normal operations (or production) activities. They are often used to determine output standards in industries where mass production is used. Such standards are essentially independent of worker performance. For example, many of today's large bakeries use sophisticated equipment to produce bread. A machine may be designed to produce a batch of dough that weighs 2,000 pounds. The machine has sensing devices that will sound an alarm if the amount of dough exceeds the machine's engineered standard for production efficiency.

Engineered standards that measure the output of individual employees or groups of employees are called **time standards** or **time study standards.** This is because time, usually measured by a stopwatch, is the element of measurement.[19] The first time studies in the United States were completed by Frederick W. Taylor in 1881 at the Midvale Steel Company, where he analyzed the productivity of hourly employees in a steel mill. Since then, time study standards have been applied to all types of production jobs as well as clerical and sales jobs. The Organizations in Action shows how sophisticated computer systems can be used to determine the amount of time required to complete transactions in various service jobs.

Engineered standards measure the output of the machine used to make these rolls. Here, an employee spot checks the quality of the output.

ORGANIZATIONS IN ACTION

In many firms, including airlines, banks, and appliance makers, "silent monitoring" is being used to examine service employees' performances. These firms use computerized devices and software programs to gather the data they need to measure employees' output. For example, silent monitoring can be used to count the keystrokes of data entry specialists or to assess the effectiveness of a telephone operator's verbal interactions with customers. This technique is called silent monitoring because employees never know when the sophisticated devices are being used to gather data about their performance. The purpose is to help employees improve their job performance. However, silent monitoring is also used to determine whether or not employees are satisfying their jobs' performance standards.

For silent monitoring to be effective, employees with whom the technique is used should (1) be selected and trained carefully; (2) be told exactly why and how their work will be monitored; and (3) view silent monitoring as a coaching and counseling tool rather than as a disciplinary tool. Although it is still controversial, some managers and consultants believe that, when used properly, silent monitoring can be beneficial for both employees and their firms.

Source: Adapted from Gene Bylinsky, "How Companies Spy on Employees," *Fortune* (November 4, 1991): 131–140.

ETHICS QUESTION
What are the ethical issues involved with the use of silent monitoring?

Companies can now use sophisticated technology to develop engineered standards to measure an individual's output. Although it is achieved through different means, the outcome of the silent monitoring technique is not significantly different from that sought by Frederick Taylor and his associates.

In establishing time standards, a standard time is determined. The **standard time** is the time required to complete the job under certain conditions. These conditions are usually defined in terms of what an average worker can do when trained in the skills of the job, working at a normal pace, and following methods prescribed for completing the job. Effort, or pace, is a matter of judgment and is measured against a standard—for example, the effort expended in walking three miles an hour on level ground. Standard times are usually developed for a normal eight-hour workday and include allowances for fatigue, unavoidable delays, personal time, and other interruptions that occur at predictable intervals. Employees who perform according to the standards set for the job are said to be working at *100 percent of standard*. However, the use of this phrase causes much misunderstanding of time study because "100 percent" normally conveys the idea of perfection, of maximum effort and maximum output.

LEARNING CHECK

Name and describe the three primary methods used to develop performance standards.

Stage 3: Measuring Actual Performance

Managers measure performances in terms of the outputs they want to control. To a degree, measurement problems are specified—and sometimes partially solved—by the manner in which performance standards are defined. It is easy to establish standards of profitability in terms of dollars, but it is not as easy to develop satisfactory standards for key result areas such as product leadership and social responsibility. The variety and number of key result areas for which standards may be set make it impossible to develop measures that are applicable to each business situation. However, through critical thinking, managers can develop measurement methods that are appropriate to specific situations.

Controls are important parts of information systems. The appropriateness of a corrective action depends almost entirely on the kind of information received. Managers can evaluate information intended to measure and describe actual performance by answering the following two questions:

1. Are the measurement units appropriate?
2. Is information being channeled to the proper authority?

These questions are addressed in the sections that follow.

APPROPRIATE UNITS OF MEASUREMENT. One of the most difficult tasks in measuring actual performance is the selection of an appropriate measure. Occasionally, the use of several different measures offers a partial solution to this problem. For example, firms can select a range of accounting-based measurements, including ROI, return on equity, and average return on sales, to evaluate their performance. They can also use several measures to evaluate an individual's performance. For a salesperson, sales volume, number of calls made, amount of repeat business, and costs incurred relative to sales earned can be used to measure performance. The use of multiple measures to describe performance is sound. Each measure serves as a cross-check on the information provided by the other measures while emphasizing a particular aspect of the performance being reviewed. At all times, managers must use organizational and individual performance measures that are relevant to the objectives, strategies, and plans being implemented.

All performance measures used in controlling organizational and individual performances should be both valid and reliable. **Validity** reflects how well a performance measure accounts for what it is supposed to measure. **Reliability** describes the consistency of a performance measure—the degree to which it yields the same results no matter how many times it is used. Managers must verify that performance measures are assessing meaningful aspects of performance (that is, the measures are valid) and that they yield the same result over time and regardless of who uses them (that is, the measures are reliable).[20]

CHANNELING INFORMATION TO THE PROPER AUTHORITY. Effective controls channel information to the right people at the right time. The proper channel for information flow varies with each firm's structure, the type of information to be interpreted, and the kind of corrective action required to attain performance standards. Even so, the following generalization can be made: Control information should be directed toward the person who has responsibility for the operation and authority to take corrective action. In other words, those held accountable for a unit's performance must receive the information required to correct deviations from the unit's expected performance levels.

Stage 4: Comparing Actual Performance with Performance Standards

This stage of the controlling process should not be difficult for managers to complete. Once the actual performance has occurred, managers have the data they need to compare that performance with the established standard. A company seeking to increase its sales volume by 8 percent over the volume for the same month last year has failed to satisfy that performance standard if sales volume has increased by only 5 percent. Similarly, a salesperson's actual performance can be measured quickly when it is compared to a sales volume performance standard.

If managers have difficulty with Stage 4 of the controlling process, it is because of poorly designed performance standards or failure to develop valid and reliable measures of actual performance. Companies should hold their managers accountable for working with employees to achieve rigorous and meaningful performance standards that tie in to measures of actual performance. For example, in setting a performance standard for customer service representatives, it is not enough to say that they should improve their interactions with customers. The standard must be spelled out in specific terms. Similarly, the training and development performance standard in a firm should be much better defined than "constantly striving to train our people as well as our resources allow." Valid standards and measurements will prevent disagreements regarding the degree to which an employee's actual performance satisfies a performance standard.

Stage 5: Evaluating Deviations

Managers must examine situations in which actual performances deviate from performance standards. For example, if the work of a salesperson goes beyond the performance standard, the manager should reward the salesperson's efforts. The manager will also want to work with the salesperson to identify the reasons for the outstanding performance. Was she particularly effective with repeat business? Did she develop techniques for closing sales that were especially effective? Did she work in a geographic area in which the business community was growing rapidly? Learning how the salesperson was effective makes it possible for the manager to teach the successful techniques to other salespeople.

More commonly, managers find that actual performance falls below performance standards. Again, they must seek to understand the causes of the deviations. Some deviations are caused by factors outside the control of an individual or a firm. For example, companies facing turbulent external environments may fail to reach performance standards that suddenly become unrealistic. They should recognize the new reality and adjust their performance standards. Managers must also work with individuals to understand the factors contributing to their failure to satisfy performance expectations.

Stage 6: Initiating Corrective Action

Several courses of action are available to managers as they deal with this stage of the controlling process. Having spotted a deviation between actual performance and a performance standard, a manager might conclude that no action is required at that point. This decision is often made when a deviation appears before a project has been completed and there is enough time to correct the deviation. The manager may want the employee to take responsibility for correcting the deviation. Such a decision may even be part of a program to develop the employee for a more responsible position in the future.

A second action managers might take when there is a deviation between performance and a standard is to help employees adjust their efforts to satisfy performance standards. A third course of action managers might take is to determine that changing conditions warrant adjustments in the performance standard itself. They should consult with the affected employees in reaching such a decision, whether they are considering the performance standard for an individual employee or for an entire corporation. Finally, it is sometimes necessary for managers to terminate an individual's employment when the person is incapable of complying with a performance standard or is unwilling to accept the standard.

Before initiating any corrective action, managers must know the difference between symptoms and causes. They must learn to recognize a symptom as just that and to devote their attention instead to the causes of various problems. Cost control, or the control of expenses, provides an example of treating symptoms rather than causes. Excessive costs indicate that something is not functioning as intended. Costs result from someone's performance, and if costs are to be brought in line with standards, it is the performance that must be corrected. First, the manager should compare the costs with the performance standard to determine whether they are indeed excessive. Next, the manager should determine the contribution of each factor to total cost. How much of the total cost is due to labor, to materials, and to overhead? Finally, the manager should study each factor separately and determine how performance could be improved in each area.

The same procedure can be applied to a decline in a product's sales volume. The solution is not necessarily to employ additional salespeople or to demand improved performances from the current sales staff. In fact, the manager may find that the sales decline has resulted from a host of other factors such as new competitive products or a key competitor's more aggressive pricing tactics.

CHARACTERISTICS OF EFFECTIVE CONTROLS

Effective controls are critical to managerial success. The characteristics of effective controls (see Figure 15-4) are discussed in the following sections. These characteristics contribute substantially to the effectiveness of a firm's controls.

FIGURE 15-4
Characteristics of
Effective Controls

Timely
Information is provided to managers when they require it.

Relevant
Outputs from control systems are relevant to the most important issues.

Appropriate
Controls being used are appropriate to a firm's actions and challenges.

Flexible
Control systems can respond quickly to changing conditions.

Accurate
Valid and reliable information is generated by the control system.

Economical
Resources are used wisely in developing and using controls.

Understandable
Controls are easily understood by all parties.

Timely

Businesses today are confronted with constant change, which is particularly dramatic in terms of customer demand. Sophisticated and particular, the 1990s customer constantly seeks new and different goods and services.

Therefore, companies must develop controls to help them monitor customers' ever-changing demands in a timely fashion. Many retailers use computerized information systems to control inventory on a daily basis, recording the sale of each product at the point of sale. At predetermined intervals, these systems automatically order goods to maintain inventory at an acceptable level. Controlling inventory in this manner reduces the retailer's costs while still satisfying customers.

The Gap, a specialty apparel retail store, uses sophisticated controls to maintain an inventory of high-quality products. These products satisfy customers' demands in terms of color, style, and detail. The firm's controls allow it to continue improving its profitability when other retailers are unable to do so.[21] Similarly, the Coleman Company now uses manufacturing systems and controls to respond to customers' needs in a timely manner. Previously, Coleman kept a two months' supply of inventory on hand to provide retailers such as Wal-Mart and Kmart with a timely shipment of

Many retailers use computerized point-of-sale inventory systems to maintain inventory at proper levels. With these systems, information on each sale is entered into the inventory system as soon as the sale is made.

lanterns or camping stoves. Today, the company can manufacture and ship products in one week. Through its new manufacturing systems and controls, Coleman has cut its inventory costs by $10 million and has raised productivity by 35 percent.[22]

Relevant

Because of their complexity, it is not possible to establish controls for each aspect of even a small- to medium-size business. However, a firm must establish controls in the key result areas of its business. It selects these points because of their strategic value. A company manufacturing products for which complete reliability is critical (e.g., component parts for commercial airline engines) must establish effective controls in its design and manufacturing processes. For example, to design its 777 plane, Boeing used a solids-modeling program, which allowed engineers to work out and correct problems on computers. Representatives from design, production, maintenance, outside supplier groups, and customer groups joined together to work on the project. A key objective of this program was to correct problems before starting the actual production process.[23]

Appropriate

As noted earlier in this chapter, some managers exercise more control than is necessary. Managers are responsible for their units' accomplishments, and they sometimes establish controls that unnecessarily restrict the freedom of individuals and work groups. These managers believe that controlling exactly how tasks will be accomplished increases the likelihood of achieving their units' objectives.

Today, however, managers must foster employees' creative and innovative abilities. They must reduce the number of controls to allow employees the freedom to produce and distribute high-quality goods or services in a timely fashion. To eliminate unnecessary controls, managers must examine each controlling method, technique, and system and adjust or eliminate those that do not contribute directly to increased productivity. Managers who use only appropriate controls set the foundation for effective coordination between the planning and controlling functions.

Flexible

The dynamic conditions in today's business environment highlight the need for flexibility in all aspects of a firm's conduct of its business. When planning, managers develop mechanisms through which the firm can take advantage of unanticipated opportunities or avoid threats. As they make adjustments to respond to such conditions, managers must also make modifications in controlling methods, techniques, and systems. An effective controlling system is one that can be updated quickly in response to changes in strategies and plans.

Accurate

Effective controls generate accurate data and information on which managers can base their decisions. Inaccurate controls cause managers to focus their energies on problems that do not exist or fail to alert managers to serious problems that do require attention.

Economical

All companies must use their resources wisely. The challenge is for managers to establish controls that are effective yet economical. If managers are not watchful, elaborate controls sometimes surface. These elaborate systems—ones that generate specific results related to virtually all of a firm's actions—appear to keep managers well informed, but it is often very expensive to develop and use them. Employees may spend too much time preparing sophisticated reports that are of marginal value. Managers themselves can devote far too much time to analyzing reports and controlling others' activities. Economical controls conserve resources while supplying first-, middle-, and top-level managers with information they actually need to carry out their control-related responsibilities.

Understandable

Effective controls are easily understood by those they affect. On the other hand, people can become frustrated if they have to cope with controls they do not understand. They may make mistakes and may ultimately choose to ignore the controls. To ensure that controls are understood, managers should ask employees for feedback regarding their perceptions of the controls that affect them. For example, a manager who is attempting to control expenses for supplies in a particular unit might ask whether the procedures established to deal with this matter are effective. The manager might discover that the controls are not clearly understood by all affected employees or that the controls are creating problems. In such instances, the manager can make appropriate adjustments to the controls. Thus, working together, managerial and nonmanagerial employees can develop and use controls that are understandable and effective.

LEARNING CHECK

Discuss the seven characteristics of effective controls: timely, relevant, appropriate, flexible, accurate, economical, and understandable.

SUMMARY

Controlling, the last of the four major functions of management, is a critical part of effective managerial practice. However, ideas about controlling are necessarily changing with the current changes in firms' environmental conditions. For example, the rapid evolution of computer-based information systems is making controlling a highly dynamic function.

Control is implemented by individuals at all levels of a firm, depending on the key result area being controlled: cash flow, costs, inventory, product quality, and so forth. Firms usually establish three types of control: operational, tactical, and strategic. Operational control, for which the first-level manager is primarily responsible, focuses on activities related to the manufacture of a firm's goods or services. With tactical control, middle-level managers attempt to determine how well the firm's goods or services are being received in the marketplace. Top-level managers use strategic control to examine the degree to which their assumptions about the impact of environmental conditions on their company have been accurate.

Because of the close relationship between planning and controlling, managers should clearly understand their firms' strategies and plans. Determining perfor-

mance standards is challenging for managers. Performance standards are established with respect to the following eight key result areas: profitability, market share, productivity, product leadership, human resources development, employee attitudes, social responsibility, and a balance between short- and long-term objectives. These performance standards may be based on statistics from past experience, managerial judgment, or engineered standards.

When measuring actual performance, managers are concerned with issues such as the appropriateness of measurement units—especially in terms of validity and reliability—and whether or not information is being given to the right people. Before they take any controlling actions to correct what appear to be problems, managers must carefully examine deviations between actual performance and performance standards. They should initiate corrective actions only after they are aware of all factors contributing to the deviations.

Controls are successful only when they are supported by most employees. Effective controls are also timely, relevant, appropriate, flexible, accurate, economical, and understandable. Thus, controls are complex and pervasive. They touch virtually every aspect of organizational life.

KEY TERMS

controlling
key result areas
operational control
tactical control
strategic control

performance standard
return on investment
  (ROI)
market share
productivity

product leadership
statistical standards
managerial judgment
  standards
engineered standards

time standards/time
  study standards
standard time
validity
reliability

QUESTIONS FOR DISCUSSION AND REVIEW

1. How is controlling defined in the chapter?
2. Discuss the differences among operational, tactical, and strategic control. In today's global marketplaces, which of these types of control do you believe is the most challenging? Be prepared to justify your answer.
3. Describe the six major stages of the controlling process.
4. Identify and discuss eight key result areas for which managers should establish performance standards.
5. Describe three methods managers often use to establish performance standards.
6. Identify and discuss five characteristics of effective controls.
7. Give an example of an ineffective control system you have witnessed or heard about. What changes would you suggest to improve the controls?

PROBLEMS FOR ACTION

A. Assume that the manager of a large city welfare department has asked you to establish controls for his department. Along with other objectives, you are expected to develop a system that will ensure that persons needing welfare services receive them and that persons not entitled to the department's services do not receive them. Furthermore, you have been asked to develop a system through which red tape and overhead costs will be minimized so that the department can allocate resources directly to servicing the requirements of people in need. Identify several points that will guide you in developing controls for this city welfare department.

B. Assume that for approximately 15 years a company has been reasonably successful as a manufacturer and distributor of different types of radios. Recently, however, foreign competitors have gained significant portions of the firm's market share. These gains have reduced the firm's sales volume and profitability. After analyzing this situation, top-level managers in the firm concluded that the quality of their radios must be improved. Based on what you have learned in the chapter, what advice would you offer the top-level managers regarding efforts to establish a successful quality-control program in their company?

CONCLUDING CASE

Controlling Sales Expenses at Deltec Dental Supplies Company

Donald Rinfrow, a district manager for Deltec Dental Supplies Company, has been in charge of the Kansas City district sales office for approximately three months. Rinfrow was transferred to Kansas City to replace Donna Kathmann, who had been in Kansas City for 15 years and had held the position of district sales manager for the last 10 years. Prior to the transfer, Rinfrow had been the assistant manager of the Portland sales district. When reviewing his new assignment with the vice president in charge of sales for the entire company, Rinfrow was told that sales volume in the Kansas City district had not kept pace with the rate of increase shown by other offices of similar size. The vice president advised him that he should first attempt to reduce the costs of operating the Kansas City office and that as soon as costs were under control he should initiate steps to increase sales volume.

Arriving in Kansas City a month prior to Kathmann's retirement, Rinfrow had reviewed the office's operations with her. Kathmann agreed that the Kansas City expenses were higher than those for offices of a similar size. She felt that the difference was due to the size of the district, which covered many more square miles than other, comparably sized offices. When Rinfrow asked to see the records of daily calls made by each sales representative, a list of potential customers, and the names of the new customers for each month, Kathmann answered:

"Donald, I do not bother very much with those kinds of records. Instead, I visit with each of my eight sales reps every morning when they come into the office. I have known every one of them since the first day they started to work here. I know that they have the best interests of Deltec Dental Supplies at heart, and I am certain that they are all working as hard as they can. I help them when asked, but otherwise I allow them to follow their own leads. This approach has made for a very comfortable and enjoyable atmosphere in our office and has not hurt the company."

Following Kathmann's formal retirement, Rinfrow had an opportunity to examine each representative's expense accounts more closely. He discovered that the average expense advance was $550, instead of the $350 maximum allowed by company policy, and that one sales representative had drawn a $1,000 expense advance. Rinfrow realized that in order to bring expenses and sales volume into line with those of other districts in the company, he would have to make a radical change in the method of managing the Kansas City office. As a first step, Rinfrow decided to offer some of his recommended changes in memo form and discuss them at the first of the new weekly meetings he had scheduled for Friday afternoons. A copy of the memorandum is shown.

1. How would you characterize Rinfrow and Kathmann with respect to their methods of exercising organizational control?
2. Is there a need for stricter controls in the Kansas City office? Why?
3. Do you agree that there is a need for the specific controls set forth in Rinfrow's memo? Do you approve of the method Rinfrow is using to establish these controls?
4. How would you have handled this situation if you were Rinfrow? Explain.

To: Sales Representatives, Kansas City District
From: Donald Rinfrow
Date: June 4, 19—
Subject: Controlling of Expenses

Each of you is aware that expenses in the Kansas City District sales office are significantly higher than those in comparable offices. Expenses in this office, for example, are 25 percent higher than those of the Memphis district, which is a district of comparable size. We must immediately bring our expenses into line with those of similar offices in the company. Procedures that will be implemented (effective next Monday) to control expenses in this office are listed below.

- Expense advances will be limited to the $350 per week allowed by company policy. Those of you who have outstanding balances of more than $350 will not be permitted to draw additional advances. Furthermore, the amount in excess of $350 must be returned to the company by the end of this month. If it is not paid by that time, authorization will be requested to deduct the balance in excess of $350 from your salary in three equal monthly installments.
- Sales representatives will no longer report to the office each morning; instead, each rep is expected to phone the office between 9:00 and 9:30 each morning and provide my secretary with a schedule of the calls you intend to make that day. You must also call the office between 1:00 and 1:30 P.M. daily so that we can relay any messages received from customers during the morning.
- Each rep is expected to report to this office in person between 4:00 and 5:00 P.M. each day to review with me the calls made during the day. At that time you will also arrange appointments for calls on large accounts so that I can join you to make the calls on these customers.
- Daily expense records will be maintained and are to be completed each afternoon when you are in the office.
- Prior approval must be obtained for any entertainment expense exceeding $75.
- Monthly time and expense reports must be completed by the 25th of each month, showing the total number of sales calls made, total expenses, and total dollar volume of orders received. These summaries will then be sent to the home office in Chicago. No salary checks will be issued until monthly time and expense reports have been received by the Chicago office.

REFERENCES

1. Lloyd L. Byars, *Strategic Management: Formulation and Implementation* (New York: Harper-Collins, 1991): 214–224.

2. "The Quality Imperative," *Business Week* (special issue for 1991).

3. Terence P. Pare, "Bankers Who Beat the Bust," *Fortune* (November 4, 1991): 159–162.

4. Robert Waterman, *The Renewal Factor* (New York: Bantam Books, 1987).

5. "Success Depends on Leadership," *Fortune* (November 18, 1991): 153–154.

6. Abraham Zaleznik, "Why Managers Lack Vision," *Business Month* (August 1989): 59–64.

7. Brian Dumaine, "Closing the Innovation Gap," *Fortune* (December 2, 1991): 56–62.

8. Judith H. Dobrzynski, "Chairman and CEO: One Hat Too Many," *Business Week* (November 18, 1991): 124.

9. Richard E. Walton, "From Control to Commitment in the Workplace," *Harvard Business Review* (March-April 1985): 76–84.

10. Peter Lorange, Michael F. Scott Morton, and Sumantra Ghosal, *Strategic Control* (St. Paul, MN: West Publishing, 1987): 11.

11. "At Cargill, the Ties That Bind Aren't Binding Anymore," *Business Week* (November 18, 1991): 92–96.

12. "Philip Morris to Restructure Food Operations," *Dallas Morning News* (November 28, 1991): 3D.

13. Peter F. Drucker, *The Practice of Management* (New York:

Harper and Row, 1954).

14. "With Tom Monaghan Back, Can Domino's Deliver?" *Business Week* (October 28, 1991): 136–140.

15. Byars, *Strategic Management: Formulation and Implementation*, 135–139.

16. Noel Tichy and Ram Charan, "Speed, Simplicity, Self-Confidence: An Interview with Jack Welch," *Harvard Business Review* (September-October 1989): 112–120.

17. William Wiggenhorn, "Motorola U: When Training Becomes an Education," *Harvard Business Review* (July-August 1990): 71–83.

18. Michael A. Hitt, Robert E. Hoskisson, R. Duane Ireland, and Jeffrey S. Harrison, "Are Acquisitions a Poison Pill for Innovation?" *The Executive* (November 1991): 22–34.

19. Joseph G. Monks, *Operations Management: Theory and Problems*, 3e (New York: McGraw-Hill, 1987); 229–234.

20. H. Kirk Downey and R. Duane Ireland, "Strategic Objectives in Policy Research," in *Advances in Strategic Management*, vol. 5, edited by Robert W. Lamb (Greenwich, CT: JAI Press, 1988): 263–275.

21. "Reading the Customer Right," *Fortune* (December 2, 1991): 106.

22. Brian Dumaine, "Earning More by Moving Faster," *Fortune* (October 7, 1991): 89–94.

23. "Boeing Knocks Down the Wall Between the Dreamers and Doers," *Business Week* (October 28, 1991): 120–121.

Chapter 16

Controlling Methods and Techniques

OPENING
CASE
. . . .
Controlling the
Construction of
Bill and Dana
Beatty's Home

Recently, Laura Steggman resigned from her job as a bank loan officer to become a partner in her father's construction company. Had she known what was in store for her, she probably would have remained at the bank. Only eight months after she joined the firm, Steggman's father suffered a severe heart attack. His poor health forced her to assume full responsibility for running the firm. Her initial experience in this role proved challenging.

Just prior to his heart attack, Tony Steggman had signed a contract to build a $500,000 "dream home" for Bill and Dana Beatty. The Steggmans personally knew and trusted all of the subcontractors they used to build the Beatty home. Laura Steggman spent many hours checking with subcontractors and suppliers to verify agreements and make certain that the appropriate materials and subcontractors would be present at the building site at the proper time.

The first unplanned event occurred when the basement excavators found a spring. One night, as the excavation neared completion, the water broke through. By morning the pond was four feet deep and rising. This necessitated a $10,000 change in foundation construction and disrupted work schedules for the remainder of the project.

Many of the materials used to build the Beatty home were of higher-than-standard quality. For example, specifications called for wallboard that was ⅝ inch thick instead of the more commonly used ½ inch. The thicker wallboard had to be special-ordered. Because of human error, the order was not placed on time, and that caused a two-week delay. Other delays were created by freezing weather that postponed bricklaying for a month, custom-made windows that did not fit properly, and cabinets that failed to meet specifications.

So painful were the frustrations of this first home-building project that Steggman considered returning to banking. Fortunately, she saw an article in a trade journal. The article described several project control techniques being used in the construction industry, including one called *Program Evaluation Review Technique (PERT)*. After reading the article, Steggman felt better about her chances of operating the Steggman Construction Company successfully.

ETHICS QUESTION
Are there ethical issues
involved with terminating
employees in order to
reduce a firm's costs?

As discussed in the previous chapter, firms must control their activities in order to be effective and efficient. Sometimes, controlling is painful for managers and workers alike. For example, as the newly appointed CEO of Warner-Lambert, one of Melvin Goodes's first actions was to unveil plans to eliminate 8 percent of the firm's workforce (or 2,700 jobs) to control expenses. Also, to better control the firm's diverse activities and its costs, Goodes decided to fold its various businesses into two core groups—pharmaceuticals and consumer products. Goodes believed these actions were necessary for his firm to cope successfully in the 1990s and beyond.[1] Similarly, when Nolan Archibald became the CEO of Black & Decker, his goal was to control costs and turn the firm around. To achieve this, he eliminated 3,000 jobs (13 percent of the workforce) and redesigned the firm's power-tool and appliance lines.[2]

Various control techniques helped Goodes and Archibald accomplish their objectives. Control techniques can also help Laura Steggman complete the Beatty home and become a successful owner/manager of the Steggman Construction Company.

In this chapter we examine the control methods and techniques used in firms today, building on the principles of control described in Chapter 15.

We discuss the nature of budgets first, followed by a review of the types of budgets used most frequently. Next we present the use of ratio analysis as a financial control technique, followed by an explanation of the appropriate use of PERT—a technique managers use to control individual projects. The chapter's final section explains how the success or failure of all controls depends on their acceptance and use by employees.

THE NATURE AND USE OF BUDGETS

A **budget** is a single-use plan expressed in numerical terms. Budgets reflect a firm's planning decisions and are the most commonly used method of organizational control.[3] Budgets are developed for a firm's activities, capital expenditures, and financial position. They provide direction and function as performance standards against which managers measure progress. Among other benefits, budgets motivate employees, coordinate individual and group activities, and provide managers with valuable insights when they assess worker performance.[4]

LEARNING CHECK

Recall from Chapter 5 that a single-use plan is one designed to deal with a planning situation that is expected to occur only once.

Certain characteristics of budgets, as presented in the following list, set them apart from other types of plans.

- A primary reason for preparing a budget is to provide a means of controlling activities.

These managers are working together to prepare their department's portion of the firm's budget. The budget will provide them with direction and performance standards.

- To control operations effectively, managers prepare a separate budget for each cost- and revenue-producing department or function of a firm (the operations or production department, for example).[5] In many instances, managers then prepare individual budgets for each of the several functions within an organizational unit. (For example, the operations department might develop individual budgets for the quality control group, purchases of raw materials, and so forth.)

- A budget covers a specific period of time. The fiscal year is often used, but the year may be subdivided into semiannual, quarterly, monthly, weekly, or even daily periods. With the increasing complexity in marketplaces, the time periods for budgets are becoming shorter. Nevertheless, certain budgets, such as capital expenditure budgets, are prepared for periods longer than a single year.

- A budget is expressed in quantitative terms to foster comparison and coordination of all phases of a firm's activities.

Budget preparation is part of the planning process. However, once prepared, budgets become part of a firm's controls. As discussed in Chapter 15, the first step in controlling is to set performance standards with respect to operations, inventory, sales, administration, and so on. These standards should guide the firm's employees in their efforts to accomplish previously established objectives, strategies, and plans. The budget itself is a set of standards expressed in quantitative terms.

Once the financial performance standards are set, actual results can be measured against these standards. If the firm detects any deviations from budgeted or expected results, it can take appropriate corrective actions. As shown in Figure 16-1, the budget control cycle is similar to the control process depicted in Chapter 15 (Figure 15-3). This highlights the fact that budgetary controls are an important part of the controlling process used by managers.

Types of Budgets

Most organizations develop operating budgets, capital expenditures budgets, and financial budgets (see Figure 16-2). We examine each of these

FIGURE 16-1 Budgets As Managerial Controls

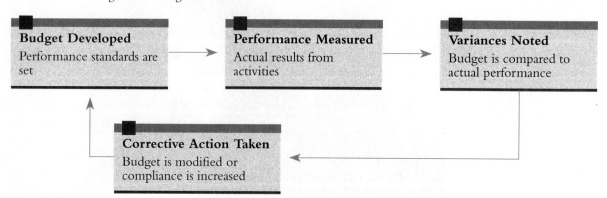

FIGURE 16-2
Types of Budgets

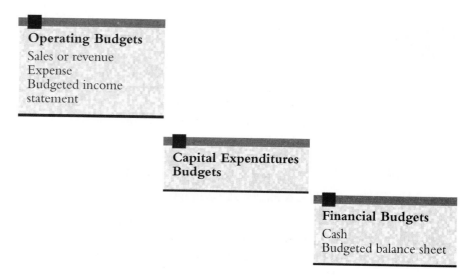

Operating Budgets
Sales or revenue
Expense
Budgeted income
statement

Capital Expenditures Budgets

Financial Budgets
Cash
Budgeted balance sheet

major budget types in the following sections, along with another budget technique—zero-base budgeting.

OPERATING BUDGETS. **Operating budgets** set the target revenues and expenses for a firm's activities over a particular time period. Two important operating budgets are the sales or revenue budget and the expense budget. These are also used to prepare the budgeted income statement.

Sales or Revenue Budget. The **sales budget** or **revenue budget** details all sales anticipated during a period of time. (Because revenues from the sale of goods or services are a firm's primary source of income, the revenue budget often is called the sales budget.) All other budgets must be coordinated with the sales budget, because revenues from sales define the upper limits of expenses and profits. Thus, this budget is the beginning point of the entire budgeting process.

When preparing a sales budget, managers must consider external environmental factors such as general economic conditions, credit availability, competitors' actions, and changes in the purchasing power of key customer groups. They must also examine conditions inside the firm, including the capabilities of its operations and marketing departments. It is difficult for managers to develop accurate sales forecasts, but their accuracy improves with experience.

Large, diversified corporations that compete in several industries develop separate sales budgets for each major good or service and then for each major business unit. For companies competing in several geographic regions with distinct characteristics, breakdowns of expected sales by individual territories are essential. Sometimes a budget will reflect anticipated sales for each type of customer. For example, customer types for a large computer company could include manufacturers, federal government agencies, and colleges and universities, among others. A local restaurant might develop a sales budget for its regular business and one for its catering services.

Expense Budget. A counterpart to the sales budget, the **expense budget** details all expenses anticipated during a period of time. This budget shows all the expenses managers expect to incur in pursuit of an organizational unit's goals. As shown in the Organizations in Action, Japanese firms view costs (or expenses) differently from the way many U.S. corporations view them. Different opinions about what to include in a cost structure affect the items included in a firm's expense budget.

ORGANIZATIONS IN ACTION

One of Japan's most significant competitive advantages is the manner in which many Japanese firms forecast, monitor, and interpret costs. Differences between Japanese and U.S. cost management systems are especially clear in terms of new product development. Typically, a U.S. firm develops a new product and then calculates its cost. If the cost is too high, the firm redesigns the product or decides to accept a reduced profit margin. Japanese firms begin the product development cycle with a target cost that is based on the price they believe the market is most likely to accept. Designers and engineers are then instructed to meet the cost target. This system causes employees to focus on eliminating costs during the planning and design stages rather than the operations stage.

Source: Ford S. Worthy, "Japan's Smart Secret Weapon," *Fortune* (August 12, 1991): 72–75.

ETHICS QUESTION
Given the costs of health care, is it ethical for companies to shift the responsibility for these costs to their employees?

Many managers believe that today's tough economic times require tough bosses.[6] They strive to cut their firms' expenses in what they believe are reasonable ways, but sometimes disagreements surface regarding expense reductions. For example, companies usually want to shift some of the costs of fringe benefits to employees. The cost of one benefit in particular—health care—is growing dramatically. To some firms, transferring more responsibility to the employee for health care costs seems to be a reasonable way to reduce expenses. However, many employees disagree with this view and feel that expenses can be reduced in less painful ways.[7]

Reducing expenses can help a firm to operate more efficiently (that is, to produce more while using fewer workers and materials). When reducing expenses, managers must be careful not to eliminate spending that is required for the firm's long-term health. For example, cutting investment in research and development is one way to reduce expenses in the short term. However, these reductions can limit a firm's future ability to develop innovative goods and services.[8]

Firms should prepare individual budgets for each organizational unit and place them in the hands of the managers of the units. For example, a firm would prepare for its production departments manufacturing budgets that become statements of expense responsibilities for the department managers. Likewise, managers of product/market divisions in the sales department are accountable for keeping the cost of sales within budgeted limits. Expense control problems often result from an ill-defined assignment of responsibility rather than an unwillingness by departmental managers to cooperate in efforts to control expenses.

The department manager is informed of his responsibilities in monitoring the expenses of his department to keep within the budget.

Budgeted Income Statement.   Once a firm has completed its revenue and expense budgets, it combines them to form a budgeted income statement. A **budgeted income statement** is a projection of a firm's revenues and expenses for a period of time. To prepare this income statement, anticipated expenses are combined and then subtracted from total expected revenues to derive projected net income. Projected net income is then compared with the desired income as a standard of acceptability. If this initial projection of net income is unacceptable, various expense and revenue items must be re-examined. Figure 16-3 shows a sample budgeted income statement.

Back to the
Opening Case

There is no information in the opening case indicating that Steggman had developed a sales budget, an expense budget, or a budgeted income statement for the Steggman Construction Company. These budgets could help substantially in her efforts to successfully operate and control the firm her father founded.

CAPITAL EXPENDITURES BUDGETS. The **capital expenditures budget** details the costs of purchasing property, plant and equipment, and other physical assets used to generate revenues over a long period of time. This budget requires the commitment of significant amounts of money for relatively long periods of time. Because of the importance of capital expenditures to development of a firm's strategic plans, top-level managers usually review decisions regarding major capital expenditures.

For large international firms, developing capital budgets is a particular challenge. Determining assets to buy for different strategic business units and operating in different countries are difficult tasks. The challenge becomes even greater when a firm reshapes its character. W. R. Grace & Company, for example, sold off 24 percent of its total assets in order to refashion itself around its core specialty chemical and health-care operations.[9]

FIGURE 16-3
Budgeted Income
Statement

Salinas Sporting Goods Company
for the year ended
December 31, 19XX

Sales		$250,000
Costs of Goods Sold		170,000
Gross Margin		80,000
Operating Expenses:		
Wages and commissions	$42,000	
Rent	9,000	
Depreciation	3,000	
Insurance	1,000	
Miscellaneous	10,000	65,000
Income from Operations		15,000
Interest Expenses		1,000
Net Income		14,000

One problem with capital expenditures is that it is difficult to evaluate their effectiveness. Many projects funded through capital expenditures require support on a continuing basis. A good deal of time may pass before their results can be assessed fully. Today's competitive environment places additional pressure on managers who must prepare capital expenditure budgets, since markets change often and dramatically. Companies that are able to introduce goods or services quickly when faced with rapid change can gain competitive advantages.[10] Therefore, managers must anticipate the future when making capital expenditure decisions.

Even though it may be difficult to evaluate the results of capital expenditure budgeting, there are several important control benefits to be gained from its use. Capital expenditure budgeting (1) improves planning by forcing managers to weigh alternative expenditures; (2) focuses attention on cash flow; and (3) increases coordination among different business units by drawing attention to large expenditures that affect everyone.

Because of the size of many capital expenditure requests, managers should examine each request carefully before providing approval and support. This type of analysis is critical today, when the ability to control costs is an important factor in competitive success.

Sometimes firms can help control costs through better use of existing facilities and current employees. It may even be possible to reduce or postpone capital expenditures. For example, some believe that the effectiveness and efficiency of a firm's manufacturing operations can be improved through frugal manufacturing rather than additional capital expenditures. *Frugal manufacturing* requires managers to do the following:

1. Get the most out of conventional plant and equipment before implementing large automation projects.
2. Maintain control over the firm's manufacturing strategy.
3. Increase a manufacturing unit's ability to modify and customize existing machinery.

ETHICS QUESTION
In your opinion, is the manager who fails to use frugal manufacturing techniques less ethical than the manager who does use these techniques?

4. Approach larger, faster machines and production lines with caution.
5. Understand that automated processes provide benefits, but at a cost—including their effects on people.[11]

Thus, managers must evaluate all capital expenditure requests carefully in order to use the firm's limited resources wisely.

FINANCIAL BUDGETS. **Financial budgets** project how a firm will acquire funds from owners and creditors and how it will manage its cash. Cash budgets and the budgeted balance sheet are parts of financial budgets.

Cash Budgets. A **cash budget** shows the cash available to and the cash needed by a business during a particular time period. This budget is derived from the data used in the revenue and expense budgets. The cash budget is extremely important because any firm, regardless of its size, operates on cash, not profits.[12]

Because of the importance of cash to a firm's activities, managers should monitor cash flow carefully. An uneven cash flow may not leave enough cash to fulfill commitments and may prevent or inhibit efficient operations. For example, if too little cash is on hand to purchase the inventory required to satisfy seasonal sales, managers could be forced to borrow money at high rates. Having sufficient cash on hand also makes it possible to take advantage of cash discounts offered by suppliers. Excess cash may be used for short-term investments, or it may permit an earlier-than-planned capital expenditure.

The traditional process of budgeting cash flow determines the amounts of cash receipts and disbursements expected during the budget period. Analysis of cash flow ensures the availability of adequate cash resources during heavy purchasing and selling seasons. Most of the data required for cash budgeting can be derived from the budgeted income statement, which displays expected revenues and expenses by year, months, or seasons. The cash budget shows planned cash outflows for capital expenditures, bond or other debt retirement, and research and development spending. The cash budget also shows expected cash inflows from issuing stocks or bonds, short-term borrowing, and sales of capital assets. With this information at hand, the firm can prepare a budgeted balance sheet.

Budgeted Balance Sheet. A **balance sheet** lists all of a firm's assets (the resources the firm owns that have value), liabilities (debts payable to outsiders), and owners' equity (the owners' claims to the firm's assets) as of a specific date. A **budgeted balance sheet** (see Figure 16-4) is a projection of a firm's assets, liabilities, and owners' equity as of a future date. This projection shows managers what the firm's financial standing should be at a particular date.

ZERO-BASE BUDGETING. Zero-base budgeting was designed to prevent the common practice of simply increasing allocations to each item based on a previous period's budget. Developed originally by Texas Instruments, the

FIGURE 16-4
Budgeted Balance Sheet

Salinas Sporting Goods Company
December 31, 19XX

Current Assets:		
Cash	$20,000	
Accounts receivable	18,500	
Inventory	41,500	
Prepaid insurance	800	80,800
Fixed Assets:		
Plant and equipment	34,000	
Accumulated depreciation	(12,000)	22,000
Total Assets		$102,800
Current Liabilities:		
Accounts payable	15,000	
Wages and commissions payable	4,000	19,000
Long-Term Liabilities		5,000
Total Liabilities		$24,000
Owner's Equity:		
Common Stock	50,000	
Retained Earnings	28,800	78,800
Total Liabilities and Owner's Equity		$102,800

technique is used extensively in both private- and public-sector organizations.

Zero-base budgeting requires managers to justify budget requests from a starting point of zero rather than from the level of previous allocations. Managers prepare a decision package for each activity under their control. This package includes an analysis of costs, purposes, alternative courses of action, measures of performance, consequences of not performing the activity, and expected benefits. In preparing the budgeted costs, two alternatives are considered: (1) develop different methods of performing the same activity, or (2) define different levels of effort in performing the activity. The focus of zero-base budgeting is to evaluate the decision packages and rank them highest to lowest in benefit to the firm. The firm then makes its funding decisions based on the rank order of the packages.[13] Allocation of resources is based on the contribution of each activity to the accomplishment of organizational objectives.

As is true with all managerial tools and techniques, zero-base budgeting has drawbacks. A serious problem arises from the fact that the judgments involved are often value based and difficult to quantify. For example, a decision as to whether a social agency should continue to be funded may rest almost solely on the philosophy of the decision makers. Those who believe in lean government and maximum private enterprise may be predisposed to cut agencies that others consider vital. In for-profit businesses, decisions to discontinue a product line or sell an entire business unit are also influenced strongly by key decision makers' philosophies. Thus, zero-base budgeting can become highly politicized in both public and private organizations. In addition, the time required for managers to develop decision packages for each of their activities can substantially increase the costs of zero-base budgeting.

Although it is expensive and difficult to apply with total objectivity, zero-base budgeting is often a useful and cost-effective control technique. Analyzing each separate function offers managers an opportunity to introduce efficiency measures that are less likely to be applied when using traditional budgeting methods. The use of zero-base budgeting in one company is described in the Manager in Action.

MANAGER IN ACTION

As the newly appointed CEO of the Campbell Soup Company, David Johnson took immediate action. Plants were closed, corporate headquarters' staff released, and hundreds of millions of dollars charged to earnings in order to restructure the firm. Johnson believed these actions were necessary to reorganize an inefficient company. A key issue was finding ways for the business units, such as soups, Swanson frozen foods, Pepperidge Farm baked goods, and Franco-American pastas and gravies, to operate more cooperatively.

To encourage cooperation, Johnson imposed the use of zero-base budgeting on each unit. During this process, he challenged every budget, including the one for the "sacred" soup division. Executives in each unit were told that they had no more dollars and that their challenge was to justify every dollar they intended to request. In preparing their budget in this manner, soup executives discovered that 10 percent of their marketing budget was being wasted. Talking about these savings, an executive said, "The 10 percent is the elimination of the stupid."

Source: Adapted from Bill Saporito, "Campbell Soup Gets Piping Hot," *Fortune* (September 9, 1991): 142–148.

Benefits and Potential Pitfalls of Budgeting

A firm cannot operate effectively without budgets. Budgets tell the firm how it intends to obtain and use resources and whether or not those intentions have been met.

However, budgets are not without weaknesses. First, budget preparation can be time consuming. Managers must make sure that employees commit appropriate amounts of time to budgeting activities. Second, when examining budgets, managers must not confuse symptoms with causes. A decline in sales revenues does not necessarily suggest the need for greater sales effort. Instead, the actual cause may be an inferior product, competitors' actions, or general economic conditions. Finally, there is a danger of rigidity. Even when used as controls, budgets are only guidelines for actions. Managers must constantly reevaluate internal and external conditions to verify that the assumptions under which their budgets were developed still apply.

FINANCIAL RATIO ANALYSIS

Financial **ratio analysis** is used by both managers and outside investors and lenders to analyze a firm's financial position. Outside investors and lenders use ratios to determine the risk involved in lending money to the firm or purchasing its stock. However, our concern here is how managers use ratio analysis as a control technique. Managers use ratios to gauge the firm's performance and to compare its performance with past years' outcomes and the performances of competitors.[14] Ratio analysis provides single figures that place a particular value—such as sales, debt, or profits—in context. Managers then can evaluate the quality of the firm's current position, how the firm's position has changed over time, and how the firm compares to competitors in terms of performance and current standing. Ratio analysis identifies areas requiring further attention.

The ratios that managers use are grouped into several categories. Four of the most prominent are liquidity, asset management, profitability, and debt management.

Liquidity Ratios

Liquidity ratios measure a firm's ability to pay off its short-term liabilities out of its liquid assets, and by doing so, remain solvent. The current ratio and the quick ratio are used most frequently to assess liquidity.

In the *current ratio*, current assets include cash, accounts receivable, prepaid expenses, marketable securities, and inventory. Current liabilities include accounts and short-term notes payable and other short-term obligations.

$$\text{Current Ratio} = \frac{\text{Current Assets}}{\text{Current Liabilities}}$$

The *quick ratio*, sometimes called the *acid test ratio*, is calculated by dividing current assets (usually cash, accounts receivable, prepaid expenses, and marketable securities, less inventory) by current liabilities.

$$\text{Quick Ratio} = \frac{\text{Current Assets} - \text{Inventory}}{\text{Current Liabilities}}$$

Although it is considered part of current assets when calculating the current ratio, inventory is excluded in the quick ratio. The reason for this is that considerable time may be required to convert a firm's inventory into cash or negotiable securities.

A poor current ratio may imply that current assets should be increased or that current liabilities should be lowered. If current liabilities are increasing faster than current assets, the current ratio will fall. By comparing current ratios over time, managers can clearly spot the financial difficulties. If the values of a firm's current or quick ratio are far below the average for its industry, managers (and creditors) should be on the alert.

Asset Management Ratios

Asset management ratios determine how effectively a firm is using its resources. These ratios are designed to answer the question: Is the amount of each type of asset owned the right amount in view of current and projected sales? Businesses usually must borrow money to acquire assets (capital expenditures). If a firm has too many assets, its interest expense will be too high and its profits will be lowered. However, if assets—especially inventory—are too low, sales may be lost. Three indicators of asset management effectiveness are the asset turnover ratio, the fixed asset turnover ratio, and the inventory turnover ratio.

The *asset turnover ratio* reflects how effectively a firm is employing its total assets. Total assets include current assets (cash, accounts receivable, prepaid expenses, marketable securities, and inventory) and net fixed assets (plant and equipment less accumulated depreciation). The asset turnover ratio is determined by dividing net sales by total assets.

$$\text{Asset Turnover Ratio} = \frac{\text{Net Sales}}{\text{Total Assets}}$$

The *fixed asset turnover ratio* is similar to the asset turnover ratio. The difference is that current assets are not included in the calculation of the fixed asset turnover ratio. The advantage of the fixed asset turnover ratio is that it shows how effectively fixed assets are being used. This is important for managers to know because fixed assets usually require major capital expenditures. The fixed asset turnover ratio is calculated by dividing net sales by net fixed assets.

$$\text{Fixed Asset Turnover Ratio} = \frac{\text{Net Sales}}{\text{Net Fixed Assets}}$$

The *inventory turnover ratio* is calculated by dividing net sales by inventory. This ratio indicates how often a firm's inventory is being turned over, or sold, during a particular time period, usually one year. Generally, firms producing small, relatively inexpensive products turn inventories over more frequently than do companies producing large, expensive products. In comparison to past years or industry averages, a low inventory turnover implies a large investment in inventory compared to the amount needed for sales. Excess inventory ties up resources. However, if inventory turnover is too high, inventories are too small and sales may be lost when customer orders cannot be filled.

$$\text{Inventory Turnover Ratio} = \frac{\text{Net Sales}}{\text{Inventory}}$$

Debt Management Ratios

Debt management ratios indicate the firm's ability to meet its short- and long-term debt obligations. *Leverage* is a measure of the extent to which a firm has financed its activities with debt. The measure of leverage used most frequently is the *debt-to-equity ratio*. A high debt-to-equity ratio indicates that a large share of financing is from debt; that is, the firm is using a great deal of leverage. Long-term creditors prefer to see a modest debt-to-equity ratio because it indicates that the owners have a significant share (equity) and the risk to creditors is lower. The debt-to-equity ratio is calculated by dividing total liabilities by owner's equity.

$$\text{Debt-to-Equity Ratio} = \frac{\text{Total Liabilities}}{\text{Owner's Equity}}$$

In general, a firm's total liabilities should not exceed its equity; that is, this ratio should not be greater than one-to-one. If liabilities exceed equity, creditors have a greater stake in the firm than do the firm's owners.

Profitability Ratios

A firm's long-term survival rests on its ability to provide satisfactory returns to its shareholders. **Profitability ratios** measure the net returns on sales and total assets. These ratios show the combined effects of liquidity, asset management, and debt management on operating results. They are overall indicators of how well a firm is being managed. Poor performance here indicates a basic failure that, if not corrected, could put the firm out of business. Two measures frequently used to examine profitability are the return on total assets ratio and the profit margin on sales ratio.

The *return on total assets ratio* measures the amount a firm earned on each dollar of assets invested in its activities. It is the total return to stockholders and lenders on the total investment they have made in the firm. Because it combines the effects of the firm's profit margin and its asset turnover, the return on total assets ratio is an important measure of the firm's profitability over a period of time. The return on total assets ratio is calculated by dividing net income by total assets.

$$\text{Return on Total Assets Ratio} = \frac{\text{Net Income}}{\text{Total Assets}}$$

The *profit margin on sales ratio* measures income per dollar of sales. The ratio shows what percentage of a firm's revenue dollars became net income. It is often useful in analyzing the possible contribution of new products or when considering the elimination of current products. Comparisons with competing firms in the same industry are also useful and advisable. A value below the industry average indicates that the firm's sales are too low, or costs are too high, or both. The profit margin on sales ratio is calculated by dividing net income by sales.

$$\text{Profit Margin on Sales Ratio} = \frac{\text{Net Income}}{\text{Sales}}$$

LEARNING CHECK   Describe the four major categories of ratios used to evaluate a firm's performance.

Recommendations for Interpreting Ratios

Financial ratio analysis is a widely used control method. However, two issues surface when these ratios are used. First, no precise means exist for determining whether a value is an acceptable or unacceptable ratio. To address this issue, ratios should be calculated over a period of time, say annually for 10 years. The ratios can be graphed against years to analyze trends. Then managers can see whether the situation is improving or worsening. In addition, it is important to compare a firm's ratios with those of its competitors or the industry average. Several sources of comparative data are available to managers. Among the most widely used are Dun & Bradstreet's *Industry Norms* and *Key Business Ratios*, Standard and Poor's *Statistical Service*, Moody's *Manuals on Investment*, the Value Line *Investment Survey*, and various federal government agencies' reports.[15]

A second issue in the use of financial ratios sometimes arises when managers infer unwarranted causal relationships. For example, a marketing manager might conclude that a decrease in the profit margin on sales ratio is due to an increase in selling expenses. However, the actual cause could be a decrease in unit price. A correlation between two variables can never be interpreted without reference to other causative data. Most faulty inferences result when managers do not closely examine the accuracy of data used to calculate a particular ratio.

When used properly, financial ratio analysis provides managers with important insights. As a tool of internal control, ratio analysis shows managers how effectively a firm is using its assets, inventories, and financial resources. Comparisons with the firm's performance in previous time periods and the performance of competitors help managers focus on areas that need attention.

PROJECT CONTROLS

Another control technique is used to manage specific projects. A **project** is a set of interrelated activities that, when completed, result in a salable product. The success of any project is influenced by effective control of resources, costs, quality, and budgets.[16] However, controlling large, complex projects is often difficult. To help control such projects, managers may use techniques that analyze *networks*, or the interrelationships among tasks. In this section, we will discuss PERT (Program Evaluation Review Technique), a project control technique often used by today's managers .

PERT was used first in the development of the Polaris Fleet Ballistic Missile for the U.S. Navy. This was an extremely complex project involving more than 3,000 agencies and contractors. PERT is credited with saving two years in the development of the Polaris missile.

PERT is widely used today in both government and industry. Recently, General Electric used PERT to upgrade the A-10 Thunderbolt II (a major ground support plane for the U.S. Air Force). PERT networks are used to design and construct major facilities, conduct research and development, and complete environmental studies, among other projects.[17] For example, GTE uses PERT to manage activities ranging from planning the project proposal through implementation of major telephone installation projects. To use PERT effectively, the following conditions must be satisfied:

1. *A starting point.* There must be an identifiable starting point for the project. Receipt of a sales order for the manufacture of a specialized piece of equipment is an example. Recall in this chapter's opening case that the Beattys had agreed to have Laura Steggman build a home for them. Signing a contract for the home was an identifiable starting point for the project.

2. *Clearly recognizable events.* An **event** is a performance milestone representing the start or finish of an activity. Events are individual points in time. In building the Beattys' home, completing the foundation and finishing the framing and roofing could be events. The actual completion of a major project, such as the Polaris missile, building a shopping center, or installing a management information system, is also an event.

3. *A series of activities.* An **activity** is work that must be completed in order to progress from one event to another. When constructing a highway interchange, many activities and events must be accomplished. Among other activities, temporary routes must be built, bridges constructed, drainage facilities installed, and service roads prepared. The completion of all activities related to a particular temporary route could be an event. In the Beattys' home, excavation and pouring concrete could be activities involved in completing the foundation. Building the entire home might involve 30 or more activities and 10 to 15 events.

4. *Time for each activity.* The time required for completion of the activities preceding each event must be calculated. For some projects, these estimates can be based on previous experience. When working on a new project, however, time estimation is more difficult.

Pouring the concrete for a new home foundation is a clearly recognizable event, or performance milestone, in a PERT network.

Figure 16-5 illustrates a PERT network. Each square in the figure represents an *event*. For this project, 10 events must be accomplished in order for the entire project to be completed. The numbers on the lines represent the days required to complete individual *activities*. The arrows indicate the sequence of activities leading to the achievement of the different events. The arrows shown in blue represent the critical path. The **critical path** is the longest chain, in time, of events and activities from start to finish. The critical path determines the duration of a project; if any activities along it are delayed, the entire project will be delayed. If the duration of a project must be shortened, it can be accomplished only by reducing the time needed to complete activities along the critical path. Reducing the time used to complete activities along another path in the PERT network will not reduce the total time required for the project; it will merely create more slack—excess time in other PERT pathways.

Consider the PERT network shown in Figure 16-5. Assume that the project is the manufacture of a complicated machine for a key customer. Notice that the network includes activities (Activity A through Activity J) and events (E1 through E10). Individual activities must be completed for events to be accomplished.

The project begins with issuance of a sales order (see E1, which is the first event in the project). The project will be completed when it passes final inspection (E10). As an activity, this inspection is estimated to take only one day after completion of the final assembly (E9). The final assembly activity requires two days (Activity I). However, final assembly cannot begin until the subassembly of all electrical components (E8) and all mechanical components (E7) is finished. (A thick arrow is drawn between E7 and E8 to show that Activity I cannot begin until Events 7 and 8 are both finished.)

To perform the mechanical subassembly, components must be released by the milling department (E4) and the lathe department (E5). The activity

FIGURE 16-5 A PERT Network

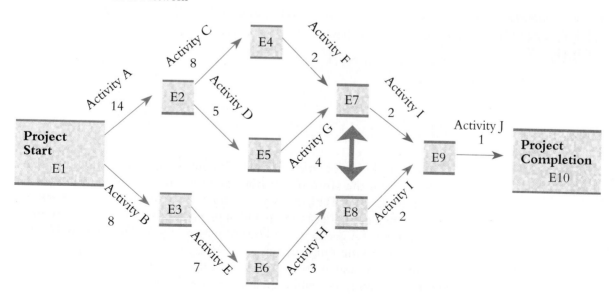

requiring the greatest time is Activity A. As shown in the figure, 14 days is the estimated time needed to obtain the mechanical components required to build the machine. In this example, the *critical path* (events E1 to E2 to E4 to E7 to E9 to E10) is 27 days long. The total amount of time for this project can be shortened only by reducing the amount of time needed to complete activities on the critical path.

Evaluation of Project Control Techniques

Three important benefits result from using PERT as a control technique. First, a PERT network requires careful planning and contributes to developing objective, structured, and flexible plans. Second, constructing a network diagram identifies a project's critical path, which is important for control purposes. Knowledge of the key events and activities in a complex project encourages managers to be forward-looking in their use of controls. These controls will prompt corrective action before serious deviations from schedules occur. Third, network analysis shows clearly the relationships among the various components of a complex project. Thus, it provides opportunities to improve both communication patterns and organizational structure.

However, project control techniques do have limitations. A PERT diagram does not show that, in cases where one activity must precede another, it might be possible to combine and work on two activities simultaneously. A second limitation is the possibility that the activities involved in a project can change over time. A network diagram developed at the start of a project could limit a manager's flexibility in dealing with later events that are created by changing conditions. Finally, experience suggests that an adhocratic (task force or project) form of organization is necessary to obtain maximum benefits from the use of PERT.

LEARNING CHECK   Describe PERT and how it is used to help control large, complex projects.

BEHAVIORAL REACTIONS TO CONTROL

Organizational controls affect people. The success or failure of controls depends more on the attitudes of those subjected to control than it does on the technique used. Responses may vary from open hostility and resentment to complete understanding and appreciation of the need for controls. In some instances, resistance to control may not be totally undesirable. Interpreted as a symptom, resistance to controls may alert managers to the need for improvements in the controls. Effective managers try to identify the sources of resistance and then address those concerns.

Why Resistance Develops

ETHICS QUESTION
Is the manager who is not
concerned with the effects
of controls on employees
less ethical than the
manager who is concerned
about these effects?

Some people resist any form of control because it poses a threat to their individuality and self-esteem. Unique problems surface when managers fail to recognize this. Problems also occur when managers develop controls without consideration of employees' needs for different types and degrees of controls. For example, controls used with research personnel should not be the same as those used with production employees because the performance standards differ for these two groups.

Several factors can cause resistance to controls. Four of these are standards that are too demanding, inaccurate measurements, controls that impede action, and aversion to corrective action.

STANDARDS THAT ARE TOO DEMANDING. Sometimes an initial reaction to control standards is that they are unreasonable or too demanding. This reaction is especially likely when managers apply controls without explanation. Often, managers can overcome these initial reactions by describing why the controls are necessary and how they will help accomplish the firm's and the employee's objectives.

However, some employees may not be committed to achieving objectives and meeting standards even if the need for both has been explained carefully. When this occurs, managers must work with employees to reevaluate the reasons for and the nature of the controls being used. After analysis, the controls may be modified. However, it is also possible that managers will conclude that the controls are legitimate. Failure to accept this decision should result in corrective actions for employees who refuse to comply with the standards.

Standards may also appear to be too demanding because of their day-to-day administration. Regardless of how carefully standards have been developed, unexpected conditions may arise that make their attainment impossible. Machine breakdowns and unsatisfactory raw materials may lower the output of production employees. Increased competition or unseasonable weather can affect the performance of a sales representative. In special cases, the effective manager notes the reasons for variances from standards and does not place undue pressure on employees to meet them.

ETHICS QUESTION
Are there any ethical issues
involved when
performance standards
continue to become more
demanding over time?

A final comment about performance standards is appropriate before completing this section. Because of increased global competition, managers and employees alike must understand the need for their performances to be measured by more-exacting standards. Even companies such as IBM and Honda, long known for lifetime employment opportunities, now find it necessary to establish and then upgrade rigorous, yet appropriate performance standards.[18] To help employees cope, managers must be certain that they have opportunities to gain the skills they need to perform effectively in a demanding, competitive environment.[19]

INACCURATE MEASUREMENTS. In some instances, performance standards are accepted even though many believe the measurements are inaccurate. Any time it is difficult to collect measurements, skepticism about their accuracy tends to be high. This is often the case with merit ratings and certain judgments of product quality. Other factors usually are involved when measurements are criticized as inaccurate. For example, a first-level manager may complain about budgetary control because the information provided by the control is not timely enough to be useful in making operating decisions.

A frequent criticism is that the performance standards used are satisfactory as far as they go, but they do not begin to measure all that the employee achieves. There is often the feeling that not all important variables are being measured. For example, a first-level operations manager may agree that physical output is an accurate indicator of what is being produced. However, he notes that it reveals nothing about the decline in the number of units that fail final inspection. A sales representative may agree that the dollar volume statement of sales is accurate. At the same time, she complains that its use as a performance standard is inappropriate because it does not reflect the number of new accounts opened or the travel time needed to contact customers. Before taking corrective action, a manager should make sure that all significant aspects of an employee's performance are being measured.

One bitter complaint regarding measurements in the control process is that they do not measure effort. For example, a student may receive a grade of C on an assignment that in her opinion was worthy of a B because of the effort expended. This problem is worsened by individual differences in ability and skill. One employee might expend significant effort yet produce less than another employee who does not work as hard. Effective managers are sensitive to each employee's ability and, as fitting, commend employees for outstanding effort. This tends to lessen the normal resistance of employees to having their work measured, especially when performance is not equal to expectations.

IMPEDING ACTIONS. Controls are necessary to coordinate a firm's actions. However, controls should not become so extensive that they burden employees unnecessarily. The challenge to managers is to develop controls that are consistent with demands from various groups (such as federal and state governments) but also permit employees some freedom in the way they complete their jobs. For example, the president of Gateway 2000, a computer producer, wants to establish the type of controls required to run a larger firm, yet maintain the flexibility needed to compete in a rapidly changing marketplace.[20]

AVERSION TO CORRECTIVE ACTION. Controls influence a firm's employees directly. Employees typically fear and dislike corrective actions taken as the result of failure to meet performance standards. However, they often believe that poor performance will be overlooked and, if detected, will be excused when they provide explanations.

One reason employees dislike corrective action is that it often takes the form of personal criticism. Criticism can never be completely impersonal, even though it may be based on an objective analysis of facts. As a result, most people tend to reject at least a part of any criticism and to interpret the criticism with some defensiveness. Effective managers always make it clear that the concern is not with the individual, but with particular behaviors that prevent the individual from meeting performance standards. Used in this manner, it is less likely that control-oriented feedback will be viewed as a criticism of the employee's character.

LEARNING CHECK Name and describe four factors that can cause resistance to organizational controls.

Effective Use of Controls

Fortunately, managers can minimize resistance to controls. A major influence on the effectiveness of a firm's controls is the leadership style of its managers. The motivational methods used by managers play an especially important role. Moreover, managers who were active in the development of a firm's controls will provide greater support to those controls than will managers who were not involved. It is difficult to conform to controls that are in no sense one's own. That is one reason why the organization-wide controls of some large, impersonal companies tend to be met with passive—and sometimes even active—resistance.

SUMMARY

Budgets are the form of control used most widely in organizations. The chapter discussed operating, capital expenditure, and financial budgets. The first two operating budgets—the sales budget and the expense budget—are summary statements of the forecasts of all the firm's subunits. The sales budget reflects managers' expectations for total sales volume over a certain time period. The expense budget shows the costs required to achieve a given volume of production and sales, along with the anticipated costs for all other departments. The third operating budget is the budgeted income statement, which shows a firm's projected net income for a period of time. It is based on the sales and expense budgets. If projected income is unacceptable, managers can reexamine the sales and expense budgets to identify areas where they can make changes.

The capital expenditures budget describes the costs of purchasing the plant and equipment needed to produce the firm's products. This budget reflects long-term financial commitments. Finally, financial budgets show how a firm intends to raise money from owners and creditors and how it will manage its cash. The cash budget describes the cash availability and cash requirements of a firm for a particular budget period. The budgeted balance sheet lists the firm's anticipated assets, liabilities, and owners' equity as of a specified date. Zero-base budgeting, which requires managers to justify budget amounts anew at the beginning of each budget period, is used in many organizations. The practice is useful, but it is also very time consuming and may become politicized.

In general, budgets provide a wide range of benefits including improved planning efforts and the expression of standards in quantitative terms. Nonetheless, managers must remember that budgets are only guidelines for action. Budgets whose contents become inflexible objectives can reduce a firm's innovativeness and ultimately hinder its success in the marketplace.

Financial ratio analysis is an important means of control. By calculating various ratios, managers can identify areas that need attention. Comparisons to previous years' ratios and to those of competing firms provide additional insight regarding a firm's performance over a particular time period.

Liquidity ratios (the current ratio and the quick ratio) provide information about a firm's ability to meet its short-term obligations. Asset management ratios describe how effectively resources are being used. Three asset management ratios are asset turnover, fixed asset turnover, and inventory turnover. Debt management ratios show the firm's ability to meet its long-term obligations. The debt-to-equity ratio is a debt management ratio. Profitability ratios are an overall measure of how effectively an organization is being managed and reflect the firm's ability to survive in the long term. The return on total assets ratio and the profit margin on sales ratio are measures of the firm's profitability.

Project controls are used in the management of special projects such as the development of a new product or service or the construction of a major office building. One widely used project control—PERT—was described in the chapter. Project controls help managers control highly complex projects such as developing an experimental model of a new automobile or aircraft. Such projects have definite starting and ending points and a series of activities and events for which time requirements can be assessed. The critical path is the longest path in the network.

Resistance to controls often develops among a firm's employees. Controls slow down action and may be viewed as too demanding or constricting. Other factors that may cause resistance are the possibility of inaccurate measurements and an aversion to corrective actions. To be successful, managers must cope with resistance in an effective manner.

KEY TERMS

budget
operating budgets
sales budget or revenue budget
expense budget
budgeted income state-

ment
capital expenditures budget
financial budgets
cash budget
balance sheet

budgeted balance sheet
zero-base budgeting
ratio analysis
liquidity ratios
asset management ratios
debt management ratios

profitability ratios
project
event
activity
critical path

QUESTIONS FOR DISCUSSION AND REVIEW

1. What are the differences among the sales, expense, capital, and cash budgets? As a top-level manager, which of these budgets would be of primary interest to you? Why?
2. Describe how zero-base budgeting might help a firm control its activities better.
3. What are the four major categories of financial ratios described in the chapter? How do managers use the results of these ratio analyses as control techniques?

4. Describe PERT. How can this technique help managers control complex projects?
5. What are four causes of resistance to organizational controls?
6. Assume that you overheard the following comment: "During the 1990s, I believe that the performance standards for managers will continue to be strengthened." Accept or reject this statement and prepare a justification for your answer.

PROBLEMS FOR ACTION

A. Late in their junior year, two students have an opportunity to take over a small pizza business located just west of the college campus. The lease on the pizza parlor can be acquired without a fee. Both students think they can work at least 30 hours per week at the parlor. They also believe many of their friends will buy pizzas from them. At a minimum, what budgets would you recommend that the two students develop before reaching a final decision about this opportunity? Explain your recommendations.

B. On many college campuses, course registration is challenging and time consuming. Some of the activities involved with registration include degree planning, examining course offerings, meeting with advisers, obtaining a registration packet, being admitted to classes, securing parking permits, paying fees, dropping and adding courses, and adjusting fees payments. List the events involved in registration at your college or university, show the approximate time spans involved in each activity, and list possible alternative paths. Using a PERT network, diagram these events and activities and trace the critical path.

CONCLUDING CASE

Control at Moreno and Associates

Life had always gone well for Jules Moreno. An excellent student, Moreno's favorite subject was mathematics. During high school, Moreno spent many hours working with his family's personal computer. Moreno's father, an electrical engineer for a local utility company, bought the PC originally to work on a few projects during the evenings. At first, Moreno was fascinated by computer games—particularly ones dealing with mathematical applications in futuristic settings. This initial interest was soon replaced by an interest in writing his own programs, using the BASIC language.

After graduating from high school, Moreno pursued a degree in computer science at the state university. Following his first two years at the university, Moreno added management information systems as a concentration. He believed the combination of a computer science degree with a working knowledge of how to use hardware and software in a business setting would serve him well.

Moreno worked hard throughout his college years. Based on his skills and excellent references from his professors, he started his career at a major software development firm. Much to his dismay, Moreno found his work in this firm unsatisfying. In fact, he quickly became disgruntled with the requirements of working in a bureaucracy. Based on what they believed was a workable business idea, Moreno and two of his co-workers started their own consulting firm.

The firm, called Moreno and Associates, specialized in helping companies develop computer systems. While their clients' needs varied, a substantial portion of the work involved controls, particularly inventory control and financial records.

Moreno and Associates was immediately successful. In only eight months, the firm had hired another nine people. Each had excellent computer skills, but like Moreno and his partners, none was an experienced business manager. Because he held the largest share of ownership and everyone considered him the key person in the firm, Moreno realized that he had to do something if Moreno and Associates were to thrive and grow.

When there were only the three partners, Moreno did not think it was necessary to establish any procedures, rules, or budgets. Everything seemed simple at first. The three partners joined forces to develop a system for each client. With increased growth, this was no longer possible. Now, with the firm working on a large number of projects simultaneously, individuals had to be assigned responsibility for entire projects and they had to file reports reflecting the progress being made.

Furthermore, the company's financial matters had become more complex. In the early days, the three partners had paid themselves minimal salaries in order to have enough left over to pay their bills and keep the business going. Now, however, they had to pay the employees reasonable wages on a regular basis. Thus, it became necessary to prepare various budgets in order to monitor expenses and determine how resources should be allocated.

Perhaps the most troubling problem was the need for the firm's employees to adopt more routine work schedules. The people employed by Moreno and Associates were creative. The nature of their work allowed them to complete some of their assignments away from the office. However, the business was becoming large and complex enough to require interactions among workers. This was impossible if employees were almost never at their desks.

In response to these issues, Moreno established a range of policies, procedures, and rules. Primarily, these controls called for employees to be more accountable for their time and expenses and for the firm to develop budgets. (The specific types of budgets to be prepared were not specified.) This information was communicated to employees through a policy manual written by Moreno.

Moreno was disappointed by the employees' neg-

ative reaction to the standards stated in the policy manual and the suggestion that formal budgets were necessary. They complained that the standards would stifle their creativity and prevent them from completing their work successfully. The resignation of two employees within a month of the manual's distribution caused Moreno to worry even more about the firm's future. How ironic it was, Moreno thought, that Moreno and Associates specialized in developing controls for other firms yet was apparently incapable of developing its own controls.

1. From information presented in the chapter, what budgets would you recommend to Moreno and Associates? Why?
2. What factors may be causing the resistance to controls described in this case?
3. In your opinion, what procedures should have been followed by Moreno to develop organizational controls in this firm?

REFERENCES

1. "Curing Warner-Lambert—Before It Gets Sick," *Business Week* (December 9, 1991): 91–94.
2. "The Screws Are Tightening at Black & Decker," *Business Week* (September 23, 1991): 61–64.
3. Charles T. Horngren and Walter T. Harrison, *Accounting*, 2e (Englewood Cliffs, NJ: Prentice-Hall, 1992): 921.
4. Horngren and Harrison, *Accounting*, 922.
5. Belverd E. Needles, Jr., Henry R. Anderson, and James C. Caldwell, *Financial & Managerial Accounting* (Boston: Houghton Mifflin, 1988): 790.
6. "Tough Times, Tough Bosses," *Business Week* (November 25, 1991): 174–185.
7. Jeremy Main, "The Battle Over Benefits," *Fortune* (December 16, 1991): 91–96.
8. Michael A. Hitt, Robert E. Hoskisson, R. Duane Ireland, and Jeffrey Harrison, "The Effects of Acquisitions on R&D Inputs and Outputs," *Academy of Management Journal* (September 1991): 693–706.
9. "The Word at Grace: If It's Not Selling, Sell It," *Business Week* (December 16, 1991): 57–58.
10. Joseph T. Vesey, "The New Competitors: They Think in Terms of Speed to the Market," *The Executive* (May 1991): 23–33.
11. Richard J. Schonberger, "Frugal Manufacturing," *Harvard Business Review* (September-October 1987): 95–100.
12. James McNeill Stancil, "When Is There Cash in Cash Flow?"

Harvard Business Review (March-April 1987): 38–49.
13. Milton F. Usry, Lawrence H. Hammer, and William K. Carter, *Cost Accounting: Planning and Control,* 10e (Cincinnati: South-Western Publishing, 1991): 475.
14. This section is based on materials included in Eugene E. Brigham, *Fundamentals of Financial Management*, 6e (New York: Dryden Press, 1991): 49–60; and Lawrence D. Schall and Charles W. Haley, *Introduction to Financial Management*, 5e (New York: McGraw-Hill, 1991): 508–522.
15. Thomas Wheelen and J. David Hunger, *Strategic Management and Business Policy,* 4e (Reading, MA: Addison-Wesley, 1992): 418–420.
16. Jay Heizer and Barry Render, *Production and Operations Management*, 2e (Boston: Allyn and Bacon, 1991): 602.
17. Everett E. Adam and Ronald J. Ebert, *Production and Operations Management*, 5e (Englewood Cliffs, NJ: Prentice-Hall, 1992): 338–339.
18. "The New IBM," *Business Week* (December 16, 1991): 112–118; and Alex Taylor, "A U.S.-Style Shakeup at Honda," *Fortune* (December 30, 1991): 115–120.
19. Peter F. Drucker, "The New Productivity Challenge," *Harvard Business Review* (November-December 1991): 69–79.
20. Andrew Kuper, "The Champ of Cheap Clones," *Fortune* (September 23, 1991): 115–120.

Operations Management and Controlling

OPENING CASE

General Motors: A Time for Change?

Over 40 years ago, the president of General Motors observed that what was good for the country was good for General Motors and vice versa. This often-repeated statement suggests the pervasive and significant effects of General Motors' operations in the United States.

Although the General Motors of the 1990s is substantially different from that of the 1950s, the company remains a dominant force in the U.S. economy. In early 1992, GM's U.S. workforce consisted of 429,000 salaried and hourly workers (its workforce world wide totaled 756,300). The firm's U.S. workforce equalled the size of the population of Fort Worth, Texas, the nation's 30th largest city. Approximately 21 percent of that workforce was made up of people from minority groups, making GM the largest private employer of minorities in the United States. The 30,000 suppliers and 10,000 dealers working with GM provided enough jobs to populate another large city. The company was the nation's largest consumer of steel, rubber, glass, plastic, and carpeting. In the eyes of some analysts, it is difficult to image a prosperous U.S. economy without a prosperous automobile industry, including a prosperous General Motors.

However, as measured by some key performance standards, GM's recent performances have been troubling. In 1991, for example, GM lost an average of $1,500 on every one of the 3.5 million automobiles and trucks it manufactured in North America. At the same time, the firm was 40 percent less productive than Ford, one of its chief rivals. GM's share of the U.S. automobile market was 35 percent in 1991, down from 46 percent in 1979.

What is needed for GM to improve its performance? Clearly, answers to this question are many and varied. But, according to some of GM's top-level managers, the firm must become more productive and efficient in its production processes. They believe that GM has to reduce the number of labor-hours required to build a car; eliminate all "fat" from its production processes; and improve coordination among designers, product engineers, and manufacturing specialists. Some of GM's managers say that because the "glory days" of traditional mass production have passed, both plants and people will have to be more flexible. Automobile workers will no longer be able to do the same job on the same type of car five days a week. Employees will have to be cross trained so they can develop multiple skills to complete a variety of tasks.

Thus, for GM to be successful during the 1990s and beyond, flexible production facilities with multiskilled and well-trained employees must become its way of doing business. With these capabilities as a foundation, it is more likely that GM will be able to respond quickly and effectively to the challenges of a global marketplace.

Source: Alex Taylor, "Can GM Remodel Itself?" *Fortune* (January 13, 1992): 26–33; "GM's Leaders Go On the Record," *Fortune* (March 9, 1992): 51-60; and "Toyota CEO Pay Appeals to Stempel," *Dallas Morning News* (March 31, 1992): 16-17D.

Alarmed by market share losses and the need to become more productive, GM is but one of many firms in which managers are reexamining how their company's operations are managed. Some companies are dealing with these challenges successfully. In other cases, managers have a great deal of work ahead of them if their firms are to compete effectively in the global marketplace.[1]

Like much of American industry, GM long relied on **mass production**—a process through which large numbers of a product are produced using standardized procedures—for its success. In more stable times, when foreign competition was not a serious threat and customers' purchasing intentions were easy to predict, mass production was an effective process to use in producing a company's products.

However, mass production is designed primarily to help firms gain ever-larger shares of an individual product's market. During the 1970s and 1980s, foreign competitors began to pursue different goals. Instead of concentrating on market share, these firms started using techniques to help them improve the efficiency of their production processes, enhance the productivity of their workers, and—perhaps most important of all—produce products that would set new standards for product quality. Decision makers in these firms believed that market share gains would come as a result of achieving the company's rigorous efficiency, productivity, and quality goals. To accomplish their goals, the firms carefully integrated their production strategies with their overall strategy. In addition, they used computer applications to find solutions to production problems.

Because of the effectiveness of global competitors (including firms in Germany, Japan, and other Southeast Asian countries) who started using new techniques to achieve different goals, many U.S. companies have changed what they do to produce their products. Some of the production goals sought by General Motors (e.g., reducing the number of man-hours necessary to produce a product and striving to develop more flexible production operations) are typical of those now being pursued in U.S. firms.

This chapter discusses management and control of a firm's operations. The term **operations** is used to describe the activities involved in making a firm's product. To examine the important process known as operations management, the chapter addresses several issues. First, operations management, operations systems, and operations activities are defined. This is followed by a discussion of a new model for operations management. The chapter examines the use of operations management in manufacturing and service firms. It considers seven types of operations systems and the techniques managers use to control the activities of some operations systems. Closing the chapter is a discussion of total quality management (TQM), an innovative approach to managing efforts directed toward continuous product quality improvements.

OPERATIONS MANAGEMENT, OPERATIONS SYSTEMS, AND OPERATIONS ACTIVITIES

Operations management is the process managers follow to develop and use effective and efficient operations systems and operations activities (see Figure 17-1). An **operations system** is a collection of activities through which a firm completes production work. Seven operations systems commonly used today are discussed later in the chapter. **Operations activities** are the individual tasks completed within different operations systems. These individual tasks are necessary to change a firm's resources into its products (goods or services).

The relationships among these three terms are important. First, managers must determine what operations systems are necessary for a firm to use its

FIGURE 17-1
The Operations
Management Process

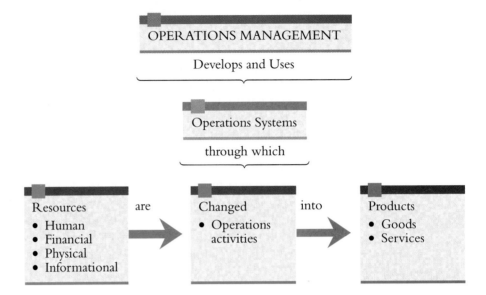

resources effectively and efficiently. Once they have identified the operations systems, managers determine the individual tasks that must be completed within each operating system. Proper integration of operations activities enables a firm to change resources into outputs effectively and efficiently.

In successful firms, all managers are involved with operations management. Top-level managers are responsible for the development and use of an appropriate operations management process. Middle-level managers must design and develop an appropriate set of operations systems. Working with inputs from middle-level managers, first-level managers have final responsibility for determining the individual production tasks to be completed.

Although it is often thought of only in terms of manufacturing firms, operations management is important in all companies. Nonmanufacturing firms also acquire human, financial, physical, and informational resources and change them into outputs. Instead of producing goods, organizations such as banks, hospitals, public utilities, libraries, universities, government agencies, and so forth produce services. In the case of both manufacturing and service firms, managers use operations systems to produce products that are valued by their customers or clients.

What customers value today in the goods and services they buy is somewhat different from what they valued in the past. A far greater variety of options, improved quality, and much faster availability are all important to today's customers.[2]

Many companies are responding to these values. For example, along with the traditional checking and savings accounts, financial institutions now offer an almost dizzying array of annuities, certificates of deposit, money-market accounts, and other financial products. Today's supermarkets feature many ethnic foods as well as items that can be cooked in minutes in microwave ovens. It is the rare automobile radio that does not have a cassette player. Customers can also choose other features, including a double cassette player (with an auto-reverse function) or a compact disc player (with multiple disk capacity). In almost all firms, continuous improvements in the quality of goods and services has become a way of life.

Like manufacturing firms, service organizations such as the public library use operations systems to provide the products their clients value.

Meeting new customer demands is a challenge operations managers must meet. In the 1990s, the key performance standard used to evaluate a firm's operations management process is the degree to which it satisfies customers' demands.[3] Because of this performance standard, some managers may use as the foundation for their operations management a model that is different from the one they used before.[4]

Two models of operations management are shown in Figure 17-2. In the left-hand column is the model that guided operations management during the mass production era. Notice that this model does not integrate operations with other functions such as marketing and finance. Notice, too, that this model calls for direct managerial control of employees and their individual production tasks. In contrast, the model described in the right-hand column calls for extensive integration among all of a firm's functions and operations. This new model involves employees in greater control of their activities and establishes operations management as a key to a firm's strategic success. In light of the challenges of today's global competition, it is important that both managerial and nonmanagerial employees accept and use the new operations management model.

ETHICS QUESTION
Are there any ethical issues involved when managers ask operations employees to change from one operations management model to another one? If so, describe those issues.

LEARNING CHECK
Define operations, operations management, an operations system, and operations activities. Be prepared to discuss the relationships among these terms.

Back to the Opening Case
Some experts suggest that General Motors could improve its overall performance if it used different processes and techniques to design and manufacture automobiles.[5] Review the new operations management model described in Figure 17-2. In your opinion, could the company improve its performance by using this new model? Why or why not?

FIGURE 17-2
Two Operations
Management Models

Old Model	New Model
Production is a stand-only activity	Production is to be integrated with all functions
Products are designed sequentially	Products are designed simultaneously by multiple parties
Long production runs	Short production runs
Control by managers and specialists	Control by self-managed work teams
Focus on quality control	Focus on zero-defects
Centralized, vertical control structures	Decentralized, horizontal control structures
Inventory used as a buffer	Inventories tied to customer demand
Standard product designs	Multiple custom-designed products

Source: Adapted from Robert O. Knorr and Edward F. Thiede, "Making New Technologies Work," *Journal of Business Strategy* (January-February 1991): 46–49; and Hamid Noori, *Managing the Dynamics of New Technology* (Englewood Cliffs, NJ: Prentice-Hall, 1990): 6–10.

OPERATIONS MANAGEMENT IN MANUFACTURING AND SERVICE FIRMS

Historically, different terms have been used to describe what is now called operations management.[6] However, each term describes the same phenomenon: processes used to change resources into products.

Manufacturing management was the first term used. This term was based on economist Adam Smith's analysis of the economic benefits of labor specialization. Smith suggested that to improve performance, firms should divide large tasks into individual subtasks. They should then train workers to become specialists in completing individual tasks.

ETHICS QUESTION
Is labor specialization an ethical foundation for the development of an operations management process? If not, why not?

Recall from Chapter 2 that the *scientific management approach* included techniques managers used to increase the efficiency of their firms' production processes. These techniques were consistent with Adam Smith's suggestions. From the early 1900s through the 1950s, these techniques, and the philosophies associated with their use, were the foundation for the way in which many managers managed their firms' production processes. Beginning around 1930 and lasting until the middle 1960s, the term used to describe these approaches was *production management*.

As we entered the 1970s, two conditions affected the way companies changed resources into outputs. First, the service sector became more prominent. Second, managers began to realize that a competitive advantage could be gained by effectively managing the process of changing resources into products. However, such a competitive advantage could be achieved only when the production process was treated as an important part of a firm's strategy. Because of these two conditions, a more contemporary and comprehensive term—*operations management*—emerged. Operations management includes systems and activities managers use in both manufacturing and service firms. However, as discussed in the next two sections, there are differences between manufacturing and service firms.[7]

Manufacturing Firms

Manufacturing firms produce physical goods such as automobiles, refrigerators, computers, and this textbook. These goods are often consumed over relatively long periods of time and are standardized in their design and manufacture. Options are available to customers, but they tend to be few and insignificant to the core design and manufacture of the goods. When purchasing a refrigerator, for example, customers can add an ice maker and a water and ice dispenser and choose from a limited range of colors. However, the focus of operations management in these firms is on the effective and efficient production of a large number of relatively standard goods.

Service Firms

Service firms produce nonphysical products such as financial, transportation, medical, legal, and educational services. Banks, airlines, physicians, lawyers, accountants, and teachers all offer services to their customers or clients. Retail stores such as Bloomingdales, JCPenney, Burger King, and Wendy's are also service firms. They provide a service to customers by selling goods that are produced by manufacturing firms. Benefits derived from services include security, comfort, convenience, and knowledge.

In contrast to manufacturing firms' production processes, customers are involved directly with a service firm's production process. Clients visit lawyers to discuss issues for which they may require legal services. Patients visit doctors for diagnosis and treatment of medical problems. Airline customers are transported from one location to another through the airline's production process. Students attend classes and take notes and examinations on lectures and assignments provided by teachers.

A second difference between products produced by manufacturing and service firms concerns physical attributes. Manufactured goods such as automobiles, refrigerators, and computers can be stored in a firm's inventory for sale at a later date. In contrast, service firms cannot store the services they provide to clients. Doctors cannot store as inventory the diagnoses they will make of patients' illnesses. Accountants cannot prepare clients' income tax forms until the clients submit all necessary data and information to them.

Nevertheless, there are similarities in the production problems faced by manufacturing and service firms. In both cases, the firm must schedule activities, purchase materials, and select a place to produce products.[8] Thus, both manufacturing and service firms develop and use the operations systems and activities discussed later in the chapter.

LEARNING CHECK

Discuss how operations management is used in both manufacturing and service firms.

The Importance of Service Firms in Today's Economy

The number of jobs in the service sector in the United States is increasing relative to the nation's shrinking manufacturing sector. During the 1980s, over 2 million jobs were lost in the manufacturing sector, while 20 million new jobs were created in service firms. In 1970, 55 percent of all jobs in the private sector were in service firms. By 1990, this number had grown to 75 percent.[9] This trend began approximately 40 years ago and, in all probability, will continue at least until the turn of the century.[10] Today, consumer expenditures continue to shift toward the purchase of the outputs of service firms.

The shift toward jobs in service firms has some worrisome aspects. In the early 1990s, approximately 42 percent of the U.S. workforce was employed in jobs requiring them to serve food; sell merchandise; perform clerical work; or clean hospitals, schools, and offices. These newly created jobs are often part time and poorly paid, and they do not provide opportunities for advancement. In addition, people holding these jobs often do not receive fringe benefits such as medical and life insurance and a pension plan.[11]

Managers of service firms should recognize the importance of developing and using an effective operations management process. Almost two-thirds of the total workforce in both private and public sectors is now employed in service firms. However, the service sector accounts for only one-half of the nation's gross domestic product. Thus, determining ways to provide services more effectively and efficiently is critical to the health of the U.S. economy.

OPERATIONS SYSTEMS

Typically, many individual tasks must be completed to change resources into outputs. Managers are responsible for developing an operations management process that is both effective (i.e., it calls for people to do the right things) and efficient (i.e., it allows available resources to be used wisely and not wasted). Individual operations systems that can be a part of a firm's operations management process are discussed next (see Figure 17-3). Although these systems are discussed individually, they must be integrated carefully if operations management is to be effective and efficient.

Product Design and Development

The purpose of the **product design and development operations system** is to determine and then develop the products a firm or agency will provide to its customers or clients. The outputs of both public and private organizations must be valued by their customers or clients. General Motors must design and manufacture automobiles customers are willing to buy at a price that provides a profit for the company. The school, college, or university you are attending must offer degree opportunities, courses, and job placement options that are consistent with your educational objectives.

FIGURE 17-3 Operations Systems

Product Design and Development
Designing and developing products customers will purchase

Facilities Location
Determining where to produce products

Inventory Management
Determining how to manage inventories

Capital Equipment
Selecting capital equipment needed to produce products

Materials Management
Purchasing and using needed materials and parts

Facilities Layout
Determining how to arrange equipment and materials

Planning and Scheduling
Coordinating operations activities

Source: Adapted from William A. Ruch, Harold E. Fearon, and C. David Wieters, *Fundamentals of Production/Operations Management,* 5e (St. Paul, MN: West Publishing Company, 1992): 21–26.

When considering design and development issues, managers think about how much it will cost to produce the product and how much customers will be willing to pay for the item. Based on feedback from other parts of the firm—the sales force, for example—managers make adjustments to this operations system.

In today's global marketplaces, customers typically have many purchasing options. Customers who are dissatisfied with a General Motors automobile can buy a car from many other domestic and foreign companies. Students who are dissatisfied with their college's offerings can transfer to another school. Customers who have a poor dining experience at a local restaurant can decide not to return there. Given the many purchasing options available today, managers must always be aware of what features of their firm's product are valued the most by customers. As indicated in our discussion of strategic management and strategic planning (Chapters 5 and 6), the features valued the most by customers should be emphasized in the design, manufacture, and distribution of a product.

Many firms make extensive use of computers in their operations systems. Some of the uses of computers in the product design and development operations system are discussed next.

COMPUTER-AIDED DESIGN (CAD). Historically, drawing boards were where a firm's new products were developed.[12] Often working somewhat in isolation, a succession of designers developed specifications for a new product. Throughout the development process, changes and improvements were made as the blueprints were moved from person to person. This manual process was time consuming, and blueprints required many modifications before being completed.[13]

Today, computers are widely used to design new products. **Computer-aided design (CAD)** is a process whereby designers use computer programs to develop new products rapidly and effectively. A designer begins by using a computer program to develop a rough sketch of a product idea. Using the computer screen as a drawing board, the designer then develops the product's shape. With CAD, alternative product designs and shapes can be developed and studied quickly. The designer also considers various properties of the different designs, such as their heat and strength transfer properties. In addition, the designer uses the CAD system to verify that all parts of the proposed product fit together correctly. Other issues the designer examines using a CAD system include production costs, the product's expected durability, and its anticipated servicing costs.

When satisfied with the product, the designer stores the design in a database. Through computer capabilities, the proposed design can be transmitted to other people—production employees, for example—for their consideration. With feedback from others, the designer then uses CAD again to improve the design of the product.[14]

CAD can be used to design almost any type of product. General Motors, for example, is using CAD to reduce the amount of time required to design new automobiles. GM also requests its suppliers to use CAD to reduce the time it takes to develop automobile components. Mars Inc. uses CAD to design its candy bars. Although the firm's candy bars have similar shapes, there are differences among them. Architects use CAD to help them design buildings that are both appealing to the eye and environmentally sound. Once new products have been designed, computers can then be used to help control the processes used to produce them.

COMPUTER-AIDED MANUFACTURING (CAM). **Computer-aided manufacturing (CAM)** is a process using computers to directly control or monitor manufacturing production processes.[15] By controlling machines, computers help increase productivity. Usually, computers provide machines in different stages of a manufacturing process instructions detailing the sequence in which activities are to be completed. Changes are made to the computers' programs as appropriate. For example, changes in a product's design that may be necessary to improve its quality are incorporated into the CAM system so the product will be manufactured according to the new specifications.

ETHICS QUESTION
Is it ethical and socially responsible for robots to take jobs away from human employees?

In some firms, industrial robots complete a number of manufacturing tasks. The work of these machines is controlled by the CAM system computers. Robots are used in a variety of tasks, especially those that are dangerous to human beings. Included among these tasks are heat treating processes, spray painting, die casting, painting and inspection, materials handling, and the loading and unloading of machines.[16] Because of their increased flexibility, robots can now complete an increasing number of tasks.

This automated machine shop uses computer-aided manufacturing to control its machines and increase productivity.

Firms gain several benefits from using CAD and CAM systems effectively. They can develop more innovative products and introduce them into the marketplace more rapidly. Similarly, they can make modifications to existing products quickly in order to respond to the unique needs of customer groups. By testing products through CAD programs, firms can eliminate design and production problems before products are produced. These early corrections improve product quality and durability.

In summary, when used together, CAD and CAM systems have the potential to help firms design and manufacture innovative products efficiently. Moreover, through constant use of CAD and CAM, companies can identify ways to improve their products one step at a time. These continuous improvements help firms maintain the loyalty of their customers.[17]

Facilities Location

The purpose of the **facilities location operations system** is to determine where a firm's facilities should be located and how they should be used. **Facilities** are physical resources in which goods or services are created, stored, or distributed. For small firms, a single facility may be used for all three activities. In contrast, large companies producing a wide range of products for sale throughout the world must make many decisions to select production, storage, and distribution facilities. For all firms—large and small, manufacturing and service, public and private—the facilities location decision is intended to select a site that will best allow the company to achieve its long-term objectives.[18]

Decisions regarding the location of facilities can have a significant impact on a firm's costs and revenues. In some cases, it takes as much as 25 percent of a product's selling price to cover the costs of shipping raw materials to a production facility and distributing the final product.[19] Managers must consider many factors when choosing sites for facilities. These include the costs of land and buildings, tax rates, access to customers, locations of competitors and suppliers, energy sources and costs, community acceptance, and quality of life in a community, among others.[20] The next section discusses a technique that can be used when selecting the location for a facility. Using this technique helps control production-related costs.

BREAK-EVEN ANALYSIS. **Break-even analysis** is a technique used to show relationships among costs, revenues, and outputs. Break-even analysis can be used to help select a production, storage, or distribution facility. In the example that follows, we apply break-even analysis only to the selection of a production facility.[21]

When break-even analysis is used to provide necessary information for deciding where to locate a production facility, it is assumed that costs and revenues increase when the facility's output increases. Costs are divided into two categories. **Fixed costs** are incurred regardless of the amount of output. Heating, lighting, and administrative expenses are fixed costs. Fixed costs remain the same whether a facility produces 10 units or 10,000 units. **Variable costs** change directly with output. Higher output results in higher variable costs, with lower output resulting in lower variable costs. Examples of variable costs are the cost of raw materials and direct labor (the wages paid to employees who complete operations activities).

Study the relationships shown in Figure 17-4 to understand how break-even analysis is used to make a facility location decision. In our example, the firm is considering two different locations for a production plant—Atlanta and Dallas. The firm has decided to use break-even analysis to identify the level of output that would have to be reached at the Atlanta and Dallas facilities so that total revenues would equal total fixed and variable costs. The quantity of output at which total revenues equal total costs is known as the **break-even point.** A break-even point depends on a product's selling price and the mix between fixed and variable costs required to produce the product. Some products have low fixed costs and high variable costs per unit produced; others have high fixed costs but low per-unit variable costs.

Many factors could cause the differences between fixed and variable costs in various locations. An obvious one is the cost of direct labor (a variable cost). Labor costs are lower in some parts of the country than others. Similarly, the amount of energy needed to heat and cool a facility (a fixed cost) varies from region to region. To complete a break-even analysis, managers must be aware of all fixed and variable costs at different locations.

As shown in Figure 17-4, the break-even point, and the size of losses and profits, would be different in Atlanta and Dallas. However, to produce a product in either facility, costs would exceed revenues up to the break-even point. Beyond the break-even point, the quantity of output produced in each facility would generate revenues in excess of costs and provide the company with profits. Notice that for products with high fixed costs and low variable costs, profitability increases rapidly after the break-even point is reached. In contrast, in Dallas, where the variable costs are higher than the

FIGURE 17-4 Break-Even Analysis and a Facilities Location Decision

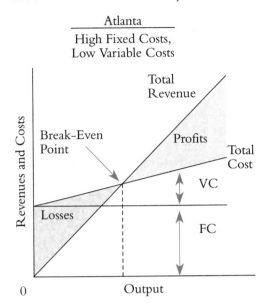

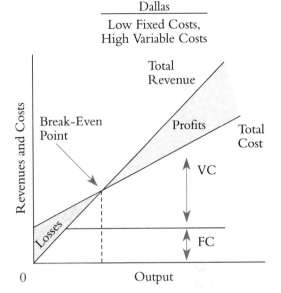

fixed costs, the increases in profits earned, based on the quantity of output, are less dramatic than in Atlanta.

Given the relationships shown in Figure 17-4, should the production facility be located in Atlanta or in Dallas? Unfortunately, break-even analysis does not provide a "correct" answer to this question. What the technique does do, however, is show how many units would have to be produced in each location in order for the company to first break even and then earn a profit. Managers can compare this information with the number of units marketing employees believe can be sold. The managers would also ask employees in finance for their opinion of the effect of incurring different levels of losses until the break-even point is reached. (Notice that the losses incurred in Atlanta are expected to exceed those incurred in Dallas.)

LEARNING CHECK   Discuss the product design and development operations system and the facilities location operations system. Describe the uses of CAD and CAM systems and break-even analysis.

Capital Equipment

The purpose of the **capital equipment operations system** is to select the physical assets (i.e., the capital equipment) needed to produce outputs. These assets normally last for long periods of time and are often expensive. Capital equipment usually has a limited number of uses. For example, a machine built to manufacture a particular part needed to assemble a key component of a firm's product is not useful for other purposes without modification.

Because of these characteristics, managers set up procedures to evaluate certain issues before making decisions about buying capital equipment. These issues include the initial purchase price, installation costs, and the costs of both routine maintenance and emergency repairs.

The importance of capital equipment varies with the goods or services a firm produces. The success of a large manufacturing firm is affected greatly by how well managers manage the purchases of capital equipment. Some service firms, such as a dentist's office, also require large capital investments. In both cases, profitability is affected by decisions to purchase and maintain capital equipment. For other firms, however, relatively few dollars are committed to capital equipment. A lumber yard is an example of a firm that spends large amounts of money to buy inventory instead of capital equipment.[22]

Facilities Layout

The purpose of the **facilities layout operations system** is to determine the physical layout of the capital equipment and materials needed to produce outputs. The basic pattern of work necessary to produce a good or a service has an important impact on how efficiently a facility is operated. In a manufacturing firm, managers want to develop a layout that ensures a smooth flow of work.

Managers in service firms are also concerned with work flow. They examine the flow of paper, information, and customers to make facilities layout decisions.[23] Service firm managers strive to develop layouts that ensure a smooth flow of traffic.[24] The objectives managers try to accomplish when designing either a manufacturing or a service facility layout are shown in Figure 17-5.

Three basic facilities layouts are used in manufacturing and service firms: process, product, and fixed-position.[25] Benefits of using the most appropriate layout include improvement of a firm's delivery rates and more productive employees.

PROCESS LAYOUT. With a **process layout,** items of equipment or departments are grouped together according to their function. For example, all stamping machines could be placed in one area while all lathes could be in a different area. A sequence of operations is established that calls for a part to travel from one area to another until the product is completed.[26] This layout is used when the flow of work is not consistent for all outputs. Hospitals use a process layout, as do distribution warehouses, automobile repair shops, and colleges and universities.

PRODUCT LAYOUT. In a **product layout,** equipment or work activities are arranged in a line so a specialized sequence of tasks can be performed on each product. A product layout is appropriate for companies producing large quantities of a standardized product. Automobile and truck manufac-

FIGURE 17-5
Facilities Layout
Objectives

Manufacturing Firms

Predictable production time
Open plant floors so all can see
Orderly handling and storage of
materials
Flexible; adapts easily to changes
A logical flow of work
Little storage of materials between
stages of production

Service Firms

A work pattern that is easy to
understand
Very little clutter
Adequate check-out locations
Easy patterns for communications
with customers
An adequate number of waiting
areas/stations
High sales volume per square foot
of space

Source: Adapted from Richard B. Chase and Nicholas J. Aquilano, *Production & Operations Management,* 6e (Homewood, IL: Richard D. Irwin, 1992): 454.

turers, computer manufacturers, cafeterias, and companies making refrigerators and dishwashers are examples of firms using product layouts.

FIXED-POSITION LAYOUT. With a **fixed-position layout,** a product remains in a single location so that required tools, equipment, and workers can be brought to it. This layout is used when weight or bulk make it difficult to move the product. Large ships, airplanes, locomotives, and houses are all built using a fixed-position layout.

Many manufacturing and service firms use combinations of layouts to produce their outputs. Frequently, product and process layouts are joined in a single firm's operations. Some activities necessary to produce certain parts of an automobile are completed through a process layout. Welding may be completed in one area and stamping in another, for example. The different subassemblies can then be used in a product layout to complete the manufacture of the automobile.

This facility follows the product layout design, with each specialized task performed in sequence on the product.

Planning and Scheduling

The **planning and scheduling operations system** is concerned with establishing the quantity and timing of outputs, coordinating individual operations activities, and balancing product demand and supply for competitive success.[27] Effective planning and scheduling anticipate the need for workers, materials, and equipment and allow for enough lead time to support any necessary changes to the original plans and schedules. [28]

A successful firm develops a number of different plans and schedules. Together, these documents make it possible for the firm to produce its outputs in a coordinated manner. A **master production schedule** specifies which products are to be produced and when.[29] It shows, on a weekly basis, how many products must be produced in order to satisfy customers' demands. Effective plans and schedules also indicate how a firm would respond to changes in demand for its products or problems with the capacity of its operations capabilities.

Materials Management

The purpose of the **materials management operations system** is to buy, move, and store the materials needed to produce outputs in an effective and efficient manner. Before buying materials, different vendors' products and prices are studied carefully. After making the purchase, managers must ensure that the materials are available to the firm's production process in a timely fashion. Given today's competitive realities, managers also try to buy the exact amount of materials necessary to produce a good or a service, and no more.

Inventory Management

Inventory is the goods a firm keeps on hand to use in its production processes. A manufacturing firm's inventory includes the raw materials, supplies, and finished goods the firm needs to produce its goods. Inventory includes different goods for service firms. In a men's retail clothing store, for example, suits, shirts, slacks, and socks are kept in inventory. Doctors keep tongue depressors, needles, suturing supplies, and a host of other items in their inventories to diagnose and treat their patients. For both manufacturing and service firms, the purpose of the **inventory management operations system** is to help the firm handle its inventories effectively and efficiently.

Firms hold items in inventory so they can produce a certain quantity of outputs when they want to produce those outputs. In addition, having ample inventory allows a firm to produce an increased number of goods or services in response to an unexpected increase in demand from customers. Buying and storing items necessary to produce a firm's products can be expensive. Because of this, firms generally try to keep inventories at minimum levels. Improved relationships with suppliers, more efficient production processes, and improved management information systems all help managers control inventory costs.[30] However, it is impossible for all items necessary to produce a firm's outputs to arrive exactly when needed. As a result, firms must keep some goods in inventory. The challenge for managers is to develop inventory management systems that strike the proper balance between too much and too little inventory. Economic order quantity, just-in-time, and materials requirements planning are three techniques used to help in the management of inventories. These techniques are discussed in the next three sections.

ECONOMIC ORDER QUANTITY. **Economic order quantity (EOQ)** is an inventory control technique used to keep a firm's ordering and holding costs as low as possible.[31] *Ordering costs* are the costs incurred in placing an order. Examples of these costs include the cost of the work necessary to process an order and expenses involved in receiving, inspecting, and inventorying items. *Holding costs* are the costs experienced when a firm retains items in its inventory. Examples of these costs are finance charges (if the items were purchased on credit) and the expenses involved in maintaining storage space.

The EOQ technique helps firms deal with the complex issues associated with different inventory costs. With large reorder quantities, average inventories grow and holding costs increase. With small reorder quantities, firms must order materials and parts more frequently, resulting in larger ordering costs. Using EOQ benefits firms by reducing both holding and ordering costs while meeting the demands of the production processes.

A manufacturer of jogging shoes must determine an effective EOQ for each of the materials and parts used to produce each of its product types. One of the parts ordered would be soles for the shoe (different soles are required for different types of jogging shoes). Assume that the ordering costs (C) for each order of soles for a certain type of running shoe are $25, the annual holding costs (H) are $8 per unit, and the annual demand (D) for the soles is 10,000 units. These data are placed into the following formula to calculate the economic order quantity:

$$EOQ = \sqrt{\frac{2DC}{H}}$$

$$= \sqrt{\frac{2 \times 10,000 \times \$25}{\$8}} = \sqrt{\frac{500,000}{8}} = \sqrt{62,500}$$

$$= 250$$

In this case, the most economic quantity of soles to order for a certain jogging shoe is 250 soles per order. The company should use EOQ to determine the optimum quantities of materials and parts to order for all items needed to manufacture each one of its shoes.

JUST-IN-TIME. **Just-in-time (JIT)** is an inventory management technique used to ensure that items needed to produce goods and services arrive at the time they are needed in a production process. JIT is actually a way of thinking about production processes and inventory levels, and not simply a technique. The system calls for employees to think continuously about what can be done to reduce the number of items that need to be stored in inventory and the length of time those items need to be stored.

JIT's primary objective is to have the necessary materials and parts delivered by suppliers *just prior to the need for them* in the production process. JIT is used most successfully in firms that produce large quantities of goods (automobiles and stereos, for examples). For JIT to be used effectively, the work of a firm's production processes must be forecast accurately. With accurate forecasts, employees can contact suppliers to inform them of the precise quantities of materials and parts that will be needed at particular times. In addition, companies must be able to develop effective relationships with their suppliers—relationships in which both parties benefit through cooperation with each other. The supplier who delivers high-quality materials to customers on time is rewarded with additional orders. The firm receiving those materials benefits because it can produce high-quality goods and services. The supplier's inventory costs are reduced substantially because it does not have to store items for long periods of time.

MATERIALS REQUIREMENTS PLANNING (MRP). **Materials requirements planning (MRP)** is a system that creates schedules identifying all materials and parts needed to produce a good or a service, when those items should be in inventory, and when they should be available to a firm's production processes.[32] Computer-based MRP systems are now used in many firms, even small ones.

The primary goal of MRP systems is "getting the right materials to the right place at the right time."[33] Through MRP systems, efforts are made to minimize the amount of money a firm invests in inventory and to improve the efficiency of operations activities. The beginning point of an MRP system is the manager's knowledge of how much output must be produced over a period of time. Next, the manager develops detailed lists of the parts and materials required to produce that amount of output and determines the exact numbers of each part and material needed. The number of items needed and those currently in inventory or on order are compared. Through computerized systems, the manager orders predetermined quantities of these parts and materials. A summary of the benefits that can be expected from using effective MRP systems is shown in Figure 17-6.

Unfortunately, some firms are not using MRP systems effectively.[34] A successful MRP system is demanding. Its development and use require significant amounts of information, extremely accurate record keeping, and strict discipline among managers and other employees. In addition, all of the firm's activities must be integrated carefully for an MRP system to work well. Design personnel must give accurate and reliable product specifications to production employees. Marketing staff should be confident of the number of units they claim can be sold over a particular period of time.

In general, MRP systems require managers and nonmanagerial employees to be more aware of how the different parts of the company work. Having such knowledge spread throughout a company's workforce is desirable,

FIGURE 17-6
A Summary of Benefits
of MRP Systems

- Improved Customer Service
- Reduced Idle Time
- Improved Responsiveness to Market Demands
- Reduced Inventories
- More Competitive Pricing Abilities
- Improved Use of Manufacturing Capacity

Source: Adapted from Richard B. Chase and Nicholas J. Aquilano, *Production & Operations Management,* 6e (Homewood, IL: Richard D. Irwin, 1992): 703.

but it does not happen in all firms. Because MRP systems leave little room for error, managers should encourage effective integration of efforts throughout the company. Firms that are able to integrate the activities of all operations systems carefully gain many of the benefits of MRP systems that are shown in Figure 17-6.

LEARNING CHECK

Discuss the facilities layout, planning and scheduling, materials management, and inventory management operations systems. Describe the use of EOQ, JIT, and an MRP system.

Back to the
Opening Case

Recent actions indicate that significant changes will continue at General Motors. Among these are changes in the firm's operations management process. To decrease the amount of time required to develop, design, and successfully introduce new products into the marketplace, several decisions have been made. Jobs have been eliminated, plants closed, innovative deals negotiated with labor unions, and individual operations activities analyzed to determine the value they add to production effectiveness and efficiency. Under John Smale, chairman of the executive committee, GM is examining its management structure. In the eyes of an analyst who studies the automobile industry, early 1992 found GM with 30 to 50 percent too many white-collar workers.[35] Viewed as a whole, the actions being taken at GM suggest that a different operations management model is emerging.

MANAGING PRODUCT AND SERVICE QUALITY

Quality encompasses all of a product's features and capabilities that affect its ability to satisfy customers' needs.[36] Thus, quality is defined by customers, not by managers or employees.[37] To understand the importance of quality to a firm's competitive success, consider the items you purchase. In general, most customers are interested in buying products they know to be of high quality. What complicates this matter for companies is that customers want to purchase these high-quality goods or services at low prices.

The History of Product Quality

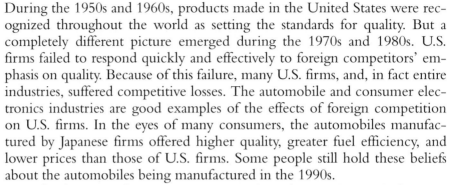

During the 1950s and 1960s, products made in the United States were recognized throughout the world as setting the standards for quality. But a completely different picture emerged during the 1970s and 1980s. U.S. firms failed to respond quickly and effectively to foreign competitors' emphasis on quality. Because of this failure, many U.S. firms, and, in fact entire industries, suffered competitive losses. The automobile and consumer electronics industries are good examples of the effects of foreign competition on U.S. firms. In the eyes of many consumers, the automobiles manufactured by Japanese firms offered higher quality, greater fuel efficiency, and lower prices than those of U.S. firms. Some people still hold these beliefs about the automobiles being manufactured in the 1990s.

Today, however, there are encouraging signs about actions U.S. firms are taking to improve the quality of their products. In fact, one of the strongest proponents of quality, J. M. Juran, suggested recently that the 1990s will be an era in which "Made in the U.S.A." again becomes a symbol of world-class quality.[38]

Many factors are contributing to these more positive views of the ability of U.S. companies to improve the quality of their outputs. For example, as many foreign companies did years ago, many U.S. firms are now establishing a position for a vice president for quality in their management structures. This position elevates the importance of quality in the minds of customers and employees alike. In addition, firms continue to make changes in what they do to produce their outputs. A primary objective of these changes is to push responsibility and authority to levels where employees have the information necessary to make quality-related decisions. Moreover, a new objective is emerging: *zero defects*. While zero defects may not be attainable in all cases, striving toward that objective focuses employees' energies in positive and productive ways. Motorola has established an objective of 60 defects or fewer for every billion components manufactured.[39] This objective may not be achieved, but Motorola is likely to become more productive and be able to reduce its costs by striving to achieve it.

ETHICS QUESTION
Describe any relationship that you believe exists between corporate social responsibility and product quality.

Total Quality Management (TQM)

Total quality management (TQM) is a firm's strategic commitment to continuously improve the quality of its products in ways that are valued by customers.[40] TQM requires that all units of a firm focus their efforts on product quality. This focus should be integrated throughout a company so each unit knows what the others are doing to improve quality. It is this approach to management that allows companies to adopt challenging, zero-defect-based production goals. TQM requires effective leadership and often changes in a firm's culture. The relationships between TQM and leadership and organizational culture are discussed in Chapter 22. As shown in the Organizations in Action, TQM can be used in all types of organizations, even colleges and universities.

ORGANIZATIONS IN ACTION

Motorola is a company known to be committed to the importance of product quality. At "Motorola University," the company teaches TQM to its own employees as well as professors from business and engineering schools.

For professors, a requirement of attending the TQM seminars is that their schools must agree to apply TQM methods to what Motorola believes are inefficient administrative systems used in colleges and universities today. Another reason for offering this opportunity to professors is that some managers, including Motorola's CEO, believe that business and engineering faculty lack the full knowledge and skills needed to teach TQM. Because Motorola and many other companies want to hire people with knowledge of quality principles and practices, these companies are willing to provide professors with the information they need to be effective teachers of total quality management. The fact that 24 universities asked to participate in the first quality seminars made available to them suggests that some top-level managers in educational institutions recognize the value of TQM programs.

Source: "B-School Faculty Quality Training," *Fortune* (January 13, 1992): 14.

An effective TQM program is based on several assumptions. First, TQM requires the training and full participation of all employees. Having even a majority of a company's employees committed to TQM is not enough. The focus of all actions must be singular—on product quality—and spread across all employees.

The second major assumption of TQM is that product quality results from controlling the process rather than inspecting the outcomes of that process. It is too expensive to correct mistakes made when producing a product. It is cheaper, and therefore more profitable, for a company to design and produce a product correctly the first time. Estimates that as much as 15 to 20 percent of every sales dollar is used to deal with quality problems indicate how expensive poor product quality is.[41] The goal of TQM is not to correct production defects quickly and effectively; rather, it is to produce a good or a service without any defects at all.

A third TQM assumption is that statistical tools and techniques are critical to efforts to control production processes. These tools and techniques are used to help organize and analyze data for the purpose of solving problems. Using these decision aids does not require employees to have a full command of statistics. However, the tools and techniques that are relevant to TQM must be used consistently and effectively.

There are several dimensions of TQM that all employees should understand fully. We consider four of these dimensions here.

CUSTOMER-DRIVEN QUALITY STANDARDS. This dimension of TQM suggests that it is the customer who determines whether or not a good is reliable or a service is fast. Companies must have marketing specialists to determine exactly what customers want and designers who can develop outputs to meet customers' specifications. Quality factors that firms examine include reliability, durability, serviceability, appearance, and esthetics.

SUPPLIER-CUSTOMER LINKS. This TQM dimension indicates that each part of a company has a customer. Often, the customer is an internal one, such as the next department in a production process. Employees completing individual operations activities are asked to be aware of the quality their customer expects. Because each person is concerned with the quality needed by the next party in the operations management process, the overall quality of the product delivered to the final customer is improved.

PREVENTION ORIENTATION. As implied by the first two TQM dimensions, producing products without defects is an important objective. This objective requires employees to design and complete all operations activities with the intent of "doing it right the first time." It is better to prevent problems or mistakes than it is to become skilled at correcting product defects. Keeping this objective in mind at all times helps to focus employees' efforts.

QUALITY AT THE SOURCE. This dimension calls for employees to be the quality inspectors of their own work. This responsibility results in employees who have more involvement with their work and are more committed to a firm's TQM program. To support employees as individual quality inspectors, managers must provide them with opportunities to gain needed skills. Often, training programs are needed for employees to master the use of statistical tools and techniques. In addition, however, training should emphasize the importance of the individual employee to a TQM program's success. This part of the training effort concentrates on philosophy and emphasizes the benefits of TQM to all parties.

Managing Quality: Past and Future

Total quality management is one approach to dealing successfully with today's competitive demands for high product quality. But why did it take so long for U.S. companies to respond to customers' demands for quality? Why didn't they try harder to reduce their costs by controlling the quality of their production processes? Using as much as 20 to 35 percent of the resources committed to a firm's production processes to correct product defects seems unreasonable, but many U.S. companies were using their resources this way in the 1970s and 1980s.

ETHICS QUESTION
How would you respond to the following statement: "Firms committed to TQM programs are more socially responsible than firms not committed to TQM programs."

Answers to these questions are not simple. Some believe that top-level managers failed to support quality-boosting efforts as they should have.[42] Rather than implement full TQM programs, a popular action was to focus on single efforts to improve quality. However, as we pointed out earlier, TQM requires an absolute, almost fanatical dedication to the pursuit of ever-increasing levels of product quality. Approaching quality on a piecemeal basis is ineffective.

It has been predicted that only companies with the highest levels of product quality will survive the latter part of the 1990s and into the 21st century. The actions of many U.S. firms today regarding TQM programs suggest that they are committed to the strategic importance of product quality. When implementing TQM programs, companies gain several benefits. In addition to increasing the quality of a firm's products, a TQM program often results in improvements in employees' productivity levels and reductions in total production costs.

Given the importance of product quality and the increasing number of companies interested in TQM programs, it is likely that one aspect of your performance as a manager will be concerned with the issue of product quality. As you consider this possibility, think of the orientation toward product quality you want to use in a managerial position. Some information that may be of value to you in this respect is presented in Chapter 22.

LEARNING CHECK

Define total quality management and describe its use. Be prepared to discuss the importance of managing quality effectively in today's manufacturing and service firms.

SUMMARY

Today, managers in many U.S. firms are reexamining their operations management process. A key reason for this is the recent success of a host of companies outside the United States. Instead of relying on mass production as the foundation for how they produce their products, these firms include operations management as a key part of their overall strategy. In addition, managers in these firms continuously seek to reduce their production costs while simultaneously increasing the quality of the product being produced.

Operations management is the process used to develop effective and efficient operations systems and operations activities. Operations systems are the groupings in which individual operations activities take place. Operations activities are the individual tasks completed in the different operations systems. Ultimately, top-level managers bear the strategic responsibility for developing an operations management process in their firm. First-level managers have the primary responsibility to develop operations activities. Middle-level managers are responsible for the development and use of appropriate operations systems.

Often, only manufacturing companies come to mind when thinking of operations management. However, operations management plays a critical role in the success of service as well as manufacturing firms. Because of the increasing importance of the service sector in today's U.S. economy, as shown by the number of people employed in this sector, it is critical that effective operations management processes be used in all types of service firms. Developing effective operations management processes calls for the use of a new model (see Figure 17-2). Basically, this new model carefully integrates operations management with all other parts of a firm's activities.

There are seven operations systems that, when combined, form the foundation of a firm's operations management process. The product design and development operations system specifies a product's design and how it will be manufactured. In all cases, a firm's outputs must be valued by customers. If they are not, customers will select products offered by competitors. Computer-aided design (CAD) and computer-aided manufacturing (CAM) are used by many companies today in designing and developing products. With these systems, it is possible to design and produce innovative goods or services rapidly.

The facilities location operations system is concerned with selecting a site that will help a firm achieve its objectives. In many instances, break-even analysis is used to assist managers in selecting a site for a production, storage, or distribution facility. To use break-even analysis successfully, it is necessary to be aware of the fixed and variable costs involved with producing a good or a service in all locations being considered.

The concern of the capital equipment operations system is the wise use of assets. Capital equipment—the physical assets required to produce a product—is expensive and lasts for a long period of time. Because of this, managers do not want to make mistakes when buying capital equipment. The facilities layout operations system determines the most effective and efficient flow of work to produce a product. Typically, one of three facilities layout patterns—process, product, or fixed-position—is used. The challenge is to select the type that is best for each set of operations activities.

The planning and scheduling operations system is concerned with the volume and timing of a firm's outputs, the effective use of a firm's production capacity, and the balancing of product demand and supply. Effective plans and schedules result in a proper amount of coordination among all of a firm's operations activities. The materials management operations system is concerned with determining how to buy, move, and store materials in the most effective and cost-efficient manner. Finally, the inventory manage-ment operations system is used to handle a firm's inventory in a manner that supports the actual production of a product. Economic order quantity, just-in-time, and materials requirements planning are techniques used in the management of inventories.

Total quality management (TQM) is a strategic commitment to the continuous improvement of a firm's products in ways that are valued by customers. Comprehensive in design and scope, TQM calls for an almost fanatical dedication on the part of all employees to the goal of continuously improving the quality of their company's outputs. To achieve this goal, employees must understand and accept the need to: (a) base quality on standards defined by customers; (b) focus on the importance of developing productive links between suppliers and customers; (c) adopt the philosophy that it is better to do one's job right the first time than it is to develop the skills required to correct defects; and (d) empower employees to be fully responsible for ensuring the quality of their work.

KEY TERMS

mass production
operations
operations management
operations system
operations activities
manufacturing firms
service firms
product design and development operations system
computer-aided design (CAD)

computer-aided manufacturing (CAM)
facilities location operations system
facilities
break-even analysis
fixed costs
variable costs
break-even point
capital equipment operations system

facilities layout operations system
process layout
product layout
fixed-position layout
planning and scheduling operations system
master production schedule
materials management operations system
inventory

inventory management operations system
economic order quantity (EOQ)
just-in-time (JIT)
materials requirements planning (MRP)
quality
total quality management (TQM)

QUESTIONS FOR DISCUSSION AND REVIEW

1. Define the terms operations, operations management, operations systems, and operations activities. As a first-level manager, which of these would be of the greatest importance to you, and why?
2. Some believe that a new operations management model should be used in today's firms. Do you agree with this position? Why or why not?
3. Prepare a response to the following statement:

"Operations management is important, but only in manufacturing firms. It is really a waste of time to be too concerned about operations management in service firms."

4. Describe the key differences between manufacturing and service firms.
5. Name and offer a concise definition of each of the seven types of operations systems used in

many companies today.

6. What are CAD and CAM systems? How are these systems used in the design and manufacture of new products?

7. What is break-even analysis? Describe how break-even analysis can be used when selecting a location for a facility.

8. Describe the differences among process, product, and fixed-position facilities layouts. In your opinion, which of these layouts should be used at your school, and why?

9. Define EOQ, JIT, and MRP and discuss their importance to today's companies.

10. How is total quality management (TQM) defined? Consider the college, school, or university you are attending. Using TQM dimensions, describe how the institution could improve the quality of the service it is providing to customers such as yourself.

PROBLEMS FOR ACTION

A. Select one of your school's service departments (food service, library or bookstore, for example) for study. Base this study on what you have experienced to date or can learn rapidly from classmates. In your opinion, are the services offered by the department you selected of high quality? Why or why not? What recommendations can you offer to increase the department's productivity and the quality of its service?

B. Jack Irons, production manager for Rader's Custom Woodworks, has asked that you assist him in efforts to install a CAD/CAM system. A large family firm that has been in business for over 35 years, Rader's Custom Woodworks attracts commercial customers from a five-state region. Historically, the firm has been quite profitable.

Recently, Irons decided that Rader's should use

CAD/CAM to improve the effectiveness and efficiency of its production processes. Irons knows that these computerized systems cannot be used to design and manufacture all of the firm's products. After all, some of Rader's jobs call for making only a few customized cabinets for a single customer. But the company also makes large numbers of standard cabinets for some of the nation's largest homebuilders. It is for these products that Irons believes CAD/CAM systems could be used successfully.

Assume that you have been asked to talk with Irons about the benefits and potential disadvantages of CAD/CAM systems. What would you say to him? In general, would you encourage Irons to use the firm's financial resources to develop and use either a CAD or a CAM system or both? Why or why not?

CONCLUDING CASE

. . . .

Workman's Manufacturing Company

David Workman, founder and president of Workman's Manufacturing Company, was worried. The past year had proved to be more difficult than the ever-optimistic Workman had thought would be the case. For the first time in its 22-year history, Workman's Manufacturing failed to earn a profit. Obviously, a number of factors resulted in the firm's poor performance. However, in thinking about this situation, it seemed to Workman that significant pressures from both foreign and domestic competitors were the principal causes of his firm's problems. Workman did not know why many of these firms had remained profitable when facing the same diffi-

cult competitive conditions affecting Workman's.

Workman's Manufacturing is a large textile manufacturer. Its primary product line includes household items—bath towels, placemats, linens, and so forth. At one time, the company also manufactured industrial grade carpets, but it never achieved much success with this product. Because Workman didn't want to waste the company's resources, he decided to stop manufacturing carpets some eight or nine years ago. Workman's was known in the trade as a manufacturer of high-quality, high-priced products. But producing high-quality products and selling them at a price that would allow the company to be profitable was becoming increasingly difficult. This confused Workman. He had always thought that customers would pay virtually any price for a product as long as it was of high quality.

Through his reading and discussions with others in the business, Workman learned that some textile manufacturers had been able to reduce their costs rather dramatically. This was accomplished primarily by closing antiquated mills, laying off excess personnel, and making massive capital investments to increase the efficiency of production processes. Workman's, too, had closed plants and laid off many employees, but unlike its competitors, it had not realized dramatic cost reductions from these actions.

As he thought about these matters, Workman wondered whether there was more to increasing a firm's effectiveness and efficiency than simply closing plants and laying off people. Although he did

not have an easy answer for this question, he knew that something had to be done. If significant changes were not made soon, the long-term survival of Workman's could be in jeopardy. What, Workman thought, should he do to turn this situation around?

1. What is your evaluation of Workman's understanding of product quality? In your opinion, is his view consistent with what most customers want today?
2. Discuss how you believe operations management could be applied at Workman's Manufacturing. Be specific in your descriptions of how individual operations systems might be of value to this firm.
3. Given the information in this case, are you optimistic about this company's future? Why or why not?

REFERENCES

1. Edmund Faltermayer, "U.S. Companies Come Back Home," *Fortune* (December 30, 1991): 106–112.
2. William K. Beckett and Khiem Dang, "Synchronous Manufacturing: New Methods, New Mind-Set," *Journal of Business Strategy* (January-February 1992): 53.
3. Beckett and Dang, "Synchronous Manufacturing," 54.
4. Robert O. Knorr, "Business Process Redesign: Key to Competitiveness," *Journal of Business Strategy* (November-December 1991): 46.
5. Scott Burns, "Through the Looking Glass on a Paradigm," *Dallas Morning News* (April 5, 1992): 1D.
6. Everett E. Adam and Ronald J. Ebert, *Production & Operations Management*, 5e (Englewood Cliffs, NJ: Prentice-Hall, 1992): 6–8.
7. Adam and Ebert, *Production & Operations Management*, 7.
8. Richard L. Daft, *Management*, 2e (Chicago: The Dryden Press, 1991): 571.
9. Stephen S. Roach, "Services Under Siege: The Restructuring Imperative," *Harvard Business Review* (September-October 1991): 82–83.
10. Leonard A. Schlesinger and James L. Heskett, "The Service-Driven Service Company," *Harvard Business Review* (September-October 1991): 72.
11. Schlesinger and Heskett, "The Service-Driven Service Company," 72.
12. Hamid Noori, *Managing the Dynamics of New Technology* (Englewood Cliffs, NJ: Prentice-Hall, 1990): 27.
13. Noori, *Dynamics of New Technology*, 27.
14. Adam and Ebert, *Production & Operations Management*, 137; and Jay Heizer and Barry Render, *Production and Operations Management*, 2e (Boston: Allyn and Bacon, 1991): 277.
15. Noori, *Dynamics of New Technology*, 23.
16. Noori, *Dynamics of New Technology*, 25.
17. Theodore Levitt, *Thinking About Management* (New York: Free Press, 1991): 51.
18. Adam and Ebert, *Production & Operations Management*, 212.
19. Heizer and Render, *Production and Operations Management*, 344.
20. William A. Ruch, Harold E. Fearon, and C. David Wieters, *Fundamentals of Production/Operations Management*, 5e (St. Paul: West Publishing, 1992).
21. This example is based on materials appearing in Adam and Ebert, *Production & Operations Management*, 212–214.
22. Ruch et al., *Production/Operations Management*, 23.
23. Adam and Ebert, *Production & Operations Management*, 252.
24. Richard B. Chase and Nicholas J. Aquilano, *Production & Operations Management*, 6e (Homewood, IL: Irwin, 1992): 454.
25. Adam and Ebert, *Production & Operations Management*, 252–256.
26. Heizer and Render, *Production and Operations Management*, 455.
27. Adam and Ebert, *Production & Operations Management*, 373.
28. Ruch et al., *Production/Operations Management*, 24–25.
29. Heizer and Render, *Production and Operations Management*, 611.
30. Ruch et al., *Production/Operations Management*, 25.
31. Chase and Aquilano, *Production & Operations Management*, 701.
32. Daft, *Management*, 581.
33. Chase and Aquilano, *Production & Operations Management*, 702.
34. M. Michael Umble and M. L. Srikanth, *Synchronous Manufacturing* (Cincinnati: South-Western Publishing Co., 1990): 8.
35. "The Board Revolt," *Business Week* (April 20, 1992): 31–36.
36. Heizer and Render, *Production and Operations Management*, 734.
37. Thomas O. Miller, "A Customer's Definition of Quality," *Journal of Business Strategy* (January-February 1992): 4.
38. "Questing for the Best," *Business Week* (October 25, 1991): 8.
39. "Future Perfect," *The Economist* (January 4, 1992): 61.
40. The discussion in this section is adapted from points appearing in Chase and Aquilano, *Production & Operations Management*, 186–225.
41. Chase and Aquilano, *Production & Operations Management*, 192.
42. "Questing for the Best," 8.

Chapter 18

Information Systems and Controlling

OPENING
CASE
Chapman's
Family
Bookstores

Chapman's Family Bookstores consists of 24 company-owned outlets in three states. Joseph Chapman is the company's owner and CEO. All of Chapman's retail outlets use cash register systems to control their inventories. These point-of-sale systems store information regarding items sold and, once every day, transfer the information to a minicomputer at the main office. That control system is working reasonably well. Still, with continuing growth, Chapman is becoming increasingly uncomfortable about a general lack of control of the business's day-to-day operations. Beyond this, he wonders whether examining other types of information would help his stores become more successful.

Among other things, Chapman wants to know which items are the most profitable and how profits are related to location, types of books in a store's inventory, size of displays, and number of store employees. He wants to understand the relationship, if any, between company sales and profits and certain external economic trends. Chapman believes that having access to these types of information would enhance profitability. Also, Chapman wants to learn more about his customers. With this knowledge, it might be possible for the firm to cater better to each customer's unique reading interests.

Chapman is convinced that computers will continue to play an important role in managing information in his firm. But after receiving conflicting opinions from vendors, he is uncertain about what to do. What kind and size of computer will be necessary? Should the firm purchase a new minicomputer, upgrade the current minicomputer, purchase a mainframe computer, or buy several powerful microcomputers that can be distributed to the 24 stores? What are the costs and benefits of these different options? What steps should be taken to determine which type of system will be the most compatible with Chapman's information needs? How soon is each of these system options likely to become obsolete? Chapman knows that the issues suggested by these questions have to be addressed before he can make a decision about managing information in his firm.

ETHICS QUESTION
What are some of the ethical issues you can think of that could be associated with the management of information?

The information issues facing Joseph Chapman are not uncommon. Today, many top-, middle-, and first-level managers recognize the importance of information and the systems used to manage that information. Managing information effectively is linked with the successful production and delivery of products to both domestic and global marketplaces.[1]

However, like Joseph Chapman, many managers find managing information a difficult challenge. Many of today's information systems are based on sophisticated computer technologies and applications. Managers are challenged to sort through many options to select the information system best suited to their needs. Like Joseph Chapman, all managers must make sure that their information systems are appropriate. Effective systems produce information that is valuable for decision-making purposes. If not managed carefully, an information system can generate invalid and unreliable information. When this occurs, resources are wasted, poor decisions are made, and operations are not controlled effectively.

In the previous three chapters, we described principles of control (Chapter 15), controlling methods and techniques (Chapter 16), and operations management practices in modern organizations (Chapter 17). With these discussions as a foundation, this chapter emphasizes the importance of having the right kinds of information available to the right people (both managers and nonmanagerial employees) at the right time. This is critical if a firm's control systems and its operations management practices are to be effective.

This chapter focuses on **information management**—the systematic control of information by managers in order to accomplish objectives and implement strategies and plans. It addresses the nature and use of information systems as instruments of control and as inputs to managerial decisions. First, we provide a description of the subtle, yet important differences between data and information. This is followed by a definition of information systems and a discussion of why they are important today. The next two sections describe different types of computers and information systems, followed by a presentation of the components that are common to many information systems. The effectiveness of any information system is influenced greatly by how well it is implemented. Following a discussion of issues critical to effective implementation of information systems, we consider several human implications. The chapter closes with a discussion of information system issues managers may face during the 1990s.

DEFINING DATA AND INFORMATION

Although the terms are sometimes used interchangeably, there are important differences between data and information. **Data** are raw facts, such as names, hours worked, and order numbers. Until they are analyzed and transformed into a usable form, data lack full value. **Information** is knowledge derived through an analysis and transformation of data. It comprises data that have been converted into forms that communicate meaning, reduce uncertainty, and have managerial value.[2] For example, as discussed in Chapter 16, cash, accounts receivable, and inventory, when combined,

To be of value to a firm, raw data must be analyzed and transformed into a form that managers can use to make decisions.

make up a firm's current assets. Current liabilities include accounts and notes payable and other short-term expenses. In these forms, current assets and current liabilities are data. However, when the current ratio (current assets divided by current liabilities) is calculated, these data are converted into usable information. Using this information, managers make decisions regarding the control of an aspect of a firm's operations. As shown in Figure 18-1, data and information play roles in the decisions made and actions taken by firms.

Information must satisfy four criteria—relevance, completeness, timeliness, and verifiability—to be of value in making decisions (see Figure 18-2).[3] Information is *relevant* when it is needed in a certain situation to help managers make decisions. The relevancy of information varies from situation to situation. For example, information about the financial performance of a firm's activities in an overseas location is not relevant to a first-level manager in the home office who is trying to find the best way to motivate workers. However, this information is quite relevant to top-level managers responsible for allocating scarce corporate resources across business units.

Information is *complete* when it provides everything that needs to be known about a particular situation. Managers considering the possibility of closing a manufacturing plant in a community would want many pieces of information before making a decision. In this situation, having information only about the effect of the plant's closing on the firm's financial performance is not complete information. Before reaching a decision, the managers would also want information about the possible effects of the plant's closing on current employees and the local community.

Information is *timely* if it is available when needed and it has not become outdated because of delay. Today's managers expect to receive information much faster than in the past. For example, Wal-Mart is connected via

Figure 18-1
Data, Information,
Decisions, and Actions

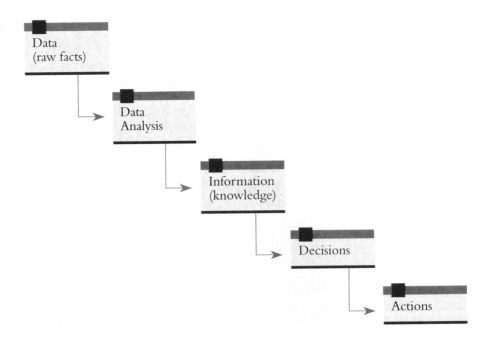

Relevant
The information is needed for a particular situation.

Complete
The information provides all that needs to be known about a particular situation.

Timely
The information is available when needed.

Verifiable
The information is accurate.

FIGURE 18-2 Criteria for Meaningful Information

computers to Procter & Gamble's distribution center. This information system reorders products automatically so that both parties benefit. Wal-Mart's shelves are stocked fully while the company maintains a minimum amount of inventory. Procter & Gamble gets "precise, timely information about buying patterns, which enables it to plan manufacturing and develop new products."[4]

Information is *verifiable* if its accuracy can be confirmed. To verify the accuracy of new information, managers either compare it with other pieces of information known to be accurate or trace the information to its original source. If information fails to satisfy one or more of the four criteria mentioned here, its decision-making value is reduced.

LEARNING CHECK   Describe the differences between data and information and discuss the four criteria information must satisfy to be valuable in a particular situation.

THE IMPORTANCE OF INFORMATION SYSTEMS

An **information system** is a set of procedures that collects, processes, stores, and distributes information to support decision making and control.[5] Information is collected from both inside and outside a firm, and it is distributed both internally and externally. An information system is an internal service function; its primary purpose is to help a firm's units operate more effectively and efficiently.[6] Through information systems, managers analyze the firm's external environments. Managers then can develop appropriate internal relationships and structures to make and implement decisions that will lead to success in those external environments.

Many think that effective management of information is linked with a firm's, and perhaps even a nation's, productivity. Jack Welch, the CEO of General Electric, believes that the success of today's firms will be significantly influenced by the degree to which information gets to people who can act effectively on that information.[7] Soon after becoming the CEO of Alcoa, Paul O'Neill decided that the company's decision-making system should be more decentralized. Critical to the success of this change was the development and implementation of information systems that allowed business units to work together more closely.[8] Some believe that, to remain competitive, U.S. industry must cooperate on a strategic vision for manufacturing in the 21st century. A key part of that vision is the shared use of information systems across many companies. Through these systems, manufacturers and their suppliers can communicate more effectively and efficiently when designing and producing products.[9]

When developed and used properly, information systems can provide two categories of benefits to a firm, as shown in Figure 18-3: improvements in productivity and competitive advantage.[10]

Improving Productivity

As defined in Chapter 15, productivity is the relationship between the inputs and outputs of a productive system.[11] Productivity is improved when fewer inputs are used to produce the same number of outputs or when a greater number of outputs is produced with the same inputs.

Typically, businesses first commit to the use of information systems in order to improve productivity. Because of their speed and storage capabilities, computers often are a part of information systems. Through computer-based information systems, workers can handle a large number of transactions with great accuracy. The results one firm achieved as it attempted to increase productivity through a computerized information system are described in the Organization in Action.

FIGURE 18-3
Information System
Benefits

Productivity Enhancements:
Resources are used more efficiently.

Competitive Advantage:
Resources are used to develop a competitive advantage.

ORGANIZATION IN ACTION

In a local dry-cleaning firm, a computerized information system was developed to keep records of customers' orders. Prior to this, orders were recorded entirely by hand. Although slow, this manual system worked acceptably until the firm's volume increased to over 10,000 customer tickets per month. With that volume, customers were forced to stand in line to drop off or pick up their garments. In addition, the recording system was incomplete, resulting in garments being misplaced or returned to the wrong customer. The firm's owner decided to install a computerized record-keeping system. Once it was installed, employees were able to receive garments and return them much faster. Of equal importance was the ability to track garments with much greater precision. In only a few months, productivity improved substantially. The new information system allowed the same number of employees to handle over 12,000 tickets per month with improved quality of service.

Gaining Competitive Advantage

Implementation of an information system is strategic if it changes how a firm competes and if, through those changes, a competitive advantage is developed. Today, many top-level managers are very interested in using information to develop competitive advantages.[12] But information and information processing technologies are not, by themselves, sufficient to develop a competitive advantage. It is through the *management* of information and information technologies that firms develop a competitive advantage. American Airlines's computerized reservation system (the SABRE system) has been a dramatically effective competitive weapon for the airline for over two decades.[13] SABRE displays American Airlines flights whenever possible, giving the firm a significant competitive advantage. In addition to

SABRE, American's computerized reservation system, is one of the airline's strongest competitive weapons.

receiving fees for processing competitors' transactions, SABRE allows American to gain a great deal of information about competitors' pricing tactics, load rates, and yields.[14] SABRE's competitive value is a product of its technological sophistication and management's ability to make effective use of the information it provides.[15]

Information systems help firms develop a competitive advantage in several ways. Information systems can help firms to:

1. reduce the time required to design, manufacture, and distribute products or services;
2. make a product more reliable or more repairable;
3. support a sales force by identifying customers and their attributes;
4. reduce the number of parts and finished goods that must be maintained in inventory; and
5. be better able to change product features in response to customers' special needs.[16]

Managers must match information system capabilities with the particular competitive advantage desired.

Back to the
Opening Case

Joseph Chapman is interested in using information systems in order to enhance productivity and develop a competitive advantage. The information system currently in use is designed to enhance productivity. Before other information systems can be developed, Chapman will have to decide what type of competitive advantage he wants to achieve.

Information Systems and Computers

There are effective information systems that are not computer based. However, because of the capabilities of computers, they are often the best foundation for an information system. Managers must decide whether an existing information system could be improved by using the processing capabilities of computers. If manual systems are performing information processing tasks efficiently and accurately, then computers may not be necessary. This may be the case in very small firms, but with success and growth, a firm's work flow often becomes more complicated and interrelated. In such a case, using computers can result in productivity gains. In both small and large firms, managers realize that computers provide the technical foundation—the tools and materials—for the development and use of an information system.[17]

In today's environment, it is reasonable to conclude that most information systems will be computer based. Thus, it is necessary for managers to select the type of computer to be used. Typically, this process involves considering the advantages and disadvantages of each type of computer and evaluating the alternatives in light of the firm's information management needs.

Define information systems, describe their importance, and discuss the value of computers to information systems.

DIFFERENT TYPES OF COMPUTERS

Information systems are designed and implemented for the benefit of end-users. An **end-user** uses the output of an information system but is not a systems specialist. Today, computers are available to a growing number of end-users. Several developments have contributed to this, but none is more important than the development of the microcomputer. A **microcomputer** (also called a *personal computer)* generally serves a single end-user, is the least expensive of all computers, and has the smallest amount of computing power.[18] Microcomputers are intended for use by people with little, if any, programming knowledge. The heart of a microcomputer is the **microprocessor,** a device that integrates the computer's memory, logic, and control on a single chip.[19] Today's microcomputers are more powerful than the mainframe computers of only a few years ago. They are capable of performing a wider range of functions at a faster pace and at a fraction of the cost.

A **minicomputer** is a medium-sized computer serving multiple end-users simultaneously. Minicomputers are more expensive than microcomputers but less expensive than mainframe computers. As with microcomputers, minicomputers are often connected or networked with large mainframe systems in order to process, store, and analyze data. Minicomputers, used extensively in universities, factories, and research laboratories, are usually about the size of an office desk.[20]

A **mainframe computer,** which usually serves 100 or more end-users simultaneously, is used to handle significant amounts of data or many complicated processes.[21] Mainframes often serve as the central computing system for major corporations and government agencies.[22]

Supercomputers have extremely large memories and rapid processing speeds and are very expensive.[23] Supercomputers are valuable in situations in which complex mathematical models and simulations are used. Examples include classified weapons research programs, weather forecasting processes, and petroleum and engineering applications.[24] The teraflops supercomputer can process a mind-boggling one trillion arithmetic operations per second. (It can do in a single second what would take a person punching one calculation per second into a hand-held calculator 24 hours a day, 365 days a year, 31,709 years to do!) This computer makes it possible to complete jobs that seemed impossible just a few years ago. For example, global climatic changes can be predicted 100 years into the future and automobile designers can use quantum mechanics to find ways to get more mileage from cars.[25]

An important outcome of the increased availability of computers to end-users is the opportunity to distribute data processing responsibilities. A

distributed processing system is a means of providing computing power throughout a firm by using microcomputers, telecommunications, and networks. Thus, managers must consider several computing options when deciding which type of computer to use as the foundation for a firm's information systems.

Back to the
Opening Case

Joseph Chapman is trying to determine what types of information systems are needed in his firm. Complicating this issue is Chapman's desire to employ the right type of computer as the foundation for the information systems. Should Chapman purchase a different minicomputer or upgrade the processing capabilities of the current minicomputer? Are the firm's information processing needs such that a mainframe computer is required? Or should microcomputers be used so the firm's data processing power could be fully distributed across the 24 stores?

TYPES OF INFORMATION SYSTEMS

There are several types of information systems used today. Seven of these are discussed in the following sections.[26]

Transaction Processing Systems

A *transaction processing system* is an organized collection of people, procedures, databases, and hardware used to record completed business transactions. These systems keep track of a firm's most basic activities, such as sales, cash deposits, the flow of materials in a factory, and payroll. The objective of these systems is to track the flow of transactions throughout the firm. Relevant data from the sale of a product that might be tracked include the customer's name, type of merchandise purchased and price paid, and payment method. Through transaction processing systems, employees can also determine where a customer's product is in the production process, whether or not an account has been paid, the number of labor hours devoted to producing a product, and so forth.

To be useful, the information provided by transaction processing systems must be available, current, and accurate. Often, these systems are used to compare outcomes across time. For example, a firm might want to know whether its salespeople sold as much this quarter as they did during the past quarter. Or it might ask whether accounts payable are being paid more rapidly than during the same period a year ago. As these examples show, these information systems focus on operational-level issues, and the information they generate is of greatest value to first-level managers.

Office Automation Systems

Office automation systems serve the needs of *data workers*—those whose jobs primarily involve the processing of data. Examples of such employees are word processing specialists, file clerks, and budget analysts. Office automation systems use data stored by transaction processing systems and support data workers' efforts to handle tasks that must be completed on a daily basis.

Knowledge Work Systems

Knowledge workers devote most of their time to the creation, distribution, or use of information.[27] Engineers, scientists, architects, and judges are knowledge workers. To complete their jobs, these people exercise judgment and creativity based on their understanding of a large body of knowledge. Through various means, including computer processing, knowledge work systems support the efforts of knowledge workers so that new knowledge and technical expertise can be integrated successfully into a firm's operations.

Management Information Systems

A *management information system (MIS)* is an organized collection of people, procedures, databases, and hardware that provides routine reports to managers and decision makers. These systems provide up-to-date information about how well a firm is performing. Satisfying the needs of first-level and, especially, middle-level managers, an MIS provides information for decision making in cases where information requirements are known in advance. Decision situations for which an MIS provides useful information tend to occur regularly. Generally, an MIS obtains its data and information from transaction processing systems. Managers use the outputs of an MIS to monitor and control activities. To display the results of these efforts, periodic reports are produced with the assistance of an MIS. Examples are annual budgets, inventory control reports, capital investment analyses, and analyses of the relationship between price and profitability for particular products.

Decision Support Systems

A *decision support system (DSS)* is an organized collection of people, procedures, databases, and hardware used to support decision making for specific problems. Decision support systems help managers with unique and relatively unstructured strategic decisions. DSSs are used by middle- and, especially, top-level managers. They are designed to deal with the information required to examine unforeseen situations. One example is the possibility of acquiring a company. Others include the sudden entrance of a powerful competitor into a firm's key market or a dramatic increase in the interest rate a firm must pay to borrow money.

Unexpected decision situations force managers to deal with many uncertain options. Through a DSS, managers engage in a series of "what-if" analyses to determine what would happen if they did X. What would happen to the value of a firm if it acquired another company? What would happen to enrollment at a college if it announced an 8 percent increase in tuition? Decision making requires managers to be able to derive informed answers to these types of questions.

Executive Support Systems

An *executive support system (ESS)* is a specialized decision support system. Designed primarily for top-level managers, an ESS evaluates both internal and external data. Inputs to an ESS come partly from the output of the information systems discussed previously. Because of the unique nature of executive support, ESSs must be easy to use. They must also support all levels of strategic decision making and be flexible in their overall approach and output presentation. These systems use advanced software applications to present information in formats (often graphs) that are meaningful for strategic decision-making processes.

Top-level managers expect an ESS to provide them with information needed to:

1. understand their firm's industry;
2. deal with multiple problems simultaneously;
3. build communications-based networks with people inside and outside the firm; and
4. maintain a viewpoint that allows them to evaluate issues pertinent to the firm as a whole.

When using an ESS, top-level managers must remain focused on key problems rather than specific details.

Expert Systems

Expert systems make it possible for computers to act like experts in particular fields. An *expert system* consists of all data, procedures, hardware, people, software, and knowledge bases needed to act or behave like a human expert in a specific field. The purpose of the knowledge base is to hold all the relevant facts and information for the specific expert system. A knowledge base is similar to the sum of an expert's knowledge gained through years of experience in a specific area.

For example, a medical expert system contains facts about diseases and symptoms as well as relationships and rules. Rules are often stored in "if-then" statements (if a certain set of medical conditions exists, then a certain diagnosis is appropriate). Doctors use expert systems to diagnose difficult medical conditions. Such a system can analyze test results and patient symptoms, diagnose the probable cause of the medical problem, and propose treatments.

Expert systems can be used to solve problems and assist in all steps of the problem-solving process. In a business setting, they are particularly useful for strategic goal setting, planning, scheduling, monitoring, and diagnosis. For example, an expert system can diagnose problems of a chemical processing facility that is not operating as expected.

ETHICS QUESTION
Are there any ethical issues involved with the use of expert systems? If so, what are they? How would you, as a manager, deal with such issues?

PRIMARY INFORMATION SYSTEM COMPONENTS

Information needs vary considerably. Because of this, each firm's information systems should be developed in light of its unique needs. Many companies, but not all, will use each of the seven types of information systems discussed in this chapter. All seven types have three components in common—hardware, software, and human resources.

Hardware

Hardware is the computer equipment required to transform data into information. **Hardware systems** include devices to input, store, and process data and provide the resulting information to end-users.

Today, firms rely less on mainframe computers as the principal source of hardware than they did in the past. Minicomputers and microcomputers have replaced mainframes in many companies. However, the mainframe is still the preferred hardware for certain applications. Mainframes process large numbers of data-intensive transactions such as those done in financial institutions and reservations departments with great speed and efficiency. Mainframes are also useful in managing large, centralized files of related information such as orders, inventory, work in progress, and shipments at a factory. They also can be used to integrate distributed computer capabilities into a single network. Integration allows significant amounts of data and information to be shared among many end-users.[28]

An information system's data processing component is concerned with the day-to-day operations of computer hardware. To process data, the hardware uses three elements: the central processing unit, input devices, and output devices.[29]

The **central processing unit (CPU)** is the "brain" of a computer. It consists of three subunits: the control unit, the arithmetic/logic unit, and the registers. The control unit monitors and regulates computer operations. It examines instructions included in a computer program, executes those instructions, and verifies that execution has occurred. The arithmetic/logic unit performs mathematical calculations and makes logical comparisons (e.g., determining whether or not one number is larger than another). Registers are high-speed storage areas used to hold small amounts of data just before, during, and after processing.

Primary storage, also called main memory, is closely associated with the CPU. It holds program instructions and data immediately before or after

This computer system includes the CPU, monitor, hard and floppy disk drives, keyboard, printer, and fax all in one workstation on wheels.

they are sent to the registers. Secondary storage is semipermanent storage on floppy or hard disks or other storage media.

Input devices feed data and instructions into the CPU. There are many types of input devices. They include microcomputers, terminals, and point-of-sale devices that can transmit data recorded on certain documents—such as sales slips—into a CPU.

An **output device** receives results from the CPU and converts them into an appropriate form for further use. A printer is a commonly used output device. An automatic teller machine (ATM) is a specialized input/output device.

Software

Software is the detailed set of instructions or programs through which computer hardware applies itself to a particular problem. Software also includes **program documentation,** the directions and descriptions designed to assist in the software's use, implementation, and operation. A **computer program** is a set of instructions or statements to the computer.[30] The instructions are written in computer language or code, stored in the computer's memory, and decoded by the control unit so the computer can perform the proper functions. An information system's software component uses two types of computer programs to complete its tasks: operating systems and applications software.

An **operating system** is a set of computer programs that supports the computer system as a whole by coordinating the activities of the hardware and the applications software.[31] There are many types of operating systems. Among other tasks, operating systems aid in the loading and execution of applications software, process input and output commands, and provide utility programs. Examples of utility program functions are listing the contents of a disk, running two or more applications programs at the same time, and allocating system resources to storage. Sophisticated information systems use several applications programs at the same time in order to provide the greatest value to end-users.

Applications software consists of programs written to solve particular problems and perform specific tasks.[32] It is the key to unlocking the potential of any computer system. Examples of applications software include word processing packages, database management software, statistical software, and presentation graphics software. Applications software is developed to perform functions that are common to most companies. Because of this, firms frequently purchase this software from developers instead of designing their own. However, it may be necessary to modify the software somewhat to satisfy the needs of a particular application.

Software's importance to information systems is increasing. Often, combinations of the capabilities provided by operating systems and applications software make it possible for a firm to develop a competitive advantage. Unique integrations of computing power through software applications help firms become more efficient and effective.

Software developers create information-based value for their customers. In fast-moving software markets, developers must provide software based on sophisticated technology.[33] Today's hardware and software customers are knowledgeable and demanding. Being a successful developer of these products during the 1990s requires a clear focus on operations and superior execution of strategies.[34]

Human Resources

Through consultation with end-users, a **systems analyst** identifies the objectives of an information system and prepares a plan to develop and implement that system. An **operating systems programmer** organizes data as needed by end-users and selects devices to store those data. An **applications programmer** develops software to generate reports, update records, and complete other transactions with the data stored in various databases.[35] These specialists will also help to develop the program documentation.

The work of systems analysts and programmers is vital to effective information systems. To complete their work, these specialists need to be technically competent, understand a firm's operations and its political realities, and possess excellent communication skills. To retain productive systems analysts and programmers, firms must offer them attractive compensation packages and stimulating work opportunities.

LEARNING CHECK   List and describe three components that are common to information systems.

All information systems should satisfy end-users' requirements. These requirements differ among firms and between managers and nonmanagerial employees. Because of these differences, changes are sometimes made in terms of various parts of the information system components we have discussed. Managers must be sure that a firm's information systems include hardware, software, and human resources (such as skilled systems and programming specialists) that can satisfy end-users' needs.

IMPLEMENTING INFORMATION SYSTEMS

In our discussions of planning (Chapters 5 and 6), we noted that the effectiveness of any plan is affected by how well it is implemented. So it is with an information system. Its value is reduced sharply if managers fail to prepare for all the tasks required to convert the plan for the information system—its description on paper—into a system that works.

Information system implementation involves many people. In addition to those who design the system, employees who will be affected by it should be a part of the implementation process. As shown in Figure 18-4, there are eight steps in implementing an information system. These steps are discussed in the following sections.[36]

Step 1: Plan the Implementation Process

In this first step, managers complete several activities. Included among these is the selection of operating systems and applications software. Given the large number of options available today, many vendors can be consulted to select software. Managers also make sure that the systems analysts and programmers needed to use the chosen software are on hand. Finally, data to be processed are converted into appropriate forms and periodic meetings are held with affected employees to describe details of the implementation process.

Step 2: Announce and Explain the Implementation Process

The cooperation of many employees is needed for an information system to be implemented successfully. To gain cooperation, managers explain employees' roles and responsibilities in the implementation process as well as the benefits of using an information system. These explanations can be offered in general terms at a single time (through a firm's in-house publication, for example). Following the global announcement, the firm can hold meetings with individual managers to detail their units' involvement. In turn, each manager should explain his or her unit's responsibilities and the role each employee will play in discharging those responsibilities.

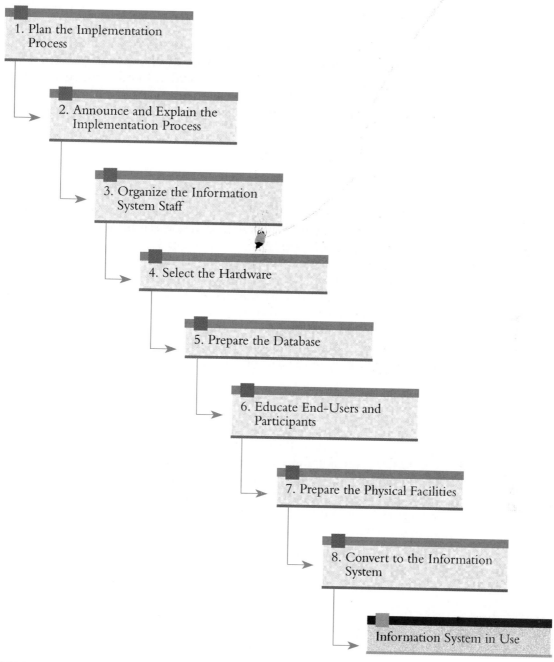

1. Plan the Implementation Process

2. Announce and Explain the Implementation Process

3. Organize the Information System Staff

4. Select the Hardware

5. Prepare the Database

6. Educate End-Users and Participants

7. Prepare the Physical Facilities

8. Convert to the Information System

Information System in Use

FIGURE 18-4 Steps in Implementing an Information System

Step 3: Organize the Information System Staff

In this step, employees are placed into various groups. Each group is assigned specific implementation objectives and tasks. Managers must form groups that include people with all the skills needed to complete assigned tasks.

Step 4: Select the Hardware

Vendors must be informed of an information system's objectives and design. They should also be told of any financial limits. In some cases, a firm might purchase all its hardware through a single vendor. In other instances, different vendors will be selected to supply particular parts of a hardware system. In this implementation step, the challenge is to purchase hardware economically.

Step 5: Prepare the Database

A **database** is an integrated collection of data and information organized for access by a computer. Database preparation can be either a simple or a complicated task. Converting hand-stored data into forms that can be used by a computer, particularly when a large database is involved, can be time consuming and difficult. For example, converting hand-stored data in the dry-cleaning firm mentioned earlier in this chapter was a sizable task. However, converting relatively small databases to a computerized system is neither complicated nor time consuming. The primary objective of data preparation is accuracy. An information system's success depends on the validity and reliability of the data being converted into information.

Step 6: Educate End-Users and Participants

An information system affects many people, including end-users and those responsible for making sure that the system is working properly. These people should be informed of their roles in the implementation process. Usually, these roles are explained by systems analysts, members of the human resources staff, or outside consultants who have assisted in the information system's design and development. Because of the dynamic nature of information systems, education for end-users and information staff members is an ongoing process.

Step 7: Prepare the Physical Facilities

If the implementation process calls for only a few additional microcomputers or one or two minicomputers, the impact on physical facilities is limited. However, adding a mainframe computer or a large number of minicomputers may require a specialized facility. In all cases, the information system staff members should be involved directly with any decisions regarding physical facilities.

Step 8: Convert to the Information System

A firm's existing information system must be usable until the new system is installed. Managers may choose one of three different approaches to the conversion step. Using the *immediate approach*, they select a time (a given day, for example) when the new system is to be used in its entirety. Although it is convenient, this approach is useful only when managers have been able to document the new system's capabilities carefully. With the *phased approach*, managers divide the unit that is to use the information system into subunits. Individual subunits begin to use the new system at various times. Companies with several plant locations often use this approach, selecting the dates on which the new system is to become operational in individual plants. Finally, with the *parallel approach*, the old system is maintained until the new system is in place and its effectiveness has been evaluated. Although it is expensive, this approach provides the greatest amount of insurance against system failure.

ETHICS QUESTION
As a manager, would ethics play a role in your selection of one of the three approaches to the conversion step? If so, describe what the role of ethics would be in this situation.

LEARNING CHECK

Name and describe each of the eight steps in implementing an information system.

HUMAN REACTIONS TO INFORMATION SYSTEMS

The effects of information technology and systems on organizational life can be pervasive and significant. Information systems create uncertainty. Employees may fear losing their jobs, and in some instances use of computerized information systems does result in loss of jobs. For example, to save $50 million annually, Sears, Roebuck & Co. spent $60 million for 28,000 custom-designed cash registers and 6,000 automated customer-service stands. This information technology eliminated approximately 1,000 non-sales positions and 5,900 part-time clerical positions.[37]

Even when jobs are not in jeopardy, employees may feel they have less influence on their jobs as they watch the introduction of new, computer-based technologies. Sometimes even a manager's rational explanation of an information system's objectives and benefits does not reduce uncertainty. The uncertainty results from being asked to cope with the unknown, and it is reduced only after the system becomes operational.

ETHICS QUESTION
Is it ethical for managers to introduce a computer-based information system knowing that employees fear the introduction and use of that system?

Often information systems affect how people perform their jobs. Some employees may feel that modern information systems require them to interact mainly with computers instead of people. This causes them to feel isolated from important personal relationships. In addition, when faced with sophisticated technologies, some employees feel incompetent. Many managers must deal with people who believe they will never acquire the skills needed to work with computers. However, through patience and practice, most employees quickly learn that they can work successfully with an information system.

Changes created by information systems also may be favorable for many employees. The modern technologies that are a key part of today's information systems can enrich jobs. Word processing packages and microcomputers have allowed clerical workers to gain skills and satisfactions well beyond the capabilities they had when using typewriters.

Distributed processing capabilities, part of many modern information systems, make it possible for increasing numbers of employees to work at home. A home microcomputer linked to computers at the firm provides a pathway to communicate actively with other employees. This option may be especially attractive for those who want to remain home with young children, avoid long commutes, or do creative work that requires solitude and quiet.

Still others may find that information system capabilities allow them to interact more effectively with employees in other parts of their firm. For example, operations, marketing, and design employees may be linked via computer networks to develop a new product. Being able to communicate actively with one another through computer networks may stimulate creativity and enhance productivity.

The total impact of modern information systems on employees is not yet known. What we do know is that the success of an information system depends as much on people as on technology. Managers, systems analysts, and programmers must understand end-users' needs, and end-users must understand the information system, believe in it, and know its benefits. Only through careful integration of technology with people can firms benefit from using information systems. Today's managers must remember that sophisticated equipment results in productivity gains and competitive advantages only when combined with superior managerial practices. Such practices are grounded in a respect for and appreciation of employees' needs and innovative capabilities.

INFORMATION SYSTEMS IN THE 1990s

Information systems are changing as a result of the evolution of computer technologies and the dynamic competition in the global marketplace. These changes suggest an interesting set of issues that managers may face in developing effective information systems during the 1990s. Three of these issues are examined in the following sections.

Managing Interdependence

Today's firms face difficult and challenging conditions. Among the factors contributing to this are the trend toward more global markets and the reduced time available to design and market products. Other factors include the continuous drive to reduce costs and the need to provide the highest quality service to customers. To deal with these conditions successfully, a firm must recognize that today its business functions are more dependent on one another than they were in the past. To sell products in global marketplaces, a firm must be able to integrate its design, engineering, operations, and marketing functions.[38]

Information systems are one means through which firms can manage interdependence effectively. Establishing common standards for data ensures that employees in different units use consistent inputs to complete tasks. Information networks and linkages among units increase the speed with which employees can interact and complete tasks. For example, information systems aid teams in completing certain assignments. Members of these teams come from various business units to work on specific, time-based projects. To function effectively, the teams must have ready access to many types of information.

Information systems also provide valuable inputs to planning activities. Data prepared using common standards, from interdependent units, yield the integrated inputs that managers need to plan successfully. As business units become even more interdependent, managers will use information systems to manage that interdependence.

Centralization Versus Decentralization

There is continuing debate regarding the relative value of centralized and decentralized information systems. Originally, most information systems were centralized. Before mini- and microcomputers became widely available, companies centralized information processing and analytical tasks around the capabilities of what was often a single mainframe computer.

But with the distribution of computing power to a larger number of end-users came the request for decentralized information systems. In a decentralized information system, mini- and microcomputers support applications in individual business units. Software is developed or purchased and maintained by local systems specialists. There are several advantages to decentralized information systems, including a reduction in telecommunications costs and immediate access to decentralized databases. However, the primary reason for decentralization is local control. With local control, individual units have control over database, hardware, and software decisions.[39]

The advantages of decentralization are significant. However, in the early 1990s, some firms began to recentralize information systems. Three factors influenced this decision:[40]

1. The high cost of multiple data processing facilities. In particular, it is expensive for firms to license software applications at several sites.
2. The changing demographics of information system professionals. Because the demand for skilled information system specialists exceeds supply, it is more cost effective to have them in a centralized location. Doing this reduces the number of information system specialists needed in a firm.
3. The emphasis on company-wide, integrated information systems. This need can be better served by a centralized information systems staff.

Integrating all of a firm's business functions through information technology is an important strategic payoff. Other benefits of centralized information systems include end-user access to computers with large-scale capacities and tighter security for databases.

Centralized and decentralized information systems each have their advantages. The managerial challenge is to develop information systems that satisfy end-users' needs. End-users should have opportunities to influence information system development and implementation. Individual business units should be able to determine their information system priorities and the number of information specialists needed. At the same time, information specialists at the corporate level should operate a consolidated computing and communications network and set standards for databases, software, and the design of applications.[41] This dual approach combines the benefits of centralized and decentralized information systems. However, achieving the integration of these benefits is a challenge.

Outsourcing

Outsourcing means obtaining needed goods, services, and/or materials from firms outside the company.[42] To trim overhead, in 1989, Kodak made a strategic decision to hire IBM and Digital Equipment to run its data processing centers and networks. According to Kodak's director of information systems, Katherine Hudson, the reason for outsourcing was simple: "IBM is in the data processing business, and Kodak isn't." Kodak was able to cut 1,000 jobs and their associated costs.

Kodak is not the only company outsourcing some or all of its computing operations. AT&T now works with Chevron employees to run the U.S. portion of Chevron's international network. J.P. Morgan will use AT&T facilities to tie its individual office computer networks in 13 countries into one large data network. GE's information services division is now running the Vatican's global data network. Outsourcing is propelled by the growing complexity of computer networking and the increasingly international scope of today's organizations. In 1990, U.S. businesses spent $7.2 billion on outsourcing. By 1995, this figure is expected to reach $15.2 billion. One analyst believes that "outsourcing is by far the biggest trend in computing since the development of the PC."

Companies give several reasons for outsourcing their computing operations. First, outsourcing may save money. The typical industrial company spends 3 to 5 percent of its operating budget on computing. Companies can sometimes save 10 percent or more of that amount by allowing others to handle their computing operations. J.P. Morgan estimates that outsourcing one of its three international data networks to British Telecommunications will save $12 million in operating costs over the next five years.

Outsourcing also provides firms with access to the most sophisticated computer and network technologies. Firms running computer systems for others assemble the best possible computing configurations. Among the largest firms engaged in this business are EDS, IBM, Andersen Consulting, Digital Equipment, AT&T, Computer Sciences Corporation, and KMPG Peat Marwick. The computing capabilities of these firms exceed what smaller companies could expect to develop for themselves. Aligning itself with one of these larger firms allows a smaller firm to benefit from the economies of scale that the large firms have in computing services.

A third outsourcing benefit is strategic in nature. Having another firm responsible for computing operations allows a company to focus its energies on what it does best. In Kodak's case, for example, computing operations are not one of its core competencies. By having IBM and Digital Equipment handle its computing and telecommunication needs, Kodak can concentrate on its core businesses.

In addition to the benefits of outsourcing, there are potential disadvantages. Not having systems specialists' expertise in house may prevent a firm from finding ways to use information systems for competitive advantage. The systems analyst of a large computing services firm does not have the intricate, company-specific knowledge that an internal systems analyst can develop. Without such knowledge, the analyst may not identify pathways to integrating functions across business units. Another possible disadvantage of outsourcing is cost. Some firms reject outsourcing because they believe they can handle their computing operations more economically. As one company official said, "Those outsourcing guys like big profit margins, which is fine. But if we can be just as efficient as they are—which I think we can— the economic benefit will go to us instead."

As this discussion suggests, outsourcing presents interesting managerial opportunities. During the 1990s and beyond, managers will continuously compare the relative benefits of in-house computing and outsourcing. They will also observe the evolution of outsourcing. It is possible that in the future outsourcing will become more of a partnership between a company and its data processing source. Two companies joining together in this manner may isolate a competitive advantage that can be exploited for mutual benefit.

ETHICS QUESTION
Are there ethical issues involved with the decision to outsource a firm's data processing tasks? If so, what are these issues, and how would you as a manager deal with them?

LEARNING CHECK

Discuss the effects of information systems on people and information system issues managers may face in the 1990s.

SUMMARY

Information systems—a set of procedures for collecting, processing, storing, and distributing information to support decision making and controlling activities—are linked with organizational success. Inputs to these systems include data and information or knowledge derived through the conversion of data. To be of maximum value, information must be relevant, complete, timely, and verifiable. The key purpose of information systems is to help firms enhance their productivity or identify a competitive advantage.

Not all information systems are computer based.

However, managers will use computers when they believe that computers will enhance the value of an information system. If managers decide to use computers, several options are available. A microcomputer is the least expensive and least powerful computer. Medium-sized minicomputers are designed to serve the needs of many end-users simultaneously. Usually, minicomputers interact with a company's mainframe computer. A mainframe computer is large and handles significant amounts of data and complicated processes. Supercomputers have extremely large memories and rapid processing speeds and are used where complex mathematical models are important.

There are seven major types of information systems used in today's firms. Transaction processing systems track a firm's most basic activities such as sales, payroll, and the flow of materials in a factory. Office automation systems serve data workers who handle tasks that are completed daily. Knowledge work systems support the efforts of those who spend most of their time creating, distributing, or using information. Managers' and decision makers' needs for routine reports are addressed by management information systems. These systems provide up-to-date information about how well a firm is performing. A decision support system helps top-level managers deal with strategic decisions that are relatively unique and unstructured. These systems allow managers to analyze a series of "what-if" statements. Executive support systems help managers evaluate both internal and external information required to make decisions regarding the management of an entire firm. Finally, expert systems allow computers to act like experts in certain fields. They are particularly useful for strategic goal setting, planning, scheduling, monitoring, and diagnosis.

All information systems include three components: hardware, software (operating systems and applications software), and human resources (systems analysts and programming specialists). To satisfy unique needs, managers develop various combinations of these components.

An information system's effectiveness is influenced by its implementation. Eight steps are followed to implement an information system successfully. These include planning the implementation process, announcing and explaining the implementation process, organizing the information system staff, selecting the hardware, preparing the database, educating end-users and participants, preparing the physical facilities, and converting to the new system. A firm's actions must be integrated carefully for the implementation process to proceed smoothly.

Human reactions to information systems are both positive and negative. Employees usually experience fear and uncertainty. In some instances, employees view information systems as an opportunity to be involved with an enriched job. The full impact of these systems on employees likely will not be known for some time to come.

Information technology and information systems are changing at a rapid pace. Issues that managers may face during the 1990s include using information systems to better manage interdependence among business units, deciding whether information systems should be centralized or decentralized, and examining the potential merits of outsourcing a firm's computing needs to a company specializing in data processing activities.

KEY TERMS

information management	minicomputer	(CPU)	systems analyst
data	mainframe computer	input devices	operating systems programmer
information	supercomputers	output device	applications programmer
information system	distributed processing system	software	database
end-user	hardware	program documentation	outsourcing
microcomputer	hardware systems	computer program	
microprocessor	central processing unit	operating system	
		applications software	

QUESTIONS FOR DISCUSSION AND REVIEW

1. If someone asked you whether data and information are the same, what would your response be?
2. What is an information system? Is it important for a firm to have information systems? Why or why not?

3. Describe the different types of computers used in today's firms.
4. What are the different types of information systems in use today? Describe how information systems have been used in companies in which you

have worked.

5. What are the primary components of an information system? Is any one component more important than the others? Justify your position.

6. What are the eight steps required to implement information systems successfully?

7. What are some of the effects of information systems on people? Describe a situation you have seen in which a person was affected by an information system.

8. In your opinion, what issues might information system managers face during the 1990s? What should managers do now to be prepared to deal with tomorrow's issues?

PROBLEMS FOR ACTION

A. Assume that your firm's top-level managers have decided to invest in a multimillion-dollar, totally integrated MIS. The MIS will use state-of-the-art technology, provide multiple reports, and include intelligent terminals allowing managers to interact electronically. Because computer applications in the firm have been minimal to date, you have expressed reservations about making such a large MIS investment. Instead, you have argued that an evolutionary approach to developing an MIS may be preferable. Top-level managers have given you 10 minutes to make a presentation to them. Prepare the presentation you would make in this situation.

B. Assume that you have earned a computer science degree and are seeking a job. During an important interview, you are asked the following question: "Why should our firm develop information systems? I think we have done quite well without them. Convince me that these systems would be a good use of our limited dollars." Use what you have learned from this chapter to answer this question.

CONCLUDING CASE

Freeman & Company's Decision Support System

Freeman & Company is a large, privately owned furniture manufacturer. Critical to its success are continuous product enhancements, service to the customer, and an aggressive sales force. Tim Freeman—the vice president for marketing and brother of the firm's sole owner and chief executive officer, James Freeman—manages the sales force. The firm has three manufacturing sites and four regional sales offices.

For many years, the firm's managers had believed in the importance of managing information effectively. Because of this, several computer-based information systems, including transaction processing, office automation systems, and management information systems, had been developed. Recently, however, James Freeman, his brother, and the firm's remaining three top-level managers (the vice presidents for finance, human resources, and manufacturing) concluded that another information system had to be developed. Competition in the furniture industry had become severe, and customers' tastes

were changing faster than ever. Competitors were introducing new products almost quicker than James Freeman could imagine. The managers concluded that they lacked the information required to respond effectively to rapidly changing conditions in what was becoming an unpredictable business environment.

At his brother's urging, Tim Freeman solicited bids from software suppliers to help the firm develop a decision support system. As it turned out, the bids were approximately the same except for the one from Century Computers. Instead of using packaged software applications, this firm proposed more expensive software that Century would develop specifically for Freeman & Company.

When the five top-level managers met to consider the alternatives, energetic discussions surfaced. Two managers, including the finance vice president, wanted to accept the lowest bid. Doing this would mean using standard hardware systems and software applications that were being used by others in the furniture industry. Another manager argued the benefits of using software tailored to their firm's information needs. Much to the group's surprise, James Freeman suggested that the firm should outsource all of its information processing activities. Based on recent readings, he believed that the firm could save money if it chose this alternative.

Tim Freeman had hoped the managers would accept one of the bids and begin discussions of how to implement the decision support system. As the meeting dragged on, he recognized that a decision would not be reached that day. If anything, the managers were farther apart in their views than they had been when the meeting started. As he left the room, after scheduling another meeting for the next week, Tim wondered what he should do. He was convinced that the top-level managers had to have a way to deal with unexpected information if the firm

was to remain successful. But choosing a system to provide them with that capability was proving to be a complicated task. That night, as he closed his office door, he was confused and concerned. Although he recognized their importance, dealing with information systems had become just about the last thing he wanted to do.

1. Evaluate the approach used by Freeman & Company to consider developing a decision support system. Was the approach effective or not? Justify your position.
2. What advice would you give Tim Freeman? What should his next steps be in developing and implementing a DSS?
3. In your opinion, does outsourcing make sense for this firm? Why or why not?

REFERENCES

1. Robert Schultheis and Mary Sumner, *Management Information Systems* (Homewood, IL: Irwin, 1992): 3.
2. James A. Senn, *Information Systems in Management*, 4e (Belmont, CA: Wadsworth, 1990): 62.
3. Senn, *Information Systems in Management*, 64.
4. David Kirkpatrick, "Why Not Farm Out Your Computing?" *Fortune* (September 23, 1991): 103–112.
5. Kenneth C. Laudon and Jane Price Laudon, *Management Information Systems*, 2e (New York: MacMillan, 1991): 5.
6. James R. Mensching and Dennis A. Adams, *Managing an Information System* (Englewood Cliffs, NJ: Prentice Hall, 1991): 19.
7. "What I Want U.S. Business to Do in '92," *Fortune* (December 30, 1991): 24–59.
8. "The Recasting of Alcoa," *Business Week* (September 9, 1991): 62–64.
9. "This Is What the U.S. Must Do to Stay Competitive," *Business Week* (December 16, 1991): 92–93.
10. This section is based on materials included in Senn, *Information Systems in Management*, 40–44.
11. Roger G. Schroeder, *Operations Management*, 3e (New York: McGraw-Hill, 1989): 662.
12. Albert L. Lederer and Raghu Nath, "Making Strategic Information Systems Happen," *The Executive* (August 1990): 76–83.
13. F. Warren McFarlan, Comments in a letter to the editor, *Harvard Business Review* (July-August 1990): 176.
14. James C. Wetherbe, Comments in a letter to the editor, *Harvard Business Review* (July-August 1990): 176–177.
15. Peter G. W. Keen, Comments in a letter to the editor, *Harvard Business Review* (July-August 1990): 177–178.
16. E. Wainright Martin, Daniel W. DeHayes, Jeffrey A. Hoffer, and William C. Perkins, *Managing Information Technology* (New York: MacMillan, 1991): 61–63.
17. Laudon and Laudon, *Management Information Systems*, 6.
18. Martin et al., *Managing Information Technology*, 645.
19. Laudon and Laudon, *Management Information Systems*, 205.
20. Laudon and Laudon, *Management Information Systems*, 207.
21. Laudon and Laudon, *Management Information Systems*, 207.
22. Martin et al., *Managing Information Technology*, 645.
23. Senn, *Information Systems in Management*, 148.
24. Laudon and Laudon, *Management Information Systems*, 214.
25. "Where No Computer Has Gone Before," *Business Week* (November 25, 1991): 80–88.
26. These materials are based on Laudon and Laudon, *Management Information Systems*, 6–12; Senn, *Information Systems in Management*, 13–19; and Ralph M. Stair, *Principles of Information Systems: A Managerial Approach* (Boston: Boyd & Fraser Publishing Company, 1992): 47–52 and 356–361.
27. John Naisbitt, *Megatrends: Ten Directions Transforming Our Lives* (New York: Warner Books, 1982).
28. Martin et al., *Managing Information Technology*, 620.
29. The discussion of hardware components is based on Stair, *Information Systems: A Managerial Approach*, 65–66 and 90.
30. Stair, *Information Systems: A Managerial Approach*, 98.
31. Stair, *Information Systems: A Managerial Approach*, 100.
32. Stair, *Information Systems: A Managerial Approach*, 100.
33. "Another Year, Another Bitter Lesson for Jim Manzi," *Business Week* (December 9, 1991): 88.
34. "Should the U.S. Abandon Computer Manufacturing?" A debate appearing in *Harvard Business Review* (September-October, 1991): 140–161.
35. Laudon and Laudon, *Management Information Systems*, 378–379.
36. This section is based on materials from Raymond McLeod Jr., *Management Information Systems*, 3e (Chicago: Science Research Associates, 1986): 736–752.
37. "Sears to Buy System from CompuAdd, Cut 7,000 Workers," *Dallas Morning News* (January 8, 1992): 1D and 2D.
38. John F. Rockart and James E. Short, "IT in the 1990s: Managing Organizational Interdependence," *Sloan Management Review* (Winter 1989): 7–16.

39. Schultheis and Sumner, *Management Information Systems*, 788.

40. Ernest M. Von Simson, "The Centrally Decentralized IS Organization," *Harvard Business Review* (July-August 1990): 159.

41. Von Simson, "The Centrally Decentralized IS Organization," 162.

42. John J. Keller, "More Firms 'Outsource' Data Networks," *The Wall Street Journal* (March 11, 1992): B1; Kirkpatrick, "Why Not Farm Out Your Computing?" 103–112; and Stair, *Information Systems: A Managerial Approach*, 473.

Controlling Operations at the ASAP Clinic

Raised on a ranch, Kerry Livesay developed an interest in medicine at an early age. In part, this interest was fueled by the location of his family's ranch in a beautiful part of a western state. The Livesay's closest neighbor was 5 miles away, with the nearest town another 18 miles from that. This location, coupled with other issues involved with running a small cattle operation, caused the Livesays to become quite independent. Kerry, along with his brother, sister, and parents, became skilled at repairing mechanical equipment and dealing with minor medical problems, particularly those concerning the cattle.

After graduating from high school, Livesay earned a degree in biology from a state university. While in medical school and during his service as a resident intern, Livesay considered several possibilities. After many discussions with classmates, teachers, and friends, he decided to establish a family practice in a medium-size community. Located approximately 150 miles from the family ranch, the town had grown rapidly in the last few years and now had a population of 170,000. Combining his interests with the town's economic base (several large manufacturing firms dominated the local economy), Livesay decided to open a minor emergency medical clinic.

The ASAP clinic started on a small scale, and Livesay was its only full-time physician during its early months. He worked long hours because the clinic was open from 9:00 A.M. to 6:00 P.M. during the week and from 9:00 A.M. to 4:00 P.M. on Saturdays. In addition to providing medical services, Livesay helped his secretary-receptionist, June Goble, develop patient files and prepare the various financial and reporting documents needed to run ASAP. The clinic's single nurse also helped with other activities when she had time. To provide some relief, Livesay hired a local physician to work some Saturdays.

Although the first year was difficult, Livesay was pleased with the clinic's success over the following three years. To handle the increased patient load, Livesay had hired a second physician to work on a full-time basis. Instead of a single nurse, the clinic now employed three nurses, and three additional people were hired to assist June Goble.

Everything appeared to be going well at the clinic. However, Livesay and his staff knew that the firm was experiencing problems that had to be addressed. Some of these were brought fully to his attention in a recent conversation with Goble. "Kerry, things are getting out of control here. We do not have enough space to handle our patients' files. It is great that we are seeing more and more clients each year, but space is a real problem for us now. We don't have a spot to prepare new files without squeezing out someone else who is trying to complete some other task.

"Even worse is the filing problem. First, we are out of space. Our cabinets simply will not hold more files. An even more serious problem is access to the files. It seems that people are always bumping into each other as they try to either pull a file or return one to its proper place. And Kerry, as you, too, have observed, even our patients are having trouble. Because of inadequate space, people who are leaving and those who are trying to pay their bills often come face to face with patients being called to the examining rooms. We simply need more space!"

Livesay listened intently to Goble. After all, she had been with him from the start and was a loyal and hard-working employee. "June, I know you are right. We do not have enough space to handle our business. I am concerned about this too, and I believe that we must find another location. I'll have more to say about this in just a few days. But tell me, are there other issues you want to talk about?"

"Yes, Kerry, there are," said Goble. "I am concerned about our records and how we keep track of things in the office. We still do not have control of our inventory. Supplies of some items—surgical gauze, for example—are excessive. But you and Dr. Grayson have found that we are completely out of other items. We need to get a much better handle on how to order and when to reorder. Furthermore, I think we must change how we deal with the financial records and documents we are required to complete for insurance companies and government agencies. Basically, we are still trying to do most of this by hand. We need computers! Can you help us with this?"

"June, I agree with everything you have said. I know that in some ways our clinic is running a bit out of control. We are going to have to do several things, including those you mentioned. There is one thing that I intended to talk with all of you about shortly, but let me mention it to you now. I have found two pieces of land in the community that I believe could be attractive to us. If we bought either one of these tracts, we would build a new clinic. With a new facility, we would be able to deal with the space issues you have talked about today.

"But I can't decide which of these locations would be best for us. One tract is more expensive than the other, but it is in a location that I believe would provide more clients. I just don't know all the information we need to gather to analyze this matter. I have an appointment with Karla Gibney early next week. She works with one of the engineering firms here in town, and I think she can help us find answers to these questions."

After his talk with Goble, Livesay knew that he had to move quickly. His clinic was in a situation re-quiring action. He knew that he had to gain more control of his firm if it was to remain successful.

1. Describe the problems of control that you believe face Livesay's clinic.
2. Seven operations systems were discussed in Chapter 18. Select those that you believe apply to the situation confronting Livesay's clinic. For each operations system you select, describe how it applies to Livesay's clinic.
3. Are there operations systems techniques that you believe could help Kerry Livesay reach decisions regarding the problems facing ASAP? If so, what are these techniques? Describe how they could benefit Livesay and the information Livesay should gather in order to use those techniques successfully.
4. What type of computer do you think could be the most effective and efficient for the management of information in Livesay's clinic? Be prepared to defend your answer.

Part VI
Managing
in
Special
Settings

Chapter 19

Entrepreneurship

Chapter Learning Objectives:

1. Define entrepreneurship and entrepreneurs.

2. Describe the characteristics of successful entrepreneurs.

3. Identify and discuss several myths about entrepreneurs.

4. Define intrapreneurship and discuss its advantages.

5. Describe the keys to successful intrapreneurship.

6. Discuss the importance of new ventures to the U.S. economy.

7. Describe several guidelines that enhance the probability that a new venture will be successful.

Raised on a family ranch, Ed Arner and his three brothers had busy childhoods. Among other chores, they fed cattle, mended fences, and repaired equipment. For the most part, Ed did not mind his busy schedule. In fact, he often thought that the busier he was, the more he managed to accomplish.

After high school graduation, Ed, along with Hal, his oldest brother, attended a junior college close to home. Because they had a streak of independence, Ed and Hal wanted to pay their own way through college. Relying on mechanical skills learned on the ranch, the two opened a car repair business. They did not have enough money to lease space, so they used the garage at the house they rented. To advertise the firm, they posted flyers throughout their school's campus.

Somewhat to their surprise, the firm became very successful. Before long, they had more customers than they could handle. They rented a garage and hired mechanics. Eventually, Ed bought Hal's share of the business. (Hal went on to complete a business degree at a four-year school and works as an accountant for a major oil company.) With continuing success, Ed Arner turned his attention to other projects.

Because he thought it was being offered at the right price, Arner purchased a locally owned and operated cookie company. The firm had been barely profitable for several years even though it was located in the town's largest mall. Although he knew nothing about operating the business, he had confidence in the store's current manager, Jill Warren. The first thing Arner did was to give Warren almost complete responsibility for running the business. Unlike the previous owner, Arner decided to offer Warren a salary plus bonuses tied to the store's profitability. After working together for a few months, Arner and Warren quickly found ways to make the firm more profitable.

With Warren solidly in charge, Arner decided to find other local companies to buy. His strategy was to buy them cheaply, then find ways to operate them more efficiently. Within 10 years, Arner owned a gas station, a video store, and a dry-cleaning firm, in addition to the garage and cookie company. In each instance, he bought the company, found a person he trusted to manage it, and then worked with that person until the business was on solid ground.

Talking about this approach with a neighbor one day, Gwen Arner, Ed's wife, commented that "Ed is happiest when he first buys a company. After he buys, he rolls up his sleeves and gets busy. He seems fascinated by the chance to learn how to operate a different type of company. Honestly, I don't think money means much to him. He's just like a little kid in a candy store when he walks into his new business. I don't think he will ever stop buying companies. Doing that is what keeps him going. But I do wish he would slow down. He's always doing something, whether working at one of his companies or trying to find another one to buy."

Ed Arner has been successful. But what is there about Arner, and others, that allows them to be successful entrepreneurs? Is a person born with entrepreneurial abilities, or can they be learned? Is entrepreneurship practiced in large corporations? How important is entrepreneurship to the health of the U.S. economy? And, will the prediction that entrepreneurs and their efforts will lead the U.S. economy into a new Golden Age come true?[1] This chapter answers these questions and considers other issues related to successful entrepreneurship.

The chapter's first section defines entrepreneurship and entrepreneurs and discusses the characteristics of successful entrepreneurs. Before describing common myths about entrepreneurs, we discuss the fact that there are different kinds of entrepreneurs. As you will learn, entrepreneurship is also practiced in some large organizations. We discuss these activities, known as *intrapreneurship*, in the next section, followed by a discussion of the importance of new ventures to the U.S. economy. This discussion includes a presentation of three different approaches entrepreneurs examine when determining how to begin their new ventures. The discussion is followed with considerations regarding properly formed business plans and guidelines for new-venture success. The chapter closes with a critique of entrepreneurship.

DEFINING ENTREPRENEURSHIP

Entrepreneurship is difficult to define. A key reason for this is that it means different things to different people. Some believe that entrepreneurs are ultimate risk-takers. Others think of entrepreneurship as an opportunity to do things differently from the way they have been allowed to do them while working for someone else. Neither of these descriptions fully captures the true meaning of entrepreneurship.

Essentially, entrepreneurship is a creative act.[2] Entrepreneurship requires perception, drive, tenacity, dedication, and hard work to pursue identified economic opportunities.[3] It also requires acceptance of **entrepreneurial risk**—risks taken with regard to one's time, financial resources, and psychological well-being. These risks are real. Approximately 50 percent of new businesses fail in their first year, and 75 to 80 percent fail within three to five years.[4] Thus, **entrepreneurship** is a process intended to create wealth. It is accomplished by gathering and managing human, financial, physical, and informational resources to pursue a business opportunity with acceptable levels of risk.[5]

When practiced successfully, entrepreneurship results in the introduction of new and often innovative goods, services, or processes into the marketplace. This in turn creates opportunities for additional goods, services, and processes. For example, the introduction of the personal computer created opportunities for the design and manufacture of software and peripheral equipment. Printers, disk drive units, and a range of systems and applications software (discussed in Chapter 18) are examples.

Entrepreneurship is instrumental in the development of any society. To flourish, entrepreneurship needs a society that encourages and supports individual initiative. The 1990s will provide a fertile ground for entrepreneurship in Eastern European economies that have long been denied the power of free enterprise. Conditions aiding entrepreneurs include readily available investment capital and a cultural acceptance of business people who sometimes operate in unconventional manners.[6] In the early 1990s, another condition—an economic recession—stimulated entrepreneurship in the United States. This is described in Entrepreneurs in Action.

ENTREPRENEURS IN ACTION

At age 43, Harvey Lewis was a 25-year Citicorp employee. Lewis had performed well, climbing the corporate ladder from his job as a back-room clerk to an assistant vice president. (He also earned his MBA degree during this time.) When Citicorp closed the New Jersey mortgage-banking office where he worked, Lewis decided to use part of his $65,000 severance pay to start his own firm. With his wife, he now operates a computer school for children. Lewis's feelings have changed dramatically in a short time: "At first I was afraid of failing and going hungry. Now I wonder why I didn't try this sooner. It's a new life."

After she left AT&T, sales executive Mary Poldruhi decided to open a restaurant serving Eastern European fare. To finance her firm, Poldruhi, who is of Polish descent, personally contacted doctors and lawyers in the local community who shared her national heritage. Through these efforts, Poldruhi found 80 people, each of whom was willing to invest $3,000 in her firm.

Ronald Wilmoth decided to buy the electronics store where he worked after the chain that owned the store went bankrupt. Facing termination by the company that had employed him for 21 years, Wilmoth obtained the financing necessary to buy the store. Wilmoth, who now employs six people, is enthusiastic about this turn of events: "I would have never tried this before. I was too comfortable to take chances."

Source: "Starting Over," *Time* (January 6, 1992): 62–63.

The responses of these three people to unexpected unemployment are not unusual. Historically, the number of new ventures created has increased with higher unemployment levels.[7] The experiences of the three first-time entrepreneurs are common. People who at first may be reluctant entrepreneurs often find their new work life to be exciting and challenging. In the next section, we define an entrepreneur more formally as a person who, like Lewis, Poldruhi, and Wilmoth, seeks to practice entrepreneurship successfully.

DEFINING ENTREPRENEURS

There are many definitions of an entrepreneur. Traditionally, economists have defined entrepreneurs as people who bring the different means of production (raw materials, labor, physical assets) together in a unique fashion to generate profits.[8] Today, entrepreneurs are also skilled at recognizing marketplace opportunities. In fact, some believe that the central task of entrepreneurs is the relentless pursuit of opportunity.[9] In the 1990s, opportunities are plentiful. Changes in domestic and foreign government policies, development of sophisticated consumer electronics, and changes in consumers' lifestyles are examples of conditions creating entrepreneurial opportunities. Thus, an **entrepreneur** is a person who recognizes a marketplace opportunity and accepts the risk of assembling resources to take advantage of that opportunity in order to create wealth.[10] Figure 19-1 summarizes our definitions of entrepreneurship and entrepreneurs.

FIGURE 19-1
Entrepreneurship and
Entrepreneurs

Entrepreneurship is:

- A process
- Concerned with creatively using a firm's resources
- Intended to create wealth

An entrepreneur is:

- A relentless seeker of opportunities
- Someone who acquires and uses resources effectively
- Someone who understands strategic management and strategic planning practices

**LEARNING
CHECK**   Define the terms entrepreneurship and entrepreneur.

Characteristics of Successful Entrepreneurs

Over the years, studies have been conducted to better understand entrepreneurs. They have identified a number of characteristics of successful entrepreneurs. A composite of these characteristics is shown in Figure 19-2.

Back to the
Opening Case

Carefully study the characteristics shown in Figure 19-2. With these characteristics in mind, reread the opening case. In your opinion, does Ed Arner possess some of the characteristics of the successful entrepreneur? If so, which ones? Be prepared to support your answers.

Knowing the characteristics of successful entrepreneurs does not provide a complete picture of what makes one entrepreneur successful while another fails. For example, we do not know how many of these characteristics a person must possess to be successful. People with only a few of these characteristics have started companies and succeeded, while others with most of the characteristics have failed.[11] Thus, it is difficult to identify a specific set of characteristics that relates to either success or failure. Steve Jobs, one of the co-founders of the Apple Computer Company and later the founder of NeXT, Inc., has been described as someone with a keen vision. **Vision** is the ability to imagine the future and the products or services that could be marketed successfully in that future. It is one of the most important entrepreneurial characteristics.[12] Another concern about the value of listing these entrepreneurial characteristics is that they also describe other successful business people. Effective managers in both large and small firms possess many of the characteristics included in Figure 19-2.

For someone who is thinking of becoming an entrepreneur, a good deal of insight can be provided by studying the characteristics of the successful

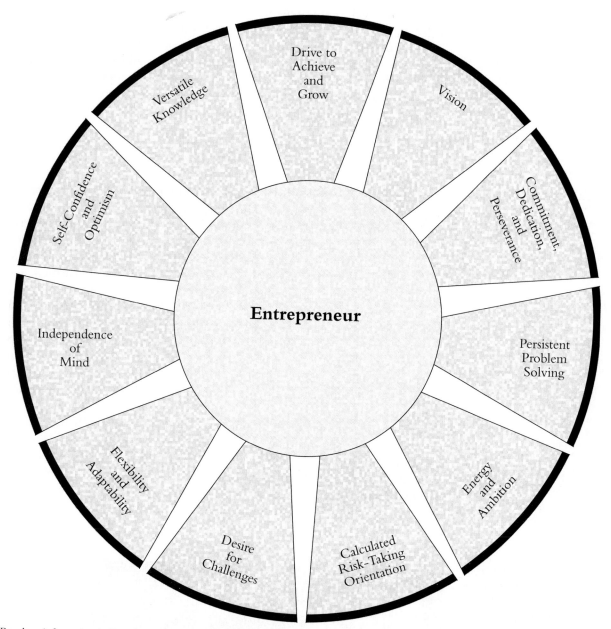

Based on information in David H. Holt, *Entrepreneurship: New Venture Creation* (Englewood Cliffs, NJ: Prentice-Hall, 1992): 8–10; and John J. Kao, *The Entrepreneur* (Englewood Cliffs, NJ: Prentice-Hall, 1991): 20–22.

FIGURE 19-2 Characteristics of Successful Entrepreneurs

entrepreneur. It would be an unusual person indeed who had all of the characteristics shown in Figure 19-2. Nevertheless, successful entrepreneurs do have many of them. It is also important to know that effective entrepreneurs surround themselves with people who possess many of the characteristics they lack. These people may be partners, members of the firm's board of directors, or investors.

Thus, successful entrepreneurs know their strengths and limitations and involve themselves with people who have skills they do not possess. Certainly in large firms entrepreneurs must rely on others. Ken Olsen, the founder of the Digital Equipment Company and the subject of a book titled *The Ultimate Entrepreneur*, follows this pattern. Olsen's approach is to provide a vision and then allow product line managers to take responsibility for the design, development, and marketing of products.[13]

Different Types of Entrepreneurs

According to Karl Vesper, a well-known entrepreneurship scholar, there are several types of entrepreneurs.[14] The most common type is the *self-employed individual*. This entrepreneur operates alone or with only a few employees. The distinguishing characteristic of this type of entrepreneur is that he or she usually performs the work personally rather than through others' efforts. Common examples of self-employed entrepreneurs are repairmen, accountants, physicians, and creative artists.

ETHICS QUESTION
Is there any reason to believe that one of these four types of entrepreneurs would be either less or more ethical than the other three types? If so, which type do you believe would be either more or less ethical, and why?

Another type of entrepreneur is the *team builder*. The team builder is a person who uses a skill acquired when working for others as the foundation for a new firm. A machinist using skills acquired during an apprenticeship program as the basis for a new business venture is an example of this type of entrepreneur. Harvey Lewis, mentioned in the opening case, is another example. The skills he used to open a computer school for children were acquired during his 25 years with Citicorp.

The *independent innovator* is an entrepreneur who thinks of better goods, services, or processes and then creates companies to produce and sell those inventions. Well-known companies such as Liz Claiborne, Federal Express, Polaroid, and Hewlett-Packard are examples of firms started by independent innovators.

Pattern multipliers are entrepreneurs who see effective business practices and then use those practices successfully in other endeavors. An example of

Self-employed individuals are the most common type of entrepreneur. This woman performs the repair work in her bicycle shop personally.

this is the people who have capitalized on the patterns used by Ray Kroc to develop the McDonald's way of doing business.

Clearly, each of these entrepreneurial types can be successful in business. The challenge to potential entrepreneurs is to recognize their own skills and tendencies and look for situations in which their entrepreneurial capabilities can be applied most profitably. For example, an entrepreneur with a capacity to see how one firm's practices could be applied effectively in other settings must think continuously about such applications.

LEARNING CHECK

List several characteristics of successful entrepreneurs and describe the differences among self-employed, team builder, independent innovator, and pattern multiplier entrepreneurs.

MYTHS ABOUT ENTREPRENEURS

In today's society, there is a considerable amount of folklore about and stereotyping of entrepreneurs.[15] To a degree, the persistence of these myths reflects our imperfect understanding of entrepreneurs and the entrepreneurial process. The following sections discuss four of the more prominent myths (see Figure 19-3).[16]

Entrepreneurs Are Doers, Not Thinkers

Some believe that entrepreneurs willingly commit their fortunes to projects that have not been planned carefully. We have all heard stories about people

FIGURE 19-3 Myths and Facts About Entrepreneurs

Myth

Entrepreneurs are doers, not thinkers.

Fact

Successful entrepreneurs carefully evaluate situations and plan their actions accordingly.

Myth

Entrepreneurs are born, not made.

Fact

Entrepreneurs develop their skills and know-how through many different experiences.

Myth

Entrepreneurs succeed with their initial venture.

Fact

Entrepreneurs learn how to be successful through trial and error.

Myth

Entrepreneurs seek power and control over others.

Fact

Responsibility, achievement and competitive results—not power and control—drive the successful entrepreneur.

who used all of their money on wild adventures only to "luck out" and become successful. Occasionally, an unplanned entrepreneurial venture *will* be successful. However, there is little chance that initial success can be maintained over time without careful planning and effective managerial practices. Effective entrepreneurs think about business decisions carefully and initiate action only after considering many alternatives. They decide not to proceed when the results of critical analyses argue against taking action.

Entrepreneurs Are Born, Not Made

Some argue that entrepreneurship cannot be learned, that a person either is born with entrepreneurial tendencies and capabilities or is not. The many characteristics of successful entrepreneurs (Figure 19-2) argue against this view, for it would be unusual for any person to be born with all of these characteristics.

In truth, entrepreneurs have always learned their trade. However, this educational process is typically informal, rather than formal. Entrepreneurs learn skills from family members and through their experiences. By developing relevant skills, know-how, and contacts over many years, a person learns to recognize patterns that result in entrepreneurial opportunities. It is through the continuous nurturing of such skills that people become successful entrepreneurs.

Entrepreneurs Succeed with Their Initial Ventures

Some entrepreneurs are successful with their initial ventures, but these people are rare. Generally speaking, entrepreneurs become successful through trial and error. Learning from mistakes is critical to entrepreneurial success. Mistakes should be examined to determine their causes. With each additional piece of knowledge, entrepreneurs are more likely to develop innovative goods, services, or processes successfully. For example, the Golden Valley Microwave Foods company's first venture into the microwave food products market was a failure. The firm's first products—vending-machine microwave entrees—spoiled after leaving the manufacturing plant. By studying this problem, the company developed an innovative packaging process. This process became the key to the firm's success with microwave popcorn.[17]

Entrepreneurs Seek Power and Control Over Others

Responsibility, achievement, and results, rather than power and control, drive the successful entrepreneur. Effective entrepreneurs want to outperform competitors. They are interested in marketplace accomplishments, not in dominating or controlling others. Success often does result in powerful and influential positions for entrepreneurs. However, these positions are by-products of the entrepreneurial process, not a driving force for the practice of entrepreneurship.[18]

INTRAPRENEURSHIP

As we have discussed in other chapters, some believe that meeting the challenges of today's global marketplace requires the rapid introduction of innovative goods and services. Are large firms—those with tens of thousands, even hundreds of thousands of employees—capable of doing this? Can they be entrepreneurial and innovative? If entrepreneurship can be practiced in both large and small firms, are there differences in those practices? These issues are addressed in the following sections.

Defining Intrapreneurship and Intrapreneurs

ETHICS QUESTION
Because of the need for corporate innovation in today's large firms, is intrapreneurship an important social responsibility for major corporations?

Intrapreneurship is the process of promoting innovation and strategic change in large organizations.[19] Intrapreneurship is an effort to diffuse a capacity to innovate throughout large firms. An **intrapreneur** assumes the responsibility for creating an innovation within a large firm and for championing it to the stage of marketability.[20]

When championing the marketability of an innovation, an intrapreneur pursues the idea behind the innovation, plans its application, acquires resources, and establishes markets. All of this is accomplished through persistence, careful planning, organization, and enthusiastic leadership.[21] Thus, effective intrapreneurs want access to corporate resources and are goal-oriented, self-motivated, self-confident, courageous, and skilled at getting others to share their vision.[22]

Evidence suggests that intrapreneurship does work. For example, intrapreneurship has been credited for the success of IBM's Personal Computer, Xerox's 2600 copier, Texas Instruments's Speak-n-Spell, DuPont's printed circuit materials, 3M's Post-it Note Pads, and GE's Gemlink.[23]

In some firms, permanent teams are created to aid intrapreneurial efforts. Sometimes called **new-venture units,** these teams are formed to inspire new ideas, nourish those ideas to marketable status, and sometimes

Members of a new-venture unit review a computer-generated design for a new car. They will follow the idea through to marketable status.

continue as the management group in charge of the venture.[24] Such teams often include designers, engineers, technicians, and others. Typically, a firm allocates financial, physical, and informational resources to a new-venture unit to support its efforts. While the team members engage in their work, other employees are busy overcoming any organizational barrier that could negatively affect the group's efforts.

Thus, entrepreneurship can be practiced successfully in large firms. Entrepreneurship and intrapreneurship are not significantly different. Entrepreneurship is practiced in the small, independent firm, while intrapreneurship calls for the use of very similar processes and efforts in the large corporation. Similarly, there is little reason to believe that there are any important differences between the personalities of the independent entrepreneur and the corporate intrapreneur.[25]

Intrapreneurship helps large firms become more innovative and responsive to new marketplace opportunities. Employees can be motivated to achieve these objectives if they are given a sense of ownership of the intrapreneurial process.[26] Firms can encourage this sense of ownership by allowing employees time to work on projects that interest them and by offering opportunities to share in the financial success of their innovations. (For example, a firm might allow employees to buy into a new venture through a stock plan.) Employees who know that their firm supports intrapreneurship may become more dedicated to the company and its objectives.

LEARNING CHECK   Discuss four prominent myths about entrepreneurs and define the terms intrapreneurship and intrapreneur.

Characteristics of Successful Intrapreneurship

Several characteristics are associated with a successful intrapreneurial environment. These are summarized in Figure 19-4. Among the most significant are managers' commitment to allow failures, support of many different projects, willingness to be patient, and encouragement of teamwork among people from different disciplines.[27] Other conditions related to successful innovation and intrapreneurship include the following:

- Constant orientation to marketplace realities.
- Use of small, flat organization structures that allow close interactions among small work teams.
- Formation of small teams to bring a product from the development stage to the marketplace.

Examples of human resources needed to complete these types of projects are engineers, technicians, designers, model makers, market analysts, and so forth.

Intrapreneurship can yield significant benefits to large firms. However, for this to occur, at least several of the characteristics mentioned must be

FIGURE 19-4
Characteristics of a Successful Intrapreneurial Environment

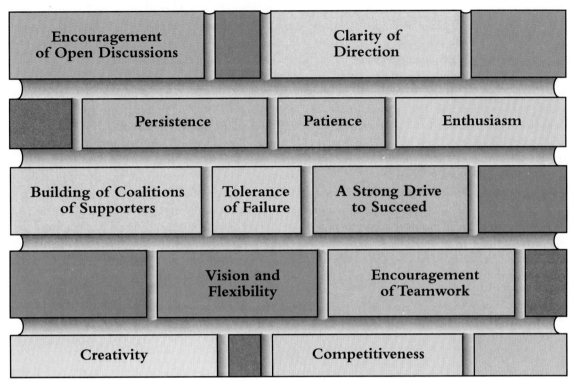

present. In the Organization in Action, efforts in one of the nation's largest firms appear to be aimed at shaping a successful intrapreneurial environment.

ORGANIZATION IN ACTION

In a recent year, General Electric had almost 300,000 employees, more people than live in Tampa, Florida, or Newark, New Jersey. Very few firms are bigger than GE, and perhaps none is as complex. GE manufactures a huge range of products, from light bulbs and home appliances to jet engines and billion-dollar power plants. Over 36 percent of the refrigerators in the United States are made by GE, and the firm manages more credit cards than does American Express.

Even with its size and diversity, Jack Welch, GE's chairman, wants to infuse the company with a sense of entrepreneurship. To do this, Welch believes, GE must develop three virtues: speed, simplicity, and self-confidence. Welch has discarded what he sees as the old ways of managing. He says, "We've got to take out the boss element." In his view, 21st-century managers will forgo their old duties—planning, organizing, implementing, and measuring—in favor of new duties. Included among these will be counseling groups, providing resources to them, and helping them think for themselves.

To move GE quickly to the point where it can succeed with its innovative ideas, the firm is now using techniques called *Work-Out*, *Best Practices*, and *Process Mapping*. Each technique encourages employee involvement and is designed to enhance productivity.

A Work-Out is a forum in which people openly try to solve problems and identify work that can be eliminated from their jobs. Proposals developed by workers are presented to their managers during the final portion of the three-day Work-Out session. Managers can either agree to a proposal on the spot, refuse the proposal, or ask for more information. One participant claims that Work-Outs, which are intended to build trust, have shown employees how to work without "bosses looking over our shoulders."

Through the Best Practices program, GE identified approximately 24 companies (none of whom were direct competitors) that had achieved faster productivity growth than GE for at least 10 years. Roughly one-half of these firms agreed to the following proposition by GE: "Let us send some peo-

ple to your shop to learn about your best management ideas; in return, we'll share the study with you and let you ask about our methods." Hewlett-Packard, Ford, and Chaparral Steel are three companies that joined in this program. According to one top-level manager, a key lesson learned from the program was that GE should focus more on *how* things are done than on *what* is done.

As a flow chart, a Process Map shows every step—no matter how small— that is involved with making or doing something. Critical to this effort is the involvement of many people. A small team of employees, suppliers, and customers work together to develop a Process Map. When a process is mapped, GE has the ability to manage an operation coherently from start to finish.

Source: Thomas A. Stewart. "GE Keeps Those Ideas Coming," *Fortune* (August 12, 1991): 41–49; and "Now for Jack Welch's Second Act," *Fortune* (November 29, 1991): 11.

ETHICS QUESTION
Is providing employees with opportunities to exercise their creative abilities an ethical challenge for today's managers? If so, why?

Although they are still relatively new, GE's Work-Outs, Best Practices, and Process Mapping techniques appear to be capable of creating an intrapreneurial environment. Small teams are formed to deal with significant issues. With all three techniques, the intent is to allow employees opportunities to exercise their creative abilities, which Welch believes are the key to GE's future.

Barriers to Successful Intrapreneurship

Certain conditions work against successful intrapreneurship. For example, without the active support of top-level managers, employees are unable to sustain the creativity linked with intrapreneurial success. Merely giving lip service is ineffective. Successful intrapreneurship requires resources, rewards, and reinforcements from top-level managers.

Another barrier to effective intrapreneurship is excessive bureaucracy. However, Art Fry, the intrapreneur responsible for the invention of 3M's Post-it Notes, says that some bureaucracy is necessary. In Fry's opinion, bureaucracy represents accumulated know-how, which provides a meaningful test for the intrapreneur's invention. The guidelines and checkpoints called for by a bureaucracy can prevent intrapreneurs from making competitive blunders.[28] Of course, too much bureaucracy can be stifling. The challenge to managers supporting intrapreneurial ventures is to arrive at the right amount of bureaucracy. Other barriers to successful intrapreneurship include inadequate planning, unrealistic corporate expectations, and operational difficulties.[29] In today's large corporations, it is vital that these barriers to innovation be reduced or eliminated.

NEW VENTURES

For the United States to compete in today's global marketplace successfully, large firms must become more innovative and entrepreneurial. However, the overall health of the U.S. economy is also affected by the performance of the thousands of new ventures started by entrepreneurs.

Importance of New Ventures

Many new ventures are started each year in the United States. In 1989, for example, 677,394 new small businesses were formed. Unfortunately, not all new businesses survive. During 1989 alone, 49,719 firms failed and another 62,449 filed for bankruptcy.[30] The annual number of formations and failures does not tell the whole story, however. Another important benefit of new ventures is their impact on employment.

New ventures consistently create more jobs each year than do large companies. Almost every year, 60 to 65 percent (and sometimes as much as 87 percent) of jobs created in the United States are the result of new ventures.[31] Thus, new ventures are an excellent source of employment opportunities for workers with all types of skills. Some people are attracted by the excitement of being a part of a new business. Although it is often risky, working in a new venture can be challenging and is rarely dull.

In addition to providing employment opportunities, new ventures create other benefits for society at large. The efforts of those working in new ventures often result in innovative products. In turn, these innovative products enhance the nation's ability to compete successfully in the global marketplace. New ventures also stimulate competition. By giving consumers innovative products, new ventures encourage other companies to improve the quality and reduce the prices of their offerings. Finally, new ventures accelerate the advance and spread of new technology. New technology upgrades the nation's defense capabilities and improves the population's standard of living.[32]

In today's business environment, all kinds of new ventures are being created. Many of these provide services. Recently, the largest share of new businesses in the United States was restaurants, business services, and retailers. In fact, between 80 and 90 percent of all new ventures created recently were pizza parlors, ice cream shops, real estate brokerages, and the like.

Some people believe that too many of the new ventures are in the service sector. Essentially, the argument is that without a strong industrial base a service economy cannot survive in the long term. Proponents of this view feel that the U.S. government and business should cooperate to develop pro-business policies. Then a more effective balance between service and manufacturing new ventures could be stimulated. This is an interesting issue that may challenge managers in the 1990s and beyond.

New Venture Formation

Entrepreneurs have three choices when considering how to establish a new venture. These are described in the following sections.

STARTING A NEW BUSINESS. The most obvious way to begin a new venture is to start one's own firm. This approach allows entrepreneurs to select the target markets they wish to serve and to develop their own relationships with suppliers, customers, employees, bankers, and so forth.

When a person starts a new business, there is little doubt as to who is responsible for its performance. While entrepreneurs often face more risk when they start a totally new venture, the psychological and financial rewards are also potentially greater. Entrepreneurs who succeed in beginning and operating their own firms rightly take pride in their accomplishments.

PURCHASING AN EXISTING BUSINESS. A second approach to beginning a new venture is to buy an existing firm. In this case, the entrepreneur knows about the company's historical and current performance. The entrepreneur can analyze the firm's financial records and talk to customers, suppliers, and bankers. Often, a great deal can be learned about a company's potential by talking with those who know about its past.

A disadvantage of this approach is that the entrepreneur inherits the firm's weaknesses as well as its strengths. When evaluating a firm for possible purchase, the entrepreneur must determine whether or not the firm's existing strengths are sufficient. Will it be possible for the new owner to "grow" the firm through continued use of its current strengths? Similarly, if weaknesses are spotted, the entrepreneur must decide whether those weaknesses are too strong to overcome. Although any weakness is undesirable, financial and human resource weaknesses tend to be the most difficult to deal with successfully.

PURCHASING A FRANCHISE OPERATION. A **franchise** is a form of ownership whereby a company grants rights to a buyer to sell its goods or services for a flat fee or a share of the resulting income.[33] A key advantage of a franchise is the opportunity to operate a firm that has proved to be a winner. Among the most successful and well-known franchise operations are McDonald's, Century 21, Burger King, Servicemaster, Computerland, H&R Block, and Budget Rent-A-Car. Examples of what the entrepreneur may receive from the parent company include use of the franchisor's brand or logo, advertising support, training in how to operate the enterprise, and use of operating procedures and systems that have proved successful.[34]

Because it involves the right to use proven operating methods, purchasing a franchise reduces entrepreneurial risk. On the other hand, a franchise

The original McDonald's hamburger stand is now a museum in Desplain, Illinois. The firm has grown into a worldwide franchising operation that has provided opportunities for many entrepreneurs to form new ventures.

is often very expensive. Buying a franchise unit from a major company can cost hundreds of thousands of dollars. Another disadvantage is that a franchisor's procedures and rules tend to be strict and rigidly enforced. From the franchisor's viewpoint, these rules are sensible. After all, it is these methods that have caused the company's success. But for entrepreneurs who want to establish their own companies and operate them in their own ways, franchises can be quite restrictive.

No one of these three approaches is always superior to the other two. Entrepreneurs must evaluate each approach carefully to determine what is in their best interests. Only careful and honest self-appraisal that includes determining how much risk is acceptable prepares an entrepreneur to select a method of starting a new venture.

After the entrepreneur decides which approach to use to start a new business venture, it is time to prepare a business plan. If developed effectively, the business plan can play an important role in the new venture's success.

LEARNING CHECK   Discuss the importance of new ventures to the U.S. economy, and describe three approaches to new venture formation that entrepreneurs consider.

Preparing a Business Plan

Not all successful entrepreneurs prepare a business plan. However, most successful new business ventures are started through the guidance provided by business plans. Even in cases in which a formal plan was not prepared, an entrepreneur has often formally developed a vision and business goals, identified a target market, and made financial projections.[35]

DEFINITION OF A BUSINESS PLAN. A **business plan** is a comprehensive set of guidelines for starting and operating a new venture.[36] A business plan should include information about "the [good] or service, the customers, the competition, the production and marketing methods, the management, the financing, and all those things necessary to enter business and make or sell the [good] or service."[37] A business plan is an entrepreneur's game plan. When prepared effectively, it shows where the entrepreneur is today, directions and objectives sought for tomorrow, and actions necessary to achieve those objectives.

. . . .

Back to the Opening Case

. . . .

Business plans are not discussed in the description of Ed Arner's entrepreneurial career. In your opinion, does Arner prepare business plans when thinking about buying a business and what he would do to run the venture successfully? Be prepared to justify your answer.

. . . .

REASONS TO PREPARE A BUSINESS PLAN. The most important reason to prepare a business plan is that doing so increases the chances of success. Recall that 75 to 80 percent of new ventures fail within five years. Preparing a business plan forces an entrepreneur to evaluate a number of issues that are critical to operating a new venture successfully. Included among these issues are the development of a business vision, identification of key competitors, and determination of how the new venture is to be managed. In specific terms, a prepared business plan:

1. improves the likelihood of securing funding for the new venture;
2. can be used to recruit employees;
3. is impressive to suppliers;
4. specifies the uniqueness of the new venture's good or service; and
5. provides benchmarks against which the new venture's performance can be measured.[38]

OUTLINE OF A BUSINESS PLAN. A business plan covers many topics. The business plan outline presented in Figure 19-5 shows the topics that are normally included. However, business plans often reflect an entrepreneur's unique personality. Bankers, venture capitalists, and others who evaluate many business plans say that no two of them are exactly alike. Determining the probability of a new venture's success by evaluating its business plan can be an exciting and challenging task.

Securing Funding for the New Business Venture

With a formal business plan, the entrepreneur is ready to obtain funding for the new venture. This type of funding is called venture capital. **Venture capital** is money invested in a high-risk, high-potential enterprise.[39] Sources of venture capital include banks, finance companies, and some savings and loan associations.[40] However, venture capital firms are a critical

FIGURE 19-5
Outline of a Business
Plan for a New Venture

1. Cover Sheet

Business name
Entrepreneur's name
Address of business

2. Summary

Highlights of key materials in the plan

3. Description of Proposed Business (or New Venture)

General description of the intended product or service
Key objectives and milestones
Significant characteristics of the industry
Unique features of the product or service

4. Market Analysis and Marketing Plan

Target market
Key customers
The competition
Market size and opportunities
Factors critical to marketing success

5. Manufacturing Plan

Characteristics of production processes
Suppliers
Equipment needs and costs
Cost of manufacturing

6. Financial Plan

Pro-forma balance sheet
Pro-forma income statements
Pro-forma cash flow statements
Break-even analysis

7. Management Plan

Description of key people's skills and responsibilities
Description of organizational structure
Compensation policies

8. Appendix of Supporting Materials (as needed)

Credit reports
Reference letters
Legal documents
Résumés
Copies of contracts and leases

Source: Based on materials included in John G. Burch, *Entrepreneurship* (New York: John Wiley & Sons, 1986.) 397–398, and Robert D. Hisrich, *Entrepreneurship, Intrapreneurship, and Venture Capital: The Foundation of Economic Renaissance* (Lexington, MA: D.C. Health and Co., 1986): 101.

source of funds for new companies. These firms provide startup money for new ventures and development funds for companies in the early growth stages. They also provide expansion funds for rapidly growing ventures with the potential to acquire other companies or become publicly traded.[41] The total amount of funds provided by venture capital firms is increasing. In 1986, venture capitalists committed just over $24 billion to new companies.[42] This figure grew to $33.4 billion in 1989.[43]

While the amount of venture capital available is growing, so is the competition for those funds. To increase their likelihood of securing venture capital, entrepreneurs must be familiar with the criteria used to determine fund allocation. The single most important criterion is the entrepreneur himself or herself. Arthur Rock, who has been involved with funding many companies such as Apple Computer, Intel, Teledyne, and Fairfield Semiconductor, says that good ideas and good products are readily available. However, this is not the case with good entrepreneurs. Based on this belief, Rock generally pays "more attention to the people who prepare a business plan that to the proposal itself."[44]

Another important funding criterion is balance among the functional areas (marketing, finance, production, and management) in the business plan. No one functional area should be over- or underemphasized if a plan is to achieve funding. In particular, finance should not be overemphasized. While they are obviously important, venture capitalists believe that financial considerations should not dominate a business plan.

Other criteria used in evaluating proposals for funding include the entrepreneur's knowledge of the target market, the anticipated growth rate for the industry, and the entrepreneur's leadership qualities.[45] Knowledge of these criteria should help entrepreneurs prepare business plans that will be more appealing to venture capitalists.

Guidelines for Successful New Ventures

Entrepreneurs face a host of potential problems as they start and operate their firms. The next sections discuss three guidelines that can help entrepreneurs operate new ventures successfully.

FOLLOW THE BUSINESS PLAN. A well-prepared business plan provides valuable direction for the operation of a new venture. To develop the plan, the entrepreneur has evaluated a number of issues. These evaluations help to determine what the firm wants to be and how it intends to accomplish its objectives. When unexpected conditions arise, the entrepreneur should not immediately discard the business plan's direction in favor of another approach. Changing conditions must be considered, but the entrepreneur should decide to alter the dictates of the business plan only after careful analysis.

CONCENTRATE ON MAJOR ISSUES. Entrepreneurs sometimes feel that they must do everything themselves if their venture is to succeed. Because of their knowledge and commitment, they often are involved with most of the firm's activities. However, the entrepreneur must allocate his or her time wisely. Running a company involves a number of relatively minor operational details. The entrepreneur should not focus on these matters at the expense of more significant issues. At the least, the entrepreneur must remain in touch with the demands of key customer groups and make sure that the new venture is meeting its financial goals. In addition, the entrepreneur must make ongoing assessments of competitors' actions in order to establish and maintain the firm's market position. Successful entrepreneurs are careful stewards of their time and energy. With experience, they learn to allocate all resources, including their own time, effectively and efficiently.

BE PERSISTENT AND TOLERANT. For most entrepreneurs, starting and operating a new venture is a dream come true. Sometimes, they have waited many years before launching their own firms, and they have an understandable tendency to want to be successful immediately. But it is rare for success to come quickly with new ventures. As a result, entrepreneurs should be persistent in the pursuit of their business goals and tolerant of setbacks. Rather than becoming discouraged, entrepreneurs should accept less than ideal situations as long as progress is being made toward the overall goal of success.

LEARNING CHECK	Define business plans and discuss their importance. Also, discuss three guidelines to new-venture success.

CRITIQUE OF ENTREPRENEURSHIP

Entrepreneurs are rightly thought of as people with drive, ambition, intuition, and vision. In this respect, "entrepreneurs have been the embodiment of our romantic view of capitalism."[46] As we have discussed, entrepreneurs have an important role in the continuing growth and development of the U.S. economy. Through successful entrepreneurship, innovative goods, services, and processes are introduced to the marketplace. An improvement in the nation's global competitiveness results from these innovations.

ETHICS QUESTION
Is there any reason to believe that the ethics of a successful entrepreneur are different from the ethics of a successful manager in a large company? If so, what would the differences be, and why do you think they exist?

It is also important to foster innovation in existing firms. Whether the process is called entrepreneurship or intrapreneurship, the core practices and key objectives are similar. Used successfully, intrapreneurship can diffuse innovative attitudes and capabilities throughout a firm.

At the beginning of this chapter, the question of entrepreneurship's ability to lead the U.S. economy into a new Golden Age was posed. This is probably not a reasonable expectation. However, successful entrepreneurship—and intrapreneurship in large companies—can result in important outcomes and stimulate innovative capabilities in the United States. But achieving global success today is a complex challenge. It will likely be through a combination of actions and relationships (such as those between government and business) that a new Golden Age will emerge.

SUMMARY

Entrepreneurship is an ongoing process intended to create wealth. Human, financial, physical, and informational resources are managed in the pursuit of a business opportunity with acceptable levels of risk. Entrepreneurship often results in the introduction of innovative goods, services, or processes into the marketplace.

Entrepreneurs recognize marketplace opportunities and are willing to accept risks to bring resources together and manage those resources to take advantage of opportunities. The main goal for entrepreneurs is to create wealth. Successful entrepreneurs have several characteristics in common, as illustrated in Figure 19-2.

There are different types of entrepreneurs. Self-employed entrepreneurs usually perform work themselves. Team-builder entrepreneurs use skills acquired through training in other companies to operate their new business firms. Independent innovators think of better products and then establish companies to produce and sell their innovations. Finally, pattern multipliers are entrepreneurs who apply to new settings the patterns of operations used effectively in other firms.

Four myths about entrepreneurs were discussed in the chapter. The first is that entrepreneurs are doers, not thinkers; the second is that entrepreneurs are born, not made; the third is that entrepreneurs succeed with their initial ventures; and the fourth is that entrepreneurs seek power and control over others. The fact that these myths survive suggests that we still do not fully understand the nature of entrepreneurs and entrepreneurship.

Intrapreneurship promotes innovation and strategic change in large firms. Its goal is to diffuse innovation throughout such firms. An intrapreneur assumes the responsibility for creating an innovation and getting it to the stage of marketability. To date, results from intrapreneurship are encouraging; many products have been created in many different firms. In some firms, permanent teams, called new-venture units, have been created to spur intrapreneurship.

New ventures are important to the health of the U.S. economy. They create employment opportunities and stimulate existing firms to improve the quality of their products. Many types of new ventures are being created today. Some believe that the nation would be better served if entrepreneurs established more manufacturing-related, rather than service-related, new ventures. Entrepreneurs choose one of three approaches—starting their own firm, purchasing an existing company, or purchasing a franchise unit—to establish a new venture.

The preparation of a business plan is critical to the successful launching of a new venture. Several issues must be detailed in the business plan, including the firm's intended marketing actions, financial practices, and management structures. Several funding sources are available to the entrepreneur, an important one being venture capital firms. The most important measure used by venture capitalists in deciding how to allocate funds concerns the entrepreneur. The logic is that good ideas are plentiful, while people who can be successful as entrepreneurs are in short supply.

Several guidelines can be followed to increase the likelihood of new-venture success. First, entrepreneurs should follow their business plans. Second, they should structure their time so they can concentrate on major issues. If they are not careful, entrepreneurs may find that focusing on significant matters has been pushed aside by their tendency to deal with daily operational problems. Finally, entrepreneurs should be persistent and tolerant in their pursuit of success. Through continued concentration on the tasks at hand and an acceptance of how long it may take, entrepreneurs increase the likelihood that their ventures will succeed.

Without doubt, both entrepreneurship and intrapreneurship play important roles in the health of the U.S. economy. Through these processes, U.S. firms can become more innovative. In turn, this outcome should help the nation as a whole regain a highly competitive position in global markets.

KEY TERMS

entrepreneurial risk	vision	new-venture units	venture capital
entrepreneurship	intrapreneurship	franchise	
entrepreneur	intrapreneur	business plan	

QUESTIONS FOR DISCUSSION AND REVIEW

1. Define the terms entrepreneurship and entrepreneur.
2. Describe at least five characteristics of a successful entrepreneur.
3. Different types of entrepreneurs were discussed in the chapter. In your opinion, which type of entrepreneur is Ed Arner? Justify your position.
4. What are four myths about entrepreneurs? What do you think caused these myths to develop?
5. Define intrapreneurship. What advantages result from the practice of intrapreneurship in today's large companies? Would you be willing to work in a large firm that does not practice intrapreneur-

ship? Why or why not?
6. Why is the creation of new ventures important to the U.S. economy and its workforce?
7. Are you interested in starting a new venture at some time in the future? Why or why not? If you do have such an interest, what type of business would you like to form?
8. Describe at least two guidelines that should be followed to achieve success with a new venture. Which of the two do you think is the most important, and why?

PROBLEMS FOR ACTION

A. Brigid Stephenson earned a degree in interior design from a respected institution. Upon graduation, she accepted a position with an interior design studio in a medium-size community. Designs by Logeman was a prominent studio serving the needs of commercial clients. After two years with the firm, Stephenson wanted to apply her talents to meeting the needs of residential clients. She talked about this interest with others in the firm. Stephenson also mentioned the matter to several of the studio's commercial clients. Everyone was encouraging and receptive to her ideas. Some even suggested that the local community needed a studio specializing in residential design work. Logeman, however, offered no encouragement at all. "Brigid, I have spent many years building this studio into what it is today. I know what my clients want and I intend to continue serving their needs. If you can't be happy with commercial design work, then you should think about doing something else. Perhaps you should start your own firm." Stephenson was confused by Logeman's comments. What should she do? Was she ready to start her own firm? Outline

a business plan for Brigid Stephenson's residential design firm.

B. Adrian Reyes worked for a large defense contractor. His job as a design engineer was enjoyable, but it did not provide the growth opportunities he desired. Reyes felt that, to reach his potential, he had to have chances to grow and develop through his work. In the recent past, he was disappointed by his manager's lack of support for an idea he had discussed with her. He had told Carol Burch that if he could take some time from his regular duties to work with people from the applications and marketing groups, he was sure they would develop an innovative product. In response to his comments, Burch said, "Look, Adrian, you have a good deal here. You're paid well, the people are pleasant to work with, and the chances of layoffs are minimal. So why don't you just do your work and stop trying to be some kind of hero?" Although disappointed, Reyes was not willing to give up. Compare the characteristics in Figure 19-4 to Reyes's situation and determine the probability of achieving intrapreneurial success in this situation.

CONCLUDING CASE

. . . .

Allan Harada: An Incurable Entrepreneur

As a youth in Athens, Greece, Allan Harada was always interested in what made products work. Some

years ago, Harada's parents were concerned when they entered his bedroom to find parts of his stereo all over the floor. "Allan, what are you doing to the stereo we just bought for your birthday?" they asked. "Well, I am trying to understand how it works, and I think I'm making great progress here." To his parent's surprise, Harada was able to put the stereo back together without too much difficulty.

This experience was the first of many. Over the years, Harada continued to take products apart. In his third year of high school, however, his focus began to change slightly; he became interested in business. He undertook his first major venture during the summer after his junior year. To finance a "sno cone" stand, Harada borrowed $3,500 from his father. The stand was so successful that he decided to open a second one in a different part of Athens, close to one of the most popular beaches. Harada's profits allowed him to pay off the loan from his father and to finance his next business, a lawn care service.

Harada's firm was able to earn money because of his management practices. He had eight of his friends working for him. Each employee was guaranteed a salary plus a commission based on the number of lawns mowed per week. Harada concentrated on selling his company's services. Through the success of the lawn care business, Harada was able to buy a car and an enviable school wardrobe.

At his family's urging, Harada went to college, and in time he earned a law degree. This was not consistent with his interests, but he felt somewhat obligated. After all, his father's law firm had been in the family for three generations. At the age of 33, Harada became the owner of the family firm. One of his first major actions was to expand the types of legal services offered by the firm. A second major undertaking was the opening of a second office in an Athens suburb.

Even though his legal practice was successful, Harada was never quite satisfied. Among other interests, he retained his fascination with personal computers. His work with PCs eventually led to the development of several computer software programs suited to the needs of legal firms. The software helped Harada increase the efficiency of his offices' operations dramatically and identify the firm's most profitable legal services. To sell these software programs to other firms, Harada organized another company. This firm proved to be successful especially as Harada developed additional pieces of software for use in other professional offices such as accounting and medical practices.

The next business Harada started was a venture into a different area still. While eating dinner out with his family one night, he decided that the Italian food they ordered had not been prepared very well. To his wife, Michi, Harada commented, "I know we could do better than this. The food is average, at best; it is cold, and the service is poor. I'm going to look into the possibility of opening a restaurant in the downtown area, near our main law office." Harada followed through with this interest, opening his first restaurant 18 months later. This business, too, was successful. After six years in the food business, Harada had opened two additional restaurants. In discussing the reasons for his success with a group of local high school students, Harada said, "The name of the game in the restaurant business is inventory control. If you can keep your food costs low by ordering the right amounts at the right time, it's really quite easy to be successful. The computer programs I have developed really help us in this area."

At age 45, Allan Harada felt that he had accomplished quite a bit, but he was still restless. Always interested in new deals, he had recently encouraged lawyers in his offices to come to him with ideas for new products or services. "I don't care if your ideas concern the legal profession or not. I want this to be an exciting place to work, and I am fascinated by considering other types of business ventures. Please exercise your full creative talents to develop new ideas. We'll all get together to work on your ideas and try to make each one of them a success."

1. What kind of an entrepreneur is Allan Harada? Be prepared to justify your answer with specific examples from the case.
2. Use factors from among those shown in the sample business plan (see Figure 19-5) to explain Allan Harada's success with his entrepreneurial ventures.
3. Refer to the four myths about entrepreneurs that were discussed in this chapter. Evaluate Allan Harada in terms of each myth. Be prepared to justify your opinions.

REFERENCES

1. Donald L. Sexton and Nancy B. Bowman-Upton, *Entrepreneurship: Creativity and Growth* (New York: MacMillan, 1991): 5.

2. Jeffry A. Timmons, *New Venture Creation*, 3e (Homewood, IL: Irwin, 1990): 5.

3. *Innovation Creativity and Capital Update* (University of Texas at Austin, Winter 1991–1992): 3.

4. R. Duane Ireland and Michael A. Hitt, "Mission Statements: Importance, Challenge, and Recommendations for Development," *Business Horizons* (May- June 1992): 34–42.

5. John J. Kao, *The Entrepreneur* (Englewood Cliffs, NJ: Prentice-Hall, 1991): 14.

6. Frederick Betz, *Managing Technology: Competing Through New Ventures, Innovation, and Corporate Research* (Englewood Cliffs, NJ: Prentice-Hall, 1987): 9.

7. David H. Holt, *Entrepreneurship* (Englewood Cliffs, NJ: Prentice-Hall, 1992): 11.

8. J. A. Schumpeter, *The Theory of Economic Development* (Cambridge: Harvard University Press, 1934).

9. Kao, *The Entrepreneur*, 18.

10. Sexton and Bowman-Upton, *Entrepreneurship: Creativity and Growth*, 11.

11. Holt, *Entrepreneurship*, 9.

12. Judith B. Kamm, Book review of "Steve Jobs: The Journey Is the Reward," *The Executive* (May 1991): 101–102.

13. Donald L. Sexton, Book review of "The Ultimate Entrepreneur: Ken Olsen and Digital Equipment," *The Executive* (May 1991): 100–101.

14. Karl H. Vesper, *New Venture Strategies*, rev. ed. (Englewood Cliffs, NJ: Prentice-Hall, 1990): 38.

15. Timmons, *New Venture Creation*, 19.

16. Holt, *Entrepreneurship*, 50–53.

17. "Entrepreneurs," *Business Week* (January 11, 1988): 152–153.

18. Timmons, *New Venture Creation*, 21.

19. Henry Mintzberg and James Brian Quinn, *The Strategy Process*, 2e (Englewood Cliffs, NJ: Prentice-Hall, 1991): 748–757.

20. Gifford Pinchot, III, *Intrapreneuring* (New York: Harper and Row, 1985): ix.

21. Holt, *Entrepreneurship*, 39.

22. Pinchot, *Intrapreneuring*, 54–55.

23. Sexton and Bowman-Upton, *Entrepreneurship: Creativity and Growth*, 270.

24. Holt, *Entrepreneurship*, 87.

25. Sexton and Bowman-Upton, *Entrepreneurship: Creativity and Growth*, 271.

26. Vesper, *New Venture Strategies*, 324.

27. Sexton and Bowman-Upton, *Entrepreneurship: Creativity and Growth*, 271.

28. "Lessons from a Successful Intrapreneur," in Arthur A. Thompson, William E. Fuller, and A. J. Strickland, III (eds.), *Readings in Strategic Management*, 4e (Homewood, IL: Irwin, 1992): 563–568.

29. Sexton and Bowman-Upton, *Entrepreneurship: Creativity and Growth*, 276.

30. *The State of Small Business: A Report of the President Transmitted to the Congress* (Washington, DC: U.S. Government Printing Office, 1990): 1315.

31. Jay B. Barney and Ricky W. Griffin, *The Management of Organizations* (Boston: Houghton Mifflin, 1992): 789.

32. Karl H. Vesper, *Entrepreneurship and National Policy* (Chicago: Heller Institute for Small Business Policy, 1983) as quoted in Charles W. Hofer and William Sandberg, "Improving New Venture Performance: Some Guidelines for Success," *American Journal of Small Business* (Summer 1987): 11–12.

33. Barney and Griffin, *The Management of Organizations*, 800; and Holt, *Entrepreneurship*, 403.

34. Vesper, *New Venture Strategies*, 217.

35. Sexton and Bowman-Upton, *Entrepreneurship: Creativity and Growth*, 143.

36. Holt, *Entrepreneurship*, 115.

37. John G. Burch, *Entrepreneurship* (New York: Wiley, 1986): 370.

38. John A. Welsh and Jerry F. White, *The Entrepreneur's Master Planning Guide* (Englewood Cliffs, NJ: Prentice-Hall, 1983): 2.

39. Welsh and White, *The Entrepreneur's Master Planning Guide*, 174.

40. *The State of Small Business: A Report of the President Transmitted to the Congress—Executive Summary* (Washington, DC: U.S. Government Printing Office, 1987): 31.

41. Holt, *Entrepreneurship*, 435.

42. *The State of Small Business: A Report of the President Transmitted to the Congress—Executive Summary*, 31.

43. *The State of Small Business: A Report of the President Transmitted to the Congress* (Washington, DC: U.S. Government Printing Office, 1990): 184.

44. Arthur Rock, "Strategy vs. Tactics from a Venture Capitalist," *Harvard Business Review* (November-December, 1987): 63.

45. Holt, *Entrepreneurship*, 437.

46. "America Expects Too Much from Its Entrepreneurial Heroes," *Business Week* (July 28, 1986): 33.

Chapter 20

International Management

OPENING
CASE

Setting Up a
Plant in a
Tropical Paradise

Several years back, Moog Inc., a manufacturer of precision systems for the aerospace industry, faced a new challenge. Chairman and founder William Moog wanted the firm to build a manufacturing plant in the Philippines. The management team was amused and cynical, but Moog was serious.

After seeing that the project was dragging, the chairman set a deadline. He gave the management team six months to develop a low-cost offshore manufacturing site. Moog wanted to lower costs and stay competitive in the aerospace business.

Although Moog Inc. had 20 years of experience in managing overseas operations, this project was different. It meant starting with a large manufacturing operation, rather than beginning with a modest sales office and progressing to small-scale manufacturing. Moreover, the company's human resources department had no experience in setting up an overseas operation. A further complication was the plant site. It was located in a mountain resort town with little industry and none of the computer-controlled machines the firm required. The skills and knowledge the firm needed would be lacking in the local population.

The challenge to the human resources department was enormous. It was necessary to develop a cost-effective, sensible plan to recruit, select, and train a workforce who could quickly learn the skills and values needed by Moog Inc.

Source: Gary Szakmary, "How HRD Can Contribute to Company Expansion," *Personnel Journal* (August 1988): 39. Adapted with permission.

The challenge faced by the managers and human resources professionals at Moog illustrates a subtle and seemingly contradictory truth about international management. Good management principles are effective when applied in different cultures, but they have to be applied or adapted with a sensitivity to cultural differences. Much of what Moog Inc. knows about recruiting, selecting, training, and motivating a workforce will apply to the small offshore island, but real differences will also be found.

In this chapter, we discuss how sound management theories and practices work cross culturally. We also look at cultural and environmental factors that require managers to adapt their practices to fit national circumstances.

The purpose of this chapter is to provide some insight about managing in an international environment. Emphasis is on the multinational corporation. In addition, the chapter shows how some already familiar concepts such as choosing an organization structure are applied in an international setting.

THE IMPORTANCE OF INTERNATIONAL MANAGEMENT

International management is the pursuit of organizational objectives in more than one nation. International management has become an increasingly important discipline in recent years as more and more corporations have become international. Improvements in transportation and communications and low production costs in many countries have made global markets easier to reach. This section describes the present scope of international trade along with prospects for the immediate future.

Scope of International Business

Firms headquartered in the United States often have immediate access to huge domestic markets. In addition, they have steadily increased their share of foreign markets. U.S. exports and imports combined are running at an annual exchange rate of about $900 billion. In 1990, exports totaled $393 billion and imports $497 billion.[1] About 10 percent of all jobs in the United States and Canada depend on export and import trade.

Other indicators, including foreign investments, profits earned overseas, and fees and royalties paid to firms abroad, point to an increase in corporate international activity. An idea of the volume of international trade can be obtained from studying the data in Figure 20-1. Observe, for example, the amount of business the United States conducts with its two major trading partners, Canada and Japan.

International trade is typically thought of in terms of manufactured goods and services such as movies and videos. However, there is now an important trend in international trade toward clerical and support services. Some U.S. insurance companies have data-entry work for domestic insurance policies performed in Hong Kong, Singapore, and China with the output shipped back to the United States. Other insurance companies ship medical claims work to Ireland. The problem these firms (including New York Life and Cigna) face is a decline in the U.S. population of young peo-

FIGURE 20-1
Top 25 Partners in Total U.S. Trade in 1990 (Expressed in Millions of Dollars)

Country	Amount of Imports, Exports, and Customs Paid
Canada	175,238
Japan	138,240
Mexico	58,548
Germany	46,946
United Kingdom	43,772
Taiwan	34,149
South Korea	32,892
France	26,776
Italy	20,711
China	20,031
Netherlands	17,988
Singapore	17,859
Hong Kong	16,328
Belgium/Luxembourg	15,027
Saudi Arabia	14,009
Brazil	13,038
Australia	12,967
Venezuela	12,554
Switzerland	10,396
Malaysia	8,697
Spain	8,518
Sweden	8,335
Thailand	8,285
Nigeria	6,529
Israel (with Gaza)	6,513

Source: U.S. Department of Commerce, 1991.

ple qualified to perform such work. In contrast, Ireland has a high unemployment rate and a growing number of high school graduates. The transfer of work to Ireland was made easier by improvements in satellite communications and fiber optic cables. With this new technology, data can be transferred across oceans almost instantaneously.[2]

Geographic Areas for Increased International Trade

International trade is also increasing because certain individual countries or groups of countries have positioned themselves for more trade. A leading example is the European Community (EC) of 1992. This 19-nation alliance has virtually turned into a single marketplace for ideas, goods, services, and investment strategies. The EC trades with member nations, the United States and Canada, and other countries throughout the world. In addition, Japanese firms are now investing rapidly in Europe. In fact, Japan now has a bigger trade surplus with Europe than it does with the United States.[3] The growing trade with Eastern European countries including Czechoslovakia, Hungary, and Poland is another force for increasing exports and imports. Examples include Suzuki of Japan's commitment of $110 million to manufacture automobiles in Hungary and Pilkinton of Britain's $140 million investment in glass manufacturing in Poland.[4]

Industrial expansion in emerging nations also contributes to increased world trade. Four of these emerging stars—Australia, Malaysia, New Zealand, and Thailand—lie in the Pacific Rim. Collectively, these countries engage in $175 billion worth of exports and imports, and all are eager to conduct business with the United States.[5]

Mexico is yet another example of a country poised for increased foreign trade. Mexico is attempting to negotiate its way into a North American free trade zone along with the United States and Canada. Many American

Industrial expansion in Malaysia had led to increasing imports of U.S. products.

manufacturers have switched their manufacturing operations from China to Mexico. In addition, many U.S. companies have established *maquiladoras*—assembly plants on the U.S.-Mexican border.[6]

Increased multinational operations lead to increased multiculturalism in businesses at home and abroad. Adjustments in managerial strategies are necessary in order to adapt to this internationalization of business. These adjustments will be described in the last several sections of this chapter.

The United States has a dilemma regarding international business and management. The United States wishes to help other, less prosperous, nations advance to a standard of living comparable to its own. At the same time, it consumes about 40 percent of the world's energy and resources even though it has only 5 percent of the world's population. If the emerging nations increase their use of resources, the United States will have to lessen its share.

CHALLENGES FACING THE INTERNATIONAL MANAGER

A host of interacting and overlapping forces create problems for managers in international settings. The manager who works for a firm that operates in only one country faces these forces infrequently. The term *infrequently* is chosen because some countries are so large that they contain radically different subcultures within their boundaries. For example, assume that a manager is transferred from corporate headquarters in New York City to a construction site on the North Slope of Alaska. In New York, the manager might supervise office workers raised in the city who speak English and some who speak Spanish. On the North Slope, the same manager might supervise some employees raised in an Eskimo culture who speak a native language such as Aleut. Thus, as this example shows, a manager working in a large, culturally diverse country could conceivably face a few challenges similar to those faced by an international manager.

Ten challenges facing the international manager are summarized in the following paragraphs.[7] The manager must deal effectively with these challenges to achieve work objectives.

Conflict of Cultural Attitudes

The most pervasive root problem in conducting business in another country is that the country's cultural values can conflict with company values. **Culture** refers to the customs, beliefs, values, and patterns of behavior of a society. An important example of conflicting cultural values relates to the need for achievement (see Chapter 12). In a society in which most people have a low need for achievement, the profit motive may not be very strong. Also, most employees may not have a strong sense of time urgency. Another example of a cultural conflict is that many countries may not wish to indulge in the "throw-away" form of marketing and packaging so prevalent in U.S. firms.

Unfavorable Political Climate

ETHICS QUESTION
How ethical is it for a company to locate a subsidiary in a foreign counry with a record of human rights abuse?

An unfavorable or even hostile political climate can increase the difficulty of conducting business in a foreign country. In extreme cases, rioting, kidnapping, and hostage taking may make it urgent for people of certain nationalities to leave a country. In some countries, terrorists justify their practices by claiming that the United States is responsible for some of their countries' problems. Political attitudes also may interfere with using the same fair and equal human resources practices that are used in the home country. U.S. companies with facilities in South Africa faced this challenge. For many firms, the solution was to divest their interests in the country. After the South African government made important strides toward decreasing racism, the U.S. government removed economic sanctions. As a result, many U.S. firms resumed trade with South Africa.

Fluctuations in the National Economy

Most national economies follow a general worldwide trend, but there are significant variations from time to time. Inflation and currency devaluation may have a severely negative impact on costs and profits. Also, if the currency of a country suddenly gains in value, it may become difficult to export products made in that country. The reason is that the products suddenly become more expensive in the importing country based solely on exchange rates, not on any changes in quality or function. In recent years, for example, the lower value of the U.S. dollar against European currencies made it possible for a surge of U.S. goods—clothing, automobiles, and electronics—to be sold in Europe. Many European companies suffered as a result. For example, the U.S.-made Chrysler LeBaron sold well against European luxury automobiles.

Currency fluctuations affect sales of goods in foreign countries. When the U.S. dollar decreases in value against the yen, U.S.-made computers become more attractive to Japanese buyers.

Another problem related to economic changes is that new democracies such as the Eastern European countries may want to avoid the prosperity-recession cycles found in the United States. To avoid such cycles, these countries might choose to not become too dependent on the U.S. economy.

Governmental Inefficiency

ETHICS QUESTION
Even if greasing is not illegal, should it be tolerated by U.S. and Canadian companies?

Governments in some underdeveloped countries are inefficient, making business transactions difficult for managers who must deal with them. For example, managers may have trouble obtaining the necessary permits to pass through customs-handling procedures smoothly. Some government officials demand payments before they will lower bureaucratic restrictions. Payments that fall within the country's law are called **greasing.** In contrast, a bribe, as defined by the Foreign Corrupt Practices Act of 1977, is a payment outside the law.

Governmental Instability

In democratic societies, the transition of power between political parties takes place in an orderly manner. In some countries, however, shifts in political power are accompanied by revolutionary tactics and bloodshed. When a political power that is unfriendly toward a foreign firm takes over, the new government may expropriate the firm. Taking over a firm or its funds by force is called **expropriation,** or nationalization. To avoid conducting business where the risk of expropriation is high, some large corporations engage in **political risk assessment.** This technique attempts to measure the risk to a firm that stems from doing business in a particular country. Among the potential risks are takeovers by foreign governments, terrorism, and sudden changes in economic or military policy. If the risk of revolution, expropriation, and heavy government regulation appears too high, the corporation will not enter the country. The Organizations in Action illustrates how political instability can threaten business.

ORGANIZATIONS IN ACTION

Political upheaval in the Soviet Union (the attempted coup d'état, followed by the republics' striving for independence) had a devastating effect on a small computer firm's efforts to develop markets. On the day of Gorbachev's "forced vacation," the president of RG Data Inc., Robert A. Giese, said, "We've tried to get on the telephone to Moscow all day and haven't succeeded." Yet Giese said he doesn't intend to surrender. "You have to

be there when problems get sorted out if you want to be there long term. If you get up and leave the table now, you've lost everything."

John Velekaken, president of Otzar Inc., an import-export firm, said the upheaval in the Soviet Union has caused a major setback to his plans to set up three-way trade among the Soviet Union, India, and companies in his cities. Most of his clients are small firms that cannot afford political risk. Velekaken anticipated that the Soviet Union would soon achieve most-favored-nation status, enabling it to trade freely with the United States. At the time of the failed coup, he thought that these hopes were dead.

Source: Phil Ebersole and William Patalon III, "Some Local Firms to Suffer Setbacks," Rochester, NY, *Democrat and Chronicle* (August 20, 1991).

Limited Education and Skill Level of Workforce

In some countries, the educational level of the workforce is too low and/or the type of education does not match the needs of the corporation. Consequently, skilled workers and potential supervisors are scarce. For instance, in many countries people are educated in the liberal arts at the exclusion of technical and business education. In less developed or nonindustrialized countries, new industrial machinery often is wasted because the workforce is untrained or unwilling to use it.

Back to the Opening Case

Human resources specialists at Moog recognized that strict selection procedures were needed to identify the right job candidates for skilled positions. The company needed applicants who had either appropriate job knowledge or the capacity to benefit from training. Both aptitude (the ability to learn) and achievement (current knowledge) tests were used. The achievement tests measured knowledge of blueprint reading, mathematics and machine tool operations. Aptitude testing included ability in English—which is taught in schools and is the official language of business—spatial reasoning, and mathematical ability.

Scarcity of Parts and Raw Material

When machinery or other equipment breaks down in a foreign country, it is sometimes difficult to repair because replacement parts are not available locally. Raw materials may also be in short supply, creating production delays. The alternative of keeping huge inventories of spare parts and raw materials can be unduly expensive.

Unfamiliar Legal Systems

The system of law in a foreign country may differ from that in a firm's home country, thus creating the need for some adjustments. In the United States, the courts are guided primarily by common law, or principles derived from previous cases. In most European and Asian countries, civil law predominates, which emphasizes civil or private rights. Thus, American managers must learn to deal with government officials to settle through diplomacy disputes that, in the United States, might be settled in court. Laws concerning taxation, banking, and human resources management also differ among countries.

Another complication is that a U.S. firm might engage in practices in another country that are legal in that country but illegal in the United States (e.g., the disposal of toxic substances). The U.S. firm then gets fined by a U.S. court for a practice that was legal in the country in which it took place.

Problems in Measuring the Contribution of Foreign Units

In an era of management by results, all units of a multinational company are expected to contribute their share to corporate profitability. But a multinational corporation cannot apply standards universally in measuring units from the home company and foreign subsidiaries. Local circumstances must be considered when setting standards. For instance, the workforce of a particular foreign subsidiary may have a weak work ethic and the local government may be siphoning off profits. It should be noted that there are also many instances in which the work ethic found among foreign employees is much stronger than that of their American counterparts. For example, some firms set up manufacturing plants in Taiwan partly because of the strong work ethic of the Taiwanese. One way of measuring the performance of foreign subsidiaries is for each of the units to justify its existence by its contribution to the total corporation.

Sex-Role Stereotyping and Other Biases

Equal employment opportunity is more advanced in the United States than in many other countries. In Japan, for example, few women are found in managerial positions in domestic firms, and most female employees are part of the temporary workforce. However, sex discrimination is gradually eroding due to a labor shortage in Japan and an equal-employment law that took effect in 1986. Japanese companies are recruiting record numbers of female graduates for jobs that lead to managerial assignments. At present, 40 percent of the Japanese workforce is comprised of women. Another sign of progress in this arena is that Nissan Motor Co. has adopted an ample child-care policy that includes a five-year parental leave.[8] Despite the lingering discrimination faced by Japanese women, Western women sent to Japan on business seem to receive fair treatment.

Another form of job discrimination in Japanese companies is that firms based in Japan rarely employ non-Japanese workers. In the U.S. subsidiaries of Japanese firms, few non-Japanese are found in top-level management positions.

THE MULTINATIONAL CORPORATION

A multinational corporation (MNC) is a firm that conducts business in two or more countries in addition to its own. Today's MNC has headquarters in one country and subsidiaries in others. However, it is more than a collection of subsidiaries that carry out decisions made at headquarters. This new type of global company develops new products in several countries and promotes key executives regardless of nationality. Furthermore, the modern MNC conducts research wherever necessary and may have shareholders on several continents.[9]

Our discussion of the multinational corporation revolves around a combination of business and managerial topics: methods of gaining entry into worldwide markets, objectives of the MNC, and special considerations about staffing, controlling, and organizing the MNC.

Methods of Entry into the International Market

Multinationalism is an evolutionary process with six identifiable stages.[10] These stages can be thought of as methods of entering the international market, with each successive stage representing stronger involvement. Not all alliances with overseas companies work smoothly. The Organization in Action describes a positive example of a healthy alliance, and the following list describes each of the six stages in entering the international market.

ORGANIZATION IN ACTION

A model strategic alliance of companies in more than one country is CFM (Commercial Fan Moteur) International. The alliance represents a 17-year equal partnership between General Electric's jet engine subsidiary and Snecma, a French firm in the same business. CFM makes engines for Boeing, Douglas, and Airbus airplanes. The alliance has received orders for 10,300 engines with a total price of $38 billion. So far, 4,000 engines have been delivered.

The success of this joint venture owes much to the friendship between the founders of the alliance, GE's Gerhard Neumann, now retired, and the late General René Ravaud. The two World War II veterans met at the 1971 Paris air show and recognized the similarity of their risk-taking styles. Ravaud, the head of Snecma at the time, proposed the joint project the day of the air show. The original rapport between the two founders has endured despite occasional friction. The general manager of aircraft operations for GE says, "The French are sometimes prickly and difficult, but they rotated good people through CFM." It also helped that the alliance was profitable.

Source: Jeremy Main, "Making Global Alliances Work," *Fortune* (December 17, 1990): 122–124.

- *Stage 1: Licensing.* Companies operating in foreign countries are authorized to produce and market products or services within limited territories for a fee. Champion Products, a manufacturer of athletic clothing, is an example of a firm that earns about one-third of its revenue from licensing arrangements in other countries.
- *Stage 2: Exporting.* Goods produced in one country are sold for direct use or resale to one or more firms in foreign countries. Many firms have been established exclusively to help other firms get into the export

business, thus serving as intermediaries who are familiar with the complexities of international trade.

- *Stage 3: Local Warehousing and Selling.* Goods that are produced in one country are shipped directly to the parent company's or a subsidiary's storage and marketing facilities in one or more foreign countries.

- *Stage 4: Local Assembly and Packaging.* Components, instead of finished products, are shipped to company-owned facilities in one or more foreign countries for final assembly and marketing. Trade regulations in a country sometimes require that a large product, such as an automobile, be assembled locally rather than shipped from the exporting country as a finished product.

- *Stage 5: Joint Venture (or Strategic Alliance).* Rather than formally merging with a firm of mutual interest, a firm in one country pools resources with those of one or more foreign companies. Together they produce, warehouse, transport, and market products. Profits or losses from these operations are shared in some predetermined proportion. The strategic alliance between GE's jet engine subsidiary and Snecma is a joint venture.

- *Stage 6: Direct Foreign Investment.* In this most advanced stage of multinational enterprise, a corporation in one country produces and markets products through wholly owned subsidiaries in foreign countries. Ford Motor Company, IBM, and Honda are among the well-known MNCs that conduct business in this manner.

Stage 1 (licensing) offers the least protection for a firm doing business in another country. Each successive stage offers more protection against political and economic risks. Among the risks is the chance that the firm in the other country will drop its affiliation with the MNC and sell the product on its own.[11] Direct foreign investment is a good way to protect the firm's technological and competitive knowledge advantage. In this way, management can directly oversee and control the firm's foreign operation.

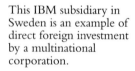

This IBM subsidiary in Sweden is an example of direct foreign investment by a multinational corporation.

Small Business Entry into International Markets

International business is not restricted to large multinational corporations. Many small businesses also participate in international trade, but usually not to the point of setting up strategic alliances with foreign firms. Two sources of help for small business owners in the United States are import-export firms and the International Trade Administration of the U.S. Department of Commerce.

A major role of import-export firms and the Department of Commerce is to help small businesses find suitable distributors to sell their products in other countries. An effective distributor serves as an extension of a small company's office. The distributor provides contacts, gathers intelligence on the competition, advises on payment terms, and sets prices.

A representative from the small company needs to familiarize the distributor and its sales agents with the product's capabilities. It is also important to describe how to sell the product and identify its target market. As the president of an export firm observed, "The essence of a successful relationship with the foreign representative lies in the ability of the exporter to instill a sense of pride and self-motivation. Close and frequent communication will provide a payback of many times the cost."[12]

Objectives of the Multinational Corporation

The goals and objectives of the MNC are similar to those of a business operating exclusively in one country. The usual goals of survival, profit, and growth apply internationally as well as nationally. The general objective of an MNC is to produce and distribute goods and services world wide in return for an acceptable return on invested capital. The MNC seeks to survive and grow by maintaining technological advantages and minimizing risks.

Conflicts Created by MNCs

An important difference between national and multinational corporations is that some of the objectives of an MNC may clash with the political and economic systems of the host country. However, there is also some overlap of objectives. The relationship between the objectives of an MNC and those of the country in which it conducts business is depicted in Figure 20-2. When the MNC achieves some of its goals, many interests of the host country may be met at the same time. For example, the MNC will create new jobs, pay taxes, train part of the workforce, and purchase goods and services from local firms. Although this arrangement is potentially harmonious, MNCs often create problems for their host countries.

Criticisms of MNCs

In pursuing their objectives, some MNCs have been criticized because they do one or more of the following things:[13]

FIGURE 20-2
Overlapping Interests of
MNC and Host
Countries

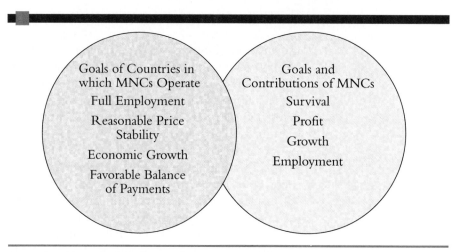

Source: R. Wayne Mondy, Robert E. Holmes, and Edwin B. Flippo, *Management: Concepts and Practices*, 2e (Boston: Allyn and Bacon, 1983): 650. Reprinted with permission.

1. Restrict or allocate markets among subsidiaries and prevent manufacturing subsidiaries from developing their own export markets.
2. Extract excessive profits and fees because they often have monopolistic advantages.
3. Take control of markets by taking over existing local firms, as opposed to developing new productive investments.
4. Finance their entry into the market primarily through debt and maintain a large share of the equity with the parent firm.
5. Redirect local savings away from productive investments by local people, hire away the most talented employees, and deplete material resources.
6. Restrict local employees' access to advanced technology. This occurs when research facilities are centralized in the home country and subsidiaries are licensed to use only existing or obsolete technologies.
7. Restrict the professional growth and development of local employees by staffing key positions with employees from the home country (expatriates).
8. Provide insufficient training and development to local employees.
9. Violate some of the host country's local customs.
10. Answer to a foreign government.

One way for international managers to deal with these problems is to recognize the potential for their existence and make adjustments when feasible. For instance, many North American firms brief their overseas employees on how to observe local customs in the host country. These customs include observation of certain times of day when one does not conduct business, protocol greetings and farewells, and national customs regarding gifts to purchasing agents.

Staffing the Multinational Corporation

With the steady growth in international business, U.S. firms have adjusted their staffing practices to fit the circumstances of doing business abroad. In the earlier days of international trade, U.S. corporations sent their top-level managers to live overseas and deal directly with foreign clients. These corporations had to learn to foster communications between two or more cultures and organizations, and the complexity of the task led to frequent failure. In response to these problems and to the unfavorable tax laws sometimes encountered, U.S. firms have increasingly hired host-country nationals for key overseas positions. A **host-country national** is an employee of an MNC who is a citizen of the country in which the foreign organizational unit is located.

To lower the failure rate of **expatriates** (managers and other workers on foreign assignments), multinational companies should take the following steps:

1. Develop a long-term orientation with regard to expatriate assignments, including performance evaluation.
2. Develop a more international orientation through such methods as emphasizing the importance of global business activity.
3. Provide more comprehensive training programs to prepare expatriate employees for cross-cultural interactions.[14] (Cultural diversity training, as described in Chapter 13, helps achieve this aim.)

Effective screening of candidates for international positions is also essential. The Organization in Action describes one such screening process.

ORGANIZATION IN ACTION

More firms are screening prospective overseas transferees and their spouses by asking them to consider issues related to living abroad. Among the questions posed at AT&T are the following:

- Would your spouse be interrupting a career to accompany you on international assignments? If so, how do you think this would affect your spouse and your relationship with each other?
- Do you enjoy the challenge of making your own way in new situations?
- Securing a job upon reentry will be primarily your responsibility. How do you feel about networking and being your own advocate?

- How able are you in initiating new social contacts?
- Can you imagine living without television?
- How important is it for you to spend significant amounts of time with people of your own ethnic, racial, religious, and national background?
- As you look at your personal history, can you isolate any episodes that indicate a real interest in learning about other peoples and cultures?
- Has it been your habit to vacation in foreign countries?
- Do you enjoy sampling foreign cooking?
- What is your tolerance for waiting for repairs?

Source: Consultants for International Living, 1992.

ETHICS QUESTION
How ethical is it for a U.S. or Canadian company to locate a manufacturing plant in another country when it results in job loss for U.S. and Canadian employees?

Managing expatriate assignments properly is becoming more important as the trend toward a global workforce becomes more pronounced. Employers are increasingly reaching across international borders to recruit for an important reason. Many of the world's skilled human resources are being trained in the developing world, whereas most of the high-paying jobs are generated in the cities of the industrialized world. As a result, well-educated workers are migrating to the cities of the developed world.[15]

Desirable Characteristics for the International Manager

The characteristics of managerial leaders described in Chapter 12 are just as important for international managers. Sensitivity to people and situations is particularly important, considering the delicate problems faced when a firm operates in a foreign culture. An example is an American manager on assignment in India who was having trouble establishing rapport with the supervisors reporting to him. Concerned about the problem, he asked one of the supervisors what he might be doing wrong. The supervisor replied candidly, "You devote too much time in staff meetings to asking us our opinion. We Indians expect the manager to exercise authority without first asking our opinion."

Part of displaying sensitivity to people of other cultures is the manager's willingness to acquire knowledge about local customs and learn to speak the native language at least passably. The multinational manager must also be patient, adaptable, flexible, and willing to listen and learn. These characteristics are part of **cultural empathy,** an awareness of and a willingness to investigate the reasons why people of another culture act as they do.[16]

Cultural empathy is so important that many multinational firms send key international employees to cross-cultural training programs they have commissioned. The programs are designed to deal with potential problems in a specific culture. For instance, the trainees learn that they should never pass documents to an Arab official with the left hand. (Muslims consider this to be unclean.) These cross-cultural training programs include role-playing exercises; language lessons; and classes on native history, politics, religion, and business customs. An intensive program developed by the University of Michigan brings together managers from diverse cultures. They learn to communicate through such means as the Outward Bound School (wilderness training).[17]

An important part of developing cultural empathy is to learn local protocol. Figure 20-3 presents a sample of dos and don'ts in several countries.

Organizing the Multinational Corporation

An appropriate organizational structure must be chosen to accomplish the mission of the MNC. The prescriptions for organization design described in Chapter 7 apply here. The organizational structure chosen must be compatible with the goals, technology, and external environment of the firm. The structure begins when the parent company appoints a top-level manager as head of the firm's international division. That manager typically reports directly to the chief operating officer of the parent firm. The three most frequent groupings of foreign organizational units are product-line, geographic, and functional, as shown in Figure 20-4.

FIGURE 20-3
Protocol Dos and Dont's
in Several Countries

Dorothy Manning, of International Business Protocol, suggests adhering to the following dos and don'ts in the countries indicated. Remember, however, that these suggestions are not absolute rules.

Great Britain

DO say please and thank you often.

DO arrive promptly for dinner.

DON'T ask personal questions, because the British protect their privacy.

DON'T gossip about British royalty.

France

DO shake hands when greeting. Only close friends give light, brushing kisses on cheeks.

DO dress more formally than in the United States. Elegant dress is highly valued.

DON'T expect to complete any work during the French two-hour lunch.

DON'T chew gum in a work setting.

Italy

DO write business correspondence in Italian for priority attention.

DO make appointments between 10:00 A.M. and 11:00 A.M. or after 3:00 P.M.

DON'T eat too much pasta, as it is not the main course.

DON'T hand out business cards freely. Italians use them infrequently.

Greece

DO distribute business cards freely so people will know how to spell your name.

DO be prompt even if your hosts are not.

DON'T expect to meet deadlines. A project takes as long as the Greeks think is necessary.

DON'T address people by formal or professional titles. The Greeks want more informality.

Source: Adapted from the *TWA Ambassador* (October 1990): 69.

PRODUCT-LINE STRUCTURE. This type of organizational structure assigns full responsibility for a line or group of products to a single unit. It is used frequently in firms with a diversified range of products and many potential customers. Each product division is responsible for marketing its own products world wide. The major advantages of this type of structure are good coordination within a specific product group and fewer communication problems.

GEOGRAPHIC STRUCTURE. This structure places all functional and operational responsibilities in specific geographic areas such as Western Europe or South America. Companies with limited product diversity favor this

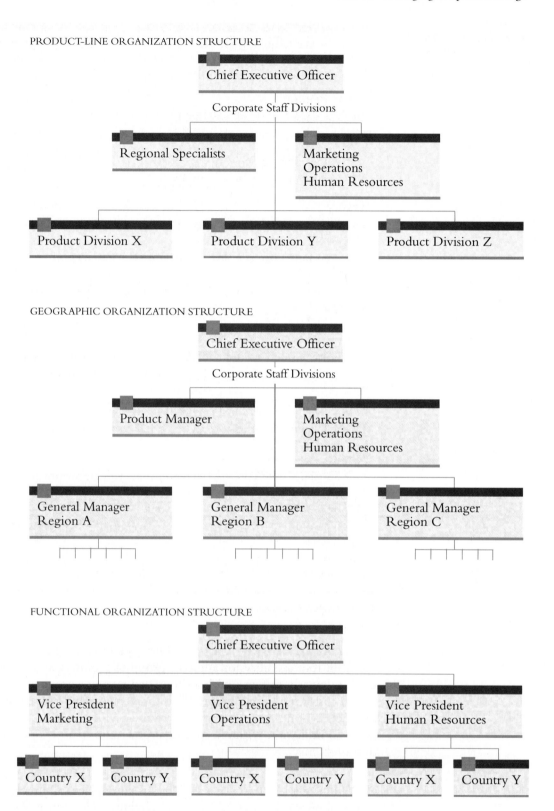

FIGURE 20-4 Organization Structures for the Multinational Firm

grouping. The geographic structure helps the MNC blend into the local culture. It also fosters company identity and employee pride (e.g., "We are Apple Computer, Inc. in France"). One problem with the geographic design is that geographic subdivisions may miss out on some important communications. One antidote to this is to create a product manager position with staff authority. Product managers are responsible for championing their products and providing operating assistance in their regions.

A challenge in designing the right geographic structure is to find the right number of geographic units. At one extreme, a geographic unit for each country served would enhance the understanding of local conditions, but most companies would find the cost prohibitive. At the other extreme, a geographic unit encompassing many different countries would lose some ability to serve local markets, but it would be less expensive.

FUNCTIONAL STRUCTURE. The functional, or traditional, structure assigns worldwide responsibilities for the major functions of a business to top-level managers in corporate headquarters. Typically, these managers report to the CEO. As illustrated in Figure 20-4, all functional vice presidents have direct line authority over worldwide operations within their functional areas. The marketing vice president, for example, has authority over the marketing activities in all foreign subsidiaries.

The major advantage of the functional structure is its ability to provide coordinated policies for each functional area. This advantage is realized most often when the firm has a limited product line and the different regions operate similarly. Nevertheless, the functional structure has important disadvantages. It conflicts with choosing an organizational structure that maximizes decentralization. Another problem is that functional departmentalization may result in a lack of direct representation of geographic areas and product lines. Also, there is some loss of coordination across functions below the top level of management. For example, when marketing and production functions are separated, each unit may make different forecasts in various geographic areas.

Choosing the right structure means applying the principles of contingency factors described in Chapter 7 to organization design. Among the most critical factors to be weighed are technology, size, goals, environmental stability, and characteristics of people. For example, one factor to consider in establishing a fully decentralized subsidiary in a foreign country is the availability of competent managers in the host country. If such help is not available, the MNC would have to choose an organizational structure that allows for more centralized control.

Managerial Controls in the Multinational Corporation

Managerial controls are important to international management because control is so difficult in a geographically dispersed corporation. Comments made by the manager of an international division of a U.S. corporation before a staff member left to visit a French subsidiary reflect this problem:

"Pick up all the information you can. We never really know what's going on over there until it's too late." For controls to be effective in a multinational corporation, all operating units must provide corporate headquarters with reports that are timely, accurate, and complete. Four types of information are vital: financial, technological, market opportunity, and political and economic.[18]

The most important financial information relates to surpluses or deficits within the subsidiaries. To keep worldwide operations running smoothly, it may be necessary to shift money from one subsidiary to another. Or the parent firm may choose to use part of a subsidiary's surplus to pay stock dividends.

Technological advances and developments must be reported back to headquarters because they may provide a competitive advantage in more than one subsidiary. If headquarters finds the new technology potentially valuable, it can move quickly to arrange licensing with its developer. A case in point is an Italian subsidiary of a U.S. wine company that found a way to reduce the vinegary flavor of inexpensive white wine. Hearing about the development, the parent firm moved quickly to use that method in its domestic white wine.

ETHICS QUESTION
What are the ethical issues involved when a foreign partner uses the other's technology to become a competitor?

It is important to note here that sharing technology can lead to cases in which today's partners become tomorrow's competitors. After a technological development leads to a successful product, one partner may go into competition with the other. One reason why this can happen is the difficulty in controlling a technological advance for long. Patents may expire quickly, because technology often moves swiftly into the public domain. Such has been the case with proprietary computer programs.

Market opportunities are the lifeblood of the multinational corporation. When an affiliate identifies a new or growing market for some product of the MNC, this should be reported quickly to the parent company. If the new market is large enough, the affiliate may begin to assemble or produce the product under a licensing agreement with the parent company or another affiliate. Other marketing information of interest to the MNC includes the subsidiary's market share, activities of competitors, and potentially valuable new products.

Political and economic information can be critical in developing managerial strategy. As an extreme example, a revolution might be fomenting in the country of a subsidiary. It might be advisable to withdraw funds from the banks in that country or even close the subsidiary until the turmoil passes. Favorable political and economic developments should be also reported back to headquarters. One example would be the appointment of government officials in the host country who favor international trade.

Control in MNCs has always been a problem. Differences of interpretation in reporting frequently arise. Today, global satellite communications systems allow for complete reporting at the close of every business day. If the widespread organizational units will comply, this may offer a solution to the control problem. Differences in time zones make 24-hour operation of communications systems necessary if instantaneous operational reporting is necessary.

**LEARNING
CHECK**

Discuss the importance of international management, the challenges and problems facing the international manager, and the basic characteristics of a multinational corporation.

MANAGING HUMAN RESOURCES EFFECTIVELY IN A CROSS-CULTURAL ENVIRONMENT

Many human resources and business problems exist in an international environment. Awareness of the potential for these problems helps point toward their resolution. In this and the following section, we describe tactics and strategies for effectively managing human problems in cross-cultural work settings. We then describe successful international business strategies.

A group of studies investigated human resources problems in international joint ventures or strategic alliances. Problems in joint ventures are likely to be pronounced because they are complex organizations with a high failure rate. The personnel issues in joint ventures can be categorized into eight areas.[19]

Staffing

A gap often exists between the actual and desired composition of the workforce of joint ventures. To help fill critical positions, some firms recruit volunteers for overseas assignments from among present employees. The lure of living and working in a new culture can attract many qualified applicants.

Promotion

Blocked promotion of host-country nationals in the joint venture and restrictions on transfers to the headquarters of either parent firm are two notable problems. The host-country nationals discover that top-level management positions usually are reserved for foreign expatriates or for parent firm transferees. Another problem cited is difficulties in returning to the parent firm following service in the joint venture. Expatriates often experience an exile syndrome characterized by the sentiment, "Out of sight, out of mind." To overcome these problems, companies should establish career development programs that increase employees' chances of being promoted within a joint venture. Opportunities for promotion to the parent companies should also be explored.

Loyalty

A conflict of loyalty to the joint venture versus the parent firm is a key problem for most employees. Employees of the joint venture notice that promoting the goals of one entity may decrease the productivity and profits of the other. It is helpful for managers to confront these issues in staff meetings.

Delegation

Parent company managers tend to limit the delegation of authority to joint venture staff. Managers working for joint ventures frequently express discontent about their dependence on headquarters staff when faced with important decisions. Parent firm managers can overcome some of these problems by reviewing their delegation practices and granting more authority when it makes sense.

Decision Making

Policy makers in joint ventures observe that decision making is complicated because the conflicting expectations of the two firms have to be reconciled. Decision making is especially complex when the goals of a venture, as stated in its documents of incorporation, are ambiguous or general. Resolving conflicting expectations can make decision making easier. For example, the parent firms need to agree on how much emphasis should be placed on enhancing quality versus minimizing costs.

Unfamiliarity

The feelings of unfamiliarity of each employee group with employees from another culture are a general problem in joint ventures. Unfamiliarity with the customs and language of employees in the foreign half of the joint venture often creates communication problems. Cross-cultural awareness training is the recommended intervention for this problem.

Communication

Both cultural differences and joint ownership are potential sources of communication problems in joint ventures. Another problem is that the two headquarters may not engage in smooth dialogue. Work unit meetings aimed at overcoming communication barriers are strongly recommended. The expatriate employees should develop adequate conversational skills in the language of the host country. Lacking such skills, they are dependent on the whims of translators.

A specific communication problem is that information is sometimes screened by one firm in the joint venture before it is sent out to the other.

One study found that difficulty in receiving exact information in Japanese firms was more of a problem in joint ventures than in wholly owned subsidiaries.[20]

Compensation

Dissatisfaction with discrepancies in compensation between employees of the two partners in the joint venture is a recurring problem. Related to this problem are the difficulties in assessing employee performance that stem from different performance standards in the parent companies. Managers involved in joint ventures should therefore give high priority to defining compensation policies. Earnings in foreign countries sometimes reflect little or no pay equity among workers on the same jobs. In many cases, lower pay is given for higher levels of work due to the caste system or personal relationships.

The human resources problems just cited sound formidable. Nevertheless, international managers who are alert to these problems and use the appropriate managerial techniques and can work around many of them. A useful perspective is that problems in joint ventures are worth tolerating because such ventures can be the best method of direct foreign investment. It is more cost effective to become involved in an equity joint venture than to own a foreign subsidiary.[21]

Back to the Opening Case

To solve staffing problems in its Philippines manufacturing plant, Moog invested heavily in testing and screening applicants. The plan worked out nicely, with 18 new employees performing well in the training program and on the job. Even more important, the foundation laid in selection and training made it possible to expand the plant rapidly.

NEGOTIATING STRATEGIES APPLIED ABROAD

Attaining objectives in international business often requires negotiation. Nancy Adler has explained that managers should negotiate when the value of the exchange and the relationship is important. Negotiating is generally the most appropriate strategy for creating win-win solutions with business people from other cultures. Specifically, business people should consider negotiation when:

- the other side has more power;
- the trust level is high;
- time is available to explore both parties' needs; and
- commitment is present to ensure that the agreement is carried out.[22]

Managerial negotiation requires significant adaptation when conducted in a foreign culture. A do-or-die attitude is often self-defeating. A list of suggestions for negotiating abroad follows. Each point includes the American attitude that could be self-defeating and explains how it can be improved.[23]

1. *Use a team approach.* Most American managers are convinced they can handle any negotiation by themselves, while other countries rely on negotiating teams. Bringing several Americans to the negotiating table may convey a seriousness of purpose and commitment.

2. *Do not push for informality.* More than any other national group, Americans value informality and equality in human relations. To negotiate successfully, Americans should not persist in using first names. They also need to pay attention to other status indicators such as the organizational rank of foreign negotiators.

3. *Speak in the native language.* In some instances, the host-country negotiators do not speak English and the Americans are left at the mercy of third-party translators. It is better to use American negotiators who speak the language of the foreign negotiators.

4. *Check with the home office.* Checking with the home office before reaching a compromise can be an effective tactic for Americans because so many foreign negotiators are accustomed to this practice.

5. *Be patient.* A striking difference between American negotiators and those in many foreign cultures concerns time. Japanese and Chinese negotiators, for example, are willing to spend many days negotiating a deal. Much of their negotiating activity seems to be ceremonial (including elaborate dining) and unrelated to the task. This often frustrates the "strictly business" American.

6. *Learn to tolerate less than full disclosure of information.* Many Americans believe that "laying one's cards on the table" is a valuable negotiating tactic. Thus, they expect honest information and are frustrated when it is not forthcoming. Because many foreign negotiators routinely practice small deceptions at the negotiating table, less than full disclosure must be tolerated.

7. *Accept silence as part of negotiating.* Unlike Asian negotiators, Americans often become uncomfortable when more than 10 seconds elapse without somebody making a task-related comment. It is sometimes fruitful to remain silent and wait for the other side to make an offer or reveal the nature of its thinking.

8. *Take no for an answer sometimes.* Americans are highly competitive in a negotiating session and take each loss personally. Foreign customers and vendors, in contrast, are often willing to lose one negotiating session to build a solid long-term relationship among people and firms.

9. *Be willing to make all concessions at the end.* Americans typically like to negotiate one point at a time. When one point is resolved (such as a delivery date), they move on to another. Far Easterners, however, prefer to settle all the issues at the end of the negotiating session. Therefore, negotiators should not think that no progress is being made when concessions are not granted along the way.

10. *Recognize that a signed contract may not settle everything.* A signed contract may have a different meaning in different countries. Therefore, Ameri-

can negotiators should not be upset unduly when a signed contract is ignored or some provisions have to be renegotiated.

11. *Be adaptable.* Negotiating tactics that are developed for use in Western countries may have to be modified to work effectively in different cultures.

A useful perspective on these suggestions is that a person is rarely on a level playing field when negotiating in another country. Adapting to the other side's negotiating tactics may help to place negotiations on an equal footing. However, Americans should not necessarily be the only group adapting their negotiating tactics to fit different cultures. Business people from around the world may have to develop a cross-cultural negotiating style.

LEARNING CHECK

Describe the human resources problems often found in international joint ventures and explain how American negotiation strategies require modification overseas.

ACHIEVING SUCCESS IN THE INTERNATIONAL MARKET

Success in international business stems from the same factors that lead to success at home. The ultimate reason for the success of any product is that it satisfies consumer needs. However, additional strategies and tactics are needed for success in the global marketplace. It is important to recognize this because internationalization of business is not always successful. Most of these strategies and tactics are a logical extension of topics discussed previously in this chapter.

Think Global, Act Local

This statement means that a competitive enterprise combines global scale and world-class technology with deep roots in local markets.[24] Local representatives of the firm behave as though their primary mission is to serve the local customer.

Diversify into Similar Product Markets

Diversification into product markets similar to markets currently served may result in several competitive advantages. First, managers understand their customers. Second, the structural characteristics of the new industry are likely to be familiar, which facilitates responding to competitive challenges. Third, some of the firm's current skills may be transferred to the new product or market, as, for example, where a fast-food chain diversifies its offerings to include a fast-food item that is popular in another culture.[25]

Diversify into Similar Technologies

Diversifying into similar technologies among business units also offers certain strategic advantages. Economies of scale can be realized, and expertise can be developed in selected production techniques. Diversification into new products that can be manufactured with an identical or similar technology leads to competitive advantage because expertise can be shared among the company units.[26]

Be Innovative in Many Spheres

Business strategist Michael Porter has shown that firms achieve competitive advantage through innovation in such spheres as a new product, a new production process, or a new way of selecting employees. Successful innovations in international markets anticipate both domestic and foreign needs. Volvo is an example of a firm that foresaw and capitalized on the growing need for safer automobiles.[27]

Be Familiar with Local Business Concepts, Laws, and Customs

Success in overseas markets is contingent upon close familiarity with the local scene. American companies that have established *maquiladoras*, or twin plants along the U.S.-Mexico border, have discovered the importance of this principle. For example, a unique aspect of Mexican labor law occurs when an officially recognized labor union declares a strike. All employees, including managers, must leave the building, and red and black flags are hung at entrances to the plant. Furthermore, employees receive full pay for all the time they are out on a legal strike.[28]

An obvious part of being familiar with the local scene is for customer contact employees to be fluent in the native language. Virtually every country doing business overseas hires host-country nationals as sales representatives.

Recruit Talented Nationals

A major success factor in building a business in another country is to hire talented citizens of that country to fill important positions. For example, Western firms have the best chance of breaking into the perplexing Japanese market if they hire top Japanese talent. A managing director at Nippon Motorola Ltd. has said about recruiting, "It's a No. 1 issue all the time. It's the one factor that could keep us from being competitive 15 years from now."[29]

Research and Assess Potential Markets

Another basic success strategy in international markets is to acquire valid information on the firm's target market. Trade statistics are usually a good starting point. If the company manufactures long-lasting light bulbs, it must find out where such bulbs are selling the best. Basic trade data are often available at foreign embassies, banks with international operations, and departments of commerce.[30]

Select the Best Method of Entry into the International Market

As described previously, small businesses often work with a distributor to begin conducting business globally. Larger companies may choose to open a subsidiary or enter a joint venture. Currently the best entrée into the European market is a joint venture. A major reason is that the European partner will understand the language and culture.[31] The Organization in Action describes an American firm that penetrated the European market successfully.

ORGANIZATION IN ACTION

Cenogenics, a small firm with headquarters in New Jersey, manufactures diagnostic tests. Founded in 1982, the firm made Europe part of its market from the outset. Michael Katz, the firm's founder and president, said, "We felt that our products had some features that were superior to the best products available in Europe." Cenogenics's product line was less expensive to manufacture at home than in Europe, giving the company a pricing advantage.

Within 10 years, the company's sales have grown tenfold to more than $3 million annually.

Foreign sales represent 51 percent of total sales. Cenogenics got its start through the matchmaker program of the U. S. Department of Commerce. This program invites American firms from a specific industry to targeted European countries and sets up interviews with potential distributors and other business partners.

"The foreign group of the Commerce Department did everything it could to beat the bushes and find companies interested in our product," said Katz.

Source: Adapted from Donna Brown, "Game-Winning Strategies for Europe's New Market," *Management Review* (May 1990): 10, 12.

Encourage Key People to Develop Foreign Language Skills

Even though English has become the official language of business internationally, overseas employees should develop skill in the language of the host country. Showing that one has made an effort to learn their native language can earn big dividends with employees, customers, prospective customers, bankers, and government officials. However, it is important to go beyond learning such obvious phrases as "Good morning," "How are you?," "Thank you," and "Please get me a taxi." Minimal foreign language skill may simply irritate the people it is intended to impress.

SUMMARY

Good management principles work well from one culture to another, but they have to be applied with a sensitivity to cultural differences. International management is the pursuit of organizational objectives in more than one nation. Because of the rapid growth in international business, international management is becoming an increasingly important discipline. U.S. foreign trade is now about $900 billion per year. The establishment of the European Community is one of several factors responsible for the current increase in world trade.

The international manager faces many challenges. Among the major ones are conflicts in cultural attitudes, unfavorable political climates, and changes in national economies and currency exchange rates. Other challenges include governmental inefficiency and instability, unskilled workforces, unfamiliar legal systems, problems in measuring the contributions of foreign units, and biases against some groups of people.

The multinational corporation (MNC) is the focal point of international business. A company can conduct international business at six different levels or stages: licensing, exporting, local warehousing and selling, local assembly and packaging, joint ventures, and direct foreign investment. The general objective of a multinational corporation is to produce and distribute products throughout the world for satisfactory return on investment. Small businesses typically enter international trade through overseas distributors.

Key positions in multinational firms are staffed largely with two types of employees, host-country nationals and expatriates. Increasing numbers of workers from other countries are being hired to work in the host country. To be effective, these expatriates must be adaptable, flexible, and sensitive to cultural differences. The three types of organizational structure used for multinational firms are product-line, geographic, and functional. The parent firm usually tries to gather four types of control information: financial, technological, marketing, and political and economic.

Managing in a worldwide environment means dealing with many human resources problems. These problems involve the following issues: staffing, promotion, employee loyalty, delegation, decision making, feelings of unfamiliarity, communication, flow of information, and compensation.

Managers need good negotiating skills to achieve their objectives in international business. North Americans must adapt their traditional negotiating tactics to fit other cultures. For example, people from other cultures may want to work more slowly than Americans on reaching agreement.

The following strategies and tactics are important for achieving success in international markets:
1. Think global, act local.
2. Diversify into similar product markets.
3. Diversify into similar technologies.
4. Be innovative in many spheres.
5. Be familiar with local business concepts, laws, and customs.
6. Recruit talented nationals.
7. Research and assess potential markets.
8. Select the best method of entry into the international market.
9. Encourage key people to develop foreign language skills.

KEY TERMS

international management	greasing	multinational corporation (MNC)	expatriates
culture	expropriation	host-country national	cultural empathy
	political risk assessment		

QUESTIONS FOR DISCUSSION AND REVIEW

1. Why is international management considered so important?
2. What are some of the key challenges facing the international manager?
3. Considering all the problems they face, should managers receive bonus pay while working in foreign countries?
4. To obtain business contracts in some countries, foreign firms must sometimes bribe government and company officials. The people accepting these bribes consider the practice to be a normal part of doing business. What is your attitude toward these bribes?
5. Should people who fly across the ocean on company business be given a day off from work to recover from the time zone differences? (For example, you might arrive back in your country at 4:00 A.M. in terms of the country of departure.)
6. At what stage of entry into foreign business are

Japanese automakers with plants in the United States?
7. Japanese automobiles are not nearly as popular in Europe as they are in the United States. Why might this be?
8. A sales representative was sent to Paris to close a business deal. The first night of her business trip, she was served pizza with what appeared to be a topping of miniature octopuses. The woman cringed inside. What should she have done to avoid getting sick or insulting her hosts?
9. McDonald's restaurants are found all over the world, including Moscow. What factors do you think account for the international success of these restaurants?
10. If English is the official language of business throughout the world, why is it important for North American international business managers and professionals to learn another language?

PROBLEMS FOR ACTION

A. You are the marketing manager for a firm that produces videos of country music entertainers. Annual sales volume in North America is now $4 million. The president of the company says he wants to expand overseas and places you in charge of the project. Sketch out your plan for going international.

B. A multinational company based in the United States wants to set up organizational structures for several of its subsidiaries. For each of the following

situations, sketch an organizational structure that will most likely result in an effective foreign unit. Use Figure 20-4 as a guide.

1. The firm wants to sell American-made tractors throughout Europe and Asia.

2. The firm plans to make inroads into the door-to-door, direct selling business, much like Amway or Avon. The intention is to begin in England, France, Italy, and Germany.

CONCLUDING CASE

Cost Containment in Chinese Exports

Recently, a Hong-Kong-based agent who sold to U.S. shoe companies received a telephone call from a Chinese manager who worked at a shoe factory in Guangdong province. The factory needed additional labor to fill the agent's sandal order, and the manager needed quick approval of a subcontractor. After a two-hour road trip, the American shoe com-

pany agent was escorted into a site of about 20 workshops producing shoes, flashlights, and hardware.

Inside, the agent saw 150 men, all shaved bald and wearing blue cotton uniforms with numbers across the chest. "This isn't a factory," the American thought, "It's a prison."

According to a *Business Week* investigation, the use of prison labor is widespread in China. Trade officials in China have crafted a secret policy to use laborers from its camps and prisons. These laborers work up to 15 hours per day and are paid nothing or close to nothing. Most of the output of these prison factories is shipped to the United States, Germany, and Japan.

Many international companies are unknowing partners with prison camps. In other situations, however, Chinese firms are open about their labor source. Officials from U.S. and European companies have been given tours of prison factories. In addition, some Japanese and Taiwanese firms are placing machinery and capital into prison production. The French cognac distributor Remy et Associés has used Chinese prison labor in the past to harvest grapes and has no plans to stop using this labor in the future. The low price of prison goods has contributed immensely to profit margins for retailers.

A U.S. State Department document uncovered by *Business Week* estimated the prison exports to be worth $100 million per year. Chinese officials deny using prison labor for exports and declined to discuss the subject with reporters.

Prison exports contribute to China's $10 billion trade surplus with the United States, the third largest after Japan and Taiwan. U.S. law forbids importing prison goods from abroad, although the practice is legal in other countries. Many of the prison workers are political dissidents who are being detained to be "rehabilitated."

Prison exports are frequently sold to American firms without the knowledge of the American managers. For example, an American firm places an order with a Hong Kong buying agent for goods made in China. The agent, in turn, makes a deal with a Chinese shipper, who then contacts a Chinese supplier. The supplier gives part of the deal to a subcontractor, who searches for the lowest bid. Often the lowest bidder is a Chinese prison.

1. Assume that you are a buyer for a large chain of department stores. It is late August, and you discover that your line of children's back-to-school backpacks were made with prison labor. How would you handle the situation?
2. Aside from being illegal, what harm is done by buying goods made with prison labor?
3. In the United States, license plates are made with prison labor. Also, a hotel chain hires prison inmates as reservation agents who work from terminals set up in the prison. Do these facts influence your thinking about the use of imported goods made with prison labor?
4. How can a firm guard against unknowingly purchasing goods made with prison labor?

Source: Facts reported in Paul Magnusson, "China's Ugly Export Secret: Prison Labor," *Business Week* (April 22, 1991): 42–46.

REFERENCES

1. *Business America: The Magazine of International Trade* (Number 2, 1991): 32.
2. Ruth Shereff, "Creative Clerical Solutions: Service Firms Open Up Satellite Global Offices," *Management Review* (August 1989): 24.
3. Peter G. Rogge, "Europe Moves Toward a Single Financial Market," *Management Review* (March 1991): 15; "The Battle for Europe," *Business Week* (June 3, 1991): 44; "Eastward, Ho! The Pioneers Plunge In," *Business Week* (April 15, 1991): 51.
4. "Eastward, Ho!", 51.
5. "Emerging Nations Earn Their Stripes," *Management Review* (February 1991): 51.
6. "Assembly Lines Start Migrating from Asia to Mexico," *Business Week* (July 1, 1991): 43.
7. Cynthia Day Wallace, *Legal Control of the Multinational Enterprise* (Boston: Martinus Nijhoff Publishers, 1982): 259–293; James A. F. Stoner and R. Edward Freeman, *Management*, 4e (Englewood Cliffs, NJ: Prentice-Hall, 1980): 775–785.
8. Karen Lowry Miller, "The 'Mommy-Track,' Japanese Style," *Business Week* (March 11, 1991): 46.
9. Sumantra Ghosal and Christopher A. Bartlett, "The Multina-tional Corporation as an Interorganizational Network," *Academy of Management Review* (October 1990): 603; "The Stateless Corporation," *Business Week* (May 14, 1990): 98.
10. Robert Kreitner, *Management*, 5e (Boston: Houghton Mifflin, 1992): 631–632.
11. Robert B. Reich and Eric D. Mankin, "Joint Ventures with Japan Give Away the Future," *Harvard Business Review* (March–April, 1986): 78–86; Jeffrey M. Hertzfeld, "Joint Ventures: Saving the Soviets from Perestroika," *Harvard Business Review* (January–February 1991): 80–91.
12. Jeremy M. Davis, "Exporting: The First Step in the Global Marketplace," *Management Review* (May 1989): 45.
13. R. Hal Mason, "Conflicts Between Host Countries and the Multinational Enterprise," *California Management Review* (Fall 1974): 6–7.
14. Rosalie L. Tung, *The New Expatriates: Managing Human Resources Abroad* (Boston: Ballinger Publishing Company, 1988).
15. William B. Johnston, "Global Work Force 2000: The New World Labor Market," *Harvard Business Review* (March–April 1991): 115.
16. Arvind V. Phatak, *International Dimensions of Management*

(Boston: PWS-Kent, 1983): 167.

17. Jeremy Main, "How 21 Men Got Global in 35 Days," *Fortune* (November 6, 1989): 71–77.

18. Donald A. Ball and Wendell H. McCulloch, Jr., *International Business: Introduction and Essentials* (Homewood, IL: Richard D. Irwin, 1982): 497–498; Phatak, *International Dimensions of Management*, 128–129.

19. Oded Shankar and Yoram Zeira, "Human Resources Management in International Joint Ventures: Directions in Research," *Academy of Management Review* (July 1987): 546–557.

20. Victoria J. Marsick, Ernie Turner, and Lars Cederholm, "International Managers as Team Leaders," *Management Review* (March 1989): 48.

21. Jafor Chowdhury, "International Ownership Modes: Strategic Options and Their Comparative Performance," *Academy of Management Best Paper Proceeding 1990* (San Francisco: Academy of Management, 1990): 101–105.

22. Nancy J. Adler, *International Dimensions of Organizational Behavior*, 2e (Boston: PWS-Kent, 1991): 183–184.

23. John L. Graham and Roy A. Herberger, Jr., "Negotiators Abroad—Don't Shoot from the Hip," *Harvard Business Review* (July-August 1983): 167.

24. William Taylor, "The Logic of Global Business: An Interview with ABB's Percy Barnevik," *Harvard Business Review* (March-April 1991): 91.

25. Michael A. Hitt and R. Duane Ireland, "Building Competitive Strength in International Markets," *Long Range Planning* (February 1987): 115–122.

26. Hitt and Ireland, "Building Competitive Strength," 115.

27. Michael E. Porter, "The Competitive Advantage of Nations," *Harvard Business Review* (March-April 1990): 74.

28. Susan S. Jarvis, "Preparing Employees to Work South of the Border," *Personnel* (June 1990): 62.

29. Robert Neff, "When in Japan, Recruit as the Japanese Do—Aggressively," *Business Week* (June 24, 1991): 58.

30. Donna Brown, "Game-Winning Strategies for Europe's New Market," *Management Review* (May 1990): 10–11.

31. Brown, "Game-Winning Strategies," 13.

It's Too Soon to Say Au Revoir to Dijon

Frazer-Dodge Inc. is an American manufacturer of personal computers, minicomputers, and printers. About 10 years ago, Frazer-Dodge established itself as an international company. The internationalization began with the hiring of a European distributor to sell its products throughout Western Europe. Frazer-Dodge's top-level managers understood that penetrating the European market would be difficult. Groupe Bulle of France and Olivetti of Italy were formidable European-based competitors. Japanese companies competing in the European computer market included Toshiba and N.E.C. In addition, Frazer-Dodge had to compete with American companies with a strong European presence such as IBM, Digital Equipment, and Unisys.

Despite the heavy competition, Frazer-Dodge computers and printers sold well in the European Market. Sales exceeded forecasts in France, Switzerland, and Italy and met forecasts in Spain and Germany. Jeff Garrison, the vice president of marketing, reasoned that the company had found a niche for its products. Frazer-Dodge computers and printers appealed to small businesses whose demands were straightforward. The typical Frazer-Dodge customer was not interested in paying for advanced technological features. Instead, customers were looking for reliable basic computer equipment that would perform ordinary functions in offices and factories.

After the computers and printers started to sell in Europe, Garrison proposed that the company create nameplate modifications to make their products more appealing in different European countries. A personal computer with the nameplate "The Cat" in the United States would be labeled "Le Chat" for sale in France and Switzerland, "El Gato" for Spain, "Lo Gatto" for Italy, and "Der Katze" for Germany. Nameplates would be added just prior to shipment to match the demand for sales in a particular country. Operating manuals for the computers were all printed in five languages: English, French, Spanish, Italian, and German.

Garrison's suggestion that the computers and printers be given names in different languages initially met with resistance from his teammates. Laurel Madison, the sales promotion manager, commented, "Jeff, I think you're being a little tacky. Our customers will feel patronized. Besides, Europeans like American labels such as Apple, IBM, Harley-Davidson, and Nike."

Garrison convinced his colleagues that the Frazer-Dodge label was American enough. He argued that giving each computer a second name in the local language would add a touch of cultural sensitivity. The multilingual operating manuals met with no resistance from the group, because such procedures are standard practice for products marketed internationally.

The group deferred to Garrison's authority, and the nameplate program was implemented. Garrison believes strongly that the foreign nameplates did increase acceptance for the Frazer-Dodge computers and printers. Many of the owners of small businesses in Europe who purchased Frazer-Dodge equipment said that they liked the warmth of the mascot names.

As sales continued to grow, Garrison and other top-level managers at Frazer-Dodge contemplated the wisdom of establishing a manufacturing plant in Europe. Garrison headed a task force to conduct a feasibility study of opening such a plant. Included in the international task force was the Frazer-Dodge director of manufacturing, the company controller, and a member of a market research firm based in Paris.

After six months of study, officials at Frazer-Dodge decided to open a manufacturing plant in Dijon, France. Dijon is located in the east-central part of France and thus is close to markets in Italy, Spain, Germany, and Switzerland. The company bought a 15-year-old plant that had been used to manufacture industrial electronic equipment.

Frazer-Dodge hired a French national, Gilles Naulleau, as the plant manager. Naulleau would have general responsibility for running the manufacturing operations, including shipping. A sales manager, Pierre Chevalier, was also hired, along with people to manage other key functions such as purchasing and finance.

Garrison and the Frazer-Dodge president wanted to grant substantial autonomy to the Dijon operation. However, they also wanted to exercise some control by establishing an American presence. The first thought was to appoint a Frazer-Dodge manager to a full-time position as director of European operations. The director would be on a full-time assignment at Dijon.

After a month spent mulling over the problem of American control, the executive group decided to create the position of "international liaison." This person would spend about five days per month in Dijon in the role of home-office representative. The liaison would exercise some control over European operations and function as the intermediary between the home office and Dijon.

Potential internal candidates for the position were evaluated carefully. The credentials of Erin Barker, a product development manager, made her a logical choice. In addition to being technically competent, Barker had good interpersonal skills and spoke French. She had studied French in high school and college and had spent one semester in France as part of her college program. In recent years she had taken two vacations in France, reflecting her interest in the French language and culture.

When Barker was offered the position, she said, "Great, this is an opportunity of a lifetime. But first I must discuss the position with my husband and son. Our family always makes big decisions together." Barker's husband and son agreed that this was an opportunity too good to pass over. They thought they could spare her one week per month if the two of them could visit Dijon with her at least once a year.

Barker still retained her position as product development manager. She planned to work at her new position about half time. Some of her responsibilities as product development manager were delegated to the two professionals in the product development department.

Barker was somewhat skeptical about occupying a liaison position, because it was by nature nebulous. The Dijon group would have to respect her authority, because she represented the Frazer-Dodge home office. However, the Dijon plant really reported to the president, not to her.

Barker prepared herself mentally for her first trip to Dijon. She gathered relevant facts and figures about Frazer-Dodge's European business and listened to French language-learning tapes intensively for two weeks. She arrived in Dijon on Sunday, after a 12-hour journey from the United States that included a commuter flight from Paris to Dijon. With a dryness in her throat, and determination in her heart, Barker walked into the Dijon conference room Monday morning for her first meeting with the French group.

Speaking French, Barker greeted the plant management team: "Bonjour mesdames et messieurs. Enchanté de faire votre connaissance. Mon séjour sera plusiers jours. Je voudrais apprendre votre operation. Aussi, je voudrais éxpliquer les operations de siège, et répondre a votre questions." ["Good day, ladies and gentlemen. It's a pleasure to meet you. My stay will be several days. I would like to learn your operation. Also, I would like to explain the operations of headquarters and answer your questions."]

"Oh, how nice. You speak a little French," said Naulleau in English. "We are happy to meet you also." Barker was taken aback that Naulleau and the other French managers seemed intent on speaking English. She interpreted it as a sign of not taking her interest in them seriously. Barker also thought that her first few days in Dijon were strictly ceremonial. She felt more like a visitor on a plant tour than an executive conducting business. When Barker touched on business topics such as sales and production forecasts, the Dijon representative would typically shrug and change the subject.

The following month, Barker revisited Dijon and again met with Naulleau and Chevalier. She opened the meeting with these words: "Ma derniere visite était très agreable. J'ai aimé l'opportunité de connaitre les cadres de Dijon. Maintenant je voudrais discuter les projèts très important pour le succes de notre affaire." ["My last visit was very pleasant. I enjoyed the opportunity to get to know the management team at Dijon. Now I would like to discuss important projects related to the success of our business."] Again, Naulleau talked mostly about superficial topics, but he did respond in a few words of French. The other managers spoke among themselves in French in her presence but held back on talking about serious business issues.

Back at headquarters, Barker met with Garrison. She discussed her seemingly slow progress in getting down to serious business with the Dijon managers. Garrison then asked whether she would like the company to assign somebody else to the job. Barker responded, "I'm not willing to say au revoir to Dijon quite yet. Give me more time to prove myself."

1. Should Frazer-Dodge management assign somebody else to the job of international coordinator?
2. How should Erin Barker handle herself in her future visits to Dijon in order to get down to serious business?

3. Is there anything inherently wrong with the job of "international liaison" from the standpoint of formal authority?
4. Would Frazer-Dodge be better off hiring a French national for the international liaison position?
5. What do you think of Frazer-Dodge's strategy for establishing success in an international market?

Part VII
Individual
and
Organizational
Development

Chapter 21

**Chapter
Learning
Objectives:**

1. Identify and explain career stages.

2. Describe what employers are doing to foster career development.

3. Summarize the manager's role in career development.

4. Describe what individuals can do to foster their own career development.

5. Explain the meaning and significance of career plateaus and "glass ceilings."

6. Specify what businesses are doing to help employees balance the demands of work and family life.

Career Management and Development

Twenty-four-year-old Robert Maser began job hunting in the spring. One of his interviews was with Frank Trujillo, a manager at International Business Machines Corporation. He startled Trujillo by stating bluntly, "I want to be clear from the start. I want a balance between career and family."

A husband and father, Maser then questioned Trujillo about his philosophy on allowing employees to spend time on family as well as work. Trujillo said he supported policies promoting a "well-balanced personal lifestyle." Among the family-friendly programs sponsored by IBM are stress reduction, flexible scheduling, leaves of absence, work-at-home programs, and child care.

Maser, a top graduate of the international business program at the University of South Carolina, was encouraged by what he heard. He ended talks with two other companies and accepted an attractive job offer from IBM.

Source: Based on Sue Shellenbarger, "More Job Seekers Put Family Needs First," *The Wall Street Journal* (November 15, 1991): B1.

The IBM programs to help meet the family needs of their employees illustrate how involved some firms have become in helping employees manage their careers. IBM helps employees achieve a balance between work and family demands. Although career management is still the primary responsibility of the individual, companies also play an important role in helping employees experience career growth. A **career** is a lifelong series of positions that form a coherent pattern. The term **career management and development** refers to a person's planned effort to achieve a more satisfying and rewarding career.

The traditional view of career management and development is geared toward maximizing promotions and financial rewards. The contemporary view is that career management and development also can help people attain a protean career. A **protean career**—which is controlled by the individual rather than the firm—emphasizes self-fulfillment, satisfaction and psychological well-being rather than external success.[1] People who achieve a protean career believe strongly in work satisfaction, depth of knowledge, and professional commitment. Although they may be high performers, they are more loyal to their own careers than to the firm.

This chapter approaches the concept of career management and development from from several perspectives. Among them are career stages, career development programs, and the manager's role in fostering career development. We also describe how individuals manage their own careers, special career challenges, and how companies help employees integrate work and family demands.

CAREER STAGES

A person's career is divided into stages, each of which has its own demands and expectations. Edgar H. Schein has developed a useful and widely recognized model of career stages.[2] These stages and their accompanying tasks are outlined in Figure 21-1 and summarized in the following paragraphs. People in different occupations move through the stages at different rates. Personal factors such as individual maturity also influence the rate of movement. For example, many 40-year-olds think to themselves, "I wonder what I'm going to be when I grow up."

Stage 1: Growth, Fantasy, and Exploration

As people begin to plan a career, they must turn fantasy into reality by obtaining an appropriate education and developing the basic skills needed for work. A few people do fulfill their actual fantasies, such as becoming a leading financier or a professional basketball player, so not all fantasies should be discouraged. Among the tasks for a person at this stage are to develop and discover his or her own abilities and talents and to engage in part-time work that helps shape career goals.

Stage 2: Entry into the World of Work

The person enters the labor market and becomes a member of a firm and an occupational field. Tasks required for entry include learning how to conduct a job search and making a realistic first-job choice. Stage 2 also can be reached through self-employment.

Stage 3: Basic Training

Early career training includes adjusting to the daily routines of work and dealing with the realities of organizational membership. (As one recent

FIGURE 21-1
Stages and Representative
Tasks of the Career Cycle

Stage	Representative Task
1. Growth, fantasy, exploration	Develop and discover one's own ability and talents
2. Entry into world of work	Make a realistic and valid first-job choice
3. Basic training	Develop confidence
4. Full membership in early career	Perform effectively and improve
5. Full membership in mid-career	Develop own performance standards
6. Mid-career crisis	Accept the present or work out a better future.
7. Late career in nonleadership role	Remain technically competent
8. Late career in leadership role	Handle high levels of responsibility and power.
9. Decline and disengagement	Find new sources of satisfaction in nonwork activities.
10. Retirement (as early as age 55)	Maintain a sense of identity and self-worth without work role

Source: Based on information from Edgar H. Schein, *Career Dynamics: Matching Individual and Organizational Needs* (Reading, MA: Addison-Wesley, 1978): 40–46.

college graduate said, "I never realized it would take three months to get anything of consequence approved.") Specific tasks at this stage include overcoming the insecurity of inexperience, developing self-confidence, and learning to get along with the manager.

Stage 4: Full Membership in Early Career

During this stage, the individual accepts responsibility and successfully carries out the first formal job assignments. The person also develops the expertise to lay the groundwork for promotion or lateral career growth. Specific tasks include performing effectively, improving skills, developing initiative, and finding a mentor and a sponsor. Although a mentor is usually somebody of higher position, this person can also be a more experienced co-worker.

Stage 5: Full Membership in Mid-Career

Here the person chooses and becomes committed to a specialty or moves toward becoming a generalist or manager. Specific tasks include gaining a measure of independence and developing personal performance standards.

Stage 6: Mid-Career Crisis

At this stage, many people reassess their progress in comparison to their early goals. If they decide they have not accomplished enough, they experience a **mid-career crisis.** These individuals choose among the options to stop climbing, change careers, or forge ahead to newer and greater challenges. Tasks at this stage include deciding whether to accept the present situation or work for whatever future is visualized. In making this choice, an individual may have to work out accommodations with family members.

Stage 7: Late Career in Nonleadership Role

A person who decides to continue to pursue a technical career must now confront the challenge of acquiring greater technical depth. For instance, an information system specialist might want to learn more about object-oriented programming (a major new software development). The individual then faces the choice of working to remain technically competent or using wisdom as a substitute for technical depth.

Stage 8: Late Career in Leadership Role

At this stage, the person must use his or her talents and skills for the long-term welfare of the firm. The person also must learn to integrate the efforts of others and to select and develop team members. Specific tasks for the person at this stage include learning how to shift from being primarily concerned with the self to becoming more responsible for the welfare of the firm. Another key task is learning how to handle high levels of responsibility and power.

Stage 9: Decline and Disengagement

At this stage, the person learns to accept reduced levels of power, responsibility, and influence and to deal with a life less dominated by work. Specific tasks include finding new sources of satisfaction outside of work and learning how to live more closely with the spouse or other partner.

Stage 10: Retirement

In this final stage, the person must adjust to drastic changes in lifestyle, role, and perhaps standard of living. Specific tasks include learning how to maintain a sense of identity without an organizational affiliation and finding outlets for one's wisdom and experience (e.g., by finding a part-time job). Learning to deal successfully with the retirement stage has increased in importance recently because so many workers are accepting early retirement.

Advantages and Disadvantages of the Career Stage Model

An advantage to this model of career stages is that it adds insights beyond simply dividing careers into the beginning, middle, and end. However, as with other career stage models, it may not consider individual differences. Schein observes that it is better to view career stages as broad sets of common issues and tasks that everyone faces rather than to link them systematically to particular ages or other life stages.[3]

CAREER DEVELOPMENT PROGRAMS

Career development programs and systems have become commonplace in businesses. This section describes the purposes and nature of these programs, including a comprehensive listing of the types of career development activities offered to employees.

Purposes of Career Development Programs

Ideally, a carefully planned career development program serves the needs of individuals, the firm, and society. The purposes and potential benefits of career development programs follow.[4]

MESHING INDIVIDUAL AND ORGANIZATIONAL GOALS. Career development helps identify the link between attaining individual and organizational goals. The career planning aspects of career development aim to match current and future needs of the firm to the hopes and plans of the individual.

SAVING MONEY. Career development programs can be cost effective. For example, the Crocker National Bank in California was able to save almost $2 million in one year through the increased productivity of career development program participants. One productivity increase was the placement of more profitable loans to customers.[5] Other cost savings may stem from reduced turnover due to improved job satisfaction. Career-minded people are more likely to stay with a firm when they see a logical career path ahead of them.

HELPING EMPLOYEES REACH THEIR POTENTIAL. One major vehicle for helping employees reach their potential is to assign them to a sequence of positions with increasing challenge.

PLANNING FOR MANAGEMENT SUCCESSION. Career development programs are useful in identifying people with potential for advanced management responsibility. At McCormack and Dodge, for example, the management resources review program is part of career development. Top-level managers review all of the employees who report to them directly and estimate their readiness for promotion into even more senior positions. In addition, the top-level managers identify the critical skills, training, and experiences each manager needs to be promotable.[6]

ETHICS QUESTION
To what extent is a firm
being socially responsible
by conducting a career
development program?

IMPLEMENTING AFFIRMATIVE ACTION PROGRAMS. With a career development program, a firm can fulfill its responsibilities toward women, selected minorities, and people with physical or mental disabilities. Without a structured program of career development, it is difficult for members of groups that have been discriminated against previously to advance into higher-level positions.

REDUCING OBSOLESCENCE AND MID-CAREER CRISIS. When employees plan their careers properly, they are less likely to experience obsolescence or an incapacitating mid-career crisis.

ENCOURAGING A STRATEGIC POINT OF VIEW. Career development involves strategic thinking. Carefully plotting a career helps a manager realize the long-term benefits of certain activities. Today's management trainee who rotates through different organizational functions is preparing for senior responsibility 15 to 20 years from now.

Describe career stages and the purposes of career development programs. Identify your own career stage.

Current Practice in Career Development

Career development programs vary extensively in both private and public organizations. One survey estimated that 50 out of the Fortune 500 firms had an active program of career development for managers.[7] At one extreme are extensive programs such as the one at Corning, Inc. This program includes in-depth evaluation of individual needs and exposure to career opportunities at Corning. An administrative and technical placement service provides information on job openings and qualifications through an electronic mail system. Previously, Corning had a closed placement system in which human resources representatives met monthly to discuss openings and possible candidates.[8] Figure 21-2 presents a diagram of the Corning program. At the other extreme are companies whose only formal career development effort is tuition refund for job-related courses.

FIGURE 21-2
Career Planning Roles in the Corning Inc. Career Development Program

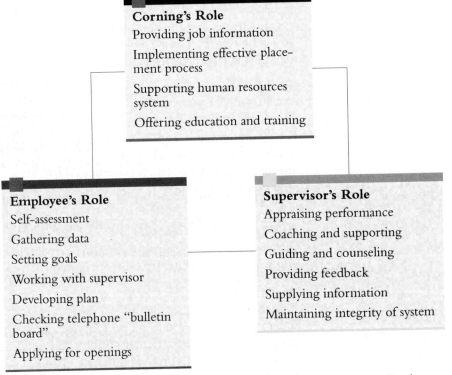

Corning's Role
Providing job information
Implementing effective placement process
Supporting human resources system
Offering education and training

Employee's Role
Self-assessment
Gathering data
Setting goals
Working with supervisor
Developing plan
Checking telephone "bulletin board"
Applying for openings

Supervisor's Role
Appraising performance
Coaching and supporting
Guiding and counseling
Providing feedback
Supplying information
Maintaining integrity of system

Source: Zandy B. Liebowitz, Barbara H. Feldman, and Sherry H. Mosley, "Career Development Works Overtime at Corning, Inc." *Personnel* (April 1990): 44.

Figure 21-3 illustrates the range of career development programs. It cites the most frequently mentioned techniques, methods, or programs of career management and development. Many of the career development programs listed are self-explanatory, such as "posting of job openings." Others are discussed in this chapter or Chapter 10. One interpretation of this listing is that career development can take many forms. Another is that no one activity is included in all career development programs. Sophisticated programs of career development combine several of the activities listed in the figure. The Organization in Action describes a representative career development program.

ORGANIZATION IN ACTION

At McCormack and Dodge, a manufacturer of industrial parts, managers can participate in a multifaceted career development program. The program examines personal values and goals along with individual strengths and weaknesses. Continuous growth through enrichment of current responsibilities (such as special trouble-shooting assignments) is another part of the program. An outside consulting firm administers this program partly because it deals with personal issues that are best handled by a professional career counselor. As one middle-level manager commented, "It's a little easier talking to an outside consultant about your real needs for development. Sure, I trust our own human resources people. Yet I don't want my limitations stored in a file located on company premises."

Company officials believe that one of the key advantages of the program is that it allows managers to focus on their personal career concerns. After they have experienced the benefits of this soul searching, they are more likely to tune in to the needs of their employees.

Source: As reported in Lorraine M. Caruli, Cheryl L. Noroian, and Cindy Levine, "Employee-Driven Career Development," *Personnel Administrator* (March 1989): 68.

THE MANAGER'S ROLE IN CAREER DEVELOPMENT

Managers make a major contribution to career development programs. Much of their contribution is tied to the related activities of counseling and mentoring.

Career Counseling by Managers

An effective career development program requires managers to be skilled in helping employees build their careers. These skills include conducting performance appraisal sessions, assisting in career goal setting, and providing feedback on performance. The manager functions as coach, appraiser, adviser, and referral agent in fulfilling the career counseling role.[9] However, not all managers are qualified by personality or training to counsel success-

FIGURE 21-3
Career Development
Programs

Rank	Technique	Percent Using
1	In-house training programs	95
2	Tuition reimbursement programs	91
3	Outside management seminars	86
4	Regular reviews of management personnel's strengths and weaknesses	67
5	Posting of job openings	67
6	Pre-retirement counseling	67
7	Counseling for terminated employees	52
8	Career pathing to help managers acquire the necessary experience for future jobs	48
9	Succession planning or replacement charts	48
10	Planned job progression for new employees	43
11	Career management seminars and workshops	38
12	Computerized skills inventories to assist with career planning	38
13	Career counseling	33
14	Five-year or other long-term career plans for management personnel	29
15	Counseling for downward transfers	24
16	Systematic job rotation of supervisors to prepare them for higher-level positions	19

Source: R. J. Aldag and T. M. Sterns, *Management,* 2e (Cincinnati: South-Western Publishing Co., 1991): 356.

fully. Those who are not so qualified are more likely to be effective in the appraiser and referral agent roles.

ETHICS QUESTION
How ethical is it for a manager to coach an employee when the manager represents the company more than the employee?

COACH. As a coach, a manager can help employees plan their careers by helping them identify strengths, areas for improvement, and job interests. Managers need counseling skills such as listening and asking probing questions to help employees acquire these insights.

APPRAISER. Observations made during the performance appraisal can help employees develop the skills and behaviors they need to achieve their career goals. During a performance appraisal, one manager was told by his superior, "You will not qualify for executive responsibility unless you learn to view your department as a profit center." These comments led the manager to become much more cost conscious, thereby conforming to company expectations.

ADVISER. The manager's role as an adviser emphasizes offering employees information that will help them set realistic career goals. Information of this type can assist employees in recognizing alternatives, limitations, and opportunities within the firm. At times it is most constructive for the manager to inform an employee that career development can take place in ways other than moving upward. Other means include transfers, temporary assignments, and sometimes a demotion to gain new skills. As adviser, the manager helps employees answer the question, "What are my alternatives and goals?"

REFERRAL AGENT. In the referral role, the manager directs employees toward activities and experiences that will help them reach their career goals. Included here are referrals to training activities, resource people, and on-the-job experiences designed to facilitate growth. To make effective referrals, the manager must be familiar with developmental activities within the firm and think creatively about which experiences are likely to prove valuable.

Mentoring

The four roles just described are often incorporated into mentoring. A **mentor** is a more experienced person who develops a junior colleague's abilities through tutoring, coaching, guidance, and emotional support. The mentor is a trusted counselor and guide who is typically a person's manager. However, a mentor can also be a staff professional or co-worker. An emotional tie exists between the protégé (or apprentice) and the mentor.

Mentoring is typically an informal relationship. However, several firms, including the Internal Revenue Service and IBM, formalize mentoring by assigning a senior manager a group of junior managers to mentor. Sometimes the junior manager is given a choice of mentors.[10] The standard approach to finding a mentor is to make oneself visible through outstanding job performance and participation in company events.

THE CONTRIBUTION OF MENTORS. Mentors enhance the careers of protégés by sponsoring them for promotions, coaching, facilitating exposure and visibility, and offering challenging work. All of these activities help

The mentor acts as role model, counselor, and friend in helping the protégé learn the ropes and advance in the firm.

the younger person establish a role in the firm, learn the ropes, and prepare for advancement. "Learning the ropes" translates into having the corporate culture, including dos and don'ts, explained by the mentor. An important function of a mentor is to encourage protégés to solve problems themselves and make their own discoveries. A comment frequently made to mentors by protégés is "I'm glad you made me think through the problem myself. You spurred my thinking."

The mentor role models, counsels, and offers friendship to help the protégé develop a sense of professional identity and competence. Mentoring also boosts morale by satisfying the basic need people have to believe in themselves and have others believe in them.[11] Furthermore, research has demonstrated that mentoring has a positive impact on promotion and rate of promotion over a 10-year period. The group chosen for study was composed of more than 600 business school graduates.[12]

Mentors also benefit from the mentoring relationship. An experienced mentor gains technical, administrative, and psychological support from the protégé. In addition, the mentor gains internal satisfaction from helping a less experienced colleague develop and gains respect from other managers for being a developer of talent.

Mentoring also benefits the firm as a whole, contributing to employee motivation, job performance, and retention rates. It adds to the vitality of the firm as a social system by passing along the values and beliefs of the firm to younger members. Another potential contribution is that by being in close touch with protégés mentors can sense trouble spots.[13] As top-level managers, they can often act on these problems. For example, mentors might notice that promising younger managers are concerned about a low level of risk taking in the firm and decide to investigate the problem.

PROBLEMS ASSOCIATED WITH MENTORING. If a person's mentor leaves the firm or falls out of power, the person's career could be set back. An antidote to this problem is for the individual to find more than one mentor, thereby decreasing the risk of losing a mentor or having the wrong mentor. A more subtle problem associated with mentoring is that the process breeds envy and resentment. Peers often look upon mentoring relationships as a form of favoritism. An advertising account executive made this comment: "Seeing other people who have a special relationship with a boss really undermines my confidence. I can't help wonder why I haven't been singled out for similar royal treatment.[14]

LEARNING CHECK   Discuss how companies contribute to career development. Include in your summary the career development and mentoring roles of managers.

CAREER DEVELOPMENT BY THE INDIVIDUAL

Despite organizational contributions to career development, the individual retains primary responsibility for managing his or her own career.[15] One reason is that the individual might change employers, either voluntarily or involuntarily. Another reason is that the employer and the individual might have different perceptions of what constitutes a satisfying and rewarding career. Career self-management is approached from four perspectives in this section: awareness of qualifications sought by employers, career planning and career pathing, career-advancement tactics, and stress management.

Qualifications Sought by Employers

An important but often overlooked early step in career planning is to understand the qualifications sought by employers. Understanding these qualifications can help job seekers prepare for opportunities. The emphasis here is on qualifications sought by employers in management and sales positions, but recent graduates in most fields would encounter the same demands. The most relevant question is often "What qualifications are sought by a particular firm at a particular time?" However, there are certain qualifications that a substantial number of employment interviewers and hiring managers look for in job applicants.[16] These qualifications are described in the following list.

1. *Appropriate education.* Many jobs leading to a career in management offer substantial on-the-job training. Consequently, prospective employers often look for a broad education related to business rather than intensive education in a subspeciality. Many other employers, however, do expect graduates to have specialized education and training. These employers want to hire people with special skills (e.g., statistical process control) so they can make an immediate contribution to productivity. In general, it is easier to find a job when you possess specific skills.

2. *Good communication skills.* Employers look for solid communication skills in candidates, particularly for jobs involving contact with people. Oral skills are judged during the employment interview. A job seeker's cover letter accompanying a résumé, as well as the follow-up letter, provides an example of written communication skills.

3. *Good interpersonal skills.* The ability to get along with other people is one of the most desirable qualities in a job candidate, and it is also a basic management skill. Interpersonal skills are often judged by how well a person interacts with the interviewers.

4. *Relevant work experience.* Work experience related to the job is helpful for two reasons. First, experienced applicants may require less training than inexperienced ones. Second, related job experience may reflect interest in the field. Many jobs in management, however, do not require comparable experience. Strength in several of the other qualifications described here can compensate for lack of relevant experience.

5. *Good problem-solving ability.* When hiring people for complex jobs, all employers seek people who have above-average intelligence. Indicators of intelligence used by employers include a candidate's grades, mental ability test scores, ability to answer questions during the interview, and quality of outside interests.

6. *Motivation and enthusiasm.* High motivation and enthusiasm are important qualifications for virtually every job. Employers often infer the

strength of a candidate's motivation from the intensity with which he or she has pursued school, sports, and other interests. Having received a job promotion in the past also could be evidence of strong motivation, as could high grades. Enthusiasm is usually inferred from the job candidate's comments and behavior during the interview. Enthusiastic candidates make many positive comments, express an interest in the company and the job, and research the company in preparation for the interview.

7. *Adaptability.* The work environment is typically fast paced and technologically complex. The workplace is constantly changing as new equipment appears. The newly hired employee must adapt to the work environment, juggle several assignments on a given workday, and be flexible. The prospective employer therefore will want to know how well applicants can adapt as shown by their ability to deal with several situations at once.[17] A student who has attended school full time and held a part-time job, as well as being an active parent, would be considered adaptable.

8. *Good judgment and common sense.* Making decisions at any job level requires both technical skill and common sense. Recruiters and hiring managers look for evidence that applicants have made practical decisions during their lives to show that they have common sense. For example, a woman who has earned part of her education expenses by operating a word-processing service for students gives evidence of good judgment and common sense.

9. *Leadership qualities.* Many entry-level positions for business school graduates lead to managerial or staff positions that require leadership. Employers routinely look for evidence of some of the leadership qualities described in Chapter 11, such as self-confidence and organizing ability. Previous work experience and school, athletic, and religious activities can reflect leadership qualities. For example, a job candidate might have worked as a restaurant manager and a class president.

Evaluate yourself against the qualifications discussed here. If you believe you are below standard in one or more of these areas, try to remedy the problem. For example, if you lack leadership experience, seek out a part-time managerial position.

Establishing a Career Plan and a Career Path

A key component of career management is to establish a career plan and a tentative career path. A **career plan** is an overall blueprint for achieving career goals by specifying those goals and accompanying action plans. A **career path** is the sequence of jobs necessary to achieve personal and career goals. A path is therefore incorporated into a career plan.

STEPS IN CAREER PLANNING. A six-step model of career planning provides a useful framework for career self-management. It updates a basic model to fit the realities of today's challenging work environment.[18]

- *Step 1: Establish a position objective.* A job candidate's first set of career plans should state a position objective or job goal for four to five years in the future. An example might be "assistant buyer for multi-store retail firm." Establishing more than one objective is useful because it increases the chance of finding a suitable position.
- *Step 2: Describe the position content.* In this step, the career planner prepares a job description of the position objective (or objectives). Identifying more than one position objective increases the chances of finding suitable employment. The description includes the major responsibilities and tasks, such as "independent responsibility for making merchandising decisions about selected retail items."
- *Step 3: Identify a portfolio of valuable skills.* The current emphasis in job finding and career switching is for the career planner to identify a portfolio of skills of value to different employers. Many top-level and middle-level managers and professionals are assembling skills they can market in different industries.[19] Identifying useful skills helps answer a question that is on the minds of many prospective employers: "What problems can this applicant solve for us?"
- *Step 4: Identify needs for personal development.* A candid self-assessment specifies the skills and characteristics needed to perform successfully in the position objective. An assistant buyer, for example, might need good negotiating skills to obtain desirable prices on products and computer skills to use databases for available items. Ideas for personal development may surface as the career planner identifies a portfolio of skills (Step 3).
- *Step 5: Set a plan for personal development.* The career planner establishes a plan of action, including a timetable, for acquiring the skills identified in Step 4. The development plan might include formal coursework, specialized workshops, or coaching by a manager.
- *Step 6: Acquire the necessary credentials.* Included here are both formal credentials such as schooling and informal credentials such as good performance on a related task. Preparing a personal portfolio that includes samples of important accomplishments is one way of documenting credentials.

Effective career planning is a continuous process. A new career plan should be developed as goals change and after each position objective is attained. Flexibility is also important, because a person may not attain the position objective he or she is seeking.

ETHICS QUESTION
Assume that you develop a career path that includes leaving your employer in five years. Are you ethically obliged to inform your employer of your plans?

ESTABLISHING A CAREER PATH. A basic career path is shown in Figure 21-4. Individual career paths will vary substantially, for not everyone aspires to become a CEO. Each step on the career path represents a position the individual would have to attain to reach a target position, the ultimate career goal sought. Each step represents more formal authority and income, although lateral movements can be included in a career path. Lateral movements, including taking on challenging special assignments while holding one's regular job, are important today. Fewer opportunities for promotion are available now than in the past, because most companies have eliminated many managerial and professional positions.

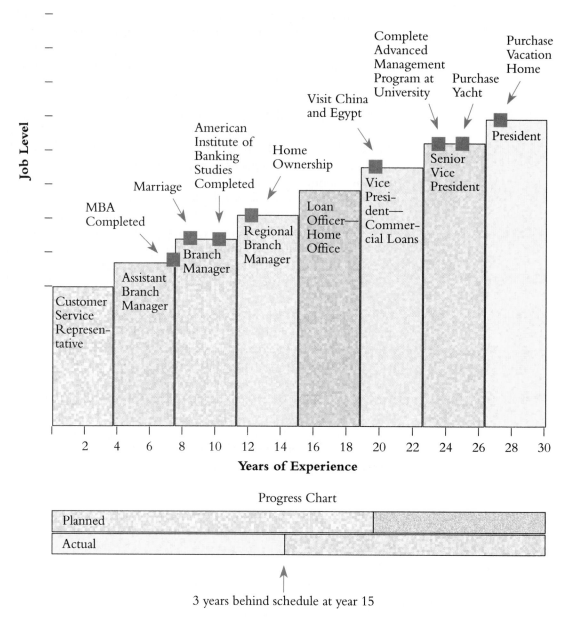

FIGURE 21-4 Career Path for a Banking Professional

An alternative to the management-oriented career path is the **parallel career track** (or **dual career ladder**). To retain valuable employees and promote professional and technical excellence, many companies have established separate-but-equal ladders for technical, nonmanagement employees. The grade levels, pay ranges, and rewards for these people correspond with positions within the management hierarchy.[20] Thus, in following a career track, professionals can receive promotions without having to become managers. A representative parallel career track is shown in Figure 21-5.

FIGURE 21-5
A Parallel Career Track

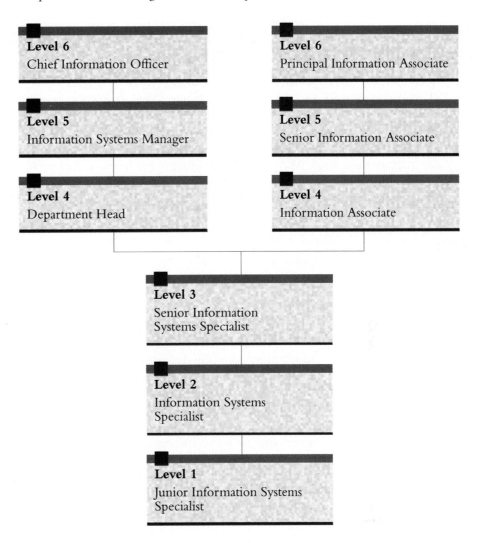

A set of personal goals, with tentative time targets, can be superimposed on the career path. Incorporating personal goals into a career path allows for a more effective integration of career and personal life. For instance, the banking professional who drew up the plan shown in Figure 21-4 might choose to work in a geographic area where home ownership would be affordable by the 10th career year.

A career path sometimes includes provisions for a **contingency plan,** which specifies what the person might do if an unfavorable event takes place. A contingency plan is often referred to as a "what-if" plan. For example, the banking professional might state, "If I am not promoted to a branch manager by age 30, I will look for a branch manager position in another bank or become a stockbroker."

Yet another emerging career path is for high-level managers and professionals to choose temporary assignments as a means of satisfying career development goals. Instead of choosing permanent positions, they seek assignments that last six months to a year, as illustrated in the Manager in Action.

MANAGER IN ACTION

Linda Pleverites joined Time Warner Inc., almost 30 years ago. She worked her way up to being controller of the magazine division. By the mid-1980s, Pleverites became bored with her corporate position. In 1988 she accepted a generous severance package from Time. After a lengthy vacation, she did some volunteer work and signed up with IMCOR, an executive temporary agency.

The agency placed Pleverites in an 11-month assignment as controller for a large advertising firm while they searched for a permanent controller. She says that she found out there is life after Time. "I learned that I could walk in and work my way through the financials of any company in any industry." She has now returned for a second one-year term at the same advertising agency, again doing financial work. Pleverites says, "It's wonderful. I can't be chained up in the corporate world anymore."

Source: Bruce Nussbaum, "I'm Worried About My Job," *Business Week* (October 7, 1991): 97.

Achieving Peak Performance

Doing exceptionally well in a demanding career requires more than high motivation, carefully developed goals, and appropriate skills and knowledge. **Peak performance** also requires a moment-by-moment poise to create the proper conditions for achieving maximum results with minimum effort. The person who achieves peak performance is mentally calm and physically at ease when challenged by difficult problems. Peak performance also requires intense focus and concentration.

The mental state achieved during peak performance is akin to a person's sense of deep concentration when immersed in a sport or hobby. For example, on days when tennis players play way above their usual game they often comment, "The ball looked so large today, I could read the label as I hit it." Focus and concentration make it possible for a person to sense and respond to information coming from within the mind and from the external environment. A peak-performing manager thus listens to his or her intuition as well as subtle messages from employees.[21]

Psychologist Charles Garfield says it is easy to detect those who have achieved or will achieve peak performance. Based on his study of more than 1,500 successful people, he observes that peak performers have a mission in their work and lives. They are fully committed to something they care about deeply.[22] Steven Jobs, co-founder of Apple Computer and founder of NeXT Computers, exemplifies a peak performer.

Career Advancement Tactics and Strategies

After establishing a career path, it is a good idea to do everything possible to increase the chance of attaining the goals specified in the path. Both the formal management literature and general-audience books and magazines have paid a great deal of attention to methods of career advancement.[23] Career advancement strategies and tactics have achieved renewed attention as baby boomers (people born between 1946 and 1964) face the likelihood of limited opportunities for promotion. Several reasons underlie this plateauing. Baby boomers comprise more than 50 percent of the workforce, thus competing with each other for good positions. The problem is intensified because the world economy has leveled off and companies are hiring managers and professionals sparingly.[24]

The following list presents 23 representative career advancement tactics and strategies based on the advice of career specialists and some empirical evidence. Some of the suggestions relate to merit, while others relate to appropriate company behavior and informal influence tactics.

1. *Develop a code of professional ethics at the outset of your career.* An ethical code determines what behavior is right or wrong (or good or bad), based on values. A code of professional ethics can help you deal with such issues as accepting bribes, backstabbing a co-worker, or engaging in sexual harassment.

2. *Make an accurate self-appraisal and stick with what you do best.* A major path to career success is to identify your best talents and build a career around them.

3. *Display good job performance consistently.* The bedrock of career advancement is professional competence.

4. *Help your manager succeed.* By doing so, you will earn a good performance evaluation.

5. *Perform with and for a top-level manager.* One study revealed that the single best chance for rapid promotions lies in the opportunity to work with a key executive.[25]

6. *Make appropriate use of networking.* The right contacts can open doors, but placing too many demands on contacts may irritate them and lead to backlash.

7. *Find the right firm for you.* Look for a fit between your personality and the organizational climate. For example, a laid-back person should try to join an easygoing firm.

8. *Recognize the potential value of growth within a job or a lateral move.* Personal and professional growth can take place through job rotation and acquiring more depth of knowledge.

9. *Become visible to influential people.* Bring favorable attention to yourself through a variety of good deeds including productive membership on task forces, cost-saving suggestions, and outstanding community service.

10. *Find a mentor or a sponsor.* Forming a relationship with people who can guide you or nominate you for promotion fosters career development. One of the major purposes of gaining visibility is to attract mentors and sponsors.

11. *Identify growth fields and growth companies.* Stay abreast of current developments to make the most of good opportunities for advancement.

12. *Practice good business etiquette.* The modern business professional is supposed to abide by unwritten rules of personal conduct such as knowing who pays for whom at a restaurant. The era of extreme informality and disregard of social niceties has passed.[26]

13. *Do not be discouraged by setbacks in your career.* A case history analysis indicates that successful people have learned to bounce back from their mistakes.[27]

14. *Document your accomplishments.* Keeping an accurate record of what you have accomplished can be valuable when you are being considered for promotion.

15. *Achieve breadth through job changes and project assignments.* Aside from the professional broadening it provides, moving to a different firm is associated with higher compensation for managers.[28] Nevertheless, job hopping and disloyalty can be damaging to a career.

16. *Avoid being constrained by a narrow job description.* Successful people often have to create their own jobs.

17. *Choose the right path to the top.* Seek a firm that is favorably disposed toward your discipline.

18. *Train a replacement for yourself.* It is difficult to be promoted if nobody is available to take your job.

19. *Compete in an environment in which you have an edge over the competition.*

20. *Plan your career jointly with your spouse or partner.* A well-managed career considers both family and professional well-being.

21. *Create a positive impression.* Look and act successful and stay physically fit. Remember, however, that dress standards have become more flexible. In many business situations, carefully chosen casual attire is in good taste. An effective use of humor is part of creating a good impression.

22. *Manage luck.* Be ready to take advantage of the right opportunities when they occur.

23. *Be ready to promote yourself tactfully and sensibly.* Inform influential people of your contributions, accomplishments, and aspirations.

Managing Work Stress

As mentioned in Chapter 14, too much negative stress may lead to ineffective performance. Stressed-out employees frequently show poor concentration and judgment. Negative stress can also lead to a wide variety of physical and mental problems such as heart disease, headaches, loss of sleep, overeating, and undereating. Handling stress effectively is therefore an important part of career management.

FACTORS CONTRIBUTING TO STRESS. Work stress is difficult to avoid because so many potential stressors exist both within the individual and in the work environment. Hostile, aggressive, and impatient people find ways of turning almost any job into a stressful experience. Such individuals are labeled Type A, in contrast to their more easygoing Type B counterparts. In addition to being angry, the outstanding trait of Type A people is a strong sense of time urgency that compels them to achieve more and more in less and less time.

A **negative lifestyle factor** is another factor within the person that contributes to stress. This factor can be any behavior that predisposes the person to stress, such as poor eating and exercise habits and heavy consumption of

Too much stress can lead to physical and mental problems and poor performance. Stressors should be controlled or eliminated in the workplace.

ETHICS QUESTION
What ethical responsibility does an employer have to guard against overstressing employees?

caffeine, alcohol, and other drugs. People who accumulate negative lifestyle factors are predisposed to work stress because they are in a weakened physical and mental condition.[29]

Organizational conditions also contribute to work stress. Under ideal conditions, workers would experience just enough stress to cause them to respond to their jobs creatively and energetically. Unfortunately, high stress levels created by adverse conditions in a firm lead to many negative stress symptoms. A major contributor to job stress today is work overload. Understaffing that results from cost cutting places heavy pressures on many employees and leads to high stress levels.

Job frustrations caused by such factors as shortages of parts, lack of promotional opportunities, or insufficient funds can also create job stress, as can extreme conflict with co-workers or managers. Another annoyance is short lead times—too little notice to get complex assignments completed. Constant assignment changes or repetition of tasks day after day are other stressors. Employees who complain, whine, and have poor attendance records create considerable stress for managers.

A SAMPLING OF STRESS MANAGEMENT TECHNIQUES. The two major strategies of stress management are controlling or eliminating the stressor and managing symptoms.[30] To manage workplace stress effectively, it is important to use some aspects of both strategies.

Controlling or Eliminating the Stressor. This stress management strategy requires the stressed person to get the difficult situation under control or leave the situation. An effective way of getting the situation under control is to improve work habits by using techniques such as preparing a "to-do" list and spending extra time catching up on paperwork. People typically experience stress when they feel they are losing or have lost control of their work assignments. Conscientious employees are especially prone to negative stress when they cannot get their work under control.

Eliminating the stressor is often the ultimate solution to escaping excessive stress. For example, a manager who is experiencing stress because of serious understaffing should negotiate to receive authorization to hire additional help. Reappraising a situation can also reduce stress because the stressfulness of an event for an individual often depends on that person's appraisal of the situation. Assume that a person experiences stress because he or she is required to learn the PERT scheduling technique. This person can reduce the stress by asking himself or herself, "Why is learning PERT so bad? I'm really pretty good at learning new techniques. With a little help, I'll be doing fine in a short period of time."

Managing Symptoms. Managing symptoms is the standard approach to stress management. Dozens of symptom-management techniques have been developed, and new ones are reported regularly. Getting physical exercise that is not too competitive or physically dangerous is a widely used and effective technique.

Making daily use of relaxation techniques is also highly recommended. The *relaxation response* is a general-purpose method of learning to relax by yourself. The key ingredient of this technique is to make yourself quiet and comfortable and think of the word *one* (or any other simple chant or prayer) with every breath for about 10 minutes. The technique slows you down both physiologically and emotionally.[31] An extremely easy relaxation method is to visualize yourself in an unusually pleasant situation such as walking by a lake, napping in a comfortable bed, or any other fantasy that is relaxing.

CAREER PLATEAUS AND THE GLASS CEILING

A substantial career challenge is dealing with the problem of being blocked for reasons beyond the individual's control. Two such blockages are career plateaus and the subtle forces that often prevent women from gaining entry into top-level management positions.

Career Plateaus

There is a labor shortage for entry-level positions in service industries and for many technical and professional positions. The shortage stems from the fact that people born between 1946 and 1964 are having only half as many children as their parents did. However, despite the current entry-level labor shortage, opportunities for promotion will be limited for the next decade. The world economy has been avoiding a depression for many years, but not enough momentum has been created to sustain the expansion necessary to generate substantial promotions. The tendency of firms to run "leaner and meaner" also dampens promotion possibilities.

Limited business expansion and the trimming down of businesses have important career consequences. A greater proportion of workers now than in the past face the prospect of plateauing. A **career plateau** is a situation in which, for either organizational or individual reasons, the probability of moving up the career ladder is low. If not taken in proper perspective and managed properly, plateaus can create enough stress to lower self-esteem and job performance.[32]

Companies can help people cope with plateaus by offering opportunities for lateral growth such as special assignments and job rotation. Managers might direct the attention of plateaued employees to the work satisfactions and achievements they will be able to experience. Discussions about an employee's plateau should point also to spheres of work and life in which the employee can win.[33]

Career plateaus become more understandable and acceptable when individuals realize that the guidelines for career progress have changed. Today, people can wait years between promotions despite good performance. A consultant notes, "Many managers are sitting in jobs longer regardless of their age, talents, or skills."[34] This problem may help to explain the slow movement of many women into key jobs.

The best response to a plateau is for the individual to control impatience and make constructive use of time. The individual might develop new skills on the job to help qualify for later promotion. Also, because there are less stringent time demands during a plateau, more time can be invested in professional self-development.

Women Moving into Upper Management

A major career development issue in many firms is the movement of women into key managerial positions. In response to the increased percentage of women in the workplace and to social and governmental pressures, many firms have moved toward equal opportunity for women in management. The number of women in middle-level close to top-level management positions has increased substantially in recent years. Women hold about 45 percent of managerial jobs in the United States. Many corporate vice presidents today are women.[35] An example is Diane Harris, the vice president of corporate development at Bausch & Lomb. Working with a staff of merger and acquisition specialists, she is responsible for buying and selling new companies and entering into new ventures for the company. Harris reports directly to the CEO of Bausch & Lomb.

Despite the considerable progress of women into management, many observers contend that women (and minorities) face a glass ceiling. A **glass ceiling** is an invisible but difficult-to-penetrate barrier to promotion based on subtle attitudes and prejudices. Fewer than 2 percent of senior executives in business are women. Furthermore, women held only 2 of the top 1,000 executive positions in 1990 and none in 1991.[36] Catalyst, a consultant in women's employment, surveyed CEOs and human resources officials about barriers facing corporate women. Among the key findings were that (a) 79 percent of CEOs acknowledged that women face barriers to reaching top-level management positions and (b) 8 percent of the companies surveyed said that more than one-fourth of top-level management positions are held by women.[37]

WHY THE GLASS CEILING EXISTS. An analysis of several factors responsible for the glass ceiling[38] points to possible solutions to the problem. A dominant factor is tradition. Men often promote men because they are more familiar with them. The glass ceiling remains a fundamental obstacle to the advancement of women into top-level management.

Another reason for the glass ceiling is lack of acceptance of women in key positions by some top-level managers. The acceptance problem is much higher in heavy industry than in service firms and consumer-oriented firms. As illustrated in the Manager in Action, the glass ceiling is fading in the advertising business. The new generation of executives, which has more egalitarian attitudes, is more accepting of women and minorities.

MANAGER IN ACTION

Earlier in her career, when Rochelle Lazarus entered meetings to formulate advertising strategy she was usually the only woman in a room filled with senior-level men. At the time, she was a junior executive for Ogilvy & Mather Worldwide, one of the country's largest advertising agencies. "For a long time most people considered Madison Avenue to be a boys' club," said 42-year-old Lazarus. "I knew it was going to take a long time for women to get the top jobs."

For Lazarus, patience has paid big dividends. In May 1991, she was appointed president and chief operating officer of the New York office of Ogilvy & Mather Worldwide, which has approximately $700 million in billings. Recently, a small group of other women has been promoted into top-level management positions at some of the country's largest agencies.

Source: Kim Foltz, "Women Are Starting to Crack the Glass Ceiling at Advertising Agencies," *The New York Times* (syndicated story, November 17, 1991).

FORMAL METHODS OF SHATTERING THE GLASS CEILING. Governmental action is one approach to overcoming invisible barriers to promotion. For example, the U.S. Labor Department investigates underrepresentation of women in top-level management positions. The focus is on subtle aspects of discrimination such as offering male executives golf club memberships but excluding women. Companies themselves may conduct periodic reviews of the progress of women and minorities into higher-level managerial positions. One such company is Honeywell Inc. Barbara Jerich, the company's director of workforce diversity, explains the process:

> "To ensure that women and minorities don't lose out more than they would otherwise [because of limited corporate growth], we have an executive talent committee. The committee reviews the progress and development of talented women and minorities who have been identified as having potential to move into significant positions. The committee meets regularly and familiarizes itself with these individuals' accomplishments, career paths, and promotions. We use high-ranking management officials to make things happen where they may not have happened with normal systems."[39]

Barbara Jerich leads Honeywell's efforts to shatter the glass ceiling by monitoring the professional development of women and minorities in the firm.

BALANCING WORK AND FAMILY DEMANDS

An important aspect of having a successful career is balancing the demands of work and personal life. For many people, achieving such a balance is difficult. Updated evidence from an older survey points to this conflict. More than one-third of workers with a spouse or children say that their jobs and family lives interfere with each other to some degree.[40] An analysis of relevant theory suggests that attempts to balance work and family roles can lead to conflict and stress.[41] This in turn can decrease productivity as workers become preoccupied with unresolved work-versus-family issues.

In the next section we describe the steps many employers are taking, or can take, to help employees achieve a balance between work and family life. We also describe the steps employees can take to achieve a better balance.

Organizational Methods of Balancing Work and Family Demands

In recent years employers have invested in developing programs to help employees meet family obligations despite full-time employment. These programs are pertinent because so many employees are working parents, single parents, and dual-career couples.

ETHICS QUESTION
To what extent do employers have a social responsibility to help employees balance the demands of work and family?

ORGANIZATIONAL PROGRAMS AND SUPPORT SYSTEMS. The discussions of job design and employee benefits (Chapters 7 and 9) included programs that help balance work and family life. Among them are child care, elder care, modified work schedules, and parental leave. Some top-level managers regard these programs as methods of productivity enhancement. William Lee, chairman and president of Duke Power, says, "No worker can be productive if he or she is worrying about a sick baby at home."[42] A review of several "family-friendly" employers identified by *Working Mother* magazine is shown in Figure 21-6.

CREATING POSITIONS FOR WORK/FAMILY PROFESSIONALS. Several large employers have created the position of work/family professional. These specialists develop (and sometimes implement) policies and programs to integrate the demands of career and personal life. Child-care programs are one example. Another aspect of the work/family professional's job is to help managers become more sensitive to conflict between work and family. An example is a workshop conducted by Ted Childs, manager of work/life programs at IBM. During the workshop, managers are informed of programs that are available to help them respond to changing demographics. The managers are also encouraged to build partnerships with employees to help them resolve work/family conflicts.[43]

FIGURE 21-6   Companies Noted for the Support They Provide to Working Parents

Company	Type of Business	Employees		Female Managers	Some Perks for Working Mothers
		Total	Female		
Beth Israel Boston	Hospital	4,984	3,489	60%	• On-site day care • Up to 12 weeks childbirth leave • Flextime, work at home, job sharing • Fitness center
Du Pont	Chemical company	103,000	24,000	7%	• Supports nearby day care • Flextime, part time • Up to 6 months childbirth leave • Work at home
FEL-PRO	Supplier to auto industry	2,127	846	12%	• On-site day care • Tuition aid • Up to 15 weeks childbirth leave • Emergency/sick child care
Hewitt	Benefits programs	2,800	1,764	37%	• Supports nearby day care • Up to 112 weeks childbirth leave • Flextime, part time, job sharing
HBO	Cable television	1,669	943	50%	• Supports nearby day care • 18 weeks childbirth leave • Flextime, work at home, part time
IBM	Computer manufacturer	205,000	60,000	21%	• Supports nearby day care • Up to 162 weeks childbirth leave • Flextime, work at home, part time
Merck	Prescription drugs	18,966	7,720	20%	• Supports nearby day care • Up to 18 months childbirth leave • Flextime, job sharing, part time
SAS	Computer software	1,437	834	46%	• On-site day care • Up to 6 weeks childbirth leave • Part time • Job sharing • Fitness/health center
UNUM	Insurance	4,197	2,923	50%	• On-site day care • Up to 3 months childbirth leave • Flextime, part time • Fitness center

Source: *Working Mother* magazine and the Associated Press (September 25, 1991). Reprinted with permission.

CREATION OF PARENT TRACKS. Some employers are making it possible for managers and professionals to choose a career track that allows more time for parenting. Investing more time in family and less in career is often referred to as **downshifting.** A person choosing a parent track would avoid positions that interfere heavily with family responsibilities, such as positions that require frequent overseas travel.

Back to the
Opening Case

Certainly, a powerful company like IBM could not be expected to create new policies and programs for one job candidate like Robert Maser. However, IBM was prepared in advance to meet the demands of outstanding job candidates who sought a family-friendly employer. Recognizing the needs of a changing labor market, IBM already had in place programs such as flexible programming that make it easier to be a full-time employee and attentive parent.

Individual Methods of Balancing Work and Family Demands

Individuals have the primary responsibility for balancing work and family demands. Aside from making use of help offered by employers, individuals can take other actions to achieve this balance. An important first step is to discuss work commitments with one's partner or prospective partner. Heavy conflict over work versus family demands can be prevented if each partner has an accurate perception of the prospective mate's work values.[44] For example, some people are prepared to work 60 hours per week to achieve their career objectives while others prefer to work no more than 40 hours. Partners who cannot agree or compromise on how much time is suitable to invest in a career may not be compatible.

Planning for family events is a helpful way of lessening conflict between work and family obligations. If parents are informed well in advance of a child's open house at school, it is sometimes possible to arrange work schedules around that date, much like a medical appointment. Dividing household chores fairly can also reduce conflict related to work versus family. In this way, neither partner feels exploited and both have more creative energy left for work demands.

SUMMARY

A career is a lifelong series of positions that form a coherent pattern. Career management and development comprise a planned effort to enhance the satisfactions and rewards associated with a person's career. A career can be divided into the following stages:

1. growth, fantasy, and exploration;
2. entry into the world of work;
3. basic training;
4. full membership in early career;
5. full membership in mid-career;

6. mid-career crisis;
7. late career in nonleadership role;
8. late career in leadership role;
9. decline and disengagement; and
10. retirement.

Under ideal circumstances, a career development program works to the benefit of individuals, the firm, and society. Career development programs vary extensively in both private and public organizations. The most comprehensive programs include an evaluation of the individual's needs and exposure to career opportunities. At the other extreme are firms whose only formal career development effort is tuition assistance. Figure 21-3 lists a full range of career development programs.

Managers have an important role in career development, particularly with respect to career counseling and mentoring. Career counseling includes four roles: coach, appraiser, adviser, and referral agent. A mentor is a more experienced person who helps a junior colleague develop through tutoring, coaching, guidance, and emotional support. A number of firms attempt to formalize mentoring by assigning a senior manager a group of junior managers to mentor.

Mentors enhance the careers of their protégés through such means as sponsoring them for promotions, coaching, facilitating exposure and visibility, and offering challenging work.

Individuals have the primary responsibility for managing their own careers. An early stage of career development is being aware of qualifications sought by employers. Among these are appropriate education, communication and interpersonal skills, motivation and enthusiasm, and leadership qualities.

A key component of career management is to establish a career plan and a career path. A career plan is an overall blueprint for achieving career goals by specifying those goals and accompanying action plans. The six steps in career planning are as follows:
1. Establish a position objective.
2. Describe the position content.
3. Identify a portfolio of valuable skills.
4. Identify needs for personal development.
5. Set a plan for personal development.
6. Acquire the necessary credentials.

A career path is the sequence of jobs necessary to achieve personal and career goals; it is therefore incorporated into a career plan.

An alternative to the management-oriented career path is the parallel career track that allows for upward growth as a specialist. This track is designed to provide pay and prestige comparable to a managerial ladder. Contingency plans are often incorporated into a career path.

Achieving peak performance is an ideal that helps the individual and the firm. The career-minded individual might consider using informal tactics and strategies for career advancement. Such methods are often necessary because of the difficulty of advancing one's career on the basis of good job performance alone. Factors such as personal preferences and imperfect systems for identifying the best performers often influence who gets ahead.

Effective stress management is another important strategy for career survival and advancement. Both personal factors such as being a Type A personality and organizational factors such as heavy workloads contribute to stress. The two major strategies of stress management are to control or eliminate the stressor and to manage the symptoms. Symptom management includes physical exercise and relaxation techniques.

A special challenge today is to deal with the career plateaus that face many managers and professionals. Much of the current plateauing is due to flattening of hierarchies and leaner firms.

A major career development issue in many firms is the movement of women into key managerial positions. Women have moved rapidly into middle-level management, including top positions in middle-level management. Yet a glass ceiling (an invisible but difficult-to-penetrate barrier) may be blocking women's progress into the top-level management positions in business. Minorities face similar barriers. Many firms are carefully reviewing the career progress of the women and minorities they employ.

A major career issue in companies today is helping employees balance work and family demands. Formal programs to deal with this problem include child care, elder care, and flexible work arrangements. Of major significance, some employers have created the position of work/family professional to help integrate work and family demands. The creation of parent tracks gives workers an opportunity to invest more time in family and less in career.

Individuals also can take actions to balance work and family demands. Such actions include discussing work commitments with a prospective partner, planning for family events, and sharing household responsibilities fairly.

KEY TERMS

career

career management and
  development

protean career

mid-career crisis

mentor

career plan

career path

parallel career track (or
  dual career ladder)

contingency plan

peak performance

negative lifestyle factor

career plateau

glass ceiling

downshifting

QUESTIONS FOR DISCUSSION AND REVIEW

1. Identify your current career stage and explain your answer. Also identify the career stage of a parent, relative, or friend.
2. Identify your primary career orientation and provide supporting evidence.
3. What risks might an employer take by running a career development program?
4. How might a CEO assist the career development of his or her vice presidents?
5. Explain how an athletic coach or music teacher can act as a mentor.
6. What is the difference between striving for peak performance and just working at full capacity?
7. What are some of the steps individuals can take to develop their own careers?
8. Why is it necessary for people to use career advancement tactics?
9. By late 1991, none of the top 1,000 corporate positions were held by women. How many women should be in this elite group by the year 2000? Explain your reasoning.
10. What implications does the presence of so many dual-career couples have for employers?

PROBLEMS FOR ACTION

A. Using Figure 21-4 as a model, draw a diagram of your career path as you envision it. Include personal goals in your path, and also establish a set of contingency plans. If you have access to the necessary equipment, use computer graphics to draw your career path.

B. Assume that you are on special assignment to the career development department of your firm. Design a work/family program for employees throughout the firm. Include some ideas for evaluating the effectiveness of your program.

CONCLUDING CASE

"What's My Next Career Move?"

John Sanderson was one of about 3,000 people attending the Franchise and Business Opportunities Expo. The exposition has been making regular stops in cities throughout the United States and Canada. Its purpose is to give franchisors an opportunity to describe their business opportunities to potential franchisees (franchise holders). Among the many franchisors on display were printing shops, soft-drink vending machine distributors, submarine shops, hot popcorn vending machine distributors, and pet care centers.

As Sanderson finished looking over the sales literature on a ceiling-cleaning franchise, he thought to himself, "Is this something I really want to do?

Leave corporate life to become the operator of a mom-and-pop business? Would I really be putting my management skills to good use?"

Five days after attending the show, Sanderson asked his boss whether the two of them could spend some time talking about Sanderson's future with the firm. His boss, Alan Goldsmith, obliged. Sanderson expressed his primary concern in these words:

"Alan, I'm getting restless. I've been the operations manager for the same product line for six years. On the one hand I'm happy to have my job. Many of my co-workers have gotten the axe in recent years. On the other hand, I'm too young to be in a career rut. Neither you nor my previous boss, Margot Petrie, has even hinted at a possible promotion for me.

"My feelings are that I'm identified with a product line that doesn't mean much to the company. It has prevented me from becoming a serious contender for the next level of management."

"You're only half right, John," responded Alan. "You have worked yourself into a niche that the company finds valuable. Your product line is making a profit, so we don't want to disturb things. The other half is that there simply aren't many opportunities for advancement these days. For you to be promoted, you would have to become a vice president. These days, the executive committee is hardly creating any new vice presidencies. The corporation is meeting its financial targets, but we are still in a period of belt tightening. I don't see any changes in the immediate future."

As Sanderson left the interview, he pondered what to do next. One thought he had was to study some of the sales literature he picked up at the Expo more carefully.

1. What would be the advantages and disadvantages of Sanderson's leaving his corporate job to become a franchise operator?
2. Which career advancement tactics should Sanderson use in an attempt to move from his plateau?
3. How representative is this case of what is happening to middle-level managers in corporate America?

REFERENCES

1. Douglas T. Hall, *Careers in Organizations* (Glenview, IL: Scott, Foresman and Company, 1976): 200–201.
2. Edgar H. Schein, *Career Dynamics: Matching Individual and Organizational Needs* (Reading, MA: Addison-Wesley, 1978): 40–46.
3. Schein, *Career Dynamics*, 48.
4. Several of the items in this list are inferred from Jack Keller and Chris Piotrowski, "Career Development Programs in Fortune 500 Firms," *Psychological Reports* (1987, 61): 920–922.
5. Abby Brown, "Career Development in 1986," *Personnel Administrator*, (March 1986): 109.
6. Lorraine M. Carulli, Cheryl L. Noroian, and Cindy Levine, "Employee-Driven Career Development," *Personnel Administrator* (March 1989): 70.
7. Keller and Piotrowski, "Career Development Programs," 920–922.
8. Zandy B. Leibowitz, Barbara H. Feldman, and Sherry H. Mosely, "Career Development Works Overtime at Corning, Inc.," *Personnel* (April 1990): 38–45.
9. Caela Farren and Associates, *Career Spark for Managers* (Darien, CT: Career Systems, Inc., 1983).
10. Margo Murray with Marna A. Owen, *Beyond the Myths and Magic of Mentoring* (San Francisco: Jossey-Bass, 1991).
11. Rick Rubow and Suzanne Jansen, "A Corporate Survival Guide for the Baby Bust," *Managment Review* (July 1990): 51.
12. William Whitely, Thomas Doughterty, and George F. Dreher, "Relationship of Career Mentoring and Socioeconomic Origin to Managers' and Professionals' Early Career Progress," *Academy of Management Journal* (June 1991): 331–351.

13. James A. Wilson and Nancy S. Elman, "Organizational Benefits of Mentoring," *Academy of Management Executive* (November 1990): 88–89.
14. "Mentor Baiting," *Executive Strategies* (September 10, 1991): 3.
15. Lewis Newman, "Career Management: Start with Goals," *Personnel Journal* (April 1989): 91.
16. Bob Weinstein, "What Employers Look For," *Business Week's Guide to Careers: How to Get a Job Guide* (1985): 10–13; survey taken by Rochester Institute of Technology Placement and Counseling Center, 1991.
17. William T. Leonard, "What the Recruiter Looks For," *Business Week's Guide to Careers* (Fall/Winter 1983): 23.
18. Frank W. Archer, "Charting a Career Course," *Personnel Journal* (April 1984): 62–63.
19. Bruce Nussbaum, "I'm Worried About My Job," *Business Week* (October 7, 1991): 91.
20. Robert W. Goddard, "Lateral Moves Enhance Careers," *HRMagazine* (December 1990): 69.
21. Ingrid Lorch-Bocci, "Achieving Peak Performance: The Hidden Dimension," *Executive Management Forum* (January 1991): 1–3.
22. Michael Rozek, "Can You Spot a Peak Performer?" *Personnel Journal* (June 1991): 77.
23. Examples include Rebecca Ellis and Herbert G. Heneman, III, "Career Determinants of Career Success for Mature Managers," *Journal of Business and Psychology* (Fall 1990): 3–22; Bruce Nussbaum, "A Career Survival Kit," *Business Week* (October 7, 1991): 98–104.
24. Douglas T. Hall and Judith Richter, "Career Gridlock: Baby

Boomers Hit the Wall," *Academy of Management Executive* (August 1990): 7.

25. Charles Garfield, *Peak Performers: The New Heroes of American Business* (New York: William Morrow, 1986).

26. Lena Williams, "Dos and Don'ts of Office Etiquette," *The New York Times* (syndicated story, May 30, 1991).

27. Andrew J. DuBrin, *Bouncing Back: How to Get Back in the Game When Your Career Is on the Line* (New York: McGraw-Hill, 1992).

28. Ellis and Heneman, "Career Determinants of Career Success," 3–22.

29. William H. Hendrix, Nestor K. Ovalle, II, and R. George Toxler, "Behavioral and Physiological Consequences of Stress and Its Antecedent Factors," *Journal of Applied Psychology* (February 1986): 99.

30. Janina C. Latack, "Coping with Job Stress: Measures and Future Directions for Scale Development," *Journal of Applied Psychology* (August 1986): 378; John S. Shepherd, "Manage the Five Cs of Stress," *Personnel Journal* (July 1990): 64–69.

31. Herbert Benson with William Proctor, *Beyond the Relaxation Response* (New York: Berkely Books, 1985): 96–97.

32. Priscilla M. Elsass and David A. Ralston, "The Stress of Career Plateauing," *Academy of Management Best Paper Proceedings 1987* (New Orleans: Academy of Management): 62–67.

33. Judith M. Bardwick, *Danger in the Comfort Zone* (New York: AMACOM, 1991): 9–10.

34. Quoted in David Kirkpatrick, "Is Your Career On Track?" *Fortune* (July 2, 1990): 39.

35. *World Almanac Book of Facts, 1990,* 122 e, ed. Mark S. Hoffman (New York, Pharos Books, 1989): 97.

36. "The Corporate Elite," *Business Week* (November 25, 1991): 185–216.

37. "Can the Feds Bust Through the 'Glass Ceiling'?" *Business Week* (April 29, 1991): 33.

38. Charlene Marmer Solomon, "Careers Under Glass," *Personnel Journal* (April 1990): 100–101; Barbara Ettore, "Breaking the Glass . . . Or Just Window Dressing?" *Management Review* (March 1992): 16–22.

39. Adapted from Solomon, "Careers Under Glass," 104.

40. Stanley D. Nollen, "The Work-Family Dilemma: How HR Managers Can Help," *Personnel* (May 1989): 26.

41. Sheldon Zedeck and Kathleen L. Mossier, "Work in the Family and Employing Organizations," *American Psychologist* (February 1990): 240.

42. Kathy Cramer and John Pearce, "Work and Family Policies Become Productivity Tools," *Management Review* (November 1990): 42.

43. Michelle Neely Martinez, "Making Room for Work/Family Positions," *HRMagazine* (August 1990): 47.

44. Douglas T. Hall and Judith Richter, "Balancing Work Life and Home Life: What Can Organizations Do to Help?" *The Academy of Management Executive* (August 1988): 213.

Chapter 22

Chapter Learning Objectives:

1. Describe the consequences and by-products of organizational culture.

2. Summarize the Japanese-style organization culture.

3. Describe the growth curve model of organization change.

4. Identify several techniques for overcoming resistance to change.

5. Describe how organization development can be used to create organization change.

6. Explain the nature of downsizing and how its negative side effects can be minimized.

7. Explain how total quality management is a strategy for organization change.

8. Describe several techniques of total quality management.

Organizational Culture and Change

Over at the chair plant in Grand Rapids they're still talking about Wayne Meuser, the night-shift manager, and his assistant, Terry VandenAkker. Still shaking their heads and smiling. Just the other night, the production crew got into a jam because their chrome vendor was having trouble getting a clean layer of chrome down on the T-line chair frames. The vendor tried everything, even sent over extras, trying to make the schedule.

Around 3:00 A.M., as they were welding and buffing out the last of the shipment, flecks of chrome started flying off. It became pretty clear that things weren't going to work out right. The night shift was going to come up a few frames short. Wayne will tell you: "Steelcase is really picky about quality. They want to make sure the customer is getting top of the line."

Well, two frames short, they got lucky. Talked a security guard into unlocking Quality Control, as a last resort. They found four masters. Took the best two, left the tags and a note—"Thanks, we needed these for schedule!" Next day, QC wasn't too happy. The plant manager even told them that if they ever pulled a stunt like that again, he'd think about giving them some unpaid vacation. Terry put it this way: "In the end he figured it would be a lot easier to replace the master frames than it would to replace the customer, if the full order wasn't received."

Understand, Steelcase has this motto: "The schedule must be met at all costs!" All those men did was take it literally.

Source: Advertisement for Steelcase, published periodically.

This informal anecdote illustrates two important topics in this chapter: organizational culture and quality. Stories such as the Steelcase anecdote are circulated throughout companies to communicate key organizational values. The Steelcase culture emphasizes product quality (only unflawed chrome) and service quality (prompt delivery). Many other firms emphasize the same values, and when they are not achieved, these firms will try to make the appropriate changes.

This final chapter begins by expanding on the concept of culture, including the Japanese-style organizational culture. It then goes on to describe the nature of change and various strategies and tactics for creating change. The final topic covered represents a strategic goal for an increasing number of private and public firms: total quality management (TQM).

ORGANIZATIONAL CULTURE

As mentioned before, **organizational culture** is a system of shared values and beliefs that influence the behavior of workers. In this chapter, our study of organizational (or corporate) culture focuses on its formation, key dimensions, and consequences.

Determinants and Dimensions of Organizational Culture

Many forces shape a firm's culture. Often its origin lies in the values, administrative practices, and personality of the founder or founders. A prime

Stew Leonard's enthusiastic personality and dedication to pleasing customers have defined the culture of his grocery store.

example is Stew Leonard, the founder of the famous grocery store bearing his name. Leonard was, and still is, almost fanatical about pleasing customers, and this is reflected in the culture of the store. Organizational culture responds to and mirrors the conscious and unconscious choices, behavior patterns, and prejudices of top-level managers. As the founders leave or become less active, other top-level managers help define the culture.[1]

The culture of the society in which a firm operates also helps determine the culture of the firm. Sooner or later, society's norms, beliefs, and values find their way into the firm. For example, the emphasis on sexual and racial equality in U.S. society has become incorporated into the value structure of most employers. Societal values are communicated through such means as the media, people's conversations, and education. Legislation such as the Civil Rights Act of 1991 reinforces such values. Stable values of a culture, such as the Japanese belief in harmony and cooperation, also influence the character and culture of a firm.[2] Thus, large Japanese firms emphasize harmony and teamwork.

The characteristics of a firm and the industry it belongs to also influence organizational culture. A public utility will have a culture different from that of a food manufacturer of comparable size. Heavy competition and low profit margins may force the food manufacturer to operate at a faster pace than the utility, which has no competition.

Businesses are founded on industry-based assumptions about customers, competitors, and society, and these assumptions help form company culture. (For example, a clothing manufacturer might assume that annual changes in style will be needed and that competition will be intense.) Based on these assumptions, the firm develops certain values concerning the right action to take. Consistent with these values, management creates the strategies, structures, and processes necessary for success.[3]

A firm's code of conduct is another key determinant of its culture. (One could also argue that the culture influences a code of conduct.) A labor law specialist has noted that the code of conduct establishes the workplace culture and communicates the employer's true attitudes.[4] For instance, a discipline system with little regard for due process leads to a harsh, threatening work environment. In contrast, a discipline system with checks and balances leads to a warmer, less threatening culture.

The dimensions, or elements, of culture help explain the nature of the subtle forces that influence employee actions. For example, a culture that values risk taking encourages employees to try new ways of doing things. The employees will do so without concern that they will be punished for failed ideas. The following list describes six influential dimensions of culture:[5]

1. *Values.* The foundation of any organizational culture is **values,** or what people consider important. A firm's philosophy is expressed through values, and values guide behavior on a daily basis.

2. *Organizational stories that have underlying meanings.* The story about the two Steelcase night-shift workers who shipped models to a waiting customer tells a lot about how much the firm values good customer service. (It also reveals a permissive code of conduct.)

3. *Myths.* Myths are dramatic narratives or imagined events about the firm's history. They contribute to corporate legends, help unify groups, and can build competitive advantages. At United Parcel Service, for example, stories circulate about drivers overcoming severe obstacles to deliver packages.

4. *Degree of stability.* A fast-paced, dynamic firm has a different culture from that of a slow-paced, stable one. Top-level managers send out signals by their own energetic or lethargic stance regarding how much they welcome innovation. The degree of stability also influences whether or not a culture can take root and how strong that culture can be.

5. *Resource allocation and rewards.* The ways in which money and other resources are allocated have a critical influence on culture. The investment of resources sends a message about what the firm values.

6. *Rites and Rituals.* Part of a firm's culture is made up of its traditions, or rites and rituals. Few companies think they have rites and rituals, yet an astute observer can identify them. Examples include regular staff meetings, retirement banquets (even for fired executives), and receptions for visiting dignitaries. More details about organizational rites are presented in Figure 22-1.

In addition to the dominant culture of a firm, the subculture also influences behavior. A **subculture** is a pocket in which the organizational culture differs from that of other pockets and the dominant culture.[6] In a bank, the consumer loan division may have a culture different from that of the mortgage group, because the consumer group has to work with much shorter time frames in processing loans.

Consequences and Implications of Organizational Culture

Depending on its strength, a firm's culture can have a pervasive impact on its organizational effectiveness. A **strong organizational culture** is one

FIGURE 22-1 Organizational Rites

Type of Rite	Example
Rite of passage	Managing restaurant at Burger King (for member of top-level management)
Rite of degradation	Firing and replacing top-level manager
Rite of enhancement	Mary Kay seminars (for sales representatives for beauty products)
Rite of renewal	Organization development activities
Rite of conflict reduction	Collective bargaining
Rite of integration	Office holiday party

Source: Adapted with permission from Harrison M. Tice and Janice M. Beyer, "Studying Organizational Cultures Through Rules and Ceremonials," *The Academy of Management Review* (October 1984): 657.

ETHICS QUESTION
What are the ethical implications of top-level managers attempting to form a culture that did not make best use of shareholders' money?

that exerts considerable influence on its employees. Members of a firm with a very strong culture will follow its values with little questioning. A weaker culture provides only broad guidelines to members. Steelcase exemplifies a firm with a strong culture. As the chapter opening case illustrates, employees at Steelcase will even risk rule violation to satisfy a dominant corporate value. Five major consequences and implications of organizational culture are outlined in Figure 22-2 and summarized in the following list.

1. *Competitive advantage and financial success.* The right organizational culture contributes to gaining competitive advantage and therefore achieving financial success. A study of 34 firms investigated the relationship between a high-involvement/participative culture and financial perfor-

FIGURE 22-2
Consequences and
Implications of
Organizational Culture

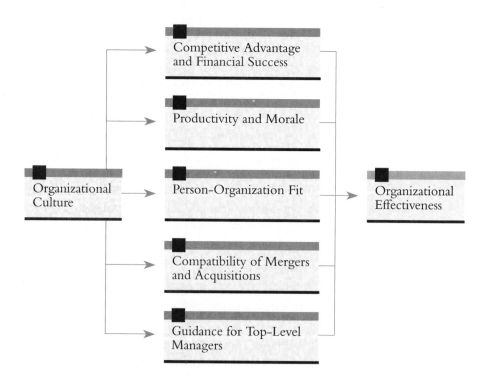

mance. Firms felt by employees to link individual efforts to company goals showed higher returns on investment and sales than firms without such linkages.[7]

2. *Productivity and morale.* A culture that stresses productivity encourages workers to be productive. A culture that values the dignity of human beings fosters high morale and job satisfaction. The opposite types of culture lead to lower productivity and lower morale and satisfaction.

3. *Person-organization fit.* In a recent study, organizations were measured on such dimensions as stability, experimenting, risk taking, and being rule oriented. The preferences of professional employees regarding culture were measured and compared to the culture of their firms. Good person-organization fits resulted in more commitment and higher job satisfaction.[8]

4. *Compatibility of mergers and acquisitions.* A reliable predictor of success in merging two or more firms is the compatibility of their respective cultures. Great American Bank found this to be true based on its experience with 16 acquisitions. The bank's most effective mergers took place with companies that had values, ethical standards, and ways of conducting business that meshed with its own.[9]

5. *Guidance for top-level managers.* Another consequence of culture is that the activities of top-level managers receive more direction than in a firm without a defined culture. Much of a top-level manager's time is spent working with the subtle forces that shape the attitudes and values of employees at all levels. A key leadership role is to establish what type of culture is needed for the firm and then shape the existing culture to match that ideal.[10]

The role of culture in improving organizational effectiveness is illustrated in the Organization in Action.

ORGANIZATION IN ACTION

Several years ago, Du Pont merged a group of well-established businesses into one large division called the Industrial Polymers Division (IPD). Among the problems facing the new division were low morale, the need for new products, and low productivity. Top-level management decided that only a cultural change could overcome these problems. A series of day-long meetings were held to outline the capabilities, functions, and cultural environment of an ideal firm. Among the culture-related principles that emerged from the meeting were the following:

- *Quality.* We embrace Total Quality Management. We will strive for continual improvement in our quality of thought, action, product and service.

- *Leadership.* We will enable people to self-manage their work toward making increasing contributions to the firm.

- *Trust.* We will foster an environment of openness and trust where:

1. Actions reinforce the belief that people can and will do the right thing.

2. Both authority and responsibility are delegated to the lowest practical level.

3. Prudent risk taking and decisive action are encouraged.

- *Communications.* We will treat each other as business partners and fully share useful and valued information throughout the organization so all people understand how their tasks relate to business performance.

Source: Bernard A. Rausch, "Du Pont Transforms a Division's Culture," *Management Review* (March 1989): 38; E. I. du Pont de Nemours & Company, Industrial Polymers Division.

. . . .

Back to the
Opening Case

The success of Steelcase can be partially attributed to a culture that encourages a high level of concern about pleasing the customer. The action of getting a security guard to provide entrance to the quality control department was thus driven by a cultural value.

. . . .

JAPANESE-STYLE MANAGEMENT AND ORGANIZATIONAL CULTURE

The cultural characteristics of large, successful Japanese firms have interested other countries in recent years because of the high productivity and quality achieved by many Japanese firms. Approximately 30 percent of the Japanese workforce is employed by firms that fit the stereotype of the Japanese organizational culture. In the following sections, we describe and evaluate the Japanese style of human resources management and culture.

Key Features of Japanese-Style Human Resources Management

The essence of **Japanese management,** and its corresponding organizational culture, is a focus on human resources development that is rooted in a general cultural belief in concern for people and harmony and cooperation (or *wa*).[11] Many Japanese people view their employers as extensions of their families.

Most of the specific practices described next stem from this general cultural belief. They also include several elements from **Theory Z management,** a human-resources-oriented Japanese style of management adapted to American firms. William G. Ouchi developed the idea of Theory Z management to contrast Japanese practices to Theory A, or typical American management practices. Ouchi believed that Japanese industrial success was the result of the superior Theory Z system, with its emphasis on long-range planning, consensus decision making, and mutual loyalty between employer and employees. According to Ouchi, many large American firms such as Motorola, Westinghouse, IBM, and Hewlett-Packard were practicing Theory Z management when he conducted his studies.[12]

EMPHASIS ON WORK GROUPS. Harmonious work groups are critical to the success of both Japanese and Japanese-style firms. These firms create

Japanese management practices reflect the high value this culture places on harmony and cooperation.

policies that foster strong work groups, including group physical exercise, quality circles, and even the singing of company songs.

THOROUGH TRAINING AND INDOCTRINATION FOR ALL EMPLOYEES. In Japan, everybody joins the firm at the bottom. Consequently, every employee is familiar with the basics of the firm's production technology. Although everybody begins at the "floor level," certain employees are placed on a managerial or professional track. Before an employee is appointed as a manager, he (or occasionally she) is thoroughly trained in management principles.

LONG-TERM EMPLOYMENT. Until recently, male employees in large Japanese firms were offered virtually lifetime employment. However, increased competition with other Asian countries such as South Korea and Taiwan has made long-term employment less frequent. Female employees and other temporary employees are used to supplement the regular workforce. Highly paid senior workers who leave a Japanese firm have limited prospects of finding employment elsewhere.

CONSENSUS DECISION MAKING. In Japanese firms, employees participate in all decisions they will be responsible for implementing. The dominant problem-solving technique is **consensus decision making.** Using this process, everybody involved in a decision places a personal stamp of approval on the outcome.

OPEN COMMUNICATION. Extensive face-to-face communication occurs in Japanese companies. Workspaces are open and crowded with employees at different levels in the hierarchy. A well-publicized feature of this open communication system is **management by wandering around,** a technique whereby managers accomplish much of their work while visiting employees in their work areas.

CONCERN FOR CLEANLINESS. The Japanese concern for cleanliness sets the stage for company-wide quality. Everything is kept in its place, even remote areas of the plant or office are kept clean, and employees dress neatly. Toward the end of the year, a day is designated for *O-Soji*, or the big cleaning. Every person in the firm is expected to clean his or her work area to start the new year with a neat and clean look.

Evaluation of Japanese Organizational Culture

The Japanese style of management and organizational culture has achieved an enviable track record. Japanese firms have met with considerable success in worldwide competition, and Japanese-owned subsidiaries in other countries have also been successful. Examples include Honda of America, Toyota of America, and NEC.

ETHICS QUESTION
Given the many instances of *karoshi* among Japanese managers and professionals, how ethical would it be for a North American executive to push his or her firm toward a Japanese style of management?

Despite these successes, the Japanese model of management is not the perfect solution for everybody. Workers who value autonomy and who are impatient for progress are not content in a Japanese-style firm. Discontent has also surfaced among middle-level managers in Japanese firms who are tired of working 60 to 80 hours per week for low pay. Many Japanese managers and professionals have been reported to be victims of *karoshi*, or death from overwork. In fact, a Health Ministry report called *karoshi* the second leading cause of death among Japanese workers (after cancer).[13]

There are other signs of disharmony in firms with a Japanese organizational culture. Managers who are not native Japanese are rarely promoted to top-level positions in a Japanese firm. Unwanted sexual advances are frequent in the workplace. About 70 percent of women have experienced some type of sexual harassment on the job, as revealed by a survey on job discrimination.[14]

Another concern is that the Japanese organizational culture receives too much credit for the success of Japanese firms. Other success factors include very selective hiring and effective use of technologies such as robotics and just-in-time inventory management. Japanese business success has also been attributed to extensive cooperation among big-business executives, elected officials, and government officials. Collusion is common in Japan, as reported by *Business Week*:[15]

> "Nowhere is this clearer than in construction bidding. Before the formal bids are submitted for a job, the Japanese contractors meet to decide whose turn it is and what the price should be. One way of quietly signaling bids to others is to write them down on the back of business cards that are exchanged during greetings. Everyone except the pre-agreed winner bids higher. Foreign contractors are not invited to these meetings."

In sum, Japanese business successes are due to a combination of factors related to organizational culture and business strategy. One analysis concludes that Japanese successes are largely the result of three factors. The first is a highly developed ability to apply technology. The second is a deep commitment to orientation and training. The third is enlightened use of modern human resources management techniques such as consensus decision making.[16]

GENERAL CONSIDERATIONS ABOUT MANAGING CHANGE

"The only constant is change" is a cliché that is frequently repeated in the workplace. To meet their objectives, managers must handle change effectively on an almost daily basis. Changes in the workplace can be grouped into four major categories. The first category is changes in organizational structure, such as mergers, acquisitions, and downsizings. Structural changes include changes in administrative practices and procedures. The second category is changes in technology and the way work is done that stem from computerization. The third category is changes stemming from worldwide competition. The fourth category is changes in the workforce profile. The new mix includes an increase in older people, minorities, and women. Also, many functionally illiterate people are found in entry-level positions.[17]

Later in this chapter we will describe organization development—a formal approach to creating change—and the challenges of managing a downsizing. Here we examine the change process itself, how people respond to change, and how to develop support for change.

Models of the Change Process

Because the topic of change in organizations is so all-inclusive, it has been studied from many different perspectives. Collectively, the two models described next help explain change from the organizational and individual standpoints.

THE GROWTH CURVE MODEL OF CHANGE IN ORGANIZATIONS. The **growth curve model** traces the inevitability of change through a firm's life cycle, as shown in Figure 22-3. According to this model, businesses pass through three phases in sequence.[18] First is the *formative phase,* characterized by a lack of structure, trial and error, and entrepreneurial risk taking. Mistakes are seen as learning opportunities, and innovation is very important. The firm focuses on its market, with the goal of becoming predictable, stable, and successful.

Second is the *normative phase,* in which stability occurs. An emphasis is placed on maintaining the existing structure and developing predictability.

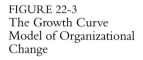

FIGURE 22-3
The Growth Curve
Model of Organizational
Change

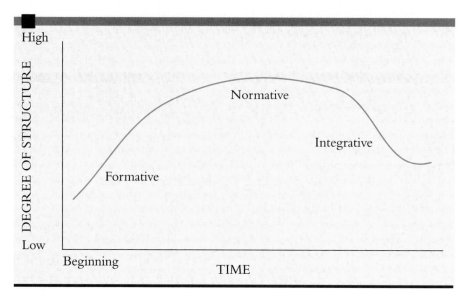

Mistakes are frowned on and perhaps punished, which leads to less risk taking. The firm becomes bureaucratized, and innovation is mostly given lip service or relegated to the research and development unit. The goal is survival, and the focus is less on the market and more on maintaining the status quo. However, changes continue to occur in the environment, which forces this phase to end.

Third is the *integrative phase*, in which the firm redefines itself and finds a new direction. During this phase, top-level managers attempt many changes such as introducing a new vision and policies. At the same time, the most resistance to change occurs as many members of the firm attempt to resist the discomfort of change. The integrative phase is associated with ambiguity and uncertainty. In addition, the firm experiences "organ rejection" of new systems. During this phase, leadership, inspiration, and interpersonal skills become more important than routine management and technical skills.

During the integrative phase, there is a pulling and tugging between forces for and against change. According to the **force-field theory,** an organization simultaneously faces forces for change (the driving forces) and forces for maintaining the status quo (the restraining forces). Forces for change include new technology, competition from other groups, and managerial pressures. Forces for the status quo include group performance norms, fear of change, employee complacency, and well-learned skills. Considerable managerial skill is required for driving forces to outweigh restraining forces. As managers push for change, there is an equal push in the opposite direction from those who want to maintain the status quo.[19]

THE UNFREEZING-CHANGING-REFREEZING MODEL. Psychologist Kurt Lewin presented a three-step analysis of the change process.[20] His unfreezing-changing-refreezing model is widely used by managers to help bring about constructive change. Many other approaches to initiating change stem from this simple model, which is illustrated in Figure 22-4.

FIGURE 22-4
The Change Process

Unfreezing ·········▶ Changing ·········▶ Refreezing

Unfreezing involves reducing or eliminating resistance to change. As long as employees oppose a change, it will not be implemented effectively. To accept change, employees must first deal with and resolve their feelings about letting go of the old. Only after people have dealt effectively with endings are they ready to make transitions.[21]

Changing or moving to a new level usually involves considerable two-way communication, including group discussion. According to Lewin, "Rather than a one-way flow of commands or recommendations, the person implementing the change should make suggestions. The changees should be encouraged to contribute and participate."

Refreezing includes pointing out the successes of the change and looking for ways to reward people involved in implementing the change. For the change process to be complete, refreezing must take place.

Responses to Change

When significant change is introduced to a firm, employees react in various ways. Some view major change so negatively that they experience job stress. This reaction is predictable, because change is a major source of stress. At the other extreme, some employees react positively to change. They welcome the excitement and challenge of a major disruption to the system.

The various employee reactions to change have been placed on a continuum with the following seven anchor points:

1. The most upset employees will *leave*.
2. Another group will show *active resistance* (e.g., a manager refusing to use electronic mail).
3. Some employees will show *opposition*, or foot dragging.
4. Another group will show *acquiescence* and comply with an unwanted change.
5. To the right of center on the continuum, some employees will show *acceptance/modification*. They will go along with the change but will attempt to negotiate details.
6. Another group of employees will show *acceptance*, even if their attitude is neutral.
7. The most positive group includes those who show *active support*. Active supporters attempt to increase a change's chance for success by, for example, encouraging others to accept the change.[22]

Why People Resist Change

Before a company's managers can gain support for change, they must understand why people resist change. People resist change for reasons they think are important, the most common being the fear of a poor outcome. This outcome could be less money, personal inconvenience, more work, and so forth. For example, many employees have resisted direct deposits of their paychecks because they think the bank will not credit their accounts properly. People also resist change for such varied reasons as not wanting to disrupt social relationships and not wanting to break well-established habits.

Even when people do not view a change as potentially damaging, they may sometimes resist it because they fear the unknown. People will sometimes cling to a system they dislike rather than change. According to folk wisdom, "People would rather deal with the devil they know."

Workers may also resist change because they are aware of weaknesses in the proposed changes that may have been overlooked or disregarded by management.[23] For example, one sales manager resisted her company's proposal to shift a key product to dealer distribution. She explained that dealers would give so little attention to the product that sales would plunge. Despite her protests, the firm shifted to dealer distribution. Sales of the product did plunge, and the company returned to direct selling.

GAINING SUPPORT FOR CHANGE. Gaining support for change, and therefore overcoming resistance, is an important managerial responsibility. The following list describes five techniques for gaining this support.

1. *Allow for discussion and negotiation.* Support for a change can be increased by discussing and negotiating the more sensitive aspects of the change. The two-way communication incorporated in the discussion helps reduce some of the concern employees might have. Discussion often leads to negotiation, which further involves employees in the change process.

2. *Allow for participation.* The best-documented way of overcoming resistance to change is to allow people to participate in defining the changes that will affect them. An application of this concept is allowing employees to set their own rules to increase compliance. A powerful participation technique is to encourage people who already favor the change to help in planning and implementation. These active supporters of the change will be even more strongly motivated to enlist the support of others.

3. *Point out the financial benefits.* Because so many employees are concerned about the financial effects of work changes, it is helpful to discuss these effects openly. If employees will earn more money as a result of the change, this fact can be used as a selling point. When Merrill Lynch went through a downsizing, managers were told that more money would be available for bonuses. Many managers quickly became converts to the importance of running an efficient operation.

4. *Use manipulation and cooptation.* **Manipulation** refers to influencing people by distorting information and engaging in other forms of deception. For example, a manager might tell employees, "If you do not accept our new rule of working every Saturday morning, we may have to close this office." (In reality, the firm has no intention of closing the office.) **Cooptation** is finding a way to get an opposing party to join

ETHICS QUESTION
What are the ethical implications of manipulating employees in order to get them to accept change?

your side. A manager might "buy off" the leader of a group opposed to the change by giving him or her a key role in the change.

As Stephen P. Robbins has observed, manipulation and cooptation will backfire once people know they have been duped. The people who know they were tricked will no longer trust the manager and may resist future changes.[24]

5. *Gain political support for change.* In practice, few changes get through firms without the change agent's forming alliances with people who will support his or her proposals. Often this means selling the proposed changes to members of top-level management before proceeding down the hierarchy. It is much more difficult to create change from the bottom up.

ORGANIZATION DEVELOPMENT AS A CHANGE METHOD

When it is necessary to bring about long-term, significant changes in a firm, a formal method of organization development is sometimes used. **Organization development (OD)** is any strategy, method, or technique for making organizations more effective by bringing about constructive, planned change. In its ideal form, organization development attempts to change the culture toward being more democratic and humanistic. At other times, organization development aims to help change the technology or structure of the firm.[25]

An appreciation of the number of OD techniques can be gained from studying Figure 22-5. Various techniques are grouped according to whether they deal primarily with individuals, small groups, or the organization as a whole. Several of these techniques, such as employee assistance programs and outplacement counseling, were described in previous chapters. Here we describe a process model of organization development, followed by examples of OD at the organization and small-group levels.

A Process Model of Organization Development

To be effective, OD methods must be made to fit a particular firm. Nevertheless, a process model has been developed that incorporates the important features of many different OD change efforts.[26] The model builds on earlier strategies for organization development. A key feature is that the OD professional and staff members are both involved in bringing about constructive change. The model, which is summarized here, is outlined in Figure 22-6. As with models of decision making and planning, this model follows the logic of the scientific method.

STEP 1: PRELIMINARY PROBLEM IDENTIFICATION. The manager recognizes that a problem exists that is interfering with work effectiveness. The problem could include the manager's own behavior.

FIGURE 22-5
A Sampling of
Organization
Development
Interventions

Individual Level

Counseling for personal problems
Employee assistance programs (EAPs)
Career development programs
Organizational behavior modification
Job enrichment
Relaxation techniques and biofeedback training (for stress)
Wellness programs
Transactional analysis training
Assertiveness training

Small-Group Level

Team development
Sensitivity training (encounter groups)
Modified work schedules
Brainstorming
Intergroup conflict resolution
Labor-management committees (LMCs)
Quality circles
Self-managing teams (work teams)

Organizational Level

Total Quality Management
Grid organization development
Employee involvement programs (or worker participation programs)
Employee stock ownership plans (ESOPs)
Gainsharing (a form of profit sharing)
Survey feedback (attitude surveys)
Scanlon Plan (profit sharing based on labor savings)
Theory Z management program (Japanese-style management)

Note: Debate exists over whether or not so many techniques and methods can rightfully be claimed as the province of OD practitioners, particularly because industrial and organizational psychologists, management scientists, and human resources specialists developed so many of these interventions.

STEP 2: MANAGERIAL COMMITMENT TO CHANGE. The manager must commit to taking the necessary steps to implement the change program. The manager is warned that the change program could involve negative feedback about his or her behavior.

STEP 3: DATA COLLECTION AND ANALYSIS. Before organization development can proceed, the climate must be assessed through interviews, observations, and a written survey. Information is obtained about such topics as the manager's alertness and open-mindedness, cooperation with other departments, problem-solving ability, and trust. This information is used to develop objectives for constructive changes.

STEP 4: DATA FEEDBACK. Data collected in Step 3 are shared with the manager and staff members. In this way staff members can compare their perceptions to those of others and the manager shows "ownership" of the problems.

FIGURE 22-6
A Process Model of
Organization
Development

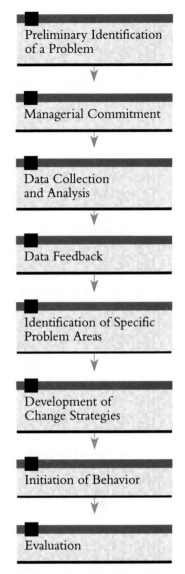

Preliminary Identification
of a Problem

Managerial Commitment

Data Collection
and Analysis

Data Feedback

Identification of Specific
Problem Areas

Development of
Change Strategies

Initiation of Behavior

Evaluation

Source: Joseph A. Young and Barbara Smith, "Organizational Change and the HR Professional," *Personnel* (October 1988): 48.

STEP 5: IDENTIFICATION OF SPECIFIC PROBLEM AREAS. The OD specialist helps staff members give the manager feedback regarding strengths and weaknesses. Although the manager may not agree with the feedback, he or she must accept the perceptions. Problem areas among the staff members can also be identified in this step.

STEP 6: DEVELOPMENT OF CHANGE STRATEGIES. The emphasis is on identifying root problems and developing action steps. A spirit of teamwork often develops as problems are identified that can be attributed to both the manager and staff members.

STEP 7: INITIATION OF BEHAVIOR. An action step is selected and implemented that seems to be the best solution to the problem. The behavioral change strategy considers who, what, when, and where. For example, the manager (who) will make sure that the planning and priority setting are accomplished (what) during staff meetings (when) in the conference room (where).

STEP 8: EVALUATION. An attempt is made to evaluate whether the behavioral changes made in Step 7 (by both the manager and staff members) have improved behavior and work results. Evaluation data may be collected through more interviews and observations, including speaking to the manager's supervisor.

Team Building

The most widely used form of organization development is **team building,** a systematic method of improving the interpersonal and task aspects of work groups. (Observe that team building was incorporated into the process model of OD just presented.) Team building has surged in popularity recently because of the growth of self-managing work teams (as described in Chapter 7). Most work teams engage in some team building. The primary objective of team building is to increase the effectiveness of people who work together as a team. It is achieved by improving problem-solving skills and interpersonal relationships within the group.[27]

Process Consultation

Closely related to team building is another standard OD technique called **process consultation**. Using this technique, the OD specialist examines the pattern of a work unit's communications. A team leader typically asks for process consultation because team meetings have not been highly productive. The process consultant (OD specialist) directly observes staff meetings. At opportune times, the consultant will raise questions or make observations about what has been happening.

The role of the process consultant is to challenge the status quo by asking questions such as the following:

- "Why doesn't anybody ever respond to Larry's questions?"
- "How come nobody challenges Jennifer's remarks when she is way off base?"
- "Why does everybody shake his or her head in agreement when the president speaks? Are you all yes-persons around here?"

Two OD experts have explained the contribution of process consultation in this way: "It points out the true quality of the emperor's new clothes even when everyone is pretending they are quite elegant." Also, the process consultant can be helpful in changing a closed communication style.[28]

Large-Scale Organization Change

At its best, organization development is a method of change aimed at breathing new life into a firm. **Large-scale organization change** is the method used to accomplish a major change in the firm's strategy and culture. The process is sometimes called *bending the frame* to indicate that the firm is changed in a significant way.[29] To accomplish such a far-reaching change, a large proportion of the workforce must be involved. If the program described in the process model of OD is used throughout the firm, large-scale change in the organization will be feasible.

Shifting from an authoritarian organizational culture to a Japanese-style culture would be one example of large-scale change in an organization. As with most other forms of organization development, an external or internal consultant is usually required to bring about large-scale change. Nevertheless, line managers sometimes bring about substantial changes themselves. The Manager in Action illustrates how managers can bring about large-scale organization change as well as how organizational culture and downsizing influence organizational effectiveness.

MANAGER IN ACTION

By the late 1980s, an unwieldy bureaucracy had slowed down innovation and flexibility at Hewlett-Packard. A network of committees designed to improve communications had in fact increased costs and slowed down product development. The HP Way (the Hewlett-Packard culture) placed too much emphasis on rapport among top-level managers and did not penalize those who missed opportunities.

John A. Young, HP's CEO, learned that the company's workstation project was slipping a year behind schedule. Young decided to change the burdensome bureaucracy to speed up delivery of Snakes (the project code name). As Young saw it, the delay was caused by endless meetings about technical decisions. He removed the project's 200 engineers from the management structure so they could work on the Snakes workstation line free of committee review.

The Snakes crisis convinced Young to revamp the entire corporate structure. HP's own laser printer operation was an example of how a strategic business unit could stay nimble and competitive. The secret of the laser unit's success was that it did not have to deal with the usual swarm of committees. Consequently, Young virtually eliminated HP's committee structure and flattened the organization. For example, a single corporate sales force existed in the past with a large, centralized management structure. Now each of the two newly formed computer units has its own sales and marketing teams. An HP executive notes, "We are doing more business and getting product out quicker with fewer people."

Source: "Hewlett-Packard Rethinks Itself," *Business Week* (April 1, 1991): 76–77.

Evaluation of Organization Development

Many organization development programs show good results in terms of such objective criteria as turnover, profits, and quality. However, many others show neutral or negative results (conditions actually worsen).[30] The results of OD are often difficult to measure. For example, if a team improves its communications it may take years before this improvement can be translated into such concrete measures as increased productivity or quality.

One problem with organization development is that its specialists are sometimes too zealous. They may impose their values and techniques on a firm that is not ready for a large-scale change. Pacific Bell experienced this problem. The OD training, with its enforced value system, was viewed as a Japanese-style "corporate religion." Pacific Bell dropped the program after two years of turmoil.[31]

LEARNING CHECK

Describe the general approaches to managing change, including overcoming resistance to change. Also, describe how organization development is used to bring about change.

DOWNSIZING AND ORGANIZATION CHANGE

The most often used deliberate organization change in recent years has been **downsizing,** which refers to reducing the size of a firm by laying off or retiring workers to decrease costs. Cost reductions are often necessary because the survival of the firm may be at stake. From a positive viewpoint, the same process is called **rightsizing,** which implies that the firm's workforce is reduced to its optimum size.

Downsizing occurs for many reasons. Improved computer systems may mean that fewer people are needed to process information. Recessions and the high cost of labor also lead to downsizing. Firms downsized in recent years include Frito-Lay, Manufacturers Hanover Trust Company, Du Pont, Arco, Wang Laboratories, Unisys, IBM, Burlington Northern, Wal-Mart, and Salt River Project (a utility). Downsizing thus includes manufacturing and service companies, and it is practiced world wide. Many managers and other employees who have been laid off in the downsizing of large firms have joined medium- and small-size firms.

In the following sections, we look at some of the advantages and disadvantages of downsizing. We also describe ways to minimize the negative impact of downsizing, or rightsizing.

Potential Advantages of Downsizing

A downsizing strategy sometimes pays handsome dividends. Above all, the reduced payroll cost may increase profits for a private company and enable a public firm to stay within budget. With a flatter structure (often a consequence of downsizing), decision making is hastened because fewer managers provide input to the same decision. Also, with fewer managers in between, top-level managers can communicate directly with their sources of information. Downsizing can increase operating efficiency by reducing duplication and overlap. For companies facing bankruptcy, downsizing may be the only route to short-term survival. Outside managers brought in to turn around a failing firm routinely begin the change process with a severe downsizing.

The fears associated with downsizing and job loss may result in a better understanding of financial realities. All members of the firm must pull their own weight. As downsizing begins, employees soon realize that slacking off today may result in losing their jobs tomorrow.

Problems Associated with Downsizing

Downsizing often backfires in attempts to achieve increased organizational effectiveness. Downsizing costs may be substantial, morale and productivity may suffer, and it may be difficult to motivate people.[32] Motivation suffers because many employees develop negative perceptions of their employer. Confusion and insecurity are rampant, leading to high levels of job stress. Employees spend considerable time conducting job searches rather than concentrating on their work.

During downsizings, confidence in top-level management plummets. Risk taking declines because employees are afraid of being fired for making a mistake. Politicking increases because employees at all levels see the importance of being in favor with influential people.

During a downsizing, many capable employees leave voluntarily, sensing that they might be laid off next. Often too many people accept early retirement, including some top performers. This places the firm in the embarrassing position of having to recruit to fill certain positions during a downsizing. The firm sometimes faces lawsuits alleging discrimination on the basis of age, race, or gender. A long aftermath of employee distrust may follow the downsizing.[33] Layoffs also hurt the national economy.

In some cases, downsizing can create severe short-term financial problems for a firm. In one quarter during 1991, it cost Digital Equipment Corporation $1.1 billion to cover the cost of cutting 10,000 positions. Among the expenses involved in downsizing are severance pay, legal fees, early-retirement bonuses, and paying workers for unused vacation.

Minimizing the Problems Associated with Downsizing

ETHICS QUESTION
What social responsibility does top-level management have to minimize downsizing?

Much has been written about dealing with the downside of downsizing, and many companies have taken action. Survivor workshops have been offered to help employees who grieve over the dismissal of co-workers or have other unresolved feelings. Sometimes these workshops include group discussions in which employees offer each other emotional support.

An important strategy for getting survivors refocused on their jobs is for management to share information with employees. Human resources consultants recommend that all employees be informed of the rationale for what is happening. Following this approach, a Bank of America manager stated, "We had senior managers showing how our changes trended with the downturn in the economy. We showed with key internal business indicators where our business was in trouble and the fact that we just could not continue operating with the same number of people."[34]

Listening to employees is another strategy for dealing with the adverse effects of a downsizing. After the Bank of America downsizing, "brown-bag" lunches were held between top-level managers and employees throughout the firm. Managers gave employees the opportunity to discuss their feelings about the layoff and concerns about their place in the firm.

Another important strategy for overcoming the problems associated with downsizing is to emphasize a merit-oriented reward system. After a downsizing, political behavior usually intensifies as employees scramble to get into favor with key managers. It is therefore to the firm's advantage to specify which types of accomplishments will lead to rewards—including surviving another cutback.

Finally, managers should apply the principles for gaining support for change that were described earlier in the chapter. One such step is to allow for discussion about the changes in the firm. Middle-level managers, for example, may wonder how they are going to handle a much wider span of control resulting from the downsizing. Top-level managers should also discuss the potential financial benefits of the downsizing, such as having more money available for bonuses.

TOTAL QUALITY MANAGEMENT AND ORGANIZATION CHANGE

A major cultural change in businesses today is a commitment to quality. For example, in one survey, 78 percent of top-level managers listed quality as a priority.[35] The basic principles of managing for quality were described in Chapter 17. In fact, most of the topics covered in this text relate to quality either directly or indirectly. Our focus in this section is on total quality management as a pervasive aspect of organizational culture. **Total quality management (TQM)** is a management system for improving performance throughout a firm by maximizing customer satisfaction. TQM also means striving for excellence and using teamwork to meet or exceed customer requirements.

In discussing TQM, we first describe quality circles—a widely used technique for improving quality—and then present examples of principles and attitudes that contribute to a culture of total quality management.

Quality Circles

A **quality circle** is a small group of employees from the same unit who meet regularly to identify, analyze, and solve work problems. Frequently, these employees are volunteers. Sometimes the group also implements its solutions. Quality circles originated in the United States and were later

Commitment to quality has become a pervasive force in organizational cultures today.

popularized by Japanese industry. While they are still used most frequently in manufacturing plants, they are also used in service firms such as banks and insurance companies. Quality circles assume that the person who performs the job is the natural expert to consult about improving the task at hand. The following sections describe the operation of quality circles and factors associated with their success.

THE QUALITY CIRCLE PROCESS: GROUP PROBLEM SOLVING IN ACTION. Quality circles are designed to gather employee suggestions about work-related topics. They are well-structured group problem-solving sessions that usually follow the steps outlined in Figure 22-7.[36]

Step 1: Problem Identification. The circle members develop a list of problems tied directly to their jobs. (Quality circles are not established to solve company-wide problems.)

Step 2: Problem Selection. The quality circle members select from the total group of problems those they choose to tackle. As one expert has suggested, "It is advisable to address simple problems initially so the circle develops confidence in the techniques that its members have been trained to use, in themselves operating as a group, and in management's endorsement of the program."

Step 3: Problem Analysis. Circle members apply analytical techniques to identify the cause of the problem, to gather information, and to sort out possible remedies. (Among these techniques are cause-and-effect diagrams

FIGURE 22-7
The Quality Circle
Operating Process

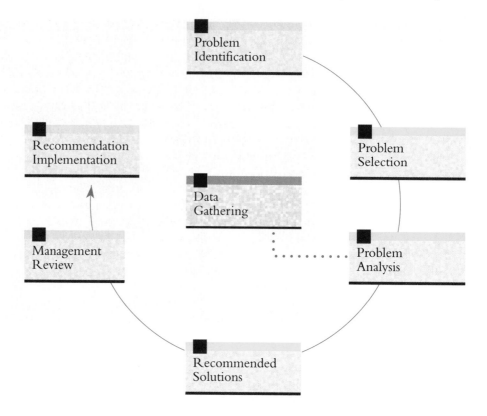

and histograms charting the frequency of specific problems.) The quality circle may need to use company data bearing on the problem. It may also be necessary to call on experts from different departments to avoid duplication of effort.

Step 4: Recommended Solutions. In most instances the quality circle will recommend a few alternative solutions. Quality circles have developed a good reputation for arriving at cost-effective solutions.

Step 5: Management Review. The output is a formal presentation to the quality circle's unit manager regarding the statement of the problem, the analysis, and recommendations. Management retains the prerogative of implementing or not implementing the recommendations.

Step 6: Implementation of the Recommendation. After a recommendation has been approved by management, its implementation usually proceeds smoothly. Employees outside the quality circle usually accept its value. They also appreciate the fact that the opinions of operating employees are incorporated into the suggestions.

KEY ELEMENTS OF A SUCCESSFUL PROGRAM. Whether a quality circle succeeds or fails depends heavily on certain contingency factors.[37] Management must clearly state the goals of the program, such as improving product quality or increasing productivity. When the organizational culture is characterized by trust between management and employees, the circle is much more likely to succeed than when there is an air of distrust. One reason is that the employees are less likely to believe that management is using the quality circle merely to squeeze extra productivity from them.

Employees accepted into the quality circle should be competent and should receive adequate training. Circle members should also receive some external rewards, including recognition and money, for outstanding suggestions. However, payments for suggestions are controversial because they may create resentment among employees who are not members of the quality circle.

An overall factor influencing the success or failure of quality circles is the issue of whether or not the method represents a true commitment to positive change. If a firm uses quality circles as a means of sham participation, paying no real attention to suggestions from members, it is unlikely to gain positive results.

Principles of Total Quality Management

Information about total quality management is accumulating rapidly, and it encompasses many topics. We approach TQM here by describing 11 of its representative principles, values, and attitudes. These ideas contribute to an organizational culture that emphasizes a concern for producing high-quality goods and services.

1. *Quality is a top priority.* A starting point in achieving TQM is for top-level managers to give top priority to quality. They must allocate resources to preventing as well as repairing quality problems. Quality should be included in organizational strategy, and every organizational unit must be responsible for quality. In short, quality is everybody's job.

2. *Quality leadership must begin with top-level managers.* As with every change effort, a shift to TQM is more likely to work if top-level managers lead the way. As W. Edwards Deming has stated, "The aim of leadership should be to improve the performance of people and machines, to improve quality, to increase output, and simultaneously bring pride of work."[38]

3. *The firm must be sensitive to customer requirements.* The essence of quality is to satisfy customer needs. To achieve this, many firms strive for zero defects in goods and services. A similar goal is to strive for zero *defections* among customers. More than two-thirds of customers defect because they find service people indifferent or unhelpful.[39] Customer defections are expensive. For example, one estimate is that a regular Domino's Pizza customer is worth more than $5,000 over a 10-year period.[40]

4. *The customer is the next process.* In TQM, a customer is not only a company outsider who pays for a product. The customer is anybody who uses the company's work output. By treating everybody as a customer, quality is enhanced throughout the firm.

5. *Quality stems from a continuous quest for improvement.* Annual improvements in quality, even if small, add up to large improvements. This approach fits well the spirit of **kaizen,** the Japanese philosophy of continuing, gradual improvements in one's personal and work life. Employees following *kaizen* will be constantly on the lookout for small improvements.

6. *It is important to attend to every detail.* The spirit of TQM is best captured by every employee's paying careful attention to every detail. (Quality expert Deming carries this spirit into his home life. He dates the eggs in his refrigerator with a felt-tip pen to make sure the older ones get eaten first.)[41]

7. *Team effort is required.* Experts agree that teamwork is basic to quality improvement. Companies that strive for total quality management almost always form quality-improvement teams. For example, the core of quality improvement at Federal Express Corp. is the Quality Action Teams. All employees are permitted to initiate and participate in these problem-solving teams. Each team is headed by a corporate officer or lower-ranking administrator. The teams search for problems in the Federal Express delivery system and then seek improvement.[42]

8. *Training in quality is essential.* To achieve TQM, employees at all levels must receive extensive training in principles of quality. The training includes problem solving in general, statistical techniques, and interpersonal skills. Quality expert Joseph M. Juran observes, "To me the major reason behind the Japanese success story is that they undertook a massive program of training managers at all levels in how to attain and improve quality. Through this training they have become the best trained managers on earth with respect to the quality disciplines."[43] The Manager in Action illustrates what a quality team can accomplish.

MANAGER IN ACTION

Carolyn McZinc is vice president of quality for Xerox's United States marketing group. She explains how a quality team dealt with a difficult customer problem:

"The customer was Burlington Northern and they had asked to receive fewer invoices. I think we were sending them something like 8,000 invoices. Each of their Xerox machines—and they had tons of Xerox machines—had individual invoices. Their accounts payable people would spend days trying to reconcile these invoices from us. We were able to reduce the number from 8,000 to 13."

Source: "In Search of Quality," *Personnel* (December 1990): 24.

9. *The firm should engage in competitive benchmarking.* Knowing how well the competition is performing is important for a company to gauge its own performance. **Competitive benchmarking** is comparing one's own quality performance to that achieved by competitive firms. As pioneered by Xerox Corporation, the idea is to quantify best performances, including average time to respond to a complaint, number of

suppliers, defect rate, and product durability. The narrow approach in benchmarking is to make comparisons to other firms in the same industry. The broad approach is to make comparisons to the best in any industry.[44] Although competitive benchmarking is basically a quantitative technique, it contributes to the cultural value of wanting to best the competition.

10. *It is necessary to believe in the 1-10-100 rule.* According to this rule, the longer a problem remains unidentified or unaddressed, the more expensive it is to repair. A problem or mistake that is identified or fixed immediately might cost $1 to correct. If the problem is caught later, it could cost as much as $10 to correct. However, if it reaches the customer, it could cost up to $100 or even put the firm out of business.[45]

11. *It is essential to emphasize the human side of quality.* Although statistical and decision-making techniques make an important contribution to quality improvement, the real thrust of TQM is for all employees to have positive attitudes toward quality. They must pay attention to detail and take pride in their work. Frederick W. Smith, the CEO of Federal Express (a Malcolm Baldridge National Quality Award winner), offers this advice:[46] "By taking a 'human side of quality' approach to empowering employees in the pursuit of service excellence and customer satisfaction, Federal Express offers a reminder that the foremost quality detail to be addressed by any service organization is not the produce or the process. It's the people. Absolutely. Positively."

Total quality management does not always lead to immediate improvements in organizational effectiveness and cash flow. An executive from the Boston Consulting Group reports that the majority of quality improvement efforts fizzle out soon after bringing about initial improvements. At Florida Power & Light, for example, the quality group swelled to 75 employees without creating a suitable return on investment.[47] As with any other program, attention to such basics as effective planning, top-level management commitment, and motivation is necessary for success.

Back to the Opening Case   By establishing a culture in which an emergency customer need can sometimes override company policy, Steelcase is practicing total quality management.

SUMMARY

Among the forces shaping a firm's culture are the values of top-level managers, the societal culture, the nature of the business and the industry, and the firm's code of conduct. The dimensions, or elements, of culture help explain the nature of the subtle forces that influence employee actions. Influential dimensions include values, organizational stories, and resource allocation and rewards.

The consequences of organizational culture include competitive advantage, productivity and morale, person-organization fit, compatibility of mergers and acquisitions, and guidance for top-level managers.

The essence of Japanese-style management and its corresponding organizational culture is a focus on human resources development. Specific Japanese management practices include emphasis on work groups and thorough training and indoctrination for all employees. Also important are long-term employment, consensus decision making, and a concern for cleanliness. Japanese business successes are best attributed to a combination of factors related to organizational culture and business strategy.

Frequent change characterizes the modern firm. The growth curve model of organizational change traces the inevitability of change through a firm's life cycle. During the integrative phase, change is rapid. During this and the next phase, there is a pulling and tugging between forces for and against change as described by force-field theory.

Another important explanation of change is the unfreezing-changing-refreezing model. It shows that attitudes must be changed before change can take place, and that the change process requires considerable two-way communication. People respond to change in various ways, including leaving the firm, active resistance, opposition, acceptance, and active support.

The most common reason for resisting change is the perception of an adverse outcome. Support can be gained for change by such means as allowing for discussion, negotiation, and participation, and explaining the financial benefits.

Organization development is any strategy, method, or technique for making firms more effective by bringing about constructive, planned change. The process model of organization development has seven steps, including managerial commitment to change, data collection and analysis, and development of change strategies.

The most widely used form of organization development is team building, a systematic method of improving the interpersonal and task aspects of work groups. A related technique is process consultation, in which the change agent examines the pattern of a work unit's communications. Large-scale organizational change attempts to revitalize the firm. A substantial proportion of the workforce must be involved to accomplish such a far-reaching change.

Downsizing is a frequently used type of organizational change. Downsizing can reduce costs and increase productivity. At times, however, downsizing creates more problems than it solves, such as a decrease in productivity and morale and the voluntary loss of many capable people. The costs of downsizing, including severance pay and defending against lawsuits, can be considerable. Survivor workshops are sometimes used to help remaining employees deal with the feelings associated with downsizing.

A major cultural change today is a shift to total quality management (TQM), a system emphasizing maximum customer satisfaction. Quality circles are a frequently used technique for enhancing quality. They have a carefully defined format and emphasize the analysis of data. Successful quality circle programs receive commitment from top-level management, reward circle members, and train participants.

Among the key principles, values, and attitudes of total quality management are the following:

- Quality is a top priority.
- Firms must be sensitive to customer requirements.
- Quality stems from a continuous quest for improvement.
- Team effort is required.
- Training in quality is essential.
- Firms should engage in competitive benchmarking.
- It is essential to emphasize the human side of quality.

KEY TERMS

organizational culture	management by wandering around	team building	quality circle
values	growth curve model	process consultation	kaizen
subculture	force-field theory	large-scale organization change	competitive benchmarking
strong organizational culture	manipulation	downsizing	
Japanese management	cooptation	rightsizing	
Theory Z management	organization development (OD)	total quality management (TQM)	
consensus decision making			

QUESTIONS FOR DISCUSSION AND REVIEW

1. How would you describe the organizational culture of the school in which you are taking this course?
2. Why do so many CEOs believe that their primary responsibility is managing organizational culture? What happened to making a profit?
3. What type of American firm is likely to have an organizational culture quite similar to that of a Japanese organization?
4. How can a concern for cleanliness actually lead to quality improvements?
5. What can managers do to help ease the pain for those who find change to be uncomfortable?
6. Would team building make much sense for the top-level management of a firm? Explain your reasoning.
7. Why might a company want to go through large-scale organizational change?
8. Downsizing is supposed to contribute to organizational productivity, yet some economists argue that downsizing perpetuates a recession. How do you explain this contradiction?
9. How do you interpret the statement that "every topic in this text is related directly or indirectly to quality"?
10. Mont Blanc fountain pens sell for around $175, and Bic ballpoint pens sell for around 39 cents. Yet both are considered to be high-quality writing instruments. Can this be explained by any of the principles of total quality management?

PROBLEMS FOR ACTION

A. At Harley-Davidson Motor Company, many of the engineers wear Harley-Davidson T-shirts, old jeans, and unpolished leather boots to work. The same attire is widespread among production employees. Suppose, as a new executive at Harley-Davidson, you decide that such attire is inappropriate. You believe that more conventional clothing should be worn by employees. What would be required to change the clothing habits of Harley-Davidson engineers and production employees?

B. Assume that you are the newly appointed manager of a large hotel. The hotel is experiencing a business decline, most likely attributable to poor-quality service. You decide that the hotel must shift to total quality management. Design a TQM program for your hotel.

CONCLUDING CASE

Quality Circles at Midwest Dental

Don Wallace, president of Midwest Dental Company, called one of his supervisors, Tom Raymonds, into his office. Raymonds was the only college-educated supervisor at Midwest, and Wallace had placed him in the position over the objections of Gerry DeSantos, the manufacturing vice president.

Wallace said to Raymonds, "Tom, I want you out on the shop floor, because we need a new direction out there. The other supervisors are not involving their people enough in making decisions. What do you think?"

Raymonds responded, "I agree. We've got 175 people out in the shop, but we're only using the brainpower of supervisors. We act as though operative employees should check their brains at the door before they punch in and pick them up again when they punch out. If we could tap their knowledge and experience, we'd really have something."

"That confirms my worst fears," replied Wallace. "It also gets to the real purpose of this meeting. I want you to be in charge of implementing a quality circle program at Midwest. By using QCs we can encourage our employees to take ownership of some of our biggest manufacturing problems. You can report to me directly on this project. I'll take care of telling Gerry and Mary Kay. [Mary Kay Benney is Raymond's immediate superior.] Furthermore, I've arranged for you to attend QC leader training at headquarters. When you're done, we should be ready to roll."

After completing the training, Raymonds made a presentation to Midwest's management committee to introduce the QC program. Although the presentation went well, Raymonds was surprised that Wallace allowed each department head to decide whether or not to use QCs. Only two departments, manufacturing and marketing, chose to implement quality circles.

Upon hearing about the circles, Benney shouted, "I guess I'll have to try these things, because Wallace wants them. I know they'll never work! There's no way those clods on the floor can tell us anything we don't already know. Besides, why are they sending a kid with six months' experience to tell me how to run my show?"

To help publicize the program, Raymonds conducted meetings with all the departments, distributed a payroll envelope stuffer about QCs, and displayed some colorful posters throughout the plant. Nevertheless, only two people from assembly showed up for the first meeting, and nobody showed up from the machine shop. Concerned about the low participation rate, Raymonds sought counsel from Benney. She said, "We've got IAM (the labor union) here. They are on public record as being opposed to QCs because they're supposedly a tool of management to bust unions. You'll have to change the name if you want to try them here. You made a mistake by not kicking the QC idea around with the IAM shop committee first."

In the ensuing months, progress came slowly. Raymonds changed the name of the program to Task Analysis Groups (TAG). He met with the union committee and finally got two pilot groups trained and operational. They met regularly and began building momentum on solving productivity and quality problems. The efforts of the TAG teams were being posted proudly on their team bulletin boards. One group even made a presentation to management about their solution to a quality problem.

Raymonds continued with the program in the following months. Even though it was sometimes difficult to get help from the functional areas that were not using quality circles, progress was encouraging. Positive feedback about the TAGs was gathered in management meetings.

Six months later, Wallace was transferred to head a troubled division of the corporation. Wanting a change in manufacturing management, he promoted Raymonds to be vice president of manufacturing at his new division. During a visit to Midwest a few months later, Raymonds noticed that all the TAG bulletin board notices had been taken down. When he asked Benney what happened, she said with a smirk, "Why don't you ask DeSantos about it?"

1. What principles of total quality management are illustrated in this case?
2. What principles of total quality management are lacking in this case?
3. How might Raymonds and Wallace have lowered the resistance to the QCs shown by DeSantos, Benney, and the labor union?

Source: Researched by Tom Price, vice president of manufacturing at Midwest Dental.

REFERENCES

1. Leonard R. Sayles and Robert V. L. Wright, "The Use of Culture in Strategic Management," *Issues & Observations* (November 1985): 2.

2. J. Steven Ott, *The Organizational Culture in Perspective* (Chicago: The Dorsey Press, 1989): 76.

3. George R. Gordon, "Industry Determinants of Organizational Culture," *Academy of Management Review* (April 1991): 396–415.

4. James R. Redeker, "Code of Conduct as Corporate Culture," *HRMagazine* (July 1990): 83.

5. Terrence Deal and Allan Kennedy, *Corporate Cultures: The Rites and Rituals of Corporate Life* (Reading, MA: Addison-Wesley,

1982): 13–14; W. Jack Duncan, "Organizational Culture: 'Getting a Fix' on an Elusive Concept," *Academy of Management Executive* (August 1989): 229–236; Sayles and Wright, "The Use of Culture in Strategic Management," 1–9.

6. Ott, *The Organizational Subculture*, 45.

7. Daniel R. Denison, *Corporate Culture and Organizational Effectiveness* (New York: John Wiley & Sons, 1990).

8. Charles A. O'Reilly, III, Jennifer Chatman, and David F. Caldwell, "People and Organizational Culture: A Profile Comparison Approach to Assessing Person-Organization Fit," *Academy of Management Journal* (September 1991): 487–516.

9. James F. Kelly, Jr., "Talk Eased Merger Stress for Great American Employees," *Personnel Journal* (October 1989): 77.

10. Duncan, "Organizational Culture," 229.

11. Richard M. Hodgetts and Fred Luthans, "Japanese HR Management Practices: Separating Fact from Fiction," *Personnel* (April 1989): 42–45; Ramesh Gehani, "The Invisible Side of Japanese Management," *Kenshu* (Summer 1988): 1–7; William G. Ouchi, *Theory Z: How American Business Can Meet the Japanese Challenge* (Reading, MA: Addison-Wesley, 1981).

12. Ouchi, *Theory Z: How American Business Can Meet the Japanese Challenge*.

13. Gail Rosenblum, "Thousands in Japan Dying Suddenly of Overwork, Stress," Gannett News Service (August 11, 1990).

14. Elaine Kurtenbach, "Sexual Harassment New Phrase, Old Story in Japan," The Associated Press (October 15, 1991).

15. "Hidden Japan," *Business Week* (August 26, 1991): 35.

16. Hodgetts and Luthans, "Japanese HR Management," 45.

17. Marcia Kleinman, "Ease the Stress of Change," *Personnel Journal*, (September 1989): 107.

18. Harry Woodward and Steve Bucholtz, *Aftershock: Helping People Through Corporate Change* (New York: John Wiley & Sons, 1987).

19. Kurt Lewin, *Field Theory in Social Science: Selected Theoretical Papers* (New York: Harper & Brothers, 1951); Edgar F. Huse and Thomas G. Cummings, *Organization Development and Change*, 3e (St. Paul, MN: West Publishing Co.,1985): 3.

20. Kurt Lewin, *Field Theory and Social Science* (New York: Harper & Row, 1964): chapters 9 and 10.

21. Woodward and Bucholz, *Aftershock*.

22. Jon L. Pierce and Randall B. Dunham, *Managing* (Glenview, IL: Scott, Foresman/Little, Brown, 1990): 428.

23. Stoner and Freeman, *Management*, 369.

24. Stephen P. Robbins, *Management*, 3e (Englewood Cliffs, NJ: Prentice-Hall, 1991): 536.

25. Robert T. Golembiewski, *Organization Development: Ideas and Issues* (New Brunswick, NJ: Transaction Books, Rutgers University, 1989).

26. Joseph A. Young and Barbara Smith, "Organizational Change and the HR Professional," *Personnel* (October 1988): 46. A forerunner to this model is Wendell L. French, "Organization Development: Objectives, Assumptions, and Strategy," *California Management Review* (No. 2, 1969): 26.

27. W. Brendan Reddy and Kaleel Jamison, eds., *Team Building: Blueprints for Productivity and Satisfaction* (San Diego, CA: University Associates, 1988).

28. Leonard D. Goodstein and W. Warner Burke, "Creating Successful Organization Change," *Organizational Dynamics* (Spring 1991): 14.

29. Goodstein and Burke, "Creating Successful Organization Change," 4; Ralph H. Kilman, Teresa Joyce Corvin, and associates, *Corporate Transformations: Revitalizing Organizations for a Competitive World* (San Francisco: Jossey-Bass, 1988).

30. For a review of these results, see Goodstein and Burke, "Creating Successful Organization Change," 15.

31. Barbara Block, "Creating a Culture All Employees Can Accept," *Management Review* (July 1989): 45.

32. Robert M. Tomasko, *Downsizing: Reshaping the Corporation for the Future* (New York: AMACOM Books, 1990).

33. Paul G. Abler and Robert B. Marshall, "Staying Afloat During Restructuring Storms," *HRMagazine* (October 1990): 68.

34. Harold P. Weinstein and Michael S. Liebman, "Corporate Scale Down: What Comes Next?" *HRMagazine* (August 1991): 36.

35. Howard Schlossberg, "U.S. Firms: Quality Is Way to Satisfy," *Marketing News* (February 4, 1991).

36. Robert J. Shaw, "Tapping the Riches of Creativity Among Working People," *Management Focus* (September-October 1981): 27–29.

37. Ricky W. Griffin, "Consequences of Quality Circles in an Industrial Setting: A Longitudinal Assessment," *Academy of Management Journal* (June 1988): 338–358.

38. As quoted in (but paraphrased and sexist language removed): G. Rex Bryce, "Quality Management Theories and Their Application," *Quality* (January 1991): 16.

39. Leonard A. Schlesinger and James L. Heskett, "The Service-Driven Service Company," *Harvard Business Review* (September-October 1991): 74.

40. Frederick E. Reichheld and W. Earl Sasser, Jr., "Zero Defections: Quality Comes to Services," *Harvard Business Review* (September-October 1990): 110.

41. John A. Byrne, "The Prophet of Quality," *Business Week* (January 28, 1991): 14.

42. *Blueprints for Service Quality: The Federal Express Approach*, AMA Management Briefing (New York: American Management Association, 1991): 71.

43. Quoted in Bryce, "Quality Management," 17.

44. Richard J. Schonberger, *Building a Chain of Customers: Linking Business Functions to Create the World Class Company* (New York: The Free Press, 1990): 24.

45. *Blueprints for Service Quality*, 77.

46. *Blueprints for Service Quality*, 80.

47. "Where Did They Go Wrong? Why Some Quality Programs Never Get Off the Ground," (*Business Week/Quality 1991*): 34, 38.

Cases
Using
Decision
Assistant
Software

INTRODUC-
TION

The *Decision Assistant* software provides five tools to assist you in analyzing data and performing financial calculations. The program was designed with pull-down menus and detailed instruction screens to help you become an effective user within minutes. A variety of other features, such as a calculator, simple file storage and retrieval, and easy data entry, aid in the overall operation of the software. The following sections cover in detail the steps to use the software and provide specific information regarding its capabilities.

START-UP PROCEDURES

For IBM PC and Tandy 1000

1. Insert a DOS system diskette (IBM PC—DOS 2.0 or higher; Tandy 1000— DOS 2.11) into Drive A and close the disk drive door.
2. Turn on the microcomputer and all peripheral devices. If the microcomputer is already on, hold down the CTRL (Control), ALT (Alternate), and DEL (Delete) keys at the same time. The prompt to enter the current date will appear on the screen.
3. Key the date and press ENTER. "Enter new time: _" will appear on the screen.
4. Key the time and press ENTER, and the prompt "A>" will be displayed.
5. Remove the DOS diskette and insert the MANAGEMENT & ORGANIZATION *Decision Assistant* into Drive A. Close the disk drive door.
6. Key the word "control" and press the ENTER key. The program will be loaded, and the opening screen for the *Decision Assistant* will appear. Press the SPACE BAR as directed to proceed to the main menu, which is shown in Figure A.

(Note: On certain monochrome monitors, it may be necessary to change the display status. If you have difficulty reading the information on the display screen, strike the letter *M* at the first opening screen to specify a monochrome monitor.)

FIGURE A
Decision Assistant Main
Menu and Tools Menu

TOOLS FILE HELP OUTPUT		
Bivariate Linear Regression		<F1>
Time Series Forecasting		<F2>
Decision Tree	<F3>	
Strategic Business Analysis		<F4>
Motivation Expectancy Theory	<F5>	

Main Menu (Selecting an Option)

The main menu, as shown in Figure A, consists of four categories: TOOLS, FILE, HELP, and OUTPUT. Each of these categories contains options that can be displayed or selected by highlighting the category title on the menu bar using the right- and left-arrow keys. Figure A shows the menu of tools that is displayed when the TOOLS category is highlighted. The up- and down-arrow keys are then used to highlight the particular option, and the ENTER key is pressed to activate your choice. Once an option is chosen, the menu bar is no longer active. The ESC (Escape) key is used to exit from the data entry mode and return to the menu bar in order to select another option.

The ESC key has another function: It is used to escape or exit from an operation and return to the data entry mode. The ESC key can be used to exit from instruction screens, the calculator, output, and graphs. The ESC key would also be used if you accidentally pressed ESC during data entry. Pressing it again would clear the menu bar and return you to the data entry mode.

As you become familiar with the program, the process of selecting choices becomes easier with the use of the command keys. The corresponding command key is located next to each option in the menu. An option can be selected easily by holding down the ALT (Alternate) key and striking the appropriate letter (such combinations are denoted in the text with a hyphen, such as "ALT- P" for the Print command). A tool can be selected by pressing the corresponding function key.

In the process of using the program, you may find that certain menus and their corresponding options will not appear when the category title is highlighted. This occurs because some options are dependent on others. For instance, the option to print data cannot be selected until a tool has been chosen and the appropriate data have been keyed. In the case of the command keys, the program will beep if an option is not available. Neither the FILE nor the OUTPUT menu is active until a tool has been selected.

Tools Menu

A tool must be selected before any operation other than the options found in HELP can be performed. After the program has been started, the TOOLS menu is displayed and the arrow keys or the appropriate function key can be used to select a tool. A new tool can be selected at any time by using the function keys or selecting one through the menu. *Note: Remember to save your current data (as described below) if you have not completed the problem you are working on or if the data will be needed at a later date. Selecting a new tool quits the current tool and erases all data.*

The five tools available on the MANAGEMENT & ORGANIZATION *Decision Assistant* are briefly described on the following page. More detailed descriptions and specific instructions are included in the software.

1. Bivariate Linear Regression
2. Time Series Forecasting
3. Decision Tree
4. Strategic Business Analysis
5. Motivation Expectancy Theory

User Option Menus

The following sections describe the user options on the FILE, HELP, and OUTPUT menus.

FILE MENU

New (ALT-N):	Erases the data for the current tool and permits new data to be entered for the current tool.
Retrieve (ALT-R):	Once a tool has been selected, data saved in a file may be retrieved from the disk. A window will appear in the center of the screen with a directory of files. Use the up- and down-arrow keys to view the file names, and press ENTER to retrieve the data. A message will appear if no files have been saved previously.
Save (ALT-S):	This option is used to save the current data if you must end a session before finishing your analysis. When it is selected, a window will appear in the center of the screen with a prompt for you to choose one of the existing file names. A new file name can be entered by using the arrow keys to scroll to the end of the directory. Key in the new file name and press ENTER. A maximum of five files can be saved per tool. To save data in a previously created file, press ENTER when the file name is displayed.
Erase (ALT-E):	Old files can be erased by selecting this option after a tool has been chosen. A window displaying the file directory will appear on the screen. Use the arrow keys to scroll through the directory until the file name to be erased is shown and press ENTER.
Quit Tool	Select this option after you have finished working with a particular tool. Another tool can be chosen at this time. *Note: Be sure to save important data before quitting a tool. All data not saved will be erased.*

HELP MENU

Instructions (ALT-I):	Context-sensitive instructions are available with the use of this option. Prior to selecting a tool, the Instructions option offers general help with respect to the proper operation of the program. The Instructions option provides detailed help with a specific application once a tool has been selected.

Calculator (ALT-C):	A calculator is available to perform mathematical operations while working with a tool. The instructions to operate the calculator appear at the same time.
Exit (ALT-X):	Use this option to exit to the disk operating system. *Note: All data not saved will be lost.*

OUTPUT MENU

Print (ALT-P):	All data keyed and the output are printed. Be sure to turn on the printer before selecting this option.
Display (ALT-D):	The output is displayed on the screen. All data must be keyed before selecting this option.
Graph (ALT-G):	Many of the tools offer the ability to view a graphic representation of the output. A color monitor is required to display some (but not all) graphs on the IBM PC. A message will be displayed if you do not have the proper hardware configuration.

Data Entry

Once a tool has been chosen, you will be required to input various parameters and data. The data entry process described below is used for every tool. The left and right brackets shown in Figure B signify that data are to be entered into the field. Use the ENTER key to proceed to the next field. The up- and down-arrow keys may be used to move from field to field during data entry in order to correct or change any data item.

You will find that the ability to edit data makes it easy to simulate "what if" types of situations. Simply enter the data and choose the Display (ALT-D) option to view the results based on the given data set. Press the ESC key to exit from the output screen, and use the arrow keys to move to a specific field, change the data, and select the Display option again.

Typical Session

When you are ready to use the *Decision Assistant,* follow these steps. After you have used the software once or twice, you should be able to use it without referring to these instructions.

FIGURE B
Data Entry Mode

Number of observations:	[5]
Observation 1:	[125]
Observation 2:	[99]
Observation 3:	[_]
Observation 4:	[ ]
Observation 5:	[ ]

Step 1   Start up the *Decision Assistant* according to the start-up instructions and proceed to the main menu.

Step 2   Because the TOOLS menu is already selected, use the down-arrow key to highlight the first tool and press ENTER.

Step 3   The title of the selected tool will appear just below the menu bar in the center of the screen.

Step 4   Before entering any data, press the ESC key to go to the menu bar. Use the right-arrow key to display the HELP menu, and highlight the Instructions (ALT-I) option by using the down-arrow key. Press ENTER to activate the option, carefully read the information, and press ESC when you have finished.

Remember, you can reach any option by simply using its command key combination. Keying "ALT-I" will activate the Instructions option without going through the menu bar. Note the key combination next to each option when following these steps.

Step 5   Depending on the tool, key the required information into each field and press ENTER. The output screen will be displayed after the information has been keyed into the last field and ENTER has been pressed.

Step 6   Review the output and press ESC to return to the data entry screen when you have finished. Press ESC a second time to go to the menu bar. Use the right-arrow key to display the OUTPUT menu; then with the down-arrow key highlight the Graph (ALT-G) option and press ENTER. A graph will now appear if the tool you are using employs a graph and you have the proper hardware configuration. Press ESC to return to the data entry mode after reviewing the graph.

Step 7   Change some of the data; then press ESC to activate the menu bar. Use the right-arrow key to display the OUTPUT menu and choose the Display (ALT-D) option to view the results of changing the data.

Step 8   Choose the Print (ALT-P) option in the same manner as described in the previous steps (or simply use the command key) to print the output.

Remember, a calculator (ALT-C) is always available if you need to perform mathematical operations.

Step 9   When you have finished, save (ALT-S) your data if it will be necessary to use the information at a later date. Select the option to quit (ALT-Q) the tool.

Step 10   Either select a new tool or exit (ALT-X) at this time.

DECISION ASSISTANT CASES

Several chapters in MANAGEMENT & ORGANIZATION cover concepts that can be reinforced or expanded by use of the tools provided by the *Decision Assistant*. The tools do the computations, allowing the user to see the effects of different variables on parameters of the question at hand. Your instructor may assign one or more of the cases that appear on the following pages when you cover the appropriate textbook chapter.

CASE 1: TRUCK TRACERS

The citizen band (CB) radio craze in the 1970s put US Antenna Systems into business. Originally, the company manufactured only a limited line of AM/FM and CB antennas. The subsequent decline in CB popularity forced the company to diversify so that it now offers a wide variety of antenna systems for special purpose and military applications. US Antenna Systems operates five manufacturing plants in the United States and two in Mexico. The U.S. plants apply either large-batch or continuous process technologies. Both of the Mexico plants are labor intensive and use the small-batch production technology with low overhead and low production capacity.

High-Tech Trucking

High technology has hit the trucking industry. Two companies, Geostar and Omninet, have developed systems that permit trucking companies to know the exact location of each truck in their fleet. Both systems are based on LORAN technology, which employs geosynchronous satellites to determine the position of portable transmitters. Ships at sea have used LORAN for years for navigation. Now this same technology is available to nationwide trucking companies. The new system can trace instantly the exact location (within 30 feet) of any truck on the North American continent. Further, it can predict arrival times and display the trucks' travel routes on a microcomputer screen.

But is it worth the cost? The cost per vehicle is $165 per month, plus about $30 for each trace. Equipping an entire fleet of several hundred trucks and tracing each one periodically can amount to a substantial cost for owner-operators. But substantial savings and other advantages are also possible. Drivers no longer need to call in their locations (which is estimated to cost about $24 in driving time). Schedules can be made more efficient, routes can be monitored, customers can be given more accurate arrival times, and drivers can report breakdowns via the system. Both Geostar and Omninet predict widespread acceptance of these new systems. Others believe it will be far less successful because truckers may feel that "Big Brother is watching" too closely.

The Opportunity

Geostar recently contacted US Antenna Systems to discuss production of the truck antenna needed to complete its new tracking system. Although prototypes had been made to test the new system, Geostar wanted to ensure sufficient supply for the expected demand. Based on Geostar's sales projections, the product justified a "state-of-the-art" continuous process production plant. Such a plant would provide the lowest per-unit cost once established but also required the greatest initial investment. If sales fell short, the company could lose money on the deal.

The company estimated the costs of producing the product using continuous process, large-batch, and small-batch methods. The computations were based on three levels of demand for the product: strong, moderate, and weak. Netting the computed costs against the expected revenues for each level of demand, the company was able to estimate annual profits for each type of production method. Those estimated profits are given in the chart shown in Figure C-1.

Project

Decide which production method to use. Consider the attributes of the tracking system and estimate a probability for each of the three states of nature (the sum of your three probabilities should equal 1.00). Then use the Decision Tree model (model #3) to determine which production method offers the highest expected profit level to US Antenna Systems.

FIGURE C-1
Estimated Profits

Production Method	States of Nature		
	Strong	Moderate	Weak
Continuous	$162,354	$38,587	−$79,238
Large–Batch	102,722	83,455	−31,994
Small–Batch	−18,977	49,845	91,331

Source: Based on information reported in William J. Cook, "Truck 54, Where Are You?" *U.S. News & World Report* (March 21, 1988): 64.

CASE 2: POTATO ICE CREAM

Bill Johnson had been in the dairy and farming business all his life. He inherited the Idaho farm from his father and purchased additional land, which was used to raise potatoes. Bill worked both operations with the help of his brother, Eric Johnson. Both brothers had homes on the land, both were married, and both had children. One of Eric's sons, Jerry, was already in college majoring in agribusiness.

The Dairy Operation

The dairy business had almost always been good. Bill Johnson had maintained the long-term relationships his father had established with three major milk producers. Demand for milk was never a problem. The key to the dairy business was controlling costs, and Bill was good at that. Success in the dairy business had allowed Bill and Eric Johnson to accumulate several hundred thousand dollars of investment capital. They had decided, however, not to expand the operation, hoping to find a more promising opportunity.

The Potato Operation

Marketing potatoes was another matter. Although they could occasionally secure contracts to supply specific customers, most of the time the entire production was sold at current market prices through the cooperative. Controlling costs was also important on this side of the business, and that had become more difficult recently with fertilizer and insecticide prices increasing. Demand for potatoes had been weak for the past four years, and this year was expected to be about the same. Both brothers would be happy to just break even on this part of the operation.

The Potato Ice Cream Idea

It was Jerry Johnson's idea. In his college studies, he had learned about the chemical composition of the potato. As part of a class project that called for the development of an "original" food product, Jerry proposed the idea of substituting processed potatoes for the whipping cream in ice cream. After a few obvious failures, he succeeded in producing a product that tasted very much like homemade ice cream. In fact, there was nothing about the look or taste of the potato ice cream that would make one think that it contained potatoes.

The class project also called for a cost analysis and an assessment of the nutritional value of the "original" food product. The potato ice cream was found to be 26 percent lower in cost and 42 percent lower in fat when compared to most other commercially prepared ice cream. Jerry served it at a family picnic the next time he went home, and no one could identify potatoes as an ingredient.

Market Analysis

Bill Johnson was convinced the product had potential. He met with one of the large milk producers who had a diversified line of dairy products and obtained a tentative agreement from the producer to market the product on a trial basis.

Bill funded a modest market study in the agricultural exhibit at the county fair. Based on the positive response in that study, a larger, more sophisticated study was funded by the Idaho Potato Growers Association. They found a somewhat mixed response to the product. It seemed that some of the people surveyed preferred a premium ice cream and did not consider price or nutritional value important. There was, however, a large percentage who considered the taste acceptable and liked the lower price and higher nutritional value.

Cost Analysis

Bill, Eric, and Jerry Johnson considered three methods of producing potato ice cream. It could be made on the farm in small batches (small-batch method), it could be produced by a local dairy in their production plant (large-batch method), or it could be produced by one of the large national operations (continuous process method). They considered the cost of each of these approaches with estimated sales volume at three levels: 5,000 gallons/month, 15,000 gallons/month, and 25,000 gallons/month. The probabilities that they assigned to each of these demand levels and the expected monthly profit for the three methods of production are presented in Figure C-2.

Project

Using the data presented in Figure C-2, determine the expected value (profit) for each method of production. Which method should be used to produce potato ice cream? Would your decision be different if the probabilities for the demand levels were different?

FIGURE C-2
Demand Level
Probabilities and
Expected Monthly
Profits for Three
Methods of Ice Cream
Production

Production Method	States of Nature		
	$p = .4$ 25,000 gal/mo	$p = .32$ 15,000 gal/mo	$p = .28$ 5,000 gal/mo
Continuous	9,769	3,474	−2,220
Large-Batch	6,658	6,123	521
Small-Batch	3,324	2,768	2,562

CASE 3: ZENTA'S HOUSE OF STEINS

Gunther Hovocost and Roy Eckjardt pooled their money and made plans to enter the Mexican import business. Having grown up in south Texas, they had seen the low-cost, unique products that had found their way into the state. They were convinced there must be a wide variety of products made in Mexico that had a ready market in the United States. The new company they had just formed was to act as a conduit between manufacturers in Mexico and wholesalers, retailers, or individual consumers in the United States. The task now was to go to Mexico and find a few initial products with high potential.

But Hovocost and Eckjardt had a lot to learn about manufacturers in Mexico. Few of the companies were very large; most were labor intensive. In many cases, the entire production was dependent on one or two key individuals. It quickly became obvious that few of the Mexican manufacturers could increase production significantly if a new market was found for their products. Furthermore, Hovocost and Eckjardt did not feel comfortable trusting their personal success to these types of firms.

The Beer Stein Business

But Germany and German beer steins were another matter. The idea hit Hovocost when he picked up one at a gift shop. The steins were works of art. Some displayed tributes to war heroes; others reproduced paintings. Many had figures carved into the sides and were tastefully handpainted. Hovocost and Eckjardt ordered a limited variety of just 200 steins, displayed them at a German festival in Cincinnati, Ohio, and sold out in two days. They were in the German import business.

Eleven years later, Zenta's House is the largest importer of German beer steins in the United States. There is only one major competitor on the West Coast. Zenta's sustainable competitive advantage is its extensive mailing list of customers. Some of them are retail businesses; many are individual collectors. Successful management of this mailing list has helped Zenta's grow because it permits distribution of an annual catalog and periodic new product release notices.

Business Units at Zenta's House of Steins

The business has expanded to offer six major lines of products, including German toys, German clothes, and inexpensive clay "decal" steins. These different lines are managed as separate business units showing separate promotional and operational costs and, therefore, separate profit contributions.

Of particular interest are the Limited Edition steins, which Hovocost and Eckjardt have a hand in designing. For these steins, they conceive of an original design, make an art presentation, and work directly with a manufacturer to have the product produced. The stein then receives the "Zenta's

House" name and is sold to collectors in limited quantities (usually 1,000 to 5,000 units).

Etched crystal steins represent the newest product line. Some are hand-blown glass; most are intricately etched with figures. Crystal steins have a more feminine appearance compared to the heavier porcelain steins and, hopefully, they will have more appeal to women. The potential for this line is great because currently the female market is virtually untapped; the vast majority of customers are male.

A Strategic Business Analysis

The most critical decisions Hovocost and Eckjardt have to make regard buying. Once a year they visit manufacturers in Germany and decide on the product mix and quantities for each of the product lines. They are now planning for a visit next month and have decided to evaluate the success of each of the business units. Specifically, they need to decide how to manage each of these lines. They need to know which segments of the business deserve expansion and which, if any, should be phased out. Figure C-3 presents the growth rates of the six business units over the past year and estimates of sales by the competing importer.

Project

Evaluate the product lines as separate business units. What strategies should Zenta's House apply to each one?

FIGURE C-3
Zenta's Product Line
Growth Rates and
Competitors' Sales

Production Line Description	Sales	Growth Rate	Competitor's Sales
1. Limited Edition Steins	$ 47,688	28%	$ 32,657
2. Porcelain Figure Steins	$ 67,565	24%	$ 43,822
3. Etched Crystal Steins	$ 12,435	26%	$ 18,783
4. Clay Decal Steins	$ 77,533	5%	$ 47,772
5. German Clothing	$ 12,764	2%	$ 25,434
6. German Toys	$ 18,511	6%	$ 27,834

CASE 4: TRI-MOLD INDUSTRIES

Tri-Mold Industries is in the toy manufacturing business. Tri-Mold was very successful in the 1980s with a line of molded plastic swimming pools, molded plastic riding toys, and a wide variety of other plastic products such as skateboards. Tri-Mold still produces these products, but when the name Tri-Mold is mentioned, most people think of only one product, Macho Dolls (and all their accessories).

The toy business is large, and managing the individual product lines of a large manufacturer requires both strategic management and operational management skills. Although the products of the company are marketed together, each product constitutes a relatively independent business within the firm. Each has its own production line, and profit contribution for each product line is computed regularly.

The rapidly changing market in the toy business makes the job of managing the corporation more difficult than in many other industries. The strategic mix of product lines must change frequently. The Boston Consulting Group (BCG) matrix is a convenient tool for tracking this mix and provides some recommended strategies, given the growth rate and market share of the business units. The corporate objective, using BCG terminology, is to ensure that there are always some "Cash Cows," always some "Stars," always some new ideas under development ("Question Marks"), and never any "Dogs." A common strategy is to use the cash flow from Cash Cows to develop new products that comply with the corporate mission. (A corporate mission statement identifies and limits the business of the firm. It provides general guidance regarding the types of products or services the company should offer.)

The data given in Figure C-4 are representative of Tri-Mold's portfolio in 1991. One year later Tri-Mold dropped Trim Computer, a low-cost microcomputer, from the portfolio and showed losses of over $140 million.

Project

According to the data given in Figure C-4, which products were Stars, Cash Cows, Question Marks, and Dogs? What went wrong with Tri-Mold's strategy of using cash flow from Cash Cows to develop the Question Marks? In your opinion, did the Trim Computer belong in Tri-Mold's mix of product lines?

FIGURE C-4
Data for Tri-Mold, 1991

Production Line Description	Sales ($mil)	Growth Rate	Competitor's Sales ($mil)
1. Swimming Pools	34.7	2%	27.4
2. Molded Riding Toys	46.8	7%	38.3
3. Misc. Molded Products	23.6	5%	19.8
4. Macho Dolls	168.4	–4%	107.5
5. Doll Accessories	56.2	22%	43.7
6. Trim Computer	7.3	24%	214.6

CASE 5: TEXAS SMOKERS, INC.

Don Blackwell entered the outdoor grill business almost by accident. He learned welding and light metal fabrication at CenTex Community College and had accepted a job with Broadlight, Inc., immediately after graduation. Broadlight manufactures a line of halogen and mercury vapor lights that are typically installed in parking lots, football stadiums, and as part of security systems. Blackwell was part of the installation crew that occasionally fabricated custom hardware. The crew also traveled to the site to install the lighting systems.

Blackwell made his first barbecue pit for himself. He simply cut a 45-gallon oil drum in half, hinged it, and welded together a set of legs. He built others of similar design on request for friends, but each time he would add a little innovation, something to make the grill unique. Some had creative smoke stacks, others sported flip-up tables. The most unique one had a smaller drum attached to the larger one. The smaller drum acted as a "fire box" that fed heat and smoke to the larger one, resulting in an excellent smoker. In the spring, Blackwell usually had more requests for barbecue pits than he could handle. In fact, the business had grown to the point that he began to think about quitting Broadlight and manufacturing the grills full time.

That was six years ago. Blackwell formed Texas Smokers, Inc., and for the past five years has been manufacturing a unique line of barbecue grills of top quality. Because of rust problems with the earlier grills, he gave up on the oil drums and now uses 1/4-inch rolled steel. The finished products are beautiful, with professionally welded seams and heavy wood handles. The top quality and unique designs of the seven basic models have kept demand increasing each year despite the premium price ($225 to $875, depending on the model).

Blackwell manufactures the grills at a site just off the interstate highway. He displays the grills there, and about 65 percent of sales are made at that site. Other sales are made through two wholesalers who have been increasing their orders each year. Peak sales are in the late fall and early spring, so most manufacturing takes place during the winter months. He does, however, have some Christmas business. Blackwell's biggest problem is estimating sales for the spring season. Quarterly sales in units for the past five years are shown in Figure C-5.

Project

Use the exponential smoothing technique of time-series analysis to estimate quarterly sales for Texas Smokers, Inc. Plot your estimates on the chart shown in Figure C-5. What is your best estimate of unit sales for next quarter (January of next year)?

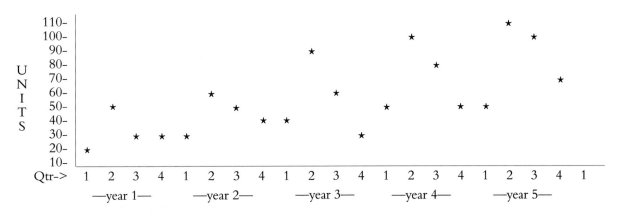

FIGURE C-5 Sales of Texas Smokers over Five Years

CASE 6: FAYETTEVILLE CABLE SYSTEMS

Fayetteville Cable Systems has been providing television cable service to Fayetteville, Arkansas, since 1977. The business has evolved from a modest operation with two satellite down-link antennas and only 1,250 subscribers to a major business with almost 50,000 subscribers. Much of this growth can be attributed to growth of the Fayetteville area. A major state university is located there, and two major poultry producers have thrived in the area. Fayetteville is growing steadily.

The current cable service is somewhat limited. Basic cable includes the major networks, three superstations, an all-sports channel, and one all-news channel. Subscribers may select from five additional channels, for which there is an extra charge.

The limited service has been the source of some customer complaints. Furthermore, the current system requires the use of a cable converter box to provide the optional channels. Modern cable systems do not require this converter box for cable-ready televisions. (Service to individual subscribers is controlled at the cable station rather than by the converter box.) The limited capacity of the converter box is the primary reason for the limited service, but to eliminate it requires a major overhaul of the entire system.

Managers at Fayetteville Cable Systems are aware of the need to renovate the system. They have been working with consultants and engineers and have had a new system designed. Plans have already been drawn for installation of two additional down-link antennas, new receivers and amplifiers, and new control equipment. A major part of the renovation is replacing almost 70 percent of the transmission cable to subscribers. The plans show that the entire process will take about one year. Costs for the renovation have been estimated.

Managers are now seeking financing for the renovation. Although long-term financing for the capital equipment can be arranged at reasonable rates, the company hopes to finance most installation expenses (labor, particularly) through operations next year. It is critical, therefore, to estimate cash flow from subscribers for the next year accurately. The average number of subscribers for the past 15 years is shown in Figure C-6.

Project

Use the moving average technique of time-series analysis to estimate the number of subscribers for Fayetteville Cable Systems. Plot your estimates on the chart shown in Figure C-6. What is your best estimate of the average number of subscribers next year?

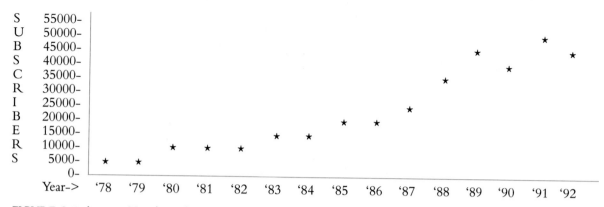

FIGURE C-6 Average Number of Cable Subscribers for Fayetteville Cable Systems, 1978–1992

CASE 7: CIRCUIT SHACK

Circuit Shack operates a chain of 1,260 electronics and stereo retail stores in the United States and Canada. The stores carry a broad assortment of products including electronic components, brand-name stereo systems, microcomputers, and cellular telephones. Most Circuit Shack stores are located in major malls, although the company has opened six large, free-standing locations to test their feasibility. The company manufactures a small percentage of the products it sells.

Corporate Strengths

A major strength of the company is its prime store locations. A highly professional real estate management group at corporate headquarters is looking constantly for new locations and has been successful at signing favorable leases for the company.

Another strength of the company is its corporate training and development office, which is directed by Matthew Inman, vice president of human resources. Representatives from this office regularly interview candidates for the company's management training program on college campuses. Traditionally, the company has interviewed only business majors for this position. Most management trainees come from this recruiting effort, although some also come from employees hired by store managers.

Management Training

The management training program is, according to most top-level executives at Circuit Shack, a successful program. It involves one year of "programmed" training at the store level and finishes with a one-week management training seminar at corporate headquarters. Most of the program involves management concepts such as hiring new employees and managing inventory, although some of the program covers basic electronics technology. Trainees are graded on their performance in the program and receive a "Readiness Score," which is used to help determine compensation.

Business Versus Technical Education

At a recent corporate management meeting, Phil Daniels, who supervises store managers in the southwest district, said, "Don't give me any more business majors, give me somebody who knows the technology." He went on to explain that he believed that sales personnel who were technically trained generally had higher commissioned sales than sales employees who were business majors.

Although Daniels had no facts to support his statement, Inman took the comment seriously and planned to investigate the matter further. He randomly sampled the personnel records and gathered the data shown in Figure C-7, which he presents to you for analysis. Specifically, he wants to know the association between (1) technical education and sales, (2) business education and sales, (3) technical education and the "Readiness Score," and (4) business education and the "Readiness Score." He would also like specific recommendations regarding the type of personnel he should be hiring and the nature of the management training program.

Project

Compute the correlation coefficients for the four associations described above. What recommendations do you have for Matthew Inman regarding (1) Circuit Shack's trainee recruiting efforts and (2) the management training program at Circuit Shack?

FIGURE C-7
Circuit Shack Personnel
Data

Trainee's Name	Hours Technical	Hours Business	Avg Monthly Sales ($)	Readiness Score
David Stair	0	60	2,620	92
Glen Gage	0	60	1,823	87
Susan Storey	0	60	1,732	97
Reggie Alexander	60	0	4,734	56
Frank Thorton	60	0	2,230	78
Ken Jenkins	58	12	2,676	83
Susan Pearson	8	52	3,435	91
Richard Webb	60	0	4,120	78
Scott Meyer	12	58	2,657	83
David Spears	0	60	1,243	86
Vicky Britten	18	36	4,804	74
Chip Albright	0	60	2,765	78
Jeff Tieken	32	18	3,124	88
Bill Soyars	36	21	4,128	67
Russell Dalton	60	0	3,878	79

CASE 8: TEMPO MUSIC

Employee turnover has always been a problem for Tempo Music Stores. Salespeople (usually high school or college students) stay on the job only a few weeks or months and then leave, frequently without giving notice. Even so, employee turnover is not considered much worse than in most similar operations. What has been concerning management over the past year is turnover of store managers. When a store manager quits, operations are disrupted severely. Company auditors must move in, inventory the store, and officially clear the manager before he or she can be discharged. The training department supplies a new manager, and the local district manager closely supervises the new manager the first week or two on the job. Last year 5 of the 18 managers working for Tempo Music quit the firm—a turnover rate of 27.8 percent. This level of turnover in management is very costly.

Top-level managers suspect that the source of the problem is related to one of the following: pay (base pay plus commissions), the amount of previous work experience, the number of weeks of supervised training, or the number of hours per week that the store is open (some stores are open Sundays, some are open nights). Fortunately, last year's performance review of store managers included the question, "How satisfied are you with your current job?"

Data that top-level managers have compiled on all store managers (including those who terminated) are presented in Figure C-8.

Project

Based on an analysis of the information given, which factor has the highest association with management turnover at Tempo Music? What action(s) would be necessary to reduce this turnover?

Manager's Name	Pay per Month★	Experience (months)	Training (weeks)	Hours Open	Satisfied? (0–10)★★
Peggy Abbott	1704	18	2	50	9
John Allen	1530	22	1	50	10
Danny Clancy	1413	16	2	58	5
Lee Ann Dye	1450	9	5	58	7
Kevin Hees	1567	12	5	58	4
Glen Heidrich	1760	15	4	50	8
Romero Lopez	1821	14	3	58	7
Rebecca Lott	1876	21	2	44	8
Mike Nash	1676	18	4	58	6
John Nunn	1435	10	3	48	10
Helen O'Keefe	1546	14	2	58	6
Bill Price	1522	16	3	42	10
Steve Sands	1765	23	3	50	8
Kelly Sawyer	1723	8	2	58	3
Katey Simms	1390	19	1	58	4
Kyle Skinner	1767	11	2	50	7
Ed Suarez	1932	27	3	48	9
Noland Winn	1298	6	2	52	10

★ Pay is average per month for the year.
★★ 0 = very dissatisfied, 10 = very satisfied

FIGURE C-8   Data on Tempo Music Store Managers

CASE 9: MERRITT'S SHOE STORE

Merritt's Shoe Store is a national chain of over 234 retail stores specializing in women's fashion shoes, handbags, and accessories. Most store managers are young college graduates and are supervised by 1 of 12 district managers. The organization chart shown in Figure C-9 depicts the organization of the retail division.

Sales and the overall financial performance of the firm have been good for the past several years, and, as a result, Merritt's has been adding five to seven stores per year. This continued expansion has resulted in a shortage of district managers within the company. Today, district managers supervise up to 20 stores. Not only does this cause inadequate supervision, it also requires the district manager to travel extensively and cover a large geographic area. Three district managers have resigned in the past two years. Many of the other district managers have been in the shoe business most of their lives, and several are approaching retirement.

The job of district manager pays at least 40 percent more than that of store manager and includes a company car; but, for some reason, few store managers apply for promotion, and some even refuse it when offered. The problem has become so acute that the corporate human resources office conducted a series of in-depth interviews with key store managers to investigate the matter. Specifically, they wanted to investigate the level of motivation store managers had to seek promotion to district manager positions.

When asked, "How motivated are you to seek promotion?" store managers typically responded with comments such as "very little" or "not much." They were asked what they felt they would have to do to obtain and keep the job of district manager. Two primary answers emerged: (1) they would have to be able to do the job and (2) they would have to be able to get along with other district managers and top-level managers.

Managers were then asked to identify the various benefits and other outcomes that would evolve if they achieved the district manager position and to place values on the importance (valence) of these outcomes. The responses of each store manager interviewed were recorded. The following results of one interview are typical of the results of all the interviews.

TABULATION OF INTERVIEW RESPONSES

Store Manager: William Porter
Store Number: 181

Case 1:   Expectancy of ability to adequately perform the duties of a district manager. (Expectancy = .8)

Outcomes If Promoted	Instrumentalities	Valences
Will have to move	0.6	−0.5
Company car	1.0	1.0
Higher pay	1.0	1.0
Will have to travel a lot	1.0	−0.4

Case 2: Expectancy of ability to work well with other district managers and top management. (Expectancy = .2)

Outcomes If Work Well	Instrumentalities	Valences
Continued promotion	0.6	0.8
Higher pay	0.5	1.0
Job security	0.5	0.6

Project

Compute the level of motivation for promotion exhibited by the store manager's responses. Assuming that these responses are typical of those of other store managers at Merritt's Shoe Store, what are the primary reasons store managers resist promotion to district manager positions? What organizational changes are suggested by this analysis?

FIGURE C-9 Organization Chart for Merritt's Retail Division

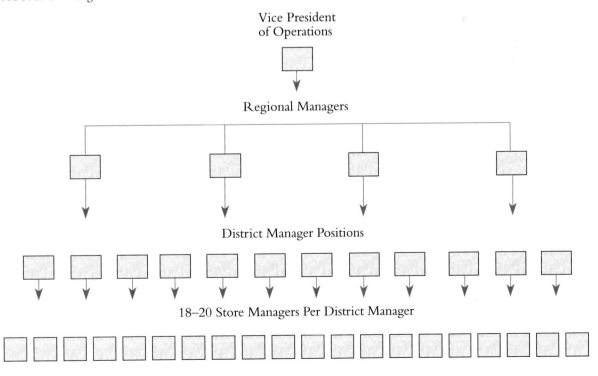

CASE 10: A GRADUATE DEGREE

Assume that within a few years you will receive your undergraduate degree. Like most students, you have no specific plans after graduation, and one of the things you may have considered (perhaps briefly) is the possibility of obtaining a graduate degree.

The following worksheet may help you decide whether or not graduate work is for you. The idea of pursuing graduate work involves more than one expectancy; it involves getting admitted (Case 1) and successfully completing the degree program (Case 2). Some outcomes for each of these are given; you may add additional ones in the spaces provided.

Project

Compute your level of motivation for pursuing a graduate degree. For what reasons are you motivated or not motivated?

Case 1:   Expectancy of ability to qualify for admission to graduate school. (Expectancy = _____).

Outcomes If Qualified	Instrumentalities	Valences
Have to study for 1–2 years	_____	_____
Will learn more	_____	_____
Can't get job and get paid	_____	_____
Cannot travel much	_____	_____
_____	_____	_____
_____	_____	_____
_____	_____	_____

Case 2:   Expectancy of ability to complete all requirements in the graduate program and receive the graduate degree. (Expectancy = _____).

Outcomes If Receive Degree	Instrumentalities	Valences
Higher paying job	_____	_____
More interesting job	_____	_____
Status	_____	_____
Greater confidence	_____	_____
_____	_____	_____
_____	_____	_____

Glossary

A

absoluteness of accountability the situation in which each person who delegates or redelegates is accountable to an immediate superior for the results.

acceptance view of authority the view that contends that authority stems from below.

accountability view of social responsibility a view suggesting that each firm should pay its own way, be fully accountable for its actions, and treat each group that has an interest in the firm with fairness and consideration.

activity work that must be com-

pleted in order to progress from one event to another.

adhocratic organizational units small, organic structures of a temporary nature.

administrative management a stream of thought concerned primarily with how organizations should be managed and structured.

administrative problem the problem of forming internal systems and structures to coordinate a firm's engineering response with its entrepreneurial problem.

agenda the grouping of the general manager's goals and plans.

applications programmer a specialist who develops software to generate reports, update records, and complete other transactions with the data stored in various databases.

applications software programs written to solve particular problems and perform specific activities or tasks.

assessment center a place for evaluating job candidates and a process that relies heavily on simulated job experiences.

asset management ratios measures that determine how effectively a firm is using its resources.

attendance training training based on behavior modification that teaches the employee to regulate his or her own attendance.

authority the right inherent in a managerial position to make decisions that guide the actions of others.

autocratic leader one who maintains most of the authority in a group by issuing orders and telling group members what to do without consulting them.

B

balance sheet a listing of all of a firm's assets, liabilities, and owners' equity as of a specific date.

behavior modeling the process of acquiring skills by imitating people who perform the skills correctly.

behavioral approach to management an approach grounded in the belief that specific attention to workers' needs creates greater satisfaction and productivity.

board of directors a group of people elected by stockholders to make sure the firm is managed well.

bounded rationality the concept that individuals' limited mental capabilities and emotions, coupled with external influences over which they have little or no control, prevent them from making completely rational decisions.

brainstorming a technique to stimulate creative thinking; free-wheeling, uninhibited thinking by group members to produce a large number of potential solutions to specific problems.

break-even analysis a technique used to show relationships among costs, revenues, and outputs.

break-even point the quantity of output at which total revenues equal total costs.

budget a single-use plan expressed in numerical terms.

budgeted balance sheet a projection of a firm's assets, liabilities, and owners' equity as of a future date.

budgeted income statement a projection of a firm's revenues and expenses for a period of time.

bureaucracy an ideal type of organization that is completely rational in its design and impersonal in the way it is implemented.

business plan a comprehensive set of guidelines for starting and operating a new venture.

business-level strategy a strategy that focuses on the question: How should we compete in each of our businesses?

C

capital equipment operations system a system for selecting the physical assets (i.e., the capital equipment) needed to produce outputs.

capital expenditures budget a plan that details the costs of purchasing property, plant and equipment, and other physical assets used to generate revenues over a long period of time.

career a lifelong series of positions that form a coherent pattern.

career management and development a person's planned effort to achieve a more satisfying and rewarding career.

career path the sequence of jobs necessary to achieve personal and career goals.

career plan an overall blueprint for achieving career goals by specifying those goals and accompanying action plans.

career plateau a situation in which, for either organizational or individual reasons, the probability of moving up the career ladder is low.

cash budget a plan that shows the cash available to and the cash needed by a business during a particular time period.

causal models models for analyzing the causes of past events and using them to predict future events.

central processing unit (CPU) the "brain" of a computer consisting of three subunits: the control unit, the arithmetic/logic unit, and the registers.

centrality closeness to power; the concept that the closer a person is to power, the greater the power that person exerts.

chain of command the steps by which authority flows downward in the organization, specifying who reports to whom.

charisma the ability to lead others based on personal charm, magnetism, inspiration, and emotion.

classical approach to management an approach consisting of two streams of thought: scientific management and administrative management.

classical view of authority the view that holds that an organization derives its authority from its stakeholders.

classical view of social responsibility a view suggesting that firms should concentrate on earning profits and should not be concerned directly with social goals and issues.

closed system a system that does not interact with and is not influenced by its environment.

code of ethics a formal statement of the values and behaviors a firm expects of its employees.

coercive power controlling others through fear of punishment or the threat of punishment.

cognitive resource theory a theory of leadership stating that competent managerial leaders possess an effective problem-solving ability by which they anticipate problems before they occur and demonstrate imagination, creativity, and a willingness to experiment in their solution.

cognitive skills mental abilities and knowledge.

common practice criterion a criterion of behavioral standards that suggests that failing to engage in certain practices results in a competitive disadvantage.

communication (or information) overload a problem that occurs when people are so overloaded with information that they cannot respond effectively to messages.

communication networks linkages that connect people and groups for sending and receiving information.

comparable worth a compensation plan whereby the firm grants equal pay for jobs that it judges to be of comparable value.

competitive advantage an advantage occurring when a firm selects markets in which it can excel or in which its unique capabilities provide an edge over competitors.

competitive benchmarking comparing one's own quality performance to that achieved by competitive firms.

complaint program a formal vehicle for listening to the concerns and problems of employees and customers.

compressed work week a full-time schedule that allows 40 hours of work to be accomplished in fewer than five days.

computer program a set of instructions or statements to the computer.

computer-aided design (CAD) a process whereby designers use computer programs to develop new products rapidly and effectively.

computer-aided manufacturing (CAM) a process using computers to directly control or monitor manufacturing production processes.

conceptual skills the ability to think in abstract terms—to simplify complex situations and determine a course of action.

consensus a state of harmony, general agreement, or majority opinion with a reasonable amount of disagreement still present.

consensus decision making a problem-solving technique whereby everybody involved in a decision places a personal stamp of approval on the outcome.

consensus leader one who encourages group discussion about an issue and then makes a decision that reflects the consensus (general agreement) of group members.

consultative leader one who solicits opinions from the group before making a decision, yet does not feel obligated to accept the group's thinking.

contingency approach to management an approach suggesting that managerial practices depend on all factors influencing a particular situation.

contingency leadership the idea that the best style of leadership depends on factors relating to group members and the work setting.

contingency plan a plan that specifies what a person might do if an unfavorable event takes place.

contingent workers people who perform work for a firm on a temporary basis but are not members of its permanent workforce.

controlling a six-stage process designed to ensure that a firm's strategies and plans will be put into effect successfully; ensuring that, through effective leading, what has been planned and organized to take place has in fact taken place.

cooptation finding a way to get an opposing party to join your side.

corporate-level strategy a strategy that is concerned with the questions of what businesses the company should be in, how headquarters should manage the businesses, and how resources should be allocated among them.

corrective discipline a positive method of improving poor performance that gives employees a chance to correct their behavior before the firm applies punishment.

critical path the longest chain, in time, of events and activities from the start to the finish of a project.

cultural empathy an awareness of and a willingness to investigate the reasons why people of another culture act as they do.

culture the customs, beliefs, values, and patterns of behavior of a society.

D

data raw facts, such as names, hours worked, and order numbers.

database an integrated collection of data and information organized for access by a computer.

debt management ratios measures that indicate a firm's ability to meet its short- and long-term debt obligations.

decentralization the extent to which executives delegate authority to lower organizational units.

decision the selection of a course of action from two or more alternatives.

decision criteria the standards of judgment used to evaluate alternatives.

decision premise the basic values and objectives followed in making a decision.

decision tree a visual representation of the analysis involved in a payoff matrix.

decision-making process the sequence of steps used to make a decision, that is, to select a particular course of action.

delegatee the person to carry out a delegated assignment.

delegation the shifting of authority from superior to subordinate.

democratic leader one who confers final authority on the group.

departmentalization the grouping of work or individuals into manageable units.

development increasing the capabilities of employees in order to improve their future job performance.

diagonal communication the sending and receiving of messages down or up the organization through different units and to people at different job levels.

differentiation the degree to which managers and specialists think and act differently, particularly with respect to goals and values.

differentiation strategy a strategy whereby the firm provides a product to customers that is differentiated in some way from others in the market.

disparate impact an adverse effect on a protected class that occurs when an employment standard is applied equally.

disparate treatment the use of personnel tests and other selection devices in such a way that protected-class members receive unequal treatment or are evaluated by different standards.

distinctive competence a strength that allows a firm to perform especially well compared to competitors.

distributed processing system a means of providing computing power throughout a firm by using microcomputers, telecommunications, and networks.

divergent thinking a risk-taking break with traditional patterns of thinking.

diversified firms firms that compete in two or more businesses.

downshifting investing more time in family and less in career.

downsizing reducing the size of a firm by laying off or retiring workers to decrease costs.

downward communication the passing of messages from higher to lower levels in an organization.

E

economic order quantity (EOQ) an inventory control technique used to keep a firm's ordering and holding costs as low as possible.

effectiveness doing the right things; that is, doing what is necessary in order to produce a good or service that is valued by customers.

efficiency the wise and economic use of resources to achieve valued outcomes without waste.

ego strength an individual's ability to manage his or her own be-

havior, particularly in tense situations.

employee assistance program (EAP) a formal organizational unit designed to help employees deal with personal problems that affect job performance.

employee benefit anything of value given to workers, in addition to their base salary, as a condition of their employment.

empowerment a manager's process of sharing power with team members, thereby enhancing their feelings of self-efficacy.

end-user a person who uses the output of an information system but is not a systems specialist.

engineered standards performance standards based on objective, quantitative analyses of specific work situations.

engineering problem the problem of developing and using an operations system through which a firm's products can be produced effectively and efficiently.

entrepreneur a person who recognizes a marketplace opportunity and accepts the risk of assembling resources to take advantage of that opportunity in order to create wealth.

entrepreneurial pay a compensation plan in which people who help found a new corporate venture share in its profits.

entrepreneurial problem the problem of determining the goods or services to be produced by a firm and the particular markets in which they will be offered.

entrepreneurial risk risks taken in terms of one's time, financial resources, and psychological well-being in order to form a new business venture.

entrepreneurship a process intended to create wealth through the gathering and efficient management of human, financial, physical, and informational resources in order to pursue a business opportunity with acceptable levels of risk.

environment all forces external to an organization that can affect its performance.

environmental adaptation an ongoing process through which a firm matches its resources and capabilities with marketplace opportunities.

environmental feedback information from the environment regarding the effectiveness of an organization's performance.

environmental opportunities the conditions in a firm's external environment that might aid in the accomplishment of its objectives.

environmental risks conditions in an organization's external environment that might prevent it from accomplishing its objectives.

equal employment opportunity a legal requirement that provides protection against all forms of employment discrimination.

ethics the moral values and standards defining desirable conduct.

event a performance milestone representing the start or finish of an activity.

exception principle a condition for effective delegation whereby the manager gets involved in the details of a group member's work only when a problem exists.

executive search firms a recruiting source for high-level positions; they conduct industry-wide searches for the right person to fill a job.

expatriates managers and other workers on foreign assignments.

expectancy a person's subjective estimate of the probability that a given level of performance will occur.

expectancy theory the idea that work motivation results from deliberate choices to engage in certain activities in order to achieve worthwhile outcomes.

expected value the sum of all possible states of nature multiplied by their individual probability estimates.

expense budget a plan that details all expenses anticipated during a period of time.

expert power the ability to influence others because of one's specialized knowledge, skills, or abilities.

expropriation taking over a firm or its funds by force.

external locus of control an individual's belief that outcomes are a product of luck, fate, or destiny.

F

facilities physical resources in which goods or services are created, stored, or distributed.

facilities layout operations system a system used to determine the physical layout of the capital equipment and materials necessary to produce outputs.

facilities location operations system a system used to determine where a firm's facilities should be located and how they should be used.

factory system a setting in which many workers join together to perform a variety of organized tasks.

false distrust a manager's erroneous belief that subordinates are trying to displace or discredit him or her.

feedback messages sent back from the receiver to the sender.

Fiedler's contingency theory of leadership a model specifying the conditions under which leaders should use task-motivated and relationship-motivated styles.

field unit a segment of an organization located away from headquarters.

filtering the coloring and altering of information to make it more acceptable to the receiver.

financial budgets plans that project how a firm will acquire funds from owners and creditors and how it will manage its cash.

financial resources the monetary resources required to support a firm's current and future operations.

first-class man Frederick W. Taylor's concept of an ambitious individual who was suited for the work he was doing.

first-level managers the people who supervise the work of all nonmanagerial, or operating-level, employees. Commonly known as supervisors, foremen, and department managers.

fixed costs costs incurred regardless of the amount of output.

fixed-position layout a facilities layout whereby a product remains in a single location so that required tools, equipment, and workers can be brought to it.

flat organization structure one that has relatively few layers of management.

flexible benefit package a system that offers a menu of benefits that can be tailored to the preferences of individual employees.

flexible working hours a modified work schedule whereby employees have flexibility in choosing their own hours.

focus strategy a strategy whereby a firm focuses on a narrow segment of an industry—a particular customer group, part of the product line, or geographic area—to the exclusion of other segments.

force-field theory the idea that an organization simultaneously faces forces for change (driving forces) and forces for maintaining the status quo (restraining forces).

forecasts predictions of future events.

frame of reference a perspective and vantage point based on past experience.

franchise a form of ownership whereby a company grants rights to a buyer to sell its goods or services for a flat fee and/or a share of the resulting income.

free association a process of producing ideas in rapid succession without censorship or control.

free-rein leader one who turns

over almost all authority to group members and does as little leading as possible.

frontload writing placing key ideas at the beginning of a memo, paragraph, or sentence.

functional authority the right to influence the activity of other employees or units outside one's chain of command.

functional-level strategies strategies used in both diversified and single-business firms to specify actions required to successfully implement business- and corporate-level strategies.

G

gainsharing a profit-sharing plan that calculates the contribution of specific groups or departments.

Gantt chart a graph that shows the relationship between work scheduled and completed and the amount of elapsed time.

general manager one who is responsible for more than a single function, such as marketing, finance, or accounting.

glass ceiling an invisible but difficult-to-penetrate barrier to promotion based on subtle attitudes and prejudices.

global essay an overall summary of an employee's performance for the period under consideration.

grapevine the major informal communication pathway in an organization.

greasing payments to officials of a foreign government that fall within that country's law.

growth curve model a model of organizational change that traces the inevitability of change through a firm's life cycle.

H

hardware the computer equipment required to transform data into information.

hardware systems computer devices to input, store, and process data and to provide the resulting information to end-users.

hearing the physical reception of sound.

horizontal (or lateral) communication sending and receiving messages between and among people at the same organizational level.

host-country national an employee of a multinational corporation who is a citizen of the country in which the foreign organizational unit is located.

human relations movement a movement based on the belief that there is an important link among managerial practices, morale, and productivity.

human resources the people through whom and with whom managers work to achieve objectives.

human resources information system (HRIS) a formal system for providing management with information about employees.

human resources planning anticipating and providing for the movement of people into, within, and out of the organization.

I

impulsive manager one who finds it difficult to delay action and tends to make hasty decisions.

Industrial Revolution the period during which mass production of goods and services, efficient transportation systems, and the substitution of machine power for human power first began to dominate business activities.

information data that have been converted into forms that communicate meaning, reduce uncertainty, and have managerial value.

information management the systematic control of information by managers in order to accomplish objectives and implement strategies and plans.

information system a set of procedures that collects, processes, stores, and distributes information to support decision making and control.

informational resources data that have been analyzed and converted into forms that help managers make effective decisions.

inplacement an approach to managing ineffective performance whereby an outside consultant works with a troubled executive, the executive's manager, and the human resources specialist to develop and implement an action plan for improvement.

input devices devices that feed data and instructions into the central processing unit of a computer.

instrumentality an individual's estimate of the probability that performance will lead to certain outcomes.

integration collaboration, or pulling together, among managers and specialists to achieve a common purpose.

integrative decisions decisions that integrate top-level managers' strategic decisions with first-level managers' operational decisions.

integrity (or honesty) test a pre-employment test designed to measure the extent of a person's integrity as it relates to job behavior.

internal locus of control an individual's belief that outcomes are a result of his or her own actions.

international management the pursuit of organizational objectives in more than one nation.

interpersonal communication sending and receiving messages between and among people through informal methods such as talking, writing, and body language.

interpersonal skills the abilities needed to work successfully with other people.

interview structure the degree to which interview questions and formats are formalized.

intrapreneur a person who assumes the responsibility for creating an innovation within a large firm and for championing it to the stage of marketability.

intrapreneurship the process of promoting innovation and strategic change in large organizations.

intuitive decisions decisions based on instantaneous analysis, personal experiences, and gut feelings.

inventory the goods a firm keeps on hand to use in its production processes.

inventory management operations system a system for handling a firm's inventories effectively and efficiently.

invisible hand the capitalistic competitive system itself, which works continually for the public's good.

J

Japanese management a style of management that focuses on human resources development and is rooted in a general cultural belief in concern for people and harmony and cooperation (or *wa*).

job (or person) specifications a description of the personal characteristics required for a particular job.

job characteristics model a method of job design that focuses on the tasks and interpersonal dimensions of a job.

job description a written statement outlining the key responsibilities of a job along with the activities required to perform the job effectively.

job design the way tasks and work are divided to form an entire job.

job enrichment making a job more motivational and satisfying by adding variety and responsibility.

job sharing a modified work schedule whereby two people share the same job, both usually working half time.

job specialization the degree to which a worker performs only a limited number of tasks.

just-in-time (JIT) an inventory management technique used to ensure that items needed to produce goods and services arrive at the time they are needed in a production process.

K

kaizen the Japanese philosophy of continuing, gradual improvements in one's personal and work life.

key result areas parts of a firm's operation that are especially critical to its success.

L

large-scale organization change the method used to accomplish a major change in a firm's strategy and culture.

lateral teams task forces or committees composed of people from different organizational units.

lead by example to influence team members by acting as a positive model.

leadership grid a framework for classifying leadership styles that examines a leader's concern for task accomplishment and people simultaneously. (Formerly called the Managerial Grid.)

leadership style the relatively consistent pattern of behavior that characterizes a leader.

leading the process of activating and directing other people's efforts toward accomplishment of organizational and personal objectives.

legality criterion a criterion for behavioral standards that suggests that the laws of the land provide all the direction required to make ethical decisions.

legitimate power power based on the manager's formal position within the organizational hierarchy.

line authority the right of a manager to allocate resources and assign tasks to employees.

line organization function one that contributes directly to the creation and distribution of goods and services.

liquidity ratios measures of a firm's ability to pay off its short-term liabilities out of its liquid assets, and by doing so, remain solvent.

listening the mental translation of sound into meaningful communications.

locus of control an individual's belief about who determines outcomes in his or her life.

long-term objectives concrete goals that ensure achievement of a firm's mission.

M

Machiavellianism a measure of deceitfulness and duplicity; manipulating others for personal gain.

machine bureaucracy an ideal organization in which activities are controlled by rules and procedures; functions are highly differentiated; the organization of offices is determined by hierarchy; behavior is regulated by rules and norms; interpersonal relationships are impersonal; promotion and selection are based on job competence; and all administrative actions are recorded in writing.

mainframe computer a computer that generally serves 100 or more end-users simultaneously and is used to handle significant amounts of data or many complicated processes.

management the process of effectively and efficiently using an organization's resources to achieve objectives through the functions of planning, organizing, leading, and controlling.

management by objectives (MBO) a technique used to determine the activities employees will complete to implement strategies.

management by wandering around a technique whereby managers accomplish much of their work while visiting employees in their work areas.

management development any planned attempt to improve the effectiveness of present or future managers.

management functions a manager's actual work-related activities.

management history an account of how management has been practiced over different periods of time and in different settings.

managerial ethics the moral values and standards that define desirable managerial behaviors.

managerial judgment standards value judgments; standards established by managers to assess employee outputs and attitudes in terms of the qualities they believe enhance productivity.

manipulation influencing people by distorting information and engaging in other forms of deception.

manufacturing firms firms that produce physical goods such as automobiles, refrigerators, computers, and textbooks.

market share the percentage of total sales volume captured by a firm's product.

Maslow's need hierarchy an explanation of motivation that arranges human needs into a pyramid-shaped model.

mass production a process through which large numbers of a product are produced using standardized procedures.

master production schedule a schedule that specifies which products are to be produced and when.

materials management operations system a system for determining how (and where) to buy, move, and store the materials needed to produce outputs in an effective and efficient manner.

materials requirements planning (MRP) a system that creates schedules identifying all materials and parts needed to produce a good or a service, when those items should be in inventory, and when they should be available to a firm's production processes.

matrix organization a project structure superimposed on a functional structure.

mentor a more experienced person who develops a junior colleague's abilities through tutoring, coaching, guidance, and emotional support.

message a purpose or idea to be conveyed.

meta-analysis a family of techniques used to combine research evidence from many studies.

methods definitions of the steps required to complete a task. Closely related to procedures but often more detailed; may specify exact arm and hand movements as well as the standard time required for each movement.

microcomputer (or personal computer) a computer that generally serves a single end-user, is the least expensive of computers, and has the smallest amount of computing power.

microprocessor a device that integrates a computer's memory, logic, and control on a single chip.

mid-career crisis a career stage in which, after assessing their progress in comparison to their early goals, people decide they have not accomplished enough.

middle-level managers the people responsible for making the visions and strategies of top-level managers fit with the operational realities faced by first-level managers.

minicomputer a medium-sized computer serving multiple end-users simultaneously.

mission the unique purpose that sets a business apart from other firms of its type and identifies the scope of its operations.

motivation the process by which behavior is mobilized and sustained in the interest of achieving organizational goals.

multinational corporation (MNC) a firm that conducts business in two or more countries in addition to its own.

N

natural soldiering Frederick W. Taylor's explanation for low worker output due to the natural instinct to take it easy.

need for achievement the desire to accomplish something difficult for its own sake.

need for affiliation the desire to establish and maintain friendly and warm relationships with others.

need for autonomy a desire for freedom, independence, and control over one's destiny.

need for power a desire to control other people, to influence their behavior, and to be responsible for them.

need for recognition the desire for attention, praise, and approval for personal accomplishments.

negative lifestyle factor any behavior that predisposes a person to stress, such as poor eating and exercise habits and heavy consumption of caffeine, alcohol, and other drugs.

network a group of people cooperating with one another to achieve organizational and personal goals.

new venture units teams formed to instigate new ideas, nourish those ideas to marketable status, and sometimes continue as the management group in charge of the venture.

noise anything that disrupts communication, including the attitudes and emotions of the receiver.

nominal group technique an approach to developing creative alternatives that requires group members to generate alternative solutions independently.

nominal groups noninteracting groups.

nonverbal communication the transmission of messages by means other than words.

norm an expected standard of conduct.

O

ombudsman a neutral person designated by a firm to help employees process complaints.

open system a system that interacts freely with and is influenced by its environment.

operating budgets plans that set the target revenues and expenses for a firm's activities over a particular time period.

operating system a set of computer programs that support the overall computer system by coordinating the activities of the hardware and the applications software.

operating systems programmer a specialist who organizes data as needed by end-users and selects devices to store those data.

operational control control of activities related to the production of a company's goods or its services.

operational decisions decisions concerned with a firm's day-to-day operations.

operational plans plans that guide an organization's day-to-day actions, specifying what is to be done, who will do it, and when it will be done.

operations the activities involved in making a firm's product.

operations activities the individual tasks completed within different operations systems to change a firm's resources into products.

operations management the process managers follow to develop and use effective and efficient operations systems and operations activities.

operations system a collection of activities through which a firm completes production work.

opportunistic decisions positive actions to take advantage of potential for growth, increased profits, or achievement of some other valued objective.

organic organization structure one that is loose and flexible and therefore highly adaptable to change.

organization design triangle an organization structure that includes cooperation (or teamwork) as well as centralization and decentralization.

organization development (OD) any strategy, method, or technique for making organizations more effective by bringing about constructive, planned change.

organization structure the arrangement of people and tasks to accomplish organizational goals; helps specify who reports to whom and who does what.

organizational behavior modification (OB Mod) a system of changing behavior by controlling rewards and punishments.

organizational communication a formal method of sending messages in the workplace by such means as memos, bulletin boards, newsletters, and suggestion system.

organizational culture a system of shared values and beliefs that actively influences the behavior of organization members.

organizational decisions decisions managers make in their official capacities on behalf of their firms.

organizational politics an influence process in which an individual or group attempts to gain advantage by using informal tactics in addition to merit.

organizational strengths internal conditions that help a firm attain its objectives.

organizational weaknesses internal conditions that make it difficult for a firm to attain its objectives.

organizing the activities concerned with how work and responsibilities are grouped; includes establishing authority relationships and coordinating human, physical, financial, and informational resources in a firm.

outplacement a method of helping terminated employees find new employment through professional career counseling and other assistance.

output device a device that receives results from the processing unit of a computer and converts them into an appropriate form for further use.

outsourcing obtaining needed goods, services, and/or materials from outside the company.

overall cost leadership strategy a strategy by which a firm works to provide a product or service with features acceptable to customers at the lowest competitive price.

P

parallel career track (or dual career ladder) an alternative to the management-oriented career path; a separate-but-equal ladder for technical, nonmanagement employees who do not wish to become managers. The grade levels, pay ranges, and rewards correspond to those given to employees within the management hierarchy.

parental leave time off for new parents with continuing benefits and the promise of a job when they return.

parity of authority and responsibility the situation in which the authority granted to a person is sufficient to carry out the assigned responsibility.

participative leader one who shares decision-making authority with group members.

pay-for-knowledge system a compensation system whereby management calculates starting pay based on the knowledge and skill level required for a given job.

payoff matrix a technique used to determine the benefits and costs associated with various alternative decisions.

peak performance doing exceptionally well in a demanding career.

performance appraisal a formal system for measuring, evaluating, and reviewing performance.

performance standard a level of performance established to serve as a model, criterion, or expectation.

personal decisions decisions that pertain to the manager as an individual rather than to the firm.

physical resources raw materials, land, building, furniture and office equipment, computers, machinery (including robots), and physical inventories used to accomplish a firm's objectives.

planning a process that identifies objectives and the commitments, resources, and actions required for their achievement.

planning and scheduling operations system a system for establishing the quantity and timing of outputs, coordinating of individual operations activities, and balancing product demand and supply for competitive success.

point-factor job evaluation a systematic method of measuring the financial worth of a job by assigning weights (capacity for earning points) to various factors that reflect the major job demands of a firm.

policies general statements (preferably written) that mirror an organization's objectives and describe the limits within which managerial decisions fall.

political risk assessment a technique for measuring the risk to a firm that stems from doing business in a particular country.

polygraph an instrument that measures physiological indicators of emotion including blood pressure, heartbeat, breathing rate, and decreases in skin temperature to test a person's honesty.

power the ability to influence decisions and control resources.

principle of management a statement that provides guidance for the practice of management.

probability the likelihood that an event will or will not take place.

probe an additional interview question suggested by the interviewee's response.

problem a situation existing when a standard or an expectation is not met or is exceeded.

problem analyzability the dimension of knowledge technology classifying the type of search process people use to analyze the exceptional cases.

problem-solving decisions decisions made to solve existing or anticipated problems.

procedures definitions of the standard sequence for completing a task, such as filling an order, paying a bill, or maintaining the proper inventory level.

process consultation a technique by which the organization development specialist examines the pattern of a work unit's communications.

process layout a facilities layout whereby items of equipment or departments are grouped together according to their function.

product design and development operations system the system whereby a firm or agency determines and then develops the products it will provide to its customers or clients.

product layout a facilities layout whereby equipment or work activities are arranged in a line so a specialized sequence of tasks can be performed on each product.

product leadership an estimate of the degree to which a firm's products are thought to set the standard for others to try to match.

productivity the relationship between total product—measured by dollar volume or units produced—and units of input.

professional bureaucracy one that standardizes skills for coordination and is composed of a core of highly trained professionals.

profitability ratios measures of the net returns on sales and total assets.

program a plan in which activities required to achieve a broader objective are specified.

program documentation the directions and descriptions designed to assist in computer software's use, implementation, and operation.

progressive discipline a system of making escalated penalties known to employees in advance and imposing them with increasing severity for repeated infractions.

project a single-use plan that describes actions necessary to achieve a concrete objective; a set of interrelated activities that, when completed, result in a salable product.

protean career a career that is controlled by the individual rather than the organization; it emphasizes self-fulfillment, satisfaction, and psychological well-being rather than external success.

Protestant work ethic a prevailing belief that humans are obligated to use their God-given talents in productive work.

public view of social responsibility a view that portrays businesses as partners with government, education, and other institutions in solving society's problems and improving the quality of life for all.

Q

quality all of a product's features and capabilities that affect its ability to satisfy customers' needs.

quality circle a small group of employees from the same unit who meet regularly to identify, analyze, and solve work problems.

quality credibility gap the difference between the message employees hear and the actual follow-through.

quantitative approach to management an approach to managerial decision making that is grounded in the scientific method. Also known as management science and operations research.

R

ratio analysis a technique used by both managers and outside investors and lenders to analyze a firm's financial position.

rational decisions decisions that are objective, logical, and designed to achieve organizational goals within specified limitations.

realistic job preview a frank discussion of all aspects of the job, both positive and negative.

recruitment the process of finding and attracting people who are capable of and interested in filling job vacancies.

referent (charismatic) power the ability to influence others that stems from the manager's desirable personal traits and characteristics.

related diversification the process by which a firm undertakes a new activity that shares some characteristic with its current products or markets.

reliability the consistency of a performance measure; the degree to which it yields the same results no matter how many times it is used.

replacement tables an important human resources planning technique specifying the number of people to be moved if a key employee retires or is removed.

resistance to planning a set of behaviors through which managers resist accepting the outputs of planning, neglect to emphasize planning, and pose threats to the continuation of planning.

resource dependence perspective the view that the organization requires a continuing flow of human resources, money, customers, technological inputs, and material to continue to function.

responsibility the obligation to perform the assigned work and to use the granted authority properly.

return on investment (ROI) a commonly used measure of profitability; a company's net income before taxes divided by net worth.

reward power controlling others through rewards or the promise of rewards.

rightsizing reducing a firm's workforce to its optimum size.

risk a situation in which the decision maker understands the available options but does not know the probability that each option will occur.

rules plans that limit individuals' discretion severely in certain areas (much more so than policies) but do not specify time sequences (as do procedures and methods).

S

sales budget (or revenue budget) a plan that details all sales anticipated during a period of time.

satisficing making decisions that are satisfactory, or good enough, instead of waiting until the optimum choice is determined to make a decision.

scientific management a stream of thought focused on the application of scientific methods to increase individual workers' productivity.

selective perception one major filter that people use to distort messages according to their needs.

self-confidence the degree to which managers trust their own judgment and are willing to take calculated risks and confront decision situations boldly.

self-determination theory the idea that people are motivated when they have a choice in initiating and regulating their actions.

semantics the varying meanings people attach to words.

service firms firms that produce nonphysical products such as financial, transportation, medical, legal, and educational services.

single-business firms firms that compete in a single business or product market.

single-use plans plans that deal with planning situations that are expected to occur only once.

situational control the degree to which the leader can control and influence the outcomes of group effort.

situational ethics an approach in which moral values and behavioral standards change from event to event.

Six Sigma a quality standard program developed by Motorola whereby errors occur only once in 3.4 per million opportunities.

skunk works a secret place where selected employees work to conceive new products.

social facilitation a process in which the productivity of each individual is increased by the stimulation group members provide.

social presence in communication, the feeling that a live person is present.

social responsibility a firm's obligation to pursue long-term goals that will serve its own interests as well as those of society.

software the detailed set of instructions or programs through which computer hardware applies itself to a particular problem.

span of control the number of employees reporting to one manager.

staff authority authority of an advisory or service nature that lacks the right of command.

staff specialists specialized staff workers who provide expertise that is not ordinarily possessed by managers.

staffing the process of ensuring that the organization has qualified employees to meet its objectives.

stakeholders individuals or groups who influence the development and achievement of a firm's mission, long-term objectives, and strategies.

standard time the time required to complete a job under certain conditions.

standing plans policies, procedures, methods, and rules that help managers deal with recurring planning issues.

states of nature uncontrollable influences on decision outcomes.

statistical standards performance standards based on an analysis of data from past experience.

strategic control control exercised by top-level managers that examines the accuracy of their assumptions about general economic conditions and the actions of the firm's competitors.

strategic decisions decisions that define the direction an organization intends to take.

strategic management a six-step process through which a firm determines actions it will take and how those actions will be implemented and evaluated.

strategic planning the process used to evaluate opportunities and risks and determine strengths and weaknesses in order to define a firm's mission, establish its long-term objectives, and formulate its strategies.

strategic plans plans that reflect organization-wide objectives and the business, or businesses, in which the firm intends to compete.

strategy the way in which the decisions and resource allocations a firm makes are used to accomplish its mission and long-term objectives.

strong organizational culture one that exerts considerable influence on its employees.

structured decisions those in which prior decisions or company policy limit the manager's latitude in decision making.

subculture a pocket in which the organizational culture differs from that of other pockets and the dominant culture.

suggestion system a written method of receiving and processing employee suggestions for job-related improvements and cost savings.

summary discipline the immediate discharge of an employee because of a serious offense.

supercomputers computers that have extremely large memories and rapid processing speeds and are very expensive.

superleadership getting group members to be self-directing.

system a set of interdependent parts that function together to accomplish an objective.

systematic approach to management one through which the practice of management is studied and then classified in a logical and orderly manner.

systematic soldiering Frederick W. Taylor's explanation for low output resulting from the workers' deliberate efforts to reduce their daily output.

systems analyst a specialist who identifies the objectives of an information system and prepares a plan to develop and implement that system.

systems approach to management an approach based on the position that an organization is a collection of parts that are both related to and dependent on one another.

T

tactical control control that concerns how well a firm's actions are being received in the marketplace.

tactical plans plans that detail the actions necessary for a firm (or a unit within a large, diversified company) to compete in its chosen business area.

tall organization structure one that has many layers of management.

task variability the dimension of knowledge technology classifying the number of exceptional cases found in the work.

team building a systematic method of improving the interpersonal and task aspects of work groups.

technical skills the skills required to complete specialized tasks.

telecommuting an arrangement by which employees perform their regular work duties from home or at another location.

Theory Z management a human-resources-oriented, Japanese style of management adapted to American firms. It emphasizes long-range planning, consensus decision making, and mutual loyalty between employer and employees.

third-party counseling an approach to managing ineffective performance whereby an outside consultant helps a manager and team member resolve a problem.

time series analysis examination of past data for trends that can be used to forecast what would happen in the future if a particular trend were to continue.

time standards/time study standards engineered standards that measure the output of individual employees or groups of employees.

time study the analysis of the amount of time needed to complete a job task.

top-level managers the people accountable for an organization's overall performance; they develop the firm's mission, strategies, and major operating policies.

total quality management (TQM) a management system reflecting a firm's strategic commitment to improve performance by continuously improving the quality of its products in ways that will maximize customer satisfaction.

training any method of increasing the level or range of employee skills in order to improve current job performance.

transformational leader one who helps organizations and people make positive changes in the way they do things.

two-factor theory of motivation a model that divides job elements into two types: motivators, or satisfiers, which can motivate and satisfy workers, and dissatisfiers, or hygiene factors, which can only prevent dissatisfaction.

U

unity of command a classic management principle stating that each subordinate receives assigned duties and delegated authority from one superior only and is accountable only to that superior.

unrelated diversification the process by which a firm undertakes a new activity that has nothing in common with its current products or markets.

unstructured decisions decisions that are relatively free from limitations imposed by prior decisions.

upward communication the passing of messages from lower-level to higher-level organization members.

upward delegation the process of assigning part of one's job to a superior.

V

valence the value a person places on a particular outcome.

validity how well a performance measure accounts for what it is supposed to measure.

value judgment an overall opinion of something based on a quick perception of its merit.

values a person's beliefs about proper standards of conduct and desired results; what people consider important.

variable costs costs that change directly with output.

variable pay an incentive plan that intentionally pays good performers more money than poor performers.

venture capital money invested in a high-risk, high-potential enterprise.

vertical job loading pushing responsibility down from the manager to the employee.

vision the ability to imagine the future and the goods or services that could be marketed successfully in that future.

W

work teams (or production work teams) small groups of individuals who work somewhat independently to complete a large task.

workaholism an addiction to work.

Z

zero-based budgeting a process by which managers justify budget requests from a starting point of zero rather than from the level of previous allocations.

zone of indifference the area in which employees will permit managers to exercise formal authority.

Organizations Index

Name Index

Subject Index